Captain Fantastic

ELTON JOHN IN THE '70S

The definitive biography by

David John DeCouto

Triple Wood Press, LLC
Chandler, AZ

Printed in the United States of America.

First Finalized Edition: May, 2018
    10 9 8 7 6 5 4 3 2 1

The Library of Congress has cataloged this edition as follows:

John, David. DeCouto
    Captain Fantastic: Elton John in the '70s / David John DeCouto.
        -1st ed.
    p.   cm.

    ISBN 9781980762485
    1.   Title
PS05242013   2018
232'.178-dd48

Cover design by David John DeCouto.

Front and back cover photographs, and various internal images © 1974, 1975, 1979 by James Fortune, James FortunePhotography.com.

Additional photographs care of Scott Segelbaum, RockArtShow.com, Richard Barnes, RbarnesPhotography.com, and Richard E. Aaron, Rockpix.com. Please visit these incredibly talented photographers' websites to purchase high-quality, hand-signed prints of Elton John, as well as many other rock stars from the '70s, '80s, '90s and beyond.

For my mom, for buying me a true treasure—the "Daniel" single, by God—one nameless summer afternoon after baseball practice.

And for my dad, for taking me to my first concert—Elton John, of course—back in that most prehistoric of years, 1976 A.D.

Oakland Coliseum, Oakland, California, September 9, 1973

TABLE OF CONTENTS

FOREWORD

∞

PART FOUR: BOTTLED & BRAINED (1975 – 1976)

PART FIVE: A SINGLE MAN (1977 – 1979)

AFTERWORD

ACKNOWLEDGMENTS

DISCOGRAPHY

CONCERTS

BIBLIOGRAPHY

ABOUT THE AUTHOR

THE PALLADIUM, NEW YORK CITY, NEW YORK, OCTOBER 18, 1979

FOREWORD

Elton John, when he first emerged, seemed to have got a niche very much for developing primarily as a writer. "Your Song" was a touching, simple, relatively unaccompanied piece, which set the tone for a very thoughtful character. From what I remember at the time, he and Bernie Taupin had got a publishing deal, and maybe Elton was singing songs in order to try his hand at it, but I think they were actually primarily about writing for other people.

It wasn't until a little later, when Elton was so established in the USA, that his performance, his modus operandi, became very theatricalized in a bouncy, energetic sort of way. As Elton's performances got more rocky and more, I suppose, filled with the extremes of onstage behavior and production values that crept in really in the first half of the '70s, when shows became more production-oriented—you spent a lot more money on lights and sound and touring around with trucks and busses—everything became of a much larger scale.

Which it hadn't been in 1969.

It was around 1972 when that really kicked off, and that was at the time that Jethro Tull started doing arenas with *Thick as a Brick*, and that was the era when Elton John was beginning to enjoy major popularity and that kind of production of large-scale, gaudy, bright, in-your-face performances which characterized him. It also characterized us, except we were a little weirder, a little more esoteric—perhaps—than the slightly almost musical presentation of Elton John. And it was that era, during '73, '74, '75, we were playing in places like Madison Square Gardens and the Forum in L.A., and we were popular enough to do multiple shows, and Elton John was doing multiple shows, and we were, I suppose, competing very much on the same level in terms of performance venues at that point. We played multiple shows per venue, as did Elton. Trying to obviously demonstrate, as artists did, that you could play three shows or five shows at the Forum in L.A., and three nights in Madison Square Gardens, and all that sort of stuff. It was all about showing-up a bit.

The weird thing was, I never got to see Elton John play live. It wasn't until one ex-tour manager of ours joined the Elton John entourage as Elton's personal assistant that I nearly got to see Elton John. We had a night off in New York at a time when Elton John was playing, I believe, at Madison Square Gardens. Our ex-tour manager said, 'Do you want to come along to the show?' We said, 'Yeah, yeah, let's do that.' We were all ready to pop along and watch for the first time Elton John play live, only to be told, a few minutes before we set off from the hotel, 'Elton's not going to play tonight.' Whatever was wrong was wrong. I suppose he wasn't feeling too good. So it was cancelled, so I never ever got to see Elton John. I *did* see him once on the other side of a restaurant somewhere, but I was too nervous to go over and say hello. Mainly because I didn't know what you call him. It's a bit like Cat Stevens. Do you call him Cat, or Mr. Stevens, or Steve, which was his real name? What do you do with Elton? Do you call him Reg? Or Mr. John? It's always a bit embarrassing as to what you do. So I didn't say hello.

I only ever once, very briefly, bumped into Elton John in person. It sounds like name dropping, but I'd been invited by a mutual friend to a Christmas party at Mr. Sting's—Gordon's— who was having a big Christmas party, and he'd invited the good and the great, and Elton John was there with David Furnish, who seemed a very nice chap. And when they were leaving, perhaps a little earlier than other people, I plucked up the courage to say, 'I just wanted to say thank you, Elton. We never met, but back in '72 you did an interview with some British music press where you praised our album *Thick as a Brick* at the time, and you said some very kind things about me, which I always remembered. And I just wanted to say thanks for the very positive words that you used.' And he looked at me kind of blankly, he obviously didn't remember it, but he was gracious and polite and went on his way. So no sign of tantrums and tiaras on the brief occasion that I had eye contact with the man.

As for my favorite Elton John song, I'm going to steer away from "Crocodile Rock" and the other up-tempo fancy songs that you have to be at a high level of energy and intensity to pull off if you're doing a big rock concert. For me, Elton is the consummate singer/songwriter. Someone who, above all, is very thoughtful. And it's difficult to do, if you're singing lyrics that somebody else wrote. It's a matter of somehow casting yourself almost like an actor. You have to take on a persona. And maybe Elton finds that easier than writing lyrics himself. Or maybe writing lyrics is a little too personal. But whatever it is, he always sounds very thoughtful—he's really singing in a way where he is considering the words, considering how to project them, how to make every nuance work. So it's the singer/songwriter Elton that I'm always going to like best. The guy who just sits downs at the piano and can mesmerize you with a calm, heartfelt rendition. So the song I come up with is "Candle in the Wind"—the original Marilyn Monroe version, not the Princess Diana version. Though he was extremely brave to do that at Diana's funeral service. It was very apt, and I think it brought tears to a lot of people, hearing him sing that. I don't know how he got through it. It must have been an enormous emotional thing for him to do that and somehow detach himself a little bit from the occasion in order to sing those words. It was such a poignant and heartfelt moment. But that's what you do when you're a performing artist and you have that skill to embed yourself in what you're doing, but also kind of just stand a little bit to one side, in the way that perhaps an actor does.

That's about it, really. I have to say, whilst Elton John has been around, he's someone who, to this day, is perhaps known not only for his music but also for his philanthropy and his position on things that matter. He's a guy who truly deserves his status in the long term. He's not just a pretty face with somebody else's hair. No, I didn't say that. Long live Elton.

Ian Anderson, June, 2016.

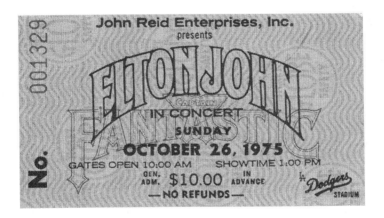

Elton John sits alone in the darkened bedroom of his Laurel Canyon manse, pale shadows converging around bare feet. The unseeing button-eyes of a dozen mute teddy bears and stuffed lizards watch in idle fascination as their superstar caretaker unscrews a bottle of ten-milligram-strength Valium, and empties a handful of pills into an unshaking hand.

"Here we go," Elton sighs, gazing blankly into a triple-mirrored vanity. Multiple faces stare dully back at him, vacant and silent and haunted.

The world's most famous pianist tosses a dozen light blue pills into his mouth, then washes them back with a quick swig of Perrier. He shakes out another handful of pills, and then another. Soon enough, the bottle is empty—eighty pills melt into his gut, quietly dispelling their insidious magic.

Clutching at the folds of his terrycloth robe, Elton rises on unsteady feet and shuffles into his backyard. All heads turn his way, easy smiles fading as the perennial Man of the Hour climbs tentatively onto a sunbaked diving board.

"I shall die within the hour," Elton announces to everyone, to no one.

Moments later, he crashes headlong into the deep end.

Into the endless depths.

Into the dark and unchartered waters where, finally, no sunlight ever dared to reach.

Forty-five hours on, Elton leaps effortlessly onto a gleaming silver grand piano, his sequined Dodgers uniform glittering ruefully beneath a bank of candy-colored stage lights.

"*Louder*," he commands, triumphantly raising a baseball bat into the panoramic sky. Standing atop his instrument, he resembles nothing so much as some fallen god reborn, a magnetic alien from a planet ten-thousand light-years away.

Elton nods at the fifty-five-thousand bodies crushed in willful supplication before him. He is the undisputed king, dominating airwaves, concert stages and the media with equal ease. His music, which accounts for a staggering *two percent* of all records sold globally, is as innovative as it is unavoidable. His tours are instant sellouts, breaking house records from London to Tokyo to Melbourne, while his albums routinely enter the charts at the Number 1 position—a feat no one in the history of recorded music has ever managed before. Not Elvis, not the Stones, not Sinatra. Not even the mighty Beatles.

Elton bounds off his piano as his high-octane band rips into the crucial chords of "Saturday Night's Alright (For Fighting)." Twin guitars lock behind a seismic backbeat, stoking a feral bonfire that rages throughout the stadium. Overcome by the insurgent maelstrom, Elton kicks his piano stool away and collapses to his knees with feverish intensity as his fingers unleash an explosive thousand-note fusillade that surges from speakers ten-stories high.

As the final thunderous notes float heavenward, a landscape of frenzied humanity writhes helplessly in the frozen twilight. Delirious and tearful, and begging for more more more.

Elton leans against his piano, soaking in the fractured apocalypse. For the moment, at least, he's safe within a cradle of mass adoration. An exalted supernova, celebrated beyond all normal human reckoning.

"All right," he says, lowering the brim of his baseball cap and allowing himself the tiniest of smiles.

He's as alone as he's ever been.

Prologue:
YOUNG MAN'S BLUES
(1947-1969)

In 1944, as World War II cracked and boomed, nineteen-year-old Royal Air Force officer Stanley Dwight met eighteen-year-old RAF clerk Sheila Eileen Harris at the Headstone Hotel in North Harrow. Sheila had come with a girlfriend to watch a local danceband, Bob Miller & the Millermen, playing alongside influential guitarist Bert Weedon, rip their way through jazz standards like "Body & Soul" and "My Funny Valentine." Stanley, who played lead trumpet with the band whenever his military schedule allowed, immediately noticed the comely Sheila standing in the crowd. By the end of the evening, romance had sparked. The officer and the svelte brunette kissed heatedly in a darkened dining hall at midnight, swearing oaths to write each other throughout the endless blitzkrieg.

Dozens of passionate letters followed. When Stanley could manage it, he would meet up with Sheila for clandestine trysts throughout the battered British countryside. Like so many other young lovers galvanized by the existential threat of annihilation, their romance took on an added dimension of gravitas which later reality would have a difficult time sustaining.

The two married the following January, exchanging vows on a leaden, snow-filled morning at Pinner Parish Church, in the sleepy northwest London suburb of Pinner, Middlesex.

Having little money, the couple moved in with Sheila's parents, Ivy and Fred Harris. The four lived in cramped nuptial stasis in a semi-detached row house—a council dwelling, government housing—at 55 Pinner Hill Road.

They were just another post-war couple, with shared hopes and dreams which would never be fully realized.

The future Elton Hercules John was born fourteen months later, in the early hours of a rain-swept Tuesday morning, on March 25, 1947. Sheila Dwight christened her only son "Reginald Kenneth." Though Stanley disliked the name and had campaigned vigorously against it in the weeks leading up to the birth, Sheila gave her husband's protests little mind.

Months later, Stanley—who had been commuting to the RAF base in Ruislip—found himself redeployed to Basra, Iraq. Not caring to be separated from her parents, Sheila refused to accompany her husband on his overseas posting.

It was already the beginning of an end which would take years still to finally conclude.

With his father thirty-five-hundred miles away, young Reg found himself being raised in a predominantly female household. The curly-haired boy's main companions were his mother, aunt, and grandmother, Nan—as well as the endless stream of popular melodies which poured forth from the family's Murphy-A46 wireless.

"We always had music in the house," Elton would later recall. "The radio was *always* on."

From morning till night, the music of Guy Mitchell, Frankie Laine, Kay Starr and Billy May would fill the impressionable youngster's head with a timeless sonic language he'd spend the rest of his life decoding and refining.

Reg grew up a mannered, overprotected child, forced to mark time alone in the small garden behind his house while the neighborhood children played Cowboys and Indians in a nearby field.

Left to his own devices, the three-year-old climbed onto the piano bench of his grandmother's King Brothers upright one nameless afternoon and began picking out the piquant melody of Waldteufel's "The Skater's Waltz" by ear.

"Mum!" he chirped, a beatific smile lighting up his normally dour countenance.

Sheila set down her vacuum and rushed over to his side, as grateful as she was amazed. Might music provide an antidote to her son's naturally downcast disposition? Indeed, she would quickly learn to place Reg in front of the piano whenever he was overtaken by a darker mood, so that he could harmlessly bang out his unspoken frustrations.

Stanley and Sheila began quarreling incessantly the moment he arrived back from Iraq. They seemed unable to agree upon much, apart from a mutual admiration for their son's musical abilities, which often proved a highlight of their frequent parties.

"We used to put him to bed in the day and get him up to play at night," Sheila said.

The prestige the youngster garnered would prove to be a double-edged sword, for while Reg enjoyed the eloquent melodies he was able to coax from the piano, from "The Sheik of Araby" to "Diamonds Are a Girl's Best Friend," he hated the forced nature of the performances themselves. "My parents always used to do it," he said. "I was wheeled out at every occasion to play the piano. It was a way of getting attention and approval. It was what I turned to for safety—music and food."

Reg's earliest musical influence came in the rotund figure of Winifred Atwell. An affable Trinidad-born pianist with a string of hits which included "Coronation Rag" and "Let's Have Another Party," Atwell routinely kept two pianos onstage—a concert grand upon which she performed theater songs and classical pieces, and a honky-tonk upright which she used to bash out a selection of rags.

"She was a huge influence," Elton said. "She was *it* for me."

Another favorite was Liberace, whose self-titled TV show was wildly popular throughout the U.K. Each week, Reg would sit transfixed before the family's tiny black-and-white telly as the flamboyant pianist tickled the ivories of a sequin-encrusted, gold-leafed Blüthner Grand.

"I don't give concerts," Liberace told his television audience. "I put on a *show*."

Stanley was promoted to RAF Squadron Leader in 1953. Now posted to RAF Lynam in Wiltshire, he could finally afford to move his young family to their own home—111 Potter Street, Northwood, a detached house only a couple miles down the road from Pinner.

Reg spent countless hours alone in his new bedroom, desperately praying for a brother or sister. But his father seemed abjectly against the idea of having another child. The situation did little to calm Reg's already delicate nerves. He would, in fact, spend the majority of his youth on tenterhooks, living in constant fear of receiving a scolding from his father for such unforgivable infractions as chewing his celery too loudly at the dinner table, or accidentally kicking a soccer ball into the rosebushes. "I was petrified of him," he later conceded. "I dreaded it when he came home."

The underlying strain of an increasingly fractured marriage inevitably metastasized. As Stanley and Sheila's

21

incessant bickering reverberated throughout the small house, Reg withdrew more deeply into himself. "My mum and dad should never have gotten married," he said. "They weren't really suited to each other. They'd both married the wrong person. Whenever my father came home, I knew there was going to be an argument with my mother. So you live in fear and you just go to your room, and basically it drove me to my music even more."

Though music would always be Reg's first—and longest-lasting—obsession, another passion soon took root in the guise of the Watford Football Club. Starting at the age of seven, Reg and his father often attended soccer games together at Vicarage Road on Saturday afternoons. Side by side they'd trundle through town, paying their sixpence and standing transfixed at the terraces on Rookery End. It was their one shared interest, they're only binding tie. "Soccer matches were the one thing my father and I did together that I used to love," Elton said. "But there was never an intimacy between the two of us. I didn't know how to communicate with him, and he didn't know how to communicate with me."

Lonely Reg found some small measure of solace at the age of seven, when he began taking piano lessons from a local teacher, Mrs. Jones, who taught him rudimentary Chopin and Bartók. "She was lovely," he said. "I could read okay, but I was never that much interested actually in becoming a classical musician, because ever since I could remember I always wanted to do something in popular music."

A few months later, young Reg gave his first official public performance, playing at the wedding of his cousin Roy Dwight, when the band booked for the reception failed to show up on time.

Though he went down a storm, Reg's narrow horizons wouldn't permanently expand until a couple years later. In August, 1956, while in Penny Green awaiting his turn for the barber's shears, Reg picked up a copy of *Life* magazine and stumbled upon a photo essay on an American singer named Elvis Presley. "I'd never seen anything like it," he said. "I thought he was from Mars."

That Friday, Reg's mother came home with a pair of 78s: "ABC Boogie" by Bob Haley & His Comets, and "Heartbreak Hotel" by Elvis himself. "I said, 'Oh Mom, I just saw this bloke in a magazine.' It was just weird that it happened the same week. That changed my life. It changed the way I listened to music forever."

Though skiffle was riding a crest of popularity throughout the British Isles at the time—with hits such as Lonnie Donegan's "Rock Island Line" clogging the charts— Reg's heart was immediately and forever taken by the rock 'n' rollers who resided on the other side of the Atlantic. "All the people I idolized were Americans," he said. "I couldn't believe how great they were."

In a vain effort to help steer his son's musical path back onto the straight and narrow, Stanley presented Reg with a copy of Frank Sinatra's just-released *Songs for Swingin' Lovers* LP on his ninth birthday. Not surprisingly, his son was unmoved by the gesture.

"I really wanted a bike, so I didn't appreciate the sentiment too much."

Reg purchased the first records of his very own soon after: "Reet Petite" by Jackie Wilson, and "At the Hop" by Danny and the Juniors. Though impressed with her son's progressive musical taste, his mother's opinion would change the day he came home from the record shop brandishing a Little Richard platter entitled "The Girl Can't Help It."

"She liked rock, but not Little Richard," Elton said, "and I was really annoyed because it was my favorite record. I was really star-struck. Pop music was my whole life."

Reg entered Pinner County Grammar School in the fall of '58. From the start, the pudgy eleven-year-old found himself an outcast. "As a kid, I was always on the fringe of everything. I wasn't part of the gang. Going to the cinema with mates, I was always the last one to be asked. I was Fat Reg to start with."

"He had…an odd little walk, special to him," classmate Gay Search would later tell author Philip Norman in *Sir Elton*. "I remember him as being totally different from the general rabble of younger boys. He had an air of being far more grown-up, more civilized."

After school let out each day, Reg would spend the balance of his free time barricaded in his bedroom, with his *Dan Dare* comics and his ever-growing record collection. "I would buy records and file them," he said. "I could tell you who published what, and then I would just stack them in a pile and look at the labels." Like all his possessions, his precious vinyl occupied a place near to his heart. "I grew up with inanimate objects as my friends, and I still believe they have feelings. That's why I keep hold of all my possessions, because I'll remember when they gave me a bit of happiness—which is more than human beings have given me."

After performing a Mozart sonata and Chopin etude for the prestigious Royal Academy of Music admissions board, Reg was awarded a Junior Exhibitioners' Scholarship to Britain's senior musical conservatory later that fall. He soon found himself taking the tube to London every Saturday for course studies in musical composition and choir. Classes were arduous, running from nine a.m. to two p.m. without a break. "When I was at the Academy," he said, "I didn't particularly enjoy it that much except, as a pianist, you love to play Chopin, because it's just beautiful. [Though] I resented some of the classical music I had to play, like Bartok and stuff like that. I didn't know whether I was playing the right notes or the wrong notes."

Reg amazed his piano instructor, Helen Piena, one day early in his training. After she performed a four-page Handel prelude for him, he immediately played it back to her, just like a gramophone. "He just had a wonderful ear, but for all that he absolutely could *not* read a note of music," she said. "So that's what I taught him first. By the end of his studies with me, he could read as well as anyone."

Reg developed a crush on Piena, bringing her presents from family beach trips. "Such a sweet boy," she said. "He would always send [me] postcards from wherever he went off to on holiday. Just so incredibly thoughtful."

Under Piena's tutelage, Reg made his first public appearance three months into his formal training, with a performance of Groylez's *Les Petites Litanies de Dieu* at the Ruislip-Northwood Music Festival in Middlesex.

"Nerve-wracking," he said. "But it was a start."

As puberty sank its hairy fangs into Reg's delicate psyche, he found himself perplexed by his burgeoning sexual feelings. "At school I used to have crushes on people, but not really any sex at all, male or female," he said. "I never had any sex education when I was at school. Sex was never discussed....The first time I masturbated, I was in pain. I was so horrified. And my parents found out because I'd used up all my pajamas. And then I got ripped apart for doing it. Sex was completely frightening. At school everyone boasted about sex. Meanwhile, I was dying to be molested by someone…just to teach me, just to find out."

Stanley Dwight blamed his son's "confusion" on pop music, which he considered a corrupting influence. "My father didn't want me to get into music, and I could never understand that because he'd been a trumpeter in a band. I mean, he *did* influence me…he used to play me his George Shearing records."

Though Reg's appreciation of Shearing and other jazz greats would grow considerably over the years, his immediate musical worship was aimed more squarely in the direction of American artists like horn-rimmed rocker Buddy Holly, who toured the U.K. in March, '58. A starry-eyed Reg attended Holly's second show at the Gaumont State cinema in Kilburn, sitting in the dark recesses, utterly transfixed.

In an attempt to emulate the "Peggy Sue" singer—who would die in a plane crash months later at the age of twenty-two—Reg took to wearing his glasses constantly. "I only needed specs to see the blackboard, but I began wearing them all the time to be like Holly," he said. "As a result, I soon became genuinely nearsighted.…I looked terrible, a fatty with glasses and with a terrible inferiority complex."

In 1960, thirteen-year-old Reg formed his first group, the Corvettes, along with bassist Geoff Dyson, a local boy he'd met at the capacious church hall around the corner from his home. Dyson was immediately impressed with Reg's musical prowess. "He really *did* change when he was playing piano," he said. "When he got down on a piano and started to sing and play rock 'n' roll, he was quite remarkably transformed into someone else."

The duo joined forces with drummer Mick Inkpen and vocalist/guitarist Stu Brown, Reg's cousin's boyfriend. At first, Brown was doubtful that the heavyset Reg was capable of properly rocking. "I was very fat," Elton admitted years later, "and when I said I played the piano, [Stu] laughed helplessly. [But] I showed him. I did my Jerry Lee Lewis bit and he stopped laughing."

(Named after a vintage brand of British shaving soap,)the Corvettes practiced after school every day, rehearsing a repertoire comprised of songs by the Beatles, the Hollies and Cliff Richard. After six weeks of rehearsal they made their public debut, performing an hour-long set at a local Scout hut, for which they earned the collective sum of £2. "We had no amplifiers," Elton said. "It all faded out after a few months. It was just a pastime."

As the Corvettes dissolved, so too—finally—did Reg's parents' strained marriage. The inciting incident came with a severe electrical shock Stanley suffered while posted to Aden. During his three-month convalescence in a British hospital, Sheila refused to visit her husband even once. While he lay helplessly in a hospital bed, troubling rumors began reaching Stanley's ears that his wife was carrying on an affair with a man she'd first met during the war, a house painter named Fred Farebrother.

When he was well enough, Stanley paid a visit to Farebrother's council house in Carpender's Park.

Farebrother's wife answered the door.

"Where's your husband?" Stanley demanded.

"I wish I knew," she replied wistfully.

Frustrated, Stanley confronted his wife that night. After a screaming row, she tearfully admitted to her infidelity. Stanley filed for divorce the next day. Soon after, he would meet a thirty-three-year-old lab technician named Edna Clough. The two quickly married, and had four children in as many years. "My pride was really snipped, because he was supposed to hate kids," Elton said. "I guess I was just a mistake in the first place."

With the marriage's dissolution, Sheila and her son moved into a two-bedroom first-floor maisonette at 30A Frome Court, Northwood Hills, along with Fred Farebrother. The change of address would put Reg more closely into the orbit of Paul Robinson, a cousin who lived several streets down. Together, the boys spent endless hours discussing their favorite band: the Beatles. "He said they were the greatest thing there'd ever been," Robinson said. "We'd sit there with an album cover and he'd tell me which one was John, Paul, George and Ringo."

Besides possessing multiple posters of the lads from Liverpool—*de rigueur* for any self-respecting pop-loving child in early-'60s Britain—Reg's bedroom walls were also covered with countless glamor shots of bouffant-coiffed soul singer Dusty Springfield. Hers was, in fact, the first fan club he ever belonged to.

"She was my idol," he said. "Dusty had a desperate desire to be needed. I could relate."

As rock 'n' roll took over Reg's life, the staid Royal Academy began to exert less and less of a hold over him. "I used to go up to Baker Street," he said, "which was where the Academy is, sit on the Circle Line train, and go round and round on the Circle Line. Then [I'd] go home and tell my mom that I've been to school."

The genial Fred Farebrother, who had quickly become a surrogate father figure to the highly insecure Reg, agreed to help him try to obtain a weekend pianist job at the Northwood Hills Hotel, a musty, dark-paneled 1930's-style tavern and inn which sat across the street from the local tube station.

"[Fred] asked me if I needed a pianist, because his boy wanted to have a go," owner George Hill said. "I said, 'All right. I don't mind having a look at him.'"

Sixteen-year-old Reg appeared the next day looking like anything but an entertainer. Dressed in a tweed sports jacket, a faded old tie and grey flannel trousers, his hair cut unfashionably short, he sat nervously before a dusty upright perched in a bay window and performed a song he'd recently written himself, a bluesy rock ballad called "Come Back Baby." The Hills were impressed enough with the performance to offer Reg a job playing every Friday, Saturday and Sunday evening. Each night, Sheila and Fred— whom the spoonerism loving Reg insisted on calling Derf (Fred backwards)—kept a close eye on him from a cramped table in the corner. "He wouldn't go into the pub by himself," Sheila said. "So [we] used to have to go with him and just sit there all evening. It was dreadful."

Reg earned £1.10s per night—a hard-won wage, as the regulars proved to be, at least at first, decidedly underwhelmed by what the portly teen had to offer. Many nights, Northwood Hills would fill with drunked shouts of "Get out of here!" and "Turn the racket down, lad!" as dozens of empty crisp packets and tin ashtrays would be thrown Reg's way. More than once, a patron well into his cups would sneak up and unplug the leads of his PA system, or dump a pint of Guiness into his piano.

Yet with dogged persistence, Reg slowly won the patrons over. After several months, people started coming into Northwood Hills specifically to hear him play. Soon enough, the bar was packed out every weekend. "It was great training," Elton said, "because I played on an old upright piano that was out-of-tune, and there were a couple of times when I had to dive out of the window when really bad fights broke out." Reg quickly learned how to placate the drunken crowd's unruly behavior through an earnest mishmash of Jim Reeves songs, Al Jolson's "Mammy," and pub house standards like "Roll Out the Barrel" and "When Irish Eyes Are Smiling."

"You *had* to play 'When Irish Eyes Are Smiling' or you'd get a pint of beer slung over you."

Derf would pass an old Punch cigar box around at the end of each evening's performance. With the tips he collected, Reg was soon earning £35 each weekend—a not-insignificant sum, given that the average weekly British salary at the time was only £12.

The young pianist saved up his money to buy a £200 Hohner Pianette electric piano and amplifier. Given his steely work ethic, money for the instrument accumulated quickly.

"During that whole period," he said, "I don't think I ever missed a gig."

On October 19, 1962, Reg saw Little Richard headline a show at the Kingston Gramade. The fifteen-year-old found himself spellbound by the flamboyant star's unrestrained theatrics. "When I saw Little Richard standing on top of the piano, all lights, sequins and energy, I decided there and then that I was going to be a rock 'n' roll piano player. Little Richard was the king for me."

Reg also got to see Jerry Lee Lewis perform several weeks later. Lewis would prove to be another colossal influence on the teenager. "This was the first time I heard someone beat the shit out of a piano," Elton said, impressed by rock 'n' roll's first great wild man. "He got me excited."

When not busy performing, going to school, or soaking up his piano-thumping idols, Reg spent what little free time he had with a twenty-year-old gypsy girl named Nellie, whom he'd met at the pub after one of his sets. "She had long blonde hair," he said. "Dyed, I think. She lived in a caravan that got moved on by the police every few weeks. When I went there, it was, 'Turn left at the third field in Southall.' The caravan was the cleanest thing I have ever seen in my life. Her parents were great. Nellie was twenty, much older than I was. People have got the wrong idea about gypsies. She was fantastic, with a great sense of humor."

Their relationship, such as it was, only lasted but a couple short months, ultimately ending the day Nellie and her caravan suddenly disappeared from sight, never to return.

Nonplussed by the whole affair, Reg accompanied his cousin Paul to London to see a schoolboy's exhibition. Bored with the display, Reg suggested they sneak off to see one of the Christmas shows that the Beatles were giving at the Hammersmith Odeon. The show had a major impact on both boys. The mop-topped pop sensations not only impressed them musically—they also seemed relatable in a way that other famous performers of the time simply were not. "Seeing the Beatles was kind of like seeing God, in a way," Elton said. "Just actually seeing them live and being in their presence. Police in the street. It was just chaos everywhere they went....Before the Beatles, pop music in England was sort of an isolated thing. It was for older people. But the Beatles were like the boys next door. We all wanted to be like them."

Though the Corvettes had long-since disbanded, Reg, Geoff Dyson, Mick Inkpen and Stu Brown reteamed in the summer of '64 to create a new unit called Bluesology. Named as an homage to three-fingered gypsy guitarist Django Reinhardt's seminal 1949 LP, *Djangology*, Bluesology was a soul band which eschewed Top 40 covers in favor of extended jams on relatively obscure songs by the likes of Mose Allison and Muddy Waters.

The band practiced every Saturday, alternating between a small reception hall at Northwood Hills and a storage room in the back of St. Edmunds's Church.

"[Reg] had an enormous personality even then," Inkpen later said. "He was an amusing bloke, and he could play the piano like nobody's business." It seemed to his band mates, in fact, that Reg could do whatever he set his mind to. "He could sit down with a stack of music and work his way through it. He could play rock 'n' roll, boogie-woogie, jazz, you name it. We couldn't have done what we did without him, really. Because of his musical knowledge, he was the only person to knit it all together."

A mere two months into their existence, Bluesology secured their first steady gig, a weekly slot at London's trendy Establishment Club. "We thought we were a cut above the local sort of groups that were playing 'Apache' and things like that still," Elton later told the BBC's Andy Peebles. "We played Jimmy Witherspoon numbers like 'Times Are Getting Tougher Than Tough' and 'When the Lights Go Out.' It didn't give us a particularly big audience, but it did wonders to our own egos, because nobody else did them."

Long out of the house, Stanley Dwight remained very much concerned with his son's questionable future. "Reggie must get all this pop nonsense out of his head," he wrote to Sheila when Reg was sixteen. "Otherwise he's going to turn into a wide-boy. He should get a sensible job with either British European Airways or Barclays Bank."

Reg was hardly surprised by the umbrage his father took. "He didn't approve of me doing what I did at all," he said.

"It made me very determined to be successful at what I was going to do, and [it] made music my life."

With Bluesology absorbing nearly all of his time, Reg decided to end his studies at the Royal Academy, much to the disappointment of his teachers. "There was so much music inside of him [that] I just couldn't bring out," Helen Piena said. "I prided myself on being able to bring out whatever gift was inside my students, but try as I might, I couldn't do it with Reg. It was the wrong kind of music. I couldn't reach him like I wanted." (Years later, after Reg had become world-famous as Elton John, a student would give Piena a tape of her star pupil's album, *Honky Château*. But she never listened to it. "I wanted to," she said. "But I just couldn't face it.")

For his part, Reg was relieved to be done with the strictures of classical training. Even so, he'd later reflect on how fortunate he was to have had the experience, as it allowed him to appreciate a wider range of music than he otherwise might have. "It also helps you as a writer, because—as a keyboard player—you tend to write with more chords than a guitar, and I think that has a lot to do with my piano playing and my love of Chopin, Bach, Mozart, and my love of singing in a choir. I think my songs have more of a classic leaning to them than other artists who haven't had that classical background, and I'm grateful for that."

Two weeks before Reg's final pre-university A-Level exams in English and Music at Pinner County Grammar School, cousin Roy Dwight told him that he knew of someone at Mills Music, a West End music publisher on Denmark Street, who was looking for a tea-boy. Though the position was not much more than that of a goffer, it immediately appealed to Reg, who saw it as a valuable inroad into the music business he so worshipped. As Roy enjoyed a certain level of local fame, having scored the first goal for the Nottingham Forest football club at Wembley Stadium in the '59 FA Cup Final, he was able to leverage his celebrity to secure an interview for Reg with office manager Pat Sherlock. "I can see him now, sitting in my office," Sherlock said. "I remember thinking what small hands he had for a piano player. He had this nervous mannerism of pushing his glasses back up his nose. And a funny little pouting look."

With Roy's endorsement, his cousin landed the job at £5 a week. Reg promptly dropped out of school. "I was probably a good enough scholar to go to university," he said, "but I never tried more than thirty percent. I was always into pop music or football, and I just squeezed through my exams. I was very lazy."

Reg attended class for the final time on March 5, 1965. History teacher Bill Johnson was flabbergasted at his decision to abandon his studies. "When you're forty," he told the boy, "you'll either be some sort of glorified office-boy or you'll be a millionaire."

With his formal education behind him, Reg spent his days at Mills Music running menial errands—posting the mail, making tea for the office, and delivering sheet music to nearby publishers.

"I'd work in the packing department," he said, "wrapping up the parcels and taking them on a wheelbarrow to the post office in Kingsway near the Oasis swimming pool." It was, admittedly, a low rung on the ladder, yet a rung nonetheless. "It was what I wanted. That was a very happy time."

That April, Reg made friends with Caleb Quaye, a messenger boy from Paxton's, a music delivery company

34

headquartered on Old Compton Street. Caleb was a handsome and genial teen, as well as a talented guitarist. (Decades later, when asked by TV host David Letterman, "So what's it like to be the best guitarist in the world?" Eric Clapton would reply, "I'm not. Caleb Quaye is.") Caleb was also an unsparing mocker who never missed an opportunity to tease Reg. "I just used to laugh at him," he said, "because he looked so much like [comic book character] Billy Bunter. Li'l Bunter."

"Caleb Quaye…used to take the piss out of me because he was a runner for another office," Elton later told *Melody Maker*'s Richard Williams. "I told him I was in a group and he'd stand there and laugh at me. I really hated him."

Despite the merciless teasing, Reg and Caleb became buddies. "He and I would hook up and spend a lot time and all our spare change going round record stores and listening to records and stuff," Caleb said. "He'd go round my house, I'd come round his house. He used to tell his mother, 'The reason Caleb is my best friend is because we like the same kind of music.' We used to scour the record stores; every last penny we had was spent buying records. We spent hours listening to music, just getting inspired. We were teenagers that dreamed together. We learned our craft together."

One rainy spring afternoon at Caleb's house, Reg watched in astonishment as his friend pounded out chords on an upright piano that sat in the parlor. "Reg had been a student at the Royal Academy of Music in London, and that's a very strict classical format, that was his training," Caleb said. "And classical players tend to use all ten fingers. And, especially when you adapt that technique to rock or jazz playing, the chords tend to sound rather dense. But I grew up with a jazz background—my dad was a jazz player—and the philosophy of that technique was 'less is more'. There was a technique of using only three notes to get the chord to sound really fat—you don't have to use all ten fingers. So one day Reg came over to my house and I played something on the piano, and he was amazed. '*How* did you get that big sound?' So I showed him what my dad showed me, just using three fingers and spreading the notes out— basically playing an octave bass line in the left hand and a three-note chord position in the right hand—and that's how you got this big sound. A rich, full sound. Reg was amazed at that. And that was the beginning of him starting to intensely change his sound from the classical training that he'd received. And it started in the living room in my house."

The technique would, in great part, help Bluesology gain a reputation as a solid blues ensemble, although in their hard-nosed attempt to appeal to minority tastes, they found they were always playing the wrong material. "We were either two months too late, or three years too early."

Even so, local businessman Arnold Tendler—who saw the group performing at a church hall in late April— immediately recognized the band's potential. "I was really bowled over," Tendler said. "At the piano there was this little roly-poly boy in clothes even *I* called square. But when he played, he was marvelous. Even then, he used to kick away the piano stool and play sitting on the floor."

Tendler signed on as Bluesology's manager, bringing a much-needed dose of discipline to the band. The businessman regimented their rehearsals and bought them proper uniforms consisting of maroon sport shirts, blue-and-white-striped dinner jackets and dark blue slacks. He even agreed to bankroll a demo recording of a potential single. With little original material to choose from, "Come Back Baby"—Reg's sole composition to date—got the nod.

"Reg wasn't a prolific writer at that time," Stu Brown later told journalist George Matlock. "It was his song, and his style completely, even though we didn't know what his style was back then,"

The recording session was held on May 13 at disc jockey Jack Johnson's four-track studio in Rickmansworth. The band ran through "Come Back Baby" twice, then committed it to recording tape. As the key proved too high for Stu Brown's voice, Reg was tasked with handling lead vocal duties. The eighteen-year-old gladly complied.

first single!

An acetate of the demo was sent to Fontana's A&R Director, Jack Baverstock, who promptly offered the band a limited recording contract. Excited at the prospect of having an honest-to-God record released, Bluesology headed into Philips Studios on June 3 and attempted to record a more polished version of the song. The band laid the song down four times, but each take was marred by an inability to properly mic Reg's piano, the song's lead instrument. Frustrated, Baverstock decided to use the original demo as the single instead.

"Come Back Baby" was released on July 23, 1965. Backed with a cover of Jimmy Witherspoon's classic blues number, "Time's Getting Tougher Than Tough," the single's chances for success seemed dubious at best, as it battled for precious radio airtime against such heavy hitters as the Rolling Stones' "Satisfaction," the Yardbirds' "For Your Love," and the Byrds' "Mr. Tambourine Man." Still, the members of Bluesology were thrilled to have any kind of official release at all. The first time Reg heard his song blaring out of a radio—during Jack Jackson's *Sunday Night Record Programme*—he was beside himself with joy. "I can remember sitting in the car and hearing the record being played on Radio Luxembourg and saying, 'Hey, that's *me* singing, folks!' I was really chuffed, because that was the very first time that I'd really sung anything."

Not surprisingly, the modest single sank without a trace—but not before Reg managed to sell the publishing rights to Mills Music for £500. The enterprising teenager then used those funds to trade in his Hohner Pianette for a transistor-based Vox AC 30 amplifier and Vox Continental organ. An archaic beast with reverse-colored keys and a metallic orange casing, the Vox quickly proved problematic for the Luddite keyboardist. Instead of taking advantage of the myriad sound settings available to him, Reg inevitably left the instrument's multiple levers stuck in the same position continuously, no matter the specific requirements of whichever song was being performed.

Worse still, the middle-C key often got stuck during performances. During one gig at the Scotch of St. James, Reg's Vox got jammed up particularly badly. Helpless to fix it, the drunken crowd was soon laughing heartlessly at his embarrassing plight.

"Hold on, mate," a thickly accented voice called out from the smoky dark. A moment later, Alan Price, keyboardist for the Animals, clomped onto stage, winked at Reg, and gave the undercarriage of the organ a mighty punch.

"I have never seen Reg look so shocked," Mick Inkpen said. "But it pleased the audience no end."

A week hence, Bluesology joined hundreds of other hopeful groups to play a "Battle of the Bands" at the Kilburn State Cinema, an enormous venue modeled after the Empire State Building which sat desolutely beneath the gray crowds of north London. The band the battle having recently gone through a lineup shift, with bassist Rex Bishop having replaced Geoff Dyson, who'd left to join a rival group called the Mockingbirds. The group also welcomed the addition of a new brass section, which consisted of trumpeter Pat Higgs and tenor saxophonist Dave Murphy.

Though Bluesology failed to place in the top three spots that afternoon, a representative from the Roy Tempest Agency was stimulated enough by their set to offer them a contract to back fading American soul acts as they traveled across Britain for two-week-long club date tours.

Exhilarated at the prospect of being a professional musician ("I simply couldn't dream of anything better!"), and with the heady prospect of earning a guaranteed £20 a week, Reg promptly tendered his resignation at Mills Music.

Bluesology's first assignment was to back soul great Wilson Pickett, who had recently scored a Top 20 hit with "In the Midnight Hour," on his upcoming U.K. tour.

"You can imagine how we felt," Elton said. "[Pickett] was such an important figure in the music we were playing, and here we were about to tour as his band." But things didn't go quite as planned. At their one and only rehearsal, Pickett's guitarist decided that he didn't care for Bluesology's drummer. "He didn't particularly like the rest of us either," Elton said.

Pickett ended up tearing Bluesology's contract to shreds.

"We were very brought down," Elton admitted.

Things went considerably better with Major Lance, a Chicago-based R&B singer who'd enjoyed several moderate hits including "The Monkey Time," "The Bird" and "Um, Um, Um, Um, Um, Um." Still feeling the sting of Pickett's rebuke, Bluesology rehearsed comprehensively before their first meeting with the physically imposing Lance. "We learnt every song he'd ever made," Elton said, "to the point where he didn't even feel the need to go through the songs more than one time....Backing Major Lance was probably the biggest thing that had ever happened to me."

After a successful tour which ended at Count Suckle's Cue Club on Praed Street, Paddington, Bluesology soon found themselves backing a succession of artists, including the Ink Spots, the Exciters, Lee Dorsey, the Original Drifters and Doris Tory. Their most memorable outing, however, came when they paired up with Patti LaBelle and the Bluebelles, a vocal group which included future Supreme Cindy Birdsong. The group was riding a wave of popularity at the time, having recently hit the charts with the Top 20 R&B hit "I Sold My Heart to the Junkman."

LaBelle's group rehearsed with Bluesology for a single rainy afternoon at the Marquee Club on Wardour Street, before tramping over to the Scotch of St. James in Mayfair for their premiere gig together. The audience was packed with a host of luminaries that night, including George Harrison, Pete Townshend, Eric Burdon, Brian Jones and Keith Richards. Unfortunately for all involved, the club's faulty stage lights cut out two songs into the set, forcing Bluesology to play in near darkness. Still, the show went down well, thanks largely to Reg's efforts. "He was a little chubby guy with glasses," Bluebelle Sarah Dash later recalled to author Mark Bego. "He was a delight. He was upbeat and he was just a delightful kid....I don't remember how good the band was, but we always remember how well he played. I remember him as being the one in the band who could pull it together."

"I didn't think [Reg] was better than we were, but he was," Patti LaBelle said. "He could play keyboards like no other white boy I have ever heard."

The band followed the Bluebelles over to their hotel room after the gig, got drunk on cheap scotch and played a Rummy-like card game called Tonk well into the wee hours. "For some reason," LaBelle said, "[Reg] thought he could play cards like he played that piano, and he wouldn't give up until I had won what little money he had. 'Come on, Patti,' he would say in his cute British accent. 'One more game of Tonk and I will win back all my pounds.' Of course, the only thing he ever won was my sympathy. I might have sent him home with an empty pocket, but I never let him leave with an empty stomach."

Life on the road for Bluesology was proving to be a grueling and less-than-glamorous grind, one that often required playing multiple shows in a single twenty-four-hour period. "Sometimes we did four gigs in one day, with someone like Billy Stewart," Elton said, referring to the portly R&B singer whose modest hits included "Sitting in the Park" and "I Do Love You." "We did the U.S. Serviceman's Club at Douglas House, Lancaster Gate, at around four in the afternoon. Then we did the Ritz and the Plaza Ballroom in Birmingham, and then we finished off by playing the Cue Club in Paddington at around six in the morning. If playing four gigs wasn't bad enough, we had to load up, unload and set up our own equipment at each gig....We used to really work our asses off."

Reg did his best to keep his band mates laughing during their endless musical marathons, with spot-on imitations of various *Goon Show* characters made famous by Spike Milligan and a pre-*Pink Panther* Peter Sellers. They were, for the most part, happy days. "I can't ever remember being miserable," he said, "even though when the van breaks down when you're on the road from Skegness to Boston at three-thirty in the morning and it's snowing, it isn't particularly cheerful. [But] I don't have any bad memories of it at all."

Bluesology released a second single on the Fontana label in February, 1966. Entitled "Mr. Frantic," and backed with a cover of B.B. King's "Everyday (I Get the Blues)," the disc—like its predecessor—was also written and sung by Reg. Unfortunately for the group, the muddled, double-tracked drums and uninspired lyrics guaranteed that "Mr. Frantic" would duplicate the failure of "Come Back Baby," making no appreciable impression upon the record-buying public.

"It was painfully obvious that though I could write a good melody, I wasn't really a words man," Elton later noted. "I never had the confidence to write down my feelings, because my feelings have never come to the surface that much. They've always been suppressed."

With the single's failure, Bluesology decided to leave the Roy Tempest Agency and sign instead with Marquee Enterprises. This move led to a string of elite gigs as the band suddenly found itself playing alongside the likes of Manfred Mann and the Who. "We did a gig with [the Who] on Brighton Pier," Rex Bishop said. "They smashed the place up, did the lights in and everything. Then we went on and we were tame in comparison. We were also on the same bill as Georgie Fame and Spencer Davis. I was just proud that our band was on the same stage as them. But when you heard a band like the Spencer Davis Group at the Flamingo, you knew they were streets ahead of you." Interestingly, Elton would later audition for the iconic Spencer Davis Group after Steve Winwood left the group, but would be summarily turned down in favor of Phil Sawyer. "Reggie *did* audition to be a member, but he didn't get the job," Spencer Davis said. "There was no reason [why], it just didn't materialize. It fizzled out of its own accord. It wasn't a slight on him or anything like that. I was looking for an image, if you like. At the time, who would have thought that a balding, bespectacled guy—and a great piano player—would morph into this huge star?"

Managing to land a series of gigs at the Cavern Club, famed birthplace of the Beatles, Bluesology felt like they had well and truly arrived. Reg, however, was unilaterally unimpressed. "It was definitely one of the worst places for getting your gear nicked," he said. "[It was] so bad, we had to keep someone posted all the time. And the overflow from the men's toilets was disgusting."

Reg seemed negatively affected by such inconveniences, which his band mates routinely shrugged off. Indeed, his temperament was markedly different—so much so, in fact, that he soon found himself an outcast in the group he'd help found. His reluctance to indulge in the same vices as the others didn't help endear him to them. There was little alcohol for Reg. No cigarettes, no drugs, and no girls. "If nothing was happening, he'd just go to sleep," Pat Higgs said. "He had a special little pillow that he used to carry round with him."

Like many bands before them, Bluesology would further attempt to emulate the Beatles' road to success by playing a month-long residency at the Top Ten Club in Hamburg. The nights were grueling—performing from seven p.m. till two in the morning, exchanging hour-long sets with another British group called the Sinners. Not having enough material to fill the required timeslot, Bluesology often jammed on extended twenty-five-minute blues improvisations, while Reg made up rude lyrics which sailed harmlessly over the heads of the German crowds.

Between sets, Reg became friends with the Sinners' lead guitarist, Pete Bellotte. In their down time, they'd often grab a bite to eat, or dance drunkenly amongst the traffic that ripped past them on the Reeperbahn.

"You've got a touch," Bellotte told him one night. "You're a great player. We should do something together sometime."

"Maybe so," Reg answered offhandedly, thinking nothing more of it.

Back on home soil that April, Bluesology played clubs like the Ricky Tick in Windsor and the Mojo Club in Sheffield. At Manchester's Twisted Wheel, they performed alongside John Mayall, sharing the stage with a baby-faced Eric Clapton. Between sets, Clapton showed Stu Brown how to use a light-gauge banjo string on his guitar, enabling him to bend notes much farther across the frets; it was a trick Brown would turn to often in the future.

During a gig at the Whisky A Go-Go, bassist Rex Bishop unexpectedly quit Bluesology. Two days later, he was replaced by the imminently more dexterous Freddy Gandy, late of Twink and the Pink Fairies. This wasn't the only lineup change the band would see—cofounding member Mick Inkpen would get ousted soon after at the behest of Patti LaBelle, who was lining up a second tour of the U.K. "You would have thought that the other members of the band, including Reg, would have stuck by me and refused to tour," a crestfallen Inkpen said. "But apparently the tour was more important."

With new drummer Paul Gale installed, the band's sophomore outing with Patti LaBelle and the Bluebelles went swimmingly. After its conclusion, Bluesology headed to Balloch, Scotland, where the youth culture seemed virulently divided between Mods and Rockers, perhaps even more so than in England proper. "We'd arrive and say, 'Why's the stage ten feet tall?'" Elton recalled. "And they'd say, 'So that the fucking people can't get to the band.' You'd see that there would be two sides to the audience. Everyone would be in two halves and you'd just wait for the fight to break out."

Violence of another sort followed Bluesology to St. Tropez, where they were scheduled to play a trio of gigs at the Papagayo Club, one of Brigitte Bardot's infamous haunts. Their dates were threatened, however, when Reg electrocuted himself on the bare wiring from a chandelier in a crumbling villa outside St. Tropez.

"I remember there was a sudden yelp and Reg was spark out," Freddy Gandy later told author Keith Hayward. A doctor was called, and a hypodermic to the derrier brought Reg around. "He recovered from the ordeal so remarkably well, even *we* were surprised," Gandy said. "The gigs we were booked to do continued with him in good form, like nothing had happened."

After a long hot summer gigging endlessly around the British Isles, Bluesology released a third single—the Kenny Lynch-produced "Since I Found You Baby," which marked Stu Brown's vinyl debut as lead singer. When the disc flopped, talks of disbanding arose. But fate took a hand in the form of twenty-five-year-old brandy-breathed soul singer Long John Baldry, who caught their act at the Cromwellian Club in South Kensington—a smoky, patchouli-scented sweatbox—and decided that they were exactly what he'd been looking for.

The six-foot-seven, immaculately dressed Baldry was something of a local legend, having featured in Alexis Korner's Blues Incorporated. Baldry had made his bones performing alongside the likes of Mick Jagger, a pre-Zeppelin Jimmy Page, and—from his short-lived band, Steampacket—a teenage Rod Stewart, whom Baldry had discovered busking on a Twickenham railway station platform.

"[Baldry] really was a fantastic blues guitarist, just him on his own, singing Leadbelly stuff," Elton said. "He was definitely a pioneer, and at the forefront of British blues music." As for his sexuality, the openly gay Baldry seemed like an exotic creature to Bluesology's organist. "I cannot believe I never realized that he was gay. I mean, I didn't realize *I* was gay at the time, but—looking back on it now—John couldn't have been any more gay if he tried. It [just] wasn't on my radar at that time."

"[Baldry] was very elegant and incredibly flamboyant, combined with this highly acute sense of humor," Eric Clapton said. "There was a darkness to him, too, that I didn't really want to know very well. I could just sense that the guy was troubled, you know?"

Baldry offered to pay Bluesology a weekly retainer to be his regular backing band. The musicians held a vote, and—feeling it a step in the right direction—unanimously accepted his offer.

Baldry got on well with his new band mates—especially with Reg, whom he found endearing. "He was taking pills to get thin," the bluesman said, "and though they worked, they also tended to make him aggressive and short-tempered. He shouted a lot, which I found amusing." Yet even with his quirks of personality, the towering Baldry had to admire the all-or-nothing manner in which Reg threw himself into performing. "A great show would make him joyous. But if anyone flubbed up or played out-of-tune, he would blow up. Music was the most precious thing to him."

One of Baldry's first decrees as Bluesology's leader was to expand the unit to a nine-piece ensemble. Only Reg, Stu Brown and Freddy Gandy agreed to this, however. Thus the rest of the band left, to be replaced by guitarist Neil Hubbard and Chevelles' drummer Pete Gavin.

"Bluesology was entirely Reg's baby at the outset," Gavin said. "He was the band leader. But then Long John

Baldry took the front line and it was a little bit odd. Reggie didn't like the way it was going by then."

Baldry then brought in soul singers Alan Walker and Marsha Hunt, to help emulate Steampacket's triple lead vocalist format. "She gave an audition down the old Studio 51 Club and she did an unaccompanied version of 'Love is a Many-Splendored Thing'," Elton said. "And she was really awful. Baldry said, 'Marvelous dear, we'll have you.' As far as Baldry was concerned, just as long as she was black and could sing relatively well, that was what he wanted. And it worked out great. She looked good and got the blokes in the audience going." (Hunt would soon go on to much bigger things, starring in the tribal hippie musical *Hair* as well as becoming the Rolling Stone's inspiration for "Brown Sugar." She would then gain further rock 'n' roll immortality when she became pregnant with Mick Jagger's first child, Karis.)

Baldry finalized his new lineup with the addition of ex-Sidewinder cornetist Marc Charig, as well as a tenor saxophonist who went by the unlikely name of Elton Dean. Dean noticed at once that Reg was a frustrated singer. "His problem was that we already had three regular singers. I never even knew he sang until I heard him do a number one day at a soundcheck. Then I thought he sounded great. Just like José Feliciano." (In time, Feliciano himself would become a fan of Elton's work. "I enjoyed his music very much," the singer reflected decades later. "Everybody told me they thought Elton sounded like me, but I really didn't hear it. Either way, simply put: I believe that Elton John will be remembered as one of the greatest performers of our era.")

That December, the new-look Bluesology was booked by Brian Epstein to play third on the bill to Little Richard at London's Saville Theatre. Reg was ecstatic to be playing with one of his idols. The gig would prove to be the first of many in support of Baldry. "We just did mediocre things," Elton later admitted. "We never starved, but it was such a mundane experience." The setup at least provided the frustrated keyboardist with a modicum of spiritual comfort, as Baldry became something of a mentor figure. Wherever Baldry went, Reg was sure to follow.

"It was really a matter of 'monkey see, monkey do'," Baldry said. "It was actually quite flattering."

On nights when the band had no shows scheduled, Reg would follow Baldry to Mike McGrath's apartment in Earls Court. McGrath, a photographer of some renown for *Rave* magazine, was a lightning rod for London's artistic underground community. "Reg had this enormous inferiority complex and he weighed two stones heavier than he was when he came to fame," McGrath said. "Reg would sit next to Baldry, lost inside his duffel coat, and not speak a single word all night long. I can't honestly remember one line that Elton ever came up with in this room, because he was just so inhibited."

In an attempt to shake off his natural reserve, Reg did what he could to better fit in with the fashionably hip artistic set, who always seemed to be decked out in the latest psychedelic, Carnaby-esque fashions of the day. Alas, no amount of flared collars or tie-dyed shirts could hide his stout figure.

"Reg was quite porky," Baldry mused. "In a caftan, he looks like a myopic nun."

His sartorial ineloquence seemed to only add fuel to his darker moods. "Reggie was prone to fits of pique," Pete Gavin said. "If something pushed his buttons, he'd just fly

tantrums
rage

off the handle. I have this one image of him just literally laying on his back on the floor, screaming and kicking his heels and bashing his elbows on the ground. He'd just come totally unglued, absolutely and completely unglued. Which was part of him. Otherwise, he was very quiet. And very kind. I remember one time when he showed up, [Bluesology] were going away for a few days and he showed up with this really nice suitcase. And I admired it and said, 'That's really nice, Reg.' And he said, 'Yeah, it was a fiver in a shop up the road.' And nothing much more was said. But a few days later we picked him up for another gig, and he'd gone somewhere and had bought me a similar suitcase and just gave it to me on the spot. I thought that was a very kind gesture. So that was Reggie. He really did have a heart of gold, but at the same time a pretty short fuse. That was just his nature."

Reg was on tour with Bluesology in Newcastle when an advertisement in the June 17 issue of *New Musical Express (NME)* caught the restless journeyman's eye. Wedged between an article on the Small Faces and a review of James Bond soundtrack discs sat an unassuming ad which featured the Statue of Liberty. Below that, the copy read:

Liberty Wants Talent—Artistes/Composers/
Singer-Musicians To Form New Group.

"I thought, 'Hello—they've put an advert in," Elton said, "and I shall answer it immediately.'"

He wrote Liberty a letter that same afternoon. Days later, it landed on the desk of Ray Williams, drafter of the *NME* ad and the label's twenty-year-old talent scout.

"When Reg wrote me, he said that he'd been in Bluesology," Ray said, "which I'd seen at the Marquee a few times. He said he was the keyboard player, so I had an image of him. So in short I said, 'Come in and say hello.'"

Reg arrived at Ray's office on Albemarle Street looking dumpy and forlorn, all of his possessions gathered together in a carrier bag.

"Immediately you noticed he didn't have your normal rock 'n' roll star potential," Ray said. "He was fairly shy, polite, so different to how he became. He said, 'I feel lost, I don't know what to do.' Basically, he was frustrated that Long John Baldry wouldn't allow him to do very much as far as singing, and that was part of the big frustration at the time. But he was an absolute enthusiast about music, and very knowledgeable about all music."

Reg informed Ray that, while he could compose melodies with ease, he was hopeless when it came to writing lyrics. Furthermore, he knew that he could be a proper vocalist if given the chance. Intrigued, Williams asked Reg to perform a few songs at the console piano which sat in his office. "He got up and sang a few songs," Ray said, "and I just thought, 'That's great.' But it wasn't obviously the sort of thing we were looking for as a label. But his voice stood out, there was something special in it—it was really warm, the kind of voice that would translate well onto record—and he obviously had ability as a keyboard player."

Williams was sufficiently impressed to book Reg into Regent Sound Studios on Denmark Street to record five songs as a vocal test. "As I never sang in the band," Elton said, "the only songs I could remember were the ones I used to sing in the public bar of the Northwood Hills Hotel. So I did some Jim Reeves material: 'I Love You Because', 'I Won't Forget You', 'He'll Have to Go'. I even sang 'Mammy'."

The acetate from the session was played for Liberty's A&R Director, Bob Reisdorf. "Bob had owned his own label, Dolton Records," Ray said, "plus he produced the enormously successful Ventures and the Fleetwoods, so he had a strong view on stuff, but he didn't really see that Reg had the talent. He didn't see it at all."

Reg was hardly surprised that Reisdorf passed on him. "I hadn't sung in years and I was awful," he confessed. "They turned me down and I don't blame them."

On the way out the door, Williams handed the dejected musician an envelope full of lyrics which had been sent in by a seventeen-year-old chicken farmer from Lincolnshire. "Basically I had a letter from this little chap called Bernie Taupin," Ray said. "And he said, 'I'm really a poet, but I think my lyrics could be set to music.' And I knew Reg said he could do music but he can't write lyrics, so a bell went off in my head: 'Let's introduce Bernie to Reg. Let's see if he could set his words to music.' If nothing else, Reg could at least say he'd tried."

Reg took Bernie's lyrics home and looked them over. They featured such mystically esoteric titles as "Smokestack Children" and "Mr. Lightning Strikerman." "I was quite impressed," he said. "[Though] I'd have been impressed by anything." In the span of only a few short hours, he'd set all fourteen lyrics to music. "They were very naïve lyrics and they were very naïve melodies. But there was a chemistry there, and I enjoyed doing it."

Bernie's later assessment of his own early work was hardly any less forgiving. "Pseudo-intellectual pre-Flower-Power trash," he said. "Before I started with Reg I'd always thought of myself as a poet, and I found it hard to write lyrics. The first stuff I ever wrote was dreadful. I mean, really disgusting, pre-*Sgt. Pepper* things about 'freaked-out teddy bears.' I'd never experienced anything, I was just a hick who thought if I wanted to make the big time I had to have freak-out lyrics. I mean, I was coming up with all of these acid-trip things, which I really had no right in writing because at the time I didn't have a clue what acid even *looked* like. What can I say? I was young and stupid."

An astute assessment, perhaps, yet Reg didn't care. "I just found my niche. I was very good at putting music around written words."

Ray Williams further assisted Reg by bringing him into the orbit of songwriters Nicky James and Kirk Duncan. "I wanted to find him some help, because I actually loved his voice," the talent scout said. "So I introduced him to Nicky and Kirk, two songwriters I was trying to help around the same time. We knew Graham Nash of the Hollies very well, so we formed a little association with Graham Nash, with Nicky and Kirk, called Niraki, which was basically Nicky, Ray and Kirk, the first two letters of each of our names. And everything started to evolve from there."

Under Gralto's auspices, Niraki existed as an independent publishing subsidiary of Dick James Music (DJM). Owned by the Beatles' publisher, Dick James—who had cofounded Northern Songs along with Brian Epstein—DJM was hallowed ground for any struggling songwriter. Reg quickly learned that one of the more immediate perks of being affiliated with Niraki was the access it provided him to DJM's in-house studio, in which he could create demos of the many new songs he suddenly found himself composing.

As fate would have it, the lead engineer and studio manager of the DJM studio was someone Reg was already well-acquainted with—his old friend from his Mills Music days, Caleb Quaye. "One day, this guy, Ray Williams...brings in this new singer-songwriter guy, Reg Dwight," Caleb recalled years later in the documentary film *A Voice Louder Than Rock.* "By this time, Reg has grown his hair longer…and he's looking a bit more hip, so I didn't actually recognize him, first of all. And he stood there in the studio kind of hunched over the piano, and I come in and I'm setting up the mics and everything to record these demos…and I can see him kind of [hiding his face in his hands], going, 'Oh no, it's *him*. Oh no'. And I suddenly went, 'Wait a minute—don't I know you?'" Caleb came away from the session more than impressed with Reg's talent. "It was so obvious [he had] got something special. Every day, a little bit more of it would come out." Caleb thus began working with Reg on a regular basis. "It was an exciting time," he said. "We were all like stable mates, there was a big community factor going. We were all friends, and we were all dipping in and out of each other's work. We were all trying to help each other." He chuckled. "All of us spent so much time at that tiny DJM studio that we'd refer to it as 'The Gaff'."

Throughout the late summer and fall of 1967, Reg would make prodigious use DJM's basement studio, where a battered Studer four-track recorder and an ancient MCI mixing board lay in a tiny white-tiled room. Securing the talents of drummer Dave Hinds and future Troggs bassist Tony Murray, Reg recorded several songs he'd written with Nicky and James—prosaic fare such as "Where It's At" and "Who's Gonna Love You"—as well as solo compositions like "Witch's House" and "I Get a Little Bit Lonely."

Reg picked up extra money over the summer by filling in for keyboardist Eric Hines, as Simon Dupree and the Big Sound toured Scotland. Consisting of Derek Shulman and his two brothers Ray and Phil, the popular psychedelic pop band was a precursor to Gentle Giant. "We didn't know Reg before this, he was sent to us through an agency," bassist Peter O'Flaherty later recalled. "We had one afternoon practice, he made a few notes, and that was it, he knew our program. He was very talented and easy to get along with....He was paid £25 a week for this tour."

After three nights in Glasgow, the band drove off to Brodick Island of Arran for several gigs. "We stayed at a small hotel in Lamlash," O'Flaherty said. "During the day, on the hotel's rundown tennis court, we played knockabout tennis, or kicked a football around. Elton was a keen Watford fan even way back then."

The tour then took in nearly a dozen more cities, including Forte William, Inverness, Aberdeen and Edinburgh.

"When it was time for Elton to leave the band and Eric [to] return," O'Flaherty said, "Elton asked us and our manager if he could stay with us. We had all become good friends with Elton and would have preferred it if he had stayed, but our manager said we had to take Eric back. In retrospect, this was for the best—Reg Dwight may have never become Elton John."

Responding to Ray Williams' off-handed comment that he should "pop in" to discuss his lyrics when he next happened to be in Mayfair, Bernie Taupin arrived unannounced in London a month later, a battered cardboard suitcase in hand. "I just turned up on the doorstep looking like the Scarecrow from *The Wizard of Oz*," he said, "and I probably felt like it too." An astonished Ray Williams took the elfin lyricist to the DJM offices at 71-75 New Oxford Street, where Reg was in the middle of a demo session for the Hollies. While they recorded, the lyricist waited anxiously in the control room, nervously picking at the sleeve of a moth-eaten jacket.

"One day this young man shows up," Caleb said, "and he's wearing sunglasses and a jacket a size or two too small for him. Straight off the farm. Reg was playing keyboards on a session when they came in. I said, 'Is he supposed to be in here?'"

"I was almost thrown out several times because they didn't know why this little hick was there," Bernie said.

Finally, Reg appeared in the control room.

"Are you the lyricist?" he asked.

"I am," Bernie admitted meekly.

"Fantastic. Come on…"

Bernie followed Reg around the corner to the Lancaster Grill on Tottenham Court Road for a cup of coffee. They immediately hit it off, finding a natural affinity in their shared love of pop music. To Bernie, Reg seemed like a competent professional who was plugged into the heart of the music scene. To Reg, Bernie—who sported a small gold hoop in his right ear after having pierced it himself with an icepick the year before—looked almost angelic. "I just adored him, like a brother," the pianist said. "I was in love with him, but not in a physical way. He was the soulmate I'd been looking for all my life."

The two decided that afternoon to partner up and make a go of it.

"We were both swimming in deep water and basically trying to find something to hang on to," Bernie said. "And we found each other." Indeed, the fledgling lyricist was grateful for the opportunity a partnership with Reg represented, especially given his highly checkered work history. "I got thrown out of one job after another," he admitted. "I was insubordinate, the typical rebellious teenager. I did work as a printer, I worked in a factory…one of those horrible Northern factory-type machine rooms with very high sky-lifts, very dark and gloomy, and little men walking around asking for their sixpence a week to join the union. I worked as an apprentice. But they said you had to be an apprentice until you're twenty-one, and when you're only like fifteen or sixteen years old, it seemed like an entire lifetime. Fuck that."

From the beginning, Bernie's partnership with Reg had an air of the inevitable about it. The fact that his lyrics had even found their way into Reg's hands at all smacked of destiny. For after happening upon the *NME* ad, writing a letter and stuffing an envelope full of lyrics, Bernie had gotten cold feet and promptly stuck the whole thing on the mantelpiece behind an old clock. One day soon after, it had disappeared—Bernie's mother had posted it, thinking he'd forgotten to mail it.

"Her innocent gesture both saved and changed my life," the lyricist later reflected.

Bernie took a train 150 miles back to Owmby-by-Spital, the small East Midlands town from whence he came, and began mailing off lyrics to his new songwriting partner in earnest. Reg quickly set them to music, despite the chaotic form they often took. "Bernie's lyrics, if you saw them, they weren't iambic pentameter at its best," he said. "There'd just be 115 lines and I'd say, 'Where the fuck do I start?' But it didn't seem that difficult, once I'd got used to it."

In short order, Reg and Bernie came up with a slew of new songs, including "A Dandelion Dies in the Wind," "The Tide Will Turn for Rebecca" ("A real John Hanson-type number," Elton would later categorize it), "Mr. Lighting Strikerman," "The Year of the Teddy Bear," "When the First Tear Shows," and the reflectively oblique "Season of the Rain," which—like most of their early efforts—evoked a general mood more than it made any kind of literal sense.

"Total rubbish," Elton said with a laugh.

The first Dwight/Taupin song committed to recording tape was a poignant ballad entitled "Scarecrow." Bernie proudly took an acetate of the piano-and-vocal demo to Putney, south London, where he had temporarily moved from Owmby-by-Spital to lodge with his aunt and uncle. That chilly October weekend was to prove a key one in the young lyricist's life.

"I just played it over and over again," he said, "thinking, 'Wow, this is living, man. This is really what it's all about.' Just to see a record going around on a turntable was a big buzz, and actually your first song going around on an acetate, 'Scarecrow', that's amazing. So exciting."

Reg's focus on his partnership with Bernie helped sever ties with Niraki, which made him ineligible to continue utilizing DJM's recording facilities. Luckily, Caleb would still sneak him in afterhours to record demos of the songs he was writing with Bernie. It was a perfect setup—at least until DJM's office manager, a straight-laced company man named Ronnie Brohn, happened to be driving past the building one rainy Sunday evening and noticed that all the lights were on.

"We were recording late at night when Ronnie Brohn shows up in the doorway," Caleb said. "Brohn was this humorless old-guard business manager. Everybody sort of froze. '*What* are you lot doing here so late?' he yells. 'Does *Dick* know about this? Well, he's *gonna* hear about it!'"

The following morning, Caleb got called into Dick James' office.

"I figured that this is it for me," Caleb said. "I'm about to lose my job. Just harrowing. But Dick was okay. He asked about the sessions and at first he said, 'I'm throwing them all out. The party's over,' that kind of thing. It became known as the Great Purge. And I said, 'You can throw them out, you can even sack me if you feel like it, but first you've got to hear these two guys, you've *gotta* listen to their stuff.' So I went and got [reel-to-reel] tapes of Elton and Bernie's songs, and I played him 'When I Was Tealby Abbey' and 'Watching the Planes Go By' and four or five others."

"I don't think [Dick] was very impressed," Elton said, "but…Caleb, who was his blue-eyed boy, said he thought it was good."

James immediately demanded to meet Reg and Bernie for himself.

"I remember them both sitting outside Dick's office," Caleb said. "Dead scared because they thought they were going to be hauled over the coals."

Reg and Bernie were thus astounded when, instead of castigating them, James offered them a contract instead. "To actually be given money for writing songs—I couldn't believe they were really serious," Bernie said. "We fell upon [the contract] like thieves. I was freer and happier than I'd ever been in my entire life."

Reg and Bernie signed with DJM on November 7, 1967, for the princely sum of £10 a week each as a guarantee against future royalties, along with a £50 down-payment, for writing fifty-four songs over the next three years. As neither were of age—Reg was still but twenty, and Bernie was only seventeen—their parents, Sheila Dwight and Robert Taupin, were required to add their signatures to the contract to make it legally binding.

"So we signed with Dick James for three years as songwriters and he guaranteed us ten quid a week each," Elton said. "That was less than I was getting in the group, but it was all I needed."

"We all went for a curry at L'Orient—which Elton called Leyton Orient, after the soccer team—all of us just ecstatic," Caleb said. "It was a great time."

Bernie moved yet again—temporarily, he hoped—into the cramped confines of Frome Court, sharing metal bunk beds in the tiny bedroom where Elton had grown up.

"We had all our records in there, all our clothes," the pianist said. "God knows how we did it."

Now officially on the payroll, Elton and Bernie were tasked with churning out formulaic pap—frothy Top 40-style pop tunes that the Engelbert Humperdincks of the world might deign to record. "We had no qualms at first," Bernie said, "because we were getting paid, and getting paid to write songs wasn't too bad because I could be driving a tractor or shoveling dead chickens into an incinerator." Reg, however, was a bit less pardoning. "Music publishers only know about yesterday's hits, so they'd say, 'Hey, you guys, you gotta quick write a tune like 'I Am the Walrus,'" or whatever else was popular at the moment. They never once wanted us to write our own kind of music."

Though prolific, the pair had little luck placing their songs with established artists. "So many times," Elton later said, "we were told that Tom Jones or Cilla Black was going to record one of our numbers, and we used to go home thinking we'd finally made it. But nothing would materialize, because basically the songs were crap." The failures hit Bernie even harder than they did his partner. "I used to get more down about it," the lyricist admitted. "Usually [Reg would] be the one keeping both our spirits up."

Making matters worse, Reg and Bernie were relentlessly mocked by DJM's stable of more experienced songsmiths, men who seemed impossibly old-fashioned to the young upstarts. "It was like the changing of the guard," Bernie said. "A lot of the guys who had office cubicles within Dick James' office were like artifacts of the music hall days. We'd hang out in the pubs and listen to all the old cronies talk about 'the good old days' and have them point fingers at us and say, 'You're not professionals, you've gotta be around a long time to be called a professional.'"

DJM's newest hire, a messenger boy named Clive Franks, would ultimately prove a more supportive force for the songwriting duo. "[Reg and I] got talking," Clive later told journalists Tom Stanton and James Turano. "I was quite mad, actually, because I had been there two months and I was earning seven pounds, ten shillings a week. He was signed up for ten pounds a week, and I thought, 'What's so special about *you?* Why are *you* getting more than me? *You're* the new boy.'" Any displeasure Clive felt quickly evaporated, however, when he was promoted to the lofty position of studio engineer. Working closely with Reg on his latest demos, the two became fast friends. "We'd go out to the pictures together," Clive said. "But I could not have foreseen what was coming, the huge international fame. In fact, his music didn't really appeal to me. It was very odd stuff."

At the same time, and quite unexpectedly, Long John Baldry scored an unlikely hit in late November with a syrupy ballad called "Let the Heartaches Begin." Instead of expanding his group's professional horizons, however, Baldry's chart success would actually set Bluesology back several steps.

"We went from playing really nice places like the Rikki Tikki and the Mojo Club," Elton said, "into playing the Cavendish Club and sort of cabaret places and sort of having to set your equipment up during bingo sessions. We were the nightclub entertainment to help the food go down nicely. The most insulting thing for a musician, if he's enjoying his work and really putting a lot into it, is to play to people that aren't interested in what he's playing."

There was a silver lining, however: Reg secured a co-writing credit—along with Baldry and Tony Macaulay—on the single's B-side, "Hey Lord You Made the Night Too Long." Yet this modest success did little to quell the keyboardist's growing dissatisfaction. Adding insult to injury, Bluesology—which was now being billed as The John Baldry Show—were forced to set down their instruments during the show's climax, while Baldry stood alone in the spotlight, miming to a pre-recorded orchestral track of "Let the Heartaches Begin."

"As competent as Bluesology was," Pete Gavin said, "John didn't want us to play on that one live. He wanted to play the prerecorded backing track through the PA, to which he would sing over it. And we'd stand like goons around on stage waiting for the track to be over, which I thought was really silly, because we could have done it justice. Nevertheless, that was what John wanted to do, so that's what he did."

Reg could clearly read the writing on the wall. Not helping matters, he was beginning to find Baldry's often illogical stage antics supremely off-putting. "I remember one gig at Haverford West," Elton said. "[Baldry] was standing there in his smart suit, singing his big hit, playing the star bit to the hilt. All the chicks were screaming and grabbing for him, and he was loving every minute of it. But then one girl pulled the microphone cable and broke it. Instead of brushing the incident aside and dismissing it with a showbiz-style gesture, he got all serious and angry, and he said to this chick, 'You've broken my microphone. That'll cost you fifty pounds,' and then he walloped her on the head with the mic. I just collapsed."

Baldry

"A lot of people didn't care for John at all," Pete Gavin concurred. "He'd get up there and he'd do his camp bit at the front of the stage, and they'd be throwing pennies and all kinds of stuff at the stage, because they didn't appreciate the camp bit at all. John really forsook the blues thing entirely, which may or may not have been a mistake, 'cause his sophisticated bit really didn't get him anywhere. The frilly shirts and the fancy neckties and whatnot just didn't work."

On Christmas Eve, 1967, after Bluesology's gig at the Cavendish Ballroom in Sheffield, Reg met the towering Linda Ann Woodrow between sets, when she came up to compliment him on his playing. The haughty, towheaded fashionista was accompanied by diminutive disc jockey Chris Crossley, who fashioned himself "The Mighty Atom." But the four-foot-tall record-spinner proved no match for Bluesology's organist. "Reg and I got on well, we clicked straightaway," said Woodrow, who, at twenty-four, was several years older than Reg. "I found him funny and I really enjoyed his company....I suppose I was flattered because of who he was, and that he took an interest in me."

"It was the oddest thing," Baldry said. "Over the week that we were up there, the relationship between her and Reg solidified, and all of a sudden the dwarf was out of the picture."

"I was with a waitress from the club that night," said Caleb, who had decided to leave Dick James' employ to join the band, which Reg was still playing with in-between his efforts with Bernie. "The four of us go back to mine and Reg's hotel room. The next day after the girls left, Reg gave me a pair of socks as a Christmas present. Those socks were all he could afford. That was really touching."

As 1968 dawned, Stephen James, Dick's twenty-year-old son and right-hand man, began shopping an acetate demo album of Reg and Bernie's songs around the London music scene. With titles such as "I Love You and That's All That Matters" and "Tartan Coloured Lady," the younger James' efforts were preordained to fail. "The songs were criticized as too airy-fairy," he said. "And no one could think of an artist to record them."

When Johnny Franz at the Philips label suggested that Reg possessed a strong enough voice to record and release the material himself, Stephen was intrigued. Mentioning Franz's assessment to his father that night, the elder James readily agreed. A couple days later, on January 10, 1968, he offered Reg a five-year recording contract. For his efforts, Reg would receive two percent of each record's retail sales price, and a £50 down-payment bonus.

Reg signed the contract with James' This Record Co. ("This" being an anagram of "Hits"—and also, as others would jokingly point out over the next several months, "Shit") to record at least four sides of seven-inch records each year. "I was sort of pushed into being a singer because nobody recorded our songs," he later was to admit. "I never thought...that I would be a singer or a performer, because I thought, 'I've had enough of this playing to people eating chicken-in-a-basket, I'll be a songwriter.' But once I got a taste of performing, I really liked it."

That weekend, Reg moved into Linda Woodrow's cold- "east end lights..." water basement flat at 29 Furlong Road, Holloway, North London, along with her two yapping lapdogs. Reg and Linda had been fairly inseparable since their first meeting, and cohabitation seemed the next logical—albeit rushed—step. "He seemed genuinely excited about the idea of moving in together," Woodrow said. "It was a decision that was made by both of us." At Elton's insistence, Bernie was to move in as well; Woodrow reluctantly agreed to the arrangement. "It was a given that where Reg went, [Bernie] did," she said. "But I didn't mind. I was in love and wanted to be with him."

The lyricist, for his part, was less than enthusiastic about the run-down neighborhood they'd relocated to. "We were in the Watts of London," he said. "We were really scraping."

If the area bothered Reg, he kept his silence about it. He had larger matters to focus on anyway. Soon after moving in, he lost his virginity to his more experienced girlfriend. "When we rolled into bed, he was clumsy and, frankly, didn't have a clue," Woodrow said. "He was a gentle person by nature, and he was that way in bed. I was so keen on him that I didn't really mind."

Not everyone was quite as acquiescent, however. Caleb, for one, found Reg's relationship with Linda nothing short of comical. "I didn't dislike her," he said, "but she was really snooty, dressing in high-fashion with a really superior upper class air. Tall and thin, and Reg always wore this huge fur coat at the time. One day the three of us all went to get a curry together, and on the way back to the studio I'm looking at Reg holding the leash to Linda's ratty little dogs, and she and Reg just looked like the numeral 10. I just lost it and fell against a lamppost in hysterics."

With the ink still wet on his recording contract, and with his first solo publicity session under his belt (photographer Val Wilmer shot a series of images on January 22, the would-be pop star looking lost inside a wolf-skin coat and leopard-skin fedora), Reg finally felt secure enough to cut the umbilical cord with Bluesology. His final performance with the band occurred in February, 1968. "We played our last gig at Green's Playhouse in Glasgow," Caleb said. "The stage had a cage around it to stop flying beer bottles, just like *The Blues Brothers* years later."

Though Reg had long contemplated leaving the group, his Vox blowing a fuse during their final Scottish gig helped him decide the matter once and for all. "Reg just got so incredibly hacked-off," Caleb said. "We were dead in the middle of this song and all of a sudden you could hear this racket going on around the back of the stage. I turned around and Reg has completely lost his bottle. Tipping his organ over, screaming, '*Fuck* this! I've had *enough!*' And meanwhile Baldry's still trying to sing." The guitarist laughed. "It was definitely time to go after that. And I decided to leave, too."

Reg gave his notice on the British Airways bus from Heathrow into London. "That was the best day in my life," he said. "When I quit the group."

Recognizing that "Reg Dwight" sounded more like an assistant librarian than a burgeoning pop star, Reg promptly began scribbling down potential stage names on the back of an envelope. None of the monikers seemed appropriate, however. Suddenly, inspiration struck hard. Walking to the back of the bus, he smiled nervously at Elton Dean, who sat staring silently out the window.

"Is it all right if I call myself Elton Dean?" he asked.

"Fuck off, Reg," the saxophonist snarled. As Dean would later reflect, "No one would be happy if someone just came up and said, 'I want your name.' But that was Li'l Bunter."

Reg shuffled back to his seat, crestfallen.

Caleb pointed toward Long John Baldry. "Why don't you take *his* name too, and mix 'em up?"

Reg thought it over. "Elton John?"

Liking the sound of it, he clapped Caleb on the shoulder. "Of course," he said. "Why the fuck not?"

In that moment, Elton John was born.

"Later," he said, "I thought about changing [my name] again, but no one could come up with anything better."

The newly christened Elton John released his first single weeks later. The Caleb Quaye-produced "I've Been Loving You"—backed with the brass-driven blues of "Here's to the Next Time" (which Elton had originally written for Marsha Hunt, and which got the nod above the quivering, never-released ballad "I Couldn't Fall In Love With Anybody Else")—hit the record shops on March 1. A four-song EP [extended play] disc of "I've Been Loving You" was also released in Portugal, and included "Thank You For All of Your Loving," a rare John/Quaye track, and "The Angel Tree," the first release of a true John/Taupin song anywhere. (For though the simplistic words to both "I've Been Loving You" and "Here's to the Next Time" belonged to him and not his partner, Elton shared the writing credits with Bernie, as the label ungrammatically testified: "EJB Taupin," allowing the lyricist to earn his first meager publishing royalties.)

Issued on the Philips label—the first of a two-single deal that Stephen James had cut—"I've Been Love You" was birthed into a pre-Internet world of Flower Power, *Lost in Space,* miniskirts and anti-Vietnam protests. Stateside, Richard Nixon and Robert F. Kennedy had thrown their hats into the presidential ring, while the Beatles' "Lady Madonna" and Louis Armstrong's "What a Wonderful World" sat high atop the pop charts. Culture was in a state of major flux, and despite ads in the London trade papers declaring that "I've Been Loving You" was "the greatest performance on a 'first' disc," and that "Elton John is 1968's great new talent," few bothered to take much notice of the song. (Interestingly, however, the band Wednesday would score a Number Six hit on the Canadian charts with a cover recording of the song years later, under the abbreviated title: "Loving You Baby.")

The disc's lack of success did little to boost any romantic illusions on the home front. "Elton did get very depressed over his music," Woodrow said. "He was also very depressed about not having any money." With the first blush decidedly off the rose, Elton and Linda Woodrow began to fight constantly—an eerie reminder of the pianist's parents' interminable discord. Adding fuel to the fire, his headstrong girlfriend had already grown wary of his failing musical ambitions, and began insisting that he follow a more conformist career path. "She didn't think that music was a good career move," Elton said. "She was trying to get me to give it all up. She didn't like my songs. It really destroyed me inside. Everything I'd write, she'd put down."

For his part, Bernie was "shit scared" of Woodrow, whose fascistically idiosyncratic house rules precluded him from even putting up posters of Simon & Garfunkel and Bob Dylan on his bedroom wall, lest he leave push-pin marks in the plaster.

With Woodrow's days spent at a secretarial job at the Evening Newspaper Advertising Bureau in Holborn, Elton and Bernie were left largely to their own devices. The two spent endless hours talking about music and poring over their prized record collections. "He turned me on to things that had grooves, like soul music, Stax, Chess, and so on," Bernie said. "In turn, I turned him onto folk music, narrative stuff like Bob Dylan, Leonard Cohen."

The duo also spent a great deal of time at the Musicland record shop at 44 Berwick Street, in London's sordid SoHo district. Elton would help out behind the counter from time to time for extra money, while Bernie investigated whichever new releases had arrived on any given week. The two novice songwriters were in heaven being amongst the endless stacks of vinyl. "We used to hang out there like people hang out in a bar," Bernie said.

"The most exciting thing was waiting for the imports to come in," Elton later recalled. "We were obsessed by American records—not just because of what was inside them, but we loved the covers. We loved the card on American records because it was harder, they didn't have that glossy sheen that English records had. It was great. It was all imports, and the biggest import album while I was working in Musicland was *Soft Machine Volume 1* in the original sleeve."

With access to an endless assortment of discs, Elton's record collection swelled to heroic proportions; soon enough it encompassed three-hundred albums, fourteen-hundred 45s, and over a hundred EPs. "My influences go back to Little Richard, Jerry Lee Lewis, Bill Halley, all those rock 'n' roll things, and then Tamla Motown," he declared a few years later. "And now my taste is everything. The only thing I really haven't got in my collection is middle of the road stuff. Englebert Humperdinck-type stuff and traditional jazz. But I've got everything from Tibetan monks playing the gong backwards to Led Zeppelin and things like that."

While Elton's vinyl assemblage flourished, his relationship with Linda Woodrow rapidly deteriorated. When their nightly arguments grew particularly heated, she took to physically attacking him.

"I was in love with her for the first three months," Elton said, "but after that she made me completely miserable."

At his wits' end, the pianist finally gave in to his girlfriend's demands and proposed to her on March 25—his twenty-first birthday.

"He didn't exactly get down on his knees," Woodrow said. "He just mumbled something about, 'Well, we may as well get married.'" Still, she readily agreed, rushing out the next day to buy her own engagement ring.

Elton wrote his father and stepmother days later, a thank you note for a leather briefcase they'd given him for his birthday. In his letter, he touched on his engagement. "We do not intend to get married yet, or at any rate not until my career takes shape," he wrote. "[Linda] is a very understanding girl, and realizes that at the moment my work comes first." He went on to say, "I have just had a record released, but I don't think that it will be a hit because none of the disc jockeys like it very much. So I will just have to wait until I can find something they do like!"

Despite Elton's cautious nuptial approach, Linda proved to be as impatient as she was insistent. Before long, a wedding was planned to be held at the Uxbridge Registry Office at 9:45 a.m., June 22, with a reception to follow at Sheila and Derf's house.

"You could see he didn't want to go through with it," Caleb said, "but he'd sort of trapped himself. But we were all teenagers. It was just one of those things."

Elton felt cornered. With his career foundering and the pressure of an upcoming marriage pressing down on him, he grew despondent and depressed. He came close to a breaking point in early June, when he walked into his tiny kitchenette and stuck his head in the oven.

"The three of us were supposed to be taking a nap," Woodrow said. "I came out of my room and Bernie came out of his, both thinking we'd heard a noise. We went into the kitchen, and there was Elton lying with his head in the gas oven."

"It was a very Woody Allen-type suicide," the pianist later admitted. "I turned on the gas and left all the windows open."

"He'd only turned the gas on to low, and left the kitchen window open," Bernie said. "And he'd thought to take a cushion to rest his head on."

The distraught lyricist quickly pulled Elton's head out of the oven. "I said, 'My God, he's tried to commit suicide!' And [Linda] said, 'Why, he's wasted all that gas.'"

With the marriage less than two weeks away, Elton and Bernie went out drinking at the Bag O'Nails on Kingsley Street with Long John Baldry.

"I was supposed to be best man," Baldry said. "So I said, 'Hey Reg, have you booked the hall yet?'" The innocent inquiry brought Elton to tears. Baldry shook his head in disgust. "It's absurd," the bluesman scalded. "You're more in love with *Bernie* than you are with this girl, dear boy. For fuck's sake, come to your senses. Why are you getting married when everyone knows you're a poove? Stop being a damn fool. If you marry this woman you'll destroy two lives—hers *and* yours."

By the time the three closed the bar, Elton had resolved to end his relationship. He and Bernie walked drunkenly up Furlong Road arm-in-arm to give themselves courage, bumping into parked cars and setting off their alarms.

When they reached their flat, Elton nodded resolutely. "I'm going to tell her now," he said.

"I'm going to throw up," the lyricist replied, stumbling toward the bathroom.

Elton headed into the kitchenette, where Linda sat fuming. Before he could get a word out, she began berating him for coming home so late, and so obviously drunk.

"Stop," he said, holding up his hand. "Listen, Linda. I don't want to get married. It's over. I'm moving out."

Woodrow broke into tears. "I was in total shock," she said.

Her crying jag soon turned into screaming accusations. With all hell breaking loose, Bernie lurched into his room and locked the door as quickly as his inebriated fingers would allow.

After a while, the flat fell eerily silent.

Moments later, a timid knock sounded at his door.

"I'm coming in there with you," Elton said. He spent the rest of the night curled up on the floor beside Bernie's bed. "I was so relieved [the marriage] was off," he said. "It was as if someone had saved my life that night."

The next morning, Linda claimed she was pregnant. When that gambit failed, she locked herself in the bathroom and threatened to kill herself by injecting her brachial artery full of air bubbles.

"I remember the two of us outside [the bathroom door]," Bernie said. "[We were] saying, 'She can't, can she? She hasn't got a syringe.'"

Having reached his limit, Elton phoned his mother. An hour later, Derf was pulling up outside their flat in his Ford Cortina. While Woodrow sat crying in the living room, Derf quickly loaded up Elton and Bernie's personal affects.

"How he managed to cram all that stuff in there, I'll never know," Elton said. "It was a narrow escape." (Within days, Woodrow would sue Elton for "Breach of Promise" for breaking the engagement, winning a not-insignificant financial reward from the courts. The legal victory did little to resolve the affair in her mind, however. "At no time during our period of engagement did [Elton] ever say that he did not want to get married," she'd maintain even years later. "We had already found a flat in Mill Hill in North London, and had even found the furniture we needed. If he did not want to go through with the wedding, he certainly did not let it show to me. It was his friends that made the decision for huh him that our relationship should end.")

Elton harnessed the massive relief he felt at dodging a matrimonial bullet by jumping head-first into a secondary musical life. Lasting well into 1970, in fact, he would pick up an enormous amount of session work on budget "sound-alike" recordings for labels such as Avenue, Music For Pleasure and Pickwick's *Top of the Pops* series—budget-priced albums sold in Woolworth's and supermarkets, with lurid cheesecake shots of smiling lasses in various stages of undress adorning their covers.

The songs were recorded across a variety of studios, including Pye Records at Cumberland Place and Decca Studios. Elton would eventually appear on over four-dozen such recordings, providing vocally dead-on facsimiles of Cat Stevens' "Lady D'Arbanville," White Plains' "My Baby Loves Lovin'," Credence Clearwater Revival's "Travelin' Band," and Norman Greenbaum's "Spirit in the Sky," among many others.

"They were a blast," Elton said years later of the sessions, which earned him £25 per. "I can remember singing the 'oohs' and 'ahhs' on a song like '(I'll Be Your) Jack in the Box.' Just a line like that would set us all off, and we'd have to stop the tapes because we'd all be laughing so hard....Of all the cheapo-cheapo cover albums that were around at that time, the ones we made were by far the best."

A new arrival at DJM in the fall of '68 was to have a powerfully lasting effect on Elton and Bernie's careers. Steve Brown, an intense, bohemian song-plugger who had been formerly employed at EMI as a promotions man for the

Beatles, was brought on as an A&R man. Brown quickly noticed that Elton and Bernie's idiosyncratic writing style left them ill-suited for churning out the type of accessible balladry Dick James expected of them. "We played Steve the commercial stuff we'd written and some of our own stuff," Elton would tell *Playboy* in 1975. "[Our songwriting] wasn't as good as we could do, and [Steve] asked us the reason why. So we told him that half of us wanted to write things that we really wanted to write, while the other half had to do what Dick wanted us to do, and that was write hit songs."

Calling the duo's attempts at commercial hit-making "fucking rubbish," Brown urged them to forget James' edict and instead write what they truly wanted to instead. The point was further driven home when Roger Cook and Roger Greenaway, a songwriting team who had penned hits for Gene Pitney and the Fortunes, gave Elton and Bernie similar advice. "You've got to quit writing what James wants and start writing the kind of songs you feel," they told their younger counterparts. "We write formula, but it works for us. Obviously, you guys need to write your own kind of material.'"

"Roger Cook and Roger Greenaway were very instrumental in helping us get on," Elton said. "We owe a lot to them."

With the words of Cook, Greenaway and Steve Brown echoing in their ears, Elton and Bernie came up with their breakthrough efforts—"Lady Samantha" and "Skyline Pigeon"—that very weekend.

"From that point on," Elton said, "we've never written a song that we haven't liked."

Freed of any commercial constraints, the songwriters began creating new work at a prolific pace—it only took Bernie an hour to come up with a complete set of lyrics, while Elton composed the music in half that time. "I think that was when the great factory syndrome of our early stuff started," Bernie said. "We had a bedroom at one end of the apartment and….I used to sit on the edge of the bunk bed writing lyrics. Then I'd walk down the corridor to the living room and put them on [Elton's] piano and go back and write some more."

The duo often tested out their new songs on Elton's mother.

"If it was one I cried at," Sheila said, "they'd say, 'Well, that's a winner, we'll have that one.'"

Within weeks, Elton and Bernie had amassed an entire LP's worth of demos. Recorded at DJM with Clive Franks engineering, the collection—entitled *Regimental Sergeant Zippo*—was never released. "There's an entire album no one's ever heard sitting somewhere," Clive said. "Maybe it's better that way."

Despondent at the fate of their first would-be album, Elton and Bernie's spirits were lifted considerably when they ran into Beatles' icon Paul McCartney at Abbey Road.

"We were talking to the Barron Knights," Bernie said. "Suddenly Paul came in, sat down at the piano, and asked us if we'd like to hear this new thing he'd written. It was 'Hey Jude'. God, we thought that was just so cool."

"It blew my fucking head apart," Elton said. "That was my first encounter with a Beatle."

Soon after, Elton and Bernie would decide that "Lady Samantha"—a cinematically expansive ode to a tortured apparition—should get the nod as their new single. They turned to Caleb Quaye to help arrange the session. "He asked me if I would record this song with him," Caleb said. "And

74

could I get a bassist and a drummer? So my job was to put a band together for the single and to arrange the music."

The chosen musicians—Roger Pope, Tony Murray, and Caleb himself—met up at DJM's studio on October 18. Though the team was initially excited at the prospect of working on such wholly original material, a technical problem quickly dampened Elton's enthusiasm. "The song was in B-flat, and the B-flat of the electric piano that we hired was out-of-tune, so I had to play a song in B-flat without playing the B-flats, which is rather difficult."

After the session, Elton was visibly brought down.

"So what do you think?" asked Steve Brown, whose turn as a sax player with Emile Ford and the Checkmates had earned him the producer's role.

The pianist shrugged as he listened to the song being played back over the studio monitors at full volume. "As a producer, you probably make a very good manager."

Brown nodded. "We thought ["Lady Samantha"] probably shouldn't be released," he said soon after.

After repeated playbacks, Elton had a change of heart.

"Okay, release it," he said with a fateful sigh. "You know, it can't do me any harm."

To help generate publicity for his new single, Elton performed before a panel of BBC judges. At stake was a decision on whether his music was "professional enough" to be broadcast over Radio 1, the BBC's fledgling pop network. Backed by Caleb Quaye on guitar, Boots Slade on bass and Malcolm Tomlinson on drums, Elton ignored a blinding migraine to sing energetic renditions of "Lady Samantha," "Skyline Pigeon," and "All Across the Havens."

BBC producer Aidan Day was impressed with the performance, calling Elton's material "highly original and inventive." Other judges, however, weren't quite as dazzled.

"Writes dreary songs and sounds like a one-key singer," one anonymous judge proclaimed, while another opined that Elton was a "wonky singer" who possessed a "thin, piercing voice with no emotional appeal."

The six-judge panel split their vote on Elton three-to-three, which allowed his performance to be later broadcast on the November 3 edition of the *Stuart Henry Show*.

Weeks after his BBC panel appearance, Elton would also appear on *John Peel's Night Ride*. Recorded at Maida Vale Studios in London, the pianist delivered a four-song set which included the as-yet-unrecorded "First Episode at Hienton," and the never-released rocker "Digging My Grave."

"Stuff the showbiz bollocks," Peel said enthusiastically after the performance's conclusion. "Elton John's a man to watch."

On December 2, Elton participated in a one-off project with a group of session musicians assembled by Apple Records assistant Tony King, a former DJM staffer, in early August. Put together as a low-rent "supergroup," the ensemble— dubbed the Bread & Beer Band after the musicians' penchant for cheese and ham rolls and pints of Guinness during recording breaks—also included Caleb Quaye, drummer Roger Pope, Hollies bassist Bernie Calvert, and Jamaican percussionists Rollo & Lennox. "It was done during a period when we were all basically starving, trying to make something happen," Caleb said. "Tony got this project together and it was great. We all earned some session fees."

With Beatles producer George Martin off on vacation, the band snuck into the studio at Abbey Road and record loose jam-band renditions of popular tunes. "We used to go down to the pub in the afternoon, have a few beers, and go back to the studio in the evening," King said. "Then we'd turn down all the lights at Abbey Road and get all moody. The Beatles had been using lots of colored lights while they were recording, and we thought it was terribly avant-garde. So we used to steal them and use them during our sessions."

The group's recording of "The Dick Barton Theme (The Devil's Gallop)" would be released the following February on Decca, with a standard 12-bar blues entitled "Breakdown Blues" as the B-side. As always, the disc failed to chart. (The Bread & Beer Band would later reconvene at Abbey Road for a pair of sessions on March 19 and April 9, 1969, to record their own unique versions of such '60s standards as "Woolly Bully," "Quick Joey Small" and "The Letter." The sessions would prove notable for being helmed by Chris Thomas, who would go on to produce the bulk of Elton's records in the '80s. An eponymous ten-song LP was pulled together from the sessions—and cover artwork created—but Decca scrapped the album's proposed June, 1969 release date, declaring the end product "rubbish." The band then pressed a dozen homemade discs on the made-up "Rubbish" label. Years later, only a single copy of the unreleased album would remain in circulation.)

"Lady Samantha" fared better, being released on the Philips label on January 17, 1969. Backed with the folksy white-soul balladry of "All Across the Havens," reviews for the gothic track were fairly positive. *NME* noted that "Lady Samantha" was "typically professional and musicianly," with lyrics which were "sensible and worthwhile....[Elton is] a promising talent." *Disc & Music Echo*, meanwhile, declared that "Elton John's 'Lady Samantha' is nice though it's much as we've heard before. Semi-Elizabethan feel, but lyrically interesting." *Melody Maker*, Great Britain's premier music paper, judged the song "an interesting guitar-ridden sound that could well create waves of interest. Very good, and a gold star." Elton himself was largely unmoved by the critical reception his single had garnered—he spent the day at the cinema, as an excerpt from his diary revealed: *Saw:—"Lady in Cement"—good, "Secret Life of An American Wife"— lousy.*

Dick James decided that his cinophile protégé should leverage the positive notices his single had garnered by appearing with Caleb Quaye, Roger Pope and bassist Dave Glover on the BBC's *Symonds on Sunday* radio program. The quartet was well-received, performing as they did hyper-energetic renditions of "Lady Samantha," "Son of Your Father" and "Sails."

"Any plans for personal appearances?" host David Symonds asked after Elton's brief but dynamic set.

"I'm getting a band together at the moment," the pianist replied. "I've got a partner who writes the lyrics to my songs. I've been very lucky. Well, I haven't had a hit yet, but I've still been lucky."

Ultimately becoming a turntable hit, "Lady Samantha" received substantial airplay on the BBC while only managing to sell a paltry 3,000 units. An import copy, however, caught the ear of Three Dog Night's lead vocalist, Danny Hutton. Hutton was impressed enough by the tune to decide that he and his band should record a cover of it. Their version would appear the following June as the second cut on their U.S. Top 10 album, *Suitable for Framing*. "Lady Samantha" would also be covered by the New Zealand band Shane, with their version quickly shooting to Number 3 on their national charts. This moderate attention proved enough for Dick James to greenlight a full album for his struggling songwriting duo.

"We just couldn't believe it," Elton said. "An album all to ourselves."

To help raise the pianist's profile, a DJM publicity press release was issued. "He is very adamant about how much talent he and other pop writers have," the one-page handout stated, "and about how seriously they should take themselves." Elton was characteristically straightforward about his career. "I'm glad things haven't gone too smoothly," the release quoted him as saying. "If I had had a hit straight after leaving [Bluesology], I'd be unbearable now. As it is, having to work for success is bringing valuable experience. I get one hell of a kick just from hearing one of our songs on the radio, and that's the way it should be."

Elton gave his first at-length print interview days later, to the music magazine *Jackie*. Admitting that he'd always wanted to be famous—"the old ego bit"—he went on to clarify that he "never wanted to be a movie star, because in fifty years' time if you mention an old film stars' name they'll just say 'Who?' But they'll still be playing Gershwin." On the subject of his increasingly bespoke wardrobe, he conceded that he enjoyed buying clothes, though due to monetary necessities, he didn't indulge his desires nearly as often as he'd like. "I've got some Noddy shirts [however]," he conceded. "They're made out of nursery curtain material. A neighbor made them for me."

With a bit of press coverage under his belt, Elton headed back into the tiny studio at DJM to record his first proper album. Again helmed by Steve Brown, musicians Caleb Quaye, Roger Pope and Tony Murray were also back on board to lend their talents, while studio engineer Clive Franks worked diligently setting up microphones and marking tape changes as they occurred.

The sessions kicked off with "Empty Sky," an insistent, Stones-influenced rocker which opened with Caleb banging away on conga drums. The strident, eight-and-a-half-minute track—about a prisoner who longs for a freedom he knows will never come—ultimately dissolved into an extended jam, with Elton doing his best breathy Jagger imitation over bluesy harmonic flourishes courtesy of Graham Vickery.

To get Caleb to play like Mick Taylor, the pianist coaxed him with Jimi Hendrix records. "We were copying the Stones on the title track," the guitarist said. "Making it a 'Gimme Shelter'-type thing, with a little 'Going Home'—off the Stones' *Aftermath* album—thrown in when [Elton] goes into those hushed vocals."

"[It's] a great rock 'n' roll track," Elton would later tell Cameron Crowe. "I love it to death. I remember doing the vocal in the stairwell to get that echo…the guitar solo was done in the stairwell as well.…'Empty Sky' has something magical about it. It came together so brilliantly.…It's hard for a piano player to write a good rock 'n' roll song. It sounded like a Stones song. I thought, 'I can do this.'"

Elton's chameleonic artistry was well on display on "Lady What's Tomorrow," an environmentally-themed song influenced by American folk musician Tim Hardin. The track was perhaps most notable for featuring a one-off performance by Plastic Penny drummer Nigel Olsson, who would soon come to play a much more significant role in Elton's career.

Next came "Valhalla," a harpsichord-accented tune steeped in Norse mythology. (Though misspelled as "Val-halla"—Bernie was a notoriously poor speller—the title was later corrected.) "'Valhalla' is Leonard Cohen," Elton admitted. "It's real easy to spot, and I think that's great. We always were, and still are, fans."

Elton then entered blues-romper territory with "Sails," a jaunty tale of dockside debauchery with a lusty lass named Lucy, while "The Scaffold" continued Bernie's obtuse lyrical inclinations. The songs all came out effortlessly, and with a growing sense of camaraderie. "The sessions...were good fun," Caleb said. "We were never sure what we were doing was going to be a hit in the commercial sense, but we knew that what we were doing was musically very interesting and relatively new for the time."

One track which *did* prove to be a bit of a challenge was "Western Ford Gateway," a tuneful slice of psychedelia which—on the face of it—seemed straightforward enough. Yet because of the limited number of tracks available, Elton was forced to sing live harmony vocals overtop previously recorded band/lead vocal tracks, as the final mix was created. "So if he messed up," Steve Brown said, "or we got the levels wrong, he would have to go back into the studio and sing live again."

The flute-laced Jethro Tull-styled "Hymn 2000" was attempted next. A futuristic tale of murder and mayhem, the song was—lyrically, at least—a "Glass Onion"-like collection of quasi-religious images which told the tale of a psycho killer. Elton was ultimately less than enthused about the finished track. "It's Bernie and I at our worst," he lamented soon after. "Bernie's lyrics were psychedelic rubbish and my song was a sort of painful type Dylan thing. It was awful."

Each night when the sessions ended, usually around four A.M., the entire group would walk over to the Salvation Army headquarters on Oxford Street. "Steve Brown's dad used to run the place, and he used to live above it," Elton said. "I used to sleep on the sofa. It's difficult to explain the amazement we felt as the album began to take shape."

The true standout track of the sessions came in the guise of "Skyline Pigeon," a pleading hymn to freedom and release. In an effort to infuse an almost palpable sense of loneliness into the recording, Clive suggested that Elton record his vocals out on the fire escape. Elton agreed, singing the pleading lyric in the chill winter starlight, his distinctive voice echoing plaintively off concrete and steel. The clever tactic worked, lending "Skyline Pigeon" an otherworldly air which melded perfectly with its aching melody.

The sessions then ended—much as the album itself eventually would—with "Gulliver," a heartfelt paean to a deceased farm dog. At its emotional height, the song gave way to a jazzy piano-and-sax jam (over the chords to the "Gulliver" chorus) called "Hay Chewed"—a tortured pun on "Hey Jude"—which itself faded into a stereophonic montage of snippets from the entire album, before closing out with the reverb-soaked screams which ended "Gulliver" proper.

"[The sessions] really blew our minds," Bernie later told *Rolling Stone*'s Bob Chorush. "We thought, 'Now we've done it. We've come up with a solution. This is what rock 'n' roll needs.' I remember…we thought: 'Watch out Rolling Stones, we're coming to get you.' Nobody else thought so."

For the briefest of moments, it seemed as if success might actually be within Elton and Bernie's grasp. As their album sessions were concluding, ebullient Scots pop star Lulu—who'd recently topped the American charts with "To Sir With Love"—sang one of their songs, "I Can't Go On Living Without You," on the February 8 edition of her weekly variety TV show, *Happening for Lulu*. The song was, in fact, one of six British submissions for the vaunted Eurovision Song Contest, in which viewers voted for their favorite tune by postcard. The winning British entry would then compete against the top contenders from a host of other nations in Madrid on a live inter-European television broadcast on March 29.

"'I Can't Go On Living Without You' was a fluke," Elton said. "It was one of our old songs that was lying around the office, and Dick entered it....I wrote all the lyrics for it, which Bernie has never forgiven me for. The same as 'I've Been Loving You'. They're entirely my lyrics, and it's credited to 'Elton John and Bernie Taupin.' But the lyrics are so fucking awful you can spot them a mile away."

Top Pops magazine was similarly unimpressed with "I Can't Go On Living Without You," noting that "it would be hard to get this title on a postcard when voting. A very unimaginative title for what is just a dull and uninteresting song." Songwriter Bill Martin concurred, expressing in the *Daily Express* how "after a promising introduction, I strained my ears to hear a nonexistent melody coupled with a pathetic lyric which consisted of the title phrase and very little else." (Years later, Martin—who would go on to write and produce for the Scottish heartthrob group the Bay City Rollers, as well as having his songs covered by the likes of Elvis Presley, Sandie Shaw and Cliff Richard, amongst many others—would reflect, "If he'd won that contest, he wouldn't be the Elton John we know today. Elton and Bernie were trying to write like the hit Tin Pan Alley songwriters of the time—Bill Martin and Phil Coulter, Greenaway and Cook, Reed and Mason—we wrote formula songs. If they had continued to try and write the way we did, Elton would not have made it. As it is, Bernie and Elton became one of the best songwriting teams in the world. The pop version of Rodgers and Hammerstein.")

Ultimately "I Can't Go On Living Without You" would come in sixth out of the six British entries, receiving only 5,087 votes. (The winner, a bouncy polka called "Boom-

Bang-a-Bang," would receive a healthy 56,476 votes. Such was the taste of the voting public in late '60s England.)

"Luckily it came last," Elton said. "My mother was very annoyed, though. She sent in reams of postcards."

Undaunted, the pianist headed to Olympic Studios in Barnes on April 10 to record a new single, "It's Me That You Need." An electric-folk hybrid stylistically reminiscent of the Moody Blues, Caleb's wailing guitar battled a cresting wave of cellos and violas arranged by Cy Payne, both exploding over a lushly emotive chorus. The B-side, a Traffic-inspired slice of acid-pop called "Just Like Strange Rain," was also recorded at the same session.

Elton and Bernie didn't apologize for their musical mimicry; it was simply part of the learning process, as they moved toward a more wholly original style.

"We were like magnets," the lyricist said. "If there were things we liked, we tried to emulate them. And I think we emulated them without realizing it."

Outside of musical ventures, April was proving to be a busy month in other ways as well: on the twelfth, Elton ran into a pair of hoodlums, as he faithfully noted in his everpresent diary: *Went into Musicland. Got "duffed up" on the way home. Went straight to bed.* His luck would take a turn for the better ten days later, however: *Got home tonight to find that Auntie Win and Mum had bought me a car—Hillman Husky Estate—Superb!!* The month then ended on an oddly confounding note: *Offer to open a carwash in Cricklewood—what!! Stayed in tonight. My glasses broke.*

Dick James was as perplexed as Elton, but for wholly different reasons. Blaming the failure of "Lady Samantha" on a lack of proper promotion, James decided to launch his own record label as a platform for any and all future Elton John releases. "It's Me That You Need" was the first beneficiary of this decision. Released on May 16 under the DJM imprimatur, the single unfortunately proved as commercially limited as its predecessors. (Though "It's Me That You Need" failed to chart in the U.K., it *would* go on to become a hit in Japan in early 1971, spending twenty-one weeks on the national charts and peaking at a more than respectable Number 13. A cover version by singer Maurizio Vandelli, released under the title "Era Lei" ["That Was Her"], would also score big overseas, becoming a Top 20 hit in Italy.)

Elton and Bernie were thus apprehensive when their first long-player, *Empty Sky,* was released in the U.K. weeks later, on June 3. Graphic designer David Larkham's album cover, a pen-and-ink rendering of Elton plunking out chords on an upright piano while floating through a haze of kaleidoscopic clouds, didn't do the disc's commercial prospects any favors.

"The cover's dreadful," Elton said simply.

The equally uninspiring back cover, meanwhile, featured a pair of endorsements from local music critics Tony Brandon and David Symonds, the latter presciently writing: "Elton John plays and pleases on this album....I too want to hear the pealing bells of distant churches sing. When it does happen, it will be a sign of tomorrow. And Elton will have a song about that as well."

Melody Maker gave the album—which toggled between pub-house rock and glitteringly confessional folk-pop—a solid review. "When I first saw it, before I heard it," the nameless reviewer wrote, "I couldn't believe that the record could be as bad as the cover design, and I was right. The record is excellent. All the numbers are original and make very pleasant listening. If you have an hour to spare, give the album a spin and 'turn on'." The *London Evening Standard* was slightly less taken with the disc, however, calling it "nicely recorded though…unadventurous," concluding that "we'd do well to watch out for Elton John. He has talent. When he gets less fanciful and less pretentious he will, I'm sure, have a worthwhile contribution to make."

The LP—which had cost £400 to record—only moved 4,000 copies, despite Dick James having sunk an additional £300 into an ad campaign which saw the back of three-dozen London Transport buses plastered with psychedelic posters proclaiming: *Elton Who? Elton John!*

Elton was cynically pragmatic about the whole mad endeavor. "Basically, I'm a writer," he said. "The solo performing and recording is really only to provide a showcase for my material, to get the songs more widely known. I'm sure the solo work won't last forever, and I don't really care if it does fall through, as long as the songwriting survives. But unless something really amazing happens, I can't see much future for myself as a solo performer."

Elton was thus in an understandably downcast mood when he ran into session-fixer Barbara Moore at Olympic Studios one rainy week later. Moore was overseeing the recording of a soundtrack album for the new Michael Winner film, *The Games*—which starred Ryan O'Neil and Michael Crawford as a pair of Olympic hopefuls—when she crossed paths with Elton, who was tickling the ivories in Studio 2.

"I heard this piano going," Moore said, "and this wailing voice. I thought, 'God, I like that.' And I poked my nose in and he stopped. And I said, 'Don't stop. Go on, it sounds really good'."

"Come sit then," Elton said, inviting Moore to perch herself beside him on the piano bench as he worked his way through a new composition called "Border Song." ("When

Elton and Bernie had written 'Border Song,'" Caleb remembered years later, "he called me up and said, 'Hey, I want you to come and hear this new song.' So I came over and we put the kettle on and had a cup of tea, and he sits at the piano and plays this gospel-infused song. I loved it. And when he gets to the last verse, he turns round and looks at me and says, 'This is for you.' It was just an expression of our friendship.")

"That has a great gospel-ish feel," Moore said after the song had ended. "What's your story, then?"

"I've brought all my songs here today to meet up with the studio owner, a man named Cliff Adams," Elton answered, "to see if he will give me a [new and better] recording contract. I'm unhappy with Dick [James]. That's what I'm looking for. A new contract."

Moore laughed. "My God, if he doesn't give it to you, he's a madman."

Wishing Elton the best of luck, Moore headed out to a nearby pub to meet up with her choir, before their afternoon recording session was scheduled to start.

"So I go over the road to the pub," she said, "where I see panic and also an ambulance leaving as I am going into the main entrance. So I said, 'What's happening? Who's in the ambulance?' And they said, 'It's Jim.' He was one of our tenors. So I said, 'Oh dear God, we're on again in three-quarters of an hour'. Then I said, '*I* know how to fill the gap. At least I'll try."

Dropping everything, Moore shot back to the studio. "It must've taken me a quarter of an hour," she said. "And by the time I get there, there's this dejected little figure standing there with his briefcase full of songs—apparently Elton had recently written fifty-odd songs—and I said, 'What's happened?' And he said, 'Cliff Adams didn't think that the songs he heard had any commercial value whatsoever, including 'Border Song.' I said, 'I think the man's mad. But meanwhile, do you want to help me out? One of my singers is ill. He said, 'No, no, I can't really read at sight.' And I said, 'You don't really need to. Come with me.'"

An hour later, Elton was laying down lead vocals on the proposed single from *The Games* soundtrack—a marimba-and-horn-fueled rocker called "From Denver to L.A." The session took less than an hour to complete. Elton earned all of £9.

With Elton's releases having died the proverbial death, he attempted to earn extra money by selling some of his tunes to music publisher David Platz, who ran Essex Music on Wardour Street. Platz was a forward-thinking businessman with a unique offer: he would purchase the publishing rights to songs outright for £50 each, with an eye toward selling them as radio jingles, or placing them in films.

One humid July morning in Essex's cramped front waiting room, Elton ran into a fellow aspiring songwriter named David Bowie, who was there with his nineteen-year-old girlfriend—and soon to be wife—the statuesque Angela Barnett. (Angela would soon become the inspiration for the Rolling Stones' ballad "Angie"—a musical apologia of sorts, necessitated after she found her husband ["An alley cat"] in bed with Mick Jagger ["A billy goat"].)

"Reg was very charming," Angela said. "When David was talking with Platz, I got to know him a bit. He was very quiet, but if you had patience and were able to draw him out, he became this incredibly witty person. He'd say the most cutting, hilarious things under his breath. Just a very clever young man, with real charisma. I liked him a lot. And when David came out of his meeting, he and Reg talked about what they'd been writing, what they'd been working on.

They talked about money and laughed, and asked each other, 'Are you playing anywhere this week?' That sort of thing."

Though Elton was unable to interest Platz in any of his songs, he *did* have better luck a fortnight later when he was asked to attend a session at Abbey Road to lay down a keyboard track for the Hollies' latest single, "He Ain't Heavy, He's My Brother."

The pianist found the band's fastidious recording habits bemusing. "They thought they were making art," he said. "I was just having a good time." (Other sessions the struggling musician attended around this time included both piano and backing vocal sessions for the Tom Jones hits "Delilah" and "Daughter of Darkness," as well as a lead vocal turn on the original demo of the Brotherhood of Man's "United We Stand." He would also appear on the 1968 U.K. chart-topping single "Lily the Pink" by the Scaffold. "We just knew him as Reg," Scaffold member John Gorman admitted years later. "He may never forgive me, but he was just one of many session men in the background.")

The highlight of that rudderless summer of '69 came on Sunday, August 31, when Elton, Bernie and Stuart Epps (who had replaced Clive Franks as the studio engineer at DJM), attended Bob Dylan's Isle of Wight concert in Wooton, where they watched the American folk artist— backed by the Band—work his wayward charms from a distance.

The songwriters, just two more faces in a sea 150,000-strong, were deeply affected by the concert.

"We've seen God," Bernie told friends the next day.

After participating in a recording session at South Harrow Market on October 27, and with the decade rapidly coming to a less-than-rhapsodic conclusion, Elton picked up a set of egg-stained lyrics that Bernie had written the week before over breakfast, and quickly read them through.

The words, which detailed a poor young man's devotion to his true love, was entitled "Your Song."

"I remember…looking at it and going, 'Oh my God, this is such a great lyric, I can't fuck this one up,'" Elton later said. "[The music] came out in about twenty minutes."

Bernie appreciated his partner's enthusiasm for "Your Song," though he himself was far less precious about the track. "I've always said that number sounds like a song about a seventeen-year-old guy who is desperate to get laid," he said. "Which, at the time, it was."

Elton's unique fusion of classical training and unerring musical instinct provided a strong foundation for the delicate lullaby. "'Your Song' is quite a complicated song as far as chord changes go," he said. "It was my first addiction to writing in the key of E-flat…I knew I'd written something that was really good. And that happens very rarely…You can't pick those songs out. They just happen."

Excited by the artistic potential "Your Song" represented, Dick James gave the okay for a follow-up album to *Empty Sky*. By this time, however, it had become apparent to all involved that Steve Brown lacked the top-tier production skills to do the duo's work justice. Further evidence of this was provided at a final Brown-helmed session at Olympic Studios, where Elton, Caleb Quaye and others laid down stylized, riff-heavy versions of several new songs that were—if not quite lackluster—at least not as innovative as the pianist and his team had wished.

"They were like rock tracks, really," said Stuart Epps, "with a three-minute 'Take Me to the Pilot' having a five-minute guitar solo in it. And it was really a step on from *Empty Sky*. But Elton had already done these demoes for the songs for the next album, and they were quite sort of classical pieces, really. So anyway, after those sessions, Steve decided he wasn't good enough to be the producer. That's how he was. He always wanted the best, even if it didn't include him."

With Brown's selfless blessing, Elton and Bernie approached famed Beatles producer George Martin. On the strength of a handful of piano-and-vocal demos for "Your Song," "Take Me To the Pilot," and "Sixty Years On," Martin agreed to helm the new album, on the condition that he also be allowed to handle the string arrangements as well. This proved a sticking point for Elton, who wanted the arranger and producer roles clearly divided. Reluctantly, he passed on Martin's offer.

Yet any worries Elton may have harbored of making a mistake by passing up on Martin's offer were set forever aside days later, when he, Bernie and Steve Brown met with curly-haired arranger Paul Buckmaster at a Miles Davis concert at Ronnie Scott's Jazz Club in London. Brown presented Buckmaster with an open-reel, two-track quarter-inch tape of Elton's demos. The Naples Conservatoire-educated arranger, who had recently scored a modest success arranging David Bowie's single "Space Oddity," liked what he heard.

"The second I heard the tapes I said, 'This is a whole different story," Buckmaster later recalled. "*This* is the game I want to get into.'"

As for a potential producer, Buckmaster recommended Gus Dudgeon, who had produced "Space Oddity" after Bowie's usual producer, Tony Visconti, decided that the song was merely a novelty and thus not worth his time. Even before the Bowie track, Gus had already enjoyed an eventful career on the British music scene, engineering sessions for the Rolling Stones ("Poison Ivy," "Fortune Teller"), the

Small Faces ("Sha La La La Lee"), the Zombies ("She's Not There"), and Marianne Faithful, as well as John Mayall's seminal *Blues Breakers with Eric Clapton* LP.

"I was told to get into producing when I was an engineer," Gus said. "I was doing a session with Andrew Loog Oldham, who used to do all the sessions with the Stones. I guess I was getting kind of lippy on sessions, saying, 'This isn't any good.' I was arguing with producers, which is not a good thing to do. Andrew was leaving the studio and said, 'Gus, go into production.' He was the second guy in two months to say it, and I thought, 'Maybe they've got a point.' And then [Andrew] stuck his head around the corner and said, 'And get a *royalty*.' I had to ask someone else what a royalty was."

"We'd heard 'Space Oddity', which for me was one of the best records of all time," Elton said, "and...we knew that we had to get [Gus] to produce the second album."

Gus' office was situated just around the corner from DJM's offices. Elton and Bernie headed over the next afternoon to play several demos for him. "I just couldn't believe it," Gus later told *Mix Magazine*'s Rick Clark. "All of [the songs] floored me. Basically, my prayers were answered. Although I'd had four hits prior to this, it was with four different artists. What I really wanted was an artist that I could work with on a consistent basis. So I was like, 'Yeah, I'm going to do this.'"

Despite Gus' initial flush of excitement, the partnership began inauspiciously. Until the end of their first meeting, in fact, the meticulously dressed producer thought that Bernie was Elton and Elton was Bernie. "I got them completely arse-about-face," he said. "Bernie had long hair and he was slim and he looked more like a singer. It was only halfway through that Steve Brown said, 'Well hang on, Elton...' and I realized I was looking at completely the wrong guy." Gus

92

laughed. "He was very quiet, and Bernie was even quieter. [Elton] always dressed like a traffic light, though."

Gus and Paul spent endless hours on the floor of the producer's office, making meticulous notes for every musical passage for the upcoming sessions. Each song was planned out as if it were a mini-film, with its own unique setting and cast of characters. "We had the demos and we had the lyric sheets, and we decided where the drums would come in, what the instrumentation would be," Buckmaster said. "We approached each song as its own individual entity. And there were no comments at all from Elton's camp. They had total confidence in what we were doing."

Great arrangements didn't come cheap, however. After triple-checking his figures, Gus informed Steve Brown that the proposed album would cost an estimated £6,000 to produce—an unheard of amount at the time—and that he demanded full and unquestioned control over the project.

Much to Steve Brown's amazement, Dick James acquiesced to all of Gus' demands. And so, as the final frozen sunbeams of the 1960s melted into the frosted skyline, Elton and his team were officially in place and ready to attack the coming decade with everything they had.

Part One:
Troubadour

It's Here.
It's Fantastic.

Elton John
Madman Across
The Water

"With the release of "Madman Across the Water," Elton John and Bernie Taupin are Britain's most important lyrical-musician team."

Eric Van Lustbader
—Crawdaddy, November 6, 1971

"On the issue of quality, John's "Madman" lives up to the highest expectations, carrying forth the expectations of his two previous U.S. studio albums."

Robert Hilburn
—The Los Angeles Times, October 31, 1971

Chapter 1:
It's A Little Bit Funny

A rusted cab rumbled to a stop at 17 St. Anne's Court in
Soho. A dented black door creaking open against a hard
January wind, and out stepped Elton John in a herringbone
coat and black trilby hat. Bernie joined him on the sleet-
filled sidewalk moments later, arms wrapped tightly around
his narrow frame.

"There you lot are," Gus Dudgeon called from the
entrance of Trident Studios.

Elton nodded to Bernie.

"Here we go," he said.

Sessions for what would eventually become the *Elton John*
album began eleven days into the new decade. The most
professionally advanced recording facility in all of London,
Trident boasted both an 8-track machine and a state-of-the-
art Ampex 3M 16-track system, as well as four massive
playback monitors. The studio also featured a felt-lined,
leather-covered Bechstein grand, which rang forth with a
sharp, rich timbre—ideal for the baroquely classical songs
Elton had recently composed. "A lot my songs were
influenced by Tchaikovsky," he said. "The guy was a genius.
I like Stravinsky as well. I like lyrical composers, and I think
Sibelius and Stravinsky are really good."

The plan of attack which Gus Dudgeon and Paul
Buckmaster had devised was simple yet formally
groundbreaking: to fuse an orchestra onto a rock rhythm

section in a wholly convincing way. "What united this diversity," Buckmaster said, "was the common continuity of all our collaborative efforts from the very beginning. So you have a natural flow, but you treat each song separately. Each one requires its own interpretation and approach."

To realize their vision, a twenty-two member orchestra was booked for the sessions. Understanding that the musicians were insufficient to properly realize the team's grand vision, Gus brought in a handful of additional session men, swelling the orchestral ranks to thirty-six. The move caused the album's initial budget to balloon up past £9,000. Dick James reluctantly absorbed the cost overrun, hopeful that he had another Beatles on his hands.

Relieved by the show of faith, Elton was still very much intimidated by the expanded group of professionally trained virtuosos which James' largesse had brought. "They had all these brilliant session musicians standing there and I had to play live," the pianist said. "I was shitting. There I was, with all these string players who could really read music, and if I made a mistake that means they went, 'Oh God, it's back to looking at the newspapers.' It was a real nightmare."

To further fill out the sonic landscape, the orchestra was augmented by Blue Mink's drummer, Barry Morgan, bassist Herbie Flowers, and guitarist Alan Parker. Caleb Quaye was also on hand to lend his sterling fret work to a few of the more rock-edged tracks, which he'd already helped flesh out with Elton. "He would sit down and run through a song in the studio and I would just sit there and play along with acoustic guitar," Caleb later told journalist James Turano. "I'm also a piano player myself, so there would be a lot of contextualizing. I'd eyeball what [chord] inversions he was using and sort of match that on the guitar, just to create this complementary sound. We didn't want the piano and the guitar to sound like two mutually exclusive things."

Recording efforts were divided into multiple three-hour sessions, running from ten a.m. till two p.m., four p.m. till six p.m., and seven p.m. till ten p.m. "We had to record three songs per session, because they [the orchestra] cost so much," Elton said. "Absolutely fucking terrifying."

"Take Me to the Pilot" was the first song attempted. Though Bernie's lyrics for the piano-based rocker were a reflective hodgepodge inspired by Michael Moorcock's science fiction novel, *Behold the Man*, the end results were so cryptic as be nearly incomprehensible. "That song means fuck-all, it doesn't mean anything," the lyricist was soon to admit. "That song proves what you can get away with.'"

Gus implored Buckmaster to write more cello parts for the track, to help underscore the half-time beat on the chorus and provide the song with a uniquely distinctive flavor.

"But that many cellos will get lost," Buckmaster argued.

"No, they won't," Gus countered. "Because if we pitch them in the right register, they're going to be perfectly audible. I can promise you that."

Buckmaster complied, dutifully writing out a powerfully linear, Dvorak-influenced arrangement which featured banks of cellos rhythmically attacking the countermelody. "['Take Me to the Pilot' has] a lot of stuff happening at the bottom of the spectrum," the arranger said. "There are only cellos in the orchestral part of that track, although at the climaxes they play towards the high-end of their range....I asked for the cellos to be phased on that. We [then] tape-flanged them." Given the extra focus the track received, it soon became one of the arranger's personal favorites. "It has this tremendous humorous quality to it," Buckmaster said. "There's a wide range of emotional expression in it. It's just wonderful."

Though Elton had supreme confidence in his producer and arranger, he wasn't quite as convinced about studio bassist Alan Weighall, who was brought in to fill out the low end on several tracks. "I took one look at the bass player and he was bald," Elton said, "and so I had this phobia about him not being able to play funky bass. But things turned out okay."

"It was a great team," Caleb said. "Not just the musicians, but Gus Dudgeon was the perfect producer for that period of time, along with the first engineer, Robin Geoffrey Cable, who was a brilliant engineer. Gus and Robin were just a great production and sound-engineering team."

With "Take Me to the Pilot" in the can, the team turned their attention to "Border Song," a fractured mood piece which Elton and Bernie were particularly keen on. "It's written in two parts," the lyricist said, "which is why it's always seemed split up to me. The first part is a gotta-get-back-to-where-I-come-from song. The second part is a peace song. We just stuck it in for no reason. We do things like that."

The lyrical schizophrenia derived, in part, from the fact that Elton had taken over lyrical chores for the brotherhood-themed final verse. Though he would soon deem his lyrical efforts "very mundane," Bernie was less critical, noting that "the great thing about Elton's last verse was that he tried to put it all into perspective."

Barbara Moore ended up arranging the choir vocals on the track. "My phone goes, and it's Reg," she said years later. "He wanted a choir, a very large choir. He said, 'I want you to do the arrangement, and it's the song you like, 'Border Song.' And that was it. He came over to my home and we ran through it, and I did the chart exactly to his specifications, and it was part of the recording sessions, and it was a success. And that was just the beginning of a long friendship. He actually ended up offering me the job as his musical director on his first tour, but I had a little girl of six years of age at the time, so I had to turn it down. I just couldn't leave my little one behind and go off traveling. So I stayed on in England. But all these years we've kept in touch, and every Christmas I get a beautiful card from him."

After recording "Border Song" in two takes, the mood lightened significantly with an exuberant jam on the raucous Jerry Lee Lewis homage "Rock 'n' Roll Madonna." Feeling the finished track was "missing an element or two," Gus turned the recording into a quasi-live track by adding audience (cheers and clapping from Jimi Hendrix's Royal Albert Hall concert) from the year before. "There was just something about [the song]," the producer said. "It had basically a loose feel to it, very much like a live recording would…It was really done sort of tongue-in-cheek. I never meant for anyone to think it was a real audience. It was meant as sort of a cartoon audience."

The team next set their sights on the sweeping grandeur of "Sixty Years On." A Spanish guitar-laced lament of a young man who rejects the warring ways of a blinded mercenary thrice his age, the song became (one of Paul Buckmaster's crowning glories.) "I transcribed the piano part for harp on 'Sixty Years On'," he said. "We had piano on every frigging track, and we wanted to do something different here. So I transcribed almost note-for-note, but changed a few notes, just to suit my tastes. And we decided there'd be no rhythm section on that. It would just be strings, vocals, harp, acoustic guitar. And at the end we introduced a Hammond organ playing a little countermelody."

Every bar of the sweeping opus was prearranged—except for the iconic rising string tone cluster which opened the track. "We were recording the strings when the 8-track machine broke down," Buckmaster said. "And then came the call from the control room from engineer Geoffrey Robin Cable, saying, 'Hey guys, can you relax for five minutes? We had a machine breakdown.' And I turned to the orchestra and asked, 'Do you want a break?' And they said, 'No, no, we'll wait, it'll only take a few minutes.' So I said, 'Okay, let's have a bit of fun.' And I told each musician, 'You play *this* note, you play *this* note, you play *that* note. I'll feed you in, I'll indicate when I want you to start vibrating wildly, in exaggerated vibrato.' And so I did. Because I'd just been listening to this great Polish conductor called Krzysztof Penderetsky—especially *Polymorphia*—and I wanted to try it out myself, so I took this opportunity. Unbeknownst to me, the machine had been fixed and was now operating, and Gus and Robin had recorded what we were doing. Afterward, I attended the mix for 'Sixty Years On', which was supposed to start with the harp, and—unbeknownst to me—Gus had tagged that rising cluster onto the front. And when I heard it, I was very pissed-off. Because that was *not* how I'd conceived the arrangement at all. But he did that, and you know what? He was right. I quickly got accustomed to it, and I thought it was a great idea in the end."

The languidly earnest "Your Song" followed. Set in binary form, with a pair of lengthy verses preceding the chorus, the musical architecture purposefully delayed—and thus heightened—the emotional payoff of the chorus. It would prove an effective template which the pianist would utilize on many future ballads.

Though beautifully performed, the future standard was not seen as anything particularly special by the musicians involved in its creation. "Not one of us at the time considered that song a future single," Caleb admitted. "We were concentrating on the harder rocking songs—'Take Me to the Pilot' and so forth. Listen to the original demo of

'Your Song'—it's a bit soft and like the Carpenters almost. No one had any idea it'd become this classic song at the time."

As with every other track recorded at these sessions, a tremendous amount of care went into the creation of "Your Song." "There's this one little nylon-string guitar phrase that Gus really loved, he kept pushing it up in the mix," Buckmaster said. "And I thought he was pushing it too far, and I told him so. But he replied that it was a nice piece and it should stand out. Everything was down to the details. Even with the bass line, we pushed things. There's actually two basses on 'Your Song'. An acoustic upright and an electric. And the drums don't come in till the second verse. It's important to hold back, to let the listener get used to the song before you introduce new elements. So you have somewhere to go." As for the main drum fill, there were no exaggerated "palm fills" cluttering up the arrangement. "It's a very discreet pat-pat-pat on the hand sort of fill," Buckmaster said. "And it was all written out. Because that's what an arranger does. It's very frustrating for me sometimes, actually, for I am, in fact, a very frustrated rhythm section disguised as a human being. My middle name is actually 'Funk Drummer': Paul 'Funk Drummer' Buckmaster." He laughed. "A friend once told me, 'Man, you have hands like concrete, but you play like a motherfucker.' And I arrange the same way."

"I Need You to Turn To" proved to be the most delicately restrained number of the entire sessions. Shifting from minor key verses to a major key chorus, the lover's plaint—much like 'Valhalla' before it—was heavily influenced by Leonard Cohen, whom both Elton and Bernie idolized.

"Recording 'I Need You to Turn To' was a really nervous moment," Elton said. "I was playing the harpsichord, [and] while the harpsichord looks very similar to the pianoforte, there's a kind of delay to how its mechanism works, so it's very easy to fuck it all up if you're not thinking ahead."

Session virtuoso Skaila Kanga was brought in to overdub a graceful harp line onto the track. After nailing her part in a single take, Elton came down from the control room, grinning madly at her.

"Do you remember me, Skaila?"

"Yes," the harpist lied, not recognizing the slender, shaggy-haired man before her.

"We were in harmony class back at the Academy," Elton said. "Reg Dwight. Remember?"

Kanga's mouth hung open in amazement.

"The Cage," a dark fantasy of sexual betrayal and emotional claustrophobia, was recorded the next morning. Powered by Barry Morgan's relentless drums, the conga-accented track's standout feature was its middle-eight solo. Originally slated to be performed by a brass section, à la the Beatles' "Magical Mystery Tour," plans were changed when a Moog synthesizer from AIR Studio arrived at the studio, along with an operator to set up the mammoth, multi-paneled machine.

Paul Buckmaster turned to keyboardist Diana Lewis, whom he was dating at the time, and asked her if she wanted to give it a shot. She did. Pleased with the result, the arranger also let her lay down an improvised, hauntingly wistful Moog line on the pensive "First Episode at Hienton"—a holdover track from 1968—while the rest of the team was off at lunch.

"She stayed behind and created it with the engineer," Buckmaster said. "I came back and listened to it and thought it was just wonderful." Lewis had, in fact, perfectly captured the somberly romantic feel of Bernie's lyrics, a reminiscence of a schoolboy crush he'd harbored for a girl named Valerie, and the long walks they'd shared around the castle ruins of poet Alfred Lord Tennyson.

"I love that one very much, the entire track," Buckmaster said. "It completely achieved what it had set out to do."

Caleb agreed. "'First Episode at Hienton' is classic Elton John. Just a perfect marriage of guitar and piano, with a classic cinematic sound about it. Very free, very poetic."

Indeed, the synergy created by Elton's gospel-cum-classical melodies, Bernie's spectral, image-laden words, Gus' singularly nuanced production, and Buckmaster's lushly angular string arrangements proved particularly effective on this atmospheric track. It was in direct counterpoint to the swaggering "No Shoestrings on Louise," a country-laced rocker about a city-dwelling harlot who has "milked the male population clean."

"That was another Stones song—three-quarter time, really emphasizing the first beat—like something off *Beggar's Banquet*," Caleb said. "Listen to Elton's vocal, he's doing his Jagger on that one."

Changing gears yet again, the team tackled "The Greatest Discovery" next. A touching vignette about Bernie's older brother discovering him as a newborn (and *not* of Bernie discovering a younger brother, as many critics—and even Elton himself—later surmised), the track featured an elliptical cello solo from Buckmaster himself.

"A perfect melody line," he said. "It's beautiful."

The epochal "The King Must Die" proved to be the centerpiece of the sessions. Beginning with a quiet D-minor piano figure, and building dynamically to a full-complement orchestral flourish, the grandiose track was an ominous tale of treasonous hearts which Bernie would be forced to publicly explain, after certain members of the press erroneously presumed that the lyrics were about recently slain civil rights activist Martin Luther King. In actuality, the lyricist had been inspired by the historical novel of the same name by Mary Renault. "It's a very famous book in England," he said. "I just thought the title was nice. People say that [the song is] not about anything, but it's about something. It's about assassination. That's it. That's all."

Though Elton was pleased with his vocal performance on the track, years later he would reflect that he "was just an infant vocally at the time. Listening now, I sound like a school boy with my balls cut off."

Though the pianist's voice may have still been in its infancy, the framework of the recording as a whole showed unusual maturity for a pop recording. "Elton and I had worked a long time on the whole concept of guitar and piano working together," Caleb said, "and then Paul Buckmaster came in on 'The King Must Die' and he just added a whole other dimension on top of what we were doing, with the strings. He's just absolutely brilliant. Paul's contribution was really remarkable, because he came in and he got involved in the songs from the ground up. Instead of taking a paint brush and putting a bank of strings here or there after the fact, Paul really paid great diligent attention to what the songs were about, the dynamics of the songs. So the arrangements have a lot of intimate dynamics involved, which paid off great. So a song like 'The King Must Die'—it's just brilliant string writing. And all of these components just sort of came together, and we just knew there was something fresh happening. We just couldn't wait to get in the studio the next day and hear what we'd done, and start working on the next tunes."

Other songs recorded during the prodigious sessions included "Thank You, Mama," "Bad Side of the Moon," "Grey Seal," "All the Way Down to El Paso," and the minimalistic "I'm Going Home"—tracks which, as often as not, explored the quotidian anxiety of the socially disenfranchised, a favored theme which Bernie would return to again and again in the coming years.

Given the intricacies of the compositions and orchestrations, the recording process ran remarkably smoothly, with an entire album's worth of material being recorded and mixed in twelve frenetic days. Yet despite the harried schedule, the endeavor proved a pleasurable test for all involved. "We never stopped grinning, twenty-four-hours a day," Gus said. "Even as we were making it, we knew it was special. What we wondered was whether anybody else would recognize it as being anything at all."

"Gus was now God," said Stuart Epps. "The arrangements, the sound, the production. Everything. He'd taken Elton's music into another realm. If you listen to *Empty Sky* and then *Elton John*, it's like chalk and cheese. Gus was stupendous."

To his credit, Elton himself recognized the salutary effect a steady hand on the tiller brought. "Gus Dudgeon produced and the team was born," he said. "It was just like Bernie and me. It was fate, basically."

With the sessions completed, a restless Elton approached Derek Shulman about joining his prog-rock outfit, Gentle Giant. An audition was organized, but Shulman ultimately passed, feeling that Elton's piano playing was too rhythmically forceful for his needs. "He played us his songs," Shulman later said, "and even though they were great songs, they weren't going in the direction we were heading. Lucky for him, we turned him down....[as] he became the most successful solo artist in the world, and we were struggling to play for two-hundred people. So great luck for him that he didn't take the job."

Elton suffered a similar setback the very next week with King Crimson. Scheduled to sing lead vocals on their second album, *In the Wake of Poseidon*—after Crimson's lead vocalist, Greg Lake, had left the group to form Emerson, Lake & Palmer—Crimson's founding guitarist, Robert Fripp, cancelled the sessions after hearing a test pressing of the *Elton John* album.

"His style didn't seem right for Crimson," Fripp said. "Simple as that."

Instead, Elton lent his piano skills to the band My Dear Watson. "We were invited down to Dick James' studio in New Oxford Street, London, to do ten tracks for an album, and an actual single," My Dear Watson's leader, Bill Cameron, said. "I was told, 'We've got a keyboard player in the company, do you want keyboards on the tracks?' And we said, 'Yes.' And it turned out to be Elton John. My first impression of him was very high. Ian, our guitarist, was in the studio doing guitar overdubs. And Elton was sitting beside me in the control room, at the back, and I was telling him the chords to a song—you know: 'C/E-minor/A-minor/D,' and so on. He wrote it down in his little book and then he went through the studio, we wired up the Steinway, and he said, 'Roll the track and give me five minutes to try it.' And then he said, 'Okay, I'm ready for a take.' And we were all in the control room listening. And what came through the speakers was quite amazing. So we knew there and then that he was destined for greater things than our little album. We thought, 'Yes, there's something there. Reg is far too good to be just a session musician.'"

Elton flew off to Switzerland the following weekend to sing "Border Song" on the March 3 episode of *Hits A Go-Go*.

Seated behind a white baby grand and dressed in a reserved gray jacket, he performed before a couple hundred well-heeled Swiss teens. It was timely promotion for the single, which—backed with the thunderously seething "Bad Side of the Moon"—was released in the U.K. on March 20. Though hopes ran high at DJM, "Border Song" followed a similar trajectory as "Lady Samantha" the year before, receiving substantial airplay yet failing to make a serious dent in the charts. ("Border Song" *did* manage to hit Number 34 in Canada—a small but not insignificant consolation which gave Elton his first Top 40 song anywhere.) In a world dominated by guitar-slinging rockers like Creedence Clearwater Revival and Deep Purple, there seemed little interest in such an unassumingly introspective tune, or its equally reflective singer.

Disappointed but determined, Elton attempted to expand his connections within the London music scene by paying the first of several visits to a communal house in Hampstead, where twenty-year-old session singer Linda Lewis lived alongside Jeff Dexter—resident disc jockey at the Middle Earth club in Covent Garden—and Ian Samwell, who was soon to produce the group America's first major hit, "A Horse With No Name."

"A lot of people would come through the house just to sit around and jam and just talk," Lewis said. "So Elton was one of them, and so was Bernie. Cat Stevens came in and out, David Bowie, Marc Bolan, all of them. It was very sort of casual. I remember Cat Stevens playing me 'Moonshadow' at the house, he was still working it out, and the bridge sounded like 'Somewhere Over the Rainbow' to me. And Marc Bolan would walk around with tap shoes and these elegant bright jackets. He was a peacock. We had a little thing, Marc and I." She sighed. "I was in a cloud in my own little world, very sort of naïve. And with all that [going on], Elton was actually quite shy and down-to-earth. Others would play their songs, but he'd sort of just sit there very quietly. David Bowie was quite shy, too. He'd come round with all this makeup on, and I asked him once why he was wearing it, and he just sort of smiled at me and didn't say a word. But Elton was the most shy of all, I'd say. Both he and Bernie."

On the other side of the Atlantic, DJM's New York-based representative Lennie Hodes began shopping Elton around for an American label release, after Bell Records' release of "Lady Samantha" had sunk without a trace the year before.

Despite his best efforts, Hodes found little interest in the unknown British singer, who was turned down by five record labels in quick succession. The only music executive to show even a scintilla of interest was Russ Regan, head of Uni Records—a small subsidiary of MCA Records—which specialized in bubblegum pop groups like the Strawberry Alarm Clock. Regan was a player in the industry, having lent an instrumental hand in the careers of both Neil Diamond and Barry White—though perhaps his single biggest accomplishment to date was having changed a certain Californian vocal group's name from the Pendletones to the much more marketable Beach Boys.

Hodes and Regan held a breakfast meeting at the Continental Hyatt House Hotel—better known within rock circles as the 'Riot House'—on Sunset Boulevard. "He was telling me about this artist who he really liked and believed in," Regan said. "That particular morning I wasn't really in the mood to sit and listen to anyone, but out of courtesy I asked to hear him."

"Here," Hodes said, handing Regan a brown manila envelope which contained copies of the *Empty Sky* album, and the "Lady Samantha" single. "You're welcome in advance."

"I just put them off on a shelf somewhere until about five o'clock that afternoon," Regan said. "Then I played the album and found that I really liked Elton as an artist, and especially liked the song 'Skyline Pigeon' from the *Empty Sky* album. It was six o'clock by then and I realized, 'My God, they're out shopping this artist. What if he's called some other record company?'"

Regan contacted DJM the next day and had them rush-ship him a white label test pressing of the *Elton John* album. "I listened to it and thought, 'Oh my God, *thank* you, *thank* you!'" Realizing at once that he'd struck gold, the label head quickly grew ecstatic. "I'd been a promotion man for five years and [I'd] promoted a lot of heavyweights and heard a lot of great products, but I'd never been overcome by an album like that."

Closing his office, Regan shut off the phones, called a company-wide meeting, and played the entire album for his thirty-strong staff. Twice. "Everybody was just freaked out by that time, because we knew we had something. I looked at the sky and said, '*Thank* you, God'. I knew we had a superstar."

As coincidence would have it, Regan was also interested in another DJM act at the time, a psychedelic pop outfit called Argosy. Led by future Supertramp founder Roger Hodgson, Argosy's debut single, "Mr. Boyd," had actually featured Elton on keyboards, along with Caleb Quaye on guitar and Nigel Olsson on drums. "They did an awesome version...of my songs," Hodgson said, "and then I sang on top...Actually it came very close to being a hit in England. It was played a lot on the radio, but never actually charted. But that was my first experience in a recording studio, and it was quite a thrill, I can tell you."

Offering $10,000 for Argosy, Dick James threw the American licensing rights for Elton's records into the deal *gratis*. Regan readily accepted.

"So I got Elton John for nothing," Regan said with a laugh. "Which is probably one of the best deals ever made."

Chapter 2:
Tumbleweed Connection

Half a world away, and oblivious to any contractual machinations happening on his behalf, Elton was heading back into Trident Studios to begin recording selections for his next LP, *Tumbleweed Connection*. "We had about three albums worth of songs stockpiled," he said. "So we split the best of those numbers into two albums. The [introspective] songs that would suit the *Elton John* album, and those [more upbeat numbers] that would suit *Tumbleweed Connection*."

The rustic tunes which would end up compromising the bulk of *Tumbleweed Connection* reflected Bernie's fascination with the American West of the 1800s, and his long-held fantasies of the Promised Land. "I've always been interested in the history of the Old West," he said. "In a way, I suppose you can say [these new songs] are cowboy songs."

Having already rehearsed a majority of the songs live with DJM label mates Hookfoot, an earthy blues-rock hybrid which had been formed by Roger Pope and Caleb Quaye during *Empty Sky*'s gestation, the sessions ran like clockwork. Hookfoot had invited Elton to air out some of his newer compositions at their Marquee Club and London Art College gigs. "What would happen was, Elton would ask if he could come and sit in with Hookfoot, to help flesh out his new songs," Caleb said. "And so we said, 'Yeah, great.' So we'd do these gigs where we'd be playing, and Genesis would be playing, and we'd work Elton's songs out. So by the time we went into the studio we had them down, because we'd already done them a million times on the road. Our rhythm section was hot. We knew those songs inside and out."

"The next album is going to be much more like we are live," Elton promised anyone who bothered to listen to him at the time. "I *swear* I'm a rocker at heart."

The pianist would prove his point from the very first bar of what would become *Tumbleweed Connection*'s opening salvo, the bluesy, sepia-toned "Ballad of a Well-Known Gun." With Caleb's modified Fender Strat tuned down to D, the bracing track—about a fugitive on the run from both the Pinkertons and a starving family—rocked out hard in an earthy 2/4 time signature reminiscent of a few of the Faces more ambitious songs. "Roger [Pope] really made that track," Gus said. "Just his fill near the end, that alone, it's such an accomplished thing. A real moment of beauty."

"Reg had been classically trained at the Royal Academy, so he always had these tightly structured songs, very piano-oriented," Caleb said. "But on songs like 'Ballad of a Well-Known Gun', Hookfoot came in and we just laid down a layer of pure funk over Elton's classical chords. It was just a great combination."

The second song attempted at these new sessions was a plaintive piano ballad entitled "Into the Old Man's Shoes." The tale of a son fighting to escape the long shadow that his late father cast, the finished recording would fail to make the final album lineup, despite being one of Elton's personal favorites.

Leslie Duncan's "Love Song" then became the first non-John/Taupin track recorded for one of Elton's albums. The track was recorded live, with Elton and Duncan sitting side by side in the vocal booth. While the songstress strummed out ethereal chords on a battered six-string, Elton kept time with his foot. Liking the intimate effect, Gus miked up Elton's boot.

Further enhancing the atmospherics, the producer faded in prerecorded sounds of parents and children laughing together at the beach throughout the final minute and a half of the track. The end result was one which greatly pleased all involved.

Elton's favorite song of the sessions, the lusty ballad "Amoreena," was cut next. His highly Americanized phrasing and lower-register vocals showed the profound influence which Van Morrison's *Astral Weeks* had on him, while his piano playing reflected the New Orleans-drenched R&B stylings of Allen Toussaint.

For Bernie, "Amoreena" was a point of pride. "It's a good song in the sense that it has a lot of natural feeling to it," he said. "It's a love song, but it's a bawdy love song."

Despite its ribald nature, the song had a bit of a familial connection, as Elton and Bernie dedicated the song to Ray Williams and his family. "My wife was pregnant," Ray said, "and Bernie said, 'If you have a girl, we want you to call her Amoreena. I have this idea for a song, and I like the name Amoreena.' And I said, 'Okay, if we have a little girl, she will be called Amoreena, and you will be the godparents.' So my little girl was born, and Amoreena was her name. That's how that song came about. It's not one of their classic songs, but it's an understated song, and of course we're all very proud." (In 1975, "Amoreena" would be featured over the opening title sequence of Sidney Lumet's Oscar-winning film, "Dog Day Afternoon." A Japanese-only release of the song would concurrently be released in a then-current *Rock of the Westies* sleeve, scoring yet another Top 20 hit for the pianist.)

115

Elton went solo on "Talking Old Soldiers," a haunting dialogue between a young man and a weathered war veteran, the latter expounding at length on the power of memory. The elegantly intimate narrative was recorded in a single take, with Elton playing saloon-like piano and singing at the same time, as the vocal line and instrumental melody were so inextricably tied together. Describing the track as "a very David Ackles-influenced song," Elton would ultimately dedicate the song to the singer ("To David with love") in *Tumbleweed Connection*'s lyric booklet.

That same night, Elton and company lit into "Burn Down the Mission," an infallibly structured gospel number about a desperate man who leads an attack on a rich man's home to help feed his family. The song's unusual rhythmic progressions—it changes keys four times—was influenced by American songwriter Laura Nyro. "She was the first person, songwriting-wise, that there were no rules," Elton said. "There were tempo changes, there wasn't a verse/chorus/verse/chorus/middle-eight. She didn't write in that kind of way. And that put in my mind that you didn't have to write in that old template that everybody else did."

Lyrically, "Burn Down the Mission" was a more straightforward proposition, the initial idea having entered Bernie's mind as he was walking down the street one day. "I just thought of it for no reason at all," he said. "I started with the first line and I followed it with something else. When it was finished, it was about something. That's how a lot of my songs happen."

The tone inside Trident's brownstone walls shifted dramatically for "Come Down in Time," an exquisite meditation on romantic illusions. Though the original take was recorded with a rhythm section, Gus felt that the percussive vibe didn't capitalize on the doleful poignancy inherent in Bernie's lyrics; subsequently, the producer brought in Paul Buckmaster to help recast the song as a symphonic piece, complete with flute, oboe and upright bass.

"I love the melancholic, and I love the sadness," Elton said. "If it were down to me, I'd write that sort of shit all the time." Indeed, he favored "Come Down in Time" because it was exactly the type of song "that a jazz singer would record. Chord-wise, it was like nothing I'd ever written before."

The requisite Stones'-style rocker for the sessions, "Son of Your Father," was a cautionary tale about family ties and the often sour milk of human compassion. Hookfoot's Ian Duck added a bluesy harmonic part to the track, for which he earned £30. "I was sent an acetate of the song and I rehearsed the harmonica part at home first, then went to the studio," Duck said. "Dudgeon would run the track and we would do it in a couple of takes....If Gus thought it was okay, then he said, 'You can go home.' It was that simple."

Like most of the other songs recorded during these sessions, "Son of Your Father" owed more than a passing debt of gratitude to the Band's watershed LP, *Music from the Big Pink*. It was a purposeful direction initially set by Bernie. "I have to admit, the Band influenced me," he told *Sounds'* Penny Valentine, "because I have so much admiration for Robbie Robertson. If you like the Band, which I do, and listen to it a lot, you can't help getting influenced. It just seeps into you."

"Where to Now, St. Peter?" was laid next. A reflective wah-wah-spiced rocker, the unusual track concerned a dead Civil War soldier who comes face-to-face with St. Peter. The soldier pleads to be shown which road he is on. Is it to be an eternity of Heaven or Hell? The question is never resolved.

Dave Glover would later recall that the session for "Where to Now, St. Peter?" was easy and relaxed. "We used to go into the studio and then go off to The Ship pub with Elton and have a few beers and then go back," the bassist said. "He was a funny guy, friendly and a good laugh. We all got on very well, and it did not feel like we were recording or rehearsing in a studio. It was more like a rehearsal in a rehearsal room."

Elton briefly left the sessions to promote his upcoming *Elton John* album in the Netherlands, thus missing basic tracking work on "Country Comfort." Session pianist Pete Robinson, a friend of Paul Buckmaster's, filled in for him on the day. Robinson provided a restrained, nondescript performance over an otherwise pastoral arrangement which featured Johnny Van Derek on fiddle, Matthews' Southern Comfort's Gordon Huntley on pedal steel guitar, and Ian Duck again on harmonica.

"We put everything you'd find on a dozen country records on it," Bernie said. "Steel guitars and fiddles. You name it."

Unhappy with the end result, Elton ended up dubbing his own piano part over Robinson's. But the feel of the song was already locked in, and there was little he could do to bring his matchless energy to the track.

"I hate it," he said later of the finished recording. "Too sugary."

Elton's displeasure was short-lived, as his childhood crush, Dusty Springfield, stepped into Trident to lend her considerable vocal talents to the choir on "My Father's Gun," alongside Madeline Belle, Kay Garner, Lesley Duncan, Tony Burrows and Tony Hazzard. The tale of a Confederate man who swears vengeance against the Yankees who killed his father in a Civil War battle, Dusty was impressed enough by the bluesy, southern-gospel-tinged track to allow the album credits to list her under her real name, and not as ("Gladys Thong," the pseudonym she usually performed under for guest appearances.)

"Dusty Springfield came along, there was just a few of us singing on it, and I was standing next to her on the night," Tony Hazzard recalled years later. "She was a lovely person. And she said, 'I don't know if I can do this.' And I was thinking, 'You're Dusty Springfield, of *course* you can.' And I told her, 'You'll be fine, don't worry.' So it was crazy, me reassuring Dusty Springfield with her great voice, because she was worried about getting it wrong, which she didn't." Hazzard laughed at the memory. "The funny thing about all this is that when you're going through it, it's just normal life, it's what I did. I sang on sessions and made albums and that's the milieu that I lived through. So you didn't think anything of it. Elton makes a record and you think, 'Good on, Elton. I hope it does well.' And then you look back and you think, 'Crikey!' I'm part of musical history."

Beyond the riveting backing vocals, "My Father's Gun" gained further sonic power from the crystalline production Gus Dudgeon lent the track. "He clearly knew what he was doing," Hazzard said. "And Elton and Gus had the same sort of humor, which helped ease things in the studio. They had this quirky humor, and they would talk in funny voices. It was a bit like the *Goon Show*. They would talk in a very sort of upper class English accent, where people slightly mispronounce words: 'Either sit *day*-own, or gait *ow*-it!' And we all used to fall about laughing. So they were relaxed sessions, and clearly Gus had a very clean aural vision, if I can mix metaphors, of what he wanted. And Elton did, as well."

The period-piece dramatics of Buckmaster's horn and string arrangements, which proved to be some of the arranger's finest work, provided added verisimilitude to the track. "Paul Buckmaster is arranging for us again and he is just totaling amazing," Elton said. "He's doing the most incredible things with straight session musicians. Half the time I just don't believe it. He has them all hitting their violins for three bars and they all love it. He is really freaky and very good. I'm so pleased that he's doing our album."

Two of the more lyrically intriguing songs of the sessions would never progress past the demo recording stage. "The Sisters of the Cross," a volatile ballad about the lonely sexual lives of nuns, and "Rolling Western Union," a full-throttle thumper which told a typically dour Taupin-esque tale of a man who spends his days laying railway tracks across America, while thinking of his wife who died a hundred miles back.

The sessions then ended with "Madman Across the Water," which featured hallucinatory guitar work from Mick Ronson, a respected session musician who was soon to join forces with David Bowie's Spiders From Mars band.

"It came out sounding like Led Zeppelin playing Elton John," Gus noted of the final recording. "A bit schizophrenic and boring."

Though the eight-minute track was temporarily shelved, it was anything but forgotten.

Dick James was impressed with Elton's most recent work; so much so, that he offered the singer an expanded recording contract which bound him to DJM's This Record Co. for five years, recording two full albums (six album-sides worth of music) per year. Elton's royalty would be four percent of the record's retail price, increasing to six percent two years down the road.

To celebrate the signing, the publisher arranged a launch party on March 26, the day after Elton's twenty-third birthday, at the Revolution Club in London's Mayfair district. Elton sipped champagne during the event and played a selection of songs to a group of invited press. David Rosner, a music manager working for Dick James in America, was in attendance that day. "The performance was good," he said. "But you couldn't really say it was spectacular. It was workman-like. He simply played some songs and that was that. His rear never left the piano seat."

Indeed, the party's highlight had nothing to do with Elton's stagecraft but rather with Dick James' grandiose presentation of a birthday present to his piano-playing charge: a state-of-the-art, lime-green 8-track stereo system.

"No expense was spared," Elton joked. "Can it get any better?"

While tracks from Elton's latest sessions were being mixed and mastered, the *Elton John* album was being released in the U.K. and throughout Europe on April 10. (Though the LP appeared uniform in most territories, "I Need You to Turn To" was swapped out for "Rock 'n' Roll Madonna" in Germany, while the Portuguese release featured an alternate mix of "The Greatest Discovery," which utilized a French horn instead of Buckmaster's cello during the song's forlorn introduction.) The work was, in every way, a quantum leap forward in quality from *Empty Sky*. Unlike its predecessor, even the cover art—a stark Rembrandt-esque portrait by fashion photographer David Bailey, which showed Elton swamped in black shadows, as if lit by a single lantern—was designed to impress.

"It was, 'Try and hide as much of his face as possible'," the pianist noted wryly.

Reviews for the disc were promising. Calling the LP "a truly great record," *Melody Maker* wondered, "Is this the year of Elton John?" The *Daily Mirror*'s Don Short took it a step further, trumpeting that it was "time to hail a new genius in the commercial folk world." *NME,* meanwhile, labeled Elton "a big talent…who sounds as if he has lived in Nashville all his life."

Industry insiders were equally as vociferous in their praise, especially in their admiration of the resonant open drum sounds Gus was able to coax from the studio. "Gus Dudgeon had phone calls in the night from producers," Elton said. "His production on that record became very influential."

Despite all the good will *Elton John* generated, the album entered the BBC charts at number 45 and promptly fell out again, unable to fend for itself amongst such major league competition as the Beatles' *Let It Be,* Simon & Garfunkel's *Bridge Over Troubled Water,* and *Led Zeppelin II.*

Wise to the realities of the music business, Dick James informed Elton in no uncertain terms that his future lay on the road.

"We were told we would have to get a band together, which was the last thing I wanted to do," the pianist said. "We came to the conclusion that I would have to go out on the road with a band and promote the record, which I'd fought against tooth and nail for a long time. And I suddenly just decided that was the only answer."

Elton rang up fellow label mates Nigel Olsson and Dee Murray, both veterans of the Spencer Davis Group, and asked if they'd be interested in doing a short promotional tour for his new album.

"He said, 'I'm doing this prestige gig," Nigel said. "Would you be interested in doing the Roundhouse?'"

The long-haired drummer was initially hesitant, having been hired mere weeks before by the hard rock outfit Uriah Heep. Still, he and Dee showed up the next night at DJM Studios to meet with Elton. The date was April 10, the day Paul McCartney officially announced to the world that the Beatles were no more.

Elton took Nigel and Dee out for an Indian meal before their test rehearsal. The news of the Beatles' split came over the radio while they sat in a tiny corner booth, silently eating their curry.

"The baton's been passed," the pianist teased.

"Right on," Dee said with a laugh; Nigel merely nodded.

The three musicians headed back to the studio around 6:30 p.m. Nigel settled himself behind a massive low-tuned drum kit, donning black racing gloves to protect his hands from cuts and callouses, while Dee dragged deeply on a cigarette before plugging his bass into a Marshall skyscraper amp.

"'Bad Side of the Moon' then," Elton said. "One...two..."

The room exploded with a Gale-Force-12 fury.

"Eight bars into the first song we played, I just thought, 'This is it, this is exactly the stuff I wanna be doing,'" Nigel said. "Something where I could play to the low end of Elton's piano...It was all so inspiring, the three of us were on the exact same wavelength." He grinned. "It was just right. The music hit me in the heart *and* in the head. I gave up on anything else after that. *This* is where I wanted to be."

Dee was equally enthusiastic. "We all had magic together, and [we] felt that we had something that could get really big. Everything felt right."

"I remember very clearly walking into Dick James Studios and there was this huge drum kit with Nigel behind

123

it—who I knew—and there was Dee, and there's Elton at the piano," Stuart Epps said. "And I thought, 'Well, where's Caleb?' And I'm looking behind the door and everything, and there's no Caleb. And Elton said, 'No, no, no, Caleb's not in this band. We don't have a guitarist.' And I just thought, 'He's mad. How can they play without a guitarist?' But they were phenomenal. They'd done these arrangements of songs like 'Sixty Years On' and 'Take Me to the Pilot', and Nigel wasn't an ordinary drummer, he was using this huge kit, this thunderous sort of orchestral kit, and Dee wasn't an ordinary bass player, he was playing chords in the songs, he was a great bass player, and because they didn't have a guitar, it left a lot more room for the piano, and we all know Elton's the most amazing pianist. It was a great sound."

No one was more pleased by the brilliant noise they created than Elton himself. "I couldn't have wished for a better band," he said soon after. "I can't say I did expect to find such good sidemen as Nigel and Dee. We all knew different styles of playing, and everything gelled very quickly. I had a pretty clear idea of the kind of group it should be, the basic, raw thing…lots of power. But knowing that, I also thought it would be nearly impossible to get just the right people for the job. When Dee came along I knew he was it, it had to be. I knew what he could do, how he would contribute, and had to have him. But Nigel was a different case. I was a little bit unsure about him at the start, but I didn't say anything because I wanted to give him a chance to prove himself. I thought I saw something there. And I did."

Elton took another step forward by appearing on the *Top of the Pops* television show. Britain's answer to *American Bandstand*—and the sole music-oriented series available in Britain—the weekly audience for *Top of the Pops* was massive, with more than a quarter of all British television sets tuned in to the show every Thursday evening.

ToTP

On April 19, Elton sang a live vocal on "Border Song" over a prerecorded backing track, per the shows rigid formatting rules. Despite the exposure *Top of the Pops* afforded, the pianist was left dissatisfied with the artificial feel of the program. "I'd really like to do a couple of gigs a week, because that's how you sell yourself to people," he said. "[But] *Top of the Pops* doesn't really give anybody an idea of what you can do. In fact, it gives them a totally wrong impression."

Elton viewed the actual broadcast the next night at the DJM offices, sweating nervously as he watched himself performing on Dick James' rarest of possessions—a color television.

"So that's me then, eh?" he joked, wiping at his brow. "What a con."

The next evening, April 21, Elton and his new band cabbed it over to the Roundhouse, a soot-covered train shed in Chalk Farm, to play the first night of a "musical fair." Hosted by popular BBC disc jockey John Peel, the six-night event also boasted a host of other groups including Mott the Hoople, Johnny Winter ("*From America!*"), Fairport Convention and Fleetwood Mac.

Elton, Nigel and Dee opened for the Marc Bolan-led folk-rock outfit Tyrannosaurus Rex, who lent Elton's group their amplifiers and drum kit for their set. (Shortly afterward, Tyrannosaurus Rex would "go glam" and change their name to the pithier T. Rex.)

A tremendously nervous, vodka-breathed Elton walked onto stage wearing a heavy afghan overcoat, which he hesitantly removed before sitting down to play.

Starting with an elegiac reading of "Skyline Pigeon," Elton was soon thrashing the keyboards with a rhythmic chord style reminiscent of his latest musical hero, Leon Russell.

"It was a terrific gig," Dee said. "We really gave it to them. We were on fire."

The set ended with the as-yet-unreleased "Burn Down the Mission." During the song's climax, Elton kicked his piano stool away and began playing standing up. Leaping about like a madman, he completely lost his mind. "Halfway through 'Burn Down the Mission', he stopped playing the piano and stood up and got hold of a tambourine and started banging it on his ass," Stuart Epps said. "I couldn't look, I had to look away. I thought, 'What the fuck is he doing?' Because he never used to do that before. He used to just sit there and play and talk to the audience a bit, but not really. And now suddenly he's up there banging this tambourine around, and I couldn't look. But the audience started to like it, and they're all clapping along and it was all right, they were obviously loving it. And that's when Elton developed into a showman. I mean, I'm sure that side of him was always there, but he'd never shown it before."

Mounting hysteria erupted as the ganja-basted crowd pushed themselves bodily against the stage.

"It was unbelievable," Nigel said afterward. "People couldn't believe that the three of us made that kind of sound."

With the band proving itself a more than reliable unit, Elton attempted again to free himself from his current contract. "Reg didn't feel like Dick James was backing him properly," Caleb said. "Dick wouldn't approve any of the songs we were doing. Elton tried to get out of his contract. He went to see Muff Winwood, Steve Winwood's brother, over at Island

Records. Muff offered to buy-out Elton's contract, but the price wasn't right and Dick James said no. Elton was furious. He felt trapped."

Undeterred, Elton decided to forge a managerial relationship with the man who'd introduced him to Bernie.

"I was living near Chelsea," Ray Williams said. "And Elton came to me with Bernie and he said, 'Let's have a drink.' And we went to the Duke of Wellington in Chester Row, Belgravia. And Elton said, 'I would like you to manage me.' He was fed up that Dick James had signed him to every imaginable contract there was, but Dick didn't really seem to understand what he had. So Elton said, 'Would you be my manager? Dick James would sell my management contract if he could get some money.' And I said, 'I've got no money; however, I'll try to find someone with some money.' So I started looking around, trying to find a money partner. The first person I tried was John French...who managed Jeff Beck. I then went to my friend Brian Morrison. Originally the agent of Pink Floyd, Brian was now working for NEMS, the old Beatles' manager's Brian Epstein's company, and [it] was run by former band leader Vic Lewis." Despite his best efforts to buy out Dick James' interest in Elton, Williams ultimately found no takers. "Vic said to me, 'Are you serious that this guy is going to earn seventy-five-thousand-dollars a night?' I said, 'Yes.' He said, 'You've got to be joking.' And the meeting was ended. Nonetheless, Brian Morrison came with me to meet Dick James, but they didn't get on very well."

Appreciating Williams' conviction, Dick James signed him to a three-year contract on May 11 to manage Elton's growing daily affairs under the auspices of DJM. The deal allowed Williams to split a twenty percent management fee with James himself, as well as earning a weekly salary of £40, plus a biweekly advance on expenses of £10.

Williams' first official action was to oversee Elton's May 22 appearance on the 13-part BBC-2 *In Concert* television series which featured a performance from a different singer/songwriter each episode. "They've got such people as Leonard Cohen and Joni Mitchell," Elton said, "so I was really knocked out when I was asked to do one as well."

Wearing a light orange shirt, a red, white and blue knitted vest, and sky-blue jeans—his unkempt ginger hair hanging down to his shoulders—Elton gave a subdued performance while Paul Buckmaster dutifully conducted a small compliment of string players behind him. Several dozen hushed teens watched politely from the bleachers, providing restrained applause for a set list which included "Your Song," "Border Song," "Sixty Years On," "Take Me to the Pilot," "The Greatest Discovery," "I Need You to Turn To" and "Burn Down the Mission."

"[The audience] were sitting on little cushions," Paul Buckmaster said. "It was meant to be informal, but actually it sort of comes across a bit stiff and stilted. But that's the BBC. They were trying to be 'groovy, baby.'" Despite the forced casualness, the arranger/conductor found the show to be a nerve-wracking experience. "It was the first time I had ever done anything like that," he said, "and I was thrown in at the deep end. You either sink or swim. I think I managed to swim…You're generally nervous before an event, but once you start you go into a professional mode. It takes over, and the next thing you know it's over and there's applause and you say, 'Oh, what happened in the middle?' You're at a different consciousness level."

A quarter way through the performance, Elton introduced the audience to Bernie, who sat shyly in the front row.

"He's my partner," the pianist said as his blushing lyricist gave a quick wave. "Actually he's more important than me, because he writes the words."

The show would air to indifferent reviews a month later, under the banal title: *In Concert: Elton John Sings the Songs of Elton John and Bernie Taupin.*

Elton hired a lone roadie, Bob Stacey, between a headlining gig at the Marquee Club on Friday, June 5, and a support slot at the Lyceum in London on June 17—the latter a gig where he and his band found themselves opening for Santana on their sole London appearance for the year. Though the Santana show proved a bit of a musical mismatch, it quickly became apparent that Elton showed a natural affinity for being the center of attention. "Once I started [touring], I really enjoyed it," he said. "Because I'd never been a front-man before, I'd just been the piano player, so in fact I was [now] in charge."

The band seemed to be gaining confidence exponentially each night as well. "It's fantastic how enjoyable it is, [it's] amazing what we can do," Dee said. "Often during a set I'll be enjoying it so much that I'll want to have a laugh with Nigel. I'll turn round and take a look at him, and he'll be working all over the place. I couldn't imagine how much [playing together has] improved our playing, plus the fact that Elton's music contains so much feeling."

Despite the band's natural affinity for performing, many early gigs still proved a trial by fire. Unable to bring his own piano with him, Elton was forced to rely on the whims of fate at each gig. Some nights he played on pianos with busted keys. Other nights, his instrument would be sorely out-of-tune. One piano rested on orange crates; another had no pedals. Though he handled it well, the unpredictability of the entire endeavor seemed to fray his writing partner's nerves. Each night Bernie could be found watching Elton anxiously from the wings, a bottle of Courvoisier in hand. "I was always nervous when Elton played," he said. "I lived vicariously through him going onstage. Because he didn't have any paranoia, I had it all for him."

"Before I go onstage, [Bernie] sort of loses a handful of hair, he goes gray," Elton joked to disc jockey Pete Fornatale. "He's really a shivering wreck. By the time I come offstage, he's lost five stone."

On June 19, midway through this makeshift tour, Elton's first non-album single of the decade, "Rock 'n' Roll Madonna," was released. Backed with the terse lunacy of "Grey Seal," the single received glowing reviews, with the *Daily Sketch* proclaiming, "As a singer/songwriter, [Elton] is emerging as one of the most fascinating new talents around." *Record Mirror's* Robert Partridge, meanwhile, asserted that Elton "is probably Britain's first real answer to Neil Young and Van Morrison." Perhaps the most positive notice of all, however, was posted by the *International Times,* which stated that "Elton John shares the distinction of creating music which strikes that rare balance between brilliance and honest originality."

Yet for all the accolades, the finely constructed single failed to chart.

Fortitude—and fortunes—seemed to brighten considerably when Elton's band scored a plum support slot on Sérgio Mendes & Brazil 66's European tour. "They aren't exactly my scene," Elton said of the Brazilian musician, famous for bossa-nova-flavored covers of such light pop fare as "The Fool on the Hill" and "Scarborough Fair." "So I just hope the audiences will accept us both. On the Continent, they are inclined to mix up the bills."

Things didn't go well opening night, however. The crowd at the Olympia in Paris hated Elton from the outset, and was soon hurling cigarette packs and bits of hot dog at him and his band. "We got booed before we even got on stage and people chucked things at us, but we played for forty-five minutes and played bloody well," he said. "And I went offstage and I went, 'Well, obviously Sérgio Mendes fans don't like me.' And then Sérgio Mendes went onstage and everyone went, 'Boooo!'" He chuckled. "*Merci beaucoup.*"

Blaming Elton for his own poor reception, Mendes severed ties with the pianist that night, paying him £60 to not complete the tour. (Sérgio would have a change of heart a few short years later, releasing a cover version of Elton's "Where to Now, St. Peter?" on his *Homecooking* LP.)

Things went infinitely better at the Speakeasy Club in London on July 4, when ex-Yardbirds blues maestro Jeff Beck turned up in the audience for Elton's set.

"I went through managers like a dose of salts at that time," Beck said, "and one of them put me on to Elton, and took me to the Speakeasy to see him play."

The guitarist was impressed with what he saw. After the show, he approached Elton and asked if he could join his band. "I was very adamant about no guitars," the pianist said, "but it was Jeff Beck and I was little Elton John." After consulting with Nigel and Dee, he invited Beck to their rehearsal at Hampstead Town Hall the next day.

"I turned up late and [Elton] gave me a terrible roasting," Beck said.

Still, he fitted in perfectly with the power trio. Despite his initial wariness, Elton grew excited, noting that "[Beck] was fine. He played very quietly and very tastefully." But it wasn't long before he and the blues guitarist found themselves at loggerheads. "[Beck] said, 'Well, I'm sorry, but I want to throw out your drummer [for Cozy Powell],' and I made it plain that he was going to meet with violent opposition from me. And then *he* wanted to employ *me*, he wanted me to come and do a tour of the States and pay me money to be in his band, ten percent of what he was going to earn, and the original idea was for *him* to join *our* band. Sod Jeff Beck."

During a brief lull in club dates, Elton's band played the Knokke Festival in Belgium on July 11. A lavish televised rock competition, the winning entrant proved to be none other than "Portrait van Elton John."

Nigel and Dee couldn't stop laughing.

"Who had any idea?" Dee said. "The Belgians [were] fucking great."

Days later, Elton entered Sound Techniques Studios—a converted barn in Chelsea—to participate in a two-day session held by Warlock Music producer Joe Boyd. Boyd's plan was to create austere versions of the most commercial tracks from his stable of songwriters—a roster which included Nick Drake, Mike Heron, John and Beverly Martin, and Ed Carter—to leverage as a promotional demo disc.

Playing alongside Traffic drummer Jim Capaldi, guitarist Simon Nicol, and bassist Pat Donaldson, Elton recorded eleven songs live, including "Way to Blue" and "Day is Done." Four of the tracks were then sung by a visibly nervous Linda Peters, girlfriend of acclaimed guitarist/singer Richard Thompson. "I don't remember much about it," she later recalled, "except that Elton had to hold me up to the microphone." The remaining seven tracks, meanwhile, were handled by Elton himself.

"He stood out at the sessions," Joe Boyd said. "Around the time we did that session, his album, *Elton John,* was being released, and I was impressed with it. And there were people talking about it. So you had the feeling already at that moment that this was a guy who wasn't going to be doing union-scale demo sessions for too much longer. He had a lot confidence, and a lot of talent."

Elton was introduced to arranger Del Newman during the sessions; Newman would later orchestrate the pianist's magnum opus, *Goodbye Yellow Brick Road*. "He was very quiet and polite, and he just got on with the task as all professionals do," Newman later recalled in his memoir, *A Touch From God*. "Elton sailed through the work.....He had a command of the material that was a delight to witness, and the calm way he approached the session told me that he had a great future ahead of him."

The fortuitous meeting with the arranger was a singular highlight for Elton in an otherwise unexceptional couple of days.

"I needed the money," he said. "So I did it."

Chapter 3:
Bad Side of the Moon

While Elton was scurrying around in circles of ceaseless motion, the *Elton John* album was quietly hitting record store shelves in America.

As was the case in the U.K., the disc—released in the U.S. on July 22, 1970—sold poorly. Still, reviews were fairly positive. A typical notice was posted by the *Village Voice*'s Robert Christgau, who noted that the album offered "at least one great lyric (about a newborn baby brother), several nice romantic ballads (I don't like its affected offhandedness, but 'Your Song' is an instant standard), and a surprising complement of memorable tracks." *Cash Box*, meanwhile, labeled the disc "one of the two or three most beautiful albums released this year." Al Kooper, Bob Dylan's organist—and the founder of Blood, Sweat & Tears—deemed the album "the perfect record." *Rolling Stone*, however, was unimpressed: "The main problem with *Elton John* is that one has to wade through so much damn fluff to get to Elton John. Here, by the sound of it, arranger Paul Buckmaster's rather pompous orchestra was spliced in as an afterthought."

Despite *Rolling Stones'* disgruntled reaction, producer Gus Dudgeon was rightfully proud of his team's first effort. "The idea of taking a rhythm section and an orchestra and doing them live at the same time, with the kind of classical overtones within Elton's piano playing and the Buckmaster arrangements on that album, added up to something

134

completely unique," he said. "It was unquestionably one of the most unique albums ever made in the history of pop."

Elton and his band were dispatched to the storm-ravaged English countryside on Friday, August 14, to play the Yorkshire Folk, Blues, and Jazz Festival in Krumlin. The poorly-organized, weekend-long gala in the north of England was plagued by severe weather. Scheduled to begin at 3 p.m., the festival wouldn't get underway until well after seven, due to torrential rains and horrendous driving conditions. Further delays were then caused when the bands involved couldn't agree on who should go on first.

Ominously, high winds caused the canvas roof above the stage to tear open before a single note had even been played, allowing gallons of cold rain to pour down on the performers. The huddled masses out in the frozen fields fared no better.

"They were carting the audience away with exposure," said Fairport Convention's Richard Thompson. "Everyone was dressed in those bin-liner things. It was great fun."

Elton ultimately took to the stage just after eight o'clock, following an opening set by the Humblebums, which featured Scottish singer Gerry Rafferty and musician-comedian Billy Connolly, who would play a part in Elton's career several years down the line.

Kicking things off with a blazing "Bad Side of the Moon," Dee strummed out combustible chords on his bass while Nigel bashed out a propulsive backbeat on his Premiere kit with primal anguish, breaking drumstick after drumstick. "Nigel suggested we try moving about on stage," Elton said. "I realized that if I jumped about, not caring about what I was doing, then at least I'd keep my ass warm. I've always been into Jerry Lee Lewis and Little Richard and all, so I started jumping about, not even really knowing what I was doing."

The frigid conditions caused his tambourine-banging performance at the Roundhouse to multiply by a factor of ten; the appreciative crowd cheered him on without reserve.

"They really went nuts," Dee said. "It was great to see."

Toward the end of an energetic hour-long set—which had the entire field clapping along enthusiastically—the pianist passed a bottle of Bernie's Courvoisier and a stack of plastic cups out to the front lines of the 2,000 rain-soaked festival-goers huddled close to the stage.

"If you're cold, come have some brandy," Elton told them. "Don't be shy. Come on." ("Elton later said, 'Peggy taught me how to drink at Krumlin,'" Fairport Convention's bassist Dave Pegg recalled years later. "That was what everyone called me: Peggy. And Elton was watching our gig, and we all spent a lot of time in the artists' bar. Anyway, we're all big Elton fans. Bless him, he deserves to be where he is.")

"[Handing out the brandy] went down really well," said journalist Chris Charlesworth, "and I was really taken with him. This guy was really trying hard here under difficult conditions to cheer everyone up. He was the star of the show, and an unknown."

"I hope this dispels the myth that I am [BBC] Radio One Club and *The Tony Blackburn Show!*" Elton shouted cheekily before returning to the stage for a rollicking encore of the Stones' recent chart-topper, "Honky Tonk Women."

"I think we are going to be hearing a lot of this man in the near future," Charlesworth wrote in *Melody Maker*. "[Elton] was fantastic."

"Border Song," which had been released in America on the Congress label, Uni Record's foreign label imprint, made it onto the charts the very next day, albeit at an anemic 93—and *that* meager success was based largely on its regional popularity in Memphis. The record stalled out one week later, at the dubious high of 92.

"Ninety-two with an anchor," Russ Regan grimly joked. "Unfortunately, we couldn't spread 'Border Song' out of Memphis."

Elton returned from the Yorkshire Moors to learn that despite his earnest efforts, his records simply weren't selling. In a last-ditch effort to salvage his investment, Dick James decided that the only course of action left was to send the pianist to America. Tasked with finding takers Stateside, manager Ray Williams had little luck. "I remember the first effort to get a gig was in New York at place called Ungano's," he said. "It was Chartwell Artists. And they offered us fifty bucks, and I said, 'No.' Then I get a call from a guy called Jerry Heller, and he said, 'Look, I can get you a gig in L.A. for $150.' And I said, 'No, this is ridiculous.'"

Russ Regan suggested that Ray talk to Doug Weston, owner of the Troubadour, a showcase club in West Hollywood. "[Uni/MCA] was looking for an anchor date on a proposed tour by this new artist," Weston said, "so I listened to about half the [*Elton John*] record and immediately got very, very excited. I then gave the go-ahead to book him into the Troubadour. There was no record play on him at the time, but we booked him in as a headliner nonetheless."

The venue offered the perfect strategic launching pad for Elton, as it boasted a proven track record of fostering young talent from James Taylor and Neil Young to Bob Dylan. Counterculture comedic duo Cheech and Chong were discovered there, as was Steve Martin. The Eagles' Don

Henley and Glenn Frey first met at the Troubadour's bar, later memorialized on the Eagles' "Sad Café." Lenny Bruce had even been arrested on the club's stage back in '64 on obscenity charges. (Bruce's audacious crime: daring to use the word "schmuck" in mixed company.)

Despite the Troubadour's storied history, Elton was dubious about the entire venture, underwhelmed at the prospect of having to travel halfway around the globe just to earn a measly $500—split three ways—for a full week's efforts. "I wanted to sort of maintain the reputation the band was getting over in England," he said. "And I sulked and became a prima donna a little bit...I thought, 'How the *hell* are they going to break a record by just playing a club for [a few] days?'"

But fifty-year-old Dick James, who was prepared to fund the £5,000 trip—was insistent. "It's make-or-break time," the avuncular publisher said, clapping a heavy hand on the pianist's shoulder. "So *make* it." He glared at the other musicians gathered in his office. "Otherwise I know of a shoe store just down the road from the Troubadour. You can all stay in California and get jobs making shoes, as far as I'm concerned. It's sink or swim, lads. Am I coming through?"

James was, in fact. Loud and clear.

Realizing that the transatlantic trip was set, Elton decided that he might as well make his foray into the unknown in style. A trip to Mr. Freedom's, a clothes boutique on Kensington Church Street, resulted in several key purchases, including a Tommy-Roberts-designed canary yellow jumpsuit with a massive piano iron-on across the back, green-winged boots, a tweed cap, and a wide leather belt adorned with oversized Texan stars. They were the first seeds of sartorial excess, the fruits of which no one could have quite imagined.

138

Seventy-two hours later, a Pan Am jumbo jet was screaming across the North Pole. Stuffed into its cramped economy-class seats sat Elton, Bernie, Nigel, Dee, Steve Brown, Ray Williams, Bob Stacey and David Larkham.

Elton stared restlessly out his tiny oval window for most of the thirteen-hour, 5,472-mile trip. Beneath his massive nerves thrummed an unchecked excitement at the thought of finally being able to visit the mecca of rock 'n' roll, the fabled land from which his favorite music had sprung. "I'm much more into American bands than British bands," he said. "Most of the British bands are hung up on loud guitars and tight trousers, they're just a flash. All the American bands stay together for such a long time and really get into each other. Bands like Spirit, Airplane, Steve Miller, the Band and the old Buffalo Springfield create so much atmosphere. They concentrate on communication rather than being pop stars."

Elton and his entourage touched down at LAX on a balmy Friday afternoon, August 21. Arriving in a land disenchanted by the Vietnam War and distrustful of their own president, the eight Brits were met—incongruously—by a bright red London Routemaster double-decker bus, upon which a giant banner shamelessly proclaimed "ELTON JOHN HAS ARRIVED." The bus was the misguided pièce de résistance of flamboyant press agent Norm Winter. Hired by Ray Williams to help spread the word about Elton in L.A., the ten-gallon-hat-wearing Winter had thrown everything he had into promoting the unknown pianist—purchasing billboards up and down Sunset Strip, making sure that Elton's eponymous album was well-stocked in every local record shop, and glad-handing disc jockeys the entire week preceding his arrival.

"We became so excited it became almost like an orgasm," Winter said. "We treated him as if an Elvis Presley was opening in Vegas, even though nobody had ever heard of Elton John."

While appreciating Winter's enthusiasm, Elton would have much preferred to have been picked up by a Cadillac. Something luxurious. Something *American*. "I found that [bus] extremely embarrassing," he said. "Everyone was sort of getting into a crouch and trying to hide below the windows. It seemed like a cheap trick. I really couldn't believe it. I didn't think it was happening. I mean, I'm a great lover of things that are done with taste…and double-decker buses *don't* qualify."

The bus struggled through the sun-dazzled traffic on the 405 for what seemed like hours, rusted gears grinding. To help pass the time, Elton kept up a running commentary on the outlandishly dressed hippies they passed out on the sunbaked sidewalks.

"*There's* a splendid lad, this one in the leopard-skin fedora, eh?" he said in his best *Goon* voice. "Me and Eccles know where he *wented*, Captain. Not likely, that. *Eh?*"

Bernie, meanwhile, gawked in disbelief at the endless landscape of neon-lit taco joints and burger stands rolling past his double-paned window.

Finally, the group made it downtown.

"We got to the Sunset Strip and it was like being on parade," Nigel later recalled in the BBC documentary, *The Making of Elton John*. "It was just unbelievable. The California sunshine and the pretty girls all over the place. It was amazing."

Elton checked into the Continental Hyatt House under the name William A. Bong—a sly reworking of billabong, an isolated lake, and the name of his imminent publishing company. As always, his tongue was planted firmly in his cheek.

Once the pianist and his entourage was settled in, they were immediately hustled back out the lobby doors and off to the Troubadour, where Longbranch Pennywhistle—which featured future Eagles coconspirators Glenn Frey and J.D. Souther—were appearing alongside cult Missouri bluegrass band the Dillards.

"They were incredible," Elton said. "Just knocked me out."

Later that night, Three Dog Night's Danny Hutton took Elton and Bernie to (the Black Rabbit) a restaurant on Melrose Avenue owned by Billy James, a publicist who had been instrumental in launching Bob Dylan's career. After dinner, Hutton drove Elton and Bernie up to his house on Lookout Mountain Avenue in Laurel Canyon, where Elton played piano for hours. Up close, Hutton was even more impressed with the Englishman's musical prowess.

"I phoned up Van Dyke Parks," Hutton told author Mark Bego, "and said, 'You had better come over and check this cat out.' So Van Dyke came up, and I remember he sat on the floor next to the piano, and...Elton just sat there playing."

For his part, Van Dyke was impressed yet skeptical, feeling that Elton "was (somewhat too imitative of Leon Russell.")

But Hutton remained wholly convinced. "It was just mind-blowing," he said.

An early highlight of the trip came the next day, when Elton and Bernie were taken to Tower Records. The songwriters were in all their glory, gladly emptying their less-than-bulging pockets to purchase as many records as they possibly could.

"The reason I came over to play the Troubadour," Elton would later tell *Phonograph Record* magazine, "was because I wanted to go to a record shop. I didn't want to play at the Troubadour, I thought it was going to be a joke. I thought it was going to be a complete hype and I thought it was going to be a disaster, and I just really wanted to go to an American record store and buy some albums."

"Elton's a musicologist," Russ Regan noted. "He appreciates other artists, which is great. Some artists are so much into themselves that they don't appreciate other artists. But *he* does. Which is just wonderful, it's a wonderful trait to have."

Back at the Hyatt House that Saturday afternoon, and in desperate need of that most essential piece of preening rock star gear—a hairdryer—Ray Williams called up an old girlfriend, Joanne Malouf. Joanne was out of the country, but her younger sister, Janis, volunteered to bring her hairdryer by. She arrived an hour later, accompanied by a lithesome, honey-voiced blonde named Maxine Feibelman. Bernie was immediately taken with the blond-tressed flower child.

"California was *it*, man," he said. "Fabulous. It was the candy store."

Janice and Maxine offered to show the newly arrived Brits the local sights. Elton demurred, preferring to explore his latest record purchases in his room. Soon enough, however, he found his self-exile less than ideal. Sitting alone in his nondescript hotel room while his compatriots raided second-hand clothing shops in Palm Springs and got drunk at the edge of the desert, Elton quickly sunk into a blue funk.

"Elton was really nervous about the Troubadour," said Ray Williams, who hadn't given a second thought about leaving his charge alone. "But of course me, considering us as friends rather than as a business thing, didn't even stop to think that he was shitting himself back at the hotel."

Feeling abandoned, Elton called Dick James back in England.

"I'm going the fuck *home!*" he howled across the international wires. "I *don't* want to be here! I've had *enough!* I'm fucking *leaving!*"

"Where's Ray?" a confused James asked. "Isn't he there with you?"

"He's in Palm-fucking-*Springs!*"

"Just calm down."

"I'm going the fuck *home!*"

Elton slammed the receiver down, kicked his bedside table over, then sat quietly on the edge of his neatly made bed and wanted impatiently for the fractious internal storm to pass.

"That's where Elton and I started to fall apart," Ray said years later. "That's where the split really started."

A recomposed Elton attended a small party at Neil Diamond's house off Coldwater Canyon that Sunday. The pianist was particularly excited, as the last album he'd purchased back in England before his trip had been Diamond's *Tap Root Manuscript.* The "I Am...I Said" singer was pleased—he was not only a fan of the *Elton John* album, but also a fellow label mate, as well as the artist who held the house attendance record at the Troubadour; given that, he readily agreed to introduce Elton onto stage opening night. By nature a generous man, Diamond was willing to do anything he could to help the introspective lad who seemingly had the odds stacked against him.

"[Elton] sat in my living room holding his cap in his lap," he said. "He was super quiet and shy. I thought to myself, 'This kid's never gonna make it.'"

Troub

Monday afternoon, the day before Elton's first show, roadie Bob Stacey began setting up Nigel's enormous drum kit on the Troubadour's tiny wooden stage. Sitting behind the house piano, Elton counted Nigel and Dee in. Together they ran through a four-song soundcheck. It was their first opportunity to play together since a London rehearsal the Thursday prior, and it felt good.

"We still had it," Dee said. "Everything was fine."

Russ Regan, who wasn't able to attend the soundcheck due to a scheduling conflict, sent Rick Frio, Uni's national sales director, in his stead. "He called me from the Troubadour," Regan later recalled, "and he said, 'You're *not* gonna believe this guy. He's got a three-piece band, but they sound like an orchestra. Elton's incredible.' And I said, 'Oh my God.'"

Tuesday night, August 25, 1970 was a muggy night. The dimly lit Troubadour was hot and smoky, music industry insiders chatting around tiny wicker tables while the bar in front bustled with activity.

When he arrived at 9081 Santa Monica Boulevard, Elton immediately noted that the Troubadour's marquee listed his name above that of folk singer David Ackles, whom he was sharing the bill with. The pianist hustled inside, found Doug Weston in his office, and insisted that Ackles name be given top-billing.

"He's a bloody living legend and I'm a nobody," Elton insisted.

But Weston refused to change the billing—*Elton* was the headliner, and that was that.

The pianist couldn't believe it. "There was no way that anyone could have convinced me that I should be above David Ackles....I was flabbergasted."

144

ador show

Stunned, Elton joined Nigel and Dee in their miniscule dressing room. He sipped a Coke. Shut his eyes. Rested his chin on his chest.

Nigel and Dee glanced at each other warily. Ten silent minutes past. When the clock on the wall hit ten o'clock sharp, Dee clapped his hands together.

"Showtime, lads," the slender bassist said with a grin. "Lord help us."

Neil Diamond took to the stage to make the introductions. "I've never done this before, so please be kind," he told the two-hundred-and-fifty in attendance. "I know Elton John's *classy* album and I love the album, and I have no idea what these people are about to do. I just want to take my seat and enjoy this with you."

A bearded Elton stepped onto stage moments later for the first show of his six-night, eight-date residency in blue jeans, his Texan star belt and a blood-red T-shirt which brazenly proclaimed: *Rock 'n' Roll*.

Many of the agents, writers and concert promoters who made up the bulk of the audience were still hanging out by the bar as the visibly uptight pianist began his set with the quietly introspective "Your Song."

"Thank you," Elton said afterward to polite applause.

"Elton appeared extremely shy and nervous," music critic Robert Hilburn later noted in his memoir, *Corn Flakes with John Lennon*. "He kept his eyes on the piano and the microphone in front of him. Someone next to me whispered that Elton had better be a good songwriter, because he certainly wasn't a very compelling performer." Ignoring his compatriot, Hilburn closed his eyes and concentrated on the music. "The tone felt wonderfully soothing after the emotional turbulence of the 1960s," he wrote. "Elton's approach, it turned out, was one of the first signs that the creative center of pop music was changing direction in the new decade."

Hilburn was one of the few inside the Troubadour's walls impressed by the lilting ballad; the boisterous conversations emanating from the bar showed no signs of abating.

"*Right!*" Elton shouted, angrily kicking his piano stool away. "If you won't listen, perhaps you'll bloody well listen to *this!*"

He and his band crashed headlong into "Bad Side of the Moon," Nigel's drums exploding like thunder as Elton's raucous piano battled with Dee's arpeggiated bass riffs.

Heads turned.

Conversations ceased.

"We just made a lot of noise," Dee said. "We had to make up for the orchestra. We hit that thing so big."

Blues-folk singer Odetta leapt out of her chair and shook her mighty torso manically to the fervent music. The entire crowd soon joined in, rising as one.

"It gave me chills," Russ Regan said. "From that point on, it was all over. Everyone in the audience knew something very, very special was happening."

A startled Carole King couldn't believe what she was witnessing. "I was blown away, like everybody else," she recalled years later. "Wow. Great songs, great performance, great presence. And then Elton just took it to an Elton level."

A couple tables over from King sat T-Bone Burnett. "This young English cat...blew the place apart," he said. "I was sitting about twenty feet from him...It was beautiful and free."

Neil Young was also impressed by the Briton's boundary-breaking set. "[Elton's music] caught my ear," he said. "It wasn't like rock 'n' roll, but it wasn't like pure pop, either. I didn't know *what* it was. That's what got me about it. It seemed like an extension of *something*. It was something I hadn't heard before."

Standing against the far wall stood a bedraggled, pre-Eagles Don Henley. "I don't know how I got in," he later told *Billboard*, "but I was among the fortunate ones who gathered there on the evening of August 25 to hear the latest rage from England....That night, Elton John forever changed the history of popular music."

"Nobody had ever seen anybody playing a piano with their feet up in the air like that," Doug Weston said. "[Elton] literally flew...In the whole eighteen years of Troubadour history, no artist had ever captured the town as completely and thoroughly. It was unique for a total unknown to have gotten such a widely positive response. The Elton John situation was nothing short of phenomenal."

"It was a charged evening," Russ Regan concurred. "Elton and Nigel and Dee just brought the house down. We knew within forty-five minutes that we had a superstar. It was electrifying. I mean, it was just an electric night." Ray Williams felt much the same. "As history will show, those shows at the Troubadour were absolutely brilliant. Nigel was super, and Dee was like the glue that held the band together. There was something very simple and strong about the way he played and joined in. He was just very melodic, a great bass player. And Elton, of course, was a wonderful performer. It was phenomenal."

Indeed, the Brit pounded restlessly on the ivories all night long, his stubby hands a blur as they hammered out one tasty legato blues phrase after another.

"I started cheering so loudly," Neil Diamond said, "[that] I spilled my drink."

 Elton and Nigel and Dee let go of any remaining inhibitions as they swung down the riotous homestretch of a fourteen-minute "Burn Down the Mission," incorporating an energetically majestic cover of the Beatles' "Get Back" into the coda.

"Suddenly, the Troubadour audience was on its feet," Robert Hilburn said. "The guy next to me wasn't whispering any longer. He joined in the thunderous applause."

"*Rock 'n' roll!*" a sweat-soaked Elton cried, doing a handstand off the keyboard and falling to his knees, his head shaking as if he were having a seizure. As the song climaxed, he leapt atop his piano and pumped his fist high into the smoky air. The crowd imitated his gesture, mesmerized by the energy he gave off.

"For the first time in my life," he said, "I felt released."

Chapter 4:
Is New York As Hip As California?

Elton compared his opening night at the Troubadour to *The Eddy Duchin Story*. "One of those old films," he said. "'Look, the boy is conducting the orchestra, he's fourteen years old and he's blind and he's got one leg and everybody's going 'Hooray!'" He laughed. "Everybody thought I was going to be a very moody person…fainting after every three songs. In fact, I came out with shorts on and flying boots…and played rock 'n' roll, and they went, 'What is *this?*'"

Music critic Robert Hilburn understood exactly what it was.

"Rejoice," he declared on page 22 of the August 27 edition of the *Los Angeles Times*. "Rock music, which has been going through a rather uneventful period recently, has a new star. He's Elton John, a 23-year-old Englishman, whose debut Tuesday night at the Troubadour was, in almost every way, magnificent." Hilburn was effusive in his praise of the pianist's "staggeringly original" music. "By the end of the evening," he presciently concluded, "there was no question about John's talent and potential. Tuesday night at the Troubadour was just the beginning. He's going to be one of rock's biggest and most important stars."

"Everything stemmed from Hilburn's article," Dee said. "[It was] just mind-blowing."

Elton felt similarly. "That one night, and that one review, saved me a year's work. It flew, word-of-mouth....It was a kind of fluke."

Yet Hilburn wasn't alone in his critical assessment of the Englishman's musical prowess. Kathy Orloff of the *Chicago Sun-Times* wrote that Elton "was a major star before the end of his first set...The future seems incredibly bright for John," while John Gibson of the *Hollywood Reporter* proclaimed "it's not often that someone gets a standing ovation at the Troubadour, but Elton John did—twice....He got the entire audience singing, clapping and stomping....Audiences don't usually join in on the enthusiasm, but he was irresistible." The *Los Angeles Free Press* noted that "recently there's been a lot of loud clatter about Elton John. And there's going to be a lot more. For once, the hype is mostly true." The *Los Angeles Herald-Examiner*, meanwhile, proclaimed Elton "a spectacular talent," while *Rolling Stone* simply declared the Brit's show "one of the great opening nights in Los Angeles rock." (Indeed, decades later, *Rolling Stone* would rate Elton's first Troubadour gig as one of "The Top Twenty Concerts That Changed The Face Of Rock 'n' Roll.)

"My whole life came alive that night," Elton said. "Musically, emotionally...everything. It was like everything I had been waiting for suddenly happened. I was the fan who had become accepted as a musician. It was just amazing. [And] there were so many people who suddenly wanted to know me. Instantly I went from being a nobody to Mr. Elton John. I must have shaken a million hands and had people slapping me on the back and calling me the Great White Wonder and all that." As to his seemingly instant success, he truly had no idea why it happened. "I think it's a matter of luck, and being in the right place at the right time. I'm a great believer in that—if you keep plugging away, you're going to make it sometime. I had to wait seven years, but no one was more surprised when it happened than me."

The spectacular evening was capped off by a telephone call from rock impresario Bill Graham, who offered Elton a pair of fall shows at his Fillmore's East and West.

"$5,000," Graham said. "It's the highest fee the Fillmore has ever paid for a new act."

"Sold!" Elton said.

Thursday afternoon, before Elton's third show, Uni Records arranged for a private VIP trip to Disneyland. It was the pianist's first ride in a limousine, and his first real taste of the star treatment, as he and Bernie and Dee and Nigel were ushered past long lines of people waiting for the bumper cars and rollercoasters. The pianist bought a pair of Mickey Mouse ears, which he threatened to wear onstage that night. Nigel and Dee thought he was joking. Hours later, they were shocked as Elton donned the ears before performing "Your Song."

"He seemed like a very quiet, subdued person," Nigel said. "All of a sudden, in front of an American audience, he started wearing Mickey Mouse ears and jumping up and down. That's where all the strange gear started."

KHJ, the big Top 40 radio station in L.A., put "Your Song" on heavy rotation.

"The new Rock Messiah is here, ladies and gentlemen," the disc jockey portentously intoned as "Your Song" became "Take Me to the Pilot." "And the new Messiah's name is Elton John."

Russ Regan, who was driving Nigel and Dee to get hamburgers at the time, pulled his car off the Hollywood Freeway, laughing through unbidden tears.

"I *love* you guys," the vindicated record head told them, genuinely moved. "I *love* you guys."

"We knew we had done something right," Nigel said.

Word of Elton's phenomenal prowess spread quickly. The subsequent nights' shows were thus packed with a litany of Los Angeles *culturati*; Graham Nash and David Crosby turned out to see the British powerhouse in action, as did the Everly Brothers, Gordon Lightfoot, Bread's David Gates, the Beach Boys' Mike Love, Quincy Jones, Henry Mancini and Elmer Bernstein.

Elton took their presence in stride. He was hardly the type to get star-struck—at least until halfway through "Burn Down the Mission" on the second night, when he noticed Leon Russell sitting in the audience, all flowing locks and aviator glasses.

"I nearly died," Elton said. "I didn't see him until the last number. Thank God I didn't, because at that time I slept and drunk Leon Russell….He was sitting there with his beautiful silver hair, looking like Rasputin…I regarded him as some kind of god. And I saw him and I just stopped."

"I had heard [Elton] with Long John Baldry," Leon said. "I sat down in the first row at the Troubadour, and he was brilliant. I wish we could have got him for Shelter [Records, Russell's U.S. label]."

Leon invited Elton and Bernie up to his house, The Mission, high up in the Malibu Canyon hills, the next afternoon. "I figured this was it," Elton said, "[Leon's] going to tie me up in a chair and whip me and say, 'Listen here, you bastard, *this* is how you play the piano.' But he was really nice instead. It was like a schoolboy's fantasies coming true….If I ever had to write one song in my life, it would be 'Song for You'."

Russell was equally enamored by Elton. "He was quite a beautiful soul singer," he said. "He had a huge blues awareness that I found interesting. I thought my career was over, 'cause he was a lot more active and a lot more showmanship. I figured I'd had it."

Elton and Bernie marveled at Russell's manse, barren except for an oversized brass bed and a massive stereo that sat by itself on a polished hardwood floor. They found it a most bizarre site. "For some reason," Bernie said, "all rock stars' houses were exactly the same."

Russell shared a gargling potion with his British counterpart, as his voice was blown out from his recent performances. "You gargle some vinegar and some honey with the hottest water you can take," Elton said. "From that day on, we've had it in the dressing room." *[handwritten margin note: throat remedy]*

The visit culminated with Russell mentioning that he wanted to record his own version of "Burn Down the Mission," and that he'd written "Roll Away the Stone" after hearing "Take Me to the Pilot." Moved by the words, Elton eagerly agreed to jam with his idol on twin pianos which sat beneath a sign reading: *Don't Shoot the Piano Player.*

"Let's record something together sometime," Russell shouted as they swung into a bluesy boogie-woogie in G-major.

Elton nodded mutely, flabbergasted.

"It's worth five-million good reviews if someone you respect as a musician comes up and tells you they like what you're doing," he said.

After his eighth and final Troubadour show, Elton found himself sitting at the end of the club's bar late Sunday night with David Ackles, sharing a bottle of scotch that Ackles had bought him as a congratulatory gift.

"It's been a real blast working with you," Ackles told him as they sipped their drinks.

Elton was moved. "David Ackles was brilliant. I made a point of watching him every night. [He] told me how much he enjoyed working with me…which is utterly incredible, because *I* had been a number one fan of his. To see the audience just chatting away while he was singing those lovely songs just tore me apart. People were there because the buzz had got around that I was the guy to see, and they didn't give a toss about a great person like him."

"To the future," Ackles said, holding his glass high.

"Do you know," Elton later reflected, "that meant most of all to me."

To help celebrate Elton's successful stand, Danny Hutton and his girlfriend, actress June Fairchild, took him and Bernie on a late-night trek to Brian Wilson's mansion in Bel Air. The reclusive creative force behind the Beach Boys was living in a house once owned by Edgar Rice Burroughs. Now painted bright purple, the driveway was lined with drum kits.

Hutton buzzed the intercom at the gated entrance. "I've got Elton with me," he said.

A moment later, Brian Wilson's unmistakable voice came singing back: "Ah, Elton. 'I hope you don't mind, I hope you don't mind…'"

The sweet-natured Beach Boy warmly embraced Elton and Bernie at the front door. Glassy-eyed and mumbling to himself, he was clearly in another land. The Brits—who'd never taken a drug in their lives—were at a loss for words.

After a quick tour of the premises—highlighted by a trip through a sand-filled dining room—they ended up in Wilson's fully equipped recording studio. He sat at an eight-octave midnight-black Bösendorfer and sang them "This

Whole World," his sole contribution to the Beach Boys' imminent LP, *Sunflower*. The moment he finished, he leapt off the piano bench, threw his large frame behind a mixing console, and started playing the master tape of "Good Vibrations." "[I had] the volume turned up and the sliders pushed down, which allowed the intricacies that are buried on the record to fly out," Wilson would recall years later in his autobiography, *Wouldn't It Be Nice*. "Elton was knocked out."

After playing the song through four times, it was Elton's turn to impress. He sat at Wilson's piano and played "Amoreena." Halfway through, Wilson stopped him.

"Great, Elton. What else have you got?"

Elton began playing 'Border Song'. Halfway through, Wilson stopped him again.

"Terrific. What else?"

Elton launched into "I Need You to Turn To."

Wilson sat back and smiled, deeply affected by the strength of the pianist's compositions. "It was the most impressive string of new material I'd ever heard," he said. "Elton asked if I were still writing and I said not much, which was hard considering how jealous I was of Elton at that moment. Listening to his songs, I knew he was hot, that he was tapped into the great source. I'd been there myself."

Local underground station KPPC took out a full-page advertisement in the *Los Angeles Free Press* to rave about Elton's talents, and to bid him a quick return to the City of Angels. His star clearly on the ascent, Viking Records decided to capitalize on the positive publicity he'd been receiving by releasing "From Denver to L.A."—erroneously crediting the disc to "Elton Johns."

Furious at the impertinence, Dick James slapped an injunction on the record and had it withdrawn from the shops.

"So if you have a copy," Elton said, "it's worth a small fortune."

Elton and his entourage decamped to San Francisco the next day for a string of shows at the Troubadour's sister club. Critic Robert Hilburn followed the caravan up, holding an interview with Elton and Bernie at a soundcheck before the first show. Unlike Janis Joplin, whom Hilburn had interviewed the year before, the critic found Elton full of energy and eager to talk. "Asked to name some of his favorite artists, he went on for several minutes, mentioning a third of the artists I had in my record collection, starting with the Beatles, Dylan, and everyone on Motown," Hilburn said. "His enthusiasm was evident when he stepped to the stage for the soundcheck. Normally, soundchecks last fifteen to twenty minutes, but Elton spent more than an hour on this one, running through not just his own songs, but also some favorites from childhood and others that were more contemporary—from "Long Tall Sally" and "In the Midnight Hour" to "The Weight" and "Long Black Veil." He was like a human computer of rock n' roll."

After the soundcheck, Elton grew even more animated when he was told that John Reid, the twenty-year-old label manager for the British division of Tamla Motown—Reid had been responsible for pulling "The Tears of a Clown" off Smokey Robinson's three-year-old *Make It Happen* album and releasing it as a Number One single in Britain in February, 1970—was in town for the label's tenth-anniversary convention. The Scotsman, who hailed from Paisley, near Glasgow, was an acquaintance of Elton's from London, having been introduced to him months before by

Harvest Records' David Crocker, who occupied the office next to Reid's in Manchester Square.

"One day," Reid said, "David came in and said, 'This is my friend Reg.' That's how I met Elton. He scrounged some Motown American singles, I can't remember what. He said, 'I made a record,' and gave me a white label of what became the *Elton John* album."

Elton gave the label manager a call.

"He rang me, a lost English soul in San Francisco," Reid said, "and he told me about how the critics had received him in Los Angeles, and he was bubbling over, he was dying to tell someone about it. I was the nearest Englishman, or the nearest thing to an Englishman."

During his first show on the Bay, Elton wore what Reid deemed to be "pretty outrageous clothes: jumpsuits with the zips up in back, bib overalls and star-spangled T-shirts, and I thought, 'What *is* this guy?'....He was something I hadn't seen before. Or since, really. He is just a one-off."

The show went down well. *The San Francisco Chronicle* concurred with their fellow critics down the coast, noting that "[Elton] had hardly opened his mouth when it was apparent that he is going to be a very, very big star."

After the performance, Elton and Reid headed back to the Scotman's room at the Japanese-style Miyako Hotel, where they became lovers.

"I was basking in my glory," the pianist later admitted. "I suddenly thought, 'To hell with it, here goes.'"

Days after his San Francisco stand, Uni Records released a full-page ad in the major music trade magazines featuring the cover of the *Elton John* album along with the headline: *Is New York As Hip As California?* With true early-'70s hyperbole, the ad copy went on to ask: "Who is Elton John? Who are you? Some of the answers to these questions are contained in Elton John's songs. Some are contained in your head."

The advertisement-cum-philosophical-treatise was timed to appear in conjunction with Elton's performance at a private midafternoon press luncheon showcase at the Playboy Club in Manhattan. Journalists sat shoulder-to-shoulder with representatives from *The Tonight Show, The Ed Sullivan Show* and *The David Frost Show*, taking detailed notes on each act and grading them for their suitability as future television bookings.

Elton was scheduled third on the three-act bill, behind McKendree Spring and Ken Lyons. By the time he took to the stage, however, lunch was well over with and nearly two-thirds of the audience had left, leaving the Brit to play to a plethora of empty seats.

"He didn't have his heart in it," Russ Regan said. "He didn't do well. He was very upset about everyone having left. What they did wasn't good, putting us on so late. We were all pissed-off."

As Eric Van Lustbader reported in *Record World*, by the end of his brief set, Elton "was beside himself, tears of rage in his eyes."

Elton stormed out of the Playboy Club, Bernie tagging along quietly behind him. After a conciliatory meal at the Carnegie Deli, Elton's mood lightened enough that he decided that he and Bernie should pay a visit to the Apollo Theater in Harlem. "It was dangerous for people to go up into Harlem, but Bernie and I wanted to go," he said. "Being white guys from England, it took us quite a few taxi drivers before we found one to take us up there. I just wanted to stand outside that theater and look at it, and think of all the great music that had come out of it."

Elton and Bernie spent the night at Lowe's Midtown Hotel on Eighth Avenue, in the urine-soaked shadows of Times Square. The Englishmen were wildly unimpressed with the city. "It really smells, the whole city seems to have gone off," the pianist said. "Everybody who lives there keeps apologizing for it. New Yorkers get really upset about what's happening to the city, but they say it just gets worse and worse."

Just past three a.m., the songwriting duo were awakened by a gun battle out in the street. They watched incredulously as a policeman shot a vandal dead before their eyes. Inspired by the incident, Bernie grabbed his notepad and began scribbling down a new lyric: "Mona Lisas and Mad Hatters," a cynical response to Ben E. King's "Spanish Harlem."

"When I first saw New York, it terrified the crap out of me," he admitted. "It actually scared me."

Elton's final gigs on his maiden trip to the United States were two nights at Philadelphia's Electric Factory, on September 11 and 12. Uni/MCA was concerned how the shows would be received, for despite Elton's recent West Coast triumphs, his eponymous album was yet to see any kind of sales spikes.

"We took the train down to Philadelphia and checked into the Marriott hotel," Russ Regan said. "And I was having a lot of people over to my suite that night—writers and the press, and various DJs—and I get a call from California, from my boss' assistant, who told me they were very upset about me going on the road, and how I was spending all this money on this 'bloody Brit'."

"We've heard you're spending money like water," his boss' assistant yelled. "You're wasting money on that Englishman."

"Well, that Englishman is gonna be a superstar," Regan retorted.

"You know what they're calling this guy at the Tower, Russ?"

"No. What are they calling him?"

"'Regan's Folly', *that's* what they're calling him."

"Go to *hell*, motherfucker! We'll show *you!*" Regan smashed the receiver down and stormed down the hall and into Elton's room.

"Don't worry," Elton told Regan after being informed of what had just transpired. "Tonight I'm gonna burn the city of Philadelphia down."

Good to his word, the uninhibited showman brought the three-thousand in attendance at the Electric Factory to the brink of pandemonium with a ferocious, twenty-five minute rendition of "Burn Down the Mission."

"Elton was on top of the piano, under the piano, he was out in the audience," Regan said. "He was everywhere. It was just electrifying. People went crazy—including me. It was ten times greater than the Troubadour. It felt like the floor was going to collapse beneath us. I mean, it was wild."

"The people were all clapping, I was up on the grand mashing about with my feet, I just gave them a signal with my hand and the whole crowd was standing," Elton said after the show. "We just steamed on. No one had a clue who we were, so we had nothing to lose. We just blew the place apart."

"It was like magic," Dee said. "That's the only word for it: magic."

"We came back to the hotel and I called room service and had three banana splits," Regan said. "The next day, all of a sudden, by 10:30 that morning, I get a call from Sam Pasmano, the local MCA distribution guy, and he wanted to order 5,000 *Elton John* LPs. I said, 'Oh my God, something happened last night.' And then, by 1:00, Sam ordered another 5,000. It was magical. So by 1:30 I called my boss' assistant and told him, 'You tell those motherfuckers that 'Regan's Folly' is coming home, and go *screw* yourself!'"

The Electric Factory gigs not only jumpstarted Elton's U.S. record sales, they also earned him yet more raves from the national press. John Mendelssohn, writing in *Rolling Stone*, summed up the critical reception succinctly, asserting that Elton's voice combined "the nasal sonority of James Taylor with the rasp of Van Morrison with the slurry intonation of M. Jagger with the exaggerated twang of Leon Russell…Elton John really is a gas.'"

Chapter 5:
Friends

Upon flying back to England, Elton's first order of business was to renew his visa. Second up was a one-off performance as the opening act for folk-rockers Fotheringay at the Royal Albert Hall on October 2. Elton was thrilled—the gig was an opportunity to show off the musical tightness he and his trio had honed on their U.S. dates. "It's a real band now," he told *Melody Maker*'s Richard Williams the day before the show, "and the boys have helped me a lot. It's so tight now, but in a year's time it'll be unbelievable. America did our confidence a lot of good, and I don't ever have to tell them what to do because we all know what we're doing. There are some songs with very broken rhythms, but [Nigel and Dee] just play them without having it said to them."

An hour before show time, Elton sat by himself on the stairs outside the historied venue, waiting for his mother, Derf, and Sue Ayton—a secretary and good friend from DJM—to arrive. No one recognized him as they passed by; the recent hysteria in America was still merely a whisper on the chilled English wind. "When Reg got back from America that first time," Caleb Quaye said, "he couldn't believe the reception he'd gotten. When he told us about their American gigs, his eyes just lit up. He couldn't believe how sudden it all was. From total anonymity to being mobbed on the street. No one could believe it, really. But back in England, it hadn't happened yet."

The pianist was determined that that situation would change soon enough. Appearing onstage that night in a gold lamé tailcoat from a 30's Busby Berkeley musical—a gift from promoter Bill Graham—Elton gave a hyper-charged performance, tearing off his tailcoat and collapsing to his knees during an incendiary finale of Elvis' "My Baby Left Me." The thousands in attendance were left begging for more.

Fotheringay watched his hypnotic performance from the wings, shell-shocked. "If we'd have known that he was going to do what he did and blow us off the stage, then we wouldn't have chosen him," guitarist Jerry Donahue later told author Keith Hayward. "When Sandy [Denny, Fotheringay's lead singer] went backstage after Elton's set had finished, she was really shaken and making comments like, '*How* are we supposed to go out there now?'...[Elton] just took control of the audience. We sounded weak compared to what they had just witnessed." Sandy Denny was so demoralized by the disastrous night, in fact, that she and her band mates would pull the plug on Fotheringay three short months later.

"Elton was amazing onstage," Sue Ayton said. "He seemed to take everything in his stride. Brilliant showmanship, beautiful voice, funny and exciting. [It was] staggering the way he reached out to everyone in the audience, with the huge Albert Hall audience on its feet."

The critics agreed. "Elton John is an exciting man to watch," noted journalist Penny Valentine the next day. "He is a man who enters into live appearances with a relish and glee that is both a change and a pleasure to watch." *London Times* music critic Karl Dallas concurred, labeling Elton "a welcome, fresh, individual voice." *Phonograph Record*'s Richard Cromelin wasn't quite as impressed however, commenting that Elton "looked like the last person you'd cast in a rockin' role…A small, stubby man, he looked as if he belonged in a physics lab or behind an accountant's desk, but surely not on a concert stage."

Elton was as displeased with the performance as Cromelin had been, but for a far different reason. "I don't think that I've heard anyone but Crosby, Stills, Nash and Young sound good there," he said of the Royal Albert Hall, which he found sonically unbalanced. "But then you learn by your mistakes. We'd never play it again."

While in London, Elton came into the orbit of director Lewis Gilbert, famed for the films *Alfie* and *You Only Live Twice*. Gilbert had fallen in love with the *Elton John* album while shooting his latest film, a teen romance cut from the same cloth as the recent box-office smash *Love Story,* and commissioned Elton to record the soundtrack for it. "They were going to call the movie *The Intimate Game,*" Elton said, "and Bernie and I said, 'No, we will not write any songs named for a movie [called that]', and we suggested *Friends,* so [they said] 'We'll settle for *Friends*.'"

Elton and Bernie wrote all of their songs in a single weekend. "I spoke with the director's son, John Gilbert," Bernie said, "and he told me what it was about. I was too lazy to read the script, so I wrote all the songs for it having never seen a cut of the film."

The soundtrack sessions took place at Olympic Studios, with Elton and his musicians watching the film unspool before them on a gigantic screen as they played. "It was an exercise in mathematics," he said. "You have to write forty seconds of music, and if you don't write forty seconds it's a disaster. I'd never do it again."

Disappointed with the overall sound at Olympic, and with constant interruptions from a myriad of film executives who attempted to commandeer the sessions, Elton decided to decamp to Trident Studios to rerecord all of his songs. "For me, a studio has to be cozy and a bit moody," he said, "and Trident's like that. Another advantage is that there the drums are contained in a little booth of their own, completely shut off from everything, so there's almost perfect separation and no leakage of sound to speak of."

Elton's faith in the studio paid off—the resulting Trident sessions produced a vastly superior set of recordings. While the film itself would utilize the original Olympic sessions, the eventual soundtrack album would feature the Trident cuts. Besides providing four original tracks ("Friends," "Michelle's Song," "Seasons," and a brief reprisal of the title track), nearly half the album would consist of Paul Buckmaster's reworkings of Elton's main themes, pastoral variations played out on woodwinds and strings.

Displeased with the "filler" aspect of the gauzy incidental score, Elton offered Gilbert a pair of additional songs—tracks which had been earmarked for his next studio LP—free of charge. "I didn't want them to release a soundtrack album with three songs on it and fill it out with garbage, motorists peeing by lakes and things like that, so we said, 'Well, we've got two spare songs, have those—"Honey Roll" and "Can I Put You On"—which we were going to put on *Madman* [*Across the Water*], and which we'd been doing on stage anyway. So they put them on [in the film] during transistor radio sequences."

Elton recorded a duet with Island Records' Cat Stevens days later at Pye Studios. "Honey Man" was a jaggedly melodic piano stomper which Stevens had co-written with Ken Cumberbatch. Though Elton and Stevens were pleased with the finished track, hopes for its release were dashed when an ongoing dispute between Uni Records and Island over royalty distribution failed to find a proper resolution. A casualty of the legal wrangling, the single was ultimately scrapped.

Even with the "Honey Man" setback, things were still progressing apace for Elton. Later that same week, in fact, he purchased a luxury flat in central London, at 384 The Water Gardens, on Tottenham Court Road. His neo-futuristic digs—replete with orange shag-pile, mirrored wallpaper, mirrored walls, and a carpeted elevator which could whisk guests from the driveway directly into the living room—fit his personality perfectly. To complete his lifestyle upgrade, the pianist traded in his clunker for a lavender Aston Martin previously owned by Maurice Gibb of the Bee Gees.

"I didn't live that far away, [in] Sussex Gardens," journalist Chris Charlesworth said years later, "and I bumped into Elton in the Edgware Road area just by chance. I remember distinctly bumping into him in a drycleaners when he was getting his stuff and I…had a drink with him in a local pub. I also met him at the Speakeasy a few times. The music business was very insular in those days."

Insular enough that—with his move to the affluent Water Gardens neighborhood—Elton decided that John Reid would make the perfect roommate. The afternoon the Scotsman moved in, Elton sat his mother down to explain the unusual living situation to her. "My mother has always said how hurt she'd be if I was ever deceitful," he said, "and so when I confided in her that I might be gay, she was very understanding about it. I was very lucky in that respect. My family was very accepting."

The pianist barely had time to unpack before Dick James hosted a lunchtime album launch party for Elton's new album, *Tumbleweed Connection*, at the Revolution Club.

"[*Tumbleweed Connection*] deals very heavily with the Civil War and a lot of my interests in America," Bernie explained during the event, which took place on October 14. "It wasn't really meant to have a theme, it was just that all the songs we did ended up having that feel to them, so it ended up being a slight concept." He glanced about with a wry grin. "Some circus, huh?"

"It's groovy," a nameless, shaggy-bearded journalist slurred.

Bernie eyed him suspiciously. "Jesus." Suddenly he noticed that the music playing from the club's sound system was from *Elton John* and not *Tumbleweed Connection.* "Hey, why aren't they playing the new album?"

Dee Murray lit a cigarette. "Don't know."

"You're on the cover of *Music Now,*" Bernie informed the bassist. "And there's an inside picture of the four of us in *Disc.* They're calling you 'smiling Dee Murray'."

Dee grinned. "I'm a star, baby," he said dreamily.

A hush fell over the room as the first indelicate notes from *Tumbleweed*'s steel-laced opener, "Ballad of a Well-Known Gun," came tumbling out of unseen speakers. When the track ended, the room broke into authentic applause. Indeed, each successive track received a warmer reception than the one before it.

Elton arrived halfway through "Country Comfort," wearing a shiny black overcoat, blue denim shirt, crimson boots and a light-up toy clown on his lapel. He was in a boundless mood, calling his new album the "funky one" and promising that "the next [album] is going to be more classical and orchestral...At the moment I am still struggling to get rid of this image that media people like Radio One have built up for me. You know, people think that I'm all cuddly and lovely and beautifully pop-star-ish. [But] I'm not, I'm really not."

As the last arpeggiated notes of the album closer, "Burn Down the Mission," faded out, Elton grabbed a microphone and stepped onto a makeshift stage. "Thank you all for coming," he told the two-hundred amassed before him. "If you listen to the album, if you dig it, you should know it's Steve Brown as much as me, Gus Dudgeon as much as me, Paul Buckmaster as much as me. It's a team effort, God knows."

After a final round of applause, the club quickly emptied out. Elton headed to a table in the corner, where *Rolling Stone* reporter Robert Greenfield awaited him. "I live, eat, sleep, breathe music," the pianist confessed. "Neil Young, the Band, the Springfield, the Dead, the Airplane. I feel more American than British, really."

5,000 miles away, Aretha Franklin—one of Elton's favorite singers—released a cover version of "Border Song." The single reached Number 37 on *Billboard*'s pop singles chart, and Number 5 on the R&B charts. It was a small but not insignificant moment: the John/Taupin team had scored their first ever U.S. Top 40 writing credit.

That the Queen of Soul deemed one of Elton's songs worthy of her time and talent spoke volumes to his quickly changing stature. Franklin's was, in fact, only one of many John/Taupin covers suddenly flooding the market. A flattering situation, perhaps, yet Elton was hardly best pleased. "Most of the stuff that has been covered has been diabolical," he said. "Brainchild have done one of our songs. Who *are* they, anyway? That's awful. Rod Stewart has done 'Country Comfort' on his new album, *Gasoline Alley*. It's still worth getting anyway, [but] we're really pissed-off about it. He sounds like he made it up as they played. I mean, they couldn't possibly have got farther away from the original if they'd sung 'Camptown Races'. It's so bloody sad, because if anyone should sing that song it ought to be him, such a great voice, but now I can't even listen to the album. I get so brought down. Every other word is wrong."

Problems of a more pressing nature arose closer to home as Ray Williams suffered Dick James' wrath at having "deserted" Elton back in L.A. An enraged James dramatically tore up Williams' management contract and threw it at him like so much confetti.

"*Sue* me if you want," the publisher snarled. "We *don't* need dead weight round here."

Williams simply hung his head.

"I totally agreed with him," he later admitted. "I could see the kind of manager [Elton] needed, and it wasn't someone like me."

Williams was given a fifteen-hundred-pound severance ("At least it was enough to pay my back rent and put some food in the fridge...") and quickly became *persona non grata* around DJM. As if in some kind of distantly-tuned karmic response, the *Elton John* album suddenly broke into the U.S. Top 40, ultimately rising to Number 4 and going Gold. (Gold records signified one million dollars' worth of sales; RIAA's prestigious Platinum designation—for albums selling a million units—wouldn't be introduced until 1976.) The album would remain in the Top 40 for twenty-eight consecutive weeks, receiving a Grammy nomination early the next year for Best Contemporary Vocal Performance, Male. (Elton would also be nominated under the Best New Artist Category, ultimately losing out to the Carpenters.) The disc also proved successful internationally, going to Number 4 in both Australia and Canada, and to Number 2 in the Netherlands.

Tumbleweed Connection's impressive performance was in no small part aided by the success of "Your Song," which was released on October 26 as the intended B-side to "Take Me to the Pilot." But DJM's U.S. label manager, David Rosner, convinced Uni Records to leave the A- and B-side designations off of the single, thus allowing disc jockeys to make up their own minds about which track they preferred. "Before you knew it," Rosner later told journalist Tom Stanton, "['Your Song' was] on the air all over the country."

"Your Song" would slowly but steadily push its way up the charts throughout the fall, ultimately topping out at Number 8 in January, alongside offerings from the Fifth Dimension and George Harrison.

Hearing the song on the radio, John Lennon was duly impressed. "There was something about his vocals that was an improvement on all the English vocals till then," he would tell *Rolling Stone* in 1975. "When I heard it, I thought, 'Great, that's the first new thing that's happened since we [the Beatles] happened.' It was a step forward. I was pleased with it." (Decades later, the song would be enshrined in the Grammy Hall of Fame, while ranking at Number 137 on *Rolling Stone*'s list of "The 500 Greatest Songs of All Time.")

The European release of *Tumbleweed Connection* took place on October 30. It would take the album two-and-a-half months to finally enter the English album charts, where it ultimately topped out at Number 2. Ultimately it would remain in the charts for five months running. Like *Elton John* before it, *Tumbleweed Connection* would also prove successful on the international market, hitting Number 7 in Spain, and Number 4 in Canada, the Netherlands and Australia.

Tumbleweed Connection's bucolic packaging was nearly as impressive as the music itself, and no doubt contributed to the album's success. Though single sleeves were industry

Tumbleweed

Packaging

standard at the time, the album—like its two predecessors—was given the deluxe gatefold treatment. Featuring a bi-fold which posited Elton and Bernie as a pair of gun-slinging vagabonds, all wide-collared leather jackets and youthful sneers, the imagery—photographed on a chilly Monday morning at the Bluebell Railway Station in Sussex—was dreamed up by Bernie himself. A 12-page rotogravure lyric booklet, meanwhile, came complete with faux nineteenth-century woodcuts of riverboats, six shooters and other Civil War-era imagery. "I've always loved Americana and I loved American Westerns," the lyricist said. "I've always said that [Marty Robbins'] 'El Paso' was the song that made me want to write songs, it was the perfect meshing of melody and storyline."

Sounds magazine was impressed with the entire production, calling the disc "a collection of strikingly strong tracks with a slight country flavor," while also noting that "Elton's piano work has gained momentum and confidence since the first album, and he lays down a rhythm that often goes into amazing complexity and fruitfulness...[It's] soulful white music at its very, very best."

Perhaps even more important than the critical acclaim the album generated, however, was the fact that the team responsible for its creation was truly pleased with the results. "*Tumbleweed* was incredible," Gus Dudgeon said. "The songs, the performances—it all came out exactly as I'd wanted it to." The normally self-critical Elton had to agree. "R&B, gospel and country—you fuse those together, and you've got a pretty soulful combination. [*Tumbleweed Connection* is] all much simpler and funkier."

Making a calculated decision not to pull any singles off the album, Elton instead decided to present the work to the public as an integrated whole. "There aren't any singles on it anyway," he said. Even so, several tracks, including "Ballad of a Well-Known Gun," "Burn Down the Mission," "Where to Now, St. Peter?" and "Country Comfort" would go on to receive massive exposure on the newly formatted album-oriented FM stations blooming across U.S. radio dials.

"I like *Empty Sky* because of its naivety, *Elton John* because it was panic stations," the pianist said. "But I'm very happy with the new album, it's much more the way I want to come over. The last album was a little too soft and too orchestrated for me."

Chapter 6:
Dylan Digs Elton!

Flush with success, Elton, Dee and Nigel returned to America in the late fall to play their first proper U.S. tour. A fifteen-city, twenty-four-date undertaking, the campaign would revisit Los Angeles, San Francisco and New York while also introducing several new destinations, including Chicago, Detroit, Minneapolis, Bridgeport and Fulton.

The tour began inauspiciously with a three-night stand at the Boston Tea Party, where Elton was introduced onto stage as "Elton Jones." "It happened every night," Russ Regan said. "I would go up to the emcee after the show and say, 'It's Elton *John*.'" And the next night: 'Elton *Jones*.' I'm not sure whether he ever got it right."

Elton, for his part, hardly cared. "I'm ready for anything," he insisted. "I'm ready to rock 'n' roll."

Believing fully in his leader, Dee was equally set to tear things up. "We had complete confidence by that point," the bassist said. "We knew we were good, we knew we belonged where we were. Nigel and I always had the freedom to improvise. And Elton was great to play with."

Robbie Robertson and the Band appeared in the audience on their third and final night in Boston. After the show, they invited Elton and Bernie up to their hotel room.

"Bernie was shaking with fear," Elton said, "but they were really sweet and we talked together for about three hours."

The Band flew off to Worcester, Massachusetts, while Elton and his entourage headed down to Philadelphia for shows at the Electric Factory. The first gig went fantastically well—Elton ended up ripping his shirt to pieces, which he gleefully flung into the frenzied crowd—despite the fact that there were still those in the audience who expected the pianist to come out with a full complement of violas and violins. "People come to see us *do* expect see an orchestra, they really do," he said. "I can't believe it, but they go away—after I've completely destroyed the piano or set fire to it—and they think, 'God, I wasn't expecting *that*.'"

When the pianist got to his dressing room after his first Electric Factory show, he found all five members of the Band waiting there. "They'd put their show forward a couple of hours and flew down in their private plane to see our act," Elton said.

Moved by their efforts, the Brit played the entirety of the *Tumbleweed Connection* album for them.

"Amazing," Robbie Robertson enthused as the record finished. "I can't believe these songs were written by someone who'd never even been to America."

Bernie allowed himself a small grin.

"It was such a compliment that I couldn't believe it," Elton said. "They asked us to go up to Woodstock to record at their place, and when Robbie Robertson asked us to write a song for them...well, I think Bernie was a bit embarrassed, because Robbie's his current idol."

Whenever and wherever Elton stepped into the spotlight, he seemed to undergo a cosmic transformation. Gone was the shy, unhappy Reg Dwight from Pinner. In his place stood the supremely confident Elton John, the screams and applause from the maddened crowds almost visibly filled his psychic sails. This ever-expanding confidence was reflected in his latest American set list, which had broadened greatly from his summer shows to include songs as far-ranging as "Honey Roll," "The King Must Die," "My Father's Gun" and "Ballad of a Well-Known Gun."

This outing also saw the power trio co-headlining with groups like the Byrds, Poco and the Kinks—the latter of whom they blew off the stage at San Francisco's Carousel Ballroom, as Elton danced gleefully against his piano to ecstatic cheers. And played beneath it. And did push-ups on top of it. "You do everything you can to make it interesting," he said. "Otherwise you're stuck behind a nine-foot plank."

One of the best-received moments each night came when Elton introduced the crowd to the stage-shy Bernie, who would give a timid nod before quickly slinking back offstage.

"Whatever Elton John is about to become, Bernie Taupin is half," Robert Greenfield opined in *Rolling Stone.* "Sweetheart, the rest is history."

On November 12, Elton, Nigel and Dee began a three-night stand at Bill Graham's Fillmore West in San Francisco.

"It's the musician's dream gig," Elton said. "Bands take it for granted they're playing the Fillmore, they don't think about the fact that they're getting the best PA system, the best sound, and the best lighting. The lighting is just incredible."

Bill Graham himself introduced the band onto stage, the audience exploding as each musician materialized out of the wings. Grinning madly at the adulation, Elton treated those in attendance to a consummate set which included a muscular rendition of Junior Walker and the All-Stars'

"Shotgun," as well as a cover of John Lennon's brotherhood anthem, "Give Peace a Chance."

The crowd's enthusiasm escalated during the encores, as they rushed past the security guards and jammed themselves tightly against the stage. For Elton, it was an unmitigated victory. "[San Francisco audiences are] like those in London, because they've seen everything, and one night it was like pushing over a brick wall very slowly, but they went in the end." He laughed. "Every audience is good, if you get at them the right way."

Elton topped the bill at the 3,000-seat Santa Monica Civic Auditorium three nights later. Though contractually obligated to return to the Troubadour when he next found himself in the Los Angeles area, Elton was able to play the infinitely large Civic Auditorium instead by buying out his contract, which he'd done at the prompting of his American agent, Howard Rose.

"You are going to be big and you ought to invest in yourself," Rose told him.

The blossoming star agreed. "We felt the momentum would justify the move." (So moved was Elton by Rose's faith in him, he agreed to become godfather to Rose's daughter, whose middle name—Umbrella—was chosen by the pianist himself.)

Elton took to the Santa Monica stage—after opening sets by Odetta and roots guitarist Ry Cooder—in a brown leather top hat, blue velvet cape, and lemon-yellow overalls. The ensemble was topped off with a flashing Santa Claus figurine—a gift from Bernie's girlfriend, Maxine, who'd recently joined the band on the road as their unofficial seamstress—placed strategically over his crotch.

Though there were some early problems with Elton's microphone, and a distracting parade of photographers shuffling about the stage, the audience didn't seem to mind—an hour in, they were nearly as bathed in sweat as the whirling dervish piano-pounder himself.

"We played for nearly two hours there," Elton said. "We seem to go on longer in America than in Britain, because the audiences are so incredible. They don't vary at all."

As the concert headed toward its dynamic finish, mass hysteria ensued. Security guards stood helplessly by as the crowd rushed the stage. Not for the last time at an Elton John concert, pandemonium reigned supreme. "The crowd, to use Elton's term, 'went mental'," David Felton noted in his *Rolling Stone* review of the show, parts of which had been filmed for inclusion in a Henry Mancini TV show entitled *The Mancini Generation*. "Sometimes he would stick out his lower lip like Stan Freberg used to do, or grit his teeth or pucker up his face like Alvin Lee. Sometimes he would recoil from the keyboard, his mouth falling open in horror as if his ass had been shot full of lightning."

Billboard's Eliot Tiegel was less impressed than Felton, however, turned off by what he felt was Elton's be-costumed gamesmanship. "Does he abandon his valid musical skills in favor of being a 'stage freak' using unnecessary physical tricks?" Tiegel wondered. The pianist was nonplussed by the critique. "I *did* get some feedback from people who thought I was being a little too much of a showman onstage. But I was just having fun, breaking out of my shell. It wasn't any desperation to be successful. I just wanted to get away from the things that everyone else was doing. I could have come out onstage in a pair of Levi's and a cowboy shirt, and everyone would have said, 'Wow.' But I would have been bored to death. I just couldn't do it."

Backstage after the show, a group of journalists and record executives tossed back complimentary champagne and congratulated themselves on their great good fortune while Elton stood by himself in a corner, still in his sweat-soaked stage clothes, spent and silent and alone.

"I was comfortable onstage," he said soon after, "but not very comfortable off it. Although I was having a ball, I was still stuck with the insecure, nervous person inside. And just being successful doesn't cure it."

While in L.A., Danny Hutton invited Elton over to his house for a late-night dinner to celebrate the Brit's ever-escalating success. June Fairchild cooked them a four-course dinner, and all three enjoyed a relaxing night of music and conversation which lasted well into the next morning.

As Elton was driving his rented Mustang back to his hotel, he thought, "I've never stayed up till 7:30 in the morning in my life. I feel really good. I must be excited."

Elation it wasn't—Hutton would later confess to having laced the pianist's dinner with cocaine.

"I might've forgotten to tell him," he said with a knowing smirk. "I think it certainly didn't hurt him."

The signature gig of Elton's second American tour happened in New York on November 17, at A&R Recording Studios' 1A Studio, located on the top floor of 799 Seventh Avenue. Elton had agreed to play a live radio broadcast on WABC, New York's premier rock station. It was to be the first FM performance broadcast live from a studio, with a hundred fans, record executives and radio contest winners—as well as Peter, Paul & Mary's Mary Travers—ushered into the spacious facility to help create a concert-like atmosphere as they listened to the musicians through massive studio speakers.

Elton, Nigel and Dee arrived at A&R Studios forty minutes before air time, quickly rehearsed a couple numbers to check for sound levels, before huddling together in a small antechamber. Nigel and Dee shared a joint while Elton sat silently, eyes downcast.

The show, only Elton's twenty-ninth American gig, was being engineered by Phil Ramone, who would go on to produce Billy Joel in the latter half of the decade and beyond. "From the start that night felt memorable," Ramone said. "The three of them were amazing. Everyone [in the studio] went nuts." As for Elton's piano playing, Ramone labeled it as exceptional. "Elton plays very cleanly, and his left hand is nonstop. Just big and precise. He's a once-a-generation talent."

Elton and his band began their performance with the gentle strains of "I Need You to Turn To" and "Your Song."

"Can you turn the piano down?" Elton politely asked the studio engineer after the latter tune had finished. "It's very loud, and I can't hear what I'm singing in the cans."

After an affecting performance of "Border Song," Elton joked that the band had "played that so much, now we call it 'The Boredom Song'."

With the levels adjusted and any lingering apathy properly exorcised, the trio were soon flexing their road muscle, ripping through energetically cymbal-crashing renditions of "Bad Side of the Moon," "Can I Put You On," "Amoreena" and "Take Me to the Pilot."

"We were all in the studio wearing headphones as if we were recording an album," Elton said, "but we were playing live. We could all hear each other extremely well. We just jammed."

Nigel particularly enjoyed playing in headphones. "I thought, 'If I could do this on gigs, this would be great, because I would hear so much better. I don't have to have monitors blasting in my ears.' The phones give me a great mix at a reasonable volume." (Not surprisingly, from that show onward the drummer would wear headphones for every gig he ever played.)

Halfway through the set, Elton told the radio audience that Bernie Taupin has just run through the studio naked.

"That's our Bernie," he joked. "Keeping the flag held high."

The audience, enraptured by every reverb-soaked moment of the virtuoso performance, laughed appreciatively.

Before debuting the epic seven-minute "Indian Sunset," Elton warned the audience, "This next number's quite long, so if anyone needs to use the toilet, now's the time. There's a method to our madness, I tell you."

The pianist then closed the show with a ferocious extended reading of "Burn Down the Mission," which incorporated portions of "My Baby Left Me" and "Get Back"—a nod to two of his rock 'n' roll forbearers—as the blistering finale brought those in attendance to their feet.

"It was magic," Nigel said. "The atmosphere in that studio was like going to a recording studio and just playing for mates."

As "Get Back" wound down, a breathless Elton told the crowd, "At this point, we'd like to thank you all for coming, and for everybody for listening. For ABC—for letting us play, for A&R Studios—for letting us have the studio. And after everybody in general, thank you and keep smiling, 'cause that's the most important thing, all right? We're just gonna do one more thing…" With that, he and his band kicked into warp-drive, edging the song into a relentless crescendo.

"The eighteen-minute jam session is some of the finest drum and bass and piano playing I've ever done," Elton was later to reflect. "We were a bloody good band."

"Elton John was a hit!" disc jockey Dave Hermann exclaimed the moment it came to a crashing end, as the rabid audience cried out for more. Elton gladly complied, obliging them with a rousing encore of "My Father's Gun."

By the end of the night, the Brit's ivories were stained red with blood—he'd been pounding the keyboard so furiously, he'd cracked his fingernails wide open.

Elton began a two-night stand at the Fillmore East on Second Avenue on November 20. The pianist was particularly pumped—not only was he playing the East Coast's premiere rock palace, but he was also opening for his idol, Leon Russell. "I went out onstage," he said, "and theoretically thought, 'Leon, you're going to have to work really hard to follow me.' And I think that's the only attitude to take if you're the underdog. I can't understand groups who go around thinking, 'Oh, it's just another gig.' I've always played my balls off."

Publicity for the shows was handled by industry pro Carol Kienfner, who was bemused by the innate innocence which both Elton and Bernie approached the event with. "They were wide-eyed, like they couldn't believe what was happening, and with being in New York," she said. "But they were very sweet, and always on time....[Elton] was incredibly professional, and a great talent."

"Elton was the undercard for Leon Russell," writer Eric Van Lustbader said. "But from the beginning, everyone was calling it 'the Elton John concert', which caused a terrible stir. Usually for the undercard, half the crowd isn't there yet, they're just walking in, they're not paying attention, they're smoking dope or whatever the heck they're doing. But for these two concerts, from the moment Elton and his band came out to play, there wasn't a seat empty in the audience. You could've heard a pin drop, which was incredible."

Elton appeared onstage in a floor-length cape and stovepipe hat, as the thousands in attendance leapt out of their velvet seats to wail out an ovation not heard since the heyday of Beatlemania.

Seated out in the audience that first night were Elton's label mates Andrew Lloyd Webber and Tim Rice, in America for the first time to promote their rock opera, *Jesus Christ Superstar*. "Elton had just broken through in America with MCA Records, just as Andrew and I had done on the same label," Rice said. "I remember an electric performance of 'Border Song' was the highlight for me. Andrew and I were very impressed, but a little worried that MCA might decide to promote his records more than ours....But we knew that we were lucky to be on the same label as a genius of contemporary music, and forgave him."

Also in the crowd was local disc jockey Dennis Elsas. "I have very, very vivid memories of that show," he said. "Elton did not disappoint. He blew the place apart."

By the end of the show, Elton was astride his Steinway, conducting a two-thousand-strong choir as he urged them to clap along to a fiery cover of Sly and the Family Stone's "I Want to Take You Higher."

"Elton seemed to acknowledge Leon Russell as an influence," said producer Joe Boyd, also in attendance at the first show. "But Elton picked up and ran with that ball, and did way more with it than Leon ever did. But then I think you can perceive a pattern here. The British approach to pop music is much more flamboyant and much more crowd-pleasing, if you will, and much more colorful than the U.S. approach. The British have that in their DNA, and that's the way they've always been. And I think in a way the contrast between Leon and Elton was a classic example of that. Although Leon tried to be British with his Uncle Sam top hat and spangles and stuff like that, it didn't really work. Whereas Elton just did it naturally, it was just the way he was. He didn't have to try."

Leon himself was perhaps most awed of all. "[Elton] was a magician," he said. "A great guy, too. If you're good, you're good, y'know?"

Bob Dylan showed up backstage after the concert in a rumpled black raincoat, holding a small briefcase. The reclusive poet complimented Elton on his muscular performing chops, and Bernie on his pictographic lyrical abilities, giving particular praise to "Ballad of a Well-Known Gun."

Unable to speak, Bernie merely nodded at Dylan.

"I was too overwhelmed," he later acknowledged. "I just couldn't take it in...I wasn't ready for it. What can I say? I mean it was like, 'Oh God,' or 'You're God,' or 'My God.'"

"I thought Bernie was going to drop to his knees and bow down," Eric Van Lustbader said, "because Dylan was his god. And to have Bob Dylan come to see them and come backstage was one of the most amazing things that I'm sure had ever happened to them. It was quite a sight."

The iconic writer of "Blowin' in the Wind" and "Like a Rolling Stone" took his leave soon after. But he showed up the next night as well, this time bringing along his wife, Sarah, as well as Paul Simon, and the Mamas and the Papas' John Phillips. Never to miss a scoop, *Melody Maker* proclaimed in their next issue, in a bold-faced headline: *DYLAN DIGS ELTON!*

"This was the first time Elton ever got a headline in a music paper," Stuart Epps said. "So basically, with the reverberation of what was happening in the States...it just all took off. It was a bit of an explosion. Suddenly all the records are in the charts, and that was the beginning of it all, really."

Elton opened for Derrick and the Dominoes in New York at the Syracuse War Memorial on December 4, just days after having brought the crowd at Chicago's Auditorium Theatre to such a pitch that police were forced to lift him out of the crowd with ropes.

The War Memorial show was, significantly, one of only two dates which Duane Allman played with the Eric Clapton-led band. "Everyone was going crazy about this kid called Elton John," Clapton said. "I was slightly threatened by all this. I *did* want to blow people off the stage, so I was working double hard, and to go on after Elton...was a big challenge."

"At the near conclusion of his performance," local reviewer Terry Lee noted, "[Elton] threw his bench to the side and played the piano standing, frantically dancing, rolling on the floor (still playing) and while jumping up in the air. The audience loved every second of it and went wild when he left."

Elton made his U.S. television debut days later, on the December 11 episode of the NBC-TV broadcast, *The Andy Williams Show.* Wearing a garish green suit, Williams officially introduced Elton to America at large. "Ladies and gentlemen," he said, "a few months ago a young man came over from England and he shot right to the top of the pop music field. His first album is a hit, his first single is a hit, and I hate him. No, I really like him. I mean, I *really* like him."

The camera pushed past Williams to show Elton seated at a black Steinway grand contemplatively playing the introduction to "Your Song" beneath a crystal chandelier.

Williams was thoroughly impressed by the young Englishman. "He was terrific," he later said. "He was terribly talented and very nice."

A group performance with fellow guest stars Ray Charles and a kaftan-draped Mama Cass Elliot was set to close out

184

the show—but it proved problematic when Charles nixed one song after another. "[Ray Charles] didn't want to sing 'Love the One You're With'," Elton said, "so then it was gonna be 'My Sweet Lord', and he didn't want to sing that [either]. They got down to 'Heaven Help Us All', and he didn't want to sing *that,* but they said it was that or nothing."

Brother Ray finally acquiesced, performing the song with Elton on matching black and white grands while Cass and Williams sang backup.

"It was the most frightening experience of my life," Elton said. "I was petrified, but Ray Charles turned out to be very nice and we got on fine." (Neither man had any way of knowing then that the final recording of Charles' storied career would be a duet with Elton on the latter's "Sorry Seems to Be the Hardest Word" three decades hence.)

The Brit also performed a brief song called "Goodbye" for the telecast, but the effort was cut from the final broadcast due to time constraints.

"It was a real drag," he said, "because I was quite good on it."

While in L.A., Elton met with director Hal Ashby, who offered him a starring role in his upcoming film, *Harold and Maude.* A black comedy about a death-fixated young man and a seventy-nine-year-old woman deeply in love with life, Elton found the future cult classic to be "*the* best script." Still, he declined the offer so that he could concentrate on his fledgling music career instead.

"We were just beginning to happen as a group," he said, "and it would have meant six months of my life without the group."

By the time Elton left America, radio stations from coast-to-coast were bombarding the airwaves with an endless selection of his deeper album tracks, from "The King Must Die" to "Love Song." Yet back in the U.K., he was still barely better known than he had been before he'd departed for the Troubadour back in August. Even so, Elton was determined to keep his spirits positive—an endeavor greatly aided by John Reid's Tamla Motown connections, which resulted in the pianist getting to meet several of his American R&B idols.

"I told Elton that Stevie Wonder and Martha and the Vandellas were coming into Britain for a tour," Reid said. "I asked if I could borrow his car to meet them at the airport because mine was out of commission at that time, and Elton wound up coming to the airport with me to meet Stevie."

"Are you the Elton John who sings 'It's a little bit funny...?'" Wonder asked, breaking into the song's chorus.

"I'm to blame," Elton replied sheepishly.

Both men fell against each other in laughter.

"That started off their relationship," Reid said.

During the lead-up to the Christmas holidays, Reid presented Elton with an advanced test pressing of the Supremes' new album, *Touch*. Elton's intense enthusiasm for the record resulted in him providing the liner notes.

"I am probably their original British fan," he wrote. "I bought their first single 'Where Did Our Love Go' in England in 1964....Since then, I have gotten every record they have ever made....Imagine my excitement when I not only received an advanced copy of this—their new album— but was also asked by Jean, Mary and Cindy to write the notes. (I felt as if I had really 'made it.')."

Elton wasn't the only one who felt that way. In a year-end article entitled "Handstands and Fluent Fusion," *Time* magazine's William Bender labeled Elton a "one-man music factory" who "plays piano with the urbane primitivism of a

Glenn Gould thumping out variations on Jerry Lee Lewis."
Bender went on to wonder if Elton might indeed be the
"superman" that young music fans needed to save them from
a desolately apocalyptic, post-Beatles landscape.

"*Yes!*" Dick James roared.

Elton merely shrugged.

"We shall see," he said.

Elton closed out his breakthrough year with a couple final
studio and stage endeavors. First he record "Make No
Mistake" at Sound Techniques in Chelsea, along with Dave
Pegg on bass, Dave Mattacks on drums, and Jimmy Page on
guitar. "Elton was one of the nicest and funniest guys I'd
ever had the good fortune to come across," Mattacks said. "I
remember thinking, 'This guy is terrific, and he's great fun.'

Elton then played the "Implosion" Christmas charity
show at the Roundhouse in London. Held on December 20,
Elton opened for the Who—who were performing their rock-
opera *Tommy* in its entirety for what would be the final time
for nearly two decades. (When they did finally perform it
again in the late '80s, Elton would actually take part in that
performance, playing the integral role of the Pinball
Wizard.)

The Who were so impressed with Elton's performance,
they decided on the spur of the moment to dedicate their
entire set to him.

"The lad's got a promising future," Townsend told the
crowd before launching into "Tommy Can You Hear Me?"

Elton would become good friends with the Who's
guitarist and creative leader in the coming years, as he would
with another rocker he got to know that same weekend.
Meeting at a Christmas party at Long John Baldry's manager
Billy Gaff's cellar apartment in Pimlico, Elton was formally
introduced to Rod Stewart, who had been a nodding

acquaintance since his days with Bluesology. Recognizing kindred spirits, the two began a laddish friendship which would last throughout the decade, and the century, and beyond.

"I loved his sense of humor," Rod later said in *Rod: The Autobiography.* "Loved the fact that he was the kind of bloke who could see the comedy value in driving thirty times around the roundabout that surrounds the Marble Arch monument in the middle of London."

The readers of *Record World* shared Rod's appreciation for the bespectacled pianist, voting Elton the Top Male Vocalist of the year. The International Music Critics Awards, meanwhile, lauded him and Bernie as Best Composers of the Year.

By any measure, Elton's star was clearly on the rise. In the U.K., he rated Number 5 on *NME's* poll of Top Male Singers, only behind the likes of Elvis Presley, Paul McCartney and Glen Campbell. He also fared well with *Record Mirror's* Pop Poll Results for Most Promising Singer/Group, coming in ahead of Led Zeppelin, Black Sabbath, David Bowie and Badfinger. Britain's *Disc and Music Echo* magazine, meanwhile, noted that Elton had been voted the act that had made "the most impact in pop during 1970" by BBC Radio 1's disc jockeys.

"Elton John will undoubtedly turn out to be the biggest discovery of 1970," Rhapsody Packard rhapsodized prophetically in the December issue of *Jazz & Pop* magazine.

Every decade could claim a single artist who eventually stood head and shoulders above the rest.

The '40s had Sinatra.

The '50s had Elvis.

The '60s had the Beatles.

The '70s were wide-open. The decade was ready for a defining musical savior. For someone exactly like Elton John.

Chapter 7:
All the Nasties

The tumultuous momentum which ended 1970 carried over into the New Year with the U.S. release of *Tumbleweed Connection* on January 4. The album entered the fray at Number 25, and hit Number 5 within weeks. Impressively, it would remain on the charts for over half a year running.

American critics were as impressed with the disc as their English counterparts had been, with the *Washington Post*'s Tom Zito describing it as being "right out of the so-called new romanticism; love songs, songs about old soldiers and inherited guns. Yet beneath all this is a real feeling for the universal." The *Village Voice*'s Robert Christgau called the album "a piece of plastic with good melodies and bad Westerns on it," while the *Saturday Review* felt that the disc brimmed over with "music that is organic, intensely human, and capable of an elusively intimate effect." *Rolling Stone*'s Jon Landau deemed *Tumbleweed Connection* "an exciting album, one that I have played endlessly for a week, but it is also something of a missed opportunity. *Tumbleweed Connection* is simpler than John's last album and next time around I hope he goes all the way and gets down to nothing but the basics. He is one of the few who is good enough not to need anything else." Writing in the *Los Angeles Times,* Robert Hilburn praised the LP as "that near-perfect album that artists often spend a whole career trying to produce."

Life's Albert Goldman, however, was determinedly unimpressed. "Meretricious copycatting," he sniffed, particularly put-off by what he felt were patently immature lyrics.

Annoyed by Goldman's brickbats, Elton sprang to his partner's defense. "People," he said, "still tend to forget that Bernie's not even twenty-one yet."

Clearly a superstar in the making, media publications began courting Elton for interviews and opinion pieces. *Melody Maker* was one of the first to land a sit-down with the pianist, asking the pianist to survey a recent batch of singles—sight unseen—for their "Blind Date" column. Correctly identifying every track played for him, Elton provided his opinions with typical forthrightness. Of Van Morrison's "Domino," he noted, "You hear this on the radio every five minutes in the States. It's the best track on the album, and it's almost certain to be a Top Five single over here...Bernie says I sound like him, but I can't see it." In response to Creedence Clearwater Revival's "Pagan Baby," he noted that "Creedence are the best rock 'n' roll group in the world...Fogerty's amazing. He's so uncomplicated. It's just simple, hard-driving rock 'n' roll with memorable melodies." When played "Saturday Miles" by Miles Davis, the pianist admitted that he liked *Bitches Brew,* "but the whole thing seems to have got a bit out of hand. The trumpet is probably my least favorite instrument, along with the clarinet, and Miles is the only trumpeter I can listen to."

Weeks later, Leon Russell would be asked to handle the "Blind Date" chores. After giving less than stellar reviews to such singles as the Allman Brothers Band's 'Hoochie Coochie Man' and Neil Diamond's 'Sweet Caroline', Leon fretted, "What can I say? Play me an Elton John record, give me a chance to say something nice."

Elton kicked off a twenty-eight date tour of the U.K. in January at Mothers, a music ballroom in the Erdington district of Birmingham. Other early dates included the Pavilion at Hemel Hempstead and Winter Gardens at Cleethropes, where anarchy descended as fans stormed the stage during a particularly flammable "Burn Down the Mission."

"Crazy times," Dee said years later. "Real music, real fans."

Two weeks in, the band detoured to France to attend MIDEM, an annual trade show gathering of music industry leaders held at Cannes. The stage seemed set for another triumph: a star-filled Sunday night on the French Riviera, rock 'n' roll beside the sparkling Mediterranean. Dick James had negotiated Elton's appearance months earlier, hoping that the event, which was being broadcast live on radio throughout Europe—would help launch his star pupil on the Continent much the same way the Troubadour shows had in America.

But it wasn't to be.

The show started late and quickly fell behind schedule. Not helping matters, Eric Burdon and his band, War, launched into an extended solo-filled jam toward the end of their set. Easily exceeding their 15-minute timeslot, the aggressive clock mismanagement was perhaps purposeful retaliation for a quote Elton had given *Melody Maker* a fortnight earlier: "Have you got Eric Burdon's new [album], *Black-Man's Burdon*? There's one track I like, but he should have been born black and given us all a rest."

Scheduled to go on directly after War, the pianist paced restlessly backstage, furious at Burdon's grandstanding, which had already run past the allocated radio time. No matter how well Elton performed now, only those in the hall would get to hear him.

"Eric Burdon, you're a *fuck-up!*" he screamed. "Get off the fucking *stage!*"

"Eric just kept playing," Eric Van Lustbader said. "He was a total shit."

With Burdon showing no sign of stopping, a furious Elton stormed out of the theater. John Reid found the pianist sulking at a bar across the street, an untouched glass of Kronenbourg 1664 set before him.

"C'mon back," Reid urged.

"*Fuck* it," the pianist muttered.

After much cajoling, Reid finally managed to coax his charge back to the theater. Richie Havens came up to Elton backstage and agreed to give him his closing slot, but Elton wouldn't hear of it. "I want you to close the show, Richie," he said. "We all should hear 'Freedom' as the last song of the evening."

Eric Burdon finally left the stage to a hearty chorus of boos. A red-faced Elton came on next and received a riotous ovation from the black-tie crowd before he'd even played a single note. But it was to be a short-lived triumph—the curtain fell on him halfway through his set.

Elton was apoplectic.

"Whoever organized this fucking thing is a fucking *idiot!*" he yelled, ripping through the curtains and vowing to never play France again. "The French are just useless," he later reflected. "The French can't organize a piss-up in a brewery."

"Your Song" was released in the U.K. on January 23, a true A-side this time. Backed with "Into the Old Man's Shoes" and fueled by Elton's ever-ascendant profile, the single quickly reached Number 7 in England, bettering its U.S. performance by a single position.

Equally as impressive, by early February the *Elton John* album had gone Gold in the British Isles. When it overtook *All Things Must Pass* in the charts, Elton received a laudatory telegram from George Harrison: "Well done, Elton. You're doing great things. Congratulations." The pianist was genuinely moved by the gesture. "It was a very thoughtful thing for him to do," he said. "It meant the whole world to me. It kick-started what I already had in my tank, which was, 'I'm having a ball here, I can compete with these guys.'"

Despite his enthusiasm and growing chart successes, however, the whirlwind touring schedule Elton found himself swept up in was beginning to have a wearing effect. Forced to cancel six February dates on doctor's orders, he claimed, "My career is gonna be very short. One and a half years, that's all. I want to quit while I'm at the top and then I'll fade into obscurity. I've got lots of obligations for this year and next, and when they're all done the group will split. Does it sound bad saying I want to quit while I'm at the top? I don't mean it arrogantly, it's just that so many artists never see the end, they never know when they've got that long slide ahead of them."

Imminent demise was the last thing the pianist had to worry about, however, as—weeks later—*Tumbleweed Connection* provided him with his second British Gold record.

Elton headed back into Trident Studios on February 27, 1971, to lay down a pair of tracks for the proper follow-up to *Tumbleweed Connection*. The first song recorded was a gospel rocker called "Levon." Borrowing the name of the Band's lead singer, Levon Helm, the song itself was a pure invention on Bernie's part, an illusory character sketch about a young man who longs to escape the paternal control which has suffocated him his whole life. "People got their knickers completely in a twist just because Levon called his son Jesus and he was a balloon salesman," the lyricist said. "Just because he didn't call his child George and he wasn't a mechanic or something. I don't know, the story's completely simple. It's just about a guy who wants to get away from his father's hold over him."

Of the esoteric lyrics, Elton could only laugh. "I really don't know what's going on in Bernie's mind," he confessed. "I ask him if a certain song is about a certain person or something like that, but I don't get any sense out of him."

The Strawbs' Rick Wakeman, who was soon to join Yes, was brought in to add organ flourishes to the track. "Elton told me that he never really enjoyed playing the organ and always considered himself a piano player," Wakeman said years later. "And indeed he was, and still is, a bloody good one, with a unique technique and style. He asked me to play Hammond on some tracks, and I was booked through a session-fixer called David Katz. The most rewarding thing was when you arrived at a session and heard songs for the first time and knew instantly they were a different class and that's what these [songs of Elton's] were....I was genuinely honored to have worked with him."

Gus also booked several Arco basses for the session, to add heft to the bottom end of the mournfully urgent track. "I knew the kind of beef that came from basses from being a tape jockey for quite a few classical sessions," he said. "I was confident I could make it work."

Gus' poise in the studio allowed for "happy accidents," one of which occurred when session drummer Barry Morgan misread his drum chart during the song's final pre-chorus and played a tom-fill in the wrong place—as Elton sang "he was born a pauper to a pawn on a Christmas day."

195

"I'm really sorry," Morgan said contritely as he shuffled into the control room, head hung low. "I screwed up."

But the producer was grinning his head off.

"Barry, that was a *superb* drum fill. What on earth made you put it there? It was a moment of genius."

Morgan insisted on doing another take, but Gus wouldn't hear of it. "Robin [Geoffrey Cable] and I played it back a couple times, and everybody agreed that it was absolutely brilliant," the producer said. "That's the kind of magic you're always looking for. But you can't force it. You've just got to be supremely patient and open to it when it arrives. And it *will* arrive."

Also recorded at this session was the reflective piano ballad "Goodbye," which had earlier been excised from the *Andy Williams Show.* At 1:48, the darkly muted, enigmatic track was the briefest song Elton had yet committed to recording tape.

Dressed in a Wonka-esque top hat and bone-white tails, Elton played London's Royal Festival Hall with a 30-piece session orchestra—along with special guests Skaila Kanga and Rick Wakeman—on March 3. Performing the first hour with just Nigel and Dee, the pianist gave fresh readings on numbers like "Where to Now, St. Peter?" and "Talking Old Soldiers," before being joined by the orchestra for a passionate selection of more expansive songs which included "First Episode at Hienton" and "Come Down in Time." The highlight of the performance, however, was an ardent "The King Must Die," which received an extended and well-deserved ovation. The show then ended, appropriately enough, with the premiere performance of the mournfully pensive "Goodbye."

Despite Elton's best efforts, *Melody Maker*'s Ray Coleman was less than impressed with the evening. "It was sad," he wrote, "the man, the living myth, darling of the Americans, the ultimate local boy makes good, struggling like a pygmy center half with just 7,000 of his own people."

Why the Brit-on-Brit hostility? Elton had an idea. "I got rave reviews from the first gig I did in America, and it snowballed," he said. "The reports began to get back to Britain, and because I hadn't done many gigs here, people assumed I was a phony. Maybe they didn't like the Americans getting to know me first...But reading anti-Elton John comments in the paper *does* depress me."

The *Friends* soundtrack album was rushed out to the shops two days later—weeks ahead of the film's release—to capitalize on Elton's cresting wave of popularity. The pianist was less than pleased by the move. "They put 'Elton John' on the front of the album cover and, in little print, 'From the film *Friends*,' and we couldn't do anything about it because that was one of the things we'd agreed to do before we'd made it. The record company are promoting it as a new Elton John album, and kids will probably think it *is* a new Elton John album...but it's not."

The LP stalled at Number 36 in the U.S., while failing to chart at all in Britain. The horrendous cover art, a garish "pink massacre" by Paramount Records' art director Ruby Mazur, was in no small part to blame. "Paramount came out with the worst album cover I've ever seen," Elton said. "It looked like a Barbara Cartland dress...[It] makes you feel ill every time you look at it. They came up with dross. I mean, it was hideous." He took off his glasses and rubbed at his face. "The whole album was a complete and utter rip-off. It should have been put out as a maxi-single, with [my] songs on it and the rest of it forgotten about."

Despite his misgivings, the album went on to receive a Grammy nomination for Best Original Score Written for a

Motion Picture. With that nomination, Elton was again lauded in the press for being a musical emancipator—praise he took with a healthy grain of salt. "Something new is gonna come along soon," he said. "I hope there is, anyway, because I think everybody needs a shot in the arm....I'm looking forward to seeing who it is."

Elton geared up for his third tour of the States, a massive ten-week, forty-five-city jaunt which commenced on April 2. The tour featured an ever-broadening set list, which now included "Ballad of a Well-Known Gun," "Friends," and the as-yet-unrecorded "All the Nasties." Elton also performed cover versions of Janis Joplin's "Mercedes Benz"—which she'd recorded just two days before her death six months prior—and a fury-saturated rendition of "Whole Lotta Shakin' Going On" which would close out the show each night in incandescent style.

The campaign again broadened Elton's reach, taking in "second tier" cities like Columbus, Cincinnati, Omaha, Portland, Seattle, Dallas, New Orleans, Oklahoma City, Denver, and Ashbury Park. While in Ohio, a roadie forgot to screw Nigel's drums together properly. "So, on the second song, the whole kit falls apart," Nigel said. "And I'm thinking, 'What would Moonie do in this situation?' So I kicked them over, and Elton stopped the show. We got backstage and fisticuffs started happening. Elton said, 'You flash bastard, don't *ever* do that again!' We started pushing each other. He pushed me, I pushed him."

Tensions had eased by the time the band reached Southern California. More than any other area on the planet, Elton was able to mark his incredible rise by the succession of venues he'd played in the sun-drenched area. In less than a year, he'd graduated from the 250-seat Troubadour to the

3,500-seat Santa Monica Civic Auditorium to the 9,100-seat Anaheim Convention Center.

The night before the May 14 Anaheim show, Russ Regan invited Elton over to his house, where he and his wife, Judy, cooked him dinner. "I was barbecuing," Regan said, "and Judy had made this phenomenal cold cherry soup. Elton just could *not* get over how fantastic that soup was." The next evening, Elton sauntered onto the Convention Center stage in a sequined cowboy suit made especially for him by famed Hollywood tailor Mr. Nudie, who had created outfits for everyone from Dean Martin to Mick Jagger.

"Before we start tonight," Elton told the crowd, "I just wanted to dedicate this concert to Judy Regan's cold cherry soup, all right? Here we go, Los Angeles..."

With this tour, Elton's popularity reached an all-time high. Yet the more his fans clamored for him, the more the press pilloried him. This was never more apparent than in critic Stephen Chensvold's emblematic review of the pianist's April 24 show at the Seattle Center Coliseum. "When John threw his long coattails into the audience in a spasmodic burst of misdirected energy," Chensvold wrote, "and when he took off his silver boots and climbed his piano, like a sophomoric cheerleader at his first big rally, the temperature of the concert began to change....If Elton John takes his performance seriously, that's one thing. But if he asks others to accept this neatly packaged, glossed-over and well-promoted garbage as anything short of ludicrous, then music has become nothing more than slick packaging and an energetic advertising campaign."

Elton read the review aloud to his next audience.

"Poor Mr. Chest Cold," the pianist teased, ripping the review to shreds and throwing the bits dismissively over his shoulder. "I think he's missing the point. And not for the first time, I'll wager. Anyway, this [concert] is for you. Any critics present may leave. We just want to rock 'n' roll. Fair enough?"

Elton's tour soon landed in New York, where he played a trio of shows at the Fillmore East.

"That's a bit of a legendary venue," Stuart Epps said. "Yet being in New York, which I didn't really like, [it was tough]. There was always this stuff in the paper about 'This person's been shot,' and 'Someone else has been shot,' or whatever. And then someone threw something at Elton onstage. It was probably only a bottle top or something, but he thought he could be shot. Still, it was an experience for everyone. The thing is, I was a complete Elton fan. I'd been rooting for him since I was fifteen. To see him doing these theater gigs and going down an absolute storm, with people whooping and yelling like American audiences do—they go out to have a good time—it was incredible. And it was emotional. And that's how everyone felt. 'Now it's all coming true,' we thought. 'It's actually happening.'"

Between gigs, the Brit sat in his midtown hotel room and admitted to *Gallery* reporter J. Marks that—despite his displeasure with certain critics—he still kept a complete book of all his reviews. Newspaper clippings and magazine articles, too. Why? "I'll look back on all of it one day, and I'll probably say, 'Wow, looky here, dearie, what I did. Look what so-and-so said about me back when.' I just think it's part of the fun. If I didn't have anything to look back on in ten years, all this wouldn't really make much sense, now would it? Because it's going by so fast that I don't hardly know that it's happening. I don't have time to enjoy it."

"Do you think that your act is going to hold up?" Marks inquired.

"No," Elton answered without hesitation. "I didn't want all of this. I'd already had enough of it. I had four years in a shitty band. I played and played and traveled and traveled. Dragging around my own huge fucking equipment. Setting it up and taking it all back down again. At the moment, I'm enjoying all of this. But I think the act will fade. I've got two or three years of performing, and then it will be completely over. I've set the deadline for 1973. That's it, as far as touring is concerned."

With an optimistic eye toward a longer-lasting future, Bernie married his "ballerina," Maxine, not long after, on a chilly late April afternoon in his hometown of Market Rasen in Lincolnshire. Paparazzi and fans swarmed the event to get a glimpse of famous wedding guests like Marc Bolan and his wife June, as well as BBC producer John Walters, who sidled up to the visibly nervous groom and serenaded him with: "If I were a bridegroom…but then again, no…"

Taking a vestiary queue from his writing partner and best man, Bernie wore a white velvet suit, lilac shirt and gold earrings to the candlelit ceremony held at Holy Rood Catholic Church. Even so, Elton still took the sartorial crown that day in a white silk suit hand-embroidered with diamanté edging, rhinestone flowers of blue and red, and a deep-silver silk top hat.

While the stars glimmered, those looking in from the outside shared their recollections. "I remember Bernie well," his former middle school teacher, Mr. Hoolton, told *The Lough Leader* paper. "In a sense he was a typical boy of the school. But he was whimsical. His writing always had character. He always seemed to write vividly about anything, stringing words together so as to make a picture for you. In a way, I wasn't surprised to find he'd gone to London, but you never really think this sort of thing is going to happen."

201

After a reception at the Market Rasen Racecourse, Dick James toasted the couple at a wedding reception at the Limes Hotel, before presenting them with a chromed-out Mark II Mini as a wedding present.

James handed Bernie the keys, which Maxine deftly plucked out of her husband's palm, as he was yet to learn how to drive.

"She was quite outrageous and very Hollywood," Stuart Epps said. "In many ways, she was leading [Bernie] around and spending his money, but she was lovely and I liked her."

Elton did his part at the festivities, playing piano as the three-hundred guests played a drunken game of musical chairs. "He was showing off all his roots," album designer David Larkham said. "Songs that influenced him, Winifred Atwell stuff interspersed with his comical impressions."

The lyricist ultimately stole the spotlight, however, leveraging a healthy share of his newly-minted royalties to surprise his bride with a stone cottage in the scenic village of Tealby. Named after a childhood character from one of his favorite authors, A.A. Milne, Bernie christened his new residence—which featured completely re-tiled floors, courtesy of Elton—"Piglet-in-the-Wilds."

As charming as the house appeared on the outside, it was equally as garish within. "I had no notion of taste," Bernie said. "What I had in the cottage at Tealby was just like any other pop *nouveau riche*—black walls, lava lamps and sand candles. Heavy Victorian furniture everywhere. Orange couches covered with Liberty prints. No coordination whatever."

Still, with his new bride—and a bloodhound pup from the Battersea Dogs Home named Cyril—Bernie confessed, "I don't wish for any more."

Bernie and Maxine honeymooned in Hawaii while Elton prepped for a concert at the Honolulu International Center. Their nuptial bliss was interrupted by a mini-crisis which erupted the day of the show, however, when the piano that the Center had promised to have ready for Elton's show never materialized. John Reid was forced to hunt down a grand piano that afternoon. After a frantic search, he finally located a foot surgeon in Waikiki who had an instrument that fit the bill. Reid dispatched several roadies to physically remove the 760-pound instrument from the good doctor's house, wrestle it onto—and then off—a flatbed truck, and then haul it onto stage.

"It's why we earn [the] big money," a long-haired roadie joked. "Didn't you know?"

Hours later, Bernie stood anxiously beside his new bride as Elton's show began. "I'm probably more nervous than anyone else in the group," he conceded. "It's very rare I can sit and watch a whole show. I have to walk around and people think I'm trying to hide."

Despite his worries, Elton gave another high-octane performance that night. By the end of the concert, the pianist was battered and bruised.

"[Touring] just kills you," he said. "I bang the piano a lot. It's hard work. My hands, by the time I go home, will be ruined."

Chapter 8:
Madman Across the Water

Elton's label decided to capitalize on the tremendous buzz surrounding his November 17, 1970 radio concert, after multiple bootlegged copies of the gig—released under such titles as *Knocking 'Em Dead Alive, Live E Jay, Radiocord, Rock and Roll Madonna, Superstar: Live* and *Very Alive*— had flooded the underground market. Elton found the situation bemusing. "It's funny to think people want to hear your stuff so desperately they'll buy a bootleg album," he said. "Or that people will go to the trouble of manufacturing a bootleg album because they know the demand is there."

Wanting to put a stop to the bootleggers efforts, the original multi-tracked tapes of the performance were rushed into production. "Gus and I mixed the tapes for the British release at Dick James' [DJM Studios]," engineer Clive Franks said. "After we played them back a few times, Gus decided to remix them again for the States. Change a few bits, tighten up the sound. He did those at Trident Studios with Dave Hentschel. They came out a lot better." After giving an attentive listen to both mixes, Elton agreed, determining that the English version was dull and dreary, while the tapes for the American market were "very good."

Taking its title from the date of the concert—*17/11/70* in the U.K. and Europe, *11/17/70* in America—the live disc was ripe for critical attack. "I'm going to get criticized for that album, because everyone will say, 'Oh, fuck, not *another* Elton John album,'" the pianist predicted. "But it *has* to come out now, because it has been released [on bootlegs] and people are playing it. So I'm just going to have to face the criticism. [But] it's a bloody good live album. What decided for me that it was a good live album was the Crosby, Stills, Nash & Young [live LP, *4 Way Street*], which I was eagerly awaiting, and I thought it was a disaster...There's two or three really nice things on it, but I think it's an unmitigated disaster. I thought, 'Well, ours is so much better than that.' It's not fair to point that out, but that's what decided that it really should come out."

While the live tracks were being mastered, the title track from the *Friends* soundtrack was released in the U.S. Backed with "Honey Roll," the single peaked at Number 34 on *Billboard*'s Top 100 chart, and at Number 17 on their Adult Contemporary chart.

Impressed with the relatively strong showings, Dick James decided to capitalize on Elton's stature by releasing a pair of instrumental demos he'd recorded back in 1969. On May 7, 1971, DJM issued a press release entitled: *Mr. Bloe meets Elton John*, dubiously announcing that the artists were teaming up "on Mr. Bloe's latest single '71-75 New Oxford Street'," despite the fact that "Mr. Bloe" was in reality the band Hookfoot. (Though the original Mr. Bloe—who had scored a Number 2 hit the year before with the song "Groovin' with Mr. Bloe"—was in actuality a motley collection of DJM session musicians led by DJM staff producer Zack Laurence, for live appearances the band Hookfoot was utilized. "The thing took off and became a Number One record," Caleb Quaye said. "When the record broke, Dick needed to put a band together to present the record on TV. We [in Hookfoot] were starving at the time, so we humbly agreed to prostitute ourselves and do *Top of the Pops* along with Zack. We ended up touring around England. It was a riot. We'd play our Hookfoot material and then we'd stick in 'Groovin' with Mr. Bloe', just to please the punters.")

"On this occasion Elton has left lyricist Bernie Taupin out of the picture," the release claimed, "for although there have been many singles using Elton John's songs this is the first one to feature one of Elton's instrumental compositions."

"71-75 New Oxford Street," and its fervent, organ-heavy B-side, "Get Out (Of This Town)"—another Elton-penned instrumental—failed to chart.

The Mr. Bloe stunt angered Elton supremely. But he had little time to stew, for days later, on May 10, *11/17/70* was hitting American record store shelves in a simple monochromatic sleeve (photographed not at the concert which gave the album its title, but rather at Elton's Troubadour shows months earlier) meant to emulate its bootleg origins, a month after its U.K. release. Initially planning to issue the disc as part of a double album in the States, along with the as-yet-unreleased *Empty Sky*, Elton was voted down by his record company. "I wanted the live album to be a free album...you know, and, of course, all the hierarchy that I'm concerned with said, 'No'. And I get so pissed-off with fighting....So we settled for *Empty Sky* not to come out [in America] yet, which is all right. They say that it's better for my 'mystique' that it should remain on import."

Free disc or no, *Rolling Stone* had misgivings with the idea of a live Elton John album. "I mean who else could ever do it in a million years but the master of preciousness?" reviewer R. Meltzer grumbled. "Like he couldn't have done it on AM, it had to be *FM.* At least it wasn't a live concert on

WNEW-FM, that might have been unbearable." Other critics were kinder. "Unquestionably a magnificent album…there is a scope revealed that one, two or three other bands today could ever hope to match," opined *Record Mirror,* while *Melody Maker* noted that the performance was "a perfect representation of the stage act worked out by the pianist and his cohorts." The *Daily Mirror,* for its part, simply state that the disc showed "Britain's runaway star in the making. His music is contagious."

Indeed, the album perfectly captured the raw energy of an Elton John performance. Perhaps more importantly, however, the album finally gave Nigel and Dee a bit of the vinyl attention they so richly deserved. The two sidemen were greatly appreciative. Seared into Nigel's memory banks, in fact, was the afternoon that his wife put the record on for him, mere minutes after having just returned from an extensive tour, jet-lagged out of his mind.

"You've *got* to listen to this," she said.

"Later, Luv."

"No, really, Nige. Listen…"

She put the record on full-blast; Nigel was blown away by what he heard.

"That is an outstanding record for me," the drummer said. "I think it's a fucking good live album in that most live albums are the result of, say, six days' recording. If you're gonna make a live recording, you get a truck to come down to two or three performances and you choose the best ones, so it really isn't a live album. It's like doing a session album. 'Which take is the best over three nights?' Ours was just totally live, we didn't know anything about it."

11/17/70 quickly shot into the American Top 10, giving Elton four albums simultaneously in the Top 40—a feat not accomplished since the Beatles. (Elton's first live disc would also break into the Top 10 in Canada, while securing the

Number 20 position in the U.K.) Additionally, several other albums on the chart featured Elton-penned songs: "Your Song" was featured on both Three Dog Night's *Golden Biscuits* and Andy Williams' *Love Story*; Mary Travers did a rendition of "Indian Sunset" on her LP *Mary*, while James Taylor's sister Kate covered not one but two Elton John songs, "Country Comfort" and "Ballad of a Well-Known Gun" on *Sister Kate.*

While some complained of an excess of Elton John material flooding the market, Russ Regan felt differently. "I had two words for them: Fuck 'em. I heard those criticisms. To some people, maybe there was a glut. But it was a damn good glut."

On May 22, Elton gave his lyricist a unique gift for this twenty-first birthday: one of Marilyn Monroe's dresses, artfully arranged in an illuminated glass display case. Bernie was pleased. Weeks later, the pianist's mentor, Long John Baldry, reached even greater heights of pleasure, however, as his album, *It Ain't Easy*—which had been recorded the winter before—was released to great fanfare.

"I was on tour in New York," Elton said, "and Long John Baldry rang me up from London and told me that Warner Brothers wanted him to do an album, and he had this idea for Rod [Stewart] to produce one side, and for me to do the other side. I hadn't ever done any producing, and the idea gave me the horrors, but nevertheless I said yes....John is one of those people I'd swim a lake full of piranha fish for, because he was great to me."

Rod was of a similar mind. "[Baldry's] done a lot for us, so why shouldn't we help him now?"

The Elton-helmed sessions took place at IBC Studios. He played piano on all the tracks he produced, alongside Caleb Quaye, Roger Pope, Dave Glover and guitarist Joshua

M'Bopo. Eschewing Baldry's suggestion to record banal tracks along the lines of Peggy Lee's "Is That All There Is?," Elton instead insisted that the bluesman work on more challenging material, including Leslie Duncan's "Mr. Rubin," Randy Newman's "Let's Burn Down the Cornfield," as well as an original song which he and Bernie had written specifically for him—an adrenaline-fueled blast called "Rock Me When He's Gone."

Baldry adjusted well to the song selection, as did the band. "You had to adapt to whatever musical paradigm you were given, and so we did," Caleb said. "I had worked with Elton since 1967 so I felt comfortable with this, and besides it was an honor to have been asked to work with Long John Baldry, as he was such a respected man, and deservedly so, in the U.K. R&B scene."

Baldry, for his part, was amused by the very different working methods of his two star pupils. "Rod loved to record well after midnight and very loosely," he said. "Elton's work ethic was to start at eight o'clock in the morning."

"Rod's side turned out raucous, with drums sounding like kettles," Elton said. "Rod's side sounds very much like *Gasoline Alley*, and my side sounds like Mantovani. I'm on that sort of thing. I'm more into choirs and things like that. It's good, because both sides of the album are different. My side is very polished and Rod's side is very raucous, and probably how John should sound. I'll probably get attacked for it."

Despite such misgivings, the bipolar *It Ain't Easy* would go on to become Baldry's biggest-selling album, featuring the impressive single "Don't Try to Lay No Boogie-Woogie on the King of Rock and Roll," and selling over a 100,000 copies—the absolute high-water mark of his career.

Elton had only the briefest moment to celebrate Baldry's triumph before having to turn his focus back to the road. June 10 and 11 were particularly important dates, as he was scheduled to appear at the famed Carnegie Hall for a pair of much-anticipated concerts.

The shows began with the pianist alone at his black grand, his rich tenor belting out reflective numbers like "Skyline Pigeon" and "Talking Old Soldiers." Halfway through the set, he was joined by Nigel and Dee for caustically urgent renditions of "Honky Tonk Women" and "Can I Put You On." "I don't want to sit down and do slow things all night," Elton explained. "I'd go to sleep. I've been a rock 'n' roll freak for a long time, but people seem to think that I have to do rock 'n' roll just to prove that I'm a hip young man. .....[But] I was brought up on rock 'n' roll. I've always been into rock 'n' roll. That's my favorite sort of music. The Rolling Stones are my idols and that's it."

Significantly, the first Carnegie Hall performance featured the world premiere of an intimate ballad called "Tiny Dancer." The song proved a challenge for Elton, who had set the lyrics to music just the day before. "I had to ring up Bernie this afternoon for the words," he admitted to the audience as he launched into the C-major plaint.

"It was just amazing to stand in the wings," noted Eric Van Lustbader, "and see the tears of the people standing there watching the show. It was pretty unusual at that point to play Carnegie Hall, and I thought it was a brilliant move, because it took Elton out of the realm of what everyone else was doing. The mood in-house was absolutely electric from the moment people started filing into the auditorium. I would say that seventy-five to eighty percent of the kids who were there had never been to Carnegie Hall before, and they felt that it was slightly transgressive for them to be there in a stately kind of place, coming to hear a guy who wasn't the least bit stately. So I think of all the places Elton played, to me that was the most special venue." Adding to the uniqueness of the event were the incredible acoustics which the hall boasted. "Of all the places that they'd played, Carnegie Hall was by far the best," Lustbader continued. "Everyone wants to play Madison Square Garden, but the acoustics are terrible. It wasn't made for music, particularly. It was made for sporting events. But Carnegie Hall was designed and built for concerts. So the sound for Elton was the most exquisite, and very, very special. And I think the band picked up on that almost immediately, and played at their highest level all the way through."

Backstage after the show, Elton was awarded his third U.S. Gold album, for the *Friends* soundtrack. "It's amusing," he told journalists Mike McGrath and Mike McQuigley from *Georgia Straight* magazine, a towel draped around his shoulders. "I'm knocked out, I'm very glad that it's a Gold record. But it's *not* an Elton John album."

The pianist was more genuinely pleased by the *New York Times* review his most recent performances had garnered. "Elton John appeared Thursday and again last night before an impassioned audience at Carnegie Hall, in what must be the best-produced rock concert there in a great long while," critic Mike Jahn noted. "Never have I heard such good sound from a rock band in Carnegie Hall. Mr. Olsson's drums were amplified perfectly, and he gave a performance that was often beyond breathtaking. Elton John and his lyricist, Bernie Taupin, clearly are deserving of their popularity."

After Elton's Sunday night performance, a celebratory party, held at the Essex House hotel on Central Park South. Journalist Henry Edwards escorted Bette Midler to the soirée, which was held in a suite which had been turned into a nineteenth-century carnival for the event.

211

Elton and the Divine Miss M embraced warmly in the center of the room, as a golde-lamé-suited Sly Stone and others applauded around them.

"I want to be you," Midler said.

"You already are," Elton cheerfully replied.

While both crowds and critics were cheering Elton in Midtown Manhattan, he was making an even bigger splash nationally, appearing on the cover of *Rolling Stone* for the first time. Pictured sitting on the floor in aluminum-colored boots and a *Bernie Taupin Funky Monkey* T-shirt, the magazine promised: "Kent State One Year After. Elton John: One Year On."

During the interview, Elton dished about hangers-on. "I don't have any trouble with groupies," he told journalist David Felton. "I couldn't stand that sort of thing. Nigel has a groupie in every town, but there's no sort of plague. Anyway, they seem to be more sophisticated now. They've become—how should I put it?—they've become less sluttish." He paused. "Bernie and I *do* seem to attract weirdos [though]. I don't know why, because we're not really weird ourselves. People give me pineapples, and some girl gave me her knickers. Yeah, in Scotland, some girl took off her knickers and threw them on stage—along with a bowler hat. Can you get that one together?" More annoying still were the spaced-out stage-monkey freaks who seemed to follow the band from town to town. "Last night there was this guy, as we were driving out he was clinging onto the car, going, 'I *must* go home with you! *Let* me be a person!' What can you do, you know?...We left him sobbing on the ground. That really disturbs me."

The interview concluded with Elton reflecting on his career. "Realistically, I don't think I can be any more popular than I am now...Who knows? When I'm forty-five years old there might be an Elton John renaissance, and I can come around doing the Hoagie Carmichael bit."

DJM struck a deal with MCA Records that summer, guaranteeing Elton a million-dollar advance, with a second million to follow the following May. For all that lucre, Elton merely had to come up with seven albums of best-selling, generation-defining music in the coming five years. The pianist felt the deal more than fair. "Dick is a straight, right-down-the-middle...publisher," he said. "To me he's been like a father. If there's any problem, Dick will sort it out for me."

Elton headlined an outdoor gig at London's Crystal Palace Bowl in south London on Saturday, July 31. An all-star affair of sorts, the bill included Yes, Fairport Convention, Hookfoot, Tir Na Nog and blues prodigy Rory Gallagher, who went on right before the pianist.

"How can I follow the blues?" Elton brooded backstage. "Look! They're leaving! They only came to see him [Gallagher]."

Despite any pre-performance anxieties, an "absolutely terrified" Elton went down well. While his eight-song set featured rarities like "Rock Me When He's Gone," "I Need You to Turn To" and "Razor Face," the clear highlight was a maniacal piano-thumping version of Jerry Lee Lewis' "Whole Lotta Shakin' Going On."

One of the screaming voices in attendance that afternoon belonged to actress Barbara Windsor, who later recalled, "Yes were on the bill, but nothing could compete with Elton. I sat on the grass and got totally lost in the music."

A bootleg LP of Elton's appearance, entitled *Live in London,* would hit the streets days later.

John Reid was asked to officially become Elton's full-time manager one week on. At first, the twenty-one-year-old Scotsman was reluctant to leave his position at EMI. "I was terrified of telling them I was leaving," Reid said. But after increased pressure from Elton, leave he did. His bosses "went bananas, saying, '*How* can you do this? We were getting you ready for great things!' So I withdrew my notice....Then after a month I thought, 'Oh shit! I really *should* do it.' [But] I was pretty scared because I'd no management experience, no legal experience, no financial experience."

Figuring Dick James would balk if he asked for an extravagant salary—thus providing Reid with a legitimate "out" for his career quandary—he asked James for £6,000 a year, nearly four times his current salary. Much to his surprise, James acquiesced. "From that experience," Reid said, "I learnt that you could never start negotiations too high."

To his credit, Dick James had no issue with the arrangement. "If he's living with his manager," the publisher reasoned, "at least he'll have someone to get him up in the morning."

John Reid quickly became a buffer for Elton. If you wanted to get to the star, you had to go through his manager first. Even Nigel and Dee lost direct access to their band leader. Unsurprisingly, the situation didn't sit well with Elton's longtime sidemen.

"We'd always been on equal terms," Dee said. "But then it all changed. Now, Elton was the star, and Nigel and I were sort of pushed to the background. We couldn't go to him like we had in the past. Now, John Reid was in the way. And he made it clear that he didn't rate us very highly. At press conferences, [Nigel and I] would just be sitting there, not saying a word. And I once said to John, 'Do we really even need to be here at all?' And he just said, 'Don't be so pedantic, Dee.' That was John. And that's how it was from that point on."

Eighteen hours after playing the International Song Festival of Vilar de Mouros in Portugal, Elton headed back into Trident Studios, on August 9, to record the bulk of his next album, his fourth studio effort in the last nineteen months.

"At this point it looked like Elton was putting out an album once every two months, which is ridiculous," Gus said. "So with [the new sessions], I decided that we ought to go back to a formula similar to when we did the first album. I wanted to make it clear to the fans that some of the things which had come in between, such as *Friends* and *11-17-70*, were not part of the official situation."

"Holiday Inn" was the first song attempted. A waltz in 6/8 time, "Holiday Inn" took a less-than-glamorous look at life on the road in America. If anything, the song in its original incarnation proved a bit too biting. Dick James' legal advisors suggested changing "motel prison" to "motel, baby." Additionally, they counseled that Bernie's final, caviling verse—which complained about broken televisions and poor room service—be cut completely.

"The lawyers made us take it out," John Reid later told *Rockline*.

The track was also notable for its featured string player, a rangy, blond-tressed native from Edinburgh, Scotland, named Davey Johnstone. Gus had worked with Davey before, having produced a pair of albums—*Seasons* and *Songs from Wasties Orchard*—for his band, Magna Carta. The producer knew that the guitarist's tasteful sense of harmonics and exquisite acoustic double-track work would perfectly complement Elton's newest songs, and was excited to bring him into the fold.

Though Davey preferred folk music to rock 'n' roll, the nineteen-year-old was more than willing to give it a go. "Honest, I didn't really know at the time who Elton John was," he said. "I'd seen him a bit in the music papers, but I wasn't into what he was doing—I was into traditional Irish music. But money's money, so I agreed to do the session. Why not, right? The day before the session, however, I saw Elton perform 'Border Song' on *Top Of The Pops*, and I went, 'Wow, this guy is good.' So I went into the session with a whole new attitude." Still, his enthusiasm couldn't quite hide the surprise he felt at how withdrawn Elton was in person. "[He] was kind of quiet at first," Davey later told *musicradar.com*. "He sort of stayed in the corner at his piano. It's funny—I wasn't intimidated at all. I *should've* been, but I was kind of a hotshot kid at the time. Elton, on the other hand, looked a little nervous. I guess he was just concentrating a lot."

Though Davey had originally been booked as a banjo player, he campaigned to play the mandolin instead, feeling that the lute-like instrument might better help accentuate "Holiday Inn." The guitarist then further suggested that Elton ditch the elaborate piano intro he'd devised for the song and instead open the song cold, with just his voice. Appreciating the feedback, Elton ultimately decided to lay it down just that way. Everyone in the studio immediately recognized the final effort as one of Elton's best to date.

"It's one of my favorite Elton songs, 'Holiday Inn'," Nigel said, despite having not played on the track himself. "We stopped staying there after a while, though. I think Dee clogged the toilet up once too many times."

● "Tiny Dancer," Bernie's dreamy paean to Maxine, was captured next. The enigmatic song was an instant classic. "Maxine was a really petite person, really into ballet dancing," David Larkham said. "She'd dance at the side of the stage while Elton was playing. That's what inspired those lyrics."

"It seemed like sunshine just radiated from the poplars," Bernie said years later. "I was trying to capture the spirit of that time [with 'Tiny Dancer'], encapsulated by the women we met…in L.A. They were free spirits, sexy in hip-huggers and lacy blouses, and very ethereal, the way they moved. So different from what I'd been used to in England. And they all wanted to sew patches on your jeans. They'd mother you and sleep with you. It was the perfect Oedipal complex."

To help add dimension to the arrangement, steel guitarist B.J. Cole—whom Elton had known since his days recording demos at DJM back in the late '60s—was brought in. "Steve Brown rang me up about four p.m. and said, 'Can you come in later this evening? We're cutting this track and we'd like you to play on it,'" Cole said. "So I went in about eleven p.m. When I arrived, Elton's band were set up in that big basement studio [at Trident]. Basically Elton put the arrangement together on the spot, with the help of the musicians in the studio, including me. We spent till about five in the morning structuring it and working out what went where, because that song has got more sections in it than almost any other pop song. It was pretty unique for me in that situation, because no other pop song had been done with the pedal steel going down with the rhythm section, where the pedal steel is part of the basic track; the pedal steel is usually added on later. If you notice, when it comes in [on the second verse], it stays in, right till the end."

The rhythm section on "Tiny Dancer" consisted of Roger Pope and Dave Glover—both of whom had come to the studio directly from their day jobs at a construction site. Roger, who had been working an industrial hopper, had cement dust in his hair. The dust mixed with his sweat as the session proceeded, hardening into a helmet against his scalp. "I even still had my work clothes on," the drummer recalled. "No time to get changed."

Roger forewent a royalty for the session, opting instead for a standard fee of £36, a decision which would cost him an untold fortune throughout the years.

"I was a daft young man," he said.

The neo-spiritual "All the Nasties" was attempted next. Featuring tasteful tambourine flourishes from percussionist Ray Cooper, a highly sought after session man, the silken, gospel-steeped tempest was the token track of these sessions to feature Nigel and Dee.

Lyrically, the song originated when Elton—fed up with the causticness of the British press—asked Bernie to pen a response to their critics.

"It's not meant to be biting," Bernie said. "It's just meant to be, we hope, subtle."

"I wasn't getting criticism, I was getting bitchiness," Elton said. "And I can't take that."

The luminous track, which featured the Cantores in Ecclesia Choir—directed by Nick Drake's arranger, Robert Kirby—was also a thinly veiled treatise on Elton's sexuality, still very much a taboo subject in the homophobic early '70s.

"Razor Face" was a far more muscular song. A character study about a young man who spends his days looking after a blind old jazz musician who's stuck inside a bottle, the recording featured memorable turns from session men Jack Engblom—who provided bluesy accordion flourishes—and

Rick Wakeman, whose atmospheric organ line lent a wistful claustrophobia to the track.

"I got [Wakeman] for that because I'm the world's worst Hammond organ player," Elton said. "I'm more used to playing my old Vox Continental, and that very badly as well. I couldn't even understand the drawbars on the Vox, and there were only six on that, but I still didn't know what they were for."

A follow-up session was held on August 14. The first track attempted this day was "Rotten Peaches," a country rocker about a repentant European who finds himself imprisoned on an American chain-gang, wasting his days picking rancid fruit. The track was notable for featuring Pentangle's drummer Terry Cox, as well as slide guitar from Chris Spedding, who would go on to produce the Sex Pistols' first demos just a few short years later. Completing the track lineup was bassist Herbie Flowers, who would feature prominently on Lou Reed's "Walk on the Wild Side" the following summer.

Written the previous October while in the U.S., "Indian Sunset"—a polemical examination of American Expansionism—was the oldest number attempted.

"That song was a case of us really having something to say," Elton noted, "and having to write a song to say it. The Indian situation in America really is appalling...but [the song] is a dramatic idea and not a social criticism. If the criticism is also part of the reaction to the song, that's just fine. But that's not our aim. We're not naïve enough to...go see a reservation for an hour and a half and think we understand all about Indians. We simply work out of our imaginations, like the old writers used to do back in the days of Tin Pan Alley. The songs are completely romantic, let's face it. You can get involved in them like you'd get involved in a story or a poem. We don't want to *say* anything in our music in the sense that people insist that Dylan said something."

"Maybe it's bad," Bernie added, "but I never read the newspaper and I never watch the news. I just couldn't get into politics because I just don't believe in anybody enough to really care. In England, life is not as freaky as it seems to be here in the States. We're more concerned with everyday things."

Opening with an urgent *a capella* turn, "Indian Sunset" quickly built to an impassioned crescendo, as it poignantly depicted the death of Apache renegade Geronimo. The song's historical inaccuracy—the real Geronimo died of pneumonia after serving over twenty years as a prisoner of war—did little to diminish the dramatic effect it achieved, and the basic tragedy behind the lyrics remained all too valid. (Perhaps thusly, the song would enjoy a second life years later, hitting Number 1 on the *Billboard* chart in 2005 when rapper/producer Eminem used the surging melody as the backbone of 2Pac's posthumous "Ghetto Gospel" single.)

Short on material, Elton decided to record his own simmering take on "Rock Me When He's Gone," the track which he and Bernie had originally written for Long John Baldry. Though this new version of the retro-soul vamp crackled with playful urgency, its party mood didn't quite fit the thematic unity shared by the rest of the tracks. As a result the song would be shelved for over two decades, before finally seeing a proper release in 1992, when it appeared as part of Elton's *Rare Masters* double-disc set.

The final song attempted at these sessions was a remake of the structurally complex "Madman Across the Water," a dark tale of a paranoid-schizophrenic trapped in an insane asylum. When it came time to record the propulsively cinematic tune, Paul Buckmaster arrived at the studio with no score in hand. "There were sixty string musicians sitting there and we had to scrap it," Elton said. "There were all those sort of disasters [during the sessions]."

Patience won the day, however, and the haunting arrangement which Buckmaster eventually came up with helped guarantee the track heavy rotation on album-oriented FM radio stations for years to come. Perhaps even more importantly, "Madman Across the Water" helped cement guitarist Davey Johnstone's place as a fixture within Elton's musical arsenal. Impressed with his fret work, which—with the aid of heavy reverb and backward echo—seemed to fit the song's yearning mood far better than Mick Ronson's showy licks had done the preceding year, Elton approached Davey about joining his band once their final touring commitments were completed for the year. The guitarist was excited for the opportunity. "That live album they did [*11/17/70*] was fantastic," he said. "I was really into the idea of getting in with the guys that made that record."

"Davey and Elton hit it off on a personal level, and that was that," Gus said. "He was one of us."

Chapter 9:
'We Literally Played in Our Overcoats'

Elton, Nigel and Dee went back on the road the moment the
sessions were over, touring the U.S. from August 26 through
September 16. Reenergized by the fruitful stint at Trident,
the Briton banged the piano so hard during their opening
dates that his nails splintered apart, causing his hands to
bleed every night. With perseverance, however, it proved a
manageable problem.

"Once you've got over the first three or four dates," he
said, "your hands harden up, the skin just hardens up."

While his partner bled beneath the spotlight, Bernie put his
relative anonymity to maximum use, releasing a self-titled
album of poetic recitations—with such obscure titles as
"Solitude" and "Ratcatcher"—over gentle folk
accompaniment provided by Davey Johnstone, Diane Lewis,
Shawn Phillips, Caleb Quaye and others. (Davey would
recall the sessions fondly years later: "Tons of laughter,
hashish, [and] beautiful acoustic jamming with Caleb....It
was all great fun. It was *too* much fun, actually.")

Bernie was hopeful that the disc's release would allow
him to begin staking out his own public identity. "I just
started to not want to be a bracket name," he said. "Like if
anyone wrote about me, they always had to put 'Elton John's
lyricist' in brackets so people knew who they were talking

about. This new album was made to get away from that....Those brackets just have to go, no matter what."

Widely seen as more of a vanity project than a legitimate musical offering, the LP was released on DJM Records in the U.K., and on Elektra in the States. Bernie only had a single contractual stipulation during the promotional phase of the album: that Elton John's name not be mentioned in any of the publicity releases. Despite—or perhaps because of—this, *Bernie Taupin* was poorly received. "Bernie Taupin is Rod McKuen in pretty British pop-star drag, and he knows it," Lester Bangs chided in *Phonograph Record.* "Just like the V.W. as a vehicle for universal brotherhood, his lyrics appeal to people who wear their sensitivity—if not their politics—on their sleeves." *Crawdaddy*'s Allan Richard concurred, asserting that "Taupin is hardly a great poet, more a better-than-average storyteller, and his interpretations are tediously monotonous. His chosen musical accompaniment also drags like a horse with a lame hoof, and I walk away from this recording a better man for never having to hear it again."

Bernie shrugged off the reviews. "It was my first shot at the spotlight," he told journalist Mary Anne Cassata. "Someone suggested that I make the album, and I foolishly accepted. It was fun while we did it."

Elton made his first foray into Japan for a six-date tour that October. Beginning at the Shibuya Kohkaido Hall in Tokyo and ending at the Shinjuku Kohsei Nenkin Hall, each show opened with "It's Me That You Need," a rare live treat performed as a special "thank you" for the superior chart performance that the island nation had granted the soaring elegy.

Pandemonium greeted each performance. The Osaka concert was particularly animated, reaching near-riot levels as hundreds of crazed teenagers broke protocol to assault the barricades which separated them from Elton, Nigel and Dee, while more athletic members of the audience simply leaped over the concrete partitions. By the end of the show, hundreds of kids crowded the stage. Yet even in their hysteria, they gave the musicians a respectful amount of space in which to play.

"Very strange, crazy people, very polite," Elton said. "I could never understand why they went to war, because they always bow." He grinned. "I quite like Japan. The only thing is, nobody talks English."

With little time built into their schedule for rest or relaxation, the band flew directly on to Australia. Minor drama occurred at the airport, when local authorities grew indignant at a few of the more risqué patches sewn into the jean jacket Elton was wearing.

"Can't let you through, mate," one burly guard said, pointing to a sexually suggestive patch on the pianist's sleeve. "Let's have it."

"No," Elton said.

The guard shrugged. "Can't let you through then."

The line behind Elton's entourage grew steadily longer and more agitated as the standoff continued.

"Hand it over," a second guard barked. "That's the kinda thing could damage our society good."

Elton grunted. "Well, I certainly can't help your society," he said.

Armed with a fresh roll of Australian dollars, John Reid intervened, quickly smoothing over the "stupid, needless hassle."

"It was always crazy on the road," Dee said. "Never a dull moment. [Just] a constant flow of madness. It was great."

Things went far more smoothly at the Subiaco Oval a couple nights later. After a thunderous show—which utilized the largest sound system Australia had ever seen—Elton, Nigel and Dee were already in their car and preparing to drive back to their hotel when the concert promoter began banging desperately on their windshield.

"*Please* come back and do us another encore," he begged. "They'll tear the place down otherwise."

Elton stared out his window and smiled—perhaps he *could* help their society after all.

The band played the Kooyong Stadium Lawn Tennis Club in Melbourne days later. The show almost didn't happen—the scaffolders had gone on strike the morning of the concert, and organizers were left scrambling to secure men to help construct the stage. In the end, however, the concert went off without a hitch; the final ovation Elton, Nigel and Dee received lasted nearly fifteen minutes.

"Elton was amazed by the crowd," the concert photographer said. "The audience just loved him. You could see he was truly moved by it all."

The pianist was equally touched by his face-to-face meeting with childhood idol Winifred Atwell the next afternoon. "[We] had a wonderful time together," he said. "She gave me a little koala bear toy....To meet her was the greatest."

After imbibing more than their fair share of complimentary backstage champagne at Western Springs Stadium, Elton reminded Nigel and Dee—as he often did—that their audience had never seen the band play live before.

"So let's give 'em hell then," he said.

Nigel and Dee nodded their agreement while compère Barry Coburn, the show's co-promoter, took to the stage.

"Please welcome that madman from across the water," Coburn said to the 20,000 in attendance. "The Captain Marvel of pop...Elton John!"

The pianist took to the stage in a star-spangled Stetson and velvet cape, white shorts, striped knee-high socks, and a long-sleeved jersey with a self-portrait emblazoned across the chest. With the merest of nods, he and his band began pounding out their set with their usual abandon.

"It was just a three-piece, and they were fantastic, phenomenal players," said Ricky Ball, drummer for the opening band, Ticket. "They rocked the whole night....[It was a] really responsive crowd. Elton went over well." As strongly as the concert was received, though, Ball was left even more impressed by the pre-show soundcheck. "I got to play on Nigel Olsson's drums....It was the most fabulous drum kit I'd ever played on."

During Elton's two-week tour of Australia, he played a football stadium, two racetracks and a speedway—during the middle of winter.

"The stage blew away on one gig, and we literally played in overcoats," he said. "It was raining on the piano....But we'll go back again. Why not?"

Elton's newest album, *Madman Across the Water*, was released soon after—on November 5 in the U.K. and ten days later in the U.S. A release party was held for the LP at Marlon Brando's house. "One of my favorite pictures of all time was taken at that party," Russ Regan said. "Neil Diamond is kissing me on this cheek and Elton John is kissing me on the other cheek. Later on I showed that picture to Elton and he said, 'You know how you got that? I was on my way to kiss Neil on the mouth and you got in the way.' I *think* he was joking. Who knows? I love the guy."

Despite overflowing with somber insights and melodic inventiveness, *Madman Across the Water* failed to trouble the upper reaches of the BBC charts, managing only a relatively dismal 41 in Elton's homeland. "I was disappointed," he acknowledged, "because I know the sales it did should have got it [higher] into the charts. I wouldn't have been worried if it didn't sell at all, but it *did* sell. Not as well as we hoped, of course." His fifth album in a year and a half fared much better in the States, instantly going Gold and reaching a lofty Number 8. The LP would also do well internationally, reaching Number 14 in Italy, Number 13 in Japan, Number 9 in Canada, and Number 8 in Australia.

The distinctive cover artwork proved as idiosyncratic as the music which it heralded. "By that time," album designer David Larkham said, "we had all visited California a few times and picked up clothes that reflected what was going on—worn denims, badges, embroidered bits and pieces. Hence my thoughts for the cover." With a flash of inspiration, Larkham cut out the back panel on his old denim jacket and drew the outline for the album's title in ball-point pen. His wife, Janis, then silk-embroidered the letters (for privacy's sake, the sleeve notes credited Janis Larkham as 'Yanis'), while Steve Brown's wife, Gill, worked on sewing in the back cover song titles."

The gatefold was equally as impressive, opening to reveal a 12-page lyric booklet featuring Victorian-era photos Larkham had picked up in Portobello Market in London. Grainy genteel images stood in for the actual band and production staff. A pair of sad-eyed urchins were labeled 'Elton John & Bernie Taupin'. A forlorn baby atop a large cracked egg was 'David Larkham'. Gus Dudgeon and Robin Geoffrey Cable were a pair of street vendors. Steve Brown was an Edwardian constable.

The ambiguous images seemed to fit well with the album's enigmatic lyrics, which received creative interpretations from their fan base. "My favorite one," Bernie said, "is 'Madman Across the Water'....Everybody thought the 'Madman' was Nixon in the White House. It had never crossed my mind for a minute, but I thought that was a fabulous idea." Indeed, the lyricist preferred that people bring their own idiosyncratic readings to his work. "I don't like to be asked what a song is about, because I think that spoils the fun. I think it's half of the fun of being able to listen to a record. Like reading a book, you visualize the characters in your own mind even if they are described in the book. You see them in your mind how they are. And I think that's how it should be with songs. I think people should interpret them in their own way."

With *Madman*'s release, Elton proclaimed that he'd gotten rid of "three years of shit. That might sound strong, but there were three years of songs and back catalogue which we've finally come to an end of....When we cut *Madman*...it was cut because we *had* to do an album. It was very painful. It was done under pressure and really tortured out of us, and I think it's remarkable that it turned out as well as it did....It's the very last album of its kind we'll ever do."

Reaction to the work was mixed. Critic Thomas Ryan maintained that Elton's emotional piano introduction to "Levon" was "enough all by itself to guarantee immortality for the song," while *Sounds'* Penny Valentine wrote that "*Madman* is a giant stride for Elton John. A powerful and decisive album from a 'full-blooded city' music man." *Rolling Stone's* Alec Dubro was less enthusiastic. "Elton John's music means a lot to me, and as a result, I'm not overjoyed with this album. 'Levon' *sounds* good, but I could listen to it for years and never know what it's about. And it does make a difference....*Madman* won't really crush any

John fans, for he sings with the same power and brilliance he's shown since he broke. But it probably won't draw any either. *Madman* is a difficult, sometimes impossibly dense record. America is worthy of a better story than this record, and Elton John needs a better story than this to sing." Writing in *Newsday,* critic Robert Christgau felt that the songs "meander. The others maunder as well. Ugh."

Elton wasn't surprised by some of the the less than glowing notices his new album generated. "Now that I've made it, it's become very hip to put me down," he told the *New York Times'* Nik Cohn. "When I was nowhere, it was hip to call me a genius. Now the same critics sneer at me. They won't share me with a mass public. The snobbery in rock is amazing."

His writing partner agreed. "I think there's a lull in everybody's career," Bernie said. "You can rise with tremendous popularity and then everybody sort of jumps on your back. They're writing everything about you, and you get to a stage where people want to see if you can maintain that popularity, and the press coverages go down slightly during a phase when you're trying to change your system of doing things and you have to come back. It's like crossing a bridge. You either cross it or you fall off it."

When *Madman* failed to live up to sales expectations, Elton began to worry that he'd oversaturated the market with too many albums too quickly.

"I was getting more and more unhappy about it," he said. "I thought, 'We've worked so bloody hard to get this far, and now we're blowing it.'" To *NME*'s Bob Randall, the star confided his determination to cut back on his work schedule. "I'll be doing less touring and putting more time aside for recording and writing. I've got the British tour to do, but next year I *must* have time to think and write."

With a U.K. tour scheduled throughout November and December, Elton had little time to lament. For this latest outing—supported by the American pop duo England Dan & John Ford Coley—the pianist opened each night with a turbocharged "Rock Me When He's Gone," which never failed to bring the crowds to their feet. The ecstatic reaction underlined a dichotomy of expectations that the pianist's audiences brought with them to his shows. "They think I'm going to be moody and pompous, like James Taylor, but I'm a rock 'n' roll freak," he said. "I always have been. People take rock so seriously, but it's just to be enjoyed. It isn't an art form." Of his ever-spiraling sartorial splendor, he noted that his clothes were simply a method to make up for lost time. "As a kid, because I was so fat, I couldn't wear the latest styles, because I could never find anything that would fit. So I suppose I'm making up for it. I didn't even start living until I was twenty-three. My life now is just an extension of things I always wanted to do. Bright clothes and shiny things. I'm catching up for all the games that I missed as a child. I'm releasing myself."

The Brit worked an emotionally raw cover of Shirley Bassey's signature tune, "This is My Life (La Vita)," into his set list. The song, with its anguished, existential lyrics, had always held special meaning for Elton. "One of my top ten," he said. "I love sad songs. ["This is My Life"] is just tremendous."

Despite the frenzied pandemonium each night's shows engendered, the internal pressure within the powerhouse trio was quickly starting to rise to dangerous levels. "The band were really getting pissed-off," Elton said, "and *I* was really getting pissed-off, because we'd done all we could really do as a three-piece unit....We were so bored, we didn't even look forward to playing anymore....It was impossible with three. It's all right if you're Emerson, Lake & Palmer and there's Hammond organs everywhere, but with just a piano." He sighed. "There's no sustaining instrument among piano, bass and drums. I can't think how we coped."

To help shake things up—as much for himself as for his fans—Elton brought T. Rex glam-rocker Marc Bolan onto stage for the encore of his show at Fairfield Hall in Croydon. Bolan, a glamorous, kohl-eyed sprite who'd recently scored a string of hits including "Hot Love" and "Ride a White Swan," took to the stage like a reigning prince, all satin cloth and Rafael curls.

"Groovy, baby," he shouted, hugging Elton at the foot of his piano as the girls in the front rows screamed and screamed. Backstage, meanwhile, a visibly stoned Bernie gave an interview for the television show *Aquarius.* "Yeah, well, I live in a fantasy world," he shyly muttered. "I'm just sort of happy the way I am. And I want to stay that way, y'know? I don't want to sort of be anything pr..." He stopped and stared out at nothing. "I mean, not that I don't want to be prolific, but I don't want to be the sort of savior of modern writing. I just want to write what I want to write, and if it's appreciated, y'know, people don't have to know me."

"Levon" was issued as a single in select territories on November 29. With little publicity yet not-insignificant airplay, the potent track eventually reached Number 24 in America, and Number 6 in Canada.

Elton was pleased by the song's relative success; at the same time, he fretted over the state of the music business as a whole. "I wish the scene would change, and people would get young idols," he told *Melody Maker.* "Rod Stewart's in his mid-twenties, Dylan and Lennon are thirtyish. Elvis is an old man—and even *I'm* twenty-four. Where *are* they? Where are the new Beatles and Stones who are going to come along and shake us all out of our complacency? It's all become so static, so solemn."

On December 7, Elton made an appearance on BBC-TV's *Old Grey Whistle Test*. Wearing a shimmering silver-and-ruby-striped jacket, he performed "Tiny Dancer" and "All the Nasties"—though not "Levon," as Dick James had deemed the song "a bit too long" for commercial release in England. Elton was displeased with this decision, seeing the rebuke as a vote of no-confidence from the person who was supposed to be his biggest backer.

"My tongue is still," the pianist said. "For the moment [anyway]."

Keeping his silence proved more difficult just one day later, when he ran into a problem at the Fortnum and Mason department store: his cashier—who instantly recognized him as Elton John, one of her favorite singers—refused to process his purchase transaction, as his checkbook read Reginald Dwight. The singer was furious.

"I'm Elton fucking *John*," he insisted, to no avail.

Though John Reid was able to smooth things over and eventually settle the matter to everyone's satisfaction, Elton had had enough; that same day, he filed a name change by deed poll with the Central Office of the Supreme Court of Judicature.

Elton ended the year by appearing with T. Rex on a spirited version of "Get It On" on the Christmas edition of *Top of the Pops*. Pummeling a white upright in a poodle-strewn jacket, the pianist allowed Marc Bolan the spotlight as he shook his long locks and swanned photogenically for the cameras.

(The song would be renamed "Bang a Gong [Get It On]" for the more delicate American market.)

The galvanizing performance left Elton thinking about the direction he foresaw himself and his band taking in the near future. "Gus and I have already talked about the next album, and we want to get back to a basic sound," he said. "I mean, I'd love to do a Rod Stewart or Neil Young type of album. It's time for a change. Adding [a] new guitarist next year will give us more scope, I think. We've proved better than anyone that piano, bass and drums can make it in a loud rock act, but there's hardly any room for solos at the moment. I have to provide rhythm *and* solos on piano, which is a bit of a drag, and I think someone fresh in the group will take a bit of responsibility off me and give us a new lease on life."

This proposed change was a daring move, considering that *Billboard* had just ranked Elton as the sixth-highest artist in the world in terms of album sales, bested only by such long-established acts as Chicago and Grand Funk Railroad. In the solo singer category, Elton tied with James Taylor for first place.

While the pianist was pleased with his musical prosperity, he was—more than anything—amazed that he'd been able to weather the tempest of fame at all.

"When I think about it," he said, "it's a wonder I've survived the last few months."

Part Two:
Silent Movies, Talking Pictures

Chapter 10:
Honky Château

1972 kicked off on a positive note, with Elton receiving official confirmation that his deed poll application had been successfully processed. Gone now forever was the lost and lonely Reginald Kenneth Dwight. In his stead, legally and forever, stood Elton Hercules John. (Elton had chosen the middle name Hercules not for its connotations to the Greek god of war, but rather because it was the name of the beaten-down cart horse on the sitcom *Steptoe and Son,* a British forerunner of *Sandford and Son.* "[I] could have called myself Fiona, I suppose," he said. "Elton Fiona John. Or Dalmation....No one ever called me Kenneth. I don't know why people bother having middle names anyway. So I thought I'd call myself Hercules. My mother had a fit. Everybody had a fit. They didn't think I was serious until it came through.")

The switch made an immediate difference to the pianist's schismatic psyche. "It was like slipping into a Superman costume," he said. "I'd grown fed up with people saying, 'This is Elton John, but his real name is Reginald Kenneth Dwight.' Reg is the unhappy part of my life. I can't bear people calling me Reg. If people send me letters as Reginald Dwight, I don't even open them."

The newly christened Elton John was advised to record his next album abroad, to escape Britain's heavy taxation rates.

"My solicitor said, 'You've got to start recording outside the country,' and I said 'Why?' And he said it would be much better financially if we recorded outside the country. I said, 'You must be joking.' He wasn't. So I said I'd go only if we could find someplace peaceful, without any interruptions."

Beyond any monetary considerations, Elton also felt that a new studio would provide the psychological freedom necessary to help expand his music in a fresh direction. "I was labeled a singer-songwriter and did four LPs in that syndrome," he said. "But I've always fought against the Elton John Syndrome. People take it too seriously. I'd like us to be a band [now]." Indeed, he was more than ready to leave behind the overly complex pocket symphonies which had exemplified his earlier releases, and move toward something simpler and more organic. "On the first albums, we used a lot of session men, but we could never do it that way now, planning it down to the last flute."

When plans to record in Nice with the Rolling Stones's sixteen-track Mobile Recording Studio fell through, Gus was dispatched to France to hunt down a conventional studio. He found just what he was looking for at the Château d'Hérouville, a secluded eighteenth-century castle thirty kilometers northwest of Paris. Hidden behind a wall of twisted chestnut trees and a four-hundred-year-old ivy-clad stone wall, the Eden-like studio overlooked the sun-dappled fields where Van Gogh had painted several of his final masterpieces, including *Wheatfield with Crows*. The impressive structure also featured, as the Castle d'Hérouville, in Balzac's 1844 novel, *Modeste Mignon*.

The property was now owned by French film composer Michel Magne, who had installed a custom-made 16-track tape machine—along with multiple tons worth of the latest electronic recording gear—into the studio. Renamed

Strawberry Studios, the facility had quickly become a much-sought-after facility by the likes of Pink Floyd and the Grateful Dead. "People said I was mad because no one would want to make the thirty kilometer journey from Paris to record in the middle of nowhere," Magne said. "But then they saw the groups arriving."

It didn't take Gus long to realize that he'd happened upon the perfect studio for Elton's purposes. "When I first walked into the studio proper, some guys from a band called Zoo were just starting a soundcheck," the producer said. "And the drummer's cymbals were nice and crisp—*ting, ting ting*—clear as a bell. And when I stepped into the control room, you could hear the exact same sound coming from the speakers—*ting, ting, ting*—even with the heavy control room door shut tight. [It was] just astounding. I'd never experienced that type of fidelity before, in any studio I'd ever been in."

The Château was comprised of two main wings—one which housed the studio facility and business offices, the other which contained spacious suites for the musicians and recording team. Boasting its own swimming pool, games room, and a five-star banquet hall, the Château's crumbling splendor offered an unparalleled creative environment. "We didn't have to pack everything away at the end of a session, and so we could work at night and sleep by day," Elton said. "It is the only way to work. You come down to a place like this and you forget about all the troubles of the outside world. Nothing matters except getting your head straight and putting the music down."

Indeed, the studio's relaxed, sleep-away-camp vibe proved invaluable in fostering a familial, us-against-the-world bond between the pianist and his band on what was to be their first full album sessions together. "The Château wasn't the most technically wonderful studio," he said, "but there was something magical about it. I'm not impressed with studios that look fantastic and then there's no atmosphere about it. I'd rather have a shitty old desk."

Besides featuring Nigel and Dee, the sessions also saw the official addition of guitarist Davey Johnstone, whose broad range of styles provided extra dimensionality to Elton's music. Interestingly, Nigel and Dee hadn't a clue that the lanky Scotsman had been invited to join the band until he suddenly joined them on the plane trip up to Paris.

"I wanted (future Procol Harum guitarist) Mick Grabham in there," Nigel confessed, "because he was a buddy from school. But we found he was the wrong type of player. Davey fitted because of his folk background."

"Surprises abounded," Dee said with a grin.

Gus and Nigel spent the first couple days at the Château working on achieving the proper drum sound, which required Nigel to bash away on his kit for hours at a time.

"Nigel and Gus, with their engineer, would spend at least two days getting a drum sound for the albums, and this was a remarkable process," Davey said. "In fact, I read *Lord of the Rings* while they were doing it. It speaks volumes for the way these records sound, because the drums sound phenomenal. They sound right-in-your-face. They sound natural."

"Within the drum kit you have every frequency you're ever going to hear," Gus noted, "from the highest high to the lowest low. Once you've got the drum sound together, someone can come in and say: 'What do you think of this bass sound?'—with it in solo. But you don't know how good it is until you've put it up against the drum kit, because it may be a great bass sound in its own right, but does it work with the bass drum?"

240

Once satisfactory drum sounds were achieved, the group quickly fell into a hyper-productive creative pattern. "We'd have all of our instruments set up at the breakfast table," Elton said. "I'd come down, have breakfast, get a lyric, and write a song at the electric piano while they'd eat....I couldn't believe how everything began to flow."

Aiding in this fluid process was the fact that Bernie's lyrics were coming to him faster than ever before. "We wanted to do some fun songs," he said. "Very simple things that people could sing along with....For the first time, I found the songs coming out naturally. I didn't have to consciously look for things to write about." Sitting upstairs in his bedroom late at night, he'd type up new lyrics, then hand them to his wife so she could correct his spelling. In the morning, Maxine would run them down to Elton and throw them on his electric piano.

"The band would join in," he said, "and by the time breakfast was over we'd written and rehearsed two songs....It was the height of our powers."

Once the band had the new songs properly locked in, they would follow Gus across the sun-drenched courtyard and into the studio proper, where they'd commit the tracks to recording tape beneath a thirteenth-century chandelier.

"The band was almost telepathic," Davey said. "We'd each know what the other one was going to play."

The third morning at the Château, Elton found a lyric which Bernie had written a week before they'd left for France. As he read the words over, his hands found a G-minor-9th chord on the keyboard, then a C-9th. "I was picking up melodies straight out on the piano and the group was right there putting everything together as complete arrangements," he said. "It was so good, so productive, that we wrote nine songs in three days. We were reeling them out."

241

Rocket Man

Elton composed "Rocket Man (I Think It's Going to Be a Long, Long Time)" in only ten minutes.

"Once he played the first chord, he would immediately sing," Davey said. "I've never really seen anybody else do that." Gus was equally as amazed. "He would start singing and playing at the same time. It was really strange. And if he ever got stuck, if he ever lost his momentum, he'd simply back up a line or two and have another go, till the logjam passed."

While Elton's speed was remarkable, it *did* give his producer a moment of pause. "I used to think, 'Does this seem great because it's coming out so fast? Am I fooling myself?' But then you'd hear the whole band fleshing it out, and it'd be, 'This actually *is*, in fact, superb.'"

Lyrically, "Rocket Man" was inspired not by David Bowie's "Space Oddity," as many critics would widely speculate, but rather by a tune composed by Pearls Before Swine's Tom Rapp. "He actually wrote a song called 'Rocket Man', which was based on a Ray Bradbury story from *The Illustrated Man,*" said Bernie, who felt little compunction in borrowing the basic idea from a fellow songwriter, or the bones of another writer's story. Bradbury's story concerned a conflicted astronaut who yearned to be home with his wife and child while out in space, yet ached to be tearing through the cosmos when he was home with his family. Bernie used the idea as the basis of his own composition. "It's common knowledge that songwriters are great thieves," he said. "And this is a perfect example." Especially, perhaps, given the unbidden manner in which the lyrics had initially come to him—the first two lines arrived while he was driving home from dinner and witnessed a shooting star in the night sky. "By the time I'd gotten home, I'd written the song in my head. I jumped out

242

of my car and ran into my parents' house, sort of shouting: '*Please* don't anyone talk to me till I've written this down!'"

Davey overdubbed four open-tuned acoustic guitars over the choruses to "Rocket Man," creating a lush harmonic soundscape underpinned by Dee's melodic bass lines. "Dee is probably the most amazing bass player," the guitarist said. "Dee Murray was a phenomenal bass player, singer, friend. If you listen to 'Rocket Man,' nobody told him what to play. That was the thing about our band...nobody told you what to play."

Happy with the instrumentation, Gus suggested that Nigel, Dee and Davey add background vocals to the track. It was a key decision, one which would introduce a trademark sound integral to Elton's signature '70s sound. It didn't come easy, however. At first, the producer found it a challenge to get a proper blend with such disparate voices huddled around a single microphone. "It's like trying to take a trombone, a triangle and a bloody string bass and...get a balance," he said. "The three of them had totally different types of singing voices. Nigel's voice is really high, he can hit those top notes really great but he doesn't have a lot of middle or bottom energy in his voice. Davey...has quite a husky voice and doesn't have a lot of energy. Dee has just pure energy, and no top and no bottom."

After a couple frustrating hours not getting anywhere, Gus decided to set up three separate microphones so he could better control the balance of their individual voices. "Suddenly we arrived at a perfect blend of voices," the producer said. "I'll be the first to admit, it was blind luck. So much of this business is down to luck."

The backing vocal sessions proved as enjoyable as they were effective. "There was always a lot of laughing going in the studio," Nigel said. "The spirit was loose and fun. Basically, we'd be left alone. Elton would sing his [lead] vocals, and then he'd say, 'OK, you guys can get on with the backgrounds.' We'd come up with our harmonies and experiment a bit. If something didn't work, we'd try another approach till we nailed it."

For the high notes, Gus would place a microphone behind Dee, who often had to sing through his legs. "He actually did," the producer said, bemused. "[Dee] couldn't get certain notes without bending over."

In stark contrast to the transcendent interplanetary ode, "I Think I'm Gonna Kill Myself" was a whimsical, down-to-earth honky-tonk romp which satirized the typical teenager's melodramatic view of the world.

After discarding the notion that Elton's stepfather Derf play a solo on the spoons, Gus brought in "Legs" Larry Smith—drummer for the outlandish Bonzo Dog Doo-Dah Band—for a tap dance solo. Smith, who'd gained notoriety in the late '60's by performing "Death Cab for Cutie" at the tail end of the Beatles' *Magical Mystery Tour* film, was all too happy to oblige, even going so far as to bring his own floor into the studio to tap on.

"He danced his ass off," Gus said. "It went down a storm."

After that night's work had been completed, Gus ambled off to his master bedroom suite, only to be awoken at four A.M. by an apparition floating at the foot of the bed that he and his wife Sheila shared. Everyone teased the couple relentlessly the next day when they'd confessed what they had seen— until the others, too, had similar run-ins. (Per local legend, the Château received visitations from the ghosts of Frédéric Chopin and novelist Amantine Lucile Aurore Dupin—who wrote under the gender-bending pseudonym George Sand—

after carrying out an illicit affair at the Château over a century before.)

"It was haunted as fuck," David Bowie's producer, Tony Visconti, later acknowledged. "David took one look at the master bedroom and said, 'I'm not sleeping in there!' [So] he took the room next door. The master bedroom had a very dark corner, right next to the window, ironically, that seemed to just suck light into it. It was colder in that corner, too." Not fearing the spirit world, Visconti ended up taking the master bedroom for himself. "What could Frédéric and George really do to me? Scare me in French?"

Ghosts or no, the recording continued apace, with the pounding "Susie (Dramas)," an angular, Move-flavored rocker which featured Davey's first-ever attempt at an electric guitar solo. "When he hit the first note and this sound leapt out of his amplifier, he nearly fell over," Gus said. "It's a very structured solo because he just didn't know how to do a free solo....Davey was an acoustic guitarist, not an electric guitarist, and this was the first solo he had ever had to play."

"Really superb tune, Reg," Gus said after the track was completed.

Elton's face darkened. He bit his lip, pushed his glasses up his nose, and left the room without a word. Everyone looked at each other, mystified.

A few minutes later, John Reid came into the control room and sat Gus and the band down.

"Listen guys, can you just call him Elton from now on? No more Reg. Just Elton, okay?"

Gus, Nigel, Dee and Davey nodded in unison.

"That was...*interesting*...shall we say," Dee later recalled. "[It was] definitely a line in the sand."

Elton was soon back in the studio, working on the gospel-soaked "Salvation," which everyone assumed would get the nod as the leadoff single for the new LP. As it turned out, the song was destined to languish in semi-obscurity as a largely overlooked album cut.

"You can only guess," Elton admitted. "You never really know which songs are going to work till you lay them down."

Jazz pioneer Jean-Luc Ponty, who'd recently gained acclaim for his cutting-edge work on the Frank Zappa-produced album *King Kong*, was brought in to add electric violin to "Amy," a rollicking Stones-like rocker of sexual awakening.

"I got an excellent impression as soon as I walked in the studio the first day," Ponty said. "Although Elton had hits in America and the U.K. already, he was not yet well-known in France, and I was not familiar with his singing. So I was very impressed as I was discovering how talented he was just hearing him alone, singing at the piano."

Elton was similarly taken with Ponty. Recording with the Frenchman was "probably the most exciting moment of my musical career," he said.

Ponty's playing proved remarkable enough, in fact, that Elton asked him to also lend his chops to "Mellow," a Leon Russell-inspired bliss-out which memorialized the sexual utopia Bernie and Maxine had found at Piglet-in-the-Wilds. Ponty was more than pleased to help out on the track. "'Mellow's an incredibly inspiring song, just beautiful," he said. "Gus asked me to plug my violin into the Hammond [organ] to get a unique sound. It really worked perfectly. I used violinistic expressions—sliding notes that cannot be played on an organ, for example—and mixed them with more usual organ-style phrasings. It came out great."

246

"Ponty was an inspiration," said Dee, who ended up altering his bass sound after every take—a habit which drove his producer crazy, but which his band mates appreciated. "There was *no* one like Dee," Nigel said. "A musical genius across the board." Davey readily agreed. "Dee was brilliant. He was a beautifully instinctual musician. His ideas were so fucking great. He'd work things out so meticulously, fiddling around. What a player."

The session's signature cut came in the guise of "Honky Cat," an idiosyncratic, New Orleans-soaked tune accented with playful Chinatown-esque piano licks. Lyrically, the song saw Bernie pining to get back to the rural countryside of his youth. Played at a daring 171 beats per minute, the syncopated stomper was fueled by a quartet of local French horn players: trombonist Jacques Bolognesi, trumpeter Ivan Jullien, and saxophonists Alain Hatot and Jean-Louis Chautemps.

Gus recorded Elton and the band playing live together as they laid "Honky Cat" down, to capture the essence of a live stage performance. But maintaining a modicum of isolation—so that he could later manipulate the piano within the framework of the entire mix—proved a bit problematic for the producer. "When I first started off," he said, "we did it the same way anybody does—you lift the lid up. I never close the lid on [Elton's] piano. It's the worst thing you can possibly do. Taking the lid off is even better, if you can get the lid physically off. The lid is only there to bounce the sound out into the hall when you're playing live with an orchestra."

The problem, as Gus quickly found out, was that separation was lost in a studio situation. "It's very unlikely you're going to be able to get the piano somewhere isolated, so with rock 'n' roll you'd like to be able to keep it shut to keep some of the noise out. But the trouble is, when you do that you've got the mics only a matter of inches from the strings, so you're going to hear all the harmonics—which you're not supposed to hear—and the sound's going to be way out of balance, because you cannot get a balanced sound across the whole keyboard unless you've got a mic every couple of feet, which would be ridiculous."

To combat this technical asymmetry, Gus commissioned a carpenter to build the shell of another piano, three times as deep and upside-down, which was then placed directly above Elton's piano. "So, physically, the piano was now about 10 feet tall, and it was padded inside. We had two holes at the side, and we just poked the mics in there, and then you could get the mics high above the strings. You could put the piano right in the middle of the rhythm section [that way], and you might just hear a little bit of low rumble from the bass—or the bass drum or something—but you could usually filter that out without spoiling the piano sound in any way."

When it came time to lay down the lead vocals on "Honky Cat," Elton knocked them out in a single take, with the volume in his headphones turned up so loud that they were literally breaking up. "How he is not deaf, I don't understand," Gus said. "He sings through this blitzkrieg of crap and sings these wonderful vocals."

"Slave" followed. An internal monologue from an indentured servant in the early 1860s who dreams of burning his master's house down, the track was initially recorded as a straight-ahead rocker, at double-speed.

"'Slave' was hilarious the way we cut it originally," Davey said. "Like the fastest rock track of all time. When we listened back we decided, after we stopped laughing, to try it totally differently."

Elton suggested that Davey attempt a swampier, largely solo, take. Laying down acoustic guitar, mandolin, slide guitar and banjo, the Scotsman's efforts truly brought the song to life.

"It makes much more sense," Bernie said of the newer, laconic version. "It makes it that sort of southern, steamy kind of thing."

"A million times better," Elton said. "Our Jean Harlow came through yet again."

The team then began working on one of the most majestic hymns in the entire John/Taupin oeuvre, "Mona Lisas and Mad Hatters." For Elton and Bernie's "first real New York song," the arrangement was simplified to just piano, acoustic guitar and mandolin, which lent the track a prayerful aura which perfectly underscored Bernie's melancholy lyrics.

Gus was more than pleased with the result, labeling it "a magic song with a magic performance, and a great lyric."

"One of my all-time favorites," Elton agreed. "I always thought it was one of my most underrated songs."

Less favored was the stark rumination "I'll Be There Tomorrow," which never made it past a single piano-only take.

Still, the sessions ended on a true party note with "Hercules," a rockabilly raver in open-G tuning. The track—which wryly canonized Elton's new middle name—was something of a milestone for Davey, who was pleasantly surprised by his new-found rhythmic precision. He credited his boss for the confidence which allowed him to so quickly expand his chops. "[Elton] has this subtle sort of control over his musicians," he said. "He doesn't actually tell you what to play, but you get to know what he wants, and he forces the best out of you."

Ecstatic with the way the sessions had gone, Elton called Nigel, Dee and Davey together into the Château's dining room their final night together for an announcement.

"This is such a great album," he said, "you guys are going to get royalties from now on."

The men were astounded.

"That was unheard of," Nigel later recalled. "It still is, to this day."

To Elton, his generous decision was the least he could do. "Everyone rose to new heights in France," he said. "Especially with Davey in the band. It was the first time we'd really got together with him, and he gave everyone such a boost."

"Tiny Dancer" hit U.S. record shops days later in a 3:38 edit of the original 6:12 album track. Though Elton had high hopes for the single, it only managed to reach a disappointing Number 41. (In due time, however, the song would go on to become a standard, and—in the digital age—the single most downloaded track of Elton's vast five-hundred-plus song catalog. Much of the track's eventual resurrection was initially due to its inclusion in a pivotal scene in Cameron Crowe's 2000 film, *Almost Famous.* As to why the song largely failed to catch fire during its initial release, critic Jim Beviglia eloquently opined in *American Songwriter* that "the radio edit for the song...took away much of what made it great. The edit robbed 'Tiny Dancer' of the subtle musical progression that takes it from John's solo piano and vocal at the beginning to the inspiring string arrangement of Paul Buckmaster that carries the song home.")

While "Tiny Dancer" was stumbling up the charts, Gus took the master tapes from the Château sessions back to Trident

Studios, where he had album engineer David Hentschel—who had recently earned plaudits for his detailed efforts on George Harrison's *All Things Must Pass* LP—record an evocatively otherworldly synth line on "Rocket Man" with a state-of-the-art ARP 2600. After laying down bongo overdubs with percussionist Ray Cooper on "Amy," Gus then began the painstaking task of sculpting a final mix of the album over the following weeks.

"It was a hell of a lot of work," he said. "But I was determined to make it as perfect as it could be."

While Gus was laboring away at his post-production duties, Elton went into rehearsals with the 80-piece Royal Philharmonic orchestra for a February concert at the Royal Festival Hall. The event, conducted by Paul Buckmaster, was being filmed for a possible theatrical release, though in the end it would instead be aired by London Weekend Television.

Rehearsals went poorly, as the classically-trained musicians openly looked down upon their rock 'n' roll counterparts.

"That was a very large orchestra and I felt very intimidated," Buckmaster said. "The orchestra sensed my uncertainty. The brass, they're the ones who will tear a conductor to shreds. The strings are always very discreet. Woodwinds are noncommittal. But the brass…they did this thing during rehearsals, they shuffled their feet on the floor, which is a sign of disrespect for the conductor, and that made things even worse. And I lacked the guts to find a proper teacher to show me how it was done."

Emblematic of the orchestra's disconnect was the moment Buckmaster cued them up to rehearse "Take Me to the Pilot."

"Can I have a bit of quiet?" he asked.

"If you got your fucking hair cut perhaps you could *hear* a bit of quiet," a heavyset trumpeter sneered.

"It was all down to that sort of scene," Elton said. "Bunch of cunts."

The pianist and the conductor gamely persevered, however, and days later Elton was taking to the stage in a glittery silver satin jacket that left little doubt which direction the compass of his artistic aspirations were pointing.

Opening the show with the premiere of his imminent single, "Rocket Man," Elton ran through a string of solo numbers before being joined by his band—augmented for the night by backing vocalists Lesley Duncan and Madeline Bell. This concert not only marked Davey's live debut, but was also notable for featuring percussionist Ray Cooper, who stood center stage bashing away on a myriad of instruments, from tubular bells to tambourines to cymbals.

As in the studio, Elton's expanded lineup clicked from the very first bar, yet a purposefully subpar performance by the capricious Royal Philharmonic left the pianist furious. "I just thought they gave a quarter of their best, and they didn't take the event seriously, and I was taking it seriously," he fumed. "That concert was a torture for me, and I was so relieved when it was over. I'd sunk a lot of bread into it. I'll never do it again." *Melody Maker* agreed. "Majestic occasion though it was…not the mindblower we perhaps expected," opined critic Ray Coleman. "And it raised the hoary question: does pop want, need, or benefit from such an uneasy hybrid?"

Chapter 11:
The Ghosts of a Hundred Songs

Now a dollar millionaire, Elton upped sticks again, trading in his Water Gardens digs for a private estate in chic Virginia Waters, Runnymede, Surrey. A Bel Air-style split-level bungalow which boasted a large swimming pool and a mini-football pitch at 14 Abbots Drive, Elton christened his new residence *Hercules*.

Elton's new home overflowed with a surplus of *objets d'art* and electronic gadgetry. A signed Andy Warhol silkscreen print, "Last Suite of the Electric Chairs," hung beside a framed Victorian poster advertising: *Exposition Internationale de Madrid, 1893-94*, which was positioned above an antique brass cash register full of emerald rings and diamond bracelets. A vintage Rock-Ola jukebox stuffed full of favorite platters from the '50s and '60s burbled beside a teal Victrola, which sat in the shadow of a *Grand Slam* pinball machine. A suit of armor, meanwhile, stood watch over multiple Old Master etchings.

"I never dreamed there were Rembrandts still to buy," Elton said. "I thought they were all in museums." (His would end up hanging in the guest bathroom.)

The sloping driveway was as ostentatious as the house itself, showing off as it did the pianist's latest infatuation: car collecting. To date, Elton owned an Aston Martin, a powder-blue Rolls-Royce Corniche hardtop, a scarlet Ferrari Boxer, a monogrammed chocolate Rolls-Royce Phantom VI (to be

253

used exclusively for touring), a vintage Bentley, and a Mini GT—which featured a minibar as well as a color television set.

Chez Hercules quickly became a revolving door of modern rock gentry. "Donovan's having a party [here] next week," Elton said, "and he's invited the whole world. Keith Moon says he doesn't want any Galactic Fairy Dust, he wants a good booze-up. Rod [Stewart] says he's not much into mushrooms and toadstools, but he'll go....David Bowie was just here. I really liked what Mott the Hoople did with his song ['All the Young Dudes'], so I rang him up and invited him for a meal."

Of his many famous guests, Elton got on best with T. Rex's Marc Bolan. "I've known Marc ever since that Roundhouse thing we did the first time," he said. "I've really got into his music a lot and I really like him, and we've been friends ever since then."

Bolan admired Elton as well, although an unmistakable touch of professional rivalry simmered just beneath the surface. "I was really envious of Elton John," the diminutive glam-rocker admitted to journalist Spencer Leigh. "He made about seventy-two sides [recordings] for those cheap labels. The idea was to copy the big hits of the moment, like 'Signed, Sealed and Delivered', as accurately as you possibly could. Elton was brilliant at it. He could do ten a day and he'd get paid £8 for each one. I also wanted to do them, but even then my voice was thought to be too distinctive. I could never impersonate anybody else."

Elton's cousin Ray Dwight was to prove slightly less begrudging. Grateful for all the help his relation had shown him in his early days, Elton gave Ray £12,000 to open a clothing boutique called Lady Samantha.

The gesture seemed to open the floodgates of familial generosity. Within weeks, the pianist had bought his mother a three-bedroom home—dubbed the 'Gingerbread House'— in nearby Ickenham, as well as a sleek white MGB sports car. When she and Derf finally married that spring, Elton volunteered to witness the union, proudly signing the marriage certificate: *Elton Hercules John.*

Not to be outdone by his more glamorous partner, Bernie splurged on a magenta Rolls, which came with all the trimmings.

"I even had a phone put in the Rolls," he said. "One of the very earliest type, when you still had to ask an operator for the number. I never called anyone on it, because of all that hassle of going through the operator. One night, we were sitting in the car outside the BBC, and we suddenly heard a beep but had no idea what it was. Then I realized, 'My God, it's the car phone! Ringing for the very first time!' I rushed to answer it, but before I could pick it up, it stopped. I never discovered who the call was from. And it never rang again."

When not missing phantom calls, Bernie often found himself hanging out at the trendy Tramp disco in St. James.

"There was me, Rod Stewart, Ringo, Gary Glitter," the lyricist recounted. "Others came and went, but Rod, Gary and I were the nucleus. You'd see our picture in *Melody Maker* with a caption saying, 'Yes, it's the same old crew again...'" He laughed. "It was just like still being schoolboys, really. You did the same thing every night: went to some club and got legless while your car waited outside...." One night he got so wasted that he couldn't figure out which of the cars parked outside the club belonged to him. Confused, he put Harry Nilsson into the back of what he thought was his car one night, and instructed the driver to take Nilsson back to his hotel. "Next day," Bernie said, "I found it hadn't been my car at all, but some Arab sheikh's. He comes out of the same club later with two hookers, and it's gone."

Sharing a similar bacchanal existence, Bernie and Rod became particularly close friends.

"Rod lived at Ascot, only a couple of miles [away]," Bernie said, "so if I'd fallen out with Maxine, I'd go back and sleep on his floor. He was always fighting with his girl, Dee [Harrington], so another night he'd come back to my place."

While Bernie and Rod were spending drunken nights passed out on each other's tiles, Elton and his band were embarking on a four-week tour of British universities. With his new guitarist's presence, the outing proved particularly rewarding. "It seems like more of a group now that we have four members," he said. "Since Davey joined on guitar, it's been like a piece of cake for me. I can really relax when I play, whereas before we had to all work at filling in the sound. It's streets ahead of anything we've ever done before."

Nigel felt much the same. "When Davey joined, it took a lot of weight off Dee and I. We had to be thinking all the time about filling it out as far as we could and making it as big as the records, but when Davey joined we could become more of a tight rhythm section and leave the fancy stuff to him. Having Davey there really helped."

Dee, however, wasn't quite as convinced. "In some ways, I preferred it when it was smaller," the bassist told *Record World.* "I didn't object to Davey joining, but I *was* a bit concerned that we might lose the image that we were in the process of building up as a three-piece. As it happened, it worked out fine."

Though Elton's new lineup was proving itself a more than reliable live unit, everything wasn't all rose petals and champagne bubbles out on the concert trail. The pianist was, in fact, becoming increasingly disenchanted by the sound emanating from the stage, as muddy mixes and feedback squalls often degraded his band's performances. Each night he had to deal with a different house engineer and a different headache. Exasperated, Elton contacted Clive Franks, DJM's studio engineer and the tape operator on the *Empty Sky* album. "I got a call from Elton saying, 'We need an engineer, we've been having problems on this European tour,'" Clive said. "The sixth one was the biggest show of the six, in a town hall in Amsterdam, Holland, and they said they really need a good sound."

Clive demurred, having never engineered a live show before. But Elton's persistence won the day, and later that same night Clive found himself manning Elton's soundboard. Not having the slightest idea how to tune a PA system—and with no independent monitoring system available—Clive soon ran into trouble. Four songs in, screeches of electronic feedback began ripping through the hall.

A fed-up Elton stopped playing halfway through "Sixty Years On," slammed his hand on the piano, and angrily kicked his piano bench over.

"Who the *fuck* is mixing the sound tonight?" he roared.

Clive did his frantic best to minimize the damage, but was in low spirits by the time the show ended.

"I sat down nearly in tears," he said. "I had let [Elton] down. He had brought me here to make it special."

John Reid found Clive sitting alone in the empty hall, and convinced him to go backstage to talk to Elton.

Reluctantly, Clive headed back, feeling like a condemned man. But Elton came up and embraced him in a bear hug. "Great job, Clivey," he said in all sincerity. "It was amazing."

Clive looked at him in shock. "Amazing? But you stopped the show. The sound was a disaster."

Elton grinned. "You should have been at the *other* shows."

Understanding the important role a competent live sound engineer played, the pianist offered Clive a full-time job that night. "Someone's creating your sound up front, which you're never going to hear," Elton said. "The element of trust is one-thousand percent, because I'm hearing what I'm hearing onstage [through stage monitors], I'm not hearing what everyone's hearing out front."

Moved by Elton's faith in his abilities, Clive accepted straightaway. He quickly got himself up to speed on the vagaries of live sound mixing, and was soon expertly mixing each of Elton's shows on a 19-channel mixing board. Being the infancy of arena rock technology, the unit Clive utilized was basic, with little equalization and absolutely no effects. "We didn't use reverb or anything like that," he said. "But I would do the best I could." The engineer's ultimate aim was to recreate onstage—as closely as possible—the aural nuances of a studio session. "So many concerts I've been to, I can't breathe because the bass drum is the loudest thing in the mix. I was into sonic balance and hi-fi. I took that knowledge from the studio and I tried to reproduce it in a live situation."

Clive would go on to work nearly every live performance Elton gave for the next four decades.

The afternoon before a concert at Shaw Theatre in Euston, an extravagantly fur-coated Elton visited a small bookshop just down the road from his house. The proprietor, Bryan Forbes, welcomed the purple-haired, green-sideburned pianist and helped him hunt down a biography on Noel Coward.

Far from being a mere book clerk, Forbes was, in fact, a major player in British cinema, having starred in such British classics as *The Quartermass Experiment* and *The Guns of Navarone*, while also directing such films as *Whistle Down the Wind* and *The L-Shaped Room*.

"You know, I'm going to a pop concert tonight," Forbes told Elton, believing the pianist to be one of the Bee Gees.

"That's funny," Elton said. "So am I."

Thanking Forbes for the Coward book, Elton left. Later that evening, he drove himself to Shaw Theatre to give a benefit concert for the Council of the National Youth Theatre, whose stated goal was to provide "good theater at prices young people can afford." Elton had initially become involved with the organization after his solicitor, who was currently serving as the group's chairman, had invited him to a production of Peter Terson's *Good Lads at Heart*. "I was so knocked out," Elton said. "It had everything in it that everything else I'd ever seen lacked. I really became involved with it. I felt completely there."

When asked if he would be willing to play a fund-raising show for the group, Elton quickly agreed to give *three* concerts: one for the general public at £1 per ticket, a second for the more well-to-do at £5 per, and a final free show for the members of the National Youth Theatre who were otherwise unable to attend. For his efforts, the pianist was invited to become vice-president of the organization, serving alongside Sir John Gielgud, Sir Michael Redgrave, and Glen Byam Shaw.

Bryan Forbes, who was the then-current president of the National Youth Theatre, visited Elton backstage after the show and toasted his performance. "I invited him to join my wife [Nanette] and I at dinner at an Indian restaurant in Hampstead, to thank him for the concert," Forbes said. "Princess Margaret came along as well. We became inseparable."

Four days later, on February 24, Elton held a concert at Watford Town Hall. The night was fraught with tension as, only forty-eight hours earlier, IRA members had blown up a car outside the UK army barracks in Aldershot, resulting in seven deaths. Known as "Bloody Sunday," the bombing was in response to twenty-six Irish protesters being shot in Derry, Northern Ireland by British soldiers. Everyone in attendance at Elton's show were well aware of the fractious political climate, so when a concert organizer came up to Elton halfway through the show and whispered nervously into his ear, a palpable buzz ran through the audience. Elton was forced to leave the stage, as the IRA had warned that a bomb had been planted somewhere in the building. Lead police officer, Inspector O'Connor, sat at Elton's piano and announced that the hall was to be evacuated at once, cutting the evening short. Fortuitously, the threat turned out to be a hoax.

"Bloody IRA," Dee Murray joked. "Everyone's a critic."

While the IRA debacle left a bitter taste in Elton's mouth, his burgeoning friendship with the charmingly self-effacing Bryan Forbes proved a comforting salve. Forbes was soon inviting the pianist over to his nearby hose, Seven Pines, regularly for dinner. It was a seemingly fated arrangement, as Elton lived only five minutes away. On these visits, Elton found himself particularly taken with Nanette—as she was with him. "He struck me as someone who was totally without conceit," she said. "And it wasn't the affectation of modesty some people put on. With Elton, it was completely genuine."

Elton was equally as impressed with the Forbes' daughters, Sarah and Emma, whom he agreed to watch over on several occasions. "I remember when *Deep Throat* was in the cinema and Elton wanted to see it, but he was babysitting Emma," Nanette told author Keith Hayward years later. "So he took her with him. Apparently the man in the box office said, 'You can't bring that child in here,' and Elton replied, 'How *dare* you! It's not a child, it's a *midget!* A forty-five-year-old *midget!*' Full of apologies, the box office clerk let them in. Emma of course went to sleep, as she didn't know what it was about anyway."

Katharine Hepburn came to stay with Bryan and Nanette Newman later that spring. Excited to meet the screen legend, Elton invited her over for a swim in his pool. Hepburn accepted, bicycling over one sunny Sunday afternoon in a bright green bathing suit. Declining the elaborate tea service Elton had set for her on his front lawn, and after politely shaking hands with Elton's gobstruck friend, Scottish comedian Stanley Baxter, the feisty star of *The African Queen* headed straight to the pool, clapped her hands together, and did an elaborate dive into the deep end.

Elton was preparing to join her when he spied a dead frog floating at the bottom of the pool.

"C'mon, already," Hepburn said.

Elton pointed at the dead frog and shook his head as Stanley Baxter doubled over in laughter.

"I wouldn't go in," the pianist later confessed. "How butch. No way was I going in that pool."

Hepburn climbed out of the pool, grabbed a large twig, dove back in, swam over to the frog, scooped it up, and nonchalantly flung it into a group of bushes.

Elton was astounded.

"How could you do that?" he asked.

"Character, dear boy," Hepburn said with a wry grin. "Character."

Having surrounded himself with movie industry insiders, it seemed only natural that Elton dip a tentative toe into cinematic waters himself. Heading off to Ascot Sound studios—located on the grounds of John Lennon's eight-acre estate in Berkshire, Tittenhurst Park—he agreed to appear in Marc Bolan's surrealistic documentary, *Born to Boogie.* Directed by ex-Beatle Ringo Starr, the three stars were soon jamming away on a barnstorming cover of Little Richard's "Tutti Frutti."

"I loved the way we did 'Tutti Frutti'," Bolan said in an affected faux-posh drawl. "Elton added a whole new thing to that song."

As well as the Little Richard performance went down, however, it was Elton's cameo appearance on "Children of the Revolution" that would ultimately prove the true highlight of the day. "The version of 'Children of the Revolution' we did is far superior to the single Marc put out, and he knows it," Elton said. "But it would be impossible to edit [it to a releasable length]."

Though pleased with the music he'd helped create for the film, the self-critical pianist was far less satisfied with his appearance. "In [*Born to Boogie*] I look like a fucking gorilla. So ugly."

Elton and Bolan would attempt to write a tune together a few days after filming had concluded. Swinging by *Chez*

Hercules with a battered guitar, Bolan and Elton sat around a piano and rocked out to songs from Bolan's *Electric Warrior* album.

Clive Banks, who had recently joined the employ of DJM, happened to be there that fateful afternoon.

"Elton had a brilliant natural voice," Banks told author Philip Norman, "but Marc's was all put-together in the studio. In real life, it wasn't much more than a little squeak. You'd get Elton playing 'Jeepster' and doing a great vocal, and this squeak going on on top of it."

With no tours imminent, an ever-restless Elton was soon joining Rod Stewart to produce a second album for Long John Baldry. Entitled *Everything Stops for Tea,* Elton recorded the tracks for his side of the disc at IBC Studios. The pianist was pleased to be working with Rod again. The feeling was mutual, as Elton's rooster-haired counterpart admired the deep musical knowledge the former Reg Dwight brought to the table. "I respected his opinions about music," he said. "[Elton] had a proper understanding of blues and soul, and if he liked something I had done, it meant a lot to me, coming from him. I quietly envied the way that gigantic-selling popular melodies seemed to come to him in such a constant flow."

Utilizing the talents of Davey, Nigel, Ray Cooper and bassist Klaus Voormann, the songs Elton produced for Baldry this time around included the Dixie Cups' "Iko Iko," Willie Dixon's "Seventh Son," and the traditional Scottish folk song "Wild Mountain Thyme." Released in April, *Everything Stops for Tea*—which featured cover artwork by Ronnie Wood—would spend six weeks on the American charts before quietly slipping away. Proving less successful than its predecessor, the LP would mark the final major release of Baldry's career.

While his partner busied himself with his former mentor, Bernie was busy completing the first draft of a book of children's poems ("They're fun. You can write a couple of songs and then some silly verse...") before heading to a Cannes studio to helm a series of recording sessions for singer David Ackles.

Producing proved a real joy for the lyricist.

"I love being in the studios anyway," he said. "I've always wanted to get behind the desk. I love the jobs which most people seem to find boring—like mixing and dubbing." His efforts ultimately yielded Ackles' highly regarded third LP, *American Gothic*, which in time would become the most celebrated album of the cultish singer's short-lived career.

"Rocket Man," the leadoff single from Elton's Château sessions, touched down in American record stores on April 14, and days later in the U.K. The song's released tied into the Apollo 16 launch, Uni Records took out an ad in *Billboard*: "On the morning of April 16, 1972, Apollo 16 was launched into orbit on a journey to the moon. A few mornings earlier Uni Records launched a new Elton John single into the worldwide orbit. What a trip! Both launchings bound ot set new records."

Indeed, "Rocket Man" proved to be an instant success, garnering massive critical praise. "While astronauts are on the moon," *Record World* wrote, "Elton John explores the outer limits of the possibilities of pop music. This should be a huge hit; it's one of his best." Across the pond, *Disc*'s John Peel determined that the single was "by far the best thing Elton John has ever done—it's quite superb....This band is great, the song is great, Bernie Taupin's lyrics are great and if the *Honky Château* LP is going to be like this you're going to have to listen to it in little doses or you'll go mad. After two hearings I was so busy singing along that I couldn't get myself organized into taking notes about the structure of the record. Consumer, not critic, that's me, and I can consume music like this for evermore."

Elton was relieved by the song's acceptance. "We were all praying it would do well," he said. "I was proud of it because it was the best single I'd ever released."

"Rocket Man" would orbit the upper reaches of the charts for fifteen weeks, ultimately soaring up to Number 6 in the U.S.—Elton's first Top 10 single since "Your Song." In England, the track was released as a maxi-single, along with a double B-side offering of "Holiday Inn" and "Goodbye." All 50,000 copies of the disc's initial printing, which incorporated a mini-LP sleeve, sold out in a matter of days. Standard printings did equally as well, powering the single to the Number 2 spot on the U.K. charts.

"['Rocket Man'] was the stepping stone, that [song] changed everything," Elton later commented. "It had an acoustic guitar on it, it was a different song for me. It was a simple sound....I was becoming successful. I was so confident musically."

Elton flew off to the States in late April to begin yet another American tour, his fifth in less than two years. Unmoved by the attention he was lavishing on the country, customs agents at LAX tore through four pairs of the pianist's stacked-heeled boots, convinced that they must contain secret drug-smuggling compartments.

After none were found, disingenuous apologies were made ("It's just that it's such a new style, we haven't caught up with it yet," one customs agent sheepishly muttered), and a frustrated Elton was finally allowed through.

"There you go," he said, running his hand through a prismatic thatch of orange and green. "'On your way,' now [that] they've naused-up me footwear. Unbelievable."

Elton's latest jaunt—which opened with an earnest "Tiny Dancer" followed by a menacingly funky "Susie (Dramas)"—saw Elton finally traveling with his own piano, a thousand-pound Steinway model "D" Concert Grand. The instrument had been customized by Elton's piano technicians—the action lightened and the hammers hardened—so that the keys responded much closer to an electric piano than to a standard acoustic piano, allowing Elton to pound away more manically than ever before.

Though the customized keyboard proved perfect for the Briton's jackhammer style, matters proved a bit less responsive offstage—at least before a May 4 gig at Jenison Fieldhouse in East Lansing, Michigan. "We had just arrived at a hotel," Clive Franks later recalled to *Radio New Zealand*'s Jesse Mulligan. "It was Greyhound buses. A special charter. We were picked up at the airport, as we did each time we came into town. It was quite a drive. A couple of guys in the band were getting hungry. And Elton didn't want to stop. An insurrection broke out. They finally stopped at a McDonald's, I think. Elton was in a foul mood."

Half an hour after the band had settled into their hotel rooms, Clive's phone rang.

"Listen, I want you to play bass tonight," Elton told him. "I've just fired the band.'"

"You can't be serious," Clive replied, dumbstruck.

"But I am. So get ready."

"You can imagine how I felt," Clive said. "I just thought, 'This can't happen.' But [Nigel, Dee and Davey] showed up for the gig. 'Don't worry, it's blown over,' Elton said. And I'll tell you, it was the *best* gig of the tour. They played a blinder."

Elton's sartorial wattage for this tour proved as outrageous as his impulsive temperament. His amped-up stage clothes

266

came courtesy of British designer Annie Reavey, who provided costumes which included a red-striped black velvet suit, a quilted lemon ensemble, and a satin two-piece featuring an intricate design of tall grass around the legs, bricks around the torso, and a bird-filled sky about the shoulders.

"I call a lot of the clothes I make for Elton 'tasteful glitter'," she said with a laugh. Indeed, her outfits perfectly captured the colorful intricacies of the pianist's personality—as he himself wanted. "I don't go up to a designer and say, 'Make me this and make me that'," Elton said. "I go up to a designer and say, 'You know who I am, you know what I am, and I'm slightly in *this* mood at the moment—make me something.' Because I feel that creative people should be allowed to do what they want to do without being told."

A free artistic hand also extended to those who designed the wide variety of specs which seemed to balance so precariously upon Elton's pug nose: heart-shaped frames, red-white-and-blue-striped frames, and hexagonal lenses of purple, blue and green. While the pianist's outrageous persona had grown in tandem with his spiraling popularity, it was intended as an ironic statement and the very opposite of tacky showbiz glamour. "I'm sending show business up," he insisted. "I mean, Rod Stewart is exactly the same—he's very flamboyant and wears pink satin suits and that's showbiz, and yet it's not. I just like to get up and have a lark. I do it tongue-in-cheek, with an 'up yours' sort of attitude. It's like an actor getting into his costume for his part. I don't really feel the part until I'm into what I'm going to wear. It's a reaction against everything I wasn't allowed to do as a kid. I wasn't allowed to wear Winklepicker shoes in case they hurt my feet. I wasn't even allowed to wear Hush Puppies. Can you imagine that? Not having had a real teenage life,

I'm living all those thirteen-to-nineteen years now. Mentally I may be twenty-five, but half of me is still thirteen."

While in Houston for a show at the Hofheinz Pavilion on April 28, the day after the Apollo 16 splashdown, Elton and his band were invited to NASA's Manned Spacecraft Center to witness the splashdown of the three-man Apollo 16 mission—America's penultimate moon-landing expedition. Afterward they lunched with Apollo 15 Command Module Pilot Al Worden, Apollo 15's Command Module pilot, before taking turns in a space flight simulator.

That night, Elton's opening band, Family, suffered an earth-bound crisis when their gear failed to show up in time for their performance. Linda Lewis, who had flown over to visit her boyfriend, Family's guitarist Jim Cregan, became the immediate center of interest backstage. (Cregan himself would soon grab his own fair share of the limelite, playing guitar for Rod Stewart in 1976 and co-writing such hits as "Passion" and "Tonight I'm Yours [Don't Hurt Me]." In the '90s, he would help form the roots-rock group Farm Dogs along with Bernie Taupin, whom he'd first met during Elton's '72 tour. "We would stay and watch [Elton's band] on most nights," Cregan said, "and they were seriously good. Bernie and I would meet backstage at various times for a quick Jack Daniels in the dressing room. He was on most of the tour just hanging out and getting into trouble.")

"I wasn't expecting to be performing or anything, especially in front of such a huge amount of people that Elton had," Linda Lewis recalled years later. "I'd only ever played in tiny clubs before, and I only knew sort of three chords as well. But Family were all panicking about their equipment not showing up, and then Jim had the bright idea, 'Why don't you go on and play the guitar and entertain them?' And I was like, 'No! You must be joking! I can't do that! No no no!' And he actually got on his knees and begged me, '*Please* go on!' And Elton said, 'You can do it, Linda. C'mon.'"

Linda finally acquiesced. It was much to Cregan's relief, especially as the tour had already proven unkind to his band's ego—they would open each night's show to universally indifferent reaction. "The only clapping in this huge stadium would be the guys doing the PA," keyboardist John "Poli" Palmer said.

Cregan kissed his visibly nervous girlfriend, and gently pushed her toward the stage.

"I went on in a kind of dream state," Linda said. "I mean, I wasn't under the influence of anything, but it was basically an out-of-body experience because I was so petrified." She chuckled at the memory. "I went on, and the next thing I knew I was coming off to rapturous applause. People were going, 'Oh my God, you're *amazing!*' And I said, 'Really? I wish I'd been there.'"

While playing the L.A. Forum, Elton attacked his keyboard with such ferocity that he split open his right index finger. His hand bled so profusely, he was forced to head backstage to have it bandaged. Minutes later, the unstoppable entertainer was back onstage.

"Even if I had only one finger left, I'd play for you," he told the crowd, who screamed out its approval with full-throated elation.

After playing a final U.S. gig at Northern Illinois University on May 13, Elton returned to Great Britain to oversee the launch of his latest album, *Honky Château*, which was set to be released on May 19—less than a month before the Watergate break-in.

Honky Chateau   reaction

The packaging for the album, which derived its title from Elton's nickname for the studio where the recording had been midwifed, was as stripped down as the music. The front cover featured a two-year-old canvas-rendered photograph of a bearded Elton as he sat backstage before his first Troubadour gig in 1970, while the back cover displayed recent portraits of Elton, Nigel, Dee and Davey, along with Bernie and Jean-Luc Ponty. The inside gatefold, meanwhile, displayed typewritten lyrics transposed over a pixilated photograph of a jacketed Bernie standing in a field outside the Château.

Elton was pleased with the record, which he'd dedicated to the Château's comely manager, Catherine Phillipe-Gérard. "I don't want to say it's the best thing I've ever done," he asserted, "because that's what I said and felt about *Madman,* but people didn't agree. It's just that with this album no one can turn around and say, 'Oh, it's Elton John with his bloody 100-piece orchestra again.'"

Indeed, the LP—transcendent in its frenzied simplicity—was a breakthrough which pointed promisingly toward the future. "John is here transmuted from dangerous poseur to likable pro," Robert Christgau wrote in *Newsweek.* "Paul Buckmaster and his sobbing strings are gone. Bernie Taupin has settled into some comprehensible (even sharp and surprising) lyrics, and John's piano, tinged with the music hall, is a rocker's delight. Also, he does have a knack for the hook. If, like me, you love 'Rocket Man' despite all your initial misgivings, try 'I Think I'm Going to Kill Myself,' [sic] about the state of teenage blues, or 'Slave'," about slavery. A-."

Creem magazine's Charles Shaar Murray opened his review by noting that "these days you have to get fashionable before you get successful or else you get resented, and, if you get too successful without first being fashionable enough to please all the little cultists, they throw the whole shitbowl at you." He went on to note that "Elton John is still growing, still playing, still creative and he's still better than James Taylor and Leon Russell put together....*Honky Château* is going to be a hit album. Make no mistake." *Rolling Stone*'s Jon Landau called the LP a "rich, warm, satisfying album that stands head and shoulders above the morass of current releases, and has now succeeded in toppling the Stones from the top spot on the charts in only three weeks. Musically more varied, emotionally less contrived, lyrically more lucid than *Tumbleweed Connection, Château* rivals *Elton John* as his best work to date, and evidences growth at every possible level." Writing for the Orlando (Florida) *Sentinentel,* critic Bill Frangus simply stated: "Listen to his piano on 'Honky Cat' and 'I Think I'm Gonna Killy Myself'. It will destroy you."

The album proved as commercially popular as it was critically adored, hitting Number 2 in the U.K. while catapulting to the vaunted Number 1 spot in America, where it remained for five weeks running. It also proved a Top 5 smash in Australia, Canada, Italy and Spain, and began a year-long residency on the *Billboard* albums chart.

Delighted with *Honky Château*'s success, Elton presented Bryan Forbes and his family with the white 1910 A-day upright he'd used to compose many of his early songs on. The piano was inscribed: *To Bryan and Nanette, Sarah and Emma with love, Elton John, May 31, 1972, original piano, lots of success with it.*

Bernie also signed the instrument: *Within this piano lays the ghosts of a hundred songs. Take care of them, they love you. God Bless from the one who writes the words, Bernie Taupin.*

Chapter 12:
⤳ Don't Shoot Me I'm Only the Piano Player

Elton headed back to the Château days later to begin work on his next album. This time, however, the unbounded excitement which usually infused the start of a new project was notably missing, thanks to a case of glandular fever. "I was very slow," the pianist said. "I said to Gus, 'I can't make this album,' so he said, 'All right, we'll do it in September.' Then I said, 'Wait, I'm going on holiday in July, it would be nice to have it over by then.'"

Mononucleosis or not, Elton was soon back to his usual practices, writing a dozen songs in two days—seven on the first, five the next. He credited his prolificacy, at least in part, to the artistic brotherhood of the era. "There was just an explosion of ideas going on," he said. "It was just the most exciting era. You could buy at least ten to fifteen great albums a week and be inspired. We were listening to bass sounds, drum sounds, piano sounds. Things that were happening technically on records. And [we were] just filled with wonder."

That sense of awe spilled over into the production realm, with the ever-perfectionistic Gus Dudgeon—now well-familiar with the Château's quirky sound system—spending more time than ever creating a pristine monitor mix for each new track. "Everybody that's working on the projects—engineers, musicians, even someone you've just brought in for an hour to do some backing vocals—it's great if they can hear a great full mix in the cans [headphones] or the monitors," Gus told *Sound on Sound*'s Sam Inglis, "and have some idea what it is that they need to project over, where they need to pitch it, how quiet or loud they need to sing or play. All the time I'm recording, everyone who's working on it knows everything that's going on and can hear everything that's being played throughout the song, and won't be saying 'Can you turn that up at that point? It's disappeared in the cans.' So, in fact, at the end of the day, the mixes aren't a massive surprise."

As with *Honky Château,* Elton and Bernie's new songs were completed quickly: rehearsed and arranged in the afternoon, and recorded in the evening. "I think that's why those songs worked so well," Davey said. "You weren't hearing things that were sitting around for years and were labored over and had no energy. What you heard was all energy."

While the community feel fostered by Strawberry Studios' paradisiacal atmosphere aided in the group's creative endeavors, its close quarters also proved the cause of an occasional flare-up. "I do remember a few arguments with Elton and Sheila, Gus' wife," Stuart Epps later recalled. "She could really wind Elton up. She would come out with, 'Don't be so fucking *stupid,*' in her broad Brazilian accent, which would have Elton raging and leaving the table. Gus was always trying to diffuse their arguments. Not very successfully."

The first song attempted at these latest sessions was a reflective C-major calypso ballad entitled "Daniel." Though some would later surmise that the track was a subtle gay love song, it was in actuality about a wounded veteran. "I was reading *Newsweek* in bed, late at night," Bernie said, "and there was a piece about the vets coming home from Vietnam.

273

"Daniel"

The story was about a guy that went back to a small town in Texas. He'd been crippled in the Tet Offensive. They'd lauded him when he came home and treated him like a hero. They just wouldn't leave him alone, they insisted that he be a hero, but he just wanted to go home, go back to the farm, and try to get back to the life that he'd led before. I just embellished that and—like everything I write—it probably ended up being very esoteric. It is a song that is important to me because it was the one thing I said about Vietnam. But when I give things to Elton, it's very important that I don't lay a big message or my innermost feelings on him, because I'm putting words in his mouth. In some ways, I had to hide it a little. Maybe in 'Daniel' I hid it too much."

Highlighted by Elton's distinctively plaintive flute-mellotron solo and Nigel's sprightly maracas, "Daniel" was recorded in just two takes. To add pathos to the lead vocals, Gus woke Elton early the next morning, so that his voice would be scratchy and sleep-worn. "It was perfect," Davey said. "It sounded great because that was the right time to record that vocal. You don't just sit there with a computer and say, 'This note's a bit sharp, this note's a bit flat.' You go for performance. *Performance*."

The track, from its inception to its completed recording, immediately became one of Elton and Bernie's personal favorites. "When you write something like 'Daniel'," the pianist said, "you instinctively know it's going to be a winner. It's one of the best lyrics Taupin's ever written."

But why did Daniel want to go to Spain?

Bernie laughed. "Because basically it rhymes with 'plane'."

The spirited French brass quartet from *Honky Château* returned to Strawberry Studios to record on three tracks steeped in piquant nostalgia for the late '50's rock 'n' roll scene: "Midnight Creeper," "I'm Gonna Be a Teenage Idol," and "Elderberry Wine."

To fill out the sound on these tracks, veteran engineer Ken Scott—who had worked closely with the Beatles for years, and who would later go on to further acclaim with Supertramp, Devo and Level 42—began double-tracking Elton's piano with the tape speed set slightly faster than normal.

"Tricks of the trade," Dee said with a laugh. "Ken was a genius. We all were for a while there."

When not busy forging new musical works, Elton, Nigel, Dee and Davey relieved tensions by holding foosball tournaments while the Mahavishnu Orchestra's *The Inner Mounting Flame* blared in the background.

The matches usually ended with Elton holding his muscular arms up in victory. His hypercompetitive nature had much to do with his unrivaled winning streak, though it didn't hurt that the rest of the band were usually as high as kites on red wine and weed.

"Our medication," Davey said. "God bless it."

"Crocodile Rock" proved an early highlight of the sessions. An exuberant shit-kicker, the song's paradoxically somber theme—which explored how time can often take a heavy toll on one's innocence—was easily missed amongst all the joyful 'la-la-la's. "This type of song is actually a very hard thing to write, because the temptation is to try too hard and go berserk," Elton said of the early-'60s pastiche. "I wanted it to be a tribute to all those people I used to go and see as a kid. That's why I used Del Shannon-type vocals and that bit from Pat Boone's 'Speedy Gonzales'. We also tried to get the worst organ sound possible. Something like Johnny & the Hurricanes used to manage to produce."

Nailing the bass part proved a bit more troublesome. "Dee kept trying all these fancy parts and everything," Gus said. "And every time I'd say, 'Why don't you play it like John Fred and His Playboy Band's 'Judy in Disguise'?' You know, just that basic root stuff that works in rock 'n' roll. And he'd pull a cheesed-off face, but he knew what I meant."

For the Van Morrison-ish "High Flying Bird"—a tale about a woman who flees from her lover's controlling affections— Davey achieved an ambrosial flutter in his acoustic Ovation by running it through a rotating speaker. "I really like the Leslie [speaker] sound and want to work it out a little more," the guitarist told *Guitar Player* magazine. "It gives such a full sound."

Elton utilized the same methodology for his piano sound on "I'm Gonna Be a Teenage Idol," for which his jubilant, pop-oriented melody proved the perfect counterbalance to Bernie's darker meditations. Dedicated to T. Rex's Marc Bolan, the song was laid in a single take.

"We wrote that song about [Marc] because that's what he wanted to be," Elton said. "We played it to him and I think he liked it. He didn't hit me, anyway."

As the sessions progressed, Quebec singer Diane Dufresne scored a minor success with the single "En Écoutant Elton John" ("Listening to Elton John"). Taken from her album *Tiens-Toé Ben J'Arrive!*, the track had Dufresne enthusing about the joys of making love while Elton serenaded her and her lover from the stereo.

"Not my type," Elton joked. "Sorry, Diane."

Bernie revisited one of his signature themes—a loner's desperate flight to freedom—on "Have Mercy on the

Criminal." A quasi-sequel to *Madman's* "Rotten Peaches," "Have Mercy on the Criminal" found Bernie's unnamed felon desperately on the run.

To help capture the desperation inherent in the track, Davey ran his acoustic six-string through a Uni-Vibe pedal, providing uniquely opaque harmonics. "'Have Mercy on the Criminal' was so exciting," the guitarist said, "because it's a very dramatic song and we wanted to keep it as wild as possible—we recorded the guitar solo live, which is unusual, but fun." Dee's bass playing, meanwhile, was as melodically nuanced and innovative as ever. He credited Davey's impassioned guitar work with freeing him up to play evermore intricate lines. Elton agreed. "I don't think Dee even realized he could play like that till [Davey] came onboard."

Paul Buckmaster, who'd recently scored massive successes arranging Harry Nilsson's "Without You" and Carly Simon's "You're So Vain," was brought in for a "sweetening session," overdubbing a string chart onto the pre-existing band recording. The exercise proved frustrating. "It's rather sad for me to be called in to do string overdubs," he said. "I'm not a string overdubber—I'm an *arranger,* for God's sake." Nonetheless, his weeping violas and violins added an element of epic grandeur to the pounding, wailing track.

"We thought it might be nice to have light strings, like on some of B.B. King's things," Elton said. "But it turned out heavier than that."

The band next tore into the gleefully perverse "Midnight Creeper," a James Brown-esque soul-stomper that came ripping out of the stalls as a unified whole—nearly. "In all the time I've worked with him," Gus said, "[Elton] only asked me to take *one* instrument off *one* song, which was a banjo that used to be on 'Midnight Creeper,' a sort of McGuiness/Flint-type banjo. For some reason, he didn't like it. But that's it."

"Blues for Baby and Me," a tale of escape and absolution, followed. To give the track a distinctive flavor, Davey again ran his Ovation through a Lesley cabinet, though this time he combined it with a Uni-Vibe pedal and a wah-wah pedal. Most notably, he then added a separate sitar line. "I ordered the sitar through an Indian magazine," the guitarist said. "It took six months to get to me from Bombay. I picked it up at the London docks. It was like Dracula. It was in a coffin. A sitar is pretty big....I'm not proficient in it. I [only] play it and use it for color."

Elton appreciated the extra effort Davey put into turning what could have otherwise been a faceless tune into a memorably sweeping musical statement. "This is a stock Elton John number," the pianist admitted. "It could have been on any of my albums."

"Teacher I Need You" proved a different case. A carelessly brilliant schoolboy fantasy, the retro rocker was equal measures Bobby Vee and the Moody Blues, with Dee's insistent yet restrained bass line adding an intriguing underpinning to Elton's sprightly piano triplets.

"You have to pick your spots and serve the song," the bassist said. "That was always my primary aim, especially in the studio."

On the alt-country ode "Texan Love Song," a Randy Newman-esque answer to Merle Haggard's "Okie From Muskogee," Elton stepped into the role of an angry southern redneck. Labeling the song "Fairport [Convention]-like," the Brit abstained from playing piano on the track, opting instead for the harmonium, which blended well with the understated arrangement of acoustic guitar, bass, mandolin and drums. To add an element of down-home atmospheric verisimilitude, Gus placed a microphone next to Davey's tapping foot, much like he had with Elton on *Tumbleweed Connection*'s "Love Song."

"[It's] a misunderstood song," Gus said years later. "But a really good one, at the same time. Davey was brilliant."

Toward the end of the sessions, Elton and his entourage huddled together in the dining hall for a late night get-together. After many bottles of wine had been demolished, the lively discussion turned to Davey's inability to secure a label to release his recently recorded solo album, *Smiling Face*; a surprising situation, given that Elton, Dee and Nigel had all played on it, and that Gus had helmed the project.

Labeling the album "like finding a box of buried treasure," Elton was determined that it see the light of day. "We were sitting around the table saying, 'What are we going to do?' And I think it was me, actually, who said, 'Start our own fucking label,' because we'd all been drinking wine—the Château produces its own wine—[and] we all said 'Yeah!' and went to bed. Next morning we all got up and said, 'Was everybody serious?' We decided that we were."

Though nothing would happen for months, the seeds for a new record label had been sewn.

Two days before Elton was scheduled to depart from the Château, Sheila Dudgeon urged him to revisit "Skyline Pigeon," a song she'd always been particularly fond of. Feeling much the same, Elton admitted that "the version on the *Empty Sky* album *is* a bit weedy."

A superlative full-band take of the lovingly crafted hymn was quickly laid down, the new version uncovering hidden depths of emotional anguish which the original had only hinted at. Besides benefiting from Elton's vocal maturation since '69, the recording was also aided by Nigel's descriptive drumming. "I always knew where to put the fills in and where to leave them out," Nigel later told *Music Radar*'s Joe Bosso. "I'd think to myself, 'All right, going into the chorus, I need to do something interesting, so I'll do *this*....You're part of the storytelling process in that way. You can't go over the top on a ballad."

Though "Skyline Pigeon" would never be issued as an A-side, the stately track would soon attain colossal success in territories as far afield as the Philippines and Brazil, where it was adopted as an unofficial national anthem after appearing on the soundtrack of the massively popular Brazilian soap opera *Carinhoso*.

Elton completed his efforts on these latest sessions with a pair of never-issued tracks: a cover of pianist Tommy Tucker's 1963 blues classic "Hi-Heel Sneakers," and a dynamic Brit-pop nugget called "Tell Me What the Doctor Said."

With his work over, Elton headed off to Paris to indulge in a bit of profligate looting at some of the finer shops up and down the Champs Elysées, while Gus and the band stayed behind to work out their backing vocals. "Elton was always a pleasure to work with," the producer said. "He always left us alone to do whatever we wanted. Once he'd done his bit, he never came [back]—which was a blessing."

Davey, Nigel and Dee were determined to take what they'd accomplished vocally on *Honky Château* and expand on it exponentially. "We were allowed to do whatever [we wanted]," Nigel said. "If anybody had an idea, we'd try it. It wouldn't be, 'Oh no, that's crap, we're not going to do that'....And mostly we didn't have to change anything."

The three singers made "a wonderful noise," Gus noted. "Individually, none of them were great. It was a total accident, but those three voices together, with their ideas and imagination and their desire to impress Elton [blended well]....Elton's chord changes had that sort of slightly classical edge, so there were always nice inversions to sing."

In most cases, the trio would create sumptuously audacious vocals across six tracks, bouncing them down as they went to leave the final four tracks free for orchestra, percussion and synthesizer overdubs.

On June 3, Elton joined the Beach Boys onstage at the Crystal Palace on a cold and rainy afternoon to help supply electric piano on "Help Me, Rhonda." Elton was more than happy to assist, as he viewed Brian Wilson as a peerless pop maestro; it hardly mattered that the pianist himself saw pop music as a highly disposable medium. "Quite honestly," he said, "I regard all pop music as irrelevant in the sense that people two-hundred years from now won't be listening to what is being written and played today. But I think they *will* be listening to Beethoven. Pop music is just fun. That's one of the reasons I don't take myself seriously. I love pop music. It's my whole life. But I love it because it's fun."

Bernie was on much the same wavelength. "Disposable songs are for the time they're in the charts and three months later they're completely forgotten and nobody bothers with them again," he said. "I think that's healthy, in a way. You should always have fresh material coming along."

Elton winged his to L.A. two days after the Crystal Palace gig for a long-overdue holiday, his first extended break since he'd broken through at the Troubadour seemingly two-million years earlier. The lack of a proper vacation showed—by the time he arrived at LAX, he was looking very much the worse for wear. "As soon as I got off the plane, people said to me, 'Hey, you're having a nervous breakdown.' I was on the verge of a crackup. Personality-wise, I was unbearable—moody and shouting at people. I'd had bouts of exhaustion before, but had never been in a nervous state like this."

The pianist unwound in a rented beach house he dubbed "Malibu de Bum Bum," along with Bernie and Maxine, John Reid, and Nanette Newman and Bryan Forbes. "MCA offered Elton a Cadillac for his holiday," Forbes said, "but Elton told them he'd rather go to Tower Records and just help ourselves to some records. MCA agreed, of course, so we all drove down to Sunset Boulevard and looted the place for maybe $70,000 worth of records and tapes. Really over the top. Wonderful."

Forbes repaid Elton by making his wide circle of Hollywood friends available to him. The pianist was enthralled by the proximity of the celluloid stars, though perhaps the pinnacle of his excitement came the night he and Bernie met aging sex-symbol Mae West in her Hollywood apartment. Now in her late seventies, West was as bawdy as ever.

"We were all taken into this room that was totally white," Bernie said. "We sat down on this big white couch, on this white shag-pile carpet. At the end of the room there was a sort of butler figure standing in front of a curtain. 'Gentlemen,' the butler said, 'Miss Mae West.' The curtain was drawn back and there she was. She looked at Elton and me on the couch and said, 'Well! Wall-to-wall men!'"

"I was trying to look for facelifts," Elton joked. "But she looks fantastic….She just looked exactly as she does. She's very interesting. She's very coherent. And she's very much into ESP. I'm into ESP. And she tells you all about her experiences. And she likes health food and carrot juice, and things like that. With people like that who are legends, [whom] you never think in your whole life you stand a chance of meeting…you just sit there and let them carry on, because you can't say anything because they're so interesting, and the stories they have to tell are fantastic."

Elton threw a party the next night. Guests included David and Angela Bowie.

"They had a huge barbecue on the beach," Angela said, "and five or six chefs preparing all this food. It was really quite beautiful, and a marvelous use of the spectacular beauty of Malibu. Just absolutely exquisite. Reg was in top form. He was with John Reid, and they seemed to be fairly happy at the time."

Another party guest was seenty-eight year old Mae West herself. "She sat there all evening at the end of the room," Bernie said, "not moving or saying anything. It was just like having a stuffed dummy of Mae West at your party."

Returning from a second record-buying outing at Tower Records the next afternoon, Elton found Bryan Forbes lighting their beach house's fireplace, despite the fact that it was over ninety degrees out.

"Someone's coming to dinner," the director told Elton. "But they insist that the fire is on."

Ten minutes later, a frail knock sounded at the front door. Elton answered it to find comedy legend Groucho Marx standing before him in an overcoat, looking every one of his eighty-one years.

"When's dinner? When the hell are we gonna eat?" Groucho whimpered, stepping infirmly into the house. "It's too damned *cold* in here."

Elton was speechless. He looked at Forbes, who merely shrugged.

With theatrical aplomb, Groucho whipped off his overcoat and laughed heartily. The whole thing had been a ruse.

"They tell me you're number one," Groucho told Elton, "but I'd never heard of you until I went into my office this morning and said I was having dinner with Elton John. They all fainted. After that, I lost what remaining respect I had for you."

Elton, Groucho and their entire group attended a performance of the rock opera *Jesus Christ Superstar* that night. As the house lights dimmed and the production began, Groucho—who had managed to commandeer a pair of teenage nymphets onto his lap—called out: "Does this have a happy ending?"

The evening concluded with Groucho presenting Elton with an autographed Marx Brothers poster, which he signed: "To John Elton, from Marx Groucho." "Because your name's backwards," Groucho explained, pointing his index finger at him like a gun. "Why the hell is that?"

The pianist held up his hands in mock-defense.

"Don't shoot me," he said, referencing French New Wave director Francois Truffaut's classic 1960 crime drama, *Shoot the Piano Player*—and perhaps recalling the sign he'd seen hanging over Leon Russell's twin pianos two years earlier. "I'm only the piano player."

Chapter 13:
'I'm Inclined to Be Extremely Moody'

Elton was awarded an RIAA gold disc for *Honky Château* on July 24, 1972. Weeks later, John Reid quit DJM and started his own incorporated company, John Reid Enterprises. Headquartered in Soho, and launched with a £5,000 loan from Barclays Bank, Reid leveraged his management contract with Elton as collateral. "I don't think I actually slept for a year," Reid said. "I must have read all of Elton's contracts about fifty times [each] to get used to them, having not read a contract before."

Reid enlisted Paul McCartney's brother-in-law, esteemed attorney John Eastman, to review the pianist's contracts. Eastman's conclusion matched that of Reid himself: Elton and Bernie's publishing deal with DJM, in which the two songwriters received only 30% of the royalties generated by their work, was indeed actionable. Though Reid decided not to pursue litigation for the time being, he filed the knowledge away for future reference.

Elton was pleased. Reid was proving to be the most loyal of watchdogs, and he had complete faith in his manager's ability to deal not only with any and all legal landmines, but also with his own mercurial nature. "It's just that [John Reid] can handle me very well," he said. "He can sort my moods out. I'm inclined to be extremely moody, and he can handle it."

With his management situation securely set, and after having taken in a Roxy Music/David Bowie concert at the Rainbow Theatre that August, Elton launched a brief eight-date U.K. tour, a low-impact preamble to the more ambitious undertaking planned for the States that fall. As was becoming increasingly the case, the majority of notices Elton received were overwhelmingly positive. "It is not all fun with Elton John," reported *The Times* in a typically glowing review. "His songs have a way of purveying the sadness of life as well. Therein lies his strength."

The day before the tour's final date at Oxford's New Theater on September 9, "Honky Cat" was released as a maxi-single. Backed with "It's Me That You Need" and "Lady Samantha," the single stalled at Number 31 in Britain; in the United States, however, it fared considerably better, peaking at respectable Number 8.

Understanding the importance of singles, Elton was ecstatic. "I'm sure singles *do* help an album," he said. "And I'm also sure you can afford to have two hit singles off an album. Singles now are getting much better. A lot more people are putting out maxi-singles, which is a good state to be in. But I won't necessarily be tied to releasing singles off albums. If I suddenly come out with a monster song, I'd probably go in the studios and work it out."

Elton's most ambitious American tour to date—a 40-city blitzkrieg—kicked off on September 26 at Barton Hall in Ithaca, New York. Foregoing the usual 4,000-seat university halls, Elton's latest foray concentrated on significantly larger 20,000-seat basketball arenas. Even with the outsized venues, the sprawling offensive easily sold out in a matter of days. "We could have done it a year and a half ago," the Brit said, "but we wanted to build up slowly. Anyway, I don't think we could have played the big halls as a trio."

Elton often made his appearance onstage in a luminous red, white and blue lamé suit, complete with matching top hat and stacked silver boots—an iridescent red "E" glittering on the right boot, a matching "J" on the left. His set list was equally as flashy, featuring an impactful assortment of musical treasures, from the pounding raw soul of "Can I Put You On" to the epic sweep of "Have Mercy on the Criminal."

Nigel drove the tightly wound band particularly hard this time around, crashing his way through one bluesy rocker after another on a fifteen-piece, double-bass Slingerland kit—*de rigueur* for any self-respecting sticksman in '72. "The reason for the massive size of the drums was because I loved the low tones I could get," he said. "The deeper and the bigger the drums, the richer and more powerful the sound. As for the double-bass setup, it was mainly for the look. A bit of flash, you know? One wanted to look impressive on stage, and a giant kit certainly helped. If you couldn't see me, you were certainly going to see my drums."

Elton poured his ceaseless energy into every performance, leaping off the piano in eight-inch heels ("It was a miracle I didn't break my fucking ankles!") and skittering manically across the lip of the stage as he clapped, mugged and shook his Technicolor thatch in time to the music. Though some critics claimed his appearance to be garish, the pianist remained untroubled, realizing that—ultimately—everything in life was comparative. "I could get out of a car...and some woman would say, 'Look at that freak, he's got green hair'," he said. "And she'd have bright blue hair and a bikini on, and be about eighty-six years old. And she'd think *I* was the freak."

With that understanding, Elton's stage clothes gained a measure of added extravagance this time around. Silken suits of gold and blue, leather suits of red and brown—nothing

was too wild for the extroverted introvert. His steadfast
writing partner, meanwhile, could still be found watching
from the wings, though his Courvoisier had been replaced by
his latest tipple of choice, Coors beer, which was now
written into his contractual rider. "I was always regarded as
part of the band, only I just didn't perform," Bernie said. "I
was just a hanger-on, man. I was sort of a groupie, I guess. It
was such a whirlwind, I don't remember ever having the
time to breathe."

Time was perhaps even more restricted for the team of
roadies who traveled with the tour. In each city, they'd
invade an empty arena at high noon, forklifting hundreds of
tons of amps, monitors, lights, drums, and the star
attraction's nine-foot Steinway onto stage. Working without
a break, they had to make sure that everything was in place
and operating properly well before Elton arrived to run
through a soundcheck several hours before the show was due
to start.

Setting monitor levels from a soundboard sat twenty-five
rows back, perched on a worn piano bench and threadbare
Oriental rug, Clive Franks would work out a proper mix as
Elton's band played to an empty hall. Once achieved, the
sound engineer would give a double thumbs-up, and the
musicians would disappear offstage.

"Soundchecks were tremendously important," Clive said.
"If you didn't get them just right, it could throw the entire
[concert] out of balance."

Elton's latest show pushed the boundaries of
audaciousness—particularly when "Legs" Larry Smith
tapped his way out of the wings during "I Think I'm Gonna
Kill Myself" dressed as a Prussian guard, replete with a
tunic-waisted jacket, a bridal train held aloft by a pair of
little people dressed as marines, and a shiny silver crash

helmet upon which bride-and-groom figurines had been glued. Matching figures were also affixed to each shoulder. (When the tour hit the Deep South, Smith stuck a black couple atop his helmet.)

With Smith's appearance, Elton would don a long trench coat before joining the tap dancer in an unhinged version of "Singin' in the Rain," the two cavorting in unison to a pre-taped instrumental version of the song—which the band had recorded live on stage in Boston at the start of the tour—while tuxedoed tour manager Marv Tabolsky sat at Elton's piano miming to the background track.

"Have you got a light, Mac?" Elton would ask Smith in his best Bogey voice.

"No, sirree!" the tap dancer would answer gleefully.

"Gee, Larry, I sure wish I could dance the way *you* do! Because then I'd be a star!"

"Gee, Elton, I wish I could play the piano the way *you* do! Because then I'd get all the boys!"

At that point, Maxine Taupin would shower the two in silver confetti.

Elton and Smith ended their act each night by whipping out magic wands from their coat pockets and firing lighted tissue paper at the audience; it was one of Stuart Epps duties to load the wands full of gunpowder before the shows. "'Legs' Larry Smith was just this mad bloke," he said. "He had all these mad tricks and weird magician's stuff in a trunk, and part of it was these magic wands, which used to explode a ball of fire. So part of my job was to load them up and make sure everything was all right. Sometimes I used to put a little bit more gunpowder than the night before, thinking, 'Well, this will be fun,' and then I'd put the magic wand in Elton's pocket. He used to put his hand in his pocket just to make sure it was there. And on one night, he set the bloody thing off. While he's standing on the side of the stage, his whole pocket turned completely fire-red and it all went up. The next minute I'm whacking him and he's going, '*What* are you doing?' And I'm saying, 'I'm putting you *out!* You're on *fire!*'"

Despite—or perhaps because of—all the explosive ammo, the "Singin' in the Rain" routine stole the show each and every night. No one was more pleased by this than Smith himself. "They were screaming for *me*, dear child," he told *Circus'* Cathi Stein in happy disbelief backstage at the San Diego Sports Arena. "Screaming for little old Bonzo Larry. It's unbelievable."

In late October, Elton was booked for multiple shows at the 18,500-seat L.A. Forum. The afternoon before his first gig, Elton invited David Bowie—deep into his Ziggy Stardust phase—over to his hotel suite.

"His entire living room was barricaded with huge stacks of record albums," Bowie later recalled in his memoir, *Moonage Daydream.* "He sat, small and bewildered-looking, in the middle, as if in some kind of bunker...I couldn't see how anyone could keep up with the amount of vinyl with which he was ensconced."

The two icons shared tea cakes and made small talk about America.

"After a polite half-hour," Bowie said, "I made my apologies, declining a further cuppa, and went for a wander down Sunset."

That night, after Elton closed the first of two Forum shows with a blistering twenty-minute, wah-wah-guitar-soaked, glam-rock/neo-soul mash-up of "Whole Lotta Shakin' Going On" and "Hercules," everyone in attendance were on their feet, emotionally spent.

"Elton got over a half-dozen standing ovations because of musicianship, not freakiness," Nat Freedland wrote in a

Billboard review of the show. "Elton is now able to consistently play it for kooky laughs, while making music that is spectacularly better than ever."

"Just before midnight," another reviewer noted, "Elton and the band finally fell off stage. Soaked with sweat and elated beyond any pitch they had known before, the only reaction they could give was to fall into each other's arms and weep."

"Crocodile Rock" was released as a single in the U.S. three days later. The self-referential homage became another Gold record for Elton, as well as his first American Number 1 single, easily knocking Stevie Wonder's "Superstition" out of the top spot. The track did well in the U.K. too, becoming Elton's second Top 5 showing in his homeland. It also hit Number 1 in Canada, Number 2 in Australia, and Number 3 in Germany, firmly cementing the pianist's status as a global superstar.

"The song...probably changed the critics' opinion of me," he was to later reflect. "My career wasn't about 'Crocodile Rock', it was just a one-off thing, but it became a huge hit record, and in the long run it became a negative for me, because people said, 'Oh, fucking "Crocodile Rock"'....*Rolling Stone* reviewed it and gave it two stars, and I said, 'Oh, fuck off.' It was a great fucking pop record. Shut the fuck up!"

Elton interrupted his U.S. tour—reshuffling several gigs and cancelling his Phoenix appearance entirely—to fly back to England for a Royal Command Variety Performance at the London Palladium before the Queen and her husband, the Duke of Edinburgh, on Monday, October 30.

"We were summoned," Elton said, "I think that's the word: 'summoned'—'If you don't play, we'll break your legs'—to do the Royal Variety Show, which is the kiss of death for anybody."

In actuality, the pianist was honored to be the first rock star since the Beatles back in 1963 to be asked to perform at the event. Others on the bill included '60's pop crooner Jack Jones, the Jackson Five, and *Hello, Dolly!* star Carol Channing.

A sleep-deprived Elton shared a dressing room with singer Jack Jones. The two were deep into a mordantly sly conversation about actress Susan George when Elton's childhood idol, Liberace, suddenly entered. Liberace ushered in several trunks full of clothes, all of them containing but a single costume: a mammoth suit covered in electric light bulbs. "I knew I was outclassed," Elton said. "How could he play the piano with all those rings on? Maybe that's why he missed some of the notes—he had fun. He said 'Fuck you' to everyone....He was the most professional person on that show."

Seated at a white grand and wearing hexaganol white frames, a lustrous red, white and blue tailcoat and matching top hat, Elton smiled in mock embarrassment at the tony crowd.

"Did I hear a snigger from the audience?" he asked before launching into a glam-bam rendition of "I Think I'm Gonna Kill Myself," during which "Legs" Larry Smith released a clutch of farting balloons. "The audience was full of the most dreadful people imaginable," he said, "and all these balloons were going *'pffft, pffft, pffft'* all over the audience, and they were all sitting there in their tiaras going, 'Ooh! Ooh!'"

Blushing hard, Nigel looked over at Dee as the song swung into its rousing final chorus.

"I hope this is a bloody dream," he shouted.

Dee just shrugged and laughed.

"This is about the rock 'n' roll records of the 1960s," Elton announced as the band launched into a turbo-charged rendition of "Crocodile Rock," Dee's rhythmic bass propelling the song ever onward. Though the quartet received the most enthusiastic ovation of the night, Elton left the Palladium wildly unimpressed with the entire enterprise. "What an awful show," he said. "As a musical event, it was the biggest nonevent of all time. The most horrendous two-day stretch I've ever had....Backstage pressures, lack of sound amplification, too many acts packed into four hours....It was carnage."

Elton and his group immediately winged their way back to the U.S. to continue on with their tour. When they hit Philadelphia for a concert at the Spectrum on September 30, the pianist rang up his old friend Patti LaBelle, whom he hadn't seen since his days with Bluesology.

"Hello, this is Elton John," he said. "Can we get together for dinner tonight?"

LaBelle chuckled. "Elton, I don't even *know* you."

"Sure you do. I'm Reg Dwight. Remember?"

"*Reggie!*" LaBelle shrieked. "What are *you* doing being *Elton John?*"

When they met face-to-face later that night, LaBelle was stunned by the transformation her former keyboard player had undergone in the intervening years. "I mean, this guy who used to play piano and I used to beat in cards was now Elton John," she said disbelievingly. "Now he's on this very high level and I thought he'd be high and mighty, but he wasn't. He's still a good person." She laughed. "I wish I could play [Tonk] with him now."

The tour soon hit Memphis. Before his gig at the Mid-South Coliseum, Elton took Bernie to the famed Stax studio on

McLemore Street to "pay homage to the…eight-track machine with the valve [amps], because the valve made a difference on the Al Jackson snare drum [sound]."

Elton bowed reverently before the eight-track machine and gave it the most reverent of kisses.

"We were and always will be fans first," Bernie said.

A bevy of winsome Rockettes joined Elton and "Legs" Larry Smith onstage for their "Singin' in the Rain" extravaganza eight days later as they performed the first of two Carnegie Hall appearances.

Critics appreciated the effort put into the show.

"There are rock singers and musicians who believe that art is enough," Ian Dove wrote in his *New York Times* review, "standing unadorned onstage, paying homage to their material as if it were the latest tablet down from the mountain. Not Elton John….With his partner Bernie Taupin, Mr. John has managed to write some of the best rock songs of the last five years….Therefore Mr. John has less need than most to decorate his concert appearances. But decorate he does, and he did at his Carnegie Hall concert on Monday evening…Mr. John does not really need the frills—his own stage dress was a glittery silver, green and red suit of lights—but it's nice that he takes the trouble."

With all of New York's finest shops laid bare, Elton's already notorious flair for shopping binges truly blossomed; indeed, the star was nearly as extravagant before a cash register as he was before an audience. From Déco figurines to samurai dolls to endless piles of records, there was little that Elton failed to open his bulging wallet for. (So unbridled were Elton's nonstop purchasing overindulgences, on his return back to England he found himself accompanied by sixty-seven suitcases and forty-two steam trunks full of shiny new acquisitions. "They needed a Greyhoud bus to take us to the airport," he said, joking but serious. Still, the star was philosophical about it all. "I *do* overspend, but you can't take it with you. So many people are miserable with success. I can't be that way....I *do* enjoy money, because tomorrow I might be knocked down by a Number Thirteen bus going to Waithamstow. If I'm successful, then I might as well enjoy it.")

His munificence extended to those in his inner circle as well. During their Big Apple stand, Davey spent several days lusting after a mandolin at Manny's music store. Priced at $800, the hand-crafted instrument was well out of the guitarist's price range. After endlessly debating it over for a day and a half, he finally decided to buy the instrument, only to find that someone had beaten him to it. Slinking dejectedly back to his hotel room, he found the mandolin waiting for him on his bed—a gift from Elton.

"He is so generous, it's unbelievable," Davey said.

Of his fabled largesse, Elton admitted that he'd read psychological deconstructions about it in the papers. "'He does it because he's insecure.'" He laughed. "Shit, I love giving people things, 'cause if I'm able to give someone something they couldn't possibly afford that I can afford to give them, it's great. I'm not doing it because I want to be Mr. Generous. But the whole point is: Christ, we're only around for a short time, and I intend to enjoy it, and the fuck with it, let's give some other people some enjoyment as well."

The charitable rocker's tour ended on a high note at Bay Front Center, St. Petersburg, on November 26. The band was well-received, being called back for *six* encores. By the evening's end, Elton was well past exhausted. Even so, his stage duties weren't quite done for the year. Barely back in

England a week, the pianist was asked by the Pinner County Grammar's Stag Society to perform at their winter dance on December 7. Elton was only too happy to oblige his alma matter. Pulling up to his old school in a bright green Ferrari—and dressed in a bright vermillion suit, blood-red specs, and a long fox cape—Elton was the prodigal son incarnate.

"This is a special night," he said as he took to the school's tiny stage. "Let's have fun."

Pounding the keys to the same Steinway he'd once played during school shows a decade earlier, Elton treated the prepubescent crowd to his entire two-hour-plus set.

"All the masters who taught me were there," he said afterward, "and they were very nice and they just said, 'Well, you've done very well. You've got on.' They looked just the same, and I thought, 'What will they think of my act?' because it was a bit wild. But they were really nice. And when I drove away, I thought, 'You've made it. You've arrived.' It was a nice feeling."

As the year drew to a close, Elton felt compelled to answer a growing charge being leveled against him: that his music was too determindely apolitical. "It's power that runs and changes any country," he said, "and you can't change things overnight with a hit song. The idea of rock singers getting into politics is rather stupid, because most of them can't even organize their own lives....Those people who scream and rant about unemployment and whatever in their songs—will they go out and vote at the next election? Probably not."

Bernie felt similarly. "What positive reaction can you get from the stoned ramblings of someone screaming a political message?"

Enough music fans seemed to agree with them. The apolitical *Madman Across the Water* was announced as the year's tenth best-selling album on the *Billboard* and *Record World* charts, while *Honky Château* sat comfortably at Number 3.

Elton was also named the top-selling male album artist of the year, as well as one of the premier singles artists and concert draws.

It seemed that he couldn't possibly get any bigger.

But looks, as the bespectacled star would be quick to point out, could often be deceiving.

Chapter 14:

Jamaica Jerk-Off

Elton kicked off 1973 by issuing "Daniel"—backed with the recently re-recorded "Skyline Pigeon"—in the U.K. on January 10. Usurping "Crocodile Rock's" originally proposed follow-up single, "Elderberry Wine," "Daniel" proved wildly successful, quickly reaching Number 4 in the British charts, Elton's highest charting single yet in his homeland. In the States, the single peaked at Number 2, held out of the top spot by Paul McCartney & Wings' "My Love." The song would ultimately remain in the Top 40 for twelve weeks—a sweet victory for Elton, who'd had to fight for its release.

"'Daniel' isn't an instant single," he said, "but most people I played it to before it was released went away whistling it. It's one of the best things Bernie and I have ever written, and I don't care if it's a hit or not. I just wanted to get it out….Dick James said he didn't want another single released to detract from sales of the new album, so I've more or less forced him to put it out. He has disowned it, so I am having to pay for all the advertising. But he said he will pay for the adverts if the single makes the Top 10. Isn't that nice?"

"We are releasing 'Daniel' as a single solely because of pressure from Elton," Dick James affirmed in a press release. "It is also against the wishes of MCA, who distribute Elton's records in America."

298

True to his word, James would eventually reimburse Elton for all advertising expenses. But his obstinacy came at a cost, exacerbating a hairline fracture in his relationship with the pianist which would eventually prove unfixable.

Interviewed backstage at a Dusty Springfield show at Carnegie Hall on January 20, Elton told *NME* that he had "never really done a major British tour, so I really would like to do one of about three and a half weeks, and do ballrooms and places like that. There's definitely going to be a big tour, either in February or March. We *do* neglect England, but it is just finding the places and the time to play. I find touring rather boring—not the gigs, but driving to Bolton isn't quite as glamorous as driving to Santiago. But we really have got to get our finger out to do it."

While the preliminary logistics for a British campaign were being sorted out, a dispute regarding the legal ownership of the Château forced Elton to find a new studio to record his next album at. When drummer Charlie Watts told Gus that the Rolling Stones had found Byron Lee's Dynamic Sounds Studio in Kingston conducive to hard work on their just-completed *Goat's Head Soup* disc, the producer decided to scout out the famed facility where Bob Marley and the Wailers had recorded their *Catch a Fire* LP.

Gus liked what he saw. "Jamaica," he told Elton.

"Let's do it," the pianist said. "Let's go."

Elton and company arrived in a land of shantytowns and turquoise beaches on January 23, the day after George Foreman's two-round heavyweight title beatdown of Joe Frazier at the National Stadium. The island was electrified, the squalid streets brimming with the threat of violence. Not helping matters, Elton had been booked into the Pink Flamingo in downtown Kingston, while the rest of the band luxuriated across the island in the resort area of Ocho Rios. "We had five or six sacks full of dope," Gus said. "We were all by the pool, doing our best to make our way through the bloody lot, but we failed." He laughed. "That was a first, actually. And probably a last."

Feeling totally shattered, Elton checked into his hotel at five in the afternoon and went straight to bed, doing his best to ignore the fact that the Rolling Stones' bassist Bill Wyman's girlfriend, Astrid Lundstrom, had been raped at knifepoint only weeks before in the very same room. A harried Elton was then awoken at 10:00 p.m. sharp. "This great noise started going on which sounded like the rising of the Third World," he said, "and we all leapt out of bed and found out that it was [jazz virtuoso] Les McCann playing outdoors to nobody. So we went and listened to him." He beamed appreciatively. "That was a saving grace. I just used to go and watch him every night."

McCann, however, would prove one of the few good things about the island. "I was afraid to go out of the room," Elton admitted, "because it was pretty funky in downtown Kingston." Instead, he stayed behind his locked door, experimenting with liquid ganja and composing music on a rusted Fender Rhodes electric piano. "Apart from the hassles, and there were a lot, Kingston was still very conducive to songwriting," he said. "I loved it because of that, and also because of all the music that I heard blaring out of all those record shacks on the street."

In three days, he'd composed eighteen songs.

"Elton goes mad if he's stuck sitting around the hotel," David Larkham said. "To alleviate his boredom—and also to give me an idea of the kind of music he'd been creating, so I could start thinking about cover designs and so on—he and I went off to the recording studio one morning after breakfast. I sat off in a corner while Elton played the piano and sang me all the songs he'd thus far written. I have to say, it was the best concert I've ever attended. So many songs, each one better than the last."

Unfortunately for Elton, the satisfaction his prolific creative streak generated was tempered by a heated workers' strike which raged at the record plant housed within Dynamic Sound's walls. On their first trip to the studio, Elton's entourage was greeted by angry protestors amassed outside a barbed wire fence, yelling obscenities at the Englishmen. As their V.W. bus passed by, picketers blew crushed fiberglass at them through crudely fashioned blowpipes.

"There were Zulu warriors leaping out of hedgerows, blowing darts at us," Gus said. "We all came out in rashes."

"There wasn't a positive vibe in the place," Bernie agreed.

Worse still, Dynamic Sound proved to be anything but dynamic. Because the facility was predominantly used for reggae records, achieving a percussive low-end proved virtually impossible. "It sounded fucking terrible," Gus said. "The Stones had just been there and they were checking out as we checked in. They told us a few slightly scary stories, like, 'Don't open the piano lid too fast or you'll upset the cockroaches that live in there.'"

To compound matters, there was nary a grand in sight. "There was never ever a sign of a good piano," Elton said. "They were always getting it the next day. There was only a five-foot Yamaha, which is fine banging away in the background of a Rolling Stones record, but for me a piano is very important."

Things went from bad to worse when the studio failed to provide a proper complement of microphones, the most basic of recording equipment.

"The guy who ran the studio said, 'Carlton, get the microphone,'" Davey later recalled. "And we went, 'Oh fuck,' y'know? Get the *microphone?* We used like twenty mics on the drums, even in those days. It was like, 'We're in deep shit here.'"

"We *need* these microphones," Gus told the studio manager.

"Don't harass me, *mon.* Tomorrow."

"The weather was beautiful and the atmosphere really fantastic," Elton said. "But the Jamaican philosophy is that anything can wait until tomorrow."

And tomorrow never came.

The only track attempted at Dynamic Sound was a frantic version of a newly written track entitled "Saturday Night's Alright (For Fighting)." When the group listened to the playback, they were disgusted. "It sounded like thirteen-million very small Japanese radios full crank," Gus said. "It was the worst sound I've ever heard in my life."

He turned to Elton.   "I think we have a problem," he said.

Elton nodded, his spirits low.

Resigned to the fact that the studio was utterly inadequate for their needs, the group decided to leave Jamaica the next day. That decision didn't go down well with the locals, however—equipment and rental cars were immediately impounded after a dispute over the band's hotel bill became a point of unresolvable contention.

"There was most definitely a very dodgy feeling in Kingston towards us," Gus said.

"It really was an escape, more or less," Bernie said. "I remember everybody sort of jumping into whatever vehicles they could get in. It was a bit like the sort of Cuban Revolution, trying to make it to the airport. I imagine it was like the scene from *The Godfather Part II*, where everybody is just racing for the airport. It was our mini version of that."

During the taxi ride to Kingston Airport, Elton and Bernie's driver mysteriously drove them through an empty sugarcane field.

"I just thought, 'They're gonna kill us,'" Elton said. "I've never been so glad in my life to leave a place."

As Elton was making good his escape, his latest album—entitled *Don't Shoot Me I'm Only the Piano Player*—was being released around the world to much fanfare. In America, it was his first LP issued on MCA's "black rainbow" label. No expense was spared advertising the disc, with tens of thousands of dollars sunk into a print ad campaign which billed the album as "The Latest Adventures of Elton and Bernie in France." Animated television commercials trumpeted the album's release in England.

As for the seven-month gap between recording and release, Elton explained, "We made the album last June, and it seemed like it would never come out. But I wanted a long gap, and we only had one LP out last year. I didn't want the situation where every few months there was an Elton John album out."

The disc's memorable cover was shot on a Universal back lot, on a '50's cinema set. The album's title glowed from a lit-up marque as a leather-clad greaser and his bobby-socked sweetheart bought tickets for a nonexistent Elton John film. Off to the side sat a poster advertising the Marx Brother's 1940 classic, *Go West*—a nod to Groucho for inspiring the work's title, and a sly reference to "Blues for Baby and Me," whose narrator sings of how he and his girlfriend are going to escape their deadend lives and go west to the sea.

The spectacular inside packaging was as detailed as the cover. It included a 12-page color libretto stuffed full of hand-tinted photographs which imbued the images—mostly taken at Elton's rented Malibu beach house—with a timeless, otherworldly feel. Created by Michael Ross and David Larkham, the booklet presented Elton as the shiny pop star he'd long-threatened to become, the Great Gatsby of Rock.

Don't Shoot Me I'm Only the Piano Player was a watershed release, moving more units in a fortnight than *Honky Château* managed in a full year. Becoming Elton's first album to feature multiple Top 5 U.K. hits, the LP would also quickly become his first transatlantic Number 1, and yet another Gold record to add to his rapidly growing collection. (The album would prove popular with the rest of the record-buying world as well, hitting Number 1 in Australia, Canada, Italy, Norway and Spain, Number 2 in the Netherlands and Finland, and Number 4 in Japan.)

"I remember being on a train, getting *Melody Maker* and seeing *Don't Shoot Me* was Number One," Davey said. "And it was like, 'Oh, that's great. It's happening."

Congratulatory telegrams poured in from all quarters. No one was more pleased—or surprised—by Elton's ever-escalating success than his old mentor, Long John Baldry. "I always knew that Rod [Stewart] was going to become something very, very special," Baldry said. "But how could one predict that a boy with an overweight problem—I mean, he *is* a bit broad across the beam, our Reg—who would have thought that this strange boy with his myopic lenses and fat arse could turn out to be one of the pop sensations of all time?"

Critics were less startled than Baldry. "It's not just geography that has affected Elton John's music," John

Pidgeon wrote in *Let It Rock* magazine. "There's a full-time guitarist, Davey Johnstone, a band unity coupled with an awareness of instrumentation previously blinkered by Paul Buckmaster's omnipresence, and a set of lyrics from Bernie Taupin that suggests he's finally thrown off his dogged obsession with Old Americana." "*Don't Shoot Me* is one nice piece of black plastic," Charles Shaar Murray opined in *NME*. "Don't listen to the nasties, Elton. You're doing all right—in fact you're doing pretty damn good—and if there's still any stigma attached to your name after this one gets out, I'll be mightily surprised. *Don't Shoot Me I'm Only the Piano Player* is a damn good album. Purchase it, glory in it, dance to it, and play it to your friends. *Comprenez?*"

Bernie saw the LP's success as yet another rung on a ladder which he envisioned stretching far into the future. "The reason we've survived and will continue to survive for a good long time," he said, "is because we've got the upper hand on everybody else and can turn our ideas into anything, any sort of music. We do things like playing rock 'n' roll, twelve bars to country material, blues....I mean, we've done every type of music. You can compile an album, taking tracks from all the things we've done, and come across with the most amazing cross-section of material."

Calling *Don't Shoot Me* his "discotheque album," Elton reflected that it was ultimately a disposable work. "It was a record that for the few months that it came out it bore a lot of relevance to that time, and I think people should just listen to it and enjoy it for that time and then put it aside and buy something else. There's so much stuff coming out that's good that you shouldn't say, 'I'm going to keep playing my *Don't Shoot Me* album and put everything else aside,' because you're probably missing out on something else."

For once, Elton's fans ignored him. *Don't Shoot Me I'm Only the Piano Player* proved a monster hit, remaining in the *Billboard* charts for a staggering eighty-nine weeks running.

Elton, Bernie, Gus Dudgeon, John Reid and Steve Brown decided to leverage the velocity *Don't Shoot Me*'s success afforded them by finally following up on their drunken idea months earlier to launch their own record label. "I always wanted to start my own record company," Elton said. "Even as a kid when I was playing my records, I'd be looking at the label spinning round and dreaming of having my own company."

Named after "Rocket Man," Rocket Records would focus on fostering the musical ambitions of those who toiled in obscurity. "Basically what we're interested in is new talent," Elton told *Disc* magazine. "There's thousands of me around in small bands—there *must* be. All I needed, initially, was the encouragement. What we're offering is our undivided love and devotion, a fucking good royalty for the artist, and a company that works its bollocks off. I'm prepared to sit in the office from dawn to midnight listening to tapes."

From the outset, Elton felt it imperative that his label not function as a vanity press for his own material, the way Swansong did for Led Zeppelin or Rolling Stones Records did for the Stones. Instead, Rocket Records would allow up-and-coming artists the breathing room necessary to create truly unique artistic works. "The whole reason for starting a record label was to get away from the 'You must record an album in fifteen hours' time' syndrome," Elton told journalist Bob Harris. "There's no real limit on to what people can do, if we're behind them. For example, there's a young guy [who] came in this week that's eighteen years old who plays the piano and we listened to his songs and [said], 'Well, they're not very good'. And then we sat down and said, 'Well, was *I* writing very good songs when I was eighteen?' I said, 'Well, I wasn't writing *any* songs when I was eighteen.' And he hadn't ever listened to any records, so we gave him some records to listen to. And we said, 'Listen, go away for six months, we'll give you wages every week for six months. And come back and see us in six months.' That's what we're looking for. Because I know how hard it was when I was trying to get publishing. It's such a hard thing."

Announcing itself in a full-page ad in the February 3 issue of *Melody Maker*, Rocket Records opened an office that same week in a small two-story house at 101 Wardour Street, London. Featuring mirrored doors painted with the Rocket Record logo—a David-Larkham-designed image of a winking *Thomas the Tank*-like train done up in childish primary colors—and walls covered in a selection of Elton's Gold records, the epicenter of the office was a massive boardroom which housed a mahogany conference table, a dozen leather swivel chairs, and a single oversized wicker peacock throne reserved for Elton himself.

Rocket's first order of business was to finalize its Board of Directors. Comprised of Elton, Bernie, Gus, Steve Brown and John Reid, each had a unique role to play. Reid was charged with looking after all business dealings and contractual negotiations, while Brown was to manage the day-to-day running of the office. Elton, Bernie and Gus, meanwhile, were left in charge of the creative end of the venture, finding and producing new talent as they came across them.

With Elton's high-profile name attached to Rocket Records, a bidding war quickly broke out for distribution rights to the embryonic company. "It was a toss-up between EMI and Island," he said, "and Island won because of their track record. Everyone was a bit worried about EMI's inability to get records in stock, and—overall throughout the country—ninety-nine percent of the stores said that Island's records were practically never out of stock. There's nothing worse than having a hit record that's out of stock."

Rocket Records quickly signed its first artist, the former Pauline Mathews, who now performed under the stage name Kiki Dee. (Interestingly, her original stagename was set to be 'Kinky Dee', before her manager decided that the slightly more anodyne 'Kiki' might prove less controversial and thus more commercial.) Twenty-six-year-old Kiki Dee possessed an enviable pedigree, having been the first white European artist ever signed to Barry Gordy's famed Motown label. She'd also served time as a backing vocalist for Dusty Springfield, while never being able to find a niche for herself as a solo artist. Elton had been impressed with her soulful voice for years. "She's been around for a long time, living in the wake of Dusty Springfield," he said. "And she could sing the balls off Rita Coolidge any day."

The pianist invited his inaugural signee over to his house for dinner, to get to know her better on a personal level.

"Neil Young was there," Kiki told journalist Richard Barber. "At one point, [Elton] asked me to go into the kitchen and fetch some wine glasses. He was already a star by then and had started investing in lovely bits and pieces. The glasses must have cost a fortune." Carefully reaching into the cupboard, Kiki promptly sent an entire row of crystal-cut glassware shattering to the floor. "I was mortified. Elton came in to see what had happened and burst out laughing. He thought it was the funniest thing he'd ever seen. I've loved him from that moment on."

Other early Rocket signees included the pub-rock unit Stackridge, the Zombies' Colin Blunstone, and the

Sunderland folk-rock group Longdancer, which featured Nigel Olsson's brother, Kai, as well as guitarist Dave Stewart, who would later rise to fame in the 1980s—along with partner Annie Lennox—as the Eurhythmics. "Their first album [*If It Was So Simple*] is gonna be good," Elton said of Longdancer. "It's not gonna be great, but then my first album [wasn't great, either]. Nobody's first album is usually great, unless you're a genius. That's not the point in signing people. You've got to have potential. The point of starting a record company is to encourage people who've got that spark of potential, to sort of encourage them onwards, because I needed that when I started off, and I really didn't get it half the time."

For his part, Dave Stewart was enthusiastic about working with one of his musical idols. "It was really like signing a record deal with the Mad Hatter," Stewart recalled in his memoir, *Sweet Dreams Are Made of This.* "[Elton] was an amazingly inspirational songwriter and performer. And also one of the sharpest wits I've ever encountered. He would always have us in hysterics by mimicking everyone from the Queen to Winston Churchill, and he could switch between the two in a nanosecond."

Elton was enthusiastic about his unknown signees. As for more established acts, he was a bit sanguine on the potential of securing their services. "We were offered Queen and Cockney Rebel," he said, "but we turned them down simply because we couldn't afford them. We were even offered 10cc—but again, they want far too much money up front to sign with the label....[But] we want to be completely open to any type of music."

Hardly stopping to catch his breath, Elton launched a winter's tour of the British Isles on February 24. Not minding the heavy effort involved, he understood how important touring was to his overall career prosperity. "People that bring albums out have really got hardly any chance if they're not on the road," he said. "If you're not on the road in England, you can't sell your albums. That's why people like Black Sabbath and Deep Purple sell a lot of albums. Not 'cause they get played on the radio, but because they go out on the road and get their following."

Elton's shows on English soil were notably different than the ones he gave in America. "We don't do 'Madman Across the Water' on stage [in the U.K.] because it's too drawn out," he said. "With an American audience you can draw it out and draw it out, but with an English audience you have to hold their attention all the time. With America, they don't mind what you do with them. In England, they really manipulate you. You can't afford to do four slow numbers together, otherwise they get really pissed-off, whereas in America you can."

The pianist gave a particularly dynamic performance at the Green's Playhouse in Glasgow, Scotland on February 25, pounding the keys like a maniac behind a diamante-encrusted, pink-satin-covered piano, driving the crowd to distraction. He may have even overshot the mark a bit, as after the show he found himself trapped inside the theater for several hours as hordes of frantic fans blocked all the exits. Promoter Peter Bowyer fought to hold the unruly throng at bay, receiving a broken ankle for his troubles. Elton finally managed to slip out of the building, only to endure a gauntlet of overwrought admirers out on the street. The maddened mob ripped his glasses off his face before chasing him down an alley. "I thought that the fans would rip us apart," he said. "I don't know what it takes for a girl to get it into her head that she must touch me. When they grab hold of you, it takes about six guys to get them off."

Similar scenes of pandemonium played out on subsequent nights, as Elton suddenly found himself elevated to teen idol status, alongside such glitter-dusted glam rockers as David Bowie, Marc Bolan, and Roxy Music. Hordes of frantic teenage girls now stood ten-deep at his shows, shrieking, screaming and flinging themselves brazenly onto stage for the chance to touch him for even a split second before burly bodyguards graded out of the wings to hurl them back into the overwrought mass of heaving flesh.

"Now Elton's a Teen Idol!" *Melody Maker* proclaimed in a bold-type front-page headline days later. "In the fluctuating world of pop," they noted, "[Elton] has made a dramatic comeback to answer the doubters. It has turned him into a teen-idol pin-up as well as a respected musician. Few artists these days can wear both crowns, and wear them with such elegance."

"It happens to anybody who has a hit," Elton philosophized, "no matter if they're the ugliest people in the world. Look at me. If they scream at me, it's probably in horror. I've not got attractive features. I'm plain."

Sharon Lawrence, a Rocket Records publicist, couldn't have disagreed more with the star. On more than one occasion, she noted, backstage lasses not only swooned over Elton—but some of the more comely ones would also spark a noticeable reaction from him, too. "I always felt that he could easily have married and had children—something he often said he wanted to do," she later told author Philip Norman. "Once or twice, I tried to encourage him in that direction. I told him, 'Don't get stuck with choices now that you'll regret for the rest of your life.'"

Indeed, the pianist *had* given thought to the idea of marriage and children, if only in the most facile manner possible.

"When I have a kid," he said, "I'm going to call my little girl Umbrella. Umbrella John is a beautiful name. Poor little girl, she'll really have the piss taken out of her. 'Umbrella, stand over there…'"

Elton's father and stepmother, Stanley and Edna, came to see the first of his two performances at the Empire Theatre in Liverpool on March 2. The three then met up after the show and made plans to have lunch together the following day at the Dwight homestead.

Elton arrived at noon in a bone-white Rolls. Dining on a home-cooked meal of roast chicken and apple pie à la mode, he sang a few songs at the family piano before playing soccer with his half-brothers out in the front yard, all of them laughing easily. Conviviality with his father proved more of a challenge, however. "There was…an awkwardness there," Elton said. "It was just two people who just didn't know how to gel together.…It's just a missed opportunity for two people to not have more love between each other."

Before taking his leave, Elton slipped a check for £2,000 into Edna's hand.

"Get dad that car he's wanted," he said.

Stanley bought the automobile in question—a Peugeot 504. Months later, however, with no explanation whatsoever, he quietly put it up for sale.

"I feel really sorry that we didn't get closer," Elton said soon after. "He has four kids now who he loves, but I don't feel that he's a shit. I just wish he could have loved me like that too."

Elton had little time to dwell on missed familial connections, for at his March 24 show at the Sundown Centre in Brixton—which began with the be-caped pianist being pulled across the stage in a silver cart by Bernie Taupin and

John Reid—dozens of fainting girls had to be lifted over the heads of concertgoers to be carried off backstage for medical attention.

"It's sort of disconcerting," the pianist said, "when you're in the middle of 'Mona Lisas and Mad Hatters' and your eyes are closed and you can sense eighteen-ton ladies being lifted past you."

Hardened concert-going critics were stunned by the sheer delirium Elton now routinely generated. "I was counting the number of fainting chicks pulled up out of the audience," Charles Shaar Murray noted in his review of the concert. "After the thirty-eighth, I gave up. The main thing is that Elton John is now one of the very, very biggest acts in the country, and all those reports you've read of hysteria and madness are absolutely true. Here is a full-scale teenage idol, just like T. Rex and Slade and all them, and you better believe it. What's more, he's done it with better music."

Rod Stewart appeared in leopard-skin pants toward the end of Elton's Brixton show to present his friend with a dozen red roses, before the latter ended the show with a rollicking rendition of Stevie Wonder's "Superstition."

"Ol' Reg," Rod laughed. "He doth rock the hardest."

Following a sold-out gig at Coventry Theatre, Elton celebrated his twenty-sixth birthday with a massive booze-up on the river Thames aboard the *John D.* Guests included Cat Stevens, Paul Simon, Ronnie Wood, Kenney Jones, Ringo Starr, Harry Nilsson, and several buxom strippers. The next day, the pianist—who had sent Marc Bolan a life-sized blow-up of himself naked but for a strategically placed briefcase for his birthday the September before—found a furniture-removal truck pulling up to his house. Inside were two items: the Silver record award for Bolan's hit 'Jeepster', and a twenty-seven-foot-high cardboard blow-up of Bolan himself.

"It was too big for the house," Elton said with a laugh. "So I kept it in the back garden."

With Bolan's image safely tucked away, Elton spent his between-gig downtime either methodically cataloging his latest vinyl acquisitions or disappearing into darkened movie theaters to escape into some fantastical alternate reality. One activity he never engaged in, however, was giving his own records a spin. "Once albums are finished, I can't bear to listen to them," he said. "I can't listen to *Don't Shoot Me* now, although I can play it onstage. The next one is always more important than the one I've just finished."

Elton's tour ended with a seven-date stand in Italy, which excited the star to no end. "I love places that have an incredible history," he said. "I love the Italian way of life. I love the food. I love the people. I love the attitudes of Italians."

While in Italy, Nigel Olsson's girlfriend, self-styled "super-groupie" Jozy Pollock, came across a local newspaper report which claimed that Elton favored the company of men. "I was reading the article and told him, 'They're talking about you being a homosexual.' He said, 'How would they know?' And I said, 'Come over to the mirror.' [Elton] was wearing silver platform boots and some outrageous outfit, and I said, 'Look in the mirror! How do you *think* they know?'"

The article did little to dampen the enthusiastic reaction Elton received. Before his show at the Palasport di Genova in Genoa, in fact, several hundred frantic kids were so desperate to get near the magnetic Brit that they overwhelmed his train coach, pleading for tickets to the sold-out show. To help calm the mob, tickets were distrubted so that the desperate fans could join the ten-thousand already in attendance for that night's show.

With the successful completion of his stage commitments for the forseeable future, Elton's next order of business was to organize a launch party for his nascent record label. Held on April 30 on the British Rail's "Football Special"—a party train equipped with its own fully stocked bar-car and discotheque—350 Rocket employees, friends and media members joined the seventy-mile rail trip from Paddington Station to Moreton-in-the-Marsh, an idyllic village nestled in the rolling hills of Gloucestershire. Upon disembarking, a brass band greeted the partygoers with a whimsical rendition of "Hello, Dolly." All and sundry were then led on a jovial march to an archaic banquet hall a mile down the road, where many bottles of *Krug Clos d'Ambonnay* were consumed. To entertain the group, Longdancer—followed by another Rocket signee, Mike Silver—blasted away from a makeshift stage. Key members of Rocket's Board of Directors soon joined in—Bernie banging arhythmically on a tambourine while Elton rocked out in a plaid safari shirt, a bottle of champagne screwed to his lips.

Despite the lingering effects of a champagne hangover, Elton found himself in an enthusiastic mood the next day over Kiki Dee's prospects. "We're trying to write a special song for her," he said. "We've never done that for anybody else, to try to get her off the ground, to try to get her publicity and everything. Bernie's task is really hard because he's got to write one as a girl. So he slips into Maxine's dresses every morning."

The results—"Lonnie & Josie" and "Supercool"—were featured on Kiki's Rocket Records debut, *Loving and Free.*

Co-produced by Elton and Clive Franks, the former contributed piano to seven of the ten tracks. "People have said that I'm risking my own reputation by writing and producing for acts who haven't made it," he said, "but I reckon that the acts have a lot more to lose. What I hope with someone like Kiki is that I can give her initial pushes, give her the benefit of my experience, help with the publicity and stand back and let her stand on her own two feet. If someone like Gamble and Huff or Burt Bacharach heard the album and said they'd like to do another one with Kiki, I'd be knocked out....Talent will always find a way in the end, but I think it criminal that so many artists have to be frustrated for so long waiting for the right break."

Kiki was eternally grateful for the special attention Elton lavished upon her. "It was his belief in me that got me started," she said, while granting that her thankfulness was perhaps enhanced by a small crush she'd harbored for him. "[Elton] was boy-next-door cute," she said. "He wasn't a sex symbol, but he had this persona and a presence about him."

Elton and Bernie sat with esteemed pop journalist Paul Gambaccini for an in-depth interview a week before they were to attempt a fresh attack on their new album sessions, which had failed so spectacularly in Jamaica. Gambaccini secured the coveted interview in a unique manner—by following Elton into the men's room during a Bee Gees concert at the Royal Festival Hall and accosting him at a urinal. "Of course, looking back now," Gambaccini later told author David Buckley, "it's beyond believability on the scale of rudeness. And he would have been forgiven if he had just whirled around in my direction. [But] he was a great gentleman and he looked at me and said, 'Call Helen Walters at DJM, she's in charge of things like that.' We didn't shake hands."

Gambaccini found Elton in a much more expansive mood on the actual day of the interview, which took place in his ornate, album-packed living room. Even so, the pianist *did* grow a bit defensive when Gambaccini mentioned a critic's charge that certain of his records sounded similar to one another. "I get fucking pissed-off at people saying, 'Their songs always sound the same,'" Elton seethed. "How can you say 'Have Mercy on the Criminal' sounds like 'Daniel'? Or 'Daniel' sounds like 'High Flying Bird'?"

As for L.A., the imminently quotable star noted: "It's a great place to arrive in, and it's a great place to leave."

Speaking of their mutual friend Alice Cooper, Bernie remarked that the Detroit-bred *enfant terrible* of rock 'n' roll was actually a "good lad" who could "really sink a few frosties." Elton agreed. "I saw him at the Hollywood Bowl," he said, "[and] it was incredible, with the helicopter, the shower of panties, the fireworks. It was the best-produced show I've ever seen. I was caught up in it myself, scrambling for a pair of panties. You *can't* do anything like that in Britain. You'd get Jobsworths backstage, saying, 'You can't do that here. Who's going to clean up the mess?'" He grinned. "[Alice] came down to the beach house the next day and his leg was all cut up where he had [a] fight. They really go into him. He must be a wreck."

Elton was less impressed with Jerry Lee Lewis. "They asked me to play on his album, but I said no," he told Gambaccini. "He was so disappointing when I saw him at the Palladium, and as far as I'm concerned he was the best rock 'n' roll pianist ever. He could have wiped the audience out, but he just sat there and played country and western numbers as if to say, 'Fuck you.' And calling himself the Killer. I could kill more people with one finger than he did when I saw him."

Of his imminent album sessions, Elton noted that "it's going to be two albums released simultaneously, or a double album, whichever works out. If we could ever record an album as good as *Abbey Road,* I'd want to retire. Even though it's not my favorite Beatles album, you hear 'Something' and 'Here Comes the Sun' and you want to fall down. Usually somebody has one good song on an album, but the Beatles had five or six mindblowers. So this is the way I feel about our next one. It's strange, you can compare us against the Beatles: *Revolver* lifted them onto a higher plane, and I think *Honky* [*Château*] did that for us, and then *Sgt. Pepper* was their most popular and *Don't Shoot Me* was ours, and then they had the *White Album,* and now we'll have a double, too."

The interview ended with Elton, Bernie and Gambaccini deciding they were famished. Handing his lyricist a fistful of pound notes, Elton instructed him to drive down to the village for some take-out.

"Ten minutes later," Gambaccini said, "we were all dining on cod and chips."

Chapter 15:
Goodbye Yellow Brick Road

John Reid officially took over exclusive management duties for both Elton and Bernie on May 10, as DJM's contract expired. Noting that James held the copyrights to Elton and Bernie's songs for the rest of their lives plus fifty years, Reid asked the cigar-chomping mogul if he would consider allowing the men who had actually created the copyrighted work to assume ownership. Having felt burnt by his interactions with the Beatles—the publisher had held the copyrights to only two of the Fab Four's songs, "Please Please Me" and "Ask Me Why," despite having published their entire catalogue—James rejected Reid's request out of hand.

The impasse was yet another point of contention in an increasingly fractious relationship between Elton and James.

Setting business matters temporarily aside, Elton and his retinue were soon reconvening at the familiar environs of the Château d'Hérouville, the facility having reopened its doors after finally resolving a legal dispute as to its true ownership.

"There was definitely the comfort of returning to a place that you really were familiar with," Bernie said. "So we basically set up camp, and everything really went pretty swimmingly." Davey shared the lyricist's optimistic feelings. "We were racking up the hits, and it was amazing," he later said of those halcyon days. "Our musical inhibitions went away. Success became our drug, and I don't just mean the financial rewards, I mean how great we felt when we played, and how we were received. The more successful we got, the better we played, and the easier it became to know what to play. It almost felt effortless."

Songs were coming with such ease, in fact, that twenty-two tracks would be completed in a mere twelve days. The genre-tripping music was earmarked for what would become Elton's crowning achievement; tentatively called *Vodka & Tonics*, the album's title would gestate during the course of the sessions into *Silent Movies, Talking Pictures*, in recognition of the widescreen sweep inherent in the new songs being laid down. Ultimately, however, Elton would decide that that title tied in too closely with the cinema on the cover of *Don't Shoot Me*, and instead would christen his latest work after a favored ballad he and Bernie had recently written. Thus, *Goodbye Yellow Brick Road* was born.

Sessions kicked off admirably on May 7, with the phantasmagoric one-two punch of "Funeral For a Friend/Love Lies Bleeding."

"Gus Dudgeon had always said I should do an instrumental," Elton said. "One day I was feeling really down and I said to myself, 'What kind of music would I like to hear at my own funeral?' I'm hung up on things like that. I really like tearful, plodding music."

The entire eleven-minute-and-seven-second-long track was recorded in a single take, with only Nigel's high-hat and additional guitar lines by Davey overdubbed afterward. "We rehearsed it a couple of times, but that was it," the guitarist said. "Elton's attention span..." The guitarist shrugged. "He's very impatient. So as soon as we knew what the song was going to be, we went in and nailed it, played it straight through. I knew I would do some layering and overdubs, but

320

still, the idea was to do as much as possible all at once. It was a lot of fun." More for the guitarist than the lyric writer. "There's a great deal of anger and torment in that song," Bernie said. "It's a very real song to me…a statement of what touring and rock 'n' roll does to the family life."

Though many would later surmise that "Funeral For a Friend/Love Lies Bleeding" was composed as it had been recorded—as a single entity—in truth they were utterly distinct creations. "The two were written completely separately and we just put them together on the spur of the moment and it worked," Elton told Robert Hilburn. "I like the instrumental better than the other one ['Love Lies Bleeding']." Davey, for his part, preferred "Love Lies Bleeding"—especially given the nouveau-retro power-pop guitar fills he'd infused into the manic outro. "I was going for a 'While My Guitar Gently Weeps' type of thing," he said. "That's why the guitar has that Clapton-esque 'waaah' with lots of vibrato. And [Elton] emulated it [vocally] to make it like we are both crying at the end."

While the entire band did yeoman's work on the track, it wouldn't actually be completed until the mixing sessions back at Trident Studios in London, when Gus suddenly had an idea. "I said to [album engineer] David [Hentschel], 'As it's a double album, it'd be nice to have some sort of intro to the whole album. To make it a bit special.'" The producer originally wanted to use Alfred Newman's iconic Twentieth Century Fox fanfare, but he quickly ran into licensing problems. Deciding that an overture would work just as well, he tasked Hentschel with creating a medley which blended prominent themes from "Candle in the Wind," "The Ballad of Danny Bailey" and "I've Seen That Movie Too" into a seamless whole. Because the only synthesizer available was a modular, monophonic ARP 2500, each electronic voicing had to be recorded separately. The task took Hentschel the better part of a day—for a minute and nine seconds worth of music. Thirty-two seconds of funereal sound effects were then tacked onto the beginning of the overture. Gus added a final element to the song—castanets—while he and Hentschel created the final mix-down. Though the song's running time would prove prohibitive for any consideration of a single release—45s could only hold a maximum of seven minutes of music per side before they suffered serious audio degradation—the epic track would go on to receive overwhelming radio-play on classic rock and album-oriented rock stations across America, quickly becoming one of Elton's most popular songs and a live staple for decades to come.

"Candle in the Wind," an introspective eulogy to doomed sex symbol Marilyn Monroe, who had died under shadowy circumstances eleven years prior, was also recorded that same day. Though the wistfully dramatic blend of music and lyrics was highly original, the title itself was not. "I had always loved the phrase," Bernie said. "Solzhenitsyn had written a book called *Candle in the Wind*. Clive Davis had used it to describe Janis Joplin, and—for some reason—I just kept hearing this term. I thought, 'What a great way of describing someone's life.'"

A misconception about the track—that the lyricist must be a Marilyn Monroe fanatic—soon arose. "It's not that I didn't have a respect for her," Bernie said, "it's just that the song could just as easily have been about James Dean or Jim Morrison...Sylvia Plath or Virginia Wolfe—basically any writer, actor, actress or musician who died young and became this iconic *Picture of Dorian Gray*....The point of the song was how the media distorts people's lives....How we abuse the living, how we abuse the dead."

Ironically, the gentle "Candle in the Wind" caused a rare moment of friction, however minor, between Elton and Davey. "When we first recorded it," the guitarist said, "I did it with electric guitar. Elton's feeling was, 'I want this to have a bit of a tougher feel.' In fact, he also had the idea for that guitar lick when he sings, 'candle in the wind...' When he sang the part to me, I went, 'That's so cheesy. You're not serious. I'm not going to play that.' It's one of the few times we've had an argument like that in the studio. And he said, 'Will you at least try it?' And I went, 'Ok.' So...being the compatible guitar player that I am, the chorus came round and I played the thing—and it worked perfectly. I was like, 'You *bastard.*'" Augmenting the track with a pair of revelatory acoustic guitar overdubs, Davey utilized open tuning to get the most evocative sound possible. "The song is in the key of E, so I tuned the guitar to E—it was a twelve-string, so it took forever—and came up with the arrangement."

Ultimately, Elton was more than pleased with the final product. "['Candle in the Wind'] is the only song I've ever written where I get goose bumps every time I play it," he said. "When in doubt, write a hymn. There's nothing more poignant than a good, melodic hymn."

One of the more unique tracks from the entire sessions—also recorded on May 7, which was turning into quite a prolific day, even by Elton's already industrious standards—was the bluesy "Bennie and the Jets." The pianist realized from the outset that the song was bound to hold a unique spot in his catalog. "When I saw the lyrics for 'Bennie and the Jets'," he said, "I knew it had to be an off-the-wall type song, an R&B-ish kind of sound or a funky sound."

Lyrically, the track was a clever send-up of the glitter-rock scene, which was then dominating the pop scene. "I'd always had this wacky science fiction idea about a futuristic rock 'n' roll band of androids fronted by some androgynous Helmut Newton-style beauty," Bernie said. "I'm not sure if it came to me in a dream, or was somehow the subconscious effect of watching Kubrick on drugs. Either way, it was totally formed as a concept." Intriguingly, the name 'Bennie' was a nod, conscious or otherwise, to one of the lyricist's early paramours, a trendy free-spirit named Sally Bennington who had lived behind the gasworks in Bernie's old village, and went by 'Bennie'. "I thought she was the most beautiful creature I'd ever seen," Bernie later confessed in his memoir, *A Cradle of Haloes.*

The idea of turning the track into a live-sounding recording came to Gus—much as it had with "Rock 'n' Roll Madonna" three years earlier—while he was mixing the track. "It was just a fluke," he said. "It just so happened before that track started [Elton] played a chord and it happened to be exactly one bar [long]. I don't know why he did it, but he just happened to do it. While we were playing the mix, it never occurred to me to make it live. But I kept hearing it and thinking I was going to have to cut that off. I was just about to say to the engineer, 'Don't forget, we need to mute that piano part.' And I kept thinking, 'This reminds me of when somebody's onstage and they go, "Ready, everybody. Okay?" And they play a chord to give themselves a starting point.' I thought this is kind of like a live thing, and it triggered this whole thought process: 'Let's try making it live.'"

To achieve the affect, Gus used audience atmospherics and applause from the beginning of Elton's 1972 Royal Festival Hall performance—specifically, when Paul Buckmaster walked out and took his place in front of the orchestra—and then adding Digital Delay Line to give the song a heavy stage-echo feel. The final elements added were multiple lines of handclaps, folded in purposefully on the wrong beat. "If you notice, it's on the on-beat, not the off-beat," Gus said. "Because English audiences *always* insist on clapping on the wrong bloody beat….English audiences always clop on the 'on' rather than the 'off' beat. Basically, they haven't got a fucking clue. And I got one of the tea boys to do one of those whistles."

Tellingly, not a single person involved in the song's creation felt that "Bennie and the Jets" held even a scintilla of commercial potential, and that the lengthy track would end up merely one more unheralded jewel upon a ceaseless musical excavator belt. "Nobody in the band thought it was going to be a hit single," Davey said. "Not *one* of us."

"I sound like Frankie Valli," Elton joked as the track faded into the ether. "Next, please…"

The album's signature rocker, "Saturday Night's Alright (For Fighting)," was tackled next. A British working-class burner, the track seemingly harkened back to the rowdy nights Bernie had spent at the Aston Arms, a Market Rasen pub of his not-so-distant youth. "I feel slightly guilty because I'm not sure that I actually *did* write it about that," the lyricist later confessed. "People say, 'Oh, Bernie wrote it about a pub he used to hang out and get into fights at.' It's quite possible there's a germ of truth in that. Did I say to myself, 'I'm going to sit down and write a song about my childhood, watching the Mods fight the Rockers?' No, I don't think that I did. With so many of my songs, the lyrical content has been misconstrued, misinterpreted, and you get to the point where you feel like you have to make something up in order to make somebody happy."

The track's musical genesis was far less confused. "Whenever a song came up," Davey said, "I'd immediately start working on what I should do. Elton would write so fast, and I had to be just as quick to keep up. As soon as I heard him writing 'Saturday Night', I knew it was a total guitar-rocking track." In the end, the fret master laid down *eight* separate lead and rhythm guitar parts, chunking out sixteenth notes on his '62 Les Paul Gold Top (the rampaging sound pouring through a customized Ted Wallace stacked amp), before adding additional tracks of serrated power chords played on a Fender Champs. "With each guitar track it sounded better and better. Elton kept saying, 'Another one! Another one!'"

Despite the lack of Caribbean drama, the song still proved tricky. "Even though we tried for hours," Elton said, "we couldn't get it down right with just the four of us as a band doing it live in the studio. It kept running away with itself, or speeding up, or disintegrating into an unruly mess."

Deciding that the only answer was to record the track sans piano, Elton roared around the studio while the rest of his band launched into a fresh take.

"Come *on* already, you lazy bastards!" he screamed. "Fucking *rock!*"

A single take was all it took. After Davey double-tracked eight separate guitar lines, Elton added a few glissando-filled piano lines. Listening to the playback of the six-minute-and-thirty-second-long recording, a visibly pleased Elton called the song "so commercial, it's ridiculous." (In post-production, the track would be edited down to a 4:57 album cut, while an even leaner 4:12 edit was later mixed for release as a single.)

Another caustic, guitar-powered rocker came in the guise of "All the Girls Love Alice." The tale of a misguided lesbian was, as Elton succinctly put it, "about youth and the dangers of being seduced. I don't think there is any danger in being seduced, but there you go." The track was a daring mix of fiercely gritty garage-rock and louche sensuality, the effective amalgam highlighted by Davey's Uni-Vibe-pedaled guitar, and flippant backing vocals from Kiki Dee, who was making her debut on an Elton John recording.

To add an atmosphere of malevolence to the outro, Nigel recorded himself roaring up and down the gravel drive outside the Château in a Mini-Cooper, while Davey double-tracked steel bottle openers sliding across the neck of his guitar to help create otherworldly atmospherics. Everything happened spontaneously, and to great effect.

The session's karmic root lay in the sweeping F-minor lament "I've Seen That Movie Too," which utilized filmic metaphors to describe a romance sabotaged by deceptions and infidelities. Though Elton's growling tenor captured the wounded lyrics perfectly, the song's focal point came with its impassioned, backward-masked guitar solo. After playing the part twice (the final result was a blend of both takes), Davey then executed a forward-tracked guitar line, playing the main theme over the latter half of the solo, which would later be embellished with a soundscape of cascading strings.

The result was an operatic requiem which would prove highly influential across multiple generations of musicians. Guns & Roses front-man Axl Rose—who would called Elton and Bernie's songs his "classical music"—would go so far as to quote the song directly on his own track, "You Could Be Mine," from *Use Your Illusion II*. ("For myself as well as for many others, no one has been there more for inspiration than Elton John," Rose would say during his speech inducting Elton into the Rock and Roll Hall of Fame in 1994.)

"Your Sister Can't Twist (But She Can Rock 'n' Roll)" offered a pleasing mélange of early-'60s rock 'n' roll steeped in swooping Beach Boys harmonies, and a torrid opening blast which recalled the Beatles' "Twist and Shout." If the point was missed, Elton drove the allusion home with a soaring organ solo which purposefully recalled Freddy Cannon's 1962 smash, "Palisades Park."

"I can't play organ, I'm the worst," the pianist confessed. "I just love messing around with shitty organ sounds and things like that."

In the final chorus, Elton substituted "surf" for "twist," a nod to the influence that the Beach Boys—especially their post-"Fun Fun Fun" recordings—continued to exert on him, while Dee, Davey and Nigel sang "Fee-Urk-Nay, Fee-Urk-Nay" in the background through stoned Icelandic accents.

"They were actual words we had invented," Davey said. "Just real juvenile stuff."

As with "Skyline Pigeon" the year before, Elton reached deep into his back catalogue to revisit another favored older tune during the sessions. This time it was "Grey Seal," which had originally appeared as the B-side to "Rock 'n' Roll Madonna" in 1970.

The new version was propelled by Dee's syncopated bass triplets and endlessly inventive chromatic Dorian-scale runs. Adding to the dynamic urgency, Davey refrained from playing except during the intro, choruses, and newly added outro—as he'd done with "Crocodile Rock" the year before. "When the verse comes in, it's just bass and drums and piano," he said. "And then the guitar comes in strong on the chorus. It would suddenly give the track a different dimension and highlight a part when it comes in....It's something I learned from George Harrison. I'm a huge Harrison fan, and if you listen to a lot of Beatles tracks, there will be songs where the guitar comes bombing in and then it will be out again."

The wildly oscillating "Grey Seal" proved to be as bipolar lyrically as it was musically.

"It's oblique," Bernie admitted. "I hadn't a clue what I was writing about. It was just images."

"Bernie hates that lyric," Elton said. "But I like it, because of the mixture of music and lyrics which is kind of Procol Harum-ish absurd, like a Dali painting."

The nonsensical mood in the studio loosened further still with "Jamaica Jerk-Off," a slice of island-flavored pop which served as a subtle kiss-off to the locale which had proven so troublesome for the Brits. Showing a stylish sense of humor, the infectious cod-reggae track was credited to the songwriting team of "Reggae Dwight and Toots Taupin," 'Toots' Hibbert and his band the Maytals being major reggae stars in the early '70s.

Elton and Bernie briefly debated about changing the title of the track to the less dubious "Jamaica Twist," but nixed the idea when it became apparent that that title wouldn't scan properly with the melody. "People [will] probably take it the wrong way and think we're having a go at Jamaica," Bernie said. "It's not rude or anything. Well, it's never *very* rude."

To fill out the sonic foreground, Gus provided various "vocal interjections" over Elton's organ solo; his enthusiastic efforts would be credited under the pseudonym "Prince Rhino." "I love rhinos, you see," the producer explained. "Jamaicans, maybe not as much. I shouldn't say that." He laughed. "At the end of the day, I can honestly tell you [that] I was more than pleased with that track."

The next song attempted was the one which would eventually provide the entire proceedings with its title: "Goodbye Yellow Brick Road." Written in Jamaica, the imagery in Bernie's lyrics were based on the iconic MGM classic *The Wizard of Oz*—the first film both he and Elton had ever seen.

Bernie's lyrics posited himself as a captive imprisoned by the bright lights and questionable lures of the big city. Elton successfully matched the inherent contemplativeness in his partner's lyrics with one of the most achingly haunting melodies he'd ever devised. "When I write, I usually get a chord sequence," he said. "And I stumbled on [the introductory chords to 'Goodbye Yellow Brick Road'] by accident. It was the intro that I got first." The simple, descending-chord preface led to a comparatively complicated melody. "Man, there are something like twenty-odd chord changes in that song," Davey said. "When Elton wrote a song, we'd rehearse it, record it and start overdubbing. So there was no time nor need to write down the chords or anything. But for 'Goodbye Yellow Brick Road' I remember thinking, 'I'd better write a quick [chord] chart here.' Because there are so many chord changes."

To complement the song's labyrinth structure, Elton employed his falsetto, imbuing the track with an intimately lilting sweep. Many critics would assume that Gus had doctored the tape speed to achieve the effect, yet that was hardly the case. "I don't know why he did it," the producer conceded in the *Classic Albums: The Making of Goodbye Yellow Brick Road* documentary. "He just went out and sung in a sort of sped-up voice....It's just the weird way he decided to do it. *That's* Elton."

While still a huge fan of Paul Buckmaster's brooding string arrangements, Elton made a conscious effort to move toward a lighter pop touch on these latest sessions by bringing arranger Del Newman into the fold. Newman, who had worked on Cat Stevens' *Tea for the Tillerman* album—as well as on Paul Simon's classic "American Tune"—added achingly melancholic orchestral flourishes which lifted "Goodbye Yellow Brick Road" to another level. "Elton told me which tracks he wanted me to be involved in," Newman said, "which was a sort of big deal for me because Gus was involved. He had a chat with me and explained what Elton wanted. He then sent me the material, which was a rough mix without orchestra....I tried to follow the vocals, as I wanted to be part of the band, rather than working against the vocals."

Unlike "Goodbye Yellow Brick Road," "The Ballad of Danny Bailey (1909-34)" was a brand-new song written at the Château. As with many of the best John/Taupin tunes, it was the result of instantaneous inspiration. "I don't know if I'd seen a movie or read a book," Bernie later told *Rolling Stone*'s Andy Greene, "but I came up with the first line....and that was it. It could have gone a number of different ways, but it ended up being a tune about a bootlegger." Indeed, the lyric would ultimately feature Bernie's fanciful amalgam of Depression-era racketeers like John Dillinger and Pretty Boy Floyd, outlaws who'd met their untimely ends at the hands of the law. "He's my composite gangster," the lyricist said. "I love creating characters."

"Now *that* is a great song," Davey said. "I love 'Danny Bailey' 'cause it's so different. It's got an interesting chord sequence and a great story in the lyric. We had a really good time with that jam at the end—especially Dee and I. Elton was really into that piano vamp [during the coda], and Dee was so good...so inventive. Elton could get to be the keyboard player he wanted. Nobody was trying to outplay anybody else, that was the beauty of it."

To achieve the ominous sound effect which followed the "Dragnet"-like piano intro, a shotgun was fired out a

Château window at four in the morning. That blast was then mixed with the sound of Nigel pummeling his snare drum while Dee stroked a delicate watercolor flourish on his Fender Jazz.

"Art, you see," the bassist said, laughing heartily.

Halfway through the sessions, Elton recorded a barrelhouse piano demo of a new song which he and Bernie had written specifically for Rod Stewart. Entitled "Let Me Be Your Car," Elton was pleased with the way the propulsive tune came out. "It's the best rock 'n' roll song I've ever done," he said. "I guess it's just an indication of our changing state of mine, because…we never really wanted to write for anyone else."

Another favored song—though in a decidedly different vein—was "Sweet Painted Lady," an accordion-accented, Noel Coward-styled cabaret number about seaside prostitutes.

"[It's] a song about the old 'say no more, say no more,'" Elton said. "If you want to pay for it, you can have it."

The morning after a fiercely drunken intra-band Ping-Pong tournament—eventually won by Dee Murray ("Elton was *pissed!*" the bassist chuckled)—the group turned their attentions to one of the strongest tracks of the entire sessions. Entitled "Screw You" (the song would be relabeled as "Young Man's Blues" for the more sensitive U.S. market), the hammering blues-drenched track—which featured Dee, Nigel and Davey's backing vocals slyly name-checking Bowie's "The Jean Genie" after the final chorus—would inexplicably fail to make the final album lineup, instead being relegated to the relative obscurity of a B-side. It was shabby treatment for a song that so completely met its aim—starting with a memorable opening guitar figure. "It was two twelve-string guitars," Davey said, "so they were slightly out of phase with one another. Then I added two guitars and tuned *every* string to the same note, which I don't think had ever been done before. All six strings were tuned to, I think, D." (In a true case of musical chairs, the group Boston would appropriate Davey's swirling guitar introduction for their 1976 hit "More Than a Feeling"—while the main riff from *that* song would later prove the basis for Nirvana's 1992 grunge anthem, "Smells Like Teen Spirit.")

Elton recorded the next song largely alone. "This Song Has No Title" was an introspective ballad detailing a young artist's yearning to find meaning in an otherwise formless existence. The enigmatic vignette featured Elton on two separate Farfisa organs, three acoustic pianos, an electric piano and a mellotron. He also provided both lead and backing vocals. "It was great because he'd know instinctively what he wanted," Davey said years later. "And I maintain to this day, you don't really need anybody else if you've got Elton John."

"Dirty Little Girl" was, by contrast, a thudding, Leslie-distorted rocker, and yet another attempt by Elton to out-Stones the Stones. "That's a filthy track...it's such good fun," Davey said. "When Gus was producing the early albums, it was great because it was like stereo piano, the whole deal, everything was really cool."

"['Dirty Little Girl' was] probably one of our better Stones' lifts," Gus said with a laugh.

During downtime in the studio, Elton busied himself with an endless string of pranks. One night he got drunk on hundred-year-old port and dialed up old acquaintances back in London at two a.m. "I *vant* to lick your body, yah? I *vant* to lick your body," he groaned in a lascivious Dr. Strangelove-

ian accent. "I *vant* to lick it now, yah? Give *unt* to me."
Early the next morning, he and the band tossed a sleeping
Clive Franks into the pool—bed and all. "I nearly bloody
drowned because I was still wrapped in the sheets," Clive
said. "I was pissed-off at the time, but I guess I can see the
funny side to it now."

More productively, Elton had Davey show him a few
basic chords on his acoustic guitar. It was a slow process for
the pianist. "I can play four chords and that's it," he said.
"The only reason I'd like to play something else is because,
when you're writing a song on a piano, you can only go so
far. And then, if you write a song on electric piano, for some
reason you write a different sort of song, because it's a
mellower sounding instrument and you write different chord
structures and you write in different keys to what you would
on an ordinary piano. And so, if I could play the guitar well,
I know I could write different songs on the guitar. It's very
frustrating. There are only so many instruments you can
write on. I think you're fairly limited. I can't see myself
picking up an oboe and writing on that. So I would like to
play guitar."

One of the band's favorite tracks, the woozy party groove
"Social Disease," was talked next. A genial, whiskey-soaked
rave-up, the song followed the drunken exploits of a
Bukowski-esque figure who paid the rent by sleeping with
his landlady and plying her with the grape.

Recorded in a single take, "Social Disease" slowly faded
up over the first verse while a bulldog barked in the
background, as if the alcoholic narrator were shaking off a
major-league hangover. Davey gave the cheery, banjo-
inflected track an additional boost by overdubbing acoustic
guitar and Uni-Vibe-phased guitar. "There's all kinds of
stuff on this track," he said. "And the barking dogs [at the

beginning] were from around the Château grounds. We just hung the mics out the window and they picked up the different sounds."

Leroy Gomez topped the whole thing off with a sleazy sax solo which lifted the entire song to another level of inebriated effervescence. Gomez's performance—indeed, the very fact that he was *at* the Château at all—was serendipitous. A struggling American-born musician living in Paris, it was only at his roommate Michael's insistence that they crash Elton's sessions, after rumors reached their ears that Elton was looking for a sax player.

"I did not see myself just barging in on Elton's recording session uninvited," Gomez later told *eltonjohnworld.com*'s Cheryl Herman. "Quite frankly, I was a little worried about being rejected. After all, this was an *Elton John* session."

After getting buzzed on Pelforth beer to calm their nerves, the two friends drove a V.W. van up to the Château. Arriving just after midnight, they climbed the backstairs which led to the top floor studio where Elton was recording. A red light shone above a soundproof door, indicating that a session was underway. "In the silence we could faintly hear someone singing on the other side of the door," Gomez told journalist Cheryl Herman. "It was Elton recording the lead vocals to the title track of the album *Goodbye Yellow Brick Road*, all those 'ah ah ahs...'"

The moment the red light dimmed, Leroy and Michael pulled the heavy door open and stepped into the studio.

"Hey Elton," Michael said breezily, pushing a nervous Leroy forward. "I heard that you've been looking for a sax player to lay down some tracks. Well, here he is."

A blushing Gomez stared at his feet. "I am sure most superstars would have been upset to have a couple of guys just barge into their recording session, but not Elton," he later recalled. "He just coolly and calmly looked at us and said, 'Great!'"

Elton nodded toward his team in the recording booth—Gus, Bernie, engineer David Hentschel and assistant engineer Andy Scott. "Okay, change of plans," he said. "Let's record some sax.'"

Gomez then laid down a raggedly melodic line for "Social Disease." "I didn't know 'Social Disease' from a monkey on the back of a dog," he said. "You just get in there, and they have this amount of space that they have to have filled-in on the song, so you listen to a little bit of what came before and what came after, and then it's, 'One-two-three, drop me in. I think I got it, I know what key we're in.' And basically that's what it is when you're a session musician. You don't get more than a couple of takes before they say, 'Thank you very much for your time.' Either they like it or that's it."

The session with Gomez ran so smoothly, Gus suggested he add his chops to "Screw You" as well. After a couple run-throughs, the saxophonist's work was completed.

Gomez and his friend were invited to remain in the studio as Elton continued recording. At five in the morning, with the session finally completed, Elton walked the two men outside and shook their hands.

"So how much do I owe you?" he asked Gomez, who quoted his normal session fee.

Elton shook his head no.

"You're worth more than that, Larry," he said. "I'm gonna make sure you get paid double." He put his hand on Gomez's shoulder. "*Never* sell yourself short. Charge more for your work, because you deserve it."

The saxophonist could only laugh. "To think that just twelve hours prior to this moment, I was worried about being rejected."

The languorous, steel-guitar-laced "Roy Rogers," which explored Bernie's love for celluloid cowboys and B-film pistoleros, provided a reflective moment. "He was my hero," the lyricist said soberly of the famous actor. "He was my savior."

Elton, who also held Rogers in high regard, sang a duet with himself on the diaphanous waltz—a vocal nod to the Everly Brothers—while Del Newman's synergistic strings elevated the choruses of the quietly riveting portrait to a sublime level seldom achieved within the depths of the pop idiom. "It was general practice for the artists to allow me to do what I thought would enhance the emotional quality of the songs, and it seemed to work very well," Newman said. "Elton was just as trusting as many other artists. I guess it was a matter of leaving things alone and wanting to be surprised."

"Whenever You're Ready (We'll Go Steady Again)" followed. Featuring Elton's most impassioned Jerry Lee Lewis stylings to date, as well as tasty fills from Davey's vibrato-drenched slide guitar, the song was, for a time, strongly under consideration by Rod Stewart as a potential single.

Next came the countrified "Jack Rabbit." Clocking in at a mere 1:52, the brief track was a double-time throwaway which featured mandolin, acoustic guitar, banjo, electric guitar and slide guitar. "It was like, 'Okay, Davey, this one's yours,'" the guitarist said. "[Elton] loved that we could take it from a piano band to a guitar band or whatever. I mean, he wrote it on piano, obviously, but then he pretty much said, 'This is a country song...no piano necessary."

"['Jack Rabbit' is] a kind of a fun bit of flak," Bernie said.

"Harmony," the final song attempted at the sessions, was a lush love song to music itself. "If you take that song and read the lyrics to it," Bernie said, "it's really, really banal. But it's got a nice tune to it and the sentiments are quite nice....I'm really a stickler for simpler songs."

The melodic elegy effectively shifted from minor key verses to major key choruses, cloaking the song in an ethereal duality. Intriguingly, the humble track took the longest to actually record, with two full days devoted to the backing vocals alone. "We just went crazy adding all these vocals at the end of 'Harmony'," Dee said. "Different parts here and there. We nicked a few ideas. [It] came out great." Davey agreed. "We stole a lot of Beach Boys ideas....Following the bass line [with our vocals] and that kind of thing....Everything was done track by track by track. By the end of it we were all destroyed, but it was worth it."

Mixing "Harmony" proved nearly as rigorous as recording it had been. "Any closed sound, like an 'Oooo'—a mellow sound—you have to change the actual EQ [equalization] on it generally to make it more present," engineer David Hentschel said. "Because it's a very warm sound that doesn't cut through, it tends to 'swamp' very easily. But then when they go to the open sound of the 'Ahhh', then it's a very bright open sound coming out of their throats, so then suddenly you have to drop the EQ settings down some."

As with most of the songs on these sessions, a potent mix was required to maximize the music's emotional impact. To that end, Gus and his engineer split the recording console duties in half, Gus commandeering the left-hand side of the board, where he could personally push Nigel's fills up and down as needed. "The drums were recorded on four tracks," Hentschel said. "The bass drum was separate. And the snare drum was also on its own track. Then all the rest of the drums and the cymbals were all recorded and mixed down to a stereo pair. So when Nigel hits the tom-toms, Gus would push that up so you get a more dynamic effect for the song. The fill actually leads you nicely into the next section of the song. Gus would do it with the piano fills as well, in between the vocal lines."

After the tracks were all properly mixed, Gus spent an enormous amount of time cutting the record, to get it as loud and vibrant as possible. "I hated the whole vinyl-cutting thing, which was one compromise from beginning to end," he said. "You have no idea how many times I had to cut albums like *Tumbleweed Connection, Madman Across the Water* or *Goodbye Yellow Brick Road* to get anywhere near the kind of dynamics I had originally planned. I knew I would have a problem when it came to mastering, but I would just deal with it then."

His intense efforts reaped immediate results. On June 29, the leadoff single from the sessions, "Saturday Night's Alright (For Fighting)," was released. With a picture sleeve featuring a photograph of Elton downing a bottle of champagne at Rocket Records' launch party a couple months prior, the song quickly shot up to the Number 7 spot in the U.K. In the States, the fiery track landed at Number 12. Backed with a double B-side of "Jack Rabbit" and "Whenever You're Ready (We'll Go Steady Again)," the 45 proved a rare instance when an Elton John single performed better in his homeland than it did in America.

Chapter 16:
Hollywood Bowl

Rocket Records' official U.S. launch was held on July 10 in L.A., on the Western Town set of Universal Pictures' back lot. Elton took the opportunity to clarify the financial situation surrounding the venture. "Everybody thinks that because I'm associated with it, there's millions of dollars pouring into the office daily," he said. "In fact, I didn't invest any of my money in it. We were given an advance from MCA in the States, so we're living off that at the moment. We are poor, and until we have hit records we're going to stay that way. It'll take about a year and a half, I think, to get us on our feet. It's going to be a struggle."

Budgetary concerns aside, no expense was spared for the launch party itself, which featured a lavish luncheon along with a stuntmen-staged Wild West shootout. Guests included disc jockey Wolfman Jack, Al Kooper, Ricky Nelson and the Hudson Brothers, along with a clutch of MCA executives.

Elton, whose hair by this point was orange, pink and green, helped bring the event to a climax by banging out scintillating renditions of "Whole Lotta Shakin' Going On" and "Crocodile Rock" on an upright piano, while Nona Hendryx and Dusty Springfield sang spirited backup.

Wolfman Jack dropped his glass of champagne as he enthusiastically applauded the pianist's efforts. "Can't touch 'im, man," he said, letting loose an appreciative whistle. "Elton's *poppin'*."

Following the party, Elton went into rehearsals for a massive forty-three-date U.S. tour, an outing which would easily shatter long-standing attendance records set by Elvis Presley over a decade earlier.

Elton chartered the *Starship 1* for this outing. A three-engine Boeing 720 with ELTON JOHN TOUR 1973 painted in gold letters across the maroon fuselage, the plane was the largest, most luxurious and expensive jetliner in the world, having been entirely retrofitted with sofas, showers, video screens, burgundy shag carpeting, a pillow-filled lounge ("The bloody 'Hippy Room', Gus joked), a faux fireplace, revolving leather armchairs, and a pair of bedrooms complete with Plexiglas showers and fur-covered beds.

"There were a pair of stewardesses who had been selected for their good looks," said journalist Chris Charlesworth. "Every detail was accounted for." Accommodating forty, the *Starship 1*—a five-star hotel in the sky—also boasted a twenty-foot mirrored bar, complete with brass trim and its own Hammond organ. "It was so glamorous," said Kiki Dee. "There was a chill-out room with a fluffy rug, and they had a bar where you could sit and have a cup of coffee. And they'd have these—so American, so early 1970s—packets of vitamins on the bar so that you could get your daily supply." Whilst sailing 30,000 feet above America, Kiki would begin a romance with Davey Johnstone. "Me and Davey got to know each other on tour," she said, "and our friendship became something more."

With New Orleans serving as home base, the *Starship 1* would fly Elton's entourage from city to city for each night's show.

"When you have your own plane," Chris Charlesworth noted, "you can run the tour from one city. So you stayed in one hotel...and from there in the afternoon they would get on the plane and go to another city to play, and the tour was planned to be within an hour's flight from the hotel city. Set off at 4:00 p.m. in the afternoon to get there and do the soundcheck and do the show, and then after the show it was into the cars, back to the same hotel. The show finished about 10:30, and you are back in your hotel by midnight. The convoys of limousines would have a police escort as well, so you would whiz through the traffic. Through red lights, too. Then they would move to another central point and start again for a couple of weeks."

The communal party atmosphere of the *Starship 1* helped ease Elton's innate fear of heavier-than-air machines. "I loathe flying," he said. "I hate it....I really don't like flying. But if you don't fly, you don't get anywhere. So you just have to keep calm."

The tour began in smaller rural cities—much like a Broadway show opening out of town before ultimately moving on to the Great White Way—so that it could be as polished as possible before hitting the major L.A./New York/Boston markets.

Starting in Mobile, Alabama, Elton provided rock 'n' roll theater at its outrageous best each night, indulging his penchant for unhinged flamboyance with a vengeance. "I felt like I could have carte blanche to do what I want—and I did," he said. "When I put my costume on, that's when I know I'm ready to go onstage. It's such a necessary thing for me. I'm putting on a show for people and I not only want to give them something to listen to, I want to give them something visual to look at as well." Bernie, for his part, was less enthusiastic about his partner's sartorial excess. "I shook my head and rolled my eyes and thought, 'Ok, maybe he'll grow out of this.' It was ridiculous."

Elton played his first American stadium gig early in the tour, selling out Kansas City's Arrowhead Stadium on

August 19. Headlining such an enormous room had the pianist's adrenaline pumping even harder than usual. "At Kansas City, I was so excited I jumped off a twelve-foot stage into the audience and I couldn't get back up again," he said. "I had to run around to the back [stage area], then lap back to the stage. Good Lord."

Each night Elton would make his entrance onto stage each night sporting a twelve-foot cape and a pair of battery-charged glasses which spelled out his name in flashing lights. The extravagant specs were created by Dennis Roberts and Hans Fiebig of Optique Boutique. "This is genius," Roberts said. "This is the most unique pair of glasses ever made in the entire history of the world. They are optically perfect. They are a masterpiece of electronics and engineering."

"[Elton] suggested that it would be nice if we could create a pair of glasses with teeth above and below each lens that would open and close like separate mouths," Fiebig said. "We have not done that yet."

After parading back and forth across the stage with his E-L-T-O-N glasses blinking into the Acapulco Gold-scented darkness, the pianist would exchange these prohibitively heavy frames for a slightly less-outrageous pair—one with working windshield-wipers, perhaps, or an ivory pair surrounded by sculpted dragons. Shrugging off his cape, he'd give a quick nod to his band before launching headlong into a hammering reading of "Elderberry Wine."

Besides the usual hits ("Your Song," "Honky Cat," "Rocket Man"), Elton dug deep into his catalog for rarer treasures such as "High Flying Bird," "Teacher I Need You" and "Hercules." He also premiered several as-yet-unreleased tracks from *Goodbye Yellow Brick Road*, including the title cut, "All the Girls Love Alice" and "Funeral For a

Friend/Love Lies Bleeding," before ending the shows with his "favorite rock 'n' roll number," the Stones' "Honky Tonk Women."

Elton's black grand was draped in a gold-trimmed pink satin cover for the tour, a string of Christmas lights flashing merrily beneath. As always, he treated the instrument like a jungle gym, thrashing the keys with his feet, throwing his leg over the keyboard, and diving beneath to play it with only one hand, lying prone next to the pedals. The rocker was unapologetic for his histrionics. "I think people expect to see a show when I come onstage, and I really enjoy doing the show," he said. "I treat my audiences with respect, and they think a lot of that, because so many bands come on and don't treat their audiences with respect....I think a lot of pop musicians take themselves seriously for no reason at all, because in a hundred years' time nobody's ever going to remember Stephen Stills, Elton John, or any of us."

The opening act chosen for Elton's latest sonic crusade was the oddly-named folk-rock combo, Sutherland Brothers & Quiver.

"We were actually in the studio one day," Gavin Sutherland—the band's bassist and lead vocalist—later recalled, "when we got a phone call, and our manager came in and he said, 'Hey! Guess what, guys? Elton John wants you to go to America. Are you into it?' And it took us about three seconds. Because Elton had just broken big. We said, 'Yeah,' and we got this long list of gigs. It was all these places steeped in the history of rock 'n' roll—words like St. Louis and Chicago and Memphis and Nashville were just like magic to us." Sutherland laughed. "And, I have to say, Elton was a really cool tour boss. He regularly came into the dressing room just to see that everybody was okay, that everything was chugging along. He was very much into a family kind of deal. These were the people on the road with him—everyone from the guys selling the T-shirts out front and the road crew and the light guys and the sound guys and us—and we were all part of the team. And he really *was* a good team player, 'cause he knew that, at the end of the day, if everybody on the tour is happy, if everybody is willing to do that extra bit, stay up that extra bit later or get up that extra bit earlier and go and do whatever needs to be done, then the tour is better. So it was great that there was no bullshit between us, no 'I'm the man' status thing. We were all sort of just British people lost in America, even though Elton was such a big deal. And we didn't realize what a different league he was in till we got over there. Playing to tens of thousands every night, it was really cool. No matter where the tour landed, we were the talk of the town. It was brilliant."

"We had a whale of time," agreed Sutherland Brothers & Quiver's guitarist Tim Renwick, who would later record with Elton on his 1978 album, *A Single Man*. "Besides visiting every major town, we also did masses of local radio promotion and interviews. Fascinating to be able to see the way that record promotion worked over there. This was proof that the music industry was actually being taken seriously—a far cry from the 'What will you do when you're twenty-five?' attitude that we had all become used to in the U.K. for so long. And it's hard to describe how massively popular EJ was in the States. I guess his music just fitted perfectly into the American way of life, people really related to it. Plus he had worked very hard, endlessly touring, to get this sort of acceptance."

Indeed, every show was met by a level of hysteria that took even Elton by surprise. "From now on, I'm only going to make one tour of America a year," he vowed. "People get more excited if you only go once a year."

Not long into the tour, "Crocodile Rock" was added to the set list. Rehearsing it with Elton on piano, the song sounded flat. "I want to play organ on this," he declared, so a Farfisa organ was quickly scared up. It sounded good, yet something was still missing. "[The song also] needs the piano," Elton determined. "What am I going to do?" He turned to Clive Franks. "Hey, *you* play keyboards, right?"

"Yeah, but I'm out here mixing," Clive replied. "What do you want me to do, set up [a keyboard] out here?"

"No, you can come up onstage and someone else can mix that song."

"You're kidding me?"

Elton just grinned.

That night, the press-ganged sound engineer found himself standing nervously behind Elton onstage, sweaty hands plunking out chords on the organ's plastic keys.

"The first night, I'm sure I wet myself," Clive later told journalists Tom Stanton and James Turano. "We'd finish the song and I would run back and carry on mixing the show."

Life on the road wasn't all music. "There were many 'never again' nights," Davey told *musicradar.com*. "Many 'never again' three-night/seventy-two-hour stretches where you literally never went to sleep. And then, what did you do? You did it all over again, twice as hard. We did as many drugs as you can imagine, and drank as much alcohol as we could possibly pour down our throats. But because of the music we played, we were never linked to the drug culture like, say, the Rolling Stones. People didn't assume we could be decadent, even though we were. We never got hassled, and we were twice as hardcore than so many other bands."

The signature concert of Elton's tour happened early in the itinerary, at the open-air Hollywood Bowl, which would serve witness to a visceral spectacle on a scale that would have made Busby Berkeley blush. For Elton, there was no other way. "I don't like to look at groups who come out looking like they've just been drowned for five years at Big Sur. A lot of English people are very theatrical—like the Faces for example, and I think that's why the American kids like it."

"Playing the Hollywood Bowl for us, you try to be cool about those sort of things, but obviously we were like little kids in a sweets shop," Gavin Sutherland said. "It was late at night and it was really warm—Tinseltown—it's kind of unreal, but it's got a magic quality about it. The whole thing was different. It was our first go over there, and it was a bit surreal."

The show—which set Elton back over twenty-thousand dollars to stage—was a true prestige gig. Twenty-four hours before he took to the boards, tickets were trading hands on the black market for up to four-hundred times their face value. Yet no one was consulting their checking accounts on the night of September 7, as multiple searchlights swept dramatically across the Californian sky. As their beams grew parallel, an eerie silence swept over the 18,000 in attendance. The house lights abruptly cut off and Tony King—whom Elton would soon hire away from Apple Records to help run Rocket Records in the U.S. as its general manager—portentously announced, "Ladies and gentlemen, this evening's hostess...the star of *Deep Throat,* Miss Linda Lovelace."

America's *fellatrix du jour* stepped onto stage dressed as a 1920's flapper as an enormous 65' x 28' backdrop of a top-hatted Elton fluttered down to reveal a stage filled with palm trees, a glittering staircase, and five grand pianos perched across a massive back riser, each instrument painted a different hue of the rainbow.

"I'd like to welcome you to the Hollywood Bowl," Lovelace nervously announced. "On this spectacular night we hope to revive some of the glamour that's all but disappeared from showbiz. In the tradition of Old Hollywood, I'd like to introduce some of tonight's guests, very important people and dignitaries from around the world who wouldn't dare have missed this gala evening."

A host of famous lookalikes paraded down the center stage staircase: Queen Elizabeth, John Wayne, Elvis Presley and Mae West. Batman and Robin. Frankenstein, Groucho Marx, Marilyn Monroe, the Pope, and, finally, the Beatles. It was the *Sgt. Pepper* album cover come to life. The star-studded crowd—which included Steve McQueen, Ali MacGraw, James Taylor, Carly Simon, Britt Ekland, Muhammad Ali, Carole King, Peggy Lee, Robbie Robertson, Bruce Johnstone, Carl and Brian Wilson, Mac Davis, Martha Reeves, the Fifth Dimension, Johnny Rivers, Lou Adler and Dyan Cannon—ate up every over-the-top moment.

"This was all Elton's idea," John Reid said. "He's been looking forward to this show for weeks. He wanted it to be a big party for everyone."

Anticipation escalated as the famous lookalikes turned in unison to await the man of the hour.

"And now," Lovelace trilled, "the gentleman you've all been waiting for. The biggest, most colossal, gigantic, fantastic man, and the costar of my next film...*Elton John!*"

Elton made his grand entrance to the triumphant strains of the Twentieth Century Fox theme. Dressed in a white-and-silver cowboy suit drenched in white plumage, a matching three-foot bolero hat, and red-tinted, white-framed specs, the pianist grinned robustly beneath the klieg lights. Raising a fist in triumph, the lookalikes lifted the lids of the five multicolored grands which littered the stage, displaying E-L-T-O-N in giant silver letters. Hundreds of white doves escaped from the instruments, fluttering wildly into the night. "Well, *some* flew out," Gavin Sutherland said. "A lot of the birds were panicked, and the road crew had to get underneath the pianos and bang them, trying to get the bloody things to fly out."

Taking off his hat, Elton sat before his own grand piano, and wordlessly began pounding out the first frenetic chords to "Elderberry Wine," as absolute bedlam descended.

"It was the most spectacular entry onto a stage I and probably everyone else at the Bowl had ever seen," *Melody Maker*'s Chris Charlesworth reported.

A chaotically supercharged "All the Girls Love Alice" soon followed. The song built to an impassioned crescendo as the former Reg Dwight rocked back and forth like a sped-up metronome.

For "Crocodile Rock," Clive Franks made his onstage appearance behind the organ dressed as the song's titular lizard. "That was my idea," he said. "I knew that the show was going to be very outrageous. I thought, 'Well, if they can do it, *I* can do it'....My hair was very long then, over my shoulders. I would pull my hair way back and put some water on it, sort of slick it back. At the Hollywood Bowl, I went to an outfitters. They had the crocodile head, but the last person who used it had ripped the body, it was all torn. I put this darn head on and said, 'Now what?' The guy said, 'We'll cover you in a black cape.' I looked totally ridiculous. I didn't tell anybody in the band about the outfit. And then Elton turned around. If you listen to that recording, he hardly sings a single word throughout the whole song. He's laughing."

During "High Flying Bird," a single dove appeared out of nowhere and slowly circled the audience for the entire song.

"The lights pointed it out," Clive said, "and everyone thought this was amazing choreography. But it was not planned. Then when the song reached its final chord, the dove came to the stage. A true story."

Elton changed outfits halfway through the carefully paced show, emerging in a brown Lurex two-piece suit covered in musical notes of yellow and orange and blue.

"Rock 'n' roll!" he cried, sending his piano bench tumbling across the stage during the crescendo to "Hercules."

Collapsing to his knees, overcome by paroxysms of musical madness, his infectious energy ignited the crowd, which rose as one. "Ninety percent of my act is music," he said later, "the heart of it is music. But the ten percent theatrics is fun. For me *and* for the audience."

The critics lavished the theatrical performance with heartfelt praise. "The crowds were in the mood for rock 'n' roll, and Elton gave it to them with 'Saturday Night's Alright (for Fighting),'" *Sounds* magazine reported, "which signaled the release of more birds as Elton jumped up on the piano to conduct the massed choir of the Hollywood Bowl Auditorium. He [even] played 'Honky Tonk Women', which cooked along like crazy."

"It wasn't so much a rock show as an event," Chris Charlesworth noted in *Melody Maker*. "An event that every ticket scout in Southern California had been anticipating for weeks....The crowd was stunned, the crowd went wild, and that was the tempo for the entire night."

Rolling Stones' David Rensin sounded the only faintly dissenting voice. "We've learned to expect different and novel things from Elton John," he opined. "[Elton] is a man, however, whose patently non-outrageous music often clashes with his glam stage show, something that has progressed from mere acrobatics to a full-blown production. But does Elton need all this? His music holds its own."

"I think we play better in America, I think we play twice as well," the pianist said. "It's this feeling you get when you're over there. Just the whole atmosphere. Bigger, somehow. Better. It all moves fast, it's big-time. England is a bit lazy, isn't it?" Regarding his stagecraft, he explained, "I like to lift them up, drop them down, lift them up again. It's the same as having an orgasm. You try to save the very best till last." He grinned. "It's like fucking for two hours and then suddenly finding out there's nothing you can do after that. It's so emotional and so physical, you don't ever want to do anything else. It's the only point in this business that gives you an adrenaline rush."

Moments after the concert ended, a swarm of screaming teenage girls descended upon Bernie as he was heading toward his limousine. "I was looking behind me to see who they were looking at and just walked straight into them," he said. "Then suddenly I was getting grabbed and kissed....It was all very strange and I was very scared, and by the time I drove away I was dazed and wondering, 'Did I enjoy that or didn't I?'"

The confused lyricist had his chauffeur drive him to an after-show party at the Roxy on Sunset Boulevard. Elton used the occasion to get to know Linda Lovelace. "She's a very nice lady, actually," he told *NME*'s Charles Shaar Murray soon after. "She was far more demure than I thought she'd be. I spoke to her for quite some time and I was very, very impressed. She's been totally misrepresented....I don't give a shit about being misrepresented. If you know down in your conscience that you're all right, you're all right. If you're misrepresented, then you have to fight against it."

The pianist retired to his darkened limousine soon after, lost inside a post-concert, post-party melancholia. Yet his massive momentum kept pushing him ever-forward, with copies of his latest single, "Goodbye Yellow Brick Road," landing in record shops that same day. Backed with "Young Man's Blues," the single reached the Number 6 spot in the U.K. and Number 2 in America, where it was to remain throughout the Christmas season.

The single would quickly prove to be one of his most admired creations ever. "He was mixing his falsetto and his chest voice to fantastic effect," piano rocker Ben Folds noted decades later. "There's that point in 'Goodbye Yellow Brick Road' where he sings: 'on the gro-o-ound...' His voice is all over the shop. It's like jumping off a diving board when he did that."

Chapter 17:
Fred Astaire and Ginger Beard

While in Denver to play the Coliseum, Elton made a brief sidetrip to check out a new studio he was considering recording his next album at. The sprawling 3,000-acre Caribou Ranch housed a state-of-the-art facility in a reconditioned barn 8,600 feet above sealevel, high up the white slopes of the Rockies. Located just north of the small town of Nederland, midway between Boulder and Denver, the cavernous, wood-paneled studio was owned by Jim Guercio, manager and producer of the brass-dominated rock group Chicago. (Intriguingly, the idea to build Caribou Ranch came to Guercio after a series of frustrating studio mishaps culminated in a portion of Blood, Sweat & Tears' "Spinning Wheel" being accidentally erased by an engineer who'd hit a wrong button. "It drove me absolutely crazy," Guercio said.)

Elton was eager to see what the studio, buried in two-and-a-half-feet of snow, had to offer; those at Caribou Ranch were equally as excited about the possibility of working with the world's biggest star. "We heard that Elton John was thinking about recording at our place," studio manager John Carsello said. "We already had Joe Walsh under our belt doing 'Rocky Mountain Way', and we had Chicago—who were a pretty mega-act in their own right—but when we heard that *Elton* was coming, it was like, 'Holy God!' It was

353

amazing. Because he was such a huge star. We were all blown away."

Carsello happily showed Elton around the studio. When he mentioned that "Rock 'n' Roll Hoochie Koo" had been recorded there, the pianist grinned.

"That's cool," he said. "'Cause that's really the sound we're going for."

Equally as impressive, there were three pianos for Elton to choose from—a 97-key Bösendorfer classic grand, a baby grand "rock 'n' roll" piano, and a mahogany 1910 Steinway from CBS Records which had an expansive history, having been used by everyone from the Benny Goodman Sextet with Charlie Christian on songs like the "The Sheik of Araby," to Simon & Garfunkel, who utilized the instrument on "Bridge Over Troubled Water."

Given that Elton's band members would be able to live in their own individual log cabins during the recording sessions, the pianist had only two stipulations—per Gus—before agreeing to book the studio: that Tannoy speakers be installed in the control room, and that Caribou's modular Olive board be replaced with a Neve 8016 recording console. Guercio and Carsello immediately agreed to both. Locating the speakers was easy enough, but the Neve board proved a bit more problematic. After scouring the globe, they were finally able to locate one at Abbey Road, through George Martin's kind assistance. "That thing was bulletproof," John Carsello said. "It was in a big huge box in London, and they had to take it out of the box to fit it on a plane to get it flown over here. So we got it flown over and hooked it up in two days, and I called Gus and told him, 'We've got a Neve, let's go.' And Gus booked the album for that coming January."

Elton was pleased—after the heavily orchestrated Trident years and the pop-flavored Château years, he felt that working in a new studio would give him a much-needed fresh perspective on the entire recording process. "It was time for a change," he said. "Even if we hadn't gone to Caribou, we would still have changed studios....[*Goodbye Yellow Brick Road*] was the finish again. After it came out, I felt exactly like I did after *Madman.* I mean, they're completely different sorts of albums, but they were both like curtains going down."

After playing a well-received show at the Pacific Coliseum in Vancouver, British Columbia—the sole Canadian gig of the current tour—Elton flew to Hawaii for a mini-vacation as well as a one-off concert at the Honolulu International Center on September 17. Though his opening band was not slated to travel with him, the pianist was adamant that they too come along.

"That was another cool thing about Elton," Gavin Sutherland said. "We weren't going to go with him to Hawaii—there was a financial element for us, 'cause obviously we weren't making the same kind of duff as Elton was. But he said, 'No, no, no, you're coming.' And he made sure everything was cool. 'The tour's fixed together,' he insisted. And we thought, 'Nice one, Elton. It was very cool."

Sporting a slight tan from the Hawaiian sun, Elton played New York's Madison Square Garden for the first time that September 23. Before the inevitable encores, Elton and Davey grabbed the stage-shy Bernie, who was standing in his normal spot in the wings, and dragged him onto stage. "I just stood there, absolutely petrified," the lyricist said. "And then someone shoved a tambourine in my hand and I had to stay there and play with them through two encores. Looking back, I suppose it was quite funny, but at the time I was so nervous I almost turned and ran."

Critical reaction to the show—less Bernie's percussive talents—was perhaps best summed up by critic Linda Solomon, who noted that it "was loaded with old and new material professionally executed with frequent casual and urbane conversational *shticks* which his ardent followers were lapping up as if it came from the Mount."

Despite his New York triumph, the protean pianist boarded the *Starship 1* the next afternoon in a foul mood. Why? No one knew. Not even Elton. He was a stranger to himself.

When someone began playing "Crocodile Rock" on the plane's organ at maximum volume, Elton had had enough.

"Shut that organ the fuck *up!*" he screamed.

Nigel Olsson came up and patted him on the shoulder.

"C'mon back," he said. "That cocktail organist is amazing. You've just gotta meet him."

"Fuck *off*, Nige!"

The drummer was persistent, however, and was finally able to convince Elton to follow him toward the back of the plane.

"He came out," Nigel said, "and it was Stevie Wonder playing. On our jet. It was just insane."

Elton hung his head in shame.

"Oh fuck," the Brit muttered. "What an asshole [I am]."

Stevie Wonder joined Elton during the encores of his Boston Gardens gig that night, the two performing energetic renditions of "Superstition," "Higher Ground," "Honky Tonk Women," and "You Are the Sunshine of My Life."

"Stevie Wonder came up to do a few numbers," Gavin Sutherland said. "So what's he gonna use, what's he gonna play? It had nothing to do with us, but we said, 'Oh, Stevie's gonna play with Elton, that's a treat, we'll have to check this out.' And they decided that Stevie was gonna play our keyboard player's Wurlitzer piano, so one of our road crew, Paul Hartley, set it up for him. And Stevie's led out onto the stage, sits down—massive, massive applause from the audience, everyone's got their cigarette lighters out—and he goes into 'Superstition'. And he's really hammering this thing. And Paul notices that, as Stevie's playing, one of the legs of the piano is working loose. So Paul crawled across the stage, thinking that a million people watching couldn't see him, then he gets under the piano and—for obvious reasons—Stevie doesn't know he's there. So Paul starts trying to tighten up the piano leg, but Stevie's swinging his foot and leg around and he's kicking Paul black and blue as he's playing. 'Cause Stevie didn't know it was a person down there. And eventually Paul crawled back off the stage. And we were killing ourselves laughing, 'cause it was hilarious. But Paul weathered the storm. Kicked around by Stevie Wonder. He said, 'I'm black and blue. But it's not so bad when it's someone like Stevie Wonder.' If you're gonna be kicked, you wanna be kicked by a superstar, right?"

The well-received performance was Stevie Wonder's first since a car accident had sent him into a coma months earlier. The Motown star would later credit that night as the beginning of his recovery.

Elton's September 30 show at the Baltimore Civic Center would prove slightly less cathartic. Trouble began early, when the pianist noticed several thick-armed security guards beating fans with flashlights and pushing them roughly to the ground.

"It was really tight security," Elton said, "and this young girl came forward, just to take a photograph, and this huge guard picked her up and threw her like twenty feet in the air. And that was it."

Elton brought the show to a halt.

"You should be home minding your babies," he snarled at the guards. "Now get the fuck outta here or the show's over!"

The guards stared up at him in disbelief.

"*Go!*" Elton ordered. "Get the *fuck* out! *Now!*"

The stunned guards complied. Moments later, the stage was swarmed by hundreds of concertgoers.

The next day, the pianist was banned from playing any Baltimore venues for the next seven years.

A week before *Goodbye Yellow Brick Road* was set to be released, and as a giant billboard of the album's cover was being coyly pieced together on Sunset Strip day by day, MCA hired out KTLA Studios, a local television facility, to hold a press conference to help build excitement for the album. "We booked a room and we decorated it like a Holiday Inn," Gus said. "We sent out special gold-embossed invites to all the top people in New York and L.A. I was going to be introducing Elton in L.A., to the people there, and in New York it was going to be Bernie doing the introducing. We told them Elton was going to be in a hotel room in Greensboro, North Carolina, and it was going to be bounced off a satellite."

In actuality, Elton was planted in a room around the corner, fifty feet from the press; there was never any satellite involved. "We put some flicker up on the screen and then Bernie and I got to say our introductions," Gus continued. "I said, 'So, gentlemen…can we get…are we in touch yet? Can anybody tell me…?' And I've got a mic in my hand and the screen sort of flickers. Some snow comes up and then a bit of Elton comes through and then it disappears again.

'Oh...oh, can you hear me, Elton? Can anybody hear me out there?' And then a voice: 'Yeah, hello, is that you, Gus?'....Elton was really playing it up. Every now and then he'd [tap his headset], 'Hello? Hello? I'm sorry, can you repeat the questions?'"

After twenty minutes of this pantomime, the "press conference" ended and the attendant journalists gathered around a buffet table. A disguised Elton slipped unnoticed into the room in a herringbone blazer and tweed cap, sans glasses.

"He'd been there for at least ten minutes, mixing with everybody," Gus said. "And somebody turned around to say something to him like, 'Can I get you a coffee?' or something. Just standing there with a plate, waiting to get some food. And they went, 'Oh my *God*...it's *Elton!*" The producer laughed. "They loved it, and the fact was we got tremendous press immediately. It paid off like a treat. It was brilliant."

The faux video conference went considerably better than an album-preview event held in Los Angeles the next day, in a private screening suite on the Universal Studios lot. The idea was to present an audio-visual show which mixed colorful slides of the album's artwork with historical photographs of Elton and Bernie as tracks from the new LP played. But things went awry, the sound emanating from the cinema's speakers coming out muddled.

Two songs in, John Reid called a halt to the proceedings.

"Can't you get this fucking thing *together?*" he barked at the lead engineer. "It's a bloody shambles!"

"It's not us, it's the tape," the engineer replied helplessly. "We're doing our best here. We really are."

"Well, your best ain't fucking good enough!"

"I'm sorry, Mr. Reid. It's not—"

Apoplectic, Reid punched the engineer.

"Jesus," the engineer groaned, blood pouring from his mouth.

Reid leapt on the engineer as he turned away, fists flying. It would take four men to finally pull the irate Scotsman off his target.

"Bloody cunts!" Reid screamed as he was bodily removed from the premises.

Days later, the fiery Scotsman attempted to explain his explosive outbursts. "They're isolated incidents," he insisted. "I don't make excuses, I'm not particularly proud of it, but any time anything like this has happened, it's been in defense of Elton or Bernie, not for personal reasons."

Goodbye Yellow Brick Road was released on October 5. The album quickly shot to the top of the charts in both England and America—Elton's second Number 1 album in a row in the U.K., and his third in the States. Even in a chart filled with such future classics as the Who's *Quadrophenia,* Marvin Gaye's *Let's Get It On,* and the Steve Miller Band's *The Joker,* Elton's sprawling, double-vinyl set proved a true sensation, knocking the Stones' *Goats Head Soup* out of the top spot in the U.S. and Canada, David Cassidy's *Dreams Are Nuthin' More Than Wishes* in the U.K., and Neil Diamond's *Jonathan Livingston Seagull* in Australia.

The cover of *Goodbye Yellow Brick Road* was a work of art unto itself, featuring a surrealistic illustration by artist Ian Beck, commissioned after an earlier fine-art portrait of Elton by world-renowned painter Bryan Organ was deemed too uncommercial. Beck had caught the eye of the Rocket Records team through the cover art he'd created months earlier for Irish folk/rock singer Jonathan Kelly's *Wait Until They Change the Backdrop* LP. "The design team at Rocket Records liked that cover," Beck said, "and wanted something similar....I was invited to listen to the master tapes of *Goodbye Yellow Brick Road*. So I spent a happy couple of hours listening to those then-unknown songs— "Candle in the Wind," "Bennie and the Jets," and so on. I was given some typed lyrics and I went away to work on some ideas, to make some rough drawings. Time was of the essence, and there was a very tight schedule indeed. I think I had ten days from beginning to end to design and draw the three outer panels [for the album]." Using his friend and fashion illustrator Leslie Chapman to stand in for Elton for some Polaroid reference pictures, Beck tapped into the recent revival of interest in '30s American design and graphics. "*Casablanca* was re-released at this time," he said, "and I tried to base what I was doing on a kind of dream of Los Angeles [as] the Dream Factory—the shadow of a palm tree, the bonnet of a 1930s car, etcetera." At Elton's request, Beck also included a Teddy Bear and a toy piano on the cover.

Beck's completed watercolor-over-pencil illustration (heightened with chalk pastel and colored pencil) ultimately showed Elton straddling the line between fantasy and reality as he stepped confidently through a poster of Oz decked out in shimmering ruby platforms and a pink silk jacket. Interestingly, a scrap of poster visible in the corner was, in fact, the "Now Showing" poster from the preceding album, *Don't Shoot Me I'm Only the Piano Player*. "That was suggested by Elton's management team," Beck said. "He was moving on from the last album, onto even bigger and better things."

"I've worked with many artists," art director David Larkham later said, "but [Beck's] *Yellow Brick Road* is still one of my favorite covers." Larkham wasn't alone—the cover art for *Goodbye Yellow Brick Road* would go on to win multiple awards, including *Music Week*'s prestigious

Album Cover of the Year. "I disclaimed it and said that the honor for the design really belonged to Mike Ross and company," Beck said. "My agent thought I was mad, but there we are. I felt I couldn't take all the credit."

The album's triple gatefold packaging was equally as impressive, featuring as it did colorful illustrations by Michael Ross, David Larkham and David Scott which helped flesh out each song's unique personality. Intriguingly, some of the imagery provided a link to both the past and the future: the drawing which accompanied "Dirty Little Girl," for one, was based on an iconic *Rolling Stone* cover photograph of Janis Joplin, while the artwork for "I've Seen That Movie Too"—a pair of silhouetted lovers seated before a silver screen—would later serve as the inspiration for '90s cult TV favorite, *Mystery Science Theater 3000.*

Calling the long-player a major pinnacle in his and Elton's career, Bernie described *Goodbye Yellow Brick Road* as "the most important album we've put out, but every album is an important album. You have to keep establishing yourself. As soon as you let go your foothold you're going to go down, and you can't scramble back up again." As for the work's *tour de force* lyrics, he admitted that he had been much more rhythmic and straightforward in the way he put things down than he'd been in the past. "Whereas before—when I was a lot younger—I tried probably to make my stuff a little too arty-farty, and tried to make it not like a lyric because it didn't impress me looking at it. You have to make up your mind whether you're going to write straight poetry or not, and if you want to write lyrics, [you have to] write very basically and make it rhyme and don't try and be clever. But that's the way I learnt, because my earlier stuff is diabolical. I mean, if you look at the stuff on the *Elton John* album—it's so sterile, so cold, because it was written by somebody who was very young and rather naïve. But I've now become a lot looser, and the stuff I write now flows a lot easier. I don't believe that everything's been written, and I don't believe it ever will be." Despite the glossy production, most of the songs on the album dealt with the underside of human nature, a theme near and dear to the lyricist's heart. "I've always been attracted to the dark side," he admitted. "I love darkness, I love sex."

For his part, Elton was rightfully proud of the LP. "*Yellow Brick Road* is like the ultimate Elton John album," he told journalist Eric Van Lustbader. "It's got all my influences from the word go. It encompasses everything I ever wrote, everything I've ever sounded like....It's the ultimate Elton John album."

Reviewers agreed, spilling a lake's worth of ink praising the work. *Record World* labeled the album "a magnificent achievement. Two records of undisputedly brilliant songs and musicianship. Few albums surpass it in spirit and fewer still in intelligence," while *Phonograph Record*'s Richard Cromelin enthused that "*Goodbye Yellow Brick Road* contains some of the most beautiful melodies and music Elton has ever made, particularly in 'Harmony', 'Roy Rogers', 'Candle in the Wind', 'Love Lies Bleeding' and the title song. He may be an incredible egotist, but with this album Elton John establishes himself as one of the leading geniuses of our pop generation. He has proven that he can do just about anything, and do it with a sense of humor and proportion."

Billboard deemed it "a superb set from the British artist who has not missed yet. As always, Elton John's keyboard playing is superb, and his vocals range from the raucous rock he has often been associated with to extremely pretty ballad material....John seems able to sing almost any type of material, from rock to country to Jamaican-flavored tunes, and this double set exposes this even more. As usual, fine words from Bernie Taupin."

Reviewing the album for *Circus*, Janis Schacht noted that "Elton John is back and stronger than he's been on record in many a blue moon. This lush two-record set moves from mood to mood with no apparent effort and a great sense of timing, class and style." John Landau, meanwhile, reported that "Elton John bridges the gap between rock bands and solo acts. He could have gone in either direction but instead chose to go in both at the same time, throwing his version of contemporary vaudeville in for good measure. He has already out-distanced his most pretentious pretender to the throne, David Bowie, as the best of Britain's self-conscious pop stars....Taken a side at a time, the four-sided *Goodbye Yellow Brick Road* is thoroughly enjoyable, the rockers moving out with more gusto than those of many bands that work exclusively in that genre, the panoramic ballads exploring his and lyricist Bernie Taupin's inherent romanticism without apology. The production (by Gus Dudgeon) and arrangement (by Del Newman) touches are almost always interesting and often engagingly excessive. In fact, no matter how far afield he wanders, I always know Elton John is a rocker because he's so damn brazen."

"Goodbye yellow brick road, and hello Elton John, all set to smash a path to the top of the album charts with this superb new collection of songs," *Melody Maker*'s Chris Welch hurrahed. "He and lyricist Bernie Taupin have surpassed themselves with a double album that is bold, adventurous and vastly entertaining....Start shipping the Gold albums and special citations. It's a corker!" *Creem*'s Wayne Robins heartily concurred. "It's a Hollywood album, both superficially and in the grooves. It's closer to the front and less presumptuous than the obsession with the American West that clearly marked John and Taupin as *foreigners* on their earliest albums....It figures that Elton and Bernie would choose Dorothy as their muse this time around. Lou Reed wishes he could relate to Dorothy, without invoking Garlands of self-pity; Bette [Midler] wishes she knew how. Elton knows *The Wizard of Oz* was a movie, and only becomes a lifestyle when you've blown all your options. While Reed couldn't find his way to or from the yellow brick road unless you shot him up with sodium pentothal, Elton's so far past that: just put on your platform shoes and let's mostly rock."

Still, not everyone was convinced. Robert Christgau deemed the album "at least three sides too long," and graded it only a C+, while—with its seemingly oft-misplaced disdain—*Rolling Stone* called the work an "exposition of unabashed fantasy, myth, wet dreams and cornball acts, an overproduced array of musical portraits and hard rock 'n' roll that always threatens to founder, too fat to float, artistically doomed by pretension but redeemed commercially by the presence of a couple of brilliant tracks out of a possible 18." The spun-sugar cascade of "Candle in the Wind" was lambasted by the magazine as "prettily solemn and unbelievably corny, a necrophilia erection for Marilyn Monroe," while "Bennie and the Jets" was deemed a "wimpy *Sgt. Pepper*ish number." As for the soaring title track? "Real wimpy too." The review churlishly concluded, "What are we going to do with Elton John? He can sing, play, emote and lead a band, but he can't get organized. This would have made a lovely, if slightly brittle, single LP. But the best tunes are obscured by drivel and peculiarly bad feelings. Not all fantasies are so rosy. Ugly ones mark a nice guy's record." (A quarter-century on, with revisionistic aplomb, *Rolling Stone* would list *Goodbye Yellow Brick Road* in the upper reaches of its "Top 500 Albums of Rock 'n' Roll" list—along with four other Elton John LPs—noting that "everything about *Goodbye Yellow Brick Road* is supersonically huge," and that, on the title track specifically, "John and his songwriting partner, Bernie Taupin, harnessed the fantastical imagery of glam to a Gershwin-sweet melody.")

Beyond the eloquent harmonies of the myriad hit singles which would eventually be pulled off the disc, a host of album tracks would also become mainstays on progressive FM rock radio. "Grey Seal," "All the Girls Love Alice," "Harmony," "The Ballad of Danny Bailey (1903-34)," and "Roy Rogers" in particular could be heard blasting forth from transistor radios from Maine to Maui, and—given Elton's unrivaled popularity—likely would have all proven Top 10 singles, had they been released in that format.

"I must say, I was sort of worried," the pianist conceded. "Not that the stuff wasn't good, but whether people would be ready for a double album from me. I was worried about the price." He needn't have concerned himself—*Goodbye Yellow Brick Road* would go Gold in its first week of release. Moreover, the LP would stay atop the American charts for two months, remaining in the Top 40 for forty-three weeks, and in the *Billboard* Top 200 for a staggering 108 weeks. Into the twenty-first century, *Goodbye Yellow Brick Road* would be certified five-times platinum in the U.K. and eight-times platinum in the U.S., selling more than thirty-one-million copies worldwide.

Before playing the Mid-South Coliseum in Memphis on October 11, Elton was visited backstage by soul singer Al Green. The pianist was elated, having been a huge Green fan for years. Excited by his visitor's presence, Elton gave a particularly exuberant performance that night, blending past triumphs with the promise of a giddier, more volcanic future.

As a result, over 3,500 fans stormed the backstage area after the show, forcing Elton to barricade himself in his dressing room for nearly two hours.

"This really is like the Beatles, isn't it?" he asked cheerily. "[It's] madness, I tell you."

After a similarly frenzied show at Auburn's Memorial Coliseum days later, Elton hopped the *Starship 1* and flew east to catch Iggy Pop and the Stooges set at Poor Richard's, a small club in Atlanta. The idea had been the brain-child of Rocket Records' Sharon Lawrence. "Elton would get so full of himself," she later recalled to journalist Tony Paris. "The world was his oyster, but he always had to have some little mood, someone didn't care about him or whatever, so I was constantly coming up with stuff [to keep him occupied]." Lawrence thus purchased a lifelike gorilla outfit at a high-end costume shop. "It was a good one, it was really good." Knocking on Elton's door, costume in hand, she informed her famous boss that she was taking him to see Iggy Pop perform. As Elton tried on the outfit, Lawrence mentioned that Dee Murray was taking a shower and might be the perfect victim to test out the veracity of his suit on. A fully done-up Elton didn't hesitate; he raced into Dee's room and burst into the bathroom. "[Dee] was washing his blond hair," Lawrence recalled. "Elton pulls back the plastic curtain, and Dee starts screaming....Elton was just out of his mind with happiness that this had happened."

Elton and Lawrence then headed over to the club where Iggy and the boys were perfoming. "When we got to the club," Lawrence said, "we had to sorta keep Elton covered with a blanket over him [until we got him] in the dressing room, where he was going to change while Iggy was onstage."

Halfway through "Search and Destroy," Elton rushed onto the tiny stage, grabbed the shrieking Iggy in a bear hug, and lifted him bodily off the stage.

Believing he was under attack by a real gorilla, Iggy scrambled desperately out of Elton's grasp and cowered behind the drum set.

"Iggy was just stunned," Lawrence said. "He simply didn't know what [was happening]….I think he was really ready to start crying and call the police or something."

"I was unusually stoned that evening to the point of barely being ambulatory, so it scared the hell out of me," Pop later acknowledged. "I look to my left and a great fucking gorilla is lumbering towards the stage. I was scared. For all I knew, it was a crazed biker on methedrine in that gorilla suit."

Stooge guitarist James Williamson raised his Strat over his head, preparing to bash the gorilla's skull in.

"[Elton] lucked out," Williamson said, "because he was smart enough to take his head off to let people know who he was, just in time."

Making sure that Iggy's drug-addled heart was still beating properly, the pianist bid the Stooges a fond farewell.

"Elton's a swell guy," Iggy enthused, while, for his part, the Brit noted, "I simply can't understand why [Iggy's] not a huge star."

The Elton juggernaut finally spun down in Gainesville, Florida on October 21. During the show, a full can of Budweiser came winging out of the darkness and smacked Elton on his upper back as "Love Lies Bleeding" was coming to its molten climax.

"Bloody Christ!" he snarled, stopping the band cold. "Hold *on!*"

368

Grabbing the beer can off the stage, he stared at it angrily for a moment, then flung it over his shoulder.

"*Saturday*," he commanded his band, who immediately launched into a scorching rendition of "Saturday Night's Alright (For Fighting)."

Gavin Sutherland was watching the incident from the wings, along with the other members of his band. To a man, they were amazed. "We were all in awe," he said. "Not only did [Elton] carry on, but he had the foresight to play a very relevant song and now had the crowd at a higher level. They were roaring."

The next day, with his tour already in the record books, Elton flew out to L.A. to contribute driving piano on Jackson Browne's "Redneck Friend," which would be released as the first single from Browne's *For Everyman* album. Because his U.S. work permit had expired the day before, Elton was forced to appear under the pseudonym Rockaday Johnnie.

"I think there are probably better session pianists around than me," he said with characteristic modesty. "My name is valuable, but there's always Billy Preston, and....I'd rather have Billy Preston playing on [my] record than me. I'd rather have Nicky Hopkins, probably, because...[he's] so good. They can fit in so easily."

While in L.A., Tony King invited Elton to a television commercial shoot at Capitol Records for John Lennon's *Mind Games* album. King, who was dressed as Queen Elizabeth for the shoot, made the formal introductions between the pianist and the ex-Beatle, who was there with May Pang, his loyal consort during his Yoko-less eighteen-month "Lost Weekend." "The two men shook hands," May later noted in her memoir, *Loving John*. "I don't know how the meeting would have progressed under more formal circumstances, but Tony's hilarious getup broke the ice. John and Elton were both very witty men and they began to tease Tony about his scepter, his crown, his dress....They laughed and quipped with each other for an hour, and at the end of an hour they were friends."

Eventually, the two Brits began talking music.

"You know, [career-wise] I'm going through my Beatles period now," Elton told Lennon. "I don't know what I'm going to do when it's over. You stopped at the top, John. You never ran down."

Lennon shrugged. "At least you're aware that you'll peak. It's going to happen, and I'm tellin' you to be prepared. It's advice nobody gave me."

The ex-Beatle took Elton out clubbing later that night.

"We just hit it off and got on like a house on fire," the pianist said. "Obviously, I was very intimidated to meet him, but he put me at ease straight away." As to what Lennon saw in Elton, he surmised, "I think outrageousness and being true to myself and not giving a fuck....I never saw the other side of John, the Harry-Nilsson-drinking side of John, where he'd turn on a sixpence. I only saw the gentle, gorgeous side of John."

"They're both fabulously warm, sympathetic, intelligent people," King said. "I felt that they would have a lot in common. And I was right."

"[Lennon's] probably the first big star who I instantly fell in love with," Elton said. "It usually takes me about six or seven meetings with someone, 'cause I'm very withdrawn. But he's so easy to get on with. The first time we met, we got a Mercedes limousine, and we were driving down past the Roxy, and the Dramatics were there, and everyone's really dressed up to the hilt to go in, all the black people, and they look fabulous. So John and I went past and started going, 'Right on! Right on!' through the roof. It was great."

The two then headed over to the Troubadour, where they ended up jamming onstage with Dr. John. The memorable evening concluded with Lennon twirling a drag queen across a dimly lit dance floor while Elton snapped Polaroids of the pair.

"Fred Astaire and Ginger Beard," Elton teased.

"I'm gonna impound those photos till I get me green card," Lennon replied.

Lennon invited Elton to a recording session days later, as the ex-Beatle was working on tracks for his *Rock 'n' Roll* album with eccentric producer Phil Spector. "[Spector] used to come over to our house to rehearse and he was carrying guns," May Pang said. "And I said to John, 'Does he have to wear these guns? Why's he coming here with guns?' 'Cause he was a short man with a Napoleonic [complex], and he would come in the night when the sun would go down, and he would leave before the sun rises. My girlfriend and I would say, 'Quick! We'd better get a mirror, he could be a vampire!'"

Despite Spector's notoriously outlandish behavior, Elton was in awe of the legendary producer. "I think he did a bloody good job for the Beatles," he said, "because he made an album out of nothing [with *Let It Be*]. If you'd heard the original tapes, you'd know what Spector did for them. The only thing I can really get against him is 'The Long and Winding Road', which was beautiful without strings and all the other rubbish."

Back in England, and with DJM's publishing contract about to expire, Elton and Bernie launched their own publishing company, Big Pig Music, on November 10. The advent of Big Pig gave the songwriters additional stores of confidence. "We want to try and write songs for other people," Elton told

Melody Maker's Chris Welch. "We've just written one for Roderick [Rod Stewart] on his new album [*Smiler*], and we've just written a couple for Kiki." More than anything, he was keen to write a song for Ray Charles, whom he considered to be one of the all-time greats. "It may be a disaster. I may send him a song and he'll say, 'Piss off, I don't want it.' But we're gonna try, because it's something we've never tried before."

Elton joined Rod Stewart at Morgan Studios in London two days later to lend his piano skills to the song which he and Bernie had created for him that spring, "Let Me Be Your Car." The first night of the two-night session—which included guitarist Ronnie Wood and drummer Micky Waller—ran late into the night, as the two friends tossed back glass after glass of brandy while performing a string of off-the-cuff soul classics.

"We just played and played," Elton said. "We spent the whole session singing old Sam Cooke numbers and didn't record anything, and got drunk. It was such a relief to be able to do that."

Elton found himself back in a studio yet again on November 19—Morgan Studios this time—with Bernie, Gus and his band in tow. Their mission: to record a just-written song of gratitude to their fans for the amazing twelve month run they'd just enjoyed. Entitled "Step Into Christmas," the song was especially tailored as a stand-alone single. "It's very echoey, and it's got a lot going on," Bernie said of the chiming track, which purposefully emulated Phil Spector's famed "Wall-of-Sound." "It's a real fun record. I guess it's that thing that everybody wants to make a Christmas single, or Christmas record, at one point in time. It *does* have a great Christmas feel to it. As soon as it begins, you can almost feel the snow falling."

"It had been in our minds for a while," Elton said. "We were going to make a semi-joke single and give it away like the Beatles used to do, but then Taupin said, 'Why don't we make a good one?' and spoilt everything. But the A-side really knocked me out more than anything I've ever done. Because it was so sudden, I suppose."

As for the flip side, "Ho! Ho! Ho! (Who'd Be a Turkey At Christmas?)," Bernie saw the recording "almost like a John Lennon kind of thing—doing all those silly things in it. We just wanted to do something for the B-side, so that was that."

"It's a loon," Elton agreed. "A jolly *larf*."

Elton, Bernie and the band shot a promotional clip for the song the next day, racing maniacally around the studio and generally having a blast, the lot of them high on single malt. It would be Elton's final cocaine-free recording of the decade.

"Step Into Christmas" was rush-released into the record shops on November 26, a mere five days after it had been recorded. In the U.K. it peaked at Number 24, an unusually high placement for a strictly seasonal song, while in America it never officially charted—because of *Billboard*'s policy of not including holiday singles on their Hot 100—though it *did* hit Number 1 on their Christmas Singles chart. Given the robust number of copies it shifted, industry insiders calculated that "Step Into Christmas" would have easily made it high into *Billboard*'s standard Top 10 as well, if not for their arcane rule.

"A smash [hit] denied," Gus said with a merry grin. "I'm bloody sure of it."

Not content to simply bask in the glow of an amazing year, Elton immediately went into rehearsals for a thirteen-show British tour. The campaign was scheduled to kick off at the

Colston Hall in Bristol, where—two years earlier—he had fallen afoul of the venue's management when he'd leapt atop their concert grand and danced wildly upon it. This time around there would be no such issues, as Elton was bringing his own piano along.

"He can bathe in it, for all we care," a Colston Hall official quipped.

Such mundane concerns had, of course, long since ceased to grab Elton's attention. His focus was now much grander, his enthusiasm unbridled. "We'll basically be doing some of the old hits, and a lot of *Goodbye Yellow Brick Road,* much more than we did in the States," he said of his upcoming campaign. "This tour we can really do what we like as long as we don't ignore some of the old ones, which people sometimes shout for. But in the States people want to hear different things—they shout for weird things like 'Levon' and also 'Amoreena' and 'Tiny Dancer,' whereas here, they want to hear 'Rocket Man.' So it's two different sets, really."

Kiki Dee, who had just scored Rocket Records' first Top 20 hit with *Loving and Free*'s "Amoureuse"—a silky love song composed by French singer Véronique Sanson, with English lyrics by Gary Osborne—joined the tour as the support act.

This brief outing would also see another enhancement to Elton's lineup, with the inclusion of noted session percussionist Ray Cooper, who had made his bones playing with everyone from the Rolling Stones and Eric Clapton to Carly Simon and Harry Nilsson. The pianist had been looking to augment his band since Greg Allman had played with them onstage in L.A. a couple months prior, and was keen on getting Ray in the band. "It was amazing, the effect one extra instrument made," he said. "Now we've got to the point where we're really playing well as a band, and we want to expand."

374

Ray Cooper, for his part, was surprised by the invitation. "I looked like something out of a dissident gulag, I just couldn't envisage myself in this band at all," he told journalist Robert Sandall. "I went to see their show in Bristol and there were screaming kids in high heels everywhere. I was mystified. Then I started to think like an actor doing a rock 'n' roll person. And without any rehearsal, at the next gig in Liverpool, I just went on and performed it." The percussionist fit in perfectly, prowling the back of the stage like a rabid panther as he vaulted from marimba to congas to cymbals. A maniac on stage, he often overshadowed Elton with his wildly theatrical behavior. "I see percussion as a watercolor," he said. "You play something, then go back into the shadow, adding color simply where it is needed, but not all over the canvas....I try to be clean, leave space, and give the music a chance to breathe." (Interestingly, Ray's innate sense of theatrics would ultimately lead him to launch— alongside George Harrison—the Handmade Films production company in 1979. Heading the Direction and Production wings of the company, Ray would oversee the production of twenty-three films, including "Time Bandits," "Mona Lisa" and "Withnail and I." He would also work as an actor, producer and/or musician on many classic Terry Gilliam films, including "Brazil," "The Fisher King," "Twelve Monkeys" and "Fear and Loathing in Las Vegas.")

"[Ray Cooper is] like an ax murderer on stage," Nigel said. "Off stage, he's the loveliest guy you would ever hope to meet. He's calm, cool and collected."

Collected or not, critic Simon Frodsham failed to be impressed by the percussionist's efforts. "New member Ray Cooper's assorted percussion fits in well, but I can't help feeling his personality doesn't," he asserted. "His continual rantings and self-obsessed exuberance led me to think he was a frustrated superstar, and therefore had no place playing with King John."

Elton himself begged to differ. "[Ray] takes a lot of work off me as far as the visuals go. I can have a rest every now and again because I know he's having a bit of a leap about."

The press—less Frodsham—proved equally taken with the whole glitzy, hard-charging affair. "Hail Elton! Rock Saviour!" *Melody Maker* proclaimed after a November 29 show at Kings Hall, Manchester. "As an act, the E.J. band has reached a peak in which both show business and musicianship blend happily without overdoing any of the departments," critic Roy Hollingworth reported. "A few flashing lights on the grand piano, a hint of dry ice and the odd taped sound effect, and that's it. The rest is down to Elton, and his right little, tight little band....Hail Elton— saviour of the British rock scene."

Such adulation fueled the pianist's desire to embark on a joint road venture with Rod Stewart. "Rod and I both think that not enough is being put back into the business, and there are lots of things we'd like to do next year," Elton told journalist Chris Welch. "It would be nice to do a package tour, just go on and everyone have a laugh. See six big groups in one night for a pound. There's always someone to say, 'Oh no, it can't be done.' But it *can* be done. Everyone else used to do it—why can't we? We don't need a massive PA system. We could go and tour the cinemas. The Who, the Faces, the Bonzos and us....If you did it for a week—could you imagine the lunatic things that would go on? It would just be insane. And wouldn't it be a great live album?" (Though the tour would never materialize, as late as four centuries later Rod was still holding out hope that he and Elton might hit the stage together. "I'd love to, before we're both in wheelchairs, go out and do a tour together," he said. "I'd love to do that.")

Bryan Forbes released a cinema verité documentary on the pop phenom that same month. Shot in stages throughout the year and entitled *Elton John and Bernie Taupin Say Goodbye Norma Jean and Other Things* (the longish title having been changed from, simply, *Reg*, when Elton balked at that title), the documentary—edited down from 18-plus hours of raw footage—covered the entire song-making process, from Elton and Bernie's initial authorship of a tune, through the process of committing it to recording tape, to its final live incarnation onstage.

Having attended a private screening of the film a week before its proper release, Elton was pleased. "It's not going to be boring," he promised. "It's not going to be like *Mad Dogs and Englishmen*. I can't stand all those films. *Woodstock* was the one good one, and that was it. They're so boring. I came out of *Mad Dogs and Englishmen* and felt I'd done an American tour...The only good thing about it was Claudia Lennear wobbling her tits around, that was the only stimulating thing. And Leon [Russell], his piano playing."

Goodbye Norma Jean and Other Things opened with Forbes' hyperbolic—though hardly off-the-mark—description of the cherubic superstar: "At twenty-six, he walks confidently on five-inch heels where lesser angels fear to tread. Sporting coats, hair and spectacles of many colors. Sometimes as bright and unyielding as the diamonds he wears on his fingers, sometimes plunged deep into self-critical gloom. A child with every toy in the shop and not a key to wind them with. Now possessing no inhibitions, now totally inhibited. Seeking fame one minute, determined to reject it the next. The life and soul of the party, the party destroyer. He does his own hoovering."

Elton proved to be a forthcoming subject for Forbes' camera. "I regard songs as postage stamps," he said. "You lick them, put them on a letter, and you never see them again. I can't remember the lyrics or some of the melodies or chords to the album I made two years ago. Like *Tumbleweed Connection*, I can't remember how any of the songs go. I'm more interested in the ones I've just written." As for concerts? "Kids want to hear noise....They just like to have their eardrums splattered....I think groups just keep going at a certain rate. I think it's very important to start up there, go down, start up. Just keep letting them down, and the final climax comes towards the end."

"One thing I've noticed about you," Forbes said, "[is] that you don't sort of talk the jargon very much."

The pianist shook his head in disgust. "Oh, I can't stand all that. Well, there *is* a jargon in pop music, and it goes sort of similar like, 'Oh man, I really dig your records. I really got spacey all night and stoned, man, and what a trip, man. And then I went 'round to the supermarket and what a bummer man, all those straights there really getting themselves together, trying to hustle some bread together for the weekend.' And that's the jargon, and I can't stand that. 'Spaced out, man. I really feel spaced out.' We've got our own language in the band anyway, I suppose." He laughed. "It's called bad language."

When asked which groups he most looked up to, Elton immediately named the Beatles, for all they'd been through. "I think they got conned and ripped-off like nobody else should have done in their position, because they're such immensely talented people," he said. "And I admire the Rolling Stones because they've been through hell and firewater as well, and they're still together. [They're] the two groups that I admire most."

As candid as Elton was, however, some of the most enlightening statements in the film were made by those closest to him. "He's had darker moods since he made it in the pop world than he ever did before," his mother confessed. "I know when he's in a mood, but I never expect him to be over the moon any time. He's just not that nature." Dick James, meanwhile, noted with a wry grin, "The artist on his way up lives with failure magnificently. I've never yet met one who could live with success."

The documentary aired that holiday season on the BBC, flickering across more than half the sets in Britain. (A longer version cut for the American market would air the following May on ABC-TV.)

Not surprisingly, critics took the opportunity to take Elton down a notch or two in their reviews. "Mr. Forbes seems to be convinced that he is reporting the Second Coming," sniffed the *New York Times'* John J. O'Connor. Of the star subject, however, O'Connor reluctantly conceded that the Englishman was "refreshingly free of trade jargon," and "a talented composer and a marvelous pianist." Critic Tony Palmer noted, "I suspect the real Elton John is neither the glittering dummy, beloved of the fashion magazines, nor a songwriting machine with a noble heart and lofty aspirations," while another reviewer opined, "One gathered little about Elton John himself—reality seemed barely discernible. Yet this young pianist singer...is skeptical enough to send up not only himself but everybody else, including Mr. Forbes."

As the year came to a close, Elton booked himself into the Hammersmith Odeon for a string of Christmas concerts, much in the spirit of the Beatles' holiday shows a decade earlier. Ticket demand was such that Elton was forced to add an additional afternoon matinee performance to the schedule. The public's interest was justified—these shows were unique events, from the set list to the staging, which featured a fully trimmed Christmas tree, special lighting, and a prominent neon sign which proclaimed *WATFORD* beside Nigel's sequined crimson drum dais.

Musically, Elton treated the crowd to seldom-played deep cuts such as "The Ballad of Danny Bailey (1909-34)" and "I've Seen That Movie Too"—along with a spirited instrumental take on "Rudolph the Red-Nosed Reindeer."

"I'm available for weddings, Christmas parties, everything—ten pounds an hour," he joked.

When a desperate roadie attempted to restring Davey's guitar halfway through the final show, Elton launched into an unscheduled solo rendition of "This Song Has No Title," which he playfully dedicated "to Dee Murray's new hairstyle." During the final encore, polystyrene snow began falling from the rafters, jamming up the pianist's keyboard and rendering his instrument useless. By that point in the evening, however, no one in the ecstatic crowd much cared.

Charles Shaar Murray noted in his review that Elton "never fails to put on a great show. Young girls adore him, probably because he reminds them of their last teddy bear. What he loses in sinuous attraction/repulsion he makes up in sheer solid lovableness." Simon Frodsham, meanwhile, wrote that "not only did the concert give the audience a memorable evening of entertainment which would be virtually impossible to equal at another rock concert, but it also reaffirmed Elton John as the country's most valuable asset since the Beatles. Long may he continue."

The feeling was universal. Not only was Elton the top concert draw in the civilized world, but by the end of the year all three major American music trades—*Billboard, Cashbox* and *Record World*—had designated him as their top singles *and* albums artist. Unsurprisingly, his December 22 show resulted in six separate bootleg albums: *Saturday Night's Alright, Christmas Concert, (No Title), Elderberry*

Wine, B-B-B-Benny, and *Rudolph the Red Nosed Reindeer,* all of which had easily sold out by New Year's Eve.

King John had well and truly arrived.

Part Three:
Ol' Pink Eyes is Back

Chapter 18:
Caribou

Elton and his band flew back to the States on January 4 to begin work on the follow-up to *Goodbye Yellow Brick Road*. Bernie already had a title set: *Stinker*. That ironic moniker would soon be dropped in favor of *Ol' Pink Eyes is Back*, with a proposed album cover featuring Elton as Sinatra, complete with a fedora and a glass of scotch, a dinner jacket flung casually over his shoulder. Other titles for the as-yet-unrecorded work were considered as well, though—as the pianist noted—"Charlie Watts' wife had the best one. She wanted to call it *Ol' Four-Eyes is Back*." Ultimately, on the advice of no less than Ringo Starr, Elton would ultimately style his latest LP after the studio at which it was to be birthed: *Caribou*. (The gesture would mean a lot to the studio's manager. "Elton was so cool, naming the album *Caribou*," John Carsello said. "It was unbelievable, it put us on the map. We all felt, 'Whoa, *thank you*.' It was a feather in our cap.")

While Elton was enthused about working at Caribou Ranch, certain members of the band had mixed feelings about their new environs. Dee and Davey at least initially preferred the sun-drenched Château; Nigel, however, immediately favored Caribou, as its extreme altitude allowed for Herculean vocal efforts. "We found that on background vocals we could sing whole octaves higher," the drummer said. "And we didn't realize that until we came down and tried to perform these songs on stage. And it was, 'Shit, I can't hit that note. What happened?'"

These sessions not only marked Elton's first studio album work on U.S. soil, they were also Ray Cooper's first outing as a full-time member of the band. While most other musicians would have given their proverbial first born to count themselves as a band mate for the biggest solo performer on the planet, the percussionist was a bit more circumspect. "Ray kept saying all the way through, 'I'm not really in the band, you know. I'm not actually in it. I'm just here,'" Gus said. "'Don't assume that because I'm here, I'm in the band.'" (So fierce was Ray's streak of independence that, as late as Elton's 2016 LP *Wonderful Crazy Night,* he refused to be listed as an official member of the band.)

After the musical feast that was *Goodbye Yellow Brick Road,* these new sessions were meant to serve as a palate cleanser of sorts. "I'm trying to get things simpler all the time," Elton said. "To get away from arrangements and make things looser. Not as loose as the Stones or the Faces. More like Joni Mitchell."

The self-imposed mandate for a more relaxed process seemed unreachable at times, as the pressure Elton found himself under was greater than ever—he and his band had only ten days to write and record an entire LP's worth of new material before jetting off to play sold-out dates in Japan, Australia and New Zealand. Following that excursion, back-to-back tours of Britain and Europe were already booked for early spring. Losing several days to technical glitches—the team had considerable trouble adjusting to Caribou's monitoring system, which was flat and non-dynamic compared to that at the Château—left only two days for Elton and Bernie to write fourteen songs, and just four days for the band to record them all.

"Our mistake," Gus said, "was to turn Caribou into an English recording studio."

Elton nodded. "I never thought we'd get an album out of it."

The superstar pianist was of two minds as the sessions began. While loving the challenge a new album represented, he was also put-off by the fact that he was back in a studio again already, his contractual hand having been forced by Dick James' ungracious refusal to accept *Goodbye Yellow Brick Road* as two separate albums. The situation caused Elton's occasional black moods to worsen dramatically; his ever-increasing alcohol consumption didn't help matters either.

"I started drinking 100-proof liquor and getting really out of it, for no reason," he said. "I used to obliterate myself....There was whisky floating all around my body."

Aiding in Elton's musical efforts this time around were the famed Tower of Power horn section, which added a fierce R&B kick to the first track attempted, a glistening tango rocker entitled "You're So Static," which Elton labeled "a send-up of groovy, trendy American ladies."

"We thought brass would be really nifty for 'You're So Static'," Gus said. "Somehow or another I came up with the idea of the Tower of Power people. I met them and I talked to Greg Adams, the lead trumpeter and arranger. I said, 'I want you to bring the band up to the office and have them play the parts to me over a backing track.' So about a week later these guys showed up. They get their horns out and I ran the track. I thought, 'Well, I'd better play it fairly loud,' because six of them stood there. I played the track really loud. I mean, the speakers were jumping off the bloody wall. And they hit the first thing and completely drowned the tape out. I'd never heard anybody play that loud or that tight [before]. It was just unbelievable.'"

Pleased by the way "You're So Static" came out, Elton considered the song one of his strongest musical accomplishments to date. "I think ['You're So Static'] could even make it as a single," he said. "It sounds like a Boots Randolph song."

Tower of Power's sax player Lenny Pickett lent his solo chops to the next two tracks as well, bringing a piquant wistfulness to the bright country ode "Dixie Lilly" and, more significantly, a sizzling slinkiness to the most unabashedly hard-edged track Elton had yet attempted, an E-flat rocker entitled "The Bitch is Back."

Far from being a slam on Elton's rock contemporaries, as many critics would soon posit, the cacophonous yet crisply melodic song was actually a tongue-in-cheek dig at himself. The title phrase, in fact, originated from an offhand comment Maxine Taupin had made the November before, when Elton stormed into the living room in a foul mood: "Oh God," she'd sighed. "The bitch is back."

"'The Bitch is Back' is a real raunchy rock 'n' roll number," the pianist said. "That's one of my favorite tracks....It's one of the best rock 'n' roll things we've ever done. We were even going to call the album *The Bitch is Back* [at one point], but we thought it was a bit too passé to call it that. It doesn't really sum up what the album is about."

The hard-hitting track was also a favorite of Davey's, who featured heavily on it. "I loved playing with out-of-phase sounds," he said. "On 'The Bitch Is Back', there are two direct guitars in the out-of-phase setting, and they're tuned to an open-G chord. Then you mix those with two

Flying Vs, and it's a great sound, the humbuckers with the single-coils. You get that bite with the attack."

Dee's "pignose bass"—in actuality a standard bass run through a phased low-end Hog 30 amp, a gift from Gus to Davey—added an additionally strident element, while backing vocals from Dusty Springfield, Jessie Mae Smith, Sherlie Matthews and Clydie King—recorded later in an L.A. studio—helped solidify the wickedly bawdy romp. Though the vocalists were all top-tier talents, the track proved a bit of a challenge for at least one of the singers. "At the time, I was very spiritual," Sherlie Matthews later recalled. "I didn't curse, and all that stuff. And Clydie was the one who contracted the session. So when we got ready to sing the song, she looked at me all apologetically and said, 'Sherlie, I didn't know we were gonna say the word 'bitch' so much,' and I said, 'It's okay, Clydie.'" She laughed. "We were all in long dresses all the way down to the floor and it was the funniest thing, we really got into the song, jumping up and down and moving to the music."

"The music was wonderful and Elton was a wonderful person to work with," Clydie King agreed. "He was all man. He is a man, he knows how to treat a woman. He handed us red roses when we finished singing. I was in heaven. Elton was the gentleman of gentlemen."

The session's signature ballad, "Don't Let the Sun Go Down On Me," came next.

"Elton was just unbelievable," John Carsello said. "My office was off the main cabin that he stayed in. There was his house and then a connecting door that locked, but we kept things open most of the time, and between my office and his house was just a tiny laundry room. So I'd open the door, and I could hear him writing songs. Bernie would show up with the lyrics, just written on notebook paper, and Elton would put them to music. And I could hear him working out songs on his piano, a 1925 Knabe baby grand. And he was cool, you could walk in there and chat. I could hear him singing songs on the piano in there like 'The Bitch is Back' or 'Don't Let the Sun Go Down On Me', which were just amazing, though of course I didn't know at the time what they were going to be."

Nigel's senses were more finely attuned to future classics than the studio manager's were. "It was early morning and I was upstairs in my room, half awake," he said, "and I could hear Elton downstairs…sort of plunking out the first few verses [of 'Don't Let the Sun Go Down on Me']. He seemed to be struggling with the first line of the chorus, when all of a sudden he got it and the whole chorus started to come out."

The drummer ran downstairs and stood beside Elton's piano.

"That's going to be a Number One," he said.

Nigel was excited at the prospect of working on a song with such obvious potential. "I knew *exactly* what I was going to play," he said. "I could hear the finished record when he was writing it."

Bernie was also thrilled by the heartrending paen, which, as far as he was concerned, had perfectly fulfilled its brief. "[Elton and I] wanted to write something big," he said. "I mean big in that dramatic Spector-y style, like 'You've Lost That Loving Feeling'. Hopefully being powerful without being pompous. I'm not sure, with this in mind, it made me fashion the lyrics any differently, although…they *do* seem to have a slightly more Brill Building flare to them, so it's entirely possible that I did."

As the band was cutting the track later that same afternoon, Gus happened upon a uniquely inventive method to add ambience to Nigel's drumming. "He was playing the straight cymbal [at the start of the song]," the producer said, "[and] I wanted to get this thing where I heard the up-close sound but also the sound I hear when I'm down the other end of the room, which is this slight delay bouncing off the walls. So I put a mic down there, cranked the mic up, and it sounded really great. But it wasn't as long a delay as I wanted. Eventually, I climbed a ladder and put the mic in the corner as far as I could away from the drums."

"The Nigel Olsson Signature Sound is basically Gus," Nigel conceded. "The key to my drum sound is the close-miking and the faraway-miking. Gus and I spent days and days on where the microphones should be, how high and far away. The cymbal sound is also the delay you get. People ask me how you get that high-hat sound. It's just the way that high-hat would go with the cymbal."

"It's [also] the way [Nigel] played," Davey added.

Gus then brought in Del Newman to add a noble brass arrangement to the track. "Del was one of the finest," the producer enthused. "[A] genius arranger and a good guy." Newman equally admired Gus' talents. "He was an absolute gentleman," Newman said. "He reminded me of an overgrown public school boy, and he always called me 'squire'. He worked quietly and was very professional in the way he approached the challenges that were presented to him." The arranger was particularly enthused for this assignment, as he felt that "Don't Let the Sun Go Down On Me" was one of Elton's best efforts to date. "It had a grandiose dimension to it, although its roots came from the southern states of America," he said. "The brass gave it weight, and this helped to build the momentum coming in late in the song and adding to the glorious finale....I take my hat off to Gus Dudgeon, for it was one of the best productions to come out of the Seventies."

"Don't Let the Sun Go Down On Me" would prove more of a challenge vocally than it had instrumentally, with the original background vocals—consisting of Billy Preston, Cat Stevens, Brian Wilson and Dusty Springfield—being scrapped after Gus deemed them "too discordant." New backing vocals were then rerecorded with the Beach Boys' Carl Wilson and Bruce Johnstone, Billy Hinsche, as well as the Captain & Tennille's Toni Tennille. "The thing that was kind of amazing," she said years later, "was that when Daryl [Dragon] and I worked in clubs and tried to make our way and tried to get noticed by the record companies, we played in some dumps. We were your friendly Top 40 band, and we did a ton of Elton songs. 'Honky Cat', a ton of them. So it was a very interesting feeling, and exciting, to sing backgrounds on a real Elton John recording."

The spectral results, arranged by Bruce Johnstone and Daryl Dragon, were much more in line with what the producer had originally envisioned for the track. But nailing the lead vocals proved an even more arduous task.

"When Elton sang the vocal track, he was in a filthy mood," Gus said. "On some takes, he'd scream it. On others, he'd mumble it. Or he'd just stand there, staring at the control room."

"I can't fucking get this!" the pianist wailed. "My fucking voice is getting blow-out up here!"

"One more time," Gus insisted. "Just one more."

"Ah, fuck *off!*"

The producer was taken aback. "It was the first time I ever had a serious quarrel with him...Eventually, he flung off the cans and said, 'OK, let's hear what we got.' When I played it to him, he said, 'That's a load of fucking crap. You can send it to Engelbert Humperdinck, and if he doesn't like it, you can give it to Lulu as a demo'....When he sang the line 'Don't discard me', he put on this really ridiculous American accent, so it came out: 'Don't *diszgard* me.' I was going to bury it in the mix, but Toni Tennille said, 'No, leave it. It sounds good.'"

The band headed off on a snowmobiling expedition near the Continental Divide while Elton labored over the next track largely alone. "Ticking" was a harrowing, emotionally complex seven-and-a-half minute mini-movie which detailed a murderous Columbine-like rampage undertaken by an unbalanced young man. Powered by Elton's highly syncopated grand piano—the only instrument to feature on the recording beside a bit of understated ARP synthesizer work courtesy of David Hentschel, who was co-engineering these sessions alongside Clive Franks—the ennui-soaked song would unfortunately prove apocryphal. "'Ticking' was probably the deepest lyric [Bernie] has ever written," Elton said. "I don't think it's pretentious, it's just a very heavy lyric."

The song's intricately aggressive music necessitated that Elton record the vocals at the same time he laid down the piano—the first time he'd had to do so since "Talking Old Soldiers" back in 1970. "I would think so much about the voice that I wouldn't play the piano right," he said. "Gus was always a stickler for separation, but I had to tell him, 'Look, the only way we're ever going to get this thing done is by doing the voice and piano together, and forget about the leakage.' It would only be the voice leaking anyway, so why care?"

The concurrent voice-and-piano methodology which "Ticking" employed was imperative, given Bernie's asymmetrically unbalanced lyrics. "['Ticking'] was just line after line," Elton said. "I've gotten so used to splitting things up into sections, I don't even think about it anymore. It helps that I can sometimes say eight words in one line whereas earlier in the song, where it's the same melody, I've said only three. It's just a matter of..." He paused. "I think I'm an expert on squeezing words into lines."

"Sick City" came next. A sauntering rocker, the track was ultimately relegated to B-side status, despite the hours of vocal experimentation the team invested in it. "We tried something weird on 'Sick City'," Gus said. "We tried doing the backing vocals backwards. We spent a hell of a long time on it and it was a complete waste of time because [Nigel, Dee and Davey] had to learn what 'sick city' sounds like backwards. In other words, we recorded it forwards, then we turned it around and listened to it. And it was coming out, 'Ahy-is-*cus*, ahy-is-*cus*.' So they were trying to sing 'ahy-is-*cus*' all together. It's difficult enough to get three people to start and end at exactly the same point in any one phrase in the best of times. But when it goes, 'Ahy-is...'? When it has to fade in? We were trying to get it to sound like it was some kind of 'sick city' weirdness. That was an experiment that didn't work."

Lyrically, this blatant critique of groupies and hangers-on was very much a product of road weariness. "It was a very cynical sort of song," Bernie admitted. "Probably another potshot at New York. I've had this love-hate relationship with New York. Actually, I *like* New York, but there's no way I could live there."

"I've Seen the Saucers" was, by contrast, an impeccably catchy tale of alien-abduction accented by Ray's delicate congas and otherworldly water-gong. The elegant track underscored how maleable Nigel's approach to drumming could be, depending on which studio he was recording at. "Caribou Ranch was the difference," he said. "The sound was so much different. Gus had me in this little box....At Caribou it was so much different from the Château, because the Château was closed in, with carpet on the floor. At Caribou, there were wood floors, glass, rock. The control room at Caribou was unheard of. Jimmy Guercio wanted this thing to look like an old western movie set, [with] a rock fireplace in the control room. The room was so much different because of the ambience."

The effect of that aural complexion was also on full display on "Grimsby," a whimsical look at a less than glamorous seaport on the Lincolnshire coast.

"'Grimsby' is the name of the town where Bernie was born," Elton said. "It's a fishing port. A very dull town. Grim. I once said to Bernie, 'Wouldn't it be nice to do a song about Grimsby?' It's such an absurd idea to write a song about Grimsby, it's one of the most putrid places. It's not romantic in the least. The song is up-tempo, I think it sounds like the Beach Boys. Anyway, Randy Newman did a song called 'Cleveland', so I thought we should do the English equivalent."

Fair to say, "Grimsby" hardly set Gus' creative heart aflame. After Elton had played it for him on the piano for the first time, the producer was flabbergasted. "I thought, 'What the fuck can I do with *this?*' You would just hope that someone else would have an inspired guitar solo. The brain just doesn't kick in. It's a bit like digging a road then." Still, Gus kept his critique to himself. He was all too well aware that—even with someone as prolific as Elton—getting a composer to execute extensive rewrites was problematic at best. "If you tell a songwriter, 'I think *this* section's great, and *this* section's great, but you could really do with a better verse,' or whatever, they always say, 'Yeah, yeah, you might have got a point, I'll do something about it.' But they never do. What they do is go off and write another song, which they think is better. So you never get from A to Z. You always get as far as K, and then they stop. It drives you mad."

Gus' complaint was ultimately a minor one, for, in general, he was ecstatic about the musical manna which Elton and his band continually reigned down on him. "The feeling that an incredible master is just around the corner is incredible," he said. "When you know it's coming, and you're encouraging it, pulling it out—that's the most exciting thing for me....When you *know* that moment is just around the bend, it's the same type of feeling that you get just before an orgasm." With a forthrightness that rivaled Elton's, the producer admitted that everything he did in the studio was done only to satisfy his own personal tastes. "If I had to constantly worry about what the public wants and what public taste is, I wouldn't want to do it....When I push the button and tell Elton he can do better than that, and he says, 'Right, I know. I'm mucking about'—it's as if he were singing for me personally. [And] when Davey plays a great guitar solo and starts roaring, it's as if he were doing it for *me*, as a friend, and that's what it's all about."

A tune which *didn't* prove particularly euphoria-inducing was the acoustic guitar-driven "Ducktail Jiver," a vintage "Hercules"-esque rocker about an aging '50's outcast desperately trying to stay relevant.

A freewheeling rhythm track and lead vocal turn were quickly recorded, yet the potentially intriguing song was shelved. "I put it to one side because I thought it wasn't anything terribly special," Gus said. "Maybe [it was] a mistake. Who knows?" (Intriguingly, Davey Johnstone would revisit "Ducktail Jiver" over forty years after the fact, laying down a guitar solo to complete the track for possible inclusion in a future retrospective release.)

The team quickly rebounded with the elliptically buoyant "Solar Prestige a Gammon," a nonsensical, Continental-steeped confection in a similar vein to the Beatles' "Sun King," and an anagram, intentional or not, of "Elton's Program is a Game." With incomprehensibly fragmented lyrics, the song was written as a direct response to the over-analysis their songs routinely received.

"I love it, because I always suggest things that Bernie Taupin's going to get knifed in the back for," Elton said of the track, which he merrily sang in a faux-operatic voice, to further confuse matters. "I thought it would be great to write a song with English words that didn't mean a thing, but that sounded fantastic when put together....It's really just a fun song, something like McCartney might do....[And] it has five fishes in it, so people might think it's religious. People are always reading things into our music. Especially in [America]. They think there's hidden meanings in everything. Bernie's going to get crucified for it."

"Pinky," a traditional John/Taupin ballad detailing the frozen frolics within Bernie and Maxine's Caribou cabin, "Running Bear," was a more straightforward offering, and a sequel of sorts to *Honky Château*'s "Mellow."

"The words are really nice on this one," Elton said. "It's very influenced by the cold winter in Caribou."

The romantic track was followed by the astoundingly inventive "Cold Highway," which—like "Sick City" before it—was doomed to end up as B-side. Featuring multiple time-signature changes which perfectly matched the darkly twisted lyrics, the slinky rocker told the story of a childhood friend of Bernie's who had lost his life on an infamously treacherous road in Lincolnshire. "It was basically a stretch of highway where I came from in England that was known as an accident 'black spot'," the lyricist said. "We used to always make jokes about it when we were teenagers. Then one day one of our friends was actually killed there, and it became a grim reality."

"Stinker" provided a tonal counterbalance, dealing as it did with a morally questionable skunk. The thumping blues tune, which featured Tower of Power's Chester Thompson on organ, was an offhand homage to the Beach Boys' "Sail On, Sailor." "The biggest influence on me from a production standpoint," Elton later told journalist Timothy White, "was Brian Wilson. I mean, I love the Beatles, I love their records, but I don't think they influenced me as songwriters. The Beach Boys sound…[was] a much bigger influence. Brian Wilson was *the* genius and always will be.…Production-wise, his idea of initially using echo vocals on a track and then using dried vocals, I mean it completely changed the face of recording vocals."

Though the band knocked out the music for "Stinker" in one take, Elton struggled with the lead vocals, ultimately having to record them six separate times—a frustrating anomaly for the normally assured Brit. "If you do the vocal more than four or five times, you start to think about it too much," he grumbled. At the end of the day, it was all part and parcel of the strange circumstances surrounding the sessions as a whole. "To be honest, for a time I thought I was going to have to redo *all* the vocals on *Caribou*. I *did* redo one: 'Dixie Lily'. Making *Caribou* was a very trying experience."

With frustration levels running high, it was a small kindness that the pianist once again made himself scarce when not actively recording his own parts. "Elton never went to *any* session other than a session that he was physically working on," Gus said. "He never went to any orchestral overdubs. No backing vocal sessions, no guitar overdub sessions, no synthesizer overdub sessions, no percussion overdubs. No mixes. Not even mastering. He didn't even get involved in the choice of running orders....Because he trusted people. He trusted people to get on with it, which was great. It's actually very unique. Not many people in this industry trust anybody to do anything properly."

Chapter 19:
Pinball Wizard

As the Caribou Ranch sessions were drawing to a close, something unexpected happened in the larger world: Detroit's leading urban station, WJLB, began playing "Bennie and the Jets" on heavy rotation. "Within three days it was our number one request item," disc jockey Donnie Simpson said. "For the three or four weeks during its airing, eighty-percent of the requests at WJLB were for 'Bennie and the Jets.' It was just phenomenal to see that whole thing, that whole scene take place."

Soon enough, other black-oriented stations began picking up on the song. Taking note of the phenomenon, MCA promotion director Pat Pipolo rang Elton up and urged him to release "Bennie and the Jets" as his next American single—instead of "Candle in the Wind," which was already sitting primly at the Number 11 spot in Britain.

The pianist was unsure, having never imagined "Bennie and the Jets" as a hit.

"Are you prepared to put your career on the line [for this release]?" Elton asked.

"Well, no, not really," Pipolo answered. "But I think we should release it as a single. You'll be an R&B artist as well as a pop artist."

That idea appealed greatly to the longtime fan of black soul music.

Released in the U.S. on February 4, 1974, "Bennie and the Jets," backed with "Harmony," slammed into the top of the charts in a matter of weeks, becoming Elton's third million-selling single in six months and his first smash record on the soul charts. "Sometimes an artist doesn't know what's good and what's bad," Elton mused. "He knows what he feels about a track, but he doesn't know how to pick singles."

The centrifugal force of Elton's ceaseless momentum carried him to every conceivable corner of the globe. After a successful jaunt through Japan, he flew straight on to Australia for a series of highly-anticipated shows. "I'm the balding Elton John now," he told waiting reporters as he leaned nonchalantly on a silver-tipped cane, over $200,000 worth of personal baggage stacked neatly behind him. His luggage was epic indeed, with one trunk dedicated solely to his glasses, while a second housed his hats and a third accommodated his stack-heeled shoes. His total excess baggage charges raced easily past the $6,500 mark.

The investment was more than justified, as Elton summarily broke attendance records up and down the coast. At the South Melbourne Football Ground alone, over 19,000 fans clamored to see the flashy superstar in action. Critic Tony Wilson was as impressed as the punters in the cheap seats, gushing how Elton's piano playing was "comparable to the venom of Jerry Lee Lewis, with at times the delicate touch of a classical pianist." In Sydney, a record-setting 25,000 souls came out to witness the Brit's concert at Randwick Racecourse, a superior performance which was soon being bootlegged as *Live in Australia*.

With hardly a moment to catch their breath, Elton and his band flew off to New Zealand for a one-off concert at the

35,000-seat Western Springs Stadium outside Auckland; demand for the show was so intense, tickets for the February 28 performance sold out in less than two hours.

The stage seemed set for another triumph. Yet the silver clouds of unstoppable success would soon reveal a very dark lining, as an afternoon press reception at a colonial pavilion in Parnell—organized by Festival Records, Elton's Australasian label—turned to custard, in the parlance of the locals. When the bar ran out of whisky, John Reid turned his not inconsiderable ire on reception organizer Kevin Williams, labeling him an incompetent fool while tossing a glassful of champagne in his face. Appalled by Reid's actions, Judith Baragwanath, a socialite and writer for Auckland's *Sunday News,* called out Elton's manager on his behavior.

"How *dare* you, you rotten little poof," she exclaimed.

Reid responded by punching her in the face, blackening her left eye.

"A reflex action," he later claimed, before adding, more reasonably, "It's a despicable thing, to hit a woman."

Elton's entourage was rushed back to their hotel, but the drama wasn't quite finished. At an after-party nightclub reception for teen heartthrob David Cassidy later that night, journalist David Wheeler, a friend and colleague of Baragwanath's, promised that Elton's group were all marked men.

Elton grabbed Wheeler by the shirt and forced him against the wall.

"Who the *fuck* do you think you are, you no good son of an Irish lephrechaun?" he growled. "*Nobody* threatens my manager!"

When Wheeler attempted to fight back, Reid interceded, knocking the journalist to the ground and chipping his tooth.

"We left the club posthaste," Elton said, "and were all physically threatened that anyone to do with the Elton John tour had better watch it. Then when we got back to the hotel we got a phone call saying, 'There's a carload of people on the lookout for you, so just stay inside your hotel.'"

Early the next afternoon, on the day of Elton's Auckland show, Reid found himself under arrest on assault charges. After a twenty-minute hearing at Auckland Magistrates Court, Reid was found guilty of assault, while Elton, dapper in a sober slate-gray suit, was charged fifty dollars and released. Refusing to take the stage with his manager in jail, the pianist was able to get Reid temporarily released. Yet as soon as the concert had ended, the Scotsman was taken back into custody and sent to Mount Eden Jail, where he began serving a 28-day prison sentence.

"We got the largest crowd in New Zealand history for one show, thirty-five thousand people, one percent of the population," Elton said. "And yet that one incident ruined it."

"I guess [Reid] was a good manager, but he had a very aggressive streak," Clive Franks later reflected. "He was a Jekyll and Hyde character. Very similar to Elton in that respect....From one day to the next they were different people. There were times when John was a friendly and loving person, but that doesn't excuse that other side....I've seen him almost strangle a hotel receptionist because his room wasn't ready."

"John certainly wasn't a normal person," Stuart Epps agreed. "He could be the best guy, incredibly generous and great. Or he could be the total opposite, and suddenly he's trying to strangle you and stuff."

Disappointed by the New Zealand incident, Elton scrapped a long-planned vacation in Tahiti and flew grimly back to England instead. Not long after landing, he impulsively canceled an imminent seventeen-date British tour which had been scheduled months before. "When all the trouble started and my manager was sent to prison, I had time to think," he said. "The thought of going on another tour, for the time being, was impossible. If we didn't stop now, I think it would have been the end....I'm the sort of person who'll say yes to things a year in advance, and then when it comes round I'll think, 'Fuck, I don't wanna *do* that.' I've been told that I've got to calm down on decisions, be told what to do for a change." Not for the first time, the superstar contemplated retirement. "Honestly, I'd really be happy to have my own record shop....My idea of happiness would be to stand behind the counter at a place like Tower Records in Los Angeles to see what people bought."

While Elton suffered through his personal dramas, Bernie found himself weathering trials and tribulations of his own. Being married to an American girl who wasn't nearly as enamored of the English countryside as he was caused a rift which the lyricist hoped to heal by selling his modest Piglet-in-the-Wilds and moving instead to the posh London suburbs. Toward that end, he purchased a Georgian mansion on the Wentworth Golf Course called *Bourne Lodge*. "I went from the sublime to the ridiculous," he later told author Philip Norman. "We'd been living in a tiny four-room cottage. Now we'd got...this enormous place...just down the road from Elton at *Hercules*. Far grander than his place. I mean, he was just living in a bungalow. I was living in a hunting lodge. I think he was a bit put out by that."

Miffed or not, Elton soon hired on a new employee, twenty-seven-year-old chauffeur Bob Halley. The first time Halley laid eyes on Elton was when he arrived at Heathrow Airport, dressed in multicolored feathers and six-inch platform boots. "I remember driving very carefully down the motorway," Halley said, "and all of a sudden I heard Elton turn to John Reid and whisper, 'Can't he go any faster?'"

In time, Halley would become one of Elton's closest friends and most trusted confidants.

Elton realized a lifelong ambition that May when he joined the Board of Directors of his beloved Watford FC. Though he'd already been a vice-president of the football club for several months, that position—an honorific, at best—didn't fire his imagination the way a directorship did. "Now I'm a vice-president, but it isn't enough," he'd noted only weeks earlier. "Anyone with £53 can become one of those. If you want to help the club you have to put money into it, and to do that you have to be a director. I'd dearly love to put some cash into the club. They are such a nice bunch of lads, and despite the problems they've been having, the morale is pretty good."

Elton's business agent, Vic Lewis, never saw the rocker as excited as he was the day he drove him to Watford to finalize the details of his directorship. "He was over the moon," Lewis said. "With a grin which spread from ear to ear and back again, [Elton] told me, 'This has to be the happiest day of my life.'"

Indeed, Watford was truly where Elton's heart lay. "I love it as much as music itself," he conceded. "It's like erasing five or six years of my life, and I'm here as if nothing had happened."

Concurrent with his increased involvement with his boyhood soccer club, Elton took thirteen-year-old Maldwyn Pope, a recent Rocket Records signee, under his considerable musical wing.

"Elton was something like a big brother," Pope said. "A lot of stuff had come out in Britain around that time about inappropriate relationships between famous people and young people, but he was just fantastic, there was nothing ever inappropriate. And he always wanted to do special things. I think he just likes promoting young talent and encouraging it, for no other reason than I think he realized he needed that support when *he* was young. I think it brings out the father-figure in him, or the big-brother-figure, and that certainly happened with me."

Between sessions for Pope's first album, produced by art director David Costa, Elton drove the pubescent singer over to Vicarage Road, home to Watford. "As we travelled," Pope recalled in his memoir, *Old Enough to Know Better,* "Elton played a copy of Paul McCartney's album, *Band on the Run.* At one point, he stopped the car and turned the volume up. He wanted to point out some out-of-tune guitars on the song 'Bluebird'. Elton couldn't believe that they had let it slip through."

Once at Watford, Elton and Pope joined the first team on the main pitch, running through drills alongside the professional athletes, and even taking their turn heading balls toward the goal from the manager's crosses. Pope was impressed. "I think the only other person Elton had taken training at Watford was Rod Stewart—who was also a massive football fan—so I was in quite a select band of people. It was fantastic."

Hours later, as they were motoring away, Elton ejected *Band on the Run* from his car's stereo and cranked up BBC Radio 1 instead.

"In which year did Elton John have a U.K. hit with 'Your Song'?" the disc jockey asked.

"1970!" Elton barked at the radio. "*1970!*"

"Wasn't it 1971?" Pope asked.

"1971," the disc jockey said.

Elton just shook his head.

Elton headed to Ramport Studios in London days later to record "Pinball Wizard," his lone contribution to the upcoming Ken Russell-helmed film, *Tommy*, based on the Who's famed rock opera.

Everyone in the pianist's camp was excited about the project. "We knew we had the best song," Gus said.

Though the rest of the soundtrack would be performed by the Who, Elton insisted on using his own band—and Gus' matchless production abilities—on "Pinball Wizard." As a special treat, he invited Maldwyn Pope along to attend the sessions. "He told me he had something unique set up, but he wouldn't tell me what," Pope said. "I was staying at a hotel in Central London, and a black cab came and picked me up and took me to this big house, and I knocked on the door, and it opens and it's Pete Townshend wearing a jumper knitted by his wife on her knitting machine, and it said: *Pete Townshend, Pete Townshend, Pete Townshend*....[There were] a lot of *Pete Townshend*s."

Not surprisingly, Elton was slightly more glamorously attired. Wearing the same tiger-skinned jacket and pink-framed glasses which would soon grace the cover of his upcoming *Caribou* album, Elton led his band through "Pinball Wizard" in just two takes. "They had a piano booth there on the left-hand-side of the studio, so it was isolated," Pope later recalled. "And they sat me above that so I could watch Elton. I can still see his stubby little fingers playing [the opening chords to] 'Pinball Wizard'. Ken Russell, the director, was there too, but the scariest thing for me was Keith Moon, because his eyes were just wild. Pete Townshend was trying to placate him all day, just to make sure he didn't go off."

Elton knocked out his lead vocals while sipping from a glass of Laphroaig single malt, completing the task in only ten minutes. Nigel, Dee and Davey then knocked out their backing vocal duties in less than an hour.

The Who were astounded by their focus and speed.

"It was a revelation," Pete Townshend later noted in his autobiography, *Who I Am*, "how quickly and efficiently Elton and his band worked, nailing a driving track with solos, lead and backing vocals in less than four hours."

Indeed, Elton's involvement in the project had more than a whiff of the inevitable about it, as he'd originally declined Russell's offer to appear in the film. "The role was originally offered to Rod Stewart," Elton said, "and he said to me, 'What do you think?' I said, 'Oh no, not a film now. Bloody hell, what are they going to do next? It will be a cartoon series soon.' Rod and I are friends and kind of rivals. Then they romanced me so much that in the end I did it, because Pete Townshend rang me up....So I told Rod not to do it and I ended up doing it. He was really furious, and rightly so. I don't think Rod's quite forgiven me for that." (Rod attempted to exact his own low-key vengeance months later. Invited over to Elton's house for dinner, Rod bought the cheapest wine he could find, emptied out a bottle of *Le Pin,* and poured the rut-gut in instead. With maximum ceremony, he presented the bottle to Elton, who spent a good ten minutes expounding on the superiority of the vintage, until Rod fell about laughing and called his friend a "right prat.")

Any potential fall-out with Rod was more than compensated by the opportunity to work with Pete Townshend, whom Elton had long admired. "Pete has always been a very big supporter," he said. "I remember Pete sitting out there when I first started, and I'm a great believer that if people have done you great favors or have been supportive, you should do things back for them."

Shooting his scenes for *Tommy* at the King's Theatre in Portsmouth a fortnight later, Elton performed in four-foot-tall Doc Martens which were attached to his legs with metal braces. "I can't stand heights—the experience was dizzying," he said. "I'm all right in an airplane if I'm 35,000 feet, but when you're sort of five feet off the ground and have to walk on them, and Ken, of course—the more I was terrified, the more he would make me walk on them."

With his *Tommy* duties completed and his fourth-division-dwelling soccer team deep in the red, Elton's first official act as a director was to volunteer his services for a benefit concert on Watford's Vicarage Road grounds to help pay off the clubs substantial debts. "I'm doing this concert in spite of canceling my British tour because I have supported Watford ever since I was a kid," he said. "I wouldn't like to see them go under, and for this reason I will do everything in my power to save them."

As a token gesture of apology for usurping the Pinball Wizard role, Elton invited Rod Stewart—whom he called "the best rock 'n' roll singer I've ever heard, as well as the greatest white soul singer"—to join him onstage on May 5, in front of 31,000 rain-soaked fans, more than quadrupling the number of fans who normally attended a Watford game.

After an opening forty-five-minute set from the Scottish hard rock outfit Nazareth, Elton took to the stage in a specially commissioned suit designed in Watford's colors of yellow and black, and sat jovially behind his Steinway grand.

Halfway through the performance, Elton unveiled a cover of the Beatles' classic, "Lucy in the Sky with Diamonds." Though he'd been debating about recording a cover of the Stylistics' soulful '73 smash "Rockin' Roll Baby"—produced and co-written by influential Philly maven Thom Bell—he decided that afternoon to instead record the Beatles song, after witnessing the tremendous ovation it received. "It went down incredibly well, staggeringly well," the pianist said. And, as he'd later point out, "the Stylistics song had a line about an 'orthopedic shoe' that wasn't natural for me to sing [anyway]."

A white-silk-suited Rod Stewart then came on to help close out the show in style.

"Good evening, sir," Elton said, grinning from behind his satin-draped piano.

"Good evening, sir," Rod replied, bowing regally. Grabbing a crumpled lyric sheet off the piano, he sang a duet with Elton on "Country Comfort" before launching into rave-up versions of Chuck Berry's "Sweet Little Rock 'n' Roller" and Jimi Hendrix's "Angel."

As Rod's brief set closed, Elton led the soggy crowd in a gleeful chorus of "Singin' in the Rain," before bringing the festivities to a proper close with a thunderously multi-textured reading of "Saturday Night's Alright (For Fighting)."

Fair to say, everyone left the muddy grounds very wet, and very satisfied.

"Don't Let the Sun Go Down On Me," the leadoff single from Elton's upcoming *Caribou* LP, was released in the U.K. a couple weeks later, on May 16. Backed with "Sick City," which would prove popular enough in its own right to garner significant radio airplay, "Don't Let the Sun Go Down On Me" peaked at an admirable Number 16 in Elton's homeland.

Two days on, the pianist performed a benefit concert at the Royal Festival Hall, which was intended to be a curated overview of his career ("An evening of semi-nostalgia") from his DJM days right up through "Don't Let the Sun Go Down On Me."

"The Festival Hall gig will be something like the History of Elton John," he promised, "and we'll go through from beginning to end. Sorry—to where we are now." As he and Gus were drawing up the set list for the show, Elton made a mental inventory of all the songs he'd played onstage over the last four years. "It came to eighty-five songs," he said. "I don't think there's any other act that can say that."

After a taped rendition of "God Save the Queen," Elton appeared on the Royal Festival stage alone at his piano.

"I'm the support act," he joked. "[And] this one is a song which was the first song that Bernie and I ever really felt excited about that we ever wrote... and it's called 'Skyline Pigeon'."

After an impassioned reading of the plaintive hymn, Elton was joined by Dee Murray and Nigel Olsson, the three recreating their original 1970 trio for a soulfully thunderous "Border Song." Davey Johnstone and Ray Cooper then filled out the ranks for such latter-day fare as "Honky Cat" and "Crocodile Rock," with the percussionist's fervent duck-call solo capably replacing an entire horn section on the former.

The performance was a success in every respect, raising more than £10,000 on behalf of the Invalid Children's Aid Society. Recorded by Gus Dudgeon, it would later become the "Here" portion of Elton's second live offering, *Here and There*, two years hence.

After the show, Elton and his entourage dined with Princess Margaret and Lord Snowdon at Kensington Palace. The unusual evening culminated with the grateful princess presenting the pianist with a pair of stuffed leopards as a "thank you" for his charity efforts.

"The whole night was very odd," Bernie said. "The thing that amazed me was that there didn't seem to be any kind of security at Kensington Palace, other than a policeman at the gate. You just rolled up, knocked at the door, and were let in.

The other thing I remember is that, getting out of the car, I split my trousers at the crotch. I had to borrow one of Lord Snowdon's dressing gowns, while a lady-in-waiting sewed them up for me."

Elton remained calm throughout his partner's embarrassing wardrobe malfunction; it was a stoicism borne from the memory of a previous royal embarrassment he had successfully weathered. While dining at Windsor Castle months earlier, the presence of the Queen Mother had overwhelmed the usually calm-nerved pianist to the point where he lost track of his actions. "I was so scared," he said, "I put sugar on my eggs hors d'oeuvre instead of salt, and then had to plow my way through it." Worse still, when asked to play piano for the Royal Family after dinner, he'd gone upstairs to a grand bedroom to change into a stage costume he'd brought along for the occasion when Princess Margaret came wandering in for a chat.

"She didn't seem to notice I was in my underwear," he said with a laugh.

Elton left Kensington Palace at three in the morning, roaring drunk. As soon as he got home, he crawled into his king-sized bed and continued drinking. It was, by now, standard operating procedure. "I'd put on forty-five pounds because I was drinking at least half a bottle of scotch each day," he said. "I just felt awful, and I looked at myself: 'At twenty-seven, your hair's going, your body's going, *you're* going.'"

After recording two of his newer songs for future broadcast on *The Old Grey Whistle Test,* "Grimsby" and "Ticking," Elton booked himself into Gardiner's Tennis Ranch on Camelback Mountain in Paradise Valley, Arizona in an attempt to stave off a premature decline. His routine included playing daily matches with six-time Wimbledon singles champ Billie Jean King, whom he'd met the summer before at a party held by Jerry Perenchio, promoter of Billie's infamous "Battle of the Sexes" exhibition match against Bobby Riggs. "Elton came over to introduce himself," the tennis star said, "and we were both embarrassed at first, but we got along from the start."

"It was the first time I'd been on my own for four and a half years," Elton said of his stay at Gardiner's. "I spent a month doing nothing but hitting a ball around, seven hours a day....The midday temperature out there on that ranch was about 112 degrees. Since then, I've lost about two stone in weight."

On one particularly auspicious afternoon, top-seeded Jimmy Connors joined in for a heated doubles match. The few times the pianist managed a winning shot, Connors would collapse onto the court in a fit of laughter. Elton hardly minded—to the inveterate sports fanatic, the company of King and Connors was Heaven-sent. "I have more heroes in sport than anywhere else," he said. "I think it's always good to have idols, people you respect, and I've got more sporting heroes than anything else. I think you need to be a special kind of person to be a top sportsman....Anyone can be a rock star. 'Wanna make a record?' There's a lot more dedication in being a tennis champion than being a rock musician. I'm sure the Stones don't get up every morning and have a band rehearsal....I can't imagine a bigger thrill than scoring a goal in the World Cup."

Elton was particularly touched when Billy Jean King presented him with a customized warm-up uniform featuring the logo of her tennis team, the Philadelphia Freedoms, designed by Englishman Ted Tinling. "We gave it to him," King said, "and as we were in the limo...he said, 'Billie, I'm going to write a song for you.' I said, 'Sure you are,' and he said, "No, I mean it. Just wait and see.'"

While Elton was racing around the courts, Gus Dudgeon was running equally as hard on a parallel track, creating detailed mixes from the Caribou Ranch sessions.

"Gus Dudgeon, I have to say, was the fifth member of our band," Elton later acknowledged. "The actual sound and the quality of the recordings are extraordinary, and that was down to him. He was our fifth member. Like the Beatles had George Martin, we had Gus." Bernie readily agreed. "It was collaborative, definitely, but Gus was holding the reins. He was brilliant in the studio, he was absolutely extraordinary. You just have to listen to those records [we did in the '70s]....Sonically, there's nothing to touch them."

The perfectionistic producer sent Elton multiple mixes of each song. "Gus does two or three different kinds of mixes and plays them for me," the pianist said. "I just pick out the one I like best and make suggestions on how to improve the most superior of the lot."

The producer understood better than anyone that the meticulous work he put into crafting and perfecting each song would eventually pay huge dividends. "Gus mixed songs so that when you're listening to it for the first time, you're always hearing something new," David Hentschel said. "Most times he'd leave the first verse and chorus alone, as you're just getting into the whole mood of the piece. But then when the second verse comes around he'd start introducing other sounds—and he'd keep adding, so by the end you've got this dynamic build going on, and the intensity of the song is peaking at the right time."

Unlike with many other bands, Gus usually culled Elton's mixes from a single master take. "With Elton and [Gus and] the band, it was as much of a performance as possible," Hentschel noted. "Not manufactured, which I have seen happen with other producers and musicians....[Most] recordings would have been one [single] take. I'm not saying the *first* take…it may have been the fourth or fifth take…but one pass straight through."

After having succeeded so well in Great Britain, "Don't Let the Sun Go Down On Me" was released in America on June 10. The harmony-soaked ballad bettered its performance in England, peaking at Number 2. Another Gold single for Elton, the mellifluent ballad would also earn him a pair of Grammy nominations, for Best Pop Vocalist of the Year—Male, and Record of the Year.

The single's mothership, *Caribou,* meanwhile, was issued in America two weeks later. The album proved beyond a shadow of a doubt that the public's appetite for all things Elton had only grown more voracious in the interceding months since his last long-player had been release. *Caribou* entered the charts at Number 5 on *Billboard*'s Top 200, only the fifth album to ever make so high a debut. (The previous LPs to achieve this feat were *Led Zeppelin III, Hey Jude,* the soundtrack from *Woodstock,* and George Harrison's *All Things Must Pass.*) Four days later, the disc was released in Elton's homeland. It quickly reached the coveted Number 1 spot in both countries, and would remain in the charts for well over a year. *Caribou* would also prove popular across the globe, reaching the Top 20 in Japan and New Zealand, Number 6 in Italy and Norway, Number 5 in Yugoslavia, and Number 1 in Australia, Canada and Denmark.

The album featured Elton's most striking cover yet: a glammed-up portrait which had been taken in a miniscule studio office above a Chinese laundry off 3rd and Sycamore in L.A., posing jauntily before a stylized Maxfield Parrish-esque backdrop in black, red-trimmed trousers, a tiger-skin bomber jacket, six-inch platform heels and oversized pink-tinted glasses. Inside the album was a pull-out sleeve with the lyrics printed on one side and a hand-tinted black-and-white portrait of the star on the other. Taken by Ed Caraeff, the pin-up-like photograph was the result of pure serendipity. "When the [photo] session finished," album art designer David Larkham said, "Ed and I followed [Elton] out to his car. And as he got into the back seat, Ed said, 'Elton', and Elton looked up just as Ed pressed the button for the last shot of the day."

Critical reaction to the album, while mostly positive, was not quite as glowing as it had been for its predecessor. "I give up," Robert Christgau wrote in the *Village Voice*. "Of course [Elton's] a machine, but haven't you ever loved a machine so much it took on its own personality? I was reminded of my first car, a '50 Plymouth. Then I decided Elton was more like a brand-new Impala I once rented on a magazine's money. Then I remembered that I ended up paying for that car myself. Yes, I hate the way he said 'don't *diszgard* me' too, but 'The Bitch is Back' is my most favorite song. B+."

"Is it as good as *Yellow Brick Road?*" *Melody Maker's* Chris Welch asked. "Well, it's different. An entertaining selection of hot ditties....Overall, an excellent compilation which shows the old firm haven't lost their ability to push forward the boundaries of the pop song, and keep close to the path of good rockin' music." Writing in *Phonograph Record,* Bud Scoppa gave the record passing marks. "For an artist with distinct limitations—vocal, compositional, and stylistic—Elton John makes awfully good records. Like the three albums before it, *Caribou* is constantly listenable, and while it places no demands on the casual listener, there's still some meat under the surface for those looking for meaning or structure. Elton pulls off a difficult stunt: he manages to be both intelligent and lighter than air."

NME's Charles Shaar Murray was considerably less impressed, however. "*Caribou* had 'product' stamped all over it," he wrote. "It came on thin and forced, with only 'The Bitch is Back' displaying the full-tilt rock 'n' roll naiveté that has characterized most of Elton's best work."

Perhaps surprisingly, Gus agreed with Murray's assessment. "*Caribou* is a piece of crap," he said. "The sound is the worst, the songs are nowhere, the sleeve came out wrong, the lyrics weren't that good, the singing wasn't all there, the playing wasn't great, the production is just plain lousy. When I got nominated for Best Produced Single/Album of the Year, I couldn't stop laughing. I thought it was ridiculous that I could be nominated for an award for the worst thing I'd ever done."

Elton, for his part, was hardly surprised by the mixed reactions his latest offering had drawn. "I'm the big cheese at the moment," he said, "so everyone feels bound to have a go at me. I read a good piece by John Tobler in *ZigZag* which said the reviews of *Caribou* were probably written before it even came out. Anyway, so what? Reviews don't mean that much, they don't really sink in. You never remember them two weeks later."

More to the point, those closest to Elton realized that with his popularity at an all-time high, critical resentment was a foregone inevitability.

"Credible artists were those who audibly suffered or were rebellious," journalist Paul Gambaccini succinctly pointed out. "And he was neither."

Chapter 20:
Whatever Gets You Thru the Night

Understanding just how fickle the glittering hand of fame could be, Elton and Bernie wasted no time in turning their attentions toward their next album.

"We came up with a science fiction concept," the lyricist said, "but we thought, 'No, people have done that, David Bowie...yawn, yawn...'"

Instead, they opted to tell their own story.

"I thought we might be accused of being conceited because writing about yourself is a bit off," Elton said, "but I just wanted people to get the idea of what really happened. [Bernie and I] are human beings. We're not machines, like everyone else thinks we are."

Bernie thus set to work on a set of highly autobiographical lyrics which detailed the duo's early lives up through the recording of their first album, *Empty Sky*. "It was very interesting to write about real incidents, and it was a good lesson because, when I write very quickly, it rolls out," the lyricist said. "With this, I took much more time. I would write something then I'd go on to something else, then go back and work some more on what I'd done previously. It was a new exercise, and I think it really paid off."

Bernie presented his work to Elton on July 20, the night before their scheduled transatlantic voyage to America. The green-haired pianist and his musicians were camped out at his house—his band getting stoned in the games room while Bernie and Maxine argued in the kitchen and he sat cross-legged in the living room, happily alphabetizing his latest album purchases.

Just after midnight, a furious pounding sounded at the door. John Reid answered to find Keith Moon and Ringo Starr standing there in their pajamas, freezing their bollocks off.

"Christ, look at you two," Reid said. "Tonight's not a good night. A bus is coming to take us to the Southampton dock in a few hours."

"Dear boy," Moon said, pushing his way inside, "you told us to drop in *anytime*."

The two drummers spent the balance of the night sitting before Elton's jukebox, drinking brandy while miming to '50s rock classics from "Johnnie B. Goode" to "Jailhouse Rock."

"An all time was had by good," Moon noted with a wry grin.

Elton and his vacant-eyed crew—along with traveling mates Julian and Cynthia Lennon, and Rocket Records' general manager, Tony King—boarded the *SS France* early the next morning. As they prepared to sail toward the westerly horizon, a brass band stood on the Southampton dock and played them off with a spirited rendition of "Yellow Submarine."

The five-day voyage passed pleasantly enough, Elton sneaking cursory glances at Bernie's latest batch of lyrics as the open sea unfolded below. "I can't write a single note without his lyrics," he admitted. "They really get me going. The energy starts flowing and I can rip off songs as fast as he can deliver the lyrics."

Though the pianist was champing at the bit to finally set to work, an opera singer had booked the Salon Debussy, the ship's sole First Class music room, for the entire trip, from dawn till dusk—except for her midday breaks, when she'd head to the dining room and scarf down her lunches. "So every two hours at lunchtime I used to go in there and nip out to the piano," Elton said. "It felt so good to be writing songs that I not only understood the lyrics to, but was a complete part of."

Davey Johnstone joined Elton in the gold-lacquered music room for several of these onboard writing sessions. "I had my trusty old Yamaha acoustic guitar with me," he said. "And I came up with that riff [on 'Captain Fantastic and the Brown Dirt Cowboy'], which was to be the first thing you hear on the record. Elton said to me, 'I need an intro,' and it was the first thing that I came up with as he was playing a G chord to an E-minor chord in kind of a lazy, country vibe. Which is just the way we do things."

Elton purposefully wrote the songs in chronological order, just as Bernie had presented them. "That made it easy to write in a way, because you had a link," the pianist said. "You could visualize what song was going to finish and when the next one was going to start."

During the brief trip, Elton managed to compose the music for not only "Captain Fantastic and the Brown Dirt Cowboy" but also "Tower of Babel," "Bitter Fingers" *("An up-tempo number, as most of the songs so far are slowsy,"* Elton noted in his diary. *"Very pleased with it..."*), "Tell Me When the Whistle Blows" and "Someone Saved My Life Tonight."

When not busy writing future classics, the restless superstar occupied himself with highly competitive games of backgammon and squash, while simultaneously monitoring the sales of *Caribou* through a ship-to-shore telephone. "You get excited by your own success," he said. "I know a lot of artists say they never look at a sales chart, but that's nonsense. They're on the phone all the time. What's the point of recording something if you don't want to know how it's going? It's great having a Number One record, don't let anybody tell you that it isn't."

Elton was chuffed by *Caribou*'s brisk sales performance; so much so that he decided to break his recently self-imposed no-carbs rule and treat himself to a warm pretzel and a glass of Mumm with the ship's captain in the Riviera Bar. *"The Chief Purser is extremely nice, but the rest of the crowd is extremely Gucci-Pucci and definitely disapproves of us,"* Elton later claimed in his diary. *"Someone says in a rather grand voice, 'That man over there is Elton John—he is very famous, but I have never heard of him.'"*

Arriving in New York, Elton's entourage was met at the New York Port Authority by John Lennon.

"Julian was a dream," Elton told the ex-Beatle. "He waited for us outside our staterooms, escorted us to the dining room, [and] always made sure we had good seats at all the events onboard."

"Julian was brilliant," Davey agreed. "He was this little guy who always had a deal going. He always had stuff in his pockets."

Elton stopped by the Record Plant studios on West 44th Street a couple nights later, on July 31, to again visit Lennon, who was recording tracks for what was to become his *Walls and Bridges* album.

"I was fiddling about one night," Lennon said. "I'd done three-quarters of ['Whatever Gets You Thru the Night']. 'Now what do we do? Should we put a camel on it or a xylophone?' That sort of thing. And [Elton] came in and said, 'Hey, I'll play some piano'....I knew him, but I'd never seen him play."

For Elton, the chance to work with the Beatles' founder was too good an opportunity to pass up. "Lennon is the only person in this business that I've ever looked up to," he said. "The *only* person. I've met people who are great, like Mick Jagger and Pete Townshend, whom I admire tremendously, but they are not in the same league, I'm sorry. He is the only person in this business who is one-hundred percent sacred to me."

After giving a listen to "Whatever Gets You Thru the Night," Elton effortlessly laid a driving piano part which brought the track to life.

"John was so impressed, all [Elton] had to do was hear it once and he knew what he wanted to put down," May Pang said. "John stared at Elton's hands while Elton played."

"I'd like to play as fast as that," Lennon said. "Elton's a fine musician, [a] great piano player....I was amazed at his ability."

When it came time to record lead vocals, the two icons huddled together around a single microphone.

"The harmony came very easily to them," May said. "Instantly, a new singing team was formed as John and Elton ripped through the vocal a couple times, getting looser each time they sang it."

When they were done, a smiling Lennon told his girlfriend, "I'd like Elton to sing harmony on 'Surprise, Surprise'."

"He knew how thrilled I'd be to have Elton perform on the song John had written for me," May said.

Elton nodded his ascent. "Let's do it," he said.

But adding co-lead vocals to "Surprise, Surprise (Sweet Bird of Paradox)" proved a bit more tricky. "[Lennon] put the vocal down first and I had to sing…double-tracked, to someone else's phrasing," Elton said. "Now, I'm very quick, but that took a long time because Lennon's phrasing was so weird. It was fantastic, but you start to understand why he was a one-off.…It was quite nerve-wracking."

"For whatever reason," May said, "it didn't work out. No reflection. Some things work and some things don't.…[Regardless,] John was overwhelmed by Elton's efforts."

Soon after, an album playback session was held; Elton was particularly impressed by the way "Whatever Gets You Thru the Night" had turned out.

"It's gonna be a Number One," he said.

Lennon, who hadn't sniffed the Top 10 since "Imagine" four years earlier, had his doubts. "Ahhh, I don't think so, Elt."

"I bet you it will," Elton insisted. "And if it *is*, you're gonna come on [stage] and sing it with me."

The famously reclusive—and painfully stage-shy—Lennon nodded. "Sure, okay," he said. "You got a bet."

Elton would later confess to having made the wager for Lennon's sake as much as for his own. "I knew it would be great fun for me," he said, "but I also did it for John. I thought it would do him good to get out of his shell."

Despite the myriad problems Elton and his team had faced at Caribou Ranch in January, he decided to utilize the studio again for his latest album sessions. Unlike *Caribou*'s hurried efforts, however, the decision was taken to devote an entire month to recording this time. Having acclimated himself to Caribou's monitoring systems, Gus wisely chose to record these new sessions flat, without any reverb or effects added—opting instead to do all the work later in the mix.

As the album had been written, so it was recorded: in running order. The sessions thus began with the title track, a bucolic rocker which recast Elton and Bernie as a pair of comic book heroes: Elton as "The Captain" and Bernie as "The Brown Dirt Cowboy." Detailing their early formative years through a gentle electric piano-accented country motif, the song shifted into hard rock overdrive for the choruses, as the duo partnered up to do battle against the heartless powers which ran the monolithic music industry.

"Tower of Babel" followed. A steely piano ballad in A-minor, the track likened the London music scene to the biblical Tower of Babel, a debauched world of sordid degeneracy where every whim was catered to, and every warped appetite indulged in to excess.

"It's about sharks in the doorway," Bernie said. "Nipping at our heels, looking for blood."

Like much of the music created during these sessions, the song's instrumental break, which hit—unusually—right after the first chorus, came about in a completely holistic way. "When the guitar part comes in, that was unsaid—it was just like, 'This is what's going to happen here,'" Davey said. "I came up with the guitar parts and the solo, and then we tracked it and I overdubbed an octave on it." Pre-arranged empty spaces were, in fact, worked into the entirety of all the new songs' arrangements, allowing the music to breathe. "Instead of having the same amount of shit on every track," Davey said, "we would instinctively know, 'Okay, I drop out there. It just doesn't need it.'"

Next came "Bitter Fingers," a cutting indictment of the churn-and-burn mentality of Denmark Street's music publishers. The track was a particularly painful one for Elton. "This is a song about having to write songs for people you don't really want to write songs for," he said. "This song is about having to write with bitter fingers. What [Bernie and I] went through when we were writing all the shit we had to write before we eventually started making records that we wanted to make. I'm glad that happened, though, because without the struggle you don't appreciate anything."

Gus double-tracked Elton's introductory piano triplets on "Bitter Fingers," vari-speeding the tape to achieve an otherworldly harmonized effect. The producer then ran Elton's piano through an Eventide Harmonizer and a rotating Lesley cabinet, a setup which B-3 organs were often fed through. Davey got in on the studio wizardry himself by manipulating his guitar's pickup selector switch and tone controls to add a pipey, trumpet-like guitar sound to the song. "And then [we] double-tracked *that*," he said. "In actual fact, there's very little going on."

After Elton recorded his lead vocals, Gus double-tracked a second lead line over the song's choruses. It was a practice they were using more and more often, to great effect. "[Double-tracking] makes the vocals pop," the producer said. "Helps it pop through the clutter." Davey felt the same. "Ours were more like Beatles overdubs. They were a bit rough and ready, but they worked better that way. That's the vibe you want. When you double-track something, the secret is you'll get something that's slightly different. That's what creates that magic."

"Tell Me When the Whistle Blows" came out in a single take. A neo-Motown groove, the track detailed the nights when Bernie would catch a train at Kings Crossing to head back to Lincolnshire for the weekend back in the late '60s, when he and Elton were first plying their songwriting craft. "I was still fresh from the sticks," the lyricist said, "and I still had tremendous ties to my friends back home in Lincolnshire. That's the song. That's it."

Noted soul arranger Gene Page later added a silk-smooth string part which meshed perfectly with Elton's sinuous clavinet and Davey's bluesy, David Gilmour-esque fret work, to add an aura of thoughtful poignancy to the bittersweet R&B shuffle.

The centerpiece of the sessions came with "Someone Saved My Life Tonight," a nearly seven-minute-long epic which recounted in painful detail Elton's near-marriage to Linda Woodrow and the resultant pressures which led to his suicide attempt.

"That would have been goodbye to the music scene for me," Elton said. "I would have been down working in Barclay's Bank or something." Musically, the song's introductory piano figure immediately set a somber mood. "There's an A-flat chord with an E-flat in the bass," he said, "which is something one would have never done without musical training. I thought about Brian Wilson and 'God Only Knows'. From the first chord you can tell that."

Nigel's idiosyncratically poignant drumming added to the overall power of the track. "Nigel had this great thing, which he couldn't control," Gus said. "As soon as he would go on a ride cymbal, he'd be tapping his hi-hat [for four steady beats]. If you notice, he just couldn't stop tapping his foot. Most drummers come off the hi-hat and go for the ride cymbal, and they might put a [fourth beat] on it. But Nigel couldn't stop. It was part of his style, but I loved it....He'd come off [the hi-hat] and it would change to a softer version in the corner while he's on the ride cymbal. It was great."

The song's structure proved as unique as Nigel's skins work, featuring as it did a middle-eight bridge and an extended coda, both relatively unusual for '70s-era pop compositions. Yet if the music was complex, the words were painfully direct. Unaware of the song's true significance,

Gus Dudgeon forced Elton to sing the lead vocal multiple times, till the superstar was nearly in tears.

"I kept telling Elton over the talkback to give the vocal more emotion, more power," Gus said. "But I didn't know what he was singing about. I never pay attention to the lyrics until later. My first concern is always the sound."

"Lay off him, Gus," Davey admonished, putting his hand on the producer's forearm. "You *do* know he's singing about killing himself, right?"

The producer was mortified. "I made him sing the most unbelievably personal things over and over again to get a bloody note right or get a bit of phrasing together. Christ."

The album's signal rocker was a guitar-riot jam entitled "(Gotta Get a) Meal Ticket," which told of the painful days when Elton and Bernie were forced to watch others grab onto the brass ring they so desperately desired. "At the time," Elton admitted, "I'd put down anybody who was making it, just because we weren't. I think a lot of artists go through a stage like that."

The song featured a uniquely off-kilter rhythm propelled by insistent syncopated guitar stabs, which helped drive the song ever-forward. The solo, meanwhile, was Davey's nod to George Harrison. "Two guitars coming in with sort of an 'octave urgency,'" he said. "Like the solo of the Beatles' 'Taxman': 'Okay: take-off time!'"

The track's background vocals were, conversely, influenced by the West Coast rock sound so recently in vogue. "The Eagles were starting to happen at that time," Davey said, "and we were big buddies with Joe Walsh already, so we took those kinds of harmonies. We kind of nicked the idea....We thought, 'What would *they* do on that?' And it worked out really well."

"Better Off Dead" proved another session highlight. A swirling pounder accented by Dee's urgent bass and Davey's double-tracked Martin D-28 acoustic guitars, the song recounted the seamy cast of roustabouts Elton and Bernie encountered as they hung out after-hours at a Wimpy Bar burger joint which sat lost inside the diesel fumes on Oxford Street. "Half the people who came in looked as if they'd be better off dead," Bernie said. "The song's really about that." Intriguingly, he left a note at the bottom of the lyric sheet, a rare musical cue for Elton, indicating that the song should sound "*á la John Prine*."

"It's nothing like John Prine," the pianist said with a laugh. "It sounds like a Gilbert & Sullivan song. Semi-operatic."

"I wrote it folky," Bernie said, "and he turned it into like a galloping major, a regimental thing."

To achieve the distinctively pounding drum sound, Gus ran Nigel's kit through a harmonizer, to achieve the most ambient sound possible. "That kind of thing dictates the way you're going to play," Davey said. "It's not like you just play any old crap and the producer puts a weird sound on it [afterward]."

"House of Cards" was undertaken the same night. The country-pop-flavored tale of cheap sex and broken hearts relied less on studio wizardry than "Better Off Dead" had, yet ultimately proved every bit as effective. Even so, the bouncy electric piano-centered track was doomed for B-side status. "Too bad," Dee said. "That was actually one of the more fun songs [to play]."

The group then turned their attention toward "Writing," a breezily insouciant remembrance of the days when Elton and Bernie learned to properly write songs together. "It's about honing your craft, about discovering each other's working patterns," Bernie said. "We were never so close as we were in those days."

Much as *Goodbye Yellow Brick Road* opened with the dual sonic punch of "Funeral For a Friend/Love Lies Bleeding," so *Captain Fantastic* closed with "We All Fall in Love Sometimes/Curtains," two separate songs recorded as a single entity. "It was done in two takes," Gus said. "I remember that Neil Sedaka walked into the control room just as we began the second take. The band actually had just started the song as he walked in. And I thought, 'Now, this is going to be interesting, to see what his reaction is.' Because it's nearly eleven-minutes long. So it got to about nine minutes and he came over to me and whispered, 'My God, are they doing this all in one go, or are they dubbing on?' And I said, whispering, 'No, it's all in one go.' He went, 'Jesus, they been going on for *hours.*'"

"The magic was there," Nigel later said of the session.

Though similar in tone and tempo, each of the songs had their own unique personality. "We All Fall in Love Sometimes" was, in particular, drenched in an atmosphere of Continental melancholia, as if it had sprung from the songbook of French crooner Charles Aznavour. "[The song] means we all find something sometimes, whether it's success, or a relationship that works out," Bernie said. "It's really a song that said there's something tomorrow." Elton's interpretation, however, varied slightly. "As far as I'm concerned, the song is about Bernie and I realizing we had a future together," he said. "Not a sexual future, but a brother relationship....It's about the realization that we could make it. Really, it says it all in that song."

"Curtains" was perhaps even more telling. A crystalline confessional brimming with references to some of the oldest songs in the John/Taupin oeuvre, the lyrical poignancy was heightened by Nigel's evocative, narrative-based artistry. "Every drum fill that I ever played is in that whole song," he said. "We were freaking out, because if we fucked-up, how were we going to be able to edit it? There were cymbals and cymbals and cymbals, and you cannot cut a cymbal…so we had to play it the whole way through and get it right. I tried to do my part in bringing the lyrics to life. You can actually do that on the drums, if you allow yourself to feel the music and let your imagination take over."

Gus was pleased with the summational track. "I got a sound on that particular track that made everything that Nigel played so well so worthwhile," he said. "It's all very well, somebody playing drums well. But if it's not recorded well—to the point that you go, 'Fuck, that is *superb!*'—then it's a bit of a waste of time."

Again, a lush layer of superior backing vocals helped add to the overall effect. "The idea [for the backing vocals on 'Curtains'] came from Gus," Davey said. "He said, 'Instead of doing your usual vocal pads and 'oohs' and 'ahhs', harmonize with him.' We thought that would be a bitch, because Elton's phrasing is amazing. He's like Frank Sinatra in that way—he phrases his own way. In 'Curtains'…to sing those lyrics was probably one of the most explosive things ever to happen to me in my music career, and I'm not really a singer. To be able to sing such words that are so beautiful, and [to] have the guys feel the same way, was really scary."

"When I listen to that record now," Nigel said years later, "it kind of brings tears to my eyes."

With the album proper in the can, John Lennon and May Pang arrived at Caribou Ranch so that John could lend his talents to Elton's remake of "Lucy in the Sky with Diamonds."

"We shared a cabin with Elton," May said. "My big thing was, 'Why are there oxygen tanks everywhere?' Because I didn't realize that we were so thin in air, when you were singing, you might need it. You needed to acclimate yourself to the thinness of the crisp air. It [soon] affected John when he sang. Because you're not getting enough air."

Thin air or no, everyone at Caribou Ranch lost their cool the moment Lennon arrived. "We couldn't get over it," John Carsello said, "because, y'know, who wouldn't be? It doesn't get any better than that. I grew up with the Beatles. And John was just so nice. Everyone was freaking out— even [Jim] Guercio—about John being up there with Elton. It was just a very cool time."

"That night after we unpacked, we joined Elton in the studio," May said. "As soon as they saw each other, John and Elton fell into each other's arms. As they did every time they met, they began to trade one-liners. They were both in rare form, and everyone stood around laughing."

Gus eventually called the session to order. But with the pressure on, Lennon lost his nerve.

"Maybe I'll just do my regular part that I did on the original," he said. "Or I could just watch you guys go at it. I'm happy just to watch."

Davey shook his head. "You've *gotta* play on this track, John."

Lennon grimaced. "You don't want me playin' on it, Davey. *You're* the guitar player."

"Just play on it," Davey insisted. "You're fucking great. You're a fucking *Beatle*."

"But I forgot me guitar, you see."

Without missing a beat, Davey handed Lennon one of his Les Paul's.

Unable to remember the chords to his own song, Lennon asked Davey to teach them to him. Together, the two

431

guitarists then brainstormed a dynamic ska break which would appear toward the end of the track.

"That was always John's thing," May said. "He loved ska music."

Dee Murray's intricately distinctive bass playing helped add another tactile layer to the song. "Dee was probably *the* finest bass player I ever got the chance to work with," Gus later reflected. "He was perfect. A really melodic player, really inventive. And just a tremendous person as well." John Carsello agreed with the producer's assessment. "Dee was just the greatest guy in the world. Just a beautiful guy. Not only was he an incredible bass player, but he was just very laid-back. Didn't raise his voice, no ego at all. Just a warm soul. And he had this personality that you could just talk to and just want to be his friend, because he was such a nice guy. Nigel and Davey were great guys too, but there was just something about Dee. And as far as his talent goes, oh my God, he was just such a phenomenal bass player. Just incredible."

Work on "Lucy in the Sky with Diamonds" lasted well into the night. "The session was a long, painstaking one," May said. "Everyone worked efficiently, the changes made sense, and each of the musicians was given precise directions. Both perfectionists, Elton and John set the pace, and everyone buckled down to make a perfect record."

For his efforts on the track, Gus received one of the greatest compliments of his career. "After he'd know me for about three days, [Lennon] said, 'You know, when I first walked into the control room and I first saw you, you totally fazed me.' And I thought, '*I* fazed *him?* Fucking hell, I can't believe it!'" The producer laughed. "I just took it as a compliment, because I think it was intended to be one."

After the vocals were laid, Gus created a rough mix of the track and played it back at full volume. Lennon listened in silence, eyes closed. As the song ended, he gave the slightest of shrugs.

"It's better than the Beatles' version," he said.

John Carsello arrived at work early the next morning and walked into the communal mess hall to grab a cup of coffee, when he ran into Lennon sitting there by himself. "May Pang was still in her room," he said. "And I went, 'Oh my God, I'm sitting here with John Lennon.' And he said, 'How are you doing?' And I shook his hand. It was so smooth and soft, I can't explain it. And here I am alone in a room with John Lennon. You can't imagine how that felt like. To be one-on-one with him was amazing. And it was around the time where his green card expired and they were trying to send him back to England. He was living in New York, and he'd just been in the news, 'They're trying to deport John Lennon, he's not a citizen,' it had just been a few days after all that started. And I said, 'I hope it works out for you, John,' and he said, 'I sure hope they let me stay here in this country. I love where I'm living, it reminds me of home.'"

Elton recorded a cover of Lennon's 1973 *Mind Games* track "One Day at a Time" the next afternoon, after John and May Pang had taken their leave. The ethereal composition was one which the pianist was particularly fond of. "I loved that song," he said. "I just wanted to choose one of [Lennon's] songs to do that was not a Beatles song, and it was my choice to do that."

"My guitar sounds like a horn on that track," Davey noted. "Gus wanted to have [my guitar] really up front on that song. I doubled them and put a harmony on them. It almost sounds like saxophones playing those lines....Just a cool little song."

Elton's second Caribou Ranch sessions concluded with a song he'd long promised Billie Jean King, who had quickly become one of his closest confidants. "She's lots of fun," he said. "I draw a parallel with her and Lennon. It's that their public image has nothing to do with what they're really like. And everyone's got preconceived ideas. You mention Lennon and they go, 'Oh, he's a real shit, isn't he?' And Billie Jean King: 'Oh, I hate her. She's so fuckin' moody.' And she's not."

Elton provided the title for his proposed King homage, "Philadelphia Freedom," to Bernie, who protested, "I can't write a song about *tennis*." So instead, the lyricist came up with a set of esoteric lyrics about being free.

"Bernie wrote the lyric in the morning and we recorded it that day," Davey said. "We double-tracked that one [intro bass] lick of Dee's. And I had a direct guitar sound...with a Telecaster plugged straight into the board to get that real clean sound....We finished it in one day."

"Before he [originally] played it for me," Gus said, "[Elton] said, 'I've written this song for Billie Jean King and her Philadelphia Freedoms tennis team. And I was going, '*What?* Where the hell does *that* come from?' Then he played me the song and I went, 'Ah, right. Okay. Fine.' I went out of my way to make a record specifically for the black market, which is why we hired arranger Gene Page, because he had done all those great arrangements for Barry White."

Page's string session went smoothly. Before it began, the arranger strode up to his podium and told his musicians, "Gentlemen, today you are going to play on an Elton John record. Now I don't want any of you to mess up, because your kids are going to hear this record. It's going to be really big. I want everybody to play the best they've ever played, okay?"

"And the most brilliant thing was that when the session was over," Gus said, "all of the players came in, and they all brought their charts, and they said, 'Can we keep our parts to show our kids that we played on an Elton John record?'"

With the sessions thus completed, Elton headed to New York with John Reid to meet up with his mother and step-father. Lennon called him that night, and offered to take them to dinner at the Russian Tea Room. "John was just the nicest man deep down," Elton said. "The kind of man who would walk into a room full of people and, instead of going up to the biggest celeb, he would go round the room talking to everyone one by one. A real man of the people."

After dinner, Lennon got up to go to the toilet. As soon as he left, Elton's mother turned to her son and, with a knowing smirk, said, "Put your money where your mouth is."

"I just looked over," May Pang said, "'cause it was all very playful, but I'm thinking, 'What's this?' So Elton asked John Reid to give him a hundred-dollar bill, and he put it on the table and [Elton] said, 'Okay, here it is.' And she took out her [false] teeth and she went around and kissed people, and it was like, 'What just happened?' It was so playful, it was just great. Elton had such a great rapport with his mom."

As the *coup de grâce*, Derf put his wife's false teeth in the ex-Beatle's water glass right before he returned to the table.

"Lennon just pissed himself laughing," Elton said.

Moving deftly from one Beatle to another, Elton visited Ringo Starr at his *Goodnight Vienna* sessions in Los Angeles days later. The pianist had agreed to play piano on "Snookeroo," a track about a North English ne'er-do-well which he and Bernie had written specifically with Starr's laddish personality in mind.

"[Ringo] said, 'Listen, make it nice and commercial,' so we did," Elton said. "Bernie wrote really simple lyrics, very Ringo-type lyrics, and I tried to write a simple sort of melody to it."

"Ringo was not himself a great songwriter," said Nancy Lee Andrews, Ringo's girlfriend throughout much of the '70s. "That's why whenever any one of his buds would write him a song, he was so grateful. And I remember, with the Elton song, the boys used to call cocaine 'snookeroo'. And then there was the billiards game snooker, too. I think it was an English thing."

The all-star band Starr assembled for the sessions included Nicky Hopkins, Robbie Robertson and future Blues Brothers band member Steve Cropper.

"I thought, 'Whoops, I've got to play well here,'" Elton said. "Then [I] realized I could play just as well as they could." He grinned. "What a silly sod."

Released as a double A-side (along with "No No Song"), "Snookeroo"—propelled in no small part by Elton's involvement—charted at Number 3 on the *Billboard* Hot 100, and became the third-highest solo success of Ringo Starr's career.

Chapter 21:
The Eight Million Dollar Man

Capitalizing on his interplanetary popularity, Elton signed the most lucrative deal ever secured by any performer in entertainment history. The fifty-five-page MCA Records contract—personally negotiated by John Reid, and signed on July 13—guaranteed the pianist an unprecedented eight-million dollars for five albums. (Elektra-Asylum label head David Geffen had crowed at a dinner party in L.A. just days before the MCA deal was struck, "I've signed Bob Dylan. Next I'm going to sign Elton, and then we're going to take over the world." Though Geffen was ultimately outbid, he *would* later secure the pianist's talents for the roster of his eponymous startup label in 1980; Elton would go on to record multiple best-selling albums under the Geffen imprimatur, including *Jump Up!, Too Low For Zero,* and *Breaking Hearts.*) Through his brilliant negotiating tactics, Reid was able to secure an unheard-of twenty-eight percent royalty for Elton for all future record sales—a rate significantly higher than the industry-standard of fifteen percent.

Besides its enormous financial benefits, the contract also provided the artist with a sense of continuity—a key advantage in Reid's eyes. "I'm superstitious about changing labels," he said. "I don't think you should do it unless something is seriously wrong....It's too hard to know what you're getting yourself into with a new company. You can't confuse a single personality with a whole company. You might know the president of a company, but you don't know all the personnel. It may take you two years to get a good working relationship with all the people in a company, and by that time it may be too late."

MCA president Mike Maitland was equally as pleased with the deal, which allowed him to keep his biggest star in-house. "The emotional effect of my having to tell the staff that we had lost [Elton] would have been tremendous," he said. "We would have survived, but it could have crippled us for a while."

Despite the backbends MCA went through to accommodate their cash cow, they *did* make one stipulation: Elton had to decrease his work rate from two albums a year to only one. To ensure their investment, MCA promptly took out a twenty-five-million-dollar insurance policy on the pianist's life. Full page ads were then placed in the June 19 editions of both the *Los Angeles Times* and the *New York Times* to announce the historic contract, which Maitland called, simply, "the best deal anybody ever got."

"I was endeavoring to make a lot of statements in one simple way," John Reid said. "[The contract] made a statement to the public, to the financial community, to the record industry, and for myself."

"It's a great deal," Elton concurred. "It gives me more flexibility, and there won't be so much product coming out. But it will give the public and me a chance to get used to the fact that I won't be around so much. I want to do other things besides music, after all."

The pianist played a rough mix of "Philadelphia Freedom"— the only song he'd purposefully written as a stand-alone single, outside of the seasonal "Step Into Christmas"—to Billie Jean King on August 25, before a World Team Tennis playoff match in Denver between her Philadelphia Freedoms and the Denver Racquets. King called the entire team around to listen to the song together as a visibly nervous Elton set a portable cassette player onto the trainer's table and hit play.

"Hear the beat?" he asked King as the tune's chorus blared out of a tiny plastic speaker. "That's *you* when you get mad on the court. Stomping up to the empire: 'PHIL-A-*DEL*-phia...'"

The tennis champion laughed, massively pleased with the song. "I don't like it, Elton," she said. "I *love* it, *love* it, *love* it."

Elton released "The Bitch is Back" on September 3. Though proving another immediate hit—and his ninth Top 10 single—many Stateside radio stations refused to play the record without bleeping out the word "bitch," which appeared forty-four times throughout the course of the song's 3:45 runtime.

Other stations refused to air the song outright. "We *will* play records that are borderline suggestive records, such as 'Disco Lady' by Johnnie Taylor," WPIX-FM's program director stated imperiously, "but we will *not* play 'The Bitch is Back' by Elton John. We won't play those types of records no matter *how* popular they get."

Even more liberal stations, which were playing the single up to twice an hour, disallowed their DJs from actually announcing the song's title on air. "At one point we were playing 'The Bitch is Back' about every hour or so because it was one of the top-selling records," said WLS-AM disc jockey Bob Sirott. "We played the hell out of that record, but we weren't allowed to say the title. He's singing it but we could say it." Despite the discrepancy, Sirott remained a steadfast fan of the Englishman. "I always loved Elton....Every new song was a special event....But even though I heard this stuff for hours every day, I never got tired of it. I always liked Elton's music."

While his latest single was causing indignation—feigned or otherwise—in America, Elton was already back in Britain, where he was busying himself signing new acts to Rocket Records. Most notable amongst them was pop crooner Neil Sedaka, who'd last hit the upper reaches of the American charts in the late '50s and early '60s with a string of hits including "Calendar Girl" and "Breaking Up is Hard to Do." Despite scoring a recent British success with "Laughter in the Rain," Sedaka was finding it tough sledding trying to secure an American label to release his new music.

"Over there, they think I'm a ghost," he told Elton.

For his part, Elton had idolized Sedaka for years. "I was a fan straightaway," he said. "I was a huge fan of *The Tra-La Days Are Over.* It was great to see someone who played the piano."

Moved by Sedaka's efforts to mount a proper comeback, Elton offered to release his new music on Rocket. Sedaka accepted straightaway. "Thank you so much," he said, stunned by the offer.

"It's okay," a pleased Elton replied. "You're handing us gold bricks."

So excited was the pianist at having one of his former idols on his label that he agreed to write the liner notes for Sedaka's upcoming album. Entitled *Sedaka's Back,* the collection—culled from Sedaka's last three British LPs—was edited down at Caribou Ranch. "I'll never forget when we left Caribou," Sedaka said, "we went together to the airport, and in those days you didn't need any ID to get on an airplane, but Elton had forgotten his ticket, and we went up to the ticket counter and Elton is dressed with the high boots and sequins, and a big hat. And the girl asked him for his ticket. He didn't have it. He said, 'I'm Elton John,' and she said, 'You have to have identification. I can't let you on the plane.' I thought she must be from another planet, between his face and his outfit, she must have known who he was, but instead he paid for another ticket in cash."

After the two pianists landed in L.A., Elton immediately headed out to various local radio stations with the specific agenda of promoting *Sedaka's Back*. Sedaka himself could hardly believe Elton's single-minded devotion. "Here was the most successful recording artist in the world," he marveled, "being the best PR man anyone could have." (Elton's faith and efforts would pay off handsomely—on February 1, 1975, "Laughter in the Rain" would top the *Billboard* charts, becoming Sedaka's first Number 1 since 1962.)

Fortunes were also looking up for Kiki Dee, who secured her second hit for Rocket soon after with the Bias Boshell-penned track "I've Got the Music in Me," an ebullient rocker produced by Gus Dudgeon at Jimi Hendrix's old studio, Electric Lady, in New York City.

The song easily zoomed up to Number 19 on the charts, belying its tortured creation. "Kiki had a bit of a studio complex, and couldn't seem to get the vocal together," Gus said. Not helping matters, Joshie Jo Armstead and Cissy Houston—the latter the mother of future R&B sensation Whitney Houston—were singing backing vocals at the session.

"They were absolutely fantastic singers," Kiki said. "And I just bottled it. I lost confidence."

"While she was doing [her vocals]," Gus said, "Elton crept in through a back door, hid behind a screen, took off all his clothes, and suddenly streaked across the studio, stark naked. Kiki nearly freaked, but kept on singing. That's why the vocal came out so great."

"All we've done is given her the confidence to do it on her own," the pianist modestly told *NME*. "And there's so many people in the business like me who can do these things for artists like Kiki Dee."

With Rocket Records finally scoring regular successes, Elton looked to expand the scope of his label's roster even further.

"I'd love to get someone like Iggy and the Stooges," he said, "but they've broken up."

Ticket demand for Elton's fall U.S. tour, a 10-week, 44-date extravaganza spread out across 31 cities, was greater than ever, with lines forming outside Ticketron offices *days* in advance of tickets actually going on sale. In L.A., ducats for three local dates at the 18,700-seat Inglewood Forum sold out in six hours, forcing the addition of a fourth show. In Landover, Maryland, an additional show had to be swiftly penciled in to avoid a near riot by unhappy, ticketless fans.

Similar scenes played out across the country. Yet despite Elton's obvious popularity, he still found himself plagued by bouts of self-doubt. On more than one occasion, he'd ring up various venues to check how ticket sales were progressing, only to find in each instance that the arenas were completely sold-out. "It's hard to believe sometimes," he said. "In all honesty, the only groups who can go to the States and sell out everywhere are Zep, the Stones, the Who, myself, and [Jethro] Tull. I can't think of any others."

Staging for Elton's latest tour was as extravagant as the public's demand for tickets, featuring as it did a cutting-edge lighting system, a mirror-paneled grand piano, and carpeted amps. Moreover, Elton's name was spelled out in luminous blue neon across a wall of speakers, stage-right, while each band member's name glowed in cherry-red neon directly above their station.

The pianist's stage clothes for this outing were, likewise, far wilder than ever before. "They're all absolutely stupid, I mean absolutely ridiculous," he said. "They've gone over the top this time, and I'm really pleased." His wardrobe included a full-length silver wizard's robe and a sleek black Lurex jumpsuit covered with fluorescent balls of orange, blue, red, yellow and green which dangled from piano wire. "Maybe I look like an idiot at times, but I've always tried to have a trace of absolute stupidity about me," he said. "Basically I'm a fucking lunatic. Or at least as much of a lunatic as a normal bloke can be."

Elton commissioned a new set of eyewear as well, including round mink-lined glasses, glasses designed as musical notes, in the shape of stars, pianos and clouds. His prized frames, however, were a special set given to him by the Four Seasons. "In fact, Frankie Valli made a special visit to come and give me the present himself," Elton said, "and when I opened it, I could see why. There were four pairs of spectacles, and across the lenses of each pair was painted a scene portraying one of the four seasons: Autumn, Summer, Winter and Spring. It absolutely knocked me out, because they'd been specially designed for me."

The most valuable pair he owned, however, were made of solid gold. "But I'm so afraid of losing them that they're strictly for my eyes only," he said with a laugh.

Each night— two hours prior to his performance, and after coating his fingers with New-Skin, a liquid bandage solution which protected his nails from cracking apart when he attacked the piano—Elton would peer out behind black backstage curtains at his audience and try to determine which of his many outfits might best please them. Then it was off to his dressing room to consult with a huge portable dresser. "You would open this wardrobe and there would be thirty pairs of shoes, two-hundred jackets to choose from, drawers and drawers of spectacles," journalist Chris Charlesworth said. "He was always very good-natured about it all. He realized it was all over-the-top and he was self-mocking about it. He thought it was all a big laugh, really."

By this point in his career, Elton's internal clock was finely tuned to the demands and exhilarations of performing before tens of thousands of rabid fans. "I start getting a little hyper late in the afternoon before a concert, and it keeps building up," he told the *Chicago Tribune*'s Lynn Van Matre before the first of two sold-out shows at the "Madhouse on Madison," Chicago Stadium. "You get to the dressing room and you hear the crowd and you finally step onstage and it's like Christmas Day and opening your presents. And then it's over and there's this feeling of release and also a definite letdown. I mean, I never go out after a show's over—what could I do that wouldn't be a drag after performing?"

Kiki Dee, who received the choice opening act slot on the tour, warmed up the audience each night with a forty-five-minute set. "She was really amazing," Elton said. "It's horrible having to support because the audience comes for the main act, but she and the band really worked hard. She got a lot of respect and she deserved it." In his zeal to see Kiki go over well, the superstar often provided uncredited backing vocals for her set, huddled around a microphone backstage with Nigel, Davey and Dee.

Seemingly every aspect of the whirlwind which Elton so effortlessly generated had Kiki's head spinning. "It was crazy," she later told *MailOnLine*'s Richard Barber. "We had a police escort everywhere we went. I felt like I was riding Elton's rainbow and it was exciting, but [ultimately] it wasn't me."

The moment Kiki and her band vacated the stage, a group of jump-suited roadies would begin pushing their equipment offstage, testing microphones and thumping away on Nigel's massive drum kit, as Elton's shimmering, sequined Steinway rose majestically onto stage by hydraulic lift. Each night, a massive roar would echo through the arena at the sight of his piano, no matter the city.

Then suddenly, without warning, the house lights would cut out.

Blackness.

Hysteria.

Massive video screens posted off to either side of the stage—a new innovation for rock concerts—would unspool a cartoon by Peggy Okeya. Set to *Don't Shoot Me*'s "I'm Gonna Be a Teenage Idol," the film showed the top-hatted superstar standing atop a giant stack of records as teenage fans toppled ecstatically into a gramophone.

The opening strains of "Funeral For a Friend/Love Lies Bleeding" would then blast forth from banks of speakers hanging bat-like above the stage, as clouds of dry ice spilled out into the audience. Taking his place behind his piano, Elton would sit silently, glittering beguilingly in the smoky darkness. A spotlight would illuminate him as he struck the first two chords of "Funeral For a Friend" proper—a simple yet evocative E-major to A-major—causing 20,000 voices to break into a sonic wail.

Gazing out at the screaming multitudes, spectacles sparkling mysteriously beneath the ever-shifting lights, Elton would invariably smirk at the hysteria his mere presence generated, as a darkened sea of faces cried out his name in fevered exaltation. Whether prepubescent or senior citizen, white, black, Hispanic or Asian, poor or wealthy, his audiences included every conceivable segment of society. "I can see four or five rows when I'm onstage," he said, "and the cross-section of people is staggering."

As always, the Brit gave his all each night. "It's the greatest thing in the world to stand on a stage and see people in the front rows smiling and know they came to see *you*," he told journalist Robert Hilburn. "The stage, in reality, is the closest you can ever get to most of the fans...that's why I get so upset if I play badly. Not only for me, but because I know I've disappointed the audience....That's what you struggle against every night."

Though his band—augmented for this tour by the contrapuntal punch of the four-piece Muscle Shoals Horns ("They're about the tightest brass section you'll ever wish to hear," Elton announced nightly)—enjoyed a higher profile than most backing bands, a certain restless displeasure *did* begin to fester during this tour, especially amongst original members Nigel and Dee. "It would have been nice," Dee said, "to have had a [band] name other than 'Elton John' that identified us, or was just a name we all created. Nigel and I kind of lost our identities along the way."

Ignoring any potentially mutinous undercurrents, Elton cheerfully cavorted about the stage each night like a royal court jester. The stage was his musical kingdom, his unquestionable dominion. Most evenings he'd end up on top of his piano, or beneath it. For Elton, it was all in a day's work. "There are so many people who think they're the big cheese," he said. "'Well, man, we played for 70,000 people.' Well, it's great, sure, but I mean, who cares? Next year someone else will be able to do it. Your next-door neighbor might do it. And that's the whole point of pop music."

Realizing that the pinnacle of rock stardom was the very slipperiest of slopes, Elton was determined to make the most of his time in the spotlight. "I've always said I don't want to be around in ten years still playing the same set I played [on this tour]," he noted. "'Cause that'd become depressing for me. 'Cause then I'd be something I set out not to be."

Though every concert was rapturously received, a few inevitable hiccups occurred as the caravan wound its way across the States.

In Mobile, Alabama, a faulty sound system sent Elton into a black mood. Kicking his stage monitor over, he refused to come back for an encore until the audience's endless chanting and stomping finally convinced him otherwise.

In Houston, a pair of security guards began throwing fans to the ground during "All the Girls Love Alice." This not only enraged Elton—it also got John Reid's back up as well. "John used to go berserk if the security men turned on the kids," Dee said. "I've seen him do some incredible things— launch himself off a lighting tower to mix it with some huge Texan bouncer built like an all-in wrestler. You couldn't fault the guy for guts."

"John Reid was quite a character," Linda Lewis concurred. "He was a great guy if you were on the right side of him, but...I saw him head-butt someone once, while on tour [back in '72]. We'd all gone to see *Beyond the Valley of the Dolls* at a private sitting, me and Elton's entourage. And they put on *Valley of the Dolls* by mistake. *Beyond the Valley of the Dolls* was much more sort of a racy kind of thing, and *Valley of the Dolls* came up [instead] and Elton wasn't pleased, so John hit the roof and just went about starting fights with everybody in this tiny little theater that he'd hired. He was quite heavy."

The manager blamed his behavior, at least in part, on the overwhelming exhaustion which befell him while on the road. "The *only* time you can relax is when Elton is back safely in his hotel room," he said. "As soon as you wake up the next day, it all starts again."

The pianist continued dominating the radio airwaves as clearly as he did the concert stage as the '70s were nearing their bespangled midpoint. This preeminence was perhaps best exemplified by *Goodbye Yellow Brick Road*'s closing track, "Harmony," which had become the most requested song on American radio stations during the summer and fall of '74. On WXLO-FM's popular "Battle of the Hits" radio program, listeners voted for the effortlessly catchy ballad over legitimate releases by major artists for a record-breaking thirty-three weeks straight.

"That has never, ever happened in the history of radio programming," RKO vice-president Paul Drew said. "Especially for an album track."

Meanwhile, WBZ-FM in Boston, which kept its own record charts, listed "Harmony" as their Number 1 song for well over a month. This phenomenon played itself out over and over again across the country.

"I never understood why ['Harmony'] wasn't a single," Gus said years later. "It was a bad mistake. It was actually a B-side twice, which is really ridiculous."

"That could have been another single," Elton conceded. "It's one of my all-time favorite songs. But I wanted to get new stuff out."

Any regrets the pianist may have had over missing out on yet another hit single were set aside long enough to arrange a surprise birthday party for his loyal sound engineer. During the L.A. leg of the tour, he insisted that Clive Franks attend a dinner party at Chasen's restaurant.

"I didn't even want to go out that night," Clive said. "I was complaining because—it being Chasen's—I had to borrow a jacket and a tie to wear. I walk in, and there's this huge table with everyone round it, and Elton's at the piano playing 'Happy Birthday to You'. Cheech and Chong are at the table, and Fred Astaire's sitting downstairs. I remember Fred Astaire said 'Hello' to Elton."

Elton spent the afternoon before the first of three sold-out shows at the L.A. Forum manning disc jockey Richard Kimball's two-hour shift on KMET-FM. Choosing his own records, and calling himself "EJ the DJ," the pianist ad-libbed comic routines between songs. A typical moment: "That's the wonderful Joe Cocker and 'I Can Stand a Little Rain', and before that you heard John Lennon and 'Nobody Loves You (When You're Down and Out),' and I think right now it's commercial time....A live advertisement from Elton John—this is me? Oh yeah? Hi, this is Elton John for Licorice Pizza. I've never had a Licorice Pizza. What're they like? Gives you a good run for your money." He let out a *Goon*-like bark of amusement. "Did you know that the largest record store in the known world is here in Tower Records? Yes, it's Los Angeles. Tower is in the heart of the Sunset Strip, and because I'm doing this commercial they're paying me seven-million. They've put a stack of my *Caribou* albums just inside the front door, and from today to Sunday midnight they're paying compensation to everyone who falls over them."

The pianist was clearly in his element, joking with listeners and spinning records by Little Feat and Aretha Franklin. "I'd like my own radio station," he told journalist Henry Edwards. "From the time I was a child, I adored watching the labels on recordings spin around. That's why I still love to play records."

449

Elton's first two Forum shows went as smoothly as his latest foray into radio broadcasting had. On the third night, however, things turned decidedly dicey. After arriving onstage upon the shoulders of his personal bodyguard, 1973's Mr. America, Jim Morris, Elton kicked the piano with his shoe and announced, "Let's rock!" as the band tore into "Saturday Night's Alright (For Fighting)." Hundreds of excited fans took him at his word, rushing the front of the stage. A cadre of security guards dispatched themselves into the fray, manhandling the teenagers and violently throwing bodies in every direction.

"Get the fuck *out* of it!" an infuriated Elton screamed in an eerie replay of his Baltimore show the year before. Then, to his fans, he announced, "This is *your* concert! Come down if you want to!"

Forum manager Jim Appel was enraged by Elton's behavior, which he saw as simple grandstanding. After the show, he threatened to have the Brit arrested if he ever caused a similar such "incitement" in the future.

"Just let him try," Elton said. "I would have loved to have been arrested on stage. I would have ground [Appel] into the floor."

On October 10, Elton took ill after eating a tainted crab omelet, forcing him to miss an "EJ the DJ" guest appearance on KFRC-FM. The station, which had heavily promoted the superstar's visit, was left feeling unduly embarrassed. To get a bit of their own back, the station's morning-drive host, Don Rose, portentously announced, "Elton is ill. I won't say gravely ill. *How* ill, we don't know. There's a doctor examining him in his suite at the Fairmont right at this very moment. We will keep you informed."

The proclomation caused a deluge of concerned calls to both the station as well as Elton's hotel. The pianist was displeased by what he saw as a vengeful stunt by the radio station. But no matter: his show that night at the Oakland Coliseum went on as scheduled.

The tour briefly snuck north of the border four days later, landing at the Pacific Coliseum in Vancouver. Elton made his entrance in grand style, riding through the venue in a convoy consisting of seven silver limousines. During "Burn Down the Mission," a fan threw a British Union Jack onstage; Elton picked up the flag with maximum reverence, and wiped a tear from his eye. "You always get emotional when you see the British flag, or when you meet Britons abroad," he'd later explain.

Draping the Union Jack over his piano, Elton finished the concert with a renewed sense of vitality. His performance elicited rapturous screams from the 17,500 in attendance, as well as glowing notices from the critics, who weren't as studiously jaded as their American counterparts. "Elton John is...one of the few real entertainers this music [rock 'n' roll] has produced since its early days," noted the *Vancouver Sun*'s Ritchie Yorke. "[Elton] is a showman, singer, and musician *par excellence,* of a class unique in rock 'n' roll. His Vancouver concert was a dynamic exercise in poise, precision and perfection attained." Yorke's only complaint was how difficult it was "to find fresh words sufficiently free of the pollution of hyperbole, but still meaningful enough to emphasize Elton's uniqueness."

Elton John's Greatest Hits was released soon after—on November 4 in the U.S., and four days later in the U.K. and Europe. The album featured an iconic cover photograph by Terry O'Neill of a white-suited Elton sitting before his living room piano. "You would not believe how many times we had to retouch the...front cover," album designer Hogie

451

McMurtrie later recalled. "I can't remember any other album where he was so picky about how this would look, and it's not like now, where it's a digital process. All the stuff was done by hand. And it would be thousands of dollars every time we'd touch it up. And he would say, 'The shadow here is a little off,' and 'My finger is wrong here,' over and over again, and of course this is *Elton,* so you'd have to do it."

The painstaking efforts proved well worthwhile, however—the disc quickly became a transatlantic smash, keeping the Rolling Stones' *It's Only Rock 'n' Roll* out of the top spot in both America and Britain. In fact, *Elton John's Greatest Hits* became MCA's fastest-selling album in their entire history, and the first "Best Of" compilation to ever top the American charts. "I thought it was unbelievable when I heard the news," the pianist said. "People said that some greatest hits albums do much better than ordinary albums, but I said I wasn't too sure, and looked at a couple of examples. *Alice Cooper's Greatest Hits* hadn't done as well as a normal album of Alice Cooper would, for example, so I just couldn't believe it. It's probably because it's a pretty strong album." Indeed, the LP would remain in the Number 1 position for ten weeks in America, and eleven weeks in Britain; it would also hit Number 1 in Canada and Australia, Number 2 in New Zealand, and Number 3 in Norway, while also proving a Top 10 hit in both Finland and France.

The critics generally applauded the release. *Circus* magazine labeled the album "a single streamlined disc," noting that "there is certainly enough fine music on *Elton John's Greatest Hits* to tempt even the most reluctant admirer of the wacky prince of piano." Robert Christgau, however, didn't agree that singles were Elton's métier. "His method is too hit-or-miss to permit such a surefire formula, and some of his best stuff ('Your Sister Can't Twist,' 'Solar

Prestige a Gammon') has proven too wild or weird....There are no clinkers here, and I suppose if you only want one of his albums this is it. But it's stylistically ragged, two of its four great cuts are also on *Honky Château,* and I'd just as soon hear the first side of *Caribou.* B+."

Elton, for his part, found the album a document well wort being proud of. "Most of it," he said, "apart from 'Border Song', which I wanted to stick on although it wasn't a sales hit, was recorded when people really started taking notice. They wanted to put a hits album out last year—you know what record companies are like when they've got product to merchandise—but we said no, because there was no point in it last year. It would have been filled with things that weren't hits. This year, I thought it would be good."

Though the LP lacked the vinyl space necessary to include such perennial favorites as "Tiny Dancer" or "Take Me to the Pilot" or "Levon"—or even more recent hits like "The Bitch is Back" or "Pinball Wizard"—it would remain in *Billboard*'s Top 200 for a staggering two years running, ultimately selling more than seventeen million copies in America alone, as well as millions more worldwide.

Chapter 22:
'Here We Go Then, Over the Hill'

"Whatever Gets You Thru the Night" reached the top spot on the *Billboard* charts on November 16. The track, a virtual duet between the most popular singer on the planet and the founder of the most popular band in the universe, easily knocked Bachman-Turner Overdrive's "You Ain't Seen Nothing Yet" out of the top spot. The song was Lennon's only post-Beatles' track to attain such lofty heights, and Elton was ecstatic—his friend had finally been awarded the success he so richly deserved, and he himself had won their wager.

"Elton was gracious," May Pang later recalled, "and said to John, 'Look, if you don't want to [appear onstage together], you're not obligated.' And John said, 'No, a bet is a bet.'"

Deciding that Elton's Thanksgiving concert at Madison Square Garden would be the ideal event for their joint appearance, Lennon and May Pang flew up on the *Starship 1* to Elton's November 20 show at Boston Garden to get a feel for the proceedings. "[His private jet] was just beautiful," May said. "You sit in a lounge. There's seating that goes around the plane, but there are places where you could just lay down. It was great, like a home away from home."

By the time they arrived at the Garden for a soundcheck, Charlie Watts was running Elton's band through an impromptu rehearsal. While "The Bitch is Back" blared, the ex-Beatle looked in awe at the massive rigging and tons of electronic equipment scattered across the stage.

"My God, is *this* what it's all about?" He turned to Nigel. "Nige, how many microphones are on them drums?"

"Maybe sixteen."

Lennon shook his head in amazement. "Fuck, we were lucky to get *three* for the vocals when we were on. And even then, one of them wouldn't work."

The ex-Beatle clearly felt out of his depth. "I was nervous watching [Elton]," he admitted of that night's performance. "I was thinking, 'Thank God it isn't me,' as he was getting dressed to go on.'"

The performance itself was, to no one's surprise, another raving success.

"John and I loved the concert from the moment Elton made his entrance," May said, "prancing onstage wearing a four-foot-high ostrich plume headdress."

After "Funeral For a Friend/Love Lies Bleeding," "Candle in the Wind" and "Grimsby," Lennon turned to his girlfriend with a droll smile. "This is exciting," he said. "This makes me wanna get up and go on tour."

By the time the finale arrived nearly three hours later, however, the ex-Beatle had had a change of heart, deciding that touring would be far too much responsibility for him to shoulder alone.

"I don't think I can do it all meself," he said in his unmistakable Liverpool dialect. "We only had to do twenty minutes, and that still used to seem like an hour to me." He turned to Elton. "There were four of us, but you do two-and-a-half hours on your own. How the fuck do you *do* it?"

Lennon and May Pang flew back to New York with Elton after the show and hung out with him in his hotel suite at the

Sherry-Netherland Hotel on Fifth Avenue, where three massive white steamer trunks worth of clothes took up half the room. Lennon and Pang busied themselves trying on various jackets, hats and glasses like children playing dress-up, while Elton sat on a couch and laughed.

"The thing I loved was trying on his glasses," May said. "What great fun. And I remember asking, 'How much could this [pair] be?' And someone said, 'Five-thousand-dollars a pair.' And that was in the *Seventies*. You go, 'Okay, *this* goes down. I'm not touching *this* one.' But John liked me in a couple of the ones that I was wearing, so it was really funny."

Less amusing was a visit several NYPD officers paid the trio later in the evening. Informing Elton that an anonymous call to the police stated that a crazed man was in the hotel looking for the pianist, they warned him to be extra vigilant.

"Just be careful," one of the policemen said. "Just in case. Okay?"

Elton thanked the officers and double-locked his door after they'd gone.

"After the policemen left," May said, "everyone became very upset. John was especially nervous, since he was about to appear live onstage for the first time in three years."

On the Sunday before the Madison Square Garden show, Lennon and May Pang joined Elton and his band at the Record Plant in New York City to practice their shared set.

"When we got there," May said, "Elton had already thoroughly rehearsed the band. He was a perfectionist, and he felt honored by John's desire to appear with him. Determined that when he and John performed they would sound exactly as they had sounded on record, he had gone to the extent of making sure that the horn section would play their parts note-for-note, like the horns on the record. The precision was astonishing."

"It was [Elton's] band and his show," Tony King said. "John came in and said, 'It's all yours,' and they routined the show and the songs. Elton was the leader of the band, and Lennon was happy for it to be like that."

Brandy and ganga made the rounds as the rehearsal proceeded, the convivial laughter flowing easily. "John was already a friend," Davey said, "and we'd had some riotous times together. The rehearsal was a blur."

The musicians began their hour-and-a-half practice session with a run-through of "Whatever Gets You Thru the Night." "I'll never forget Elton saying that he wanted everything to go right for John, knowing that John hadn't been onstage for a long time," May said. "There's even a part in the horns where Bobby Keys normally takes the lead in 'Whatever Gets You Thru the Night' [on the original recording], and it sounds a little flat. And Elton made sure that note was just the way it was [in rehearsals], he didn't want to make it perfect, because that may not have been the way John wanted it, and he went as true as he could to the record, to how it was."

After tearing through the song twice, the band next rehearsed "Lucy in the Sky with Diamonds," which Elton had just released as his latest single that November 18. Realizing that the fans would want at least one more song together, Elton suggested doing "Imagine" as their final number. But the ex-Beatle, who was wearing a curly blonde wig for absolutely no reason at all, was having none of it.

"Boring," he said with a yawn. "The last thing I wanna do is come on like Dean Martin doing his classic hits. I've done it before. Let's do a rock 'n' roll song. We've done a song of Elton's and a song of mine. Let's pick a neutral number." He paused. "Let's go all the way back."

"So I thought of 'I Saw Her Standing There', which was the first track on the first Beatles album," Elton said. "And he had never sung it. It was McCartney who sang it. John was so knocked out, because he'd never actually sung the lead before."

"Bootleg number five-thousand-sixty-nine," Lennon joked as he counted in the number. "This is dedicated to the One-Eyed Git…"

After the rehearsal ended, Elton and Lennon retreated to the Sherry-Netherland and methodically became as high as was humanly possible.

"We were so naughty together," the pianist said. "We laughed our heads off."

Sometime after midnight, Elton tripped over a coffee table and plummeted to the rug. With unsure hands, he adjusted a pair of giant metal frames as Lennon burst into hysterics.

"For fuck's sake, Elton! Take those glasses off and *face* the world already!"

They both started laughing uncontrollably again. The hilarity continued for some time, until "Time in a Bottle" came on the radio. The two Brits suddenly fell silent. Since Jim Croce's untimely death in a plane crash the year before, his songs had been in heavy rotation. When "Time in a Bottle" faded into "Rocket Man," Lennon snapped off the radio with an acidic groan.

"Christ, you're played enough," he said. "If you ever die, I shall throw my radio out the window."

The two superstars partied into the small hours of the night. At three a.m., a knock sounded at the door.

Lennon arched a paranoid eyebrow. "The police?"

"Fuck knows."

"Go to the door and look through the thing, Elt!"

Nervously, they both crept up to the door and to staring through the peephole. Out in the hallway sto Warhol, impatiently adjusting the lens of his Nikon.

"So we were trying to work out how Andy got to be a policeman," Elton said. "He was standing there for what seemed like hours, banging on this door. And we just couldn't work it out."

The night of the Madison Square Garden concert, November 28, found Lennon more apprehensive than ever.

"He grimly got up and dressed in his black suit," May Pang said. Around his neck, he'd chosen to wear a pendant from Van Cleef & Arpels which Elton had given him the month before. ("During John's birthday," May said, "Elton sent over a pendant. John looked at it and said, 'Oh, lovely,' and he put it on the floor. Then Tony King calls up and says, 'Well, how do you like your necklace?' And [John] said, 'Oh, it's nice. Rhinestones, you know.' And Tony goes, '*Rhinestones?* Darling, those are *diamonds.*' You've never seen anybody [move so fast], he jumped over the bed and took it off the floor. It was a wall and bridge in gold and platinum, and on the back it was [inscribed to] 'Winston O'Boogie' in diamonds.")

"Numbly," May continued, "we went to the limousine. John was numb during the ride to the Sherry-Netherland, where we picked up Elton and went to Madison Square Garden. All of us were very quiet in the limousine. It was as if we were going to a wake."

The quiet inside the limo was in stark contrast to the electric buzz which had built up around the entire city, as rumors flew that the Beatles' founder was going to make a special guest appearance at Elton's concert. Yoko Ono thus decided to attend the show, arranging to be seated near enough to the stage as to have a good view, yet not so close that Lennon might pick her out of the crowd.

An hour before the show, Ono sent two wrapped boxes backstage—matching white gardenia corsages for Elton and her ex. ("There's been many rumors about what actually happened," May said years later. "But *I* was the one who told Yoko that John was performing, and she wanted tickets. So Tony King actually arranged for the tickets, for where she wanted to sit...People don't realize, [but] she called us every day. We saw her. There's a myth going, let me put it that way. She called us, she visited us when we were out in L.A. But the myth goes on.")

"Thank *God* Yoko's not here tonight," Lennon said backstage. "Otherwise I know I'd never be able to go out there."

Except for a charity gig in 1972, the icon hadn't performed live since the Beatles' rooftop concert back in January, '69. The lack of recent stage experience showed: Lennon was a nervous wreck, shaky and sweaty and vacant-eyed.

"I know I've done this before, but Christ," he said, wiping his face on a grease-stained towel. In a dumbstruck fog, he grabbed his guitar and wandered into a special backstage room reserved for musical acts to tune up their instruments. Davey Johnstone sat there alone, adjusting his guitars for the evening.

"In those days we didn't have guitar techs, I did it all myself," Davey recalled years later. "John Lennon came into the room and said, 'Will you tune my guitar for me?' I went, 'Yeah, sure, John.' And he was totally white."

"You okay, John?'

"I'm nervous."

"It'll be great. It'll be fine."

The ex-Beatle stared at the floor. "How long before go on?"

"About fifteen minutes."

Lennon nodded distractedly. "We used to get a bit of fanny around about now."

"Excuse me?" Davey asked in confusion.

"We used to get a bit of fanny around about now," Lennon repeated.

Davey laughed hard. "That was probably the coolest thing I'd ever heard."

Elton opened the concert dressed as the Mad Hatter incarnate, in a purple jacket and oversized top hat. "He looked for all the gawking world...like the bastard offspring of some unthinkable tryst between Leon Russell and Liberace," noted *Rolling Stone*'s Ed McCormack.

As always, the pianist was in complete—almost psychic—control of his audience. They rose when he wanted them to rise, and sat quietly when he wanted them to pay total attention. The ebbs and flows of his performance were perfectly calibrated, so that, two hours later, every person in the arena was as emotionally drained as he was.

I went into a backstage bathroom to wash up," author Eric Van Lustbader said, "and I hear somebody projectile-vomiting in one of the cubicles, and going on and on. And I had no idea who it was. And finally I said, 'Are you all right?' And someone said, 'Yeah' in this very weak voice. And then the door opens and it's John Lennon, and he's as green as grass. He just looked terrified. And I said, 'John, I think it's going to be okay. Elton has your back and it's going to be great.'"

Out onstage, Elton was grinning madly at his spent audience. "Seeing it's Thanksgiving, and Thanksgiving's a joyous occasion," he said, exhausted yet exhilarated, "we thought we'd make tonight a little bit of a joyous occasion by inviting someone up with us onto stage." The already charged air became electrified with raw anticipation. "And I'm sure he will be no stranger to anybody in the audience when I say, it's our great privilege, and *your* great privilege, to see and hear...Mr. John Lennon!"

Backstage, Lennon clung desperately onto Bernie.

"You *gotta* come on with me, Bern, or I'm gonna be sick all over you."

Bernie walked his frightened comrade to the stairs which led to the stage.

"You're on your own now," the lyricist said, giving Lennon the gentlest of pushes.

"Oh shit." Sighing fatalistically, the ex-Beatle raised his black Fender Telecaster like a rifle. "Here we go then, over the hill."

The Garden detonated as he took to the stage.

Chewing nervously on a stick of gum, Lennon stuck out his tongue at the crowd as he mock-nonchalantly tossed one of Ray's tambourines into the blackened frenzy. "When I walked on, they were all screaming and shouting," he said later in bewilderment. "It was like Beatlemania. I was thinking, 'What *is* this?' 'Cause I hadn't heard it since the Beatles....The place was really rocking."

"[Lennon] hadn't played live onstage for a long time," Elton said, "and he was almost ordinary again, at least as a person. So when he came onstage with us at Madison Square Garden, I watched him go, 'Oh Christ, what the hell is *this?*' Because he'd forgotten what it was like....The amount of love from people just happy to see him on a stage was overwhelming."

Playing the riff from "I Feel Fine" to help make Lennon feel at ease, Davey shook his head in disbelief as the entire venue swayed back and forth. "We were actually getting dizzy," he said. "It felt like an earthquake. It was unbelievable. It wasn't just a feeling—you could actually *see* the balconies moving a little bit. It was unreal."

"When he hit the stage, the whole place was rocking," Nigel concurred. "We thought it was going to fall down….[The crowd] went mental. It was unbelievable."

David Larkham, who was in the photographer's pit in front of the stage, was equally as astounded. "Normally, when taking pictures at any concert," he said, "you have no recollection of the music, [the] performance, or the atmosphere. You're just totally concentrating on getting the right framing in your camera viewfinder and pressing the button. That particular night was one exception, probably the only occasion I stopped for a few moments to take in the whole spirit and feel of the evening….Not only was the crowd noise overwhelming, but the whole building was shaking. The crowd appeared to be bouncing, and it felt like the Garden floor was moving up and down with it. I'd never encountered a performance atmosphere like it before. Or since."

Out in row 11, Ono was in tears. "I knew he was getting a wonderful reception," she said. "But when he bowed, it was too quickly and too many times. And I suddenly thought, 'He looks so lonely up there.'"

The thunderous reception kept rolling on and on. It was an ear-shattering ovation that seemed to gain energy from itself.

It lasted three minutes.

Six minutes.

Eight minutes.

Ten minutes.

Gus, who was recording the show in a mobile studio deep within the bowels of the arena, literally thought a seismic shock had taken place. "I was about five or six floors down," he said. "[And] the truck was just floating on its suspensions. I've never heard human beings make a noise like that. It was just incredible."

"I don't think anyone in history has ever had an ovation like that," Clive Franks agreed. "I was like everyone else. I was shaking."

Lennon leaned patiently against Elton's piano as the ovation continued, visibly moved by the genuine outpouring of love. "I was quite astonished that the crowd was so nice to me," he said, "because I was only judging by what papers said about me, and I thought I may as well not be around."

At Lennon's insistence, May Pang stood behind Elton's piano during his appearance. "I've never felt anything like that, being on that stage," she said. "It was just amazing. You could see John just turning and looking to see if I was okay, and it was very interesting because everyone's screaming and clapping, and you could feel the stage going up and down. I felt like I could go through the floor. It's an amazing feeling to be a performer, that much energy and feeling and ruckus. It has to be a rush."

"A-one, two...a-*one*, two, three, four!" Elton shouted as he and the band ripped into "Whatever Gets You Thru the Night."

Bashing away behind his kit, Nigel had to reimagine his drum fills as the song rolled along. "Because the cymbals were actually moving away from the drums," he said, "rocking to the drums and back from the drums. I had to plan where I was going to hit the cymbal. It had to be on the inward swing."

"When they actually launched into the first song, for me it was just like the Beatles," said Stuart Epps, who was serving as Kiki Dee's band manager for the tour. "There was only one of them there, but it might as well have been the four of them. Although Madison Square Garden is a massive, massive room, that night it was like a club. You felt the floor pounding away, and the PAs were sort of bouncing up and down with people banging on the floor, and I'm looking at the ceiling, at the PAs bouncing up and down, and I'm thinking, 'Is it going to hold?' It was exciting as well as frightening, but that's the way it was. Like a small club with 20,000 people, everyone going absolutely bananas."

"The difference between the private and public John was startling," May said. "John was nervous when he first began to sing and play, but he quickly picked up steam. Occasionally he turned and looked at me. I sang and danced and gave him reassuring smiles, and with each note he grew stronger and stronger."

After a fluidly enigmatic rendition of "Lucy in the Sky with Diamonds," Lennon stepped nervously up to his microphone center stage.

"Hi. I'd like to thank Elton and the boys for having me on tonight," he said. "We tried to think of a number to finish off with so I can get out of here and be sick, and we thought we'd do a number of an old estranged fiancé of mine called Paul. This is one I never sang, it's an old Beatles number, and we just about know it."

"Here we go!" Elton cheered as the band tore into a heated version of "I Saw Her Standing There."

"*Boogie*, baby!" Lennon screamed as the song swung into a frenzied solo. The crowd responded in kind, finding hidden reserves of energy as the historic performance climaxed before them.

"The audience went wild," May said. "I thought the building would collapse during 'I Saw Her Standing There'."

By the end of his brief appearance, Lennon was overcome. "The emotional thing was Elton and I together," he said. "It meant a lot to me and it meant a hell of a lot to

Elton, and he was in tears. It was a great high night, a really high night."

Davey felt similarly. "The whole thing was actually so dream-like," he said, "that I don't actually remember anything specific about it. I *do* remember I broke a string and played the solo [on 'I Saw Her Standing There'] on five strings. It didn't sound that bad when I heard it back. I really didn't care."

"John did well that evening," Dee agreed. "The lad's got a future."

The magic continued flowing even after Lennon left the stage.

"Everyone was just standing there in amazement," Elton said. "I was halfway through 'Don't Let the Sun Go Down On Me', which I always do with my eyes closed, and suddenly there were all these lighted matches in the audience...A little tear did run down me eyes. It's impossible not to be touched by that sort of thing."

"A galaxy of match-stick torches erupted in schlock-symbolic tribute," *Rolling Stone*'s McCormack noted sarcastically in his review of the concert, "glowing from the very apron of the stage to the remotest Siberias of the Puerto Rican wrestling-night bleachers to Godspeed Elton over the quavery inspirational soars."

"It was the first time I'd seen everybody strike lighters and matches in the darkness," Tony King's personal secretary, Margo Stevens, said. "By that time, you as a spectator were completely wrung out and drained, so God knows what it must have felt like for Elton."

"That was probably one of the best shows we've ever, ever done," Bernie said. "The emotion generated in that building that night, you'll never see that again."

Elton encored with "Your Song" before Lennon again joined in on guitar and backing vocals on "The Bitch is Back." "The very next day after the concert," May Pang said, "Gus sent over an acetate direct from the [sound] board, [music that] hadn't been mixed. It was direct, with flaws and all—just so John could hear the sound and how everything went. And I listened to it and I turned to John and somebody had hit some bum notes [on "The Bitch is Back"], because you could hear it, and John said, 'Don't look at me,' laughing....'That's not my fault. That ain't me.'"

After the show, the ex-Beatle ran into Yoko backstage. The two sat quietly for a few moments, holding hands.

"John was like he wanted to eat me up or something," Yoko said.

"Well, *there's* two people in love," a roadie joked as he passed by the blushing pair.

"That's probably when we felt something," Lennon said. "It was very weird."

Their time reconnecting would prove short-lived, however, as Lennon had to prepare to meet Elton at an elaborate after-party being held in the ballroom of the luxurious Pierre Hotel. Guests at the fête included Patti LaBelle, Neil Sedaka, Andy Warhol, Angela Lansbury and Elliott Gould. A mystified correspondent from the *New Yorker* attended as well, reporting that "Elton John was sitting at a table and the crowd was watching him eat. He was dressed in white, and he had short blond hair. John Lennon was trying to elbow his way through the crowd to get to Elton John's table, and that did not accord with our idea of reality. Our idea of reality would be Elton John trying to elbow his way to get to John Lennon's table."

Psychic Uri Geller, famous for his ability to bend spoons and restart broken watches with just the power of his mind, was also in attendance. Geller had been an admirer of

Elton's for a long time, ever since a rainy Tel Aviv afternoon several years before, when—on the way to his future-wife Hanna's house—he'd noticed a vinyl record stuck in a drainage grill, a 45 of "Daniel." Taking the record to Hanna, he told her, "If we ever have a son, we will name him Daniel." When their first child was later born, he *was*, indeed, a Daniel. "I believe so much in synchronicity and a higher power," Geller said.

As the party burned on into the wee hours, Geller asked Lennon to draw a picture, claiming that he would draw the same picture without looking. A minute later, Lennon held up a doodle of a rowboat.

"And sure enough," Stuart Epps said, "Uri is also drawing a boat. I mean, not the exact same one, but they were both drawing a boat. It was wild."

"A night to remember," Lennon laughed.

He would never appear live onstage again.

Davey Johnstone had trouble getting back into his hotel room after the party, as Uri Geller had used his mind powers to bend his room key out of shape. Finally, with the help of a front desk clerk, the guitarist managed to make his way inside. The moment he did, Elton phoned him.

"John would like to come and hang out with you and Kiki," the pianist said. "Is that cool?"

"*Cool?* Are you kidding? Send him over!"

Davey watched in disbelief as John Lennon and May Pang walked down the hotel corridor, the ex-Beatle dressed all in black: black jacket, black cape, black hat.

"I thought I had died and gone to Heaven," Davey said. "We proceeded to drink lots of wine, and I turned him on to some of my favorite music of the day: Ry Cooder, Al Green, the Band, the Meters, Little Feat..."

As wine and other substances flowed, Lennon tried to persuade Kiki to change her stage appearance. "Start wearing black leather," he said. "Like Suzi Quatro."

An embarrassed Kiki demurred. Still, she found herself enthralled by Lennon's presence. "[Davey and I] spent the whole night in our hotel room with them," she said. "It was a real thrill for us both."

"At the beginning of the tour," May said. "[Kiki] was there as the opening act, and somewhere in the middle of the tour, next thing you know, they [Davey and Kiki] were together. I don't drink and I don't take drugs, but after a while those nights were beginning to be the same. But I liked Davey a lot, and Kiki. It was good."

The main topic of the evening was, not surprisingly, music. Davey was delighted that Lennon spoke openly about the epic catalog he'd helped create with his former band mates. "He was totally cool about discussing some of the Beatles recording techniques and our mutual love of studio 'accidents'," he said. "Like the feedback at the beginning of 'I Feel Fine'."

As the night edged its way toward morning, Lennon began removing paintings off the walls, turning them over and drawing doodles on the back sides before carefully hanging them up again.

"I was in such a rush to get to the airport [the next morning]," Davey said, "I totally forgot these hidden masterpieces. I like to think some maid discovered them and is now living in St. Tropez."

Elton stopped by WNEW-FM on Fifth Avenue and Forty-Sixth Street the next afternoon and spent over an hour on the air with disc jockey Dennis Elsas, during his four o'clock show entitled *Things From England*.

"Elton had been at the station earlier in the week as well," Elsas said. "And we had arranged for him to return on Friday. He very much enjoyed coming to WNEW—he felt comfortable there, and we put him on very often. I was a huge Elton fan."

After the show, Elton hopped a limo down to the Bottom Line on Fourth Street, where he had drinks with Led Zeppelin's Robert Plant. "Let's face it," Plant said. "Elton's fearsome. He's the whole spectrum, really." It was a sentiment Black Sabbath's front-man, Ozzy Osbourne, would later echo. "[Elton's] got a great talent, he does great songs, he does great shows," the Ozzman said. "There's nobody else that sounds like Elton John. You know Elton John as soon as you hear his voice."

The American ticket-buying public felt much the same. Despite being in the depths of an economic recession, Elton's 1974 tour, which had been witnessed by over a million people, ended up grossing a record-breaking 6.7 million dollars—an enormous sum in a world where the average American home cost only $37,000, and the median household income was $9,900.

Elton performed a pair of close-out gigs at the Spectrum in Philadelphia. The pianist invited Billie Jean King onto stage during the final show, on December 3; terrified at the prospect, the stage-shy tennis star took off running down the backstage hallway. But an adamant Elton chased her down, scooped her up in his arms, and carried her bodily onto stage. Though she sang with gusto during "The Bitch is Back," she'd later joke, "I'm not even sure they were brave enough to turn [my] microphone on!"

Elton arrived back in Britain soon after; he didn't even attempt to hide how glad he was to be back on English soil. "I thought seriously about staying in the States," he said, "but had to accept the reality that I simply couldn't face it. Anyway, I've now made enough money to live happily in Britain…whatever the taxman may take from me."

The pianist's love of country was hardly an affectation. When Rod Stewart stopped by his house later that week and admitted that he was thinking of becoming a permanent tax exile, Elton became enraged.

"He called me a traitor," Rod said, "and put on Elgar's 'Pomp and Circumstance Marches' at a volume so high that we couldn't talk over it."

Having properly chastised his compatriot, Elton decided to add to the British GNP by spending a little of his hard-earned money Christmas shopping at some of England's finer auction houses. Yet because of his high profile, the joy he might have felt in this endeavor was slightly usurped, as he was forced to submit all of his bids by proxy.

"It upsets me a bit that I can't actually go and bid for [art pieces] myself," he said, "but if I appear at Sotheby's, it immediately puts the price up, I'm told." Still, his assigned intermediaries did well enough on his behalf, allowing him to furnish his home with French Art Déco pieces, Lalique sculptures, and paintings by Pablo Picasso and Francis Bacon.

"[My house] would look like the British Museum," he said, "except that I've got Gold records on the ceiling."

One who had little need of devoting ceiling space to Gold records was teenager Maldwyn Pope; an album he'd cut with David Costa—upon which all his career hopes rested—had its release date permanently scrapped. "That record was just about to come out when there was a big falling out with everybody at Rocket," he said. "So a lot of artists were cut. *I* wasn't cut, but a single came out and didn't chart. But in the meantime my voice had taken nature's course and my voice was getting lower. So Gus said, 'I'm going to take control, we're going to start again.' And I did a 24-track recording at the studios at Wardour Street. It was Roger Pope on drums, Davey Johnstone on guitar, Freddy Gandy played bass, and a guy called Mike Moran was on piano. He was a great piano player, and Gus was a great producer. His sessions went on and on and on. He'd picked the best musicians he could and then he created this atmosphere. And he used to tell these stories all night. We'd play a bit and then he'd tell a little bit of a story—Gus was a great storyteller, he always had another story to tell—and then we'd go and record again and again. And he'd just get it down to the level where it was perfect. Gus was just so much fun to be with. He knew the right ingredients to put into a record; everything was just perfect, everything was just in the right place."

While they were in the studio, tapes of the Elton/Lennon performances at Madison Square Garden arrived special delivery. "The tapes were brought straight to the studio, but they didn't get there till two o'clock in the morning," Pope later recalled. "So Gus got the tapes up and he started mixing the tracks straight away. It's three o'clock in the morning and I fell asleep on the sofa in the back of the studio while they mixed 'I Saw Her Standing There'." He laughed. "I was like the *Forest Gump* of Elton John's career."

Elton finished off his triumphal year with yet another series of holiday concerts at London's Hammersmith Odeon, with part of the December 21 show being aired on the BBC-2 on Christmas Eve. (The performance would never reach American shores, despite a fierce bidding war which broke out amongst the major broadcasting networks. Unmoved by the astronomical figures being bandied about, John Reid steadfastly refused to cut a deal, as he still felt burnt by some of the negative critical reaction which the Bryan Forbes' documentary had drawn the year before.)

The memorable gig opened with a lifelike dummy of Elton dressed in a white-feathered jumpsuit sliding down a guide wire from the balcony. Zipping across the heads of the fans, the faux-Elton landed stage-right and disappeared into the wings—at which point the real Elton materialized in an identical suit.

The audience roared its approval.

"That was Elton at his absolute peak in terms of energy, flamboyance, stage presentation and warmth," the show's presenter, Bob Harris, said. "I was at the side of the stage throughout most of the concert. Most of the audience were bathed in light, partly from the lights from the stage but also because of television lights used so that the cameras can pick up people's faces. So I was looking out across the stage toward Elton and then out across the whole crowd into the auditorium, and everyone had a smile on their face. The warmth that was being generated toward Elton that night— you could cut it, you could hold it."

Despite suffering from a bad cold which sapped a bit of his considerable energy, Elton still gave a galvanizing performance.

Toward the end of the concert, a pair of high-heeled snow-bunnies emerged from the wings to present Elton with a Christmas cake. Rod Stewart and Gary Glitter joined in on the festivities, lending their voices to a rousing sing-a-long on "White Christmas" as loads of polystyrene snow fell from the rafters. The crowd's collective vocal chords shred themselves in unchecked appreciation as they stomped and clapped in unison.

"Altogether, a night to remember," John Tobler trumpeted in *ZigZag*. "Elton John is no way a here-today-gone-tomorrow performer—he's a consummate professional who, apart from writing extraordinarily memorable and enduring songs, is able to stage a live concert which few, if any, of the audience would dare to leave without a contented smile….Say no more, squire."

Melody Maker felt similarly, maintaining that Elton had packed "more solid entertainment into one show than most artists put into half a year's work," adding that "apart from the showmanship, the costumes and special effects, the lasting impression was of Elton turning his voice, with its wide range and unpretentious style, to a whole gamut of stand-out songs. There are few singers in rock who could sustain interest in this fashion, or cope with such demanding material, without cracking up or resorting to vocal gimmicks. Thank you E.J. for giving us one of the best concerts of 1974, and keeping rock music alive and well."

Elton hosted a star-studded party after his Christmas Eve concert at 7 Dials Studio on Shelton Street, Covent Garden. Guests included Bryan Ferry, Brian Eno, Radio 1's Noel Edmonds, the Monkees' Micky Dolenz, Cat Stevens, Ringo Starr and Monty Python's Graham Chapman.

As the clock struck midnight, Elton and Rod Stewart exchanged Christmas presents.

"A fucking Rembrandt!" Rod exclaimed as he opened Elton's gift, an etching from the Dutch master entitled *The Adoration of the Shepherds.*

In return, Rod presented Elton with a mini-fridge.

"An ice bucket," the pianist groused, shaking his head ruefully. "Thanks a fucking lot."

"I felt pretty small," Rod admitted.

As the holidays arrived, the world's top music trade magazines—*Billboard, Record World* and *Cash Box*—again named Elton the world's most popular artist. He was the top draw in concert, and the undisputed master in shifting units of vinyl. *Billboard* christened *Goodbye Yellow Brick Road* the album of the year, while *Record World* named Elton the top singles artist.

The '70s may have been half in the books, yet in many ways Elton John was still just getting started.

Part Four:
Bottled & Brained

Chapter 23:
Dogs in the Kitchen

1975 opened with Elton's cover of "Lucy in the Sky with Diamonds" having ascended to the top of the American charts, Lennon's contributions to the single coyly credited on the label to 'the reggae guitars of Dr. Winson O'Boogie'. In the U.K., the single reached a less lofty, albeit still respectable, Number 10.

"[The single's success] didn't surprise me in England," Elton said, "but it surprised me [in America]. *Sgt. Pepper* is a revered album in England—it's like the Bible. So all the kids knew it anyway, even the very young kids that I attract to concerts. They all knew it. But over here, it was a different ballgame. People went nuts when I did 'Lucy' from that album. Some kids hadn't even heard it. And that really floored me. I thought, 'Oh my God, there's a new generation coming up somewhere."

Elton headed back to the future nine days later—and a mere twelve hours after jamming onstage with the Average White Band on a cover of the Motown classic "I Heard It Through the Grapevine" at the Marquee Club in London—by officially releasing his 1969 long-playing debut, *Empty Sky*, in the States. Featuring a brand-new cover—the artist Folon's Picasso-esque painting of a blue Sphinx, the original of which hung proudly on the wall of the pianist's study— the U.S. release of Elton's freshman effort was a greatly anticipated event. New liner notes had been composed for the package by author Eric Van Lustbader, while a center-spread photograph showed, incongruously, the wide-open turquoise sky above Caribou Ranch. "*Empty Sky* is as crude an album in its way as *Meet the Beatles,* but therein lies the charm," Lustbader noted. "Greatness, thank God, has nothing whatsoever to do with elegance."

The LP, which had originally sunk without a trace in Britain six years prior, now quickly ascended to the Number 6 spot in Elton's adopted country; it would ultimately remain in the *Billboard* album charts for eighteen weeks straight.

Elton was pleased that the disc had finally gotten its due. "I can remember more about making *Empty Sky* than later albums," he said. "It's such a great feeling to be able to make a record. The first one is never the best, but it's always the most memorable."

Elton appeared on television sets across America on February 12, on the pilot episode of a variety show entitled, simply, *Cher*. A dour, Sonny-less affair, the production—which had actually been shot several weeks earlier—aired as a standalone special. Standing before CBS-TV cameras in cloud-shaped platinum specs encrusted with 103 diamonds, the Brit sang a duet with the hostess on "Bennie and the Jets" before offering a reflective rendition of "Lucy in the Sky with Diamonds." After several imminently forgettable comedy sketches, the show then ended with a white-tuxedoed Elton, seated behind a mirrored baby grand, dutifully pounding out the chords to a medley of "Mockingbird," "Proud Mary, "Ain't No Mountain High Enough" and "Never Can Say Goodbye," while Cher, Flip Wilson and Bette Midler harmonized around him.

Things were far less harmonious behind the scenes.

"He said some very unkind things [during rehearsals]," Cher admitted. "I got very upset and I began to cry. 'Damn it, Elton,' I said. 'Who needs this aggravation?'"

Though the finished show left Cher in much higher spirits, especially after Elton made amends with the gift of a star sapphire on a 24-karat gold chain, Bette Midler was left glum about the direction her career might take moving forward. To that end, she asked Elton to help her pick out songs to record for her next album, which he agreed to do. "She's always down in the dumps," the pianist said. "Seems most ladies are like that. I haven't met one female singer who's really on the ball. [Though] I *do* have a feeling Joni Mitchell might be different."

The critics, fortuitously, were slightly less desultory than Bette Midler. "Television hasn't seen so much glitter and flash since NBC did a special on Liberace's closet," *Newsweek* noted, while the *Woodmore TV Review* opined, "Best show of the week (year?) by a country mile. More Elton, please. And soon."

The Englishman's appearance was enough to guarantee a viewership of 40 million, and a Top 10 placement in the all-important Nielson ratings. Months later, without the assistance of rock's most famous man, the *Cher* show would be summarily canceled.

While the former Cherilyn Sarkisian was doing her best to forge a solo television identity, and while Elton was performing a solo benefit for Johnny Williams at Baileys nightclub in Watford on February 18, John Reid was busy chiseling out space in his hectic schedule to take over the management reins of the rock group Queen. The first question he had for Freddie Mercury and company: Could they play live? "All I'd heard was 'Killer Queen' and 'Seven

Seas of Rhye'," Reid said, "but they actually set up a full rig show…just for me."

Reid liked what he saw of the band, which had been in negotiations with Led Zeppelin's manager Peter Grant. While Grant advised Queen to go on an extended tour while he sorted out the financial quagmire they'd found themselves in courtesy of their prior manager, Norman Sheffield (who would soon become the target of Freddie acerbic "Death On Two Legs [Dedicated To…]"), Reid simply told them to "go into the studio and make the best record you can make." This was exactly what the four members of Queen wanted to hear. "We knew we were in a difficult position management-wise, but we were in a good position overall," guitarist Brian May later told author Mark Blake. "So we went around and saw everybody that we could, and the only situation that was suitable for us, really, was John Reid."

After signing with the Scotsman, the band immediately began work on what would become their *pièce de résistance*, *A Night at the Opera*.

"Philadelphia Freedom" was released on February 24. Bearing the inscription: *With love to BJK and the music of Philadelphia*—and credited, for the first (and last) time, to "The Elton John Band"—the single was notable for its unique B-side, the Elton/Lennon live duet on "I Saw Her Standing There."

In a matter of weeks, "Philadelphia Freedom" reached the Number 12 spot in the U.K., and Number 1 in America— Elton's third chart-topping single in twelve months. The pounding anthem would also help break down the barriers between rock, soul and the burgeoning disco scene, as it became his second single in less than a year to break into *Billboard*'s R&B charts. Elton was so pleased with its performance that he sent Billie Jean King a framed copy of the 45, along with the *Billboard* chart which showed the song sitting pretty in the top spot.

Six days on, Elton hosted a seventy-five-minute show on BBC Radio 1 as his "EJ the DJ." Playing a wide variety of music which ranged from Archie Bell & the Drells to Little Feat, the pianist truly rose to the occasion, filling the airwaves with a constant stream of comic asides in a host of his well-practiced *Goon* voices. The broadcast proved predictably popular; so many people called into the studio during the show, in fact, that the overwhelmed switchboards collapsed, causing local telephone lines to go down for the balance of the afternoon.

Similar mayhem ensued during the premier of Ken Russell's film *Tommy* on March 19. Attending the premiere on the mezzanine level of New York's 57th Street subway station in a striped suit and *John Lennon: Rock 'n' Roll* button, Elton posed for the paparazzi alongside costars Tina Turner, Ann-Margret and Pete Townshend. Thousands turned up to witness the affair, including pop-art maestro Andy Warhol and *Psycho* actor Anthony Perkins.

When a television reporter tried to conduct an interview with the pianist, a horde of screaming fans attacked, causing them both to retreat as the cameraman got trampled.

"I'm a natural disaster, I tell you," Elton joked.

Elton's professional successes seemed to know no bounds—although *Tommy* ostensibly starred Jack Nicholson, Eric Clapton, Oliver Reed, and the Who, his five-minute cameo as the Pinball Wizard would earn him top billing on many of the movie house marquees across the country. Still, he felt in need of a brand-new direction. The pianist thus spent a large part of the new year brooding under stormy English skies.

"I couldn't understand why I was feeling so depressed," he said. "In the end I just had to own up that it was because I wanted a change. I've always wanted to be part of a good, driving, rock 'n' roll band. [Nigel, Dee and I] used to rattle along. Whenever we played anything live, it was always twice the tempo of the recording, and it was a bit off-putting to me. I wanted to chug rather than race. I wanted to rock 'n' roll in a laidback manner."

The axe came down later that spring, on April 19.

"Both members took it very hard," Elton said. "I did them both by phone. Nigel was in L.A...[and] he actually took it worse than Dee....He's a little hurt, and I can understand that....It's an impossible sort of situation saying to someone after five years that they're out and that's it. But give it a little time and things will work out."

Lennon, for his part, was shocked when he learned of Nigel and Dee's sacking. "You're a fool for breaking up that band," he told Elton pointblank. John Reid agreed with the ex-Beatle. "I nearly had a heart attack...when [Elton] said he was going to change the band," he said. "It was actually inconceivable to me that it would happen so suddenly, and that it would work."

Yet despite Lennon and Reid's input to the contrary, Elton had made up his mind. "I felt that we had gone as far as we could," he said. "After the [*Captain*] *Fantastic* album and the tour and everything, I felt we got to a point where we could go stale, and if I just added some other members to the band, I don't think the older members would have liked it very much. Also, I don't think Dee wanted to do much this year. He was getting a bit fed-up with the touring, so that was another factor."

Gus was at Elton's house when he placed the fateful calls to Nigel and Dee. Like Lennon, the producer thought he was fucking crackers. "It's funny how [Elton] can be the warmest bloke in the world," the producer said, "but there are times when he just doesn't seem to connect with people who genuinely care about him over and above music or anything else to do with music. Just as a bloke. And I think he's brilliant, I absolutely love the guy. But he pisses me off sometimes, because he's sometimes so removed."

No one knew that better than the musicians he'd just dismissed.

"[Elton] hadn't told us what was going on," Nigel said. "In fact, he called me the week before and he was raving about the fact that we were going to do Dodger Stadium....The next week I got this call....I was floored. We were totally devastated. It was out of the fucking blue."

"It was a disappointment, because there were things going on that I didn't know about," Dee later confided to authors Susan Crimp and Patricia Burstein. "If people had the courage to just come out in the open with it, then it would have been more understandable....Too many people take the easy way out."

Nigel and Dee were quickly hired on by Billy Joel, who was recording his *Turnstiles* album at Caribou Ranch.

"I heard those recordings," drummer Liberty DeVitto said years later. "Elton actually sent flowers to Nigel and Dee with a card that said, 'I heard you're working with another piano player.' Their version of the song 'James' was great. Nigel and Dee were [also] involved in the backing vocals— they are both great singers, but the rest [of their playing] was a bit too Elton-esque."

"Billy, in those days, was like an Elton freak," Nigel said. "He would sing all his songs on his record that we were going to cut *exactly* like Elton would sing them. And then Dee and I couldn't help but play like we did with Elton."

Deeming the results far too close to Elton's signature sound, Joel's management scrapped the sessions. Soon after, the "Piano Man" singer tried out new musicians. "When I was asked to audition for Billy," DeVitto said, "I asked what can I listen to or what is he into that I should know about. I was told, 'Get Elton John's *Caribou.*' So I learned all of Nigel Olsson's licks. You know on 'Don't Let the Sun Go Down On Me', where he kept time on the ride cymbal? I thought that was brilliant, so I did it on 'New York State of Mind', 'Honesty', 'Leningrad' and a few others. I still love how it sets up a verse."

Due to the enormous amounts of money Elton was now earning—even without a functioning band in place—John Reid decided that it would be in his best interest to establish the pianist as a "resident alien" within the United States. The move would allow Elton to avoid double taxation on his earnings—a key concern, especially in light of Britain's eighty-three percent taxation rate.

Agreeing that the plan had merit, Elton reluctantly purchased a Moorish-style six-bedroom palace high up in the Benedict Canyon hills, at 1400 Tower Grove Road. The mansion had enjoyed an infamously storied past, having been owned by a succession of notable movie people—from silent-screen heartthrob John Gilbert to *Gone With the Wind* producer David O. Selznick. Amongst its many dubious charms, the customized house featured a master suite bathtub with a trapdoor which once disposed eager starlets to a bedroom below, while the garden held a gazebo where movie legend Greta Garbo often slept when it rained.

Situated near the scene of the Sharon Tate murders several years before, Elton's new digs were full of gloomy corridors and darkened rooms which perfectly mirrored the city itself. "Good ol' L.A.," he said. "There are a bunch of weirdos around this town, like Charles Manson. I never got that feeling from any other town, even New York. There, the weirdness is different."

To help make the place feel a bit less eerie, Elton quickly stuffed his new home full of Gold records, vintage Rockola jukeboxes and blinking pinball machines. His efforts to ward off the creepier aspects of the city proved futile, however, for, a mere week into his residency, the superstar awoke to find a stranger in bed with him.

"Who are *you?*" he asked, fumbling around for his glasses.

The buxom blonde beside him grinned. "Oh, you don't know me."

Elton was aghast. Somehow this intruder had managed to bypass an elaborate security system and sneak beneath his covers.

"The CIA should have the sources these kids have," he mused. "She could have been somebody with a gun."

It spoke volumes about L.A.'s inherent lunacy. that Elton wasn't even the wildest resident on the block—that honor fell to his next door neighbor, Alice Cooper. One day, Alice's home caught fire, bringing a herd of stoned hippies onto Elton's driveway to watch the flames as they licked at the sky. On another occasion, Elton held a garage sale at his house. "He was selling things like pairs of his platform shoes," the shock-rocker told author Mark Bego. "There were normal platform shoes—and then there were *Elton's* platform shoes, which had five-inch heels on them. They weren't my size, but I was with my father, who's a preacher, and they were his size. He bought a pair of Elton's shoes and I said to him, '*What* are you going to do with those?' He said, 'I'm not quite sure, but I am going to work them into a sermon and announce the fact that I am wearing Elton John's shoes.'"

While Elton's footwear became a bemusing point of doctrinal intrigue, it was his myriad spectacles—closing in on two-hundred pairs, and valued at more than $40,000—which seemed to best define his persona within the public's consciousness. Recognizing this, the American Optical Society bestowed its "Eyes Right" award to the pianist in recognition of his efforts to give glasses a more positive image.

"Many people, particularly entertainers, had rather stumble around half-blind than wear glasses," the Society's president, Cecil H. Byrd, noted. "By making his specs his trademark, Elton John has proven that glasses can be glamorous as well as useful."

On May 17, the bespectacled pianist found himself the first major white entertainer to be invited onto *Soul Train*, black America's answer to *American Bandstand.* Host Don Cornelius opened the show—taped at KTLA Studios in Hollywood—standing beside a transparent Plexiglas piano. "This is especially for a very, very gifted young man," Cornelius announced suavely, "who has combined absolute genius as a musician, composer and singer with a sort of psychedelic outlook on life that causes everybody that comes near him to have a lot of fun besides being thoroughly entertained. If you will, gang, a warm welcome for one of the world's greatest: Mr. Elton John."

The pianist came onstage dressed like a Martian pimp, in a wide-lapeled pinstriped suit, vermilion shirt, glittering specs and a feathered fedora.

"*All right!*" Cornelius said with a knowing grin. "Where'd you get that suit, brotha'?"

The Brit laughed. "Sears and Roebuck."

"Elton, it's really a pleasure to have you with us," Cornelius continued, "and I understand that you've been quite a fan of these kids for some time. Is that right?"

Elton glanced shyly around the two dozen dancers who encircled him—collectively known as the Soul Train Gang—and nodded his ascent.

"[*Soul Train* is] the only thing that you can look forward to on a tour, apart from the sports programs, on American television," he said. "I just watch it every week. And the whole band watches it, it keeps us amused and it's great. We've been watching it for a long time."

Members of the Soul Train Gang then asked the pianist a few questions.

Where did he get his funky frames?

"Well, it's not far from here. Optique Boutique is the name of the place, and it's on Sunset Strip. Just go in there and ask for a pair of glasses."

Which was his favorite song he'd recorded?

"That's a difficult one. I sort of like the ones that I've written most recently. I like 'Don't Let the Sun Go Down On Me', and I like 'Bennie and the Jets'." The dancers cheered loudly. "I don't know, it's difficult. You ask anyone what's their favorite song and they always dry up, because it's usually the one they've written this morning or something, y'know?"

Did he start singing from childhood?

Elton looked down shyly at his hands.

"No, I've only been singing for about five or six years. I used to be a pianist in a band. When I first started professionally, I used to back Patti LaBelle and Major Lance and people like that. And I didn't sing until about five years ago, and so I'm just learning to sing." He grinned. "I'm having a good time."

Elton then proved his point by providing relentlessly percolating renditions of "Bennie and the Jets" and "Philadelphia Freedom," singing live over a pre-recorded backing track. Everyone got down. It was a stone gas.

Elton's turn on *Soul Train* proved much smoother than a proposed appearance on *Top of the Pops* back in his homeland. A Musicians' Union rule which compelled artists to rerecord their songs utilizing the show's infamously underwhelming in-house orchestra was anathema to the perfectionist star. Elton simply refused to promote "Philadelphia Freedom" on the show. John Reid released an official statement the next day: "The Elton John Band and their producer Gus Dudgeon are in the habit of spending a great deal of time and love perfecting each number they record. It is completely impossible to reproduce such labor at short notice."

It was all just as well, for even if Elton had decided to play by the *Top of the Pops'* arcane rules, Gus already had his hands full finishing his meticulous months-long post-production work on what would become the *Captain Fantastic and the Brown Dirt Cowboy* album. As to why it had taken so long to complete, Gus explained to *Beat Instrumental's* Steve Turner, "We always prefer to leave the tracks for two to three months before we mix them down. It's always a good policy to leave the material for a short period before mixing, because after having been so intensely involved with the recording, it's difficult to see things objectively."

Finally pleased with the mixes he'd achieved, the producer played the finished album for Elton and Bernie. The lyricist nodded his appreciation after each track, meditatively sipping from a can of Coors. Elton's reaction, especially to one track in particular, was markedly stronger.

490

"He'd been enjoying it a whole lot," Gus said, "and then I played 'Someone Saved My Life Tonight' and he was just overcome, he had to leave the room....He just couldn't take it."

A listening party for Elton's latest LP was held the next afternoon at Media Sound Studios on West 57th Street. Sipping Dom Pérignon and cracking an endless string of jokes for the select rock journalists in attendance, Elton would bow in mock-embarrassment as his guests enthusiastically applauded each new song was played. The heartiest ovation of the day was saved—intriguingly enough—for "Bitter Fingers."

One of the journalists invited to the party was *Melody Maker's* Chris Charlesworth, who had missed the album's playback due to a magazine deadline commitment. "The phone rang at about 1:30," he later recalled, "and it was one of Elton's assistants, who told me Elton had noticed I wasn't at this party and he wanted to know why." By the time Charlesworth arrived, many people had already come and gone. "[Elton] came running over and gave me a great big hug and said he thought I wasn't coming. I said I had to write about people other than him, you know, and he said, yes, he knew that. It sounds silly now, but that's how he felt....I was actually astonished that my absence had worried him, that he was worried I was no longer an ally, as it were. He didn't need me or any other journalists by then, so it was reassuring to realize that for all the success he'd achieved, he didn't want to lose touch with those from his past who'd helped him a bit."

Captain Fantastic and the Brown Dirt Cowboy was released in America on May 19, and four days later in the U.K. (A limited-edition, autographed version of the disc was also issued on brown vinyl, and became an instant collector's item.) Anticipation for Elton's newest LP ran high, causing it to amass more than 1.4 million advanced orders before the master tapes had even been shipped to the pressing plants, thus guaranteeing the disc a Number 1 debut. It was a staggering feat that no other album had ever managed before. (Unlike in the twenty-first century, where albums routinely enter the charts in pole position—due to a less exacting tabulation process which relies heavily on amorphous multi-metric consumption figures such as track equivalent albums [TEA] and stream equivalent albums [SEA], as well as estimated radio airplay—in the twentieth-century, album placements were more strictly determined by actual sales, which is why the feat of entering the charts at Number 1 had never been realized in all the decades leading up to *Captain Fantastic*'s release.)

The iconic album cover, painted by Alan Aldridge—the graphic artist responsible for *The Beatles Songbook*—was a Bosch-esque maelstrom of demonic imagery which gleefully depicted the savagery of the music industry. A masked Elton bravely charged through the melee like a conquering hero upon a wildly rearing, stead-like piano, while Bernie resided in his own little Eden on the back cover, safely encapsulated in a protective glass bubble.

The most intriguing image of the entire cover, however, belonged to a satanic figure which bore an unmistakable likeness to Dick James, a sick-faced creature who mockingly held the figurative key to the kingdom. Whether for this slight or not, DJM refused to pay the bill Aldridge presented them for his cover painting, which they deemed "too introverted and indulgent." Rocket Records was thus forced to pick up the tab, and then lease the artwork back to DJM. To add insult to injury, DJM priced the disc as a double in

England, making it the costliest single album in British history.

"It's their decision, not mine," Elton told *Melody Maker*. "There's only one album left to do in the DJM contract. After that, I'm free."

The disc's lavish packaging was as phenomenal as its sales figures, including as it did a full-sized poster of the cover art, a scrapbook full of ancient press clippings and assorted memorabilia—compiled by Bernie himself—and an illustrated lyric booklet which included the words to the unrecorded "Dogs in the Kitchen," a scathing attack on corporate lechery which spoke of be-suited vultures and vampires. Who were these monsters, exactly? "The people who wanted us to be successful without being prepared to put any effort in to help us, or give us any support," Elton explained. "You get executives going to give one of their artists a Gold record, but you know they're wishing they were somewhere else. Listening to Mozart, probably. There are very few record executives who are into the music, and that makes me really mad."

The music contained within the grooves of the self-mythologizing disc proved to be united and mature; a purposefully noncommercial work intended to be consumed as an integrated whole. Having achieved exactly what they'd set out to do, the producer was rightfully proud of the work. "The whole thing is perfect, it's absolutely perfect," Gus said. "I can't fault it. It's the best that they've ever played, it's the best that Elton's ever played, and it's the best collection of songs. There's not one song on there that's less than incredible....I've managed to get the best sound I've ever got, and it's the loudest album I've ever cut, despite its being twenty-five-and-a-half minutes long on one side."

The critics were equally as beguiled. "Reg Dwight is the biggest phenomenon in modern-day rock," *Phonograph Record's* Greg Shaw noted in his review. Shaw went on to praise "the remarkable process by which Elton John transforms mere lyrics (however sophisticated) and mere musicians (however brilliant they may be—and certainly are) into a gestalt that defies analysis….[Elton's] best songs don't merely set words to music, they use both lyrics and basic melody as a starting point from which elaborately constructed moods are explored, often culminating in tonal crescendos that completely overshadow the songs' origins. Elton John's music has become refined now to the point where almost every song he does achieves that kind of impact, helped along by producer Gus Dudgeon and the rest of the team that, with *Captain Fantastic and the Brown Dirt Cowboy,* should finally receive proper recognition for their part in creating (we may as well face it) the only true pop phenomenon of our times." To prove his point, Shaw conducted an experiment, randomly flipping through the radio dial for six hours straight and finding an Elton John song playing, on average, every two minutes. Moreover, he noted, at least one FM station per each major American market labeled itself "the official Elton John station." "Reg Dwight is the biggest phenomenon in modern-day rock," Shaw concluded. "His songs are on every radio station, every hour of every day; the old ones as well as the new. If the singles charts were based solely on airplay, the Beatles' long-standing record of eight songs in the Hot 100 during one week would be quickly forgotten; it's been over a year since Elton had less than that many on the air."

The *Los Angeles Times'* Robert Hilburn was equally as impressed with *Captain Fantastic and the Brown Dirt Cowboy,* noting that "the arrangements, vocals and lyrics are as controlled and finely honed as anything they've yet done." Wayne Robins, reviewing the disc for *Creem,* asserted that "in this thoroughly autobiographical album, The Captain (Elton) and the Cowboy (Bernie Taupin) achieve a unity as a songwriting team that they've been striving for....For the first time, Elton does not seem to be speaking someone else's words." *Sounds'* Penny Valentine similarly opined, "For once, Elton is singing about himself and not simply giving voice to images and emotions which ostensibly are drawn from Bernie's experience alone....He is more exposed than ever on this album."

The plaudits didn't stop there. "This is one of Elton John's best albums," Jon Landau claimed in his *Rolling Stone* review. "It isn't weighted down with the over-arranging and over-production that marred so much of *Goodbye Yellow Brick Road.* It sounds more relaxed than *Caribou.* His voice sounds rough, hoarse, almost weary. But that only helps make him sound more personal and intimate than in the past....There's no illusion of saying something, they *are* saying something; there's no illusion of superb performance but a superb performance itself; no imitation of quality but rock of a very high caliber." *ZigZag's* John Tobler had much the same reaction. "I've played it several times, particularly the first side, which I marginally prefer, and no way am I disappointed by what I hear," he wrote. "'Bitter Fingers' is the best track for me, coming into the same class as 'Tiny Dancer', my absolute fave Elton track, and 'Someone Saved My Life Tonight' isn't far behind....If you like Elton John, this is well up to standard. If you don't like Elton John, then you bloody well should."

Despite the glowing reviews, a few dissenters still seemed determined to cling to their anti-authoritarian, success-hating bias. Chief amongst them was the *Village Voice's* Robert Christgau, who wondered "what's happening to our children *lol yes!*

when a concept album about the hard times of a songwriting team hits Number One on all charts the week it's released? Does it matter that the five good songs on this one aren't as catchy as the five good songs on the last one? Probably not." More dire still was Charles Shaar Murray, who argued thusly in his *NME* review: "*Captain Fantastic* seemed like an album that Elton actually deeply wanted to make. It was somewhat excruciating to listen to." The *Village Voice's* Greil Marcus concurred, deriding Elton's latest work as "flat, painfully slow, and filled with the kind of self-awareness that in rock 'n' roll so often comes off as mere self-pity."

Yet far more important than the mutable whims of the critics, the creative team behind the disc were deeply satisfied with what they'd achieved. "For me, *Captain Fantastic* will always remain an entirely satisfying work," Bernie said. "Possibly the only album we have ever made where every track fits into a cohesive pattern free of any corrupting elements....It's time in a bottle, a potent capsulated snapshot of a crucial period in our lives that helps to remind me that nothing comes easy....[Elton's] turn with a melodic phrase is unbeatable. When Elton's on the ball, man, nobody writes melodies like Elton, and I'm proud to be the one who sticks the lyrics in there."

"Elton's a spoiler," Gus told *Circus Raves'* John Tiven. "He really *is* a bloody nuisance. He writes these songs in twenty minutes, we do the track, and then he does the vocal track in about half an hour. Then I go in the studio with some other group that I'm working with and spend four or five hours on a vocal—which is quite normal—and I think, 'Christ, these people are so *slow*'....When you work with people who aren't quite that together, it makes you appreciate [Elton] even more."

The pianist, for his part, was succinct. "I think [*Captain Fantastic*] wipes the floor with *Yellow Brick Road.*"

Captain Fantastic and the Brown Dirt Cowboy would go on to be nominated for a Grammy for Album of the Year. Elton would also be nominated for Best Vocal, Male, for "Someone Saved My Life Tonight." Beyond its phenomenal awards and sales success in England and America, the album would also land at—or near—the top of the charts in Australia, Austria, Britain, Canada, Finland, France, New Zealand, Norway and Spain, eventually going on to sell well in excess of ten-million copies globally.

Chapter 24:

Chameleon

With his latest LP sitting pretty atop the charts, Elton finally began the task of pulling a new band together. Deciding to keep guitarist Davey Johnstone and percussionist Ray Cooper, his first new acquisition was drummer Roger Pope. (A snarling maniac, Roger's wild onstage antics helped inspire Jim Henson—whom Roger had known in Sausalito—to base the Muppet drummer "Animal" on him, with touches of Ginger Baker and Keith Moon thrown in for good measure.) Roger was no stranger to Elton's work, having played on the "Lady Samantha" single, as well as on sessions for *Empty Sky, Tumbleweed Connection,* and *Madman Across the Water.*

Elton called Roger the day after he saw him drumming behind Kiki Dee on *Top of the Pops.*

"I'm shutting Kiki's band down," he said. "Consider yourself out of work."

"Cheers, ya bastard. Thanks a fucking lot."

The pianist laughed. "Hang on, Rog. I'm putting a new band together and *you're* gonna be in it. Come over to the office so we can talk about it."

Two hours later, Roger arrived at Rocket Records' headquarters in London. The office had a different feel to it of late, as Steve Brown, Elton's longtime champion and head of Rocket's U.K. operations, had recently left the company. "John [Reid] and Steve were often having fights," Stuart

498

Epps said. "And though Steve was sort of meek and mild, he still wanted to run things. So there would be clashes. Eventually, Steve got fed up with that and more or less wanted to retire. He was a real sort of country guy—he liked country life and everything—and he just wanted to get out. And so he did…and John started running the show, which is what he always wanted to do, I suppose."

As Roger came crashing through Rocket's front door, John Reid uncorked a bottle of twenty-five-year-old Johnnie Walker Blue and pulled out a vial of coke. After indulging a bit, he and Elton and Reid embraced.

"So who do we want?" the pianist asked the drummer. "We can get anyone at all."

The drummer shrugged. "Caleb, of course. He's the greatest fucking guitarist in the world."

Elton placed a call to Caleb, who had been keeping himself busy over the years with high-level session work, including sessions with Lou Reed on his self-titled post-Velvet Underground album.

"I was living in Chicago at the time," Caleb said. "I'd heard something about the other band breaking up. Something had exploded or they'd gotten fired. 'What's going on here?' Then out of the blue I got a phone call from Elton, he told me that Nigel and Dee were always complaining, they were never satisfied with the way things were. And more to the point, Elton wanted a bigger band, and he wanted it to be more rock-oriented—to rock a little harder—and he said, 'Popey's in there already, and you're the only guitar player in the world. It's up to you.' So I said, 'Okay, fantastic.' Of course I was freezing in Chicago, so that was great." He let out an easy laugh. "Elton told me what he wanted to do—he wanted his band to be looser, funkier."

"So that's it," the pianist concluded. "You in?"

"Sounds great. I'd love to do it, but on one condition."

"What's that?"

"That we don't play 'Crocodile Rock.'"

Elton groaned. "Fine."

"I hated that song, and he knew I hated it," Caleb said. "Too mainstream, too commercial. But he agreed to it, and that was that."

While having two lead guitarists in the same band could prove problematic, any potential rivalry between Caleb and Davey was diffused by the former's easy-going personality and the latter's magnanimous nature. More than anything, the Scotsman was glad to have Elton's original fret man back in the fold. "Caleb's one of my favorite guitar players," he said. "He's a brilliant player, capable of playing almost any kind of music."

Elton next decided that a synthesizer player was necessary to help flesh out the soundscapes he imagined his new band creating. "I needed the keyboard player to do Moog and things like that," he said. "There's a lot of orchestration-type stuff on [*Captain*] *Fantastic,* and I just can't fiddle around with knobs and all that. I just want to stick to playing piano and singing."

The pianist turned to twenty-four-year-old multi-keyboardist James Newton Howard, a highly regarded session man who'd recorded with everyone from Art Garfunkel and Ringo Starr to Carly Simon and Melissa Manchester. "I didn't play a note for Elton," James said. "I just went up to his house and we sat on the couch together. We couldn't talk—we were both very nervous—so instead he played me *Captain Fantastic.*"

As the album ended, Elton turned to Howard and held out his hands.

"You've got the gig if you want it," he said. "We're leaving for Amsterdam in four days. We're gonna rehearse for two weeks, and then we have a concert at Wembley Stadium in front of 80,000 people, with the Eagles and the Beach Boys opening for us."

"Okay," a stunned James said. "I'm in."

Elton wrote out a set list—the keyboardist had three days to learn thirty-five songs.

As he stumbled numbly toward the front door, a member of Elton's management team stopped James and wrote down the figure he'd be earning as a member of the band.

"It was like fifty-five-thousand times what I had ever made in my life," James said. "I went outside and just screamed my heart out."

Last into the fold came twenty-six-year-old bassist Kenny Passarelli. A classically trained trumpeter who had played fretless bass with Joe Walsh in Barnstorm, Kenny had already tasted success with the 1973 hit "Rocky Mountain Way," which he'd co-written along with the perpetually-stoned future Eagle, and keyboardist Rocke Grace. Still, an invitation from the world's biggest star to join his new lineup was startling.

"One day Joe Walsh calls me up," Kenny said, "and he tells me, 'Hey man, Elton's breaking up his original band and he wants you to be part of his new group.' I liked Elton's first album, and 'Your Song' and 'Levon'—and I loved the *Goodbye Yellow Brick Road* album—but that was kind of it. But I wasn't gonna turn that gig down. He was the biggest star on the planet. He was fucking huge. He was fucking *everywhere*."

Connie Pappas, Rocket Records' executive vice-president, called the bassist and asked if he could fly over to Paris to audition. "And she told me what I'd earn," he said.

"It was some astronomical number. And I was on tour at the time with [guitarist] Joe Vitale, so I said, 'Can Elton call me himself?' 'Cause you never know, man. But sure enough, Elton calls me the next day, and that was it. I left Vitale, who was really fucking pissed at me at the time. I just split. There were bad vibes. Someone even stole my bass. I just got out of there."

Arriving in Paris days later, Kenny went from his plane straight to Elton's Corniche Rolls. "And I'll never forget it, he kept playing that 10cc song, 'I'm Not in Love', just looping it, playing it over and over as we drove from Charles de Gaulle [Airport] out to the Château. And forty minutes later, there it was: the Honky Château. It was un-fucking-believable." Kenny laughed. "So I'm sitting in the back of this Corniche and I'm going, 'This is really far out', and Elton doesn't say a word. I swear to God, he was so shy."

When Elton's Rolls pulled up the Château's gravel drive, Kenny turned to him and asked how the audition process would go.

Elton shrugged. "You know what? I'm jet-lagged. I'm gonna go to bed. Talk to the band.'"

Davey Johnstone came over to the bewildered bassist.

"You wouldn't be here if there was an audition," Davey said. "There's not a problem here. You're already in the band.'"

Kenny was flabbergasted. "And then Davey said, 'Elton John is bisexual.' I looked at him kind of funny and I said, 'Okay, well what does *that* mean? Am I gonna have to audition for him *that* way?' I mean, I'd been around Stephen Stills and Joe Walsh, you couldn't really get any more macho than the people I'd been around most of my life, all these rock 'n' rollers. But Davey said, 'Elton is cool, man. He's got his own scene, he's got his own entourage. He's incredible, man, he's the ultimate professional, you're gonna love working with him, he's fucking unbelievable. But that's the scene and nobody knows about it, because the record company knows that he's got such a huge audience of young girls that it's not good business as far as that's concerned.' And I said, 'I understand.'"

The plan was for Kenny to hear a playback of *Captain Fantastic* the next day, before beginning work on a solo album for Davey. "And that was gonna be the first rehearsals with the new band, Davey's solo record, breaking in the new band. But we had problems with the studio. We couldn't even play *Captain Fantastic*. Bad Company had just recorded there and some bullshit stuff had gone down, so we ended up just canceling the session. That was it. Elton said, 'Fuck this.'"

Before the group left the Château, Elton and Kenny jammed one-on-one on "Bennie and the Jets" and a couple other tunes. "I'm not gonna lie, I was pretty intimidated the whole time," the bassist said. "But it was obvious there were no problems, and that's how it started. He said, 'You're very heavy', and that was it, I was in the band." (One potential hitch *did* exist to Kenny's joining ranks with Elton, however: Peter Frampton had just offered the bassist a spot in *his* band as well. "Peter was pretty pissed-off that I bailed on him," Kenny said. All would end well, however, after Kenny turned Frampton on to bassist Stanley Sheldon, who would become an integral part of his upcoming *Frampton Comes Alive* project.)

Flying to Amsterdam, Elton put his new band through their paces. The entire ensemble—including backup singers Brian and Brenda Russell, and Donny Gerard—rehearsed for ten hours a day for two weeks straight, in a barren film studio soundstage by a canal.

The group meshed beautifully from the very start.

"Practice went well," Caleb said. "We all jelled from the first bar. It was a tight band."

"Things that Nigel used to do, I've kept in," Roger said. "There's a few drum parts he had worked out with Ray. It's fairly logical, what you have to play. It all came pretty quickly."

Brenda Russell was impressed not only by how easily the new band came together as a cohesive unit, but also—particularly—by her new employer's work habits. "We're in this sort of arena," she said, "and Elton came out into the rehearsal and started playing like there was 20,000 people in the arena. And that was the kind of energy he put into the rehearsal. And we were up-and-coming artists, and Elton is playing like there's thousands of people in this arena, which was completely empty. And we looked at each other and went, 'Shit. Is *that* what you have to do to be a star?' We were blown away by his intensity. It was a great lesson, to be giving it up at all times."

Each night after rehearsals, the musicians would retire to the Amsterdam Hilton—infamous as the setting for John Lennon and Yoko Ono's "bed-in" several years earlier—and partied with abandoned.

"Davey and I just hung out and got high and learned all the tunes," Kenny said. "I got to know Davey. I love Davey Johnstone. We had the greatest time. Partying like there was no tomorrow." The band and road crew managed to quickly rack up a bar bill which ran into the thousands. "We didn't know how we were gonna pay it," Kenny said, laughing at the memory. "But then Elton, y'know, he just writes out a check for the entire thing. Pretty fucking cool."

Three days in, Keith Moon—who had been best man at Roger Pope's wedding—walked into the rehearsals with his girlfriend, unannounced.

"He sat himself down on Roger's drums," Caleb said, "and started doing this whole Who concert, top to bottom, just all by himself. He was going all over the place, bashing the hell out of everything. And then he just threw the sticks down and stood up. 'Okay. That feels better,' he said. And he and his girl just walked off."

Not to be outdone, Ringo Starr showed up the next day. "We were all on a three-day cocaine binge at the time," Caleb said, "and I asked Ringo about *Sgt. Pepper*, and he was so stoned that he couldn't even remember the album."

"Could I sit in on a few songs with you?" the ex-Beatle asked the band. "You guys sound great."

Everyone readily agreed. Climbing behind Roger's drum kit, Ringo picked up a pair of sticks. Before a single bar was played, he noticed that he was holding his own customized 'Ringo Starr' drumsticks.

"Own up, you're a fan," Ringo said to Roger with a laugh. "Many thanks."

Roger simply chuckled.

"I'd bought up all three-hundred pairs of Ringo Starr drumsticks from this music shop in London," he later admitted. "Not because of Ringo, who was great—not a great drummer, but a great *Beatle,* if you know what I mean—but because I really liked the weight of his sticks. They were nice and heavy. Great heft. Great for bashing away."

With Ringo in the driver's seat, the band ran through "Pinball Wizard" and "Lucy in the Sky with Diamonds."

"You know, I'm not doing anything at the moment," he said afterward. "How about I come on tour with you guys?"

"We stayed up all night racking our brains as to what to do," Caleb said. "Poor Roger was going totally crazy, figuring he might lose the gig to the world's most famous drummer."

"How do you say no to the Beatles' drummer without upsetting him?" Roger wondered. "It was a very strange situation."

In the end, it was left to John Reid to deliver the bad news to Ringo.

"I remember," said Nancy Lee Andrews, Ringo's paramour, "the song that was famous then, 'I'm Not in Love'. And we were up in Elton's room that night, and all he did was play that song over and over and over. And I said, 'Elton, you have a broken heart.' And he said, "I do, man. I do. And this song just breaks my heart.' And I said, 'Who's the lucky guy?' And he said, 'I'll never tell.' I remember then I got up and went into the bathroom to put on some lipstick, and Bernie Taupin walks in and slams the door and says, 'I'm so *sick* of that fucking song. It's been going on for weeks.' Elton had a lot of crushes that I think might've been unrequited."

Pleased with his revamped lineup, Elton silently celebrated. The heavier sounds his new band managed to generate put to rest any lingering doubts he'd had about changing personnel in the first place. "It's fulfilling one of my lifelong ambitions—this band *chugs*," he said. "Technically, Caleb and Davey—and, to a certain extent, Ray—can play anything. And, what with Kenny and James, it's worked out that I'm literally the worst musician in the band. I've got to work hard to keep up with them, which is going to make me play harder and better."

As for having his new band debut at Wembley in front of eighty-thousand people, the pianist admitted that "it's really jumping in at the deep end, but we're looking forward to it, nerves and all. Every detail must be right. Every note, every chord. When you are on top of the tree—and I suppose we are at the moment—you are always the target for cynics. But I will not give them the opportunity to tumble me."

During the run-up to the Wembley concert, Bernie had been introduced to Kenny Passarelli, whom he found a natural affinity with.

"Bernie came out for that gig," Kenny said, "and Davey told me, 'Don't be surprised if he doesn't say two words to you. Bernie's really shy.' But he and I just hit it off. We just clicked, we ended up doing everything together. So Bernie and I are hanging out and we're having a grand old time, and I remember Bernie called Maxine in L.A. and told her, 'You gotta come out here and meet Kenny, I think you guys would really hit it off.'" Kenny grunted. "Bernie and I were best friends. And then Maxine showed up in London before the Wembley gig. I said like two words to her. I thought she was a stuck-up chick. And that was it."

On the day of the Wembley gig, June 21, the *London Times* labeled Elton "the most popular single performer in the ephemeral history of rock 'n' roll. Britain's true successor to the Beatles." The paper, which also included a full-color 16" x 25" poster of the superstar in all his sequined glory, sold-out in less than an hour.

That same day, *Melody Maker* featured an interview he'd given to journalist Caroline Coon, who noted that Elton "was born with the ability to make sounds feel like an electronic fix of warm opium squirted directly into the pleasure center of the brain."

"Women fascinate me because they are harder to get to know than men," Elton confessed to Coon a couple days prior, stretched out on his king-sized bed at the Amsterdam Hilton in a dark blue tracksuit. "They are so confused, and that fascinates me. Kiki [Dee] and Bette [Midler] don't seem to have had anybody who really believes in them, to sit down and talk to and really show an interest in what they want to do. Ladies are so messed up. You get the wrong person behind a lady and it ruins them. I can't think of a female artist I've met who seems at all secure or confident. There is so much more to find out about women than men."

The superstar admitted to enjoying his unparalleled success; at the same time, he blamed it for having created a backlash against his music. "In America I've got 'Philadelphia Freedom' going up the charts again. I wish the bloody thing would piss off. And 'Pinball Wizard' is being played to death. I can see why people get sick and tired of me. In America, *I* get sick and tired of hearing myself on AM radio. It's embarrassing."

As for his seemingly self-destructive streak, the star turned reflective. "I get terribly depressed," he confessed. "It's my desperate craving for affection coming out. I'll get in a mood and I'll sit at home for two days in bed, getting more and more depressed, wondering if it's all worth it....I can be very happy and then, all of a sudden, I'm on a comedown....I consider myself slightly insane, in a funny way."

Elton's Wembley gig—dubbed MidSummer Music—proved to be the single biggest musical event in England during that hazy summer of '75. (The concert broke an attendance record set by daredevil Evel Knievel just weeks earlier, for his ill-fated attempt to clear thirteen double-decker busses on a three-hundred-pound Harley-Davidson XR-750.) In an era before charity concerts became fashionable, it was notable that Elton chose to divide the massive proceeds from this outing amongst nine separate organizations, including the Institute for the Blind and the Lady Hoare Trust for Physically Handicapped Children. "That, too, was an example of the compassionate nature within him," arranger Del Newman said. "I met many artists who—with all their wealth—would never have considered helping anyone less fortunate than themselves. Some were so wrapped up in their own importance that they weren't conscious of the needs of others."

Elton had handpicked the artists for the daylong concert. The bill included Rocket signees Stackridge, as well as Joe Walsh, the American funk band Rufus—which featured R&B singer Chaka Khan—and the Eagles, whom Elton called "the best band I've seen onstage the last couple of years."

"It was awesome," Eagles' guitarist Don Felder said of the summer solstice show. "The place and the people just made us high. We didn't need anything else."

Stevie Wonder, who had originally been slated to appear directly before Elton, was forced to back out at the last minute when health issues precluded his appearance. John Reid rang up the Beach Boys, who agreed to appear in the Motown star's stead.

The Beach Boys made the most of the opportunity, opening their set with a spirited rendition of "Wouldn't It Be Nice." From the outset they had the entire stadium on its feet, singing along to one golden oldie after another, from "Little Deuce Coupe" to "Surfer Girl" to "Fun, Fun, Fun."

Taking their leave after five encores, the audience was forced to sit through a lengthy intermission during which the stage was adorned with potted palms and an electrified thirty-three-foot-long *Captain Fantastic* emblem. At the same time, the sun dipped behind the lip of the stadium, causing the temperature to drop nearly thirty degrees.

"Everyone was really uncomfortable and they had had such a long day," Clive Franks said. "That was probably one of the most difficult shows for all of us."

At just after seven p.m., compere Johnny Walker took to the specially commissioned 150' x 70' stage to introduce the superstar. "It's been a beautiful day," he said to the cheering mob. "Are you ready for the big finish? Are you ready for Elton John? Elton John with his new musicians!"

Appearing in an aquamarine jumpsuit, Elton began his set with a 60,000-watt opening salvo of "Funeral For a Friend/Love Lies Bleeding," "Rocket Man" and "Candle in the Wind." His new band—augmented on the day by Doobie Brothers fret ace Jeff "Skunk" Baxter—then treated the fans to a string of classic hits which included "The Bitch is Back," "Rocket Man" and "Philadelphia Freedom."

If the musicians were at all apprehensive about premiering in front of such a massive crowd, they weren't showing it.

"Nerves weren't an issue for this band," Roger said. "We all knew we could play. If I was personally nervous about *anything*, it was meeting John Robinson, Rufus' drummer. We came toward each other backstage, right before we went on. You should have seen him. He just laughed and fell to his knees, and I said, 'What the hell are you doing?' He said he was bowing to the world's greatest living drummer.' That made my whole day right there."

Chugging from a bottle of *Pouilly-Fuissé,* Elton unveiled an expressive new ballad called "Chameleon," which the Beach Boys had originally asked Bernie and him to write for them. "The Beach Boys came to us," Elton later recalled, "and said, 'Write us a song, baby.' When I write a song, normally it takes me twenty minutes, half an hour—top whack—and I'm finished. With 'Chameleon', I spent six months on it, and I finished it, I always remember, in

Honolulu, Hawaii. I rang Taupin up and said, 'I've done it, I've done it, I've finished it.' And it was, for me, what the Beach Boys were all about. And they didn't like it.'

Though the Beach Boys turned the song down, feeling it too introspective, the massive Wembley audience had no such reservations—they greeted its poignant G-major melody with a particularly enthusiastic cheer.

After delivering a trio of insurance hits ("Bennie and the Jets," "Lucy in the Sky with Diamonds" and "I Saw Her Standing There"), Elton took the daring risk of playing the entirety of *Captain Fantastic*.

"We have a new album out called *Captain Fantastic and the Brown Dirt Cowboy*," the pianist said. "I'm sorry it's £3.25, but I'll tell you about that later." He grinned into the upper decks of the stadium. "We're gonna do the whole of the album, and usually it bores everyone to tears if you play things that people don't know, but we're gonna take the chance anyway. This is the whole of the *Captain Fantastic* album. Here we go. One, two, three…"

"No one had done that before," Kenny Passarelli later told journalist Luc Hatlestad. "Only Elton could pull it off."

Paul McCartney and Wings cheered on Elton's artistic gamble from the Royal Box. Other voices shouting out their approval that night belonged to Harry Nilsson, John Entwistle, Ringo Starr, Derek Taylor, Jimmy Connors, Billie Jean King, Martina Navratilova and Candice Bergen.

Elton fed on their approbation. It was his lifeblood, his *raison d'être*.

Interestingly, a seemingly agenda-driven report by *Melody Maker* ("Beach Boys' Cup Runneth Over. Elton Left To Pick Up The Empties") had half the fans racing for the exits as the pianist's set progressed. Several Elton John biographers would later pick up on this article, parroting it back and helping set in stone a fundamental misunderstanding of the reception that Elton and his new band actually commanded. Photographs of the concert, however—as well as a stereophonic recording released decades later—testify to the fact that this was absolutely not the case. While a few thousand casual spectators *did* leave when the temperature dipped dramatically before Elton's set began, the overwhelming majority stayed in place to cheer on England's favorite son to yet another triumph.

Arranger Paul Buckmaster, who had been in attendance, efficiently analyzed the situation. "That was a classic case of British media," he said. "When somebody finally makes it, they start to tear him down. It was a great concert. It was very exciting. That's the only thing that I can attribute it to. And the fact that Elton had changed his band, his formula. This just kind of fuels whatever that negative thing is with the British media, where they say, 'Okay, we've had enough. It's time to start tearing you down.'"

Caleb agreed. "I think it went down well," he said. "One critic said the audience was walking out on us, but I certainly didn't see that. There's a photo that Roger actually took of me playing, and you could see the crowd behind me, and I happened to look round, and he took the picture. And the place is *packed*. I don't remember seeing anybody leave—or maybe if they did leave, it didn't make any difference. We were just on cloud nine, 'cause for us it was the first rock concert ever to be held at Wembley Stadium at that time. It was a huge deal. To be English lads at Wembley Stadium, the shrine of English soccer, it was just amazing."

As for the small percentage of spectators who *did* perhaps bail, the pianist took it in stride. "People don't like to go and sit at concerts, perhaps, and hear a whole album full of new stuff," he told the BBC's Andy Peebles. "I mean, I know when I go to a Joni Mitchell concert and she does some new songs, I think, 'Oh go on, do one I know.' But as artists, I thought I had to do it, it was a new band and as a new album—the previous band had made and recorded the album—the new band was playing it. I had to do it."

After the final chords of "We All Fall in Love Sometimes/Curtains" disappeared into the frigid British skyline, frantic fans called the band back for a double encore of "Pinball Wizard" and "Saturday Night's Alright (For Fighting)."

"Amazing!" Elton told the cheering crowd as the song's triple guitar assault came to an electrified climax. "We'll see ya soon! *Thank* you!"

"Someone Saved My Life Tonight" was released a week later. Backed with "House of Cards," MCA had wanted to edit the six-minute-and-forty-four-second A-side down to a more manageable length, fearing it far too long for radio consumption; Elton unwaveringly refused.

Despite its prohibitive running length, "Someone Saved My Life Tonight" managed a modest Number 22 placement in the U.K. charts, while making it all the way up to the Number 4 spot in the U.S.

Critics were unified in their praise. "As long as Elton John can bring forth one performance per album on the order of 'Someone Saved My Life Tonight,' *Rolling Stone*'s Jon Landau noted, "the chance remains that he will become something more than the great entertainer he already is and go on to make a lasting contribution to rock." Other notices were similarly glowing. Yet the person who in large part inspired the song's creation, ex-fiancé Linda Woodrow, had mixed emotions about the track. "'Someone Saved My Life Tonight' was a great song," she said. "However, it made me very sad to hear it…because it sounded like Reg was not happy with me, and that was not so."

To help promote *Captain Fantastic*, Elton appeared with journalist Paul Gambaccini on BBC Radio 1. With the tape rolling, Gambaccini asked Elton to pick a track to play to the patients of a nearby cancer hospital.

"Better Off Dead," the pianist replied without missing a beat.

Gambaccini turned off the tape.

"You can't say *that*. This is for a cancer hospital."

Elton nodded. "Okay, I'll choose a different one."

Gambaccini cleared his throat and turned the recorder back on.

"Elton, could you choose a track from the album that the patients might enjoy hearing?"

"Let's hear the new single, 'Someone Saved My Life Tonight'," he answered in all innocence.

Realizing what had just been said, the two men broke into peals of laughter.

"Let's forget the question," Gambaccini said.

Chapter 25:
Rock of the Westies

Elton soon found himself back in America to begin work on the follow-up to *Captain Fantastic*. At the same time, his smiling visage could be seen beaming out from the cover of *Time* magazine on newsstands coast to coast.

"When I met Bernie, I wanted to sit home and write records," Elton reflected to *Time*'s journalist David DeVoss. "But it was easy to give in to the image. Things shiny and clean came so quickly. But in the winning, something was lost. Five years ago I wondered if I'd ever get to Spain for a holiday. Now, I whiz around the world. I regret losing touch with reality."

"We never want to write songs that tell an audience what to do," said Bernie, who was also interviewed for the piece. "We don't know enough about the world to preach to people. We take ourselves seriously, but the music has to be listenable."

Sessions for the new album began back at Caribou Ranch in early July, with a track-suited Elton writing songs at 6:30 a.m. each day, hours before the rest of his band awoke.

Gus Dudgeon arrived at the studio twenty-four hours later to find Elton hard at work at the studio's Steinway.

"Had a good flight, Gus?" Elton asked, grinning at his producer. "I've written six songs already, all rock 'n' roll. Got some great riffs."

"Yeah?"

Elton nodded, sipped a Perrier. "Davey's written some bits, [and] Caleb's unreal."

The pianist began banging out the percussively brutal "Street Kids" for his producer. Halfway through, Davey arrived, picked up a guitar, and joined in. Soon enough, the entire band was jamming away, Caleb letting loose volcanic solos on an Epiphone guitar which had once belonged to B.B. King.

"They sounded brilliant," Gus said. "They had 'it', whatever 'it' was."

Indeed the group was remarkably tight, despite the copious amounts of cocaine and LSD which were making the rounds. "I remember standing in the middle of a garden trying to teach [Caleb] the chords to a song, and he was tripping off his head," Elton said. "It was all very strange."

"There were a lot of drugs in those times," Caleb later recalled. "It was a crazy time and we all had money to spend, so we spent it. All the excesses of rock 'n' roll were at our disposal."

The first song attempted at these latest sessions was the lacerating stadium rocker "Grow Some Funk of Your Own." Davey would receive a co-writing credit, for his work on the sizzling intro riff. "I had zero recollection [of] writing that one," the guitarist admitted. "I'd been so drunk, the whole thing just escaped me till Elton played it for me the next day."

Next came the Beale Street funk of "Dan Dare (Pilot of the Future)." A flippant interplanetary tale centering on England's comic book answer to Flash Gordon, the song gained a distinctively garage-glam flavor through Davey's use of a guitar voice-bag, soon to be made famous by Peter Frampton on his live version of "Do You Feel Like We Do?"

Adding to the playful nature of the track, during the coda a coked-up Elton gleefully hissed, "But I liked the Mekon" during the coda, confusing American listeners unfamiliar with the green-skinned, round-skulled alien who was Dan Dare's sworn enemy.

Elton then attempted a rerecording of an outtake from the *Captain Fantastic* sessions called "Planes." The compelling song, originally slated to appear between the title track and "Tower of Babel," saw Bernie—stuck in Lincolnshire with his border terrier, Jessie—watching airplanes roar past overhead, helplessly imagining the exotic locales those lucky travelers were destined for. "In my utopian ideology," he said, "those planes touched down only in the most romantic places." Despite a superior reading, the song would—for a second time—fail to make the final album cut. ("Planes" would finally see the light of day a year later, when it was given to Rocket Records' own Colin Blunstone, who released a successful single version of the song.)

With the group firing on all cylinders, these early sessions proved incredibly productive. "There was new energy," Kenny said. "Elton's got a new band, he's got a bunch of new people around him, he's got his old mates from a long time ago. And the way Elton just wrote those songs, he'd just pick up one of Bernie's lyrics and go. It was weird, man. It was magic. He has something very few people have. I remember when Davey first played me 'Chameleon', before the Wembley gig. I heard it and I thought, 'Jesus, what a songwriter.'"

When not recording, the band took to hanging out in their individual log cabins on the Caribou Ranch premises. Kenny, who had a house in Boulder, was the exception. Late one afternoon, Caleb and his wife Patricia went to visit the bassist—only to find Bernie's wife Maxine there. "It was like, 'Well, okay,'" Caleb later recalled. "Bernie was drinking pretty heavily then and keeping to himself even more than he usually did, but I don't remember any tension." He laughed. "It was the Seventies, after all. Free love."

"Bernie and Maxine, their thing was that they'd married young, Maxine was way too young," Kenny said. "Too much money and too much fame. It's enough to fuck up anybody. But it was what it was. And Maxine and I really hit it off, and it turned into an affair. We were covert, but Bernie eventually found out."

John Carsello, for one, was hardly surprised. "I love Kenny," the studio manager said. "He can play a fretless bass like nobody could play—he was one of the innovators of the electric fretless bass—but, y'know, guard your wife or girlfriend when he's around. Women liked him, and he and Maxine—they hit it off."

Group harmony was further tested when a helicopter came whirling out of the azure Colorado sky just as the sessions were kicking into high gear. Landing directly outside the studio, the chopper deposited several stern-faced attorneys outfitted in mirrored shades and Brooks Brothers suits.

"Hang on, boys," one of them said, unsnapping a briefcase. "We need to get your signatures on these contracts for the fall tour before anything else can happen." Another lawyer forced an unctuous grin. "Now step right up and sign your lives away."

"Can't this wait a bit?" Caleb asked. "We're in a bit of a creative mode at the moment."

But the attorneys were insistent.

"It was an incredible amount of pressure," Caleb later admitted. "It really hit me that we were stuck inside this huge machine."

Gus successfully harnessed that stress, capturing the raw vitality of Elton's young band on the propulsive "Billy Bones and the White Bird." The song was to introduce yet another of Bernie's trademark characters, a seafaring scoundrel who owed more than a little to Herman Melville's Billy Budd, while its musical DNA traced back to a band jam on Bo Didley's "Cadillac," which Elton had debated about recording and releasing as a standalone single that fall.

"Billy Bones and the White Bird" featured richly textured sonics, courtesy of Elton's matchless sonic architect. "Gus was just the greatest producer," John Carsello said. "He got such sounds out of the bands he was recording, and out of our studio. If you didn't know him, you'd think he was kind of high-strung, just that British kind of high-strung, standoffish bit. So we thought we needed to step around this guy, give him what he wants. But once you got to know him, he was so sweet, and so incredibly talented. And his wife, Sheila, they were just so British—really heavy British accents—they were just amazing." Carsello sighed. "And Jeff Guercio, Jimmy's younger brother, he was just learning to engineer. So we asked Gus, 'Will you take Jeff under your wing, give him some pointers?' And he did. That was a major thing, getting a guy like Gus teaching you to engineer. Because he did sounds that were so clean and so incredible. He was a producer who was electronically inclined. But he wasn't a musician—he was a scientist. An electronics genius getting the greatest sounds. Just listen to Elton's piano sounds and Davey's guitar sounds—especially the rhythms in the background. You could just hear everything Gus did. His talent in the control room was just unbelievable."

The session's signature ballad came in the form of "I Feel Like a Bullet (In the Gun of Robert Ford)." The seemingly straightforward track would prove one of the more difficult ones attempted. "Just because of the sensitivity, and the dynamics in the music," Caleb said, referencing the song's tonal shifts, which moved from open G-major verses to sweepingly cinematic F-minor choruses. "It required a bit more concentration."

Lyrically, the allegorical track drew parallels between Robert Newton Ford—the notorious coward who shot outlaw Jesse James in the back while hanging a picture in his living room—and a guilt-ridden man dealing with the aftermath of a failed love affair.

"[It's] a knife-in-the-back love song," Bernie said.

After the song had been completed to everyone's satisfaction, Gus and Sheila took one of the studio's Chevy Blazers into town for dinner. They came tearing back through the complex a couple hours later, their car sliding wildly around the corners, sending stones flying everywhere.

"Holy shit!" Ray Cooper yelled, leaping out of the car's path. The percussionist was hardly amused—his wife and new baby were both with him at the Ranch. "Gus is gonna kill himself, or someone else."

Responsible for the safety of the studio complex, John Carsello was having none of it. "I freaked out," he said. "Gus drove like a racecar driver. He was a wild man. So I called Gus' cabin and I said, 'I don't give a shit *who* you are, or *who* you're here with—you either slow down or you're not driving here anymore!' I was screaming. 'You've gotta *stop* this, Gus! You're driving like a maniac and that ends *now!*' And he didn't say anything. After we hung up I see him walking up to my office, and I thought, 'Oh-oh, this is it. This is where he goes, "Who do you think you are, talking to me like that?"' And so I started talking first. I said, 'Gus, first of all I wanna apologize for yelling at you, I really don't do that, but I freaked out when I saw you flying past in the car.' But he said, 'Nope, John, I deserved it. And I just came up here personally to apologize. And I will never drive like that around here again. You were doing your job, you did the right thing. And I'm really sorry.'" (Sadly, Gus and Sheila would both lose their lives when their car skidded off the M4 motorway in England in the early morning hours of July 21, 2002. "When I heard that he'd been killed," Carsello said, "I thought back to that time at Caribou Ranch. And I wish I could've been around to yell at him before he drove that night. He was probably driving too fast. I miss him so much.")

Elton would record only one more ballad at these sessions: "Sugar on the Floor," a song penned by Kiki Dee. The pianist channeled his inner Ray Charles for the spare breakup track, which featured only acoustic piano, lead vocals, and elegiac electric guitar flourishes courtesy of Davey Johnstone.

After laying down the jazzy, vibes-driven heroin addiction serenade "Feed Me," which featured James Newton Howard, and not Elton, on lead electric piano, Elton briefly halted the sessions to helicopter over to Fort Collins, where he was to join the Rolling Stones onstage for their July 20 show at Hughes Stadium. Accompanying the pianist on the trip were Gus, Roger, Kenny and Caleb.

Elton was excited to be playing with his compatriots. "They're perfect," he said. "I mean, Jagger is the perfect pop star, there's nobody more perfect than Jagger. He's rude, he's ugly, attractive, he's brilliant. The Stones are the perfect pop group, they've got it all tied up."

But the feeling, at least on that overcast afternoon, proved to be anything but mutual. All too aware that Elton had usurped their place as Britains favortive musical export, the

Stones felt that, by choppering in, Elton was trying to upstage them.

"The Stones were treating [Elton] like shit," Roger said. Watching the show alongside Gus high above the back of the stage, the drummer was disgusted by the shabby treatment his boss was receiving at the hands of Britain's bluesy bad boys. "Belittling him, everything. Fuckers. He was the biggest star in the world—bigger than *they* were by that point—and they couldn't handle it."

A gaunt, mascara-heavy Mick Jagger introduced Elton, who was dressed casually for the event in a cowboy hat and L.A. Dodgers windbreaker, as "Reg from Pinner." It was a subtle dig which Elton gamely ignored as he and the Stones tore through a raggedly unbridled "Honky Tonk Women," his impassioned backing vocals soaring easily past Jagger's strained warble.

As soon as the song ended, Elton waved to the crowd and gambled off stage. Not long after, however, a roadie told him that Billy Preston, the Stones' keyboardist for the tour, wanted him to come back and play some more. Happy to oblige, Elton was soon jamming away on "Tumbling Dice," "Brown Sugar" and "It's Only Rock 'n' Roll (But I Like It)."

With the pianist commanding the crowd's attention, the Stones initial jealousy turned into unmasked anger.

"It was a little odd," Caleb said. "There was some drama going on back there. And on that particular gig, I remember watching the Stones and they weren't that hot. They weren't having a good day for whatever reason."

After a smoldering "Midnight Rambler," Elton bid the crowd adieu to rapturous applause and cries of "Don't go! Don't go!"

"We should have kicked him off the stage," Jagger said later, "but we didn't. It's because we're both English."

"Elton was just sitting in," Kenny said. "But he was such a big star that Jagger and Richards got pissed. Elton was laidback, and he was just sitting there playing piano. They said he overstayed his welcome, but he wasn't taking the limelight at all. But the Stones were pissed-off. What I found out later was—'cause I was getting high with [Keith] Richards and we were backstage and this chick was taking pictures, and I said, 'Who the fuck is taking pictures of us?', and Keith said, 'Don't worry about it, she's with us.' And it was Annie Leibovitz, she's probably got a whole volume worth of people getting high in her collection—and we went back to say hello, and Mick Jagger was really nervous [because] it was one of Ronnie Woods' first gigs. *Richards* wasn't nervous, but apparently Jagger was. He was afraid that Elton was throwing Woods off-balance, so they kicked everybody out. We're backstage and next thing I know they say, 'Anyone to do with Caribou Ranch, please leave now!'"

Elton threw himself dejectedly into the back of a stretch limousine.

"I get in a limo with Davey and Elton," Kenny said, "and Elton was *really* depressed. He just sat there and he didn't say a fucking word. And [Atlantic Records label head] Ahmet Ertegun and all these people were scheduled to have a big barbecue at Caribou the next day with everybody, and it was all cancelled. The Stones said, 'We're not going up there anymore, *fuck* Elton.' And it was really a drag. Elton didn't do *anything*, man. But he took it really hard."

Arriving back at Caribou Ranch, Elton remained despondent. "He comes out of the bathroom of his cabin and he's got a mouthful of Valium," Kenny said. "Davey and I wrestle him to the ground, but Elton, man—that fucker was strong, we could barely get him down, the two of us. But we finally did, and we're pulling pills out of his mouth." He groaned. "It was fucked-up. It was crazy, crazy stuff."

523

A day after his second suicide bid, Elton effortlessly knocked out the Hawaiian-flavored "Island Girl." Highlighted by Davey's open B-flat acoustic chords, as well as Caribbean-accented percussive flourishes from Ray, the song followed the exploits of a six-foot-three Jamaican whore in New York City.

Bernie was unusually confident of his work on this track. "I knew I'd written a hit even before I heard the melody," he said.

A couple days later, Elton played a concert with Chicago and the Beach Boys on their self-styled "Beachago" tour. This appearance went infinitely better than the Stones' gig had.

"Elton sat in with the Beach Boys on 'Good Vibrations' and so did I," Caleb said. "And Davey, too. I was playing alongside Carl Wilson. It was all last minute: 'Okay, Carl, what key is this in? All right, Carl, I'll watch you.' And then Elton sat in with Chicago too. It was a lot of fun."

Chicago's keyboardist, Robert Lamm, recalled the concert fondly. "I had broken my leg while performing in Washington, D.C., a couple nights before the Colorado show," he said. "We had been expecting Elton to visit, and the crowd went bonkers when he took the stage for the encore. It was quite exciting. Elton is so gifted as a player and singer, but he obviously figured out how to grab the audience emotionally and visually as well."

Patti LaBelle, who'd recently scored a massive hit with the slinky party anthem "Lady Marmalade," was brought into the sessions—along with partners Nona Hendryx and Sarah Dash—to provide backing vocals on several tracks, including "Medley (Yell Help, Wednesday Night, Ugly)," a synthesis of three short songs co-composed by Davey Johnstone. "'Medley' was written in Elton's cabin during a night of complete drunken/substance abuse and was based on my love of the great J.J. Cale," the guitarist said. "Elton really loved what I was playing, and we found the lyric in Bernie's stack of papers."

The tune, which exchanged pop niceties for maximalized guitar thunder, wouldn't truly come to life until Roger impulsively reversed the beat during the band's second take. "We all just looked at each other," Kenny said, "and we were like, 'What the hell is *that?*' Just fucking fantastic. He completely changed the beat around, turned it inside out. Just by feel. Roger was the best drummer on the planet."

While LaBelle, Hendryx and Dash provided soulful backing vocals on the inverted, groove-based track, it wasn't until they'd left the studio for good that Gus realized he'd made an uncharacteristic oversight and forgotten to record the trio on the final chorus.

"So I made myself an enormous joint, walked into the studio and imitated LaBelle," Gus said. "Nobody's spotted it—not even Elton."

Elton revisited a year-old song with the driving "Hard Luck Story," which he and Bernie had originally written for Kiki Dee under the pseudonym "Ann Orson/Carte Blanche"—the names a pun on "a horse and cart." Kenny's driving bass anchored the song, while Elton's keyboard work lifted it into the funkified stratosphere.

"His piano playing was always phenomenal," James Newton Howard said. "He's one of the finest pianists I've ever worked with, and I didn't know how good he was till I worked with him. His playing was always underplayed a little in the mixes, I think intentionally so. Gus Dudgeon made him another member of the band, rather than the featured soloist."

Deciding to forego the cuisine offered at Caribou's five-star dining hall that night, Elton announced that he was in the mood for some burgers. "So we went down to Boulder in this thirty-three-foot GMC motorhome we had," John Carsello said. "Me and Elton and Kenny and Davey and Jeff Guercio. And we pulled into the parking lot of Red Barn—it was a hamburger stand like McDonald's almost, but in a barn, a Colorado fast food chain—and I said, 'Well, I'll go in and order burgers.' And Elton goes, 'No, *I'll* go in.' So Elton takes everybody's order and then he goes in there by himself. And we're all watching through the window. And nobody noticed him right away. But then people started freaking out in there. He signed autographs for a long time, and then he brought out all the burgers. He loved it. He was that kind of guy."

That night, Elton and his band feasted on their greasy fast food treats while enjoying a private screening of Steven Spielberg's *Jaws*. "Elton had a lot of pull with movie companies like United Artist," Carsello said, "and we could convert the studio room into a private theater. We had a screen that would electrically come down, and we had two 35mm cameras. So Elton called up United Artists, and I'd gone down to Denver just the day before and picked up a 35mm print of *Jaws*. We ran it in the studio, we had everybody in there—even Guercio's parents were there, there were like thirty people in there, everybody laying around the floor—and it was great. We were all screaming."

Stevie Wonder stopped by the studio the next day to socialize with the band.

"I loved your horn arrangement on 'Honky Cat'," the Motown wunderkind told Gus, who was moved by the compliment.

"Really incredible," the producer said years later. "Stevie was a gentleman. And he'd done 'Superstition', so his words meant a helluva lot."

Stevie brought along an analogue tape which held several tracks under consideration for his masterwork-in-progress, *Songs in the Key of Life.* "He came and played me some stuff that was just unreal," Elton said. "I don't think there's any of it on the album, though."

Still, the highlight of Stevie's visit was nonmusical in nature. Jim Guercio was driving him around the premises in a restored four-wheel drive military Jeep, along with Larry Fitzgerald, Chicago's manager. "They were going down to Bernie's cabin," Carsello said. "So they put Stevie behind the wheel. Jimmy sat next to him, and he had a stick that he used to work the gas pedal, and he was steering under the dashboard, operating the bottom of the steering wheel, and Stevie was pretending to be driving. So they drove past Bernie, and Bernie was like, 'Whoa! What's going *on?*' It totally blew his mind." Carsello laughed. "He truly thought Stevie was driving."

After Stevie's departure, the sessions concluded with the searing squall of "Street Kids," a raging lament about British punks marking time in an East End gang. Elton played bluesy barrelhouse piano on the track, belying the long-held influence Little Feat's Bill Payne had on him. Attempting to live up to Payne's intricate style brought out Elton's competitive best. "There was a piano riff in triads starting up on an A-D-F and going down in sixteenth notes, all the way to the bottom of the piano," James said. "[Elton] developed the riff, then turned around at the piano, looked at me, and said something like, 'Check *that* one out.'"

Besides housing some of Elton's most corrosively elegant piano licks ever committed to tape, "Street Kids" also boasted a flamethrower guitar solo, the longest ever to be featured on an Elton John recording. "We stretched that out," Caleb said. "That was done live, it wasn't an overdub. That track is a good example of the tightness of the band. It flew."

The sessions were completed ten short days after they began—or so Kenny Passarelli thought.

"We finish recording all the songs," he said, "and I'm ready to get out of there and party, and Gus pulls me aside and tells me that he couldn't get a decent sound off my fretless bass, and that I'm gonna have to replay the entire thing, overdub the entire thing. I could *not* fucking believe it. It burst the bubble for me."

The bassist tried talking Gus out of it, but the producer was adamant.

"What am I gonna do, man?" Kenny asked.

Gus grimaced. "Well, don't you have any other basses?"

"No."

"Well...find one."

At a loss, Kenny scrounged a few basses from his friends—including Paul McCartney's Hofner, which Paul had given to Jim Guercio in gratitude for Guercio's having mixed his *Ram* album.

"I brought everything I had to the studio," Kenny said, "and I'll be damned, the hardest one to play—and the only one that Gus could get a sound on—was the Hofner. The action on it was horrible. But Gus kept insisting. I just fucking hated his guts. I just could *not* believe what this guy was doing to me, 'cause I just know how great those live tracks were. As a matter of fact, there were only two songs Gus kept that have fretless bass on them that were the live bass tracks—'Feed Me' and 'Street Kids'. If you listen to those two real close, you can hear that it's a fretless bass. Anyway, we got it done. And I was just so pissed-off."

Chapter 26:
'Elton Could Shit Bricks and People Would
Go Out and Buy Them'

With the new Caribou Ranch sessions thus completed, a black-bereted Elton joined the Doobie Brothers and the Eagles at their joint concert at the Oakland Coliseum. Pounding a dented black grand, Elton—who, thanks to a diet of avocados and Diet Dr. Pepper, was at his thinnest—added his chops to the Doobies' "Listen to the Music," as well as to a spirited cover of Chuck Berry's "Carol" with the Eagles.

Gus, meanwhile, took the master tapes from the recently concluded sessions back to England for mixing and mastering. Though such a large band could have easily gotten cluttered in the surging soundscape, Gus was able to carve out a space for each individual musician within the larger whole. While such exacting efforts could easily take its toll on one's senses, the producer had a self-prescribed cure for such matters. "[Gus] used to ring me up, as he liked smoking a bit of dope and in those days I knew every dealer on every street corner," Freddy Gandy—one of Bluesology's ex-bassists—later told author Keith Hayward. "So whenever Gus came back from America, he would go straight into the studio—because he just loved getting back to the tapes— give me a call, and I would go and meet him with some stuff....We'd spend time together rolling joints and playing music. When [the new Caribou Ranch tracks were] finished, Gus turned to me and said, 'This is going to go straight to

Number One in the album charts in a couple of months' time'....Gus *made* the sound of Elton John."

When Kenny Passarelli heard the finished tracks, he began to gain a better understanding of Gus' methodology. "When he brought those mixed tracks back, they sounded so incredible," the bassist said years later. "I mean, to this day, people say, 'Man, that bass, it sounds fucking unbelievable, it's so *forward.*' And so I had to say to Gus afterwards, 'Man, I gotta tell you, I was really pissed-off with what happened, but man, the record sounds unbelievable.' Gus was a brilliant engineer and producer."

After the new songs were properly mixed and mastered, the long struggle to properly sequence the album began. It was an indispensable step often overlooked by other recording acts. "I can't believe how many people put two similar tracks next to each other [on an album]," Gus later told *East End Lights'* John F. Higgins. "In the same key, with the same tempo and the same sort of instruments. I guess that's actually probably the secret for me: I always used to try to go, 'Okay, so here's the first song...' And you get a vibe off it. And then you shouldn't know what to expect when the next thing happens. Hopefully, it will either be a surprise or it will be a logical thing....There is the odd track that you think, 'Well, this is not a great track.' The classic 'elephant's graveyard,' as we used to call it, was usually the second-to-last cut on one of the sides. Either second-to-last or third-to-last on, usually, side two...[though] I rarely found myself in that situation [with Elton]. It's very rare that I recorded something that I felt that uncomfortable about."

A song the producer *may* have felt less than completely satisfied with, had he been directly involved, was a comic record by Clive Baldwin entitled "Now It's Paul McCartney

Stevie Wonder Alice Cooper Elton John." In an era where oddball records like "Mr. Jaws," "Junk-Food Junkie" and "Disco Duck" flourished, Baldwin's single imagined vaudeville singer Al Jolson awakening from a state of suspended animation to learn that the music of his time has been irrevocably displaced.

The single was soon followed by another howler, Yugoslavian songbird Zdenka Kovacicek's disco offering, "Hallo [sic] Mr. Elton John."

"I suppose this means I've made it," Elton joked about the profusion of novelty 45s. "What a world, I tell you."

The pianist was much more impressed by a test pressing John Reid played him of Queen's upcoming single, an operatic phantasia entitled "Bohemian Rhapsody."

"Are you fucking mad?" Elton said. "You *can't* release that. It's brilliant, but…it's too much. Nobody's gonna play that thing, not in a million fucking years. Play it again."

Reid went back to Queen the next day.

"We're onto something, boys," he said with a Cheshire grin. (So impressed was Freddie Mercury with Reid's guidance that he soon composed an ebulliently baroque extravaganza entitled "The Millionaie's Waltz" specifically for the manager.)

Not pausing to catch his breath, Elton cohosted the first annual telecast of the *Rock Music Awards,* on August 9. Broadcast live from the Santa Monica Civic Auditorium, the production was the brainchild of rock impresario Don Kirshner, who'd originally gotten the idea for the show while attending the Grammy Awards. "I said to myself [that] it's absolutely incredible that there are no awards for such groups as Led Zeppelin, the Rolling Stones and other progressive rock musicians," Kirshner said. "It was so blatantly obvious that these groups hadn't been recognized....If country music can have its own awards program, why not rock?"

Decked out in a gold lamé suit and rhinestone-studded glasses, Elton appeared at the top of the show alongside hostess Diana Ross.

"Good evening, everybody in TV Land," Elton said. "I'm Captain Fantastic."

"And I'm General Delivery," a very pregnant Ross replied. "Better known as Big Bird."

"So I can tell her to 'cluck off' during the program," Elton retorted, wincing at the painfully lame script. "Stay tuned," he extemporized. "It gets worse."

During the broadcast, Elton and Ross handed out awards to Bob Dylan, the Eagles, Joni Mitchell and Bad Company. Nominated himself in multiple categories—including Best Group and Best Pop Male Vocalist in a Rock Movie (Gus Dudgeon was also nominated for Best Producer)—Elton would win Best Rock Single for "Philadelphia Freedom," as well as being named Outstanding Rock Personality of the Year.

"It might seem odd," critic John Rockwell sniped in the *New York Times,* "that Mr. John was considered the year's 'outstanding personality' when he wasn't chosen the best male vocalist or the producer of the best single or album....For the best group, it seemed peculiar to include Mr. John's band among the nominees, since he is such a strong solo artist and has disbanded his old group."

Elton, for his part, was less put-off by any vagaries of the nominating process than by the overall tenor of the show itself. "We had a script meeting with CBS and it was the most disgusting thing I've ever heard in my life," he said. "They wanted all shark jokes [because of *Jaws*], so they could reach the middle-aged in Peoria. I mean, they had David Janssen and Brenda Vaccaro and Michael Douglas presenting awards. What a joke. I was gonna get out, but I'd asked Diana Ross to be hostess on the show, and she was pregnant, and someone pointed out it would be harmful to her if I left her in the lurch."

Despite Elton's misgivings—and in large part directly thanks to his presence—the show pulled in over 40 million viewers, easily landing itself in Nielson's Top 10. (The next year's broadcast, sans Elton, would languish in Nielson's bottom 50.) The success of the broadcast gave the pianist an idea for an "all-time great" TV special. "Just have music all the way through and no bullshit," he said. "With just people like Grand Central Station, and then you'd cut to the Ohio Players, and then you'd cut to the Who or something. Just go *Bang! Bang! Bang! Bang! Bang! Bang!*—[and] with great sound. So we're going to try and work on that."

Elton quickly turned his attention back to the performing stage. Making a pilgrimage of sorts to the site of his initial breakthrough, the Troubadour, he played a handful of five-year anniversary shows on August 25, 26 and 27. Demand for tickets was so high, a special postcard lottery raffle had to be held; with more than two-hundred-thousand entries received, Elton and Bernie personally drew the winners by hand.

The opening night gala performance was a true event, which forced Santa Monica Boulevard to be closed off to traffic, to keep the thousands of onlookers away. Those lucky enough to be inside dined on a complimentary lobster and champagne dinner. As had been the case half a decade earlier, Neil Diamond was again on hand to introduce the Brit onto stage. And again, as with five years earlier, Elton was bearded for the occasion.

Leading his band through a ninety-minute set which featured a plethora of hits—as well as the premiere of "Street

Kids"—Elton's efforts were rewarded by multiple standing ovations from the celebrity-studded crowd, which included Tony Curtis, Hugh Hefner, Helen Reddy, Ringo Starr, Joe Walsh, Cher, and Elton's original drummer, Nigel Olsson.

"Now I *know* he's the greatest," Nigel said. "I've never been able to see him from [the audience] before. It's weird being out here rather than on stage, but he's just fantastic. Fantastic."

Promoter Bill Graham was also impressed with the performance, proceeds for which benefited the Jules C. Stein Eye Institute at UCLA. (Intrestingly, Dr. Stein, who had established the Research to Prevent Blindness organization, was also the founder of MCA Records. When asked his thoughts on Elton, Dr. Stein labeled him "a wonderful man with no artistic pretensions, and he's one hell of a showman.") Calling Elton's new group the best band he'd ever seen in support of a vocalist, Graham went on to claim that their "fullness is something you just never get outside of a studio. It was an absolutely brilliant set. [Elton] is number one."

Robert Hilburn, whose original Troubadour review was so instrumental in helping launch Elton's career back in 1970, noted the pianist's outstanding growth as both a writer and performer. "He has not only created a major body of work," the critic wrote, "but his light, good-natured manner on stage has helped kick much of the pompousness out of rock." Still, Hilburn was disconcerted when he met up with the pianist after the show in a small trailer behind the club. "Uncharacteristically, he didn't want to say hello to all the well-wishers. Elton pulled me aside and said he wanted to tell me something just as a friend. The man who I thought was the anti-Joplin said his life was spinning out of control and that he had tried to commit suicide. All the joy in him seemed to have vanished."

A special limited edition hardcover book, entitled *Five Years of Fun,* was created especially for those lucky enough to find themselves in attendance at the opening night performances. Written by Robert Hilburn and art directed by David Larkham, its yearbook-like pages provided a kaleidoscopic overview of Elton's life from August 1970 to August 1975. Within the pages were photographs of Elton at the Troubadour, at the Santa Monica Civic Auditorium, at Madison Square Garden. Elton with Annie Leibovitz, Tatum O'Neal, Richard Chamberlain and Candice Bergen. Elton posing beside Harry Nilsson, Martina Navratilova, John Lennon and Steve McQueen. Elton signing his eight-million-dollar contract, and Elton clowning around with Bernie at the *Caribou* album cover shoot—Bernie pretending to relieve himself against the bucolic backdrop while a monocle-wearing Elton stared vacantly off into space, both of them swigging from bottles of Coors.

"The simplest and safest thing to say now," Hilburn wrote in summation, "is that [Elton] has dominated pop music in the 1970s. He has not only helped reintroduce the element of *fun* to pop music through his stage shows, but he has, with the help of lyricist Bernie Taupin and record producer Gus Dudgeon, given us a body of work that has touched a wider and more celebrative pop audience than anyone since the day earlier in 1970 when Paul McCartney announced the end of another era was over. The consummate rock fan has, in short, become the consummate rock star."

The Troubadour shows served as an extended rehearsal of sorts for Elton's 15-date *West of the Rockies* tour. Opening on August 29 at the San Diego Sports Arena, multiple stadiums' worth of tickets sold out as fast as overburdened Ticketron computers could spit them out. Unsurprisingly, hysteria reigned in each city where the tour was to land. In Las Vegas, when a local deejay announced that tickets were about to go on sale at the Cinerama Dome—instead of at the expected Convention Center box office—a throng of desperate fans already lined up at the Convention Center raced madly across the desert. Once at the Cinerama Dome, one girl passed out in the 102-degree heat. Her friends dragged her limp body beneath the shade of a palm tree, then immediately got back in line, even as hundreds more converged on the cinema.

"It looked like something out of a disaster movie," fan Bob Bell said.

Though the shows themselves were as highly anticipated as ever, the core feeling of the production had shifted. Swapping glitz for a steelier edge, the gigs—powered by Roger's deep-in-the-pocket drumming, and the cannonading twin-guitar assault of Davey Johnstone and Caleb Quaye— pushed the outer limits of rock 'n' roll lunacy. "It was the closest Elton had to a real zapping rock 'n' roll band," Ray Cooper said. "This was a hard-edged band. Caleb doesn't take any prisoners."

Each concert was a marathon event, a thirty-song, three-hour-plus spectacle encompassing every stage of Elton's career. Opening with the gentle strains of "Your Song," "I Need You to Turn To" and "Border Song," Elton and his new band were soon dishing up shattering live-wire performances of "Dan Dare (Pilot of the Future)," "Island Girl" and "(Gotta Get a) Meal Ticket," while also brocading their set with rare treats which included an extended workout on "Empty Sky" and a sinewy revamp of *Caribou*'s countrified pastiche, "Dixie Lily." "Harmony" would also make its live debut during the tour. "It's our most requested song, so we thought we'd better start doing it," Elton said.

"Because people came up to us and said, 'Why don't you sing it? It's the only happy song on *Yellow Brick Road.*'"

Elton's band was augmented for this campaign by a trio of backup vocalists. "I worked a lot with Bruce Johnstone, and was actually signed to a production deal with him in '72," singer Jon Joyce recalled years later. "Bruce was going to form a group called California Music, because things weren't going so well with the Beach Boys at the time, things were going in different directions. He was my introduction into rock 'n' roll. And Elton's management came to Bruce for recommendations for a background group. They wanted to do a three-voice Beach Boys-like background group. And so it was me, my friend Jim Haas, and Carol Parks, who was [session guitarist] Dean Parks' wife. But then Elton met Cindy Bullens and they were just instant buds, so Carol was out. But that worked out fine. Cindy has been a lifelong friend."

"I crashed a press party for Neil Sedaka, hosted by Rocket Records, at Cherokee Recording Studios in Hollywood on Wednesday, September 17," Cindy Bullens said of her fortuitous meeting with Elton. "I had been hanging out at Cherokee, recording with Bob Crewe and singing backup on occasional sessions there. I had become friends with the owners, the Robb Brothers, and had heard that Elton was going to be at the studio for the party. The brothers and I were watching the party from the control room of Studio One when I suddenly decided I was going to go in." Bullens headed straight for the food table and did her best to mingle. "After a few minutes, Elton walked up to me and asked me my name. I was in shock. He was the last person I expected to talk to. We chatted for a few minutes and then someone led him away. I thought I might get kicked out, but I didn't. A few minutes later, one of his management team asked me what I did. I told her I was a singer. A few minutes after that, she came back up to me and asked me what I was doing for the next two months, and that Elton wanted to know if I wanted to go on the road with him. Two weeks later, I was on the road with Elton John. True story."

The first time all three backing vocalists worked directly with Elton was at a rehearsal stage at Columbia Pictures days later.

"We'd been given a set list and told to learn our parts," Jim Haas said. "Strange as it sounds, I sang top, Cindy sang the middle part, and Jon sang the bottom. Because [for] most of Elton's stuff back in that time, Nigel's was the high voice. So we got a real edgy, kind of Brian Wilson/Frankie Valli sound going on up high, and everything else beneath it to fill it out. We all just learned our parts and then we added things that we felt were essential, or good to do. The music was so good, it was a blast to work on. I mean, Davey was still there, he was still playing. But we also had Caleb and James Newton Howard, for Christ's sake. You don't get any better than that. It was a remarkable group of musicians, and Elton was so musically gifted. Every piece of music was a joy to work on. It never got old."

Rolling Stone's Ben Edmonds was effusive in his praise of an early show at the Las Vegas Convention Center, one of the few non-stadium gigs on the tour. "On a musical level," he wrote, "Elton delivered, and the 6,000 people who packed the Las Vegas Convention Center got more than three hours of Elton's best. On this night, Elton gave his people everything they wanted."

"I remember the first time we walked out onstage," Jon Joyce said, "and I could not believe what a huge reception Elton got. We did like thirty-six songs, and they were all stone hits. 'Bennie and the Jets', 'Lucy in the Sky with Diamonds'…it was just one thing after another. I was just pinching myself. That was a highpoint for me."

The euphoria which Elton felt from performing a great show was unrivaled. Yet the highs couldn't erase the darker moments which still haunted him. "I saw a couple occasions on the road—and he never took it out on anyone else—but Elton would just lock himself away and he would go into this really deep, dark place," Jim Haas said. "And nobody in the band even tried to approach him then. He just took things out on himself, he just stuck to himself and got very moody. But when he was fine and in a good mood, which was ninety-five percent of the time, we'd fly back from shows— we'd stay in one city and do, say, the southern part of the tour—and then if we were in Phoenix and did Tucson or Denver, someplace close, and we got back relatively early, he would invite me up to his place to play baccarat. So just he and I would sit around and talk and play baccarat. He would disappear occasionally, and I'm sure he was back there doing a line or two, and he drank pretty heavily as well. He either had Southern Comfort or Jack Daniels. I remember a couple times watching him down a whole quart of one or the other and then just taking off his clothes and diving into the pool. And it was time for me to go home, but I was worried that he was going to hit his head or drown in there, so I always stayed and made sure that he was okay, because by then everyone else was conked out. But the combination of the little white powder and booze—he was always a very alert, awake drunk. And he could play the shit out of baccarat. Very few times did I win. But we had a great time, and he was always very kind to me. Always interested in what I did for a living outside of when I was around with him, and what my goals were. He was a very nice guy."

As always, Bernie joined the caravan as it lit out for territories both old and new.

"I don't sing and I don't play anything, yet somehow I get treated like a rock 'n' roll star," he said. "But I couldn't live with the pressures Elton has. I hate going onstage, even when Elton makes me come on and wave. I prefer to stand aside and absorb the excitement."

Whether on the road or off, Elton's streak of musical achievements seemed unstoppable. The latest proof came that October, when "Bad Blood"—a single from Neil Sedaka's Rocket Records album, *The Hungry Years* (which boasted Bernie Taupin on the cover, dressed as a hobo)— reached the top spot on the *Billboard* charts. The effervescent track, featuring prominent backing vocals from Elton, became the most successful single of Sedaka's career. The crooner was hardly surprised. "Within seven takes, [Elton had] put his voice on 'Bad Blood' perfectly. I knew then it would be a big hit. It was full of energy." While in Clover Studios on Santa Monica Boulevard, Elton also lent his vocal talents to a bouncy Sedaka-penned trifle entitled "Steppin' Out." "I played him three or four songs," Sedaka told *East End Light*'s Kevin Bell. "I played him 'Your Favorite Entertainer', [and] I said, 'Do you want to do background on that?' He said, 'Maybe not'....Then I played him 'Steppin' Out', [and] he said, 'I want to do that.' And 'Bad Blood'. He said, 'I want to do that.' He was kind enough to accept both of them....I will be indebted to Elton forever....He's a genius of all time. Everything he touches is perfection."

Elton then lent a hand in the resurrection of Cliff Richard, helping shepherd "Devil Woman" into the American Top 10, thus securing a Gold disc for the Peter Pan of British pop. The pianist was only too glad to help. "I admire Cliff very much," he said, "as he's kept a hold on what he believes in and also makes very good music."

Yet despite the faultless Midas Touch Elton displayed with others, his attempts at releasing his own "Dan Dare (Pilot of the Future)" as the leadoff single from his upcoming album proved futile. Manager John Reid— supported by a corps of MCA executives—insisted that "Island Girl" get the nod instead. And so it did. Backed with "Sugar on the Floor," the rhythmic A-side, released on September 19, quickly stormed up the charts. Within weeks, "Island Girl" was knocking "Bad Blood" out of the top spot to become Elton's third U.S. Number 1 single of the year. (In the U.K., "Island Girl" had to make do with a slightly more modest Number 14 showing.)

"Island Girl" proved a mere appetizer for the main feast, when, on October 4, the unapologetic guitar crunch of *Rock of the Westies* was released. The album, which had gone through various title changes during its brief gestation— from *Bottled and Brained* to *Street Kids* to *It's Banana Time Again*—hit record store racks with a preorder sale in excess of one million copies. Seemingly a *fait accompli*—and abounding as it did with casual stunners—the collection became, after *Captain Fantastic and the Brown Dirt Cowboy*, only the second album to ever enter the *Billboard* charts at Number 1 (Stevie Wonder would enter at the Number 1 position a year later with *Songs in the Key of Life*; after that, no other artist would even come close to managing that feat for well over a decade), as well as Elton's seventh consecutive chart-topping studio LP, a feat never accomplished before. (*Rock of the Westies*—the title a play on "west of the Rockies," and a perfect summation of the West Coast rock sound on full display within its grooves— would also hit Number 1 in Canada, as well as proving to be a Top 10 smash in Spain, Sweden, Australia, France, New Zealand and Norway.)

"We were elated and devastated all at once," Bernie said. "We thought, 'Well, we've finally done it.' But then we thought, 'Where to now?'"

"Elton could shit bricks and people would go out and buy them," the Who's Pete Townshend wryly noted.

The packaging for *Rock of the Westies*—Elton's final studio album owed to DJM (though a "floater" disc consisting of either hits or live recordings still remained contractually due)—featured the matchless photographic work of Terry O'Neill. "I set up the back cover picture of the band on one of the log cabin verandas," he said. "The front cover shot was just a casual shot snatched of Elton while he was having breakfast al fresco. Nothing posed, just an off-the-cuff shot." Each band member was also featured on the inner sleeve, their individual portraits boasting cheeky bio write-ups— Elton was "a boring little musician" who was "prone to getting fat at Christmas," while Bernie was "a small, almost midget-sized Lincolnshire Imp whose main interest in life is trying to pass wind while suffering from the acute runs. Has succeeded in this with his second-form lyrics."

"Elton John was great," the Tubes' lead singer, Fee Waybill (aka Quay Lewd), said. "And on *Rock of the Westies,* under the picture of the guitar player, Caleb Quaye, it said, 'Caleb Quaye, not to be confused with Quay Lewd of the Tubes'. I just thought that was really cool. So yeah, I've always loved Elton John. Great singer, great songs. He's the real deal. I've always been a fan."

The LP, which featured handwritten lyrics courtesy of Denise McMurtrie, wife of Rocket Records' art designer Hogie McMurtrie, was dedicated to Nigel and Dee. Though neither musician particularly appreciated the gesture, the general public certainly didn't seem to mind—*Rock of the Westies* would stay atop the U.S. charts for the better part of a month.

While pleased with the album's commercial success, Caleb, for one, was disappointed with the final musical results, feeling that Gus had denuded the band's high-octane sound. "Gus Dudgeon was a fantastic producer," the guitarist said, "but he mixed the guitars too low on that album. Even the basic tracks would've knocked the walls down, but to me the final mix sounded thin. We kicked much harder live than what you ever heard on the records."

While understanding Caleb's complaint, Gus nonetheless stood by his production decisions. "When you're mixing piano in with a lot of heavy guitars, it can be a challenge," he said, "because the instruments tend to live in the same mid-spectrum range. Now, loud drums and bass will work with a piano, but not guitar. It's an either/or. If you have them both, things get muddy. It doesn't come together."

Reviews for the album were mostly positive. Under the churlish heading: "Elton John: The Little Hooker That Could," the *Village Voice*'s Robert Christgau contended that "despite his considerable commercial skill and fabulous commercial success, John does not suit my (rather permissive) notions about how an artist should behave, and although (or perhaps because) he is five years younger than me, he is not a child of the '60s the way I am. He threatens me, and like most people I know I tend to fear and distrust him, so I write him off all the time." To his credit, Christgau would go on to admit in his review how he had laid down in a bad mood one night and read along with the lyrics as he listened to *Rock of the Westies*. "The next day, you guessed it, I found myself singing not one but three or four of the tunes—the "Take Me to the Pilot" effect, in a way, although rather than leading me to gibberish, the music was, in effect, the gibberish itself. 'I'll shake this off,' I said to myself, but I could not resist playing the record again…and again. Both sides. Hooked again."

Rolling Stone's Stephen Holden began his review on an unmistakably smarmy note: "Already the most commercially successful solo rock act since Elvis, Elton John continues to grow in popularity and there's no end in sight." Observing that the pianist was a "great live entertainer, his records, while commercially essential to his career strategy, have come to seem more and more artistically inconsequential." Labeling Elton's sound "seamlessly mechanistic," Holden concluded that the superstar's "only work that is likely to last is *Honky Château* and a handful of singles."

The *Los Angeles Times'* Robert Hilburn, meanwhile, found *Rock of the Westies* "as festive and well-designed instrumentally as anything else John has done. It's simply good-time rock 'n' roll: highly infectious and fervently energetic." Hilburn went on to note that the pianist's new band "not only sharpens the texture of Elton's music, but also helps expand its boundaries. Despite the album's slick professionalism, it is an adventurous work musically. One can sense the exploration and interchange between musicians."

"It's more an album of good licks than good songs," declared Ben Edmonds in *Phonograph Record.* "It's not that the members of the band are outstanding soloists—though you know they are if you've seen Elton on his current tour—but how smoothly they hold together as a unit….The album's best power songs, 'Street Kids' and 'Billy Bones', point in a direction worth developing heavy-duty expectations for. *Rock of the Westies* should be taken as a good first album from a new band. I can't wait to hear what they're capable of after they've played an entire tour together; I suspect that it will only please."

Not every review was quite as florid, however. *The New York Times'* Janet Maslin—then married to critic and producer Jon Landau—called the album "an embarrassingly flat and slipshod quickie, flailing in the wake of the relatively interesting *Captain Fantastic,*" while rating the disc only one star, and that "strictly for the *whooooosh!* noise on 'Island Girl', the title spoonerism, and old times' sake." *NME*'s Charles Shaar Murray voiced similar disdain. "Elton has been making an awful lot of records recently. The last couple have shown severe signs of strain, and *Rock of the Westies,* which will undoubtedly be Number One in every available chart by the time you've turned round three times and counted to a hundred, is so rickety it'd collapse if you breathed heavy on it." Allowing that "everybody's playing superbly, including E.J. himself," Murray went on to surmise that "unfortunately, *Rock of the Westies* sounds like it was made to meet a quota; just another Elton John album. Which is cool; lotsa people like Elton John albums. I've been known to dig a few of 'em myself, and hopefully I will again. But this one…simply doesn't do the man justice."

Sensing a lockstep unfairness in many of the notices *Rock of the Westies* was garnering, *ZigZag*'s John Tobler took it upon himself to mount a one-man defense of the LP. "Several reviews have numbered this album on the grounds that it's not well thought out, rushed, substandard and various other uncomplimentary things," he wrote. "I wonder, I really wonder, if those people really listened to the album, or instead prepared a review on non-aural evidence, because I have to tell you that I do indeed like this album, and in fact I like it better on a similar number of hearings than I liked *Captain Fantastic*….Don't believe the doubters, check it out with your own ears. In the case of an obscure record, a review is often the only way to find out what's what, but where someone of the stature of Elton is concerned, you owe it to yourself to find out for yourself. Go on, before they're sold out."

Chapter 27:
Dodger Stadium

In a year marked by oversized events, perhaps none proved larger than Elton's tour-closing gigs, a two-day stand at L.A.'s Dodger Stadium on October 25 and 26. The shows caused a box office frenzy, with 110,000 seats being snapped up in just an hour-and-five minutes. "He could've probably sold it out twenty days running," a bemused Ticketron official said. "He's the biggest draw in the world, it's not even close."

To help Elton share in this triumphant milestone, he paid £50,000 to charter an international Pan Am 707—dubbed *The Rock of the Westies Express*—to fly 130 family members, friends, journalists and Rocket Record employees from Heathrow to LAX to witness the shows firsthand. Nannette Newman and Bryan Forbes, who were already in a celebratory mood—the latter having just directed the hit film *The Stepford Wives*—were also part of the extended entourage.

Elton met the plane on the tarmac at LAX, along with several spangled gymnasts and circus performers from a local troupe. The group was then loaded into a fleet of vintage Rolls-Royces and Cadillacs, which brought them in true mid-70s rock star style to their rooms at the Beverly Hills Holiday Inn.

The large collection of Brits was then divided in two. One group would attend the show on one night, while the other group was given VIP treatment at Universal Studios, taking in the sets of *Earthquake, The Sting,* and other recent films. The next day, the groups would swap roles. All of them were treated to an extravagant party on John Reid's luxury yacht. A birthday gift from Elton—along with an Appaloosa racehorse—the 60-foot boat had been christened, appropriately enough, *Madman.* It was a lavish gift, especially in light of the fact that the pianist had little use for boats. "I'd rather play tennis," he told London Weekend Television's Russell Harty. "I mean, after five minutes, I say, 'Well, what else does it do? So it floats? Ducks float.'" He smiled enigmatically. "I'm very restless."

The Dodgers' president was fully invested in the Brit's scheduled appearances at his oversized venue. "Elton John is a very special act," said Peter O'Malley, who had personally disallowed any rock acts from playing Dodger Stadium since the Beatles back in '66. (Interestingly, the Beatles had played an eleven-song, twenty-seven-minute set to 45,000 fans; Elton would perform for six times as long, two nights in a row, to well over twice as many people.) "I doubt if we're going to find many who can match his standards. When someone else comes along like the Beatles or Elton John, we might do it again. But we want to hold it at that level. Dodger Stadium was built for baseball."

In advance of the shows, October 20-26 was officially declared Elton John Week by L.A.'s mayor, Tom Bradley. Festivities culminated with the pianist receiving his own star on Hollywood's vaunted Walk of Fame on October 23, alongside the likes of Clark Gable, Marilyn Monroe, Humphrey Bogart and John Wayne.

A record-setting crowd of more than 6,000 turned out for the event, necessitating Hollywood Boulevard be completely shut down—a first in the 1,662 ceremonies which had been held at the site.

Elton appeared at high noon in a golden golf cart which came replete with bowtie headlights and metallic lapel mudguards. Wearing a lime-green satin suit covered with its own Walk of Stars, and a matching *Clockwork Orange*-esque bowler, the pianist seemed unnaturally subdued as the ceremony got under way. "I now declare this supermarket open," he joked. "Oh sorry, wrong place. This is more nerve-wracking than doing a concert." Taking to one knee, the man of the hour posed dutifully beside his star. "It's hard to think of things to say to the bloody pavement," he mused.

Minutes later, the superstar disappeared into a waiting Rolls, as helplessly enamored throngs of mostly teenaged fans screamed and waved at the idol they all felt they understood so well.

"Everyone knows everything about me." Elton sighed. "And everyone knows nothing."

His star now forever agleam outside Grauman's Chinese Theatre, Elton John had truly been embraced as the legend he'd always wished to become. The adulation, however, did little to help close the chasm of darkness growing inside of him.

"I felt lonely," he said. "There was an incredible drive and passion, but all I had in my life was my music. Not a bad thing to have, but there was a loneliness." As for any praise he'd received in the press—that was to be taken with a massive grain of salt, as the pundits clearly had no idea what defined the true parameters of his existence. "There's one guy who writes for *The Daily Express,* he's got a gossip column. He's printed a couple things about me—they've not been nasty or anything, they've just been absolute rubbish. When Evel Knievel was supposed to jump that canyon in the rocket, I was supposedly by his side, singing the National Anthem. And I'm in my house, going 'Oh yeah?'....[And] *The National Star* wrote that I'd become an egomaniac when I broke up the band and said I believed after my role in *Tommy* that I was the world's biggest film star. At that time, I was hiding behind the walls of my Hollywood mansion. Not even my servants knew where I was."

There was little doubt that Elton's meteoric rise had taken him from an emotionally excitable aspirant to an erratically volatile mega-celebrity. Rocket Records' Sharon Lawrence noted similar danger signs in the pianist as she had years earlier with Jimi Hendrix. "I remembered this person who was mildly temperamental, who could be a bit neurotic and difficult, but who was basically happy and organized," she told author Philip Norman. "Now [Elton] looked ghastly, he was incredibly strung up, anxious and panicky. In the few months since I'd seen him, he seemed to have become a complete wreck....He put [*Rock of the Westies*] on at full volume and sat there staring at me, waiting for me to say it was brilliant....I said it was, because he seemed to need that so desperately."

Elton's private agony led him to drop eighty ten-strength Valium later that same afternoon.

"Well, that's it," he said, stumbling out to the pool, where his family sat basking in the sunshine. "I've ended it all. I shall die within the hour."

The pianist's seventy-five-year-old grandmother Ivy shook her head in disbelief.

"I suppose we've all got to go home now," she said.

"I regret what I did," Elton later reflected. "It was a very selfish thing to do....I was an immature little schoolboy craving attention on a totally different level than I was getting as Elton John. I was very, very untogether."

"It was a terrible, terrible time, those days," his mother, Sheila, admitted years later in the David Furnish-directed documentary, *Tantrums & Tiaras.* "It's an awful thing to see someone you love unhappy. I couldn't get near him at all. It was a different lifestyle and he'd got in with a different crowd of people. There were drugs, which he denied frantically, but I'm not daft....He looked terrible. I thought he was going to die."

"This was a total shock," Caleb said of Elton's latest suicide attempt. "Everything [he] touched turned to gold. The gigs were going great. We didn't have bad gigs. It was all stadium stuff. He seemed really pleased with the band, musically everything was gelling nicely. So from my perspective, I didn't see it coming. The medics came and pumped his stomach."

Elton was rushed to the hospital, where he spent the night in a coma.

"He was in and out of consciousness all night," Caleb said. "We sat up all night with John Reid, we were all in shock, going, 'Okay, what are we going to do? Is he going to make it? If he doesn't make it, what in the world are we going to do?' It was an incredibly emotional night. We didn't know what was going to happen. It was eleventh-hour stuff. It was all very intense."

"My fantasies about being a rock 'n' roll star were broken after seeing how difficult life could be for Elton," backup singer Cindy Bullens admitted to journalist Miquel Sala.

Miraculously, Elton showed few ill effects from his actions. Twenty-four hours after coming out of his coma, he was preparing to take the stage for the first of his two Dodger Stadium concerts. At the sound check before the first show, he and the band engaged in an impromptu soccer match on the enormous field. When Kenny Passarelli tried to pass him with the ball, Elton vigorously tackled him. "I thought he'd broken my nose, he elbowed me so hard," Kenny said. "I was on the ground going, 'What just happened?' Elton doesn't want to lose at anything. I mean, *anything*. He's the most competitive guy you'll ever meet."

Shunning the pre-show glamor of showbiz well-wishers like Hollywood leading man Cary Grant and comedian Charles Nelson Reilly, Elton opted to instead wait out the final hours before he was due to take the stage sitting alone in his trailer, a terse handwritten note outside his door warning: *Absolutely no one but Elton.*

Security personnel at Dodger Stadium began allowing fans in two-and-a-half-hours earlier than the scheduled 9 A.M. gate opening, to accommodate the ten thousand fans who had amassed outside,impatiently chanting: "One, two, three four: Open up the fucking door! Five, six, seven, eight: Open up the fucking gate!" They were indeed let in, stampeding across the Dodger Stadium infield and jockeying for position before the stage, which was situated in deep centerfield. Even hours before the show, the crowd was already in a frenzy—dancing in their seats, making-out in the shadows, and blanket-tossing each other high into the cloudless sky.

Dealers, executives, high school kids, jugglers, acid freaks and millionaires all joined together in a feeling of communal anticipation, a true sense of occasion permeating the ganja-filled air. Onstage, Cecil, a lion from the Los Angeles Zoo, prowled the stage alongside local car dealer Calvin "Cal" Coolidge Worthington. After several laps around the stage, Cecil was taken back to his cage—and promptly escaped. "At one point, these roadies start running around, screaming that the lion had somehow escaped his cage and was roaming free," Caleb said. "I was in my trailer, completely out of my mind, just falling about, rolling hysterically on the floor. They finally cornered the lion and got him back into his cage." The guitarist smirked. "*That was the Seventies.*"

Country-pop singer Emmylou Harris took to the stage at one o'clock. Backed by her Hot Band—which included guitarist James Burton and Elvis' pianist, Glen D. Hardin— Harris played a forty-five-minute set. Joe Walsh went on next. The audience reacted to both artists with polite indifference, as beach balls bounced across the giant cement bowl like so much popcorn. Neither artist was called back for even a single encore.

Elton's mother, who was watching the scene unfold from the from the upper deck, along with husband Derf, smiled benignly at the whole mad spectacle. "I have butterflies," she told documentarian Russell Harty, who was on hand to film portions of the show for a BBC special, "but then I know that [Elton] doesn't worry about anything. If I thought that *he* was nervous, then I would be a bundle of nerves. But...let's face it, he loves what he's doing, he doesn't have to worry about it."

Moments later, a deafening roar erupted as white curtains parted to reveal Elton seated at his grand piano—the instrument covered in silver Mylar for the occasion, gleaming like a sacred dagger. As he rolled toward the massive crowd on a hydraulic platform, the first delicate notes of "Your Song" came tinkling down over the stadium like so much silver rain. Any demons that may have haunted Elton days before were abandoned as fifty-five-thousand hysterical voices screamed out their worshipful commendation.

Several lines into the song, Elton raised his left fist in triumph, causing the frantic crowd to break into a fresh roar of cheers.

"It must have been an amazing feeling for Elton...and the band, because it was an unbelievable feeling for me, and I was just the photographer," Terry O'Neill later recalled in his photo-book, *Two Days That Rocked the World*. Stationed on Ray Cooper's percussion podium, O'Neill was on hand to snap many epochal images of the pianist as he held court before the massive hordes. "He was like Elvis at the height of his career. It is *impossible* to try to explain to people today what it was like."

"How are ya?" Elton asked the hysterical throng. "We're gonna play as long as you want us to play for, all right?"

After an artfully delicate "I Need You to Turn To," the band joined in on "Border Song." From that point on, there was no looking back. The concert was a release of pure emotion, a cathartic exorcism on pop's biggest stage. "It was surreal," Caleb said. "Such a rush of emotions. Every emotion: happiness, relief, anger—you name it. To be onstage there, the crowd's just roaring and we can't hear ourselves. We really had to know those songs, because once the crowd got going, the massive cheers from all angles, we couldn't say, 'What key are we in?' We were screaming at each other just to hear ourselves talk. It was surreal. A highly adrenalized experience."

Kenny agreed. "When there are 55,000 people…singing the lyrics of [an] entire song, it's a pretty amazing experience."

Elton performed the first half of the show in rhinestone-studded overalls and a mirrored shirt, while a bejeweled bowler hat twinkled upon his head. After a white-knuckled ten-minute jam on "Empty Sky," he chucked his hat into the crowd before leaving the stage for a brief intermission.

Twenty minutes later, Elton reemerged wearing a silver-and-blue Dodgers uniform—a Bob Mackie original which had cost over two-thousand dollars. ("But that's just a ballpark figure," Elton quipped to *Time* magazine.) Across the back, it read, simply: *Elton, 1*. Grabbing a silver baseball bat, he wacked a few tennis balls deep into the crowd as the riotous synth intro to "Funeral For a Friend" blared.

"He was completely in control," Caleb said. "The heart and soul of every fan belonged to him that day. Just superb."

Waves of uncut energy poured continuously from the silvered stage. As "Love Lies Bleeding" reached its giddily thrumming crescendo, it was clear that the Elton John carnival was in full-gear. The pristine acoustics achieved at the massive venue only added to the manic energy.

"Usually, outdoors, the sound is lost and you lose the atmosphere," the pianist later said, "but for some peculiar reason at Dodgers it stayed in the arena. At Wembley, for example, there seemed to be a tremendous gap between me and the audience, where I felt very close to them at Dodgers."

"Different members of Toto came backstage to tell us how amazing the sound was," Kenny said. "That meant a lot. Elton spent a lot on the best sound systems, the best equipment. No expense was spared, the way he staged his shows. When other musicians notice how good you're sounding, that really means something."

A true highlight came with the first ripping chords of "Bennie and the Jets." "The crowd was huge," backup singer Jim Haas said, "and when we played 'Bennie and the Jets', it hit some visceral point with everybody, and the crowd absolutely went berserk. People really dug it, and Elton played it longer and louder than anything else. People were just going nuts."

Elton's ardent performance of "Don't Let the Sun Go Down On Me" truly captured the essence of the day. The song was perfectly timed, the sun falling from the sky as the final chorus kicked into overdrive. Thousands of cigarette lighters flickered like tiny suns; the effect was so overwhelming, the usually stoic Bernie was nearly driven to tears. And he was far from the only one. "The concert at Dodger Stadium was a magical experience," Cindy Bullens said. "Everything about it was amazing. The atmosphere was electric, Elton was particularly *on* that evening, and the band was completely in sync....It was a truly spiritual experience."

Wearing an Esso gas station uniform, Billie Jean King joined in on the festivities, lending her spirited, if atonal, voice to "Philadelphia Freedom." Like everyone else in attendance, the tennis champion was fundamentally moved by the event. "It was one of the best nights of my life," she said, "seeing 55,000 fans with candles in their hands, swaying back and forth to the music and being totally involved in the moment."

"That stadium was just, I don't know, sort of *vibrating* when we were playing," Kenny said. "It was crazy. I'd never experience that kind of energy before with an audience, really. Before or after. There was just an intensity that you couldn't believe. Elton was just *on*. He and the whole band, we were just one with the audience."

The Reverend James Cleveland's forty-five-member Institutional Baptist and Southern California Choir took to the stage toward the end of the evening to lend their voices to "We All Fall in Love Sometimes/Curtains," while Elton did his best to choke back the tears.

"I was tired," he admitted, "and the choir sounded so beautiful."

The show then ended with the triple assault of "Tell Me When the Whistle Blows," "Saturday Night's Alright (For Fighting)" and "Pinball Wizard," the last song the clear emotional pinnacle of the night. "You can't properly describe the feeling in the air," Roger said. "It sent tingles up and down your spine. Truly. I was in tears. If I never did anything else in my life, and if I just had those two days, it'd be enough. [It was] just a perfect thing."

Ray Cooper was of a similar mind. "It would be wrong to say that up to that point I hadn't fully comprehended how much Elton's music meant to the American public," the percussionist said. "But that day at Dodger Stadium I bore witness to such an unforgettable affirmation of his rightfully stellar place in the pantheon of musical gods."

The Dodger Stadium stand was, without question, a high-water mark for Elton, especially in light of his most recent suicide attempt. "I didn't think I'd ever perform again," he said. "Yet it was the most magical gig I've ever done."

The critics were universal in their praise.

"While the spark of pop star image was present in satisfying doses," *Cashbox* reported, "the vast majority of pleasure derived came from getting inside the consistently creative flow of John and the music people he surrounds himself with...It was four hours of pure music that showcased the light and dark of Bernie Taupin's lyrical mind as a fertile songwriter of this age. His pennings, coupled with Elton's almost preternatural ability to match music to words, is the perfect meshing of musical minds. And this day it showed in spades." Not the least of the pianist's many capabilities was his almost hypnotic effect on his audience, the nameless reviewer noted in summation. "As the music unfolded, a powerful force was making its presence felt in the crowd. Almost as if guided by psychic cue cards, the masses rose, swirled, swayed and danced. It was in unison. It was one thought controlling many."

"For the first time in recent memory," Ben Edmonds wrote in *Rolling Stone,* "an Elton John concert wasn't as much a glittering extravaganza. Elton and band performed...without the neon signs, spangled keyboards, and peacock costumes of recent tours....On this night, Elton gave his people everything they wanted." Robert Hilburn concurred, noting that the Brit's appearance was "akin to a World Series for rock music fans. The 55,000 fans Saturday reacted to the key moments of John's show with the kind of enthusiastic abandon that Dodger President Peter O'Malley and his staff had probably thought was limited to a series-winning bottom-of-the-ninth Steve Garvey double. The Dodgers may not have made it even to the playoffs this year, but Dodger Stadium got its World Series after all. At least, it did for 110,000 rock fans."

"After two days in that stadium, he was wiped out," Terry O'Neill said. "I don't think I've ever seen anyone work so hard in my life, [and] be so dedicated to putting on a show that the crowd would remember for the rest of their lives."

Indeed, the highly-charged concerts cemented Elton's reputation as the most popular and relevant artist of the decade. In a manner of weeks, he and his new band had played to over a quarter-million people—more than many upper-echelon bands would engage over the course of their entire *careers*—becoming purveyors of the largest-grossing tour ever undertaken. The outing was a genuine phenomenon, a high-decibel apotheosis that could, perhaps, only fully be understood in retrospect.

Two days after the triumphant stand, Elton disappeared halfway through a party John Reid was throwing in L.A. Photographer Terry O'Neill found the superstar shedding tears in an empty alleyway—he and Reid's volatile relationship had finally ended once and for all.

"My arguments with Elton get so bad that we've ended up knocking one another around," Reid confessed. "I've given him more than one black eye."

"He was more unfaithful than I liked," Elton said simply.

The strain Elton and Reid had been under had caused the superstar's experimental drug use to shift into overdrive. Perennial favorites like marijuana and scotch were now superseded by cocaine, which quickly became Elton's drug of choice. "With coke, you get rid of so many inhibitions," he said. "You have a hundred thoughts in a minute, but other people can't follow you. And then when I'd come down, I'd be a complete monster....Any relationship that you bring drugs into is doomed to failure."

Even with the breakup, Elton and Reid decided to keep their professional relationship together. It was a decision which would see both men successfully through the decade and beyond.

Alone now but determinedly resilient, Elton turned his sites to American soccer, investing in a twenty-five-percent ownership of the L.A. Aztecs.

"The people that got the Aztecs together approached me to sort of do some publicity for soccer in America in general and for the Aztecs, because I sort of regard L.A. as my hometown in America," he said. "So I actually support all the L.A. teams, and I thought it'd be great [if] we could have a team in Los Angeles."

The pianist proved his worth from the outset, helping secure the services of international soccer great George Best.

"I don't think I can take hardly any credit for that," Elton said. "But I know George knew I was involved with the club, and he came out here. I'm so glad. It was great for him because George came out of retirement, came out here, got himself fit, and then went back to play in English soccer as well. And I think it's improved him as a player as well. It's incredible."

Aztec manager John Chaffetz was more than pleased with the situation. "With Elton off the field and Best on the field," he said, "if we can't make it, we ought to buy a drugstore, [for] we're in the wrong business."

As the holidays loomed, Elton retreated back to the comforting, green-sided hills of England. Though the U.K.'s tax rate remained prohibitively high, he'd come to the decision—after his recent sojourn to L.A.—that England was where his heart truly lay. "There is nowhere like Britain, and I will pay through the nose to live here," he said. "I love America, but there is no way to describe the feeling you get when the plane touches down in England. Within minutes you are back into a British environment."

Having been forced to erect electric gates around his Virginia Water home to dissuade overzealous fans from continually storming the barricades, the pianist realized that it was well past time to move to a place which offered more seclusion. "I made up my mind to move after visiting Ringo Starr's house," he said. "When I walked through the grounds, I suddenly had this feeling of complete freedom and privacy."

Elton settled on Woodside Manor, a £415,000 Berkshire estate nestled off a serene country lane near Windsor Castle. Built in the sixteenth-century, the three-story, eight-bedroom mansion had originally belonged to King Henry VIII's private physician. Sitting on thirty-seven acres of wooded land, Elton's new home featured a swimming pool, tennis court, private cinema, elevator and gym. It also boasted an outsized garden, three lakes, a vineyard, a coach house with stabling, multiple garages, a staff cottage and a groom's flat.

"It's home," the pianist said. "That's it."

Woodside's wide halls were soon filled with Rembrandts and Renoirs, while hundreds of Gold and Platinum records lined the walls, ceilings and floors which led to an enormous climate-controlled room dedicated to Elton's prized record collection—now over 50,000 strong, his was rumored to be the largest private collection in the world. "I listen to practically every new album that comes out," he said. "Not because I'm trying to pinch ideas, but because I'm interested in finding out what's happening. If you take the standard of our albums compared to other people, the standard is so much higher. I read a great review of an album in a music paper and I immediately rush out and buy it. And some of those albums wouldn't even grace making into an ashtray. It just seems that people are drastically searching for something red-hot and they're not really finding it, and they're turning to crap and saying, 'That's good.'"

Within weeks, Elton invited his chauffeur, Bob Halley, to move into the staff cottage, along with his wife, Pearl. In time, after Pearl ran off with Elton's landscaper, the ever-cheerful Halley would be moved into the mansion as the pianist's trusted aide-de-camp.

"I think Elton liked me because I didn't suck up to him," Halley said. "I was always honest, and we shared the same sense of humor."

On November 8, as Elton was busy remodeling his new digs, John Lennon and Yoko Ono called to tell him that they'd named him godfather to their first and only child, Sean Ono Lennon. The honor was at least partly in recognition of the key role he'd played in helping them reconcile the year before.

"I was moved," Elton said. "He re-met Yoko [the night of the Thanksgiving concert at Madison Square Garden]. It changed the course of his life again. Maybe I was put into John's life to reinstate him with Yoko."

Elton closed out 1975 much as he had begun it, as the most popular artist on Earth. *Billboard* not only announced that he was the first solo artist to ever sell more than a million audiocassette albums in Britain—he'd also sold far more tickets, and shifted far more records, than anyone else had ever managed to do before.

"He seems to have mastered the art of doing a thousand different things within a twenty-four-hour day," Tony King said. "That's what makes Elton John so successful and unique....He's doing things that no one else in his position has ever done, and that's what makes him so interesting. He isn't like your everyday rock 'n' roll star. He's an intelligent, aware person who's interested in what's going on, and then gets out there and into areas outside of his own career."

Record World, Cashbox and *Billboard* agreed with King's assessment, unanimously dubbing Elton as the Best Selling Record Artist of the Year. His *Greatest Hits* collection was the Best Selling Album of the Year, according to *Record World* and *Cashbox,* while *Billboard* bestowed that honor upon *Captain Fantastic and the Brown Dirt Cowboy. Rolling Stone*, meanwhile, listed "Philadelphia Freedom" as the Single of the Year.

What was there left to accomplish?

Only Elton knew for certain.

Chapter 28:
Blue Moves

Elton flew off to the white sand beaches of Barbados for the holidays. The lush West Indies island appealed to his nationalistic tendencies, existing as it did within the British Commonwealth, tea and cricket were as much a part of daily life as scuba diving and waterskiing.

The pianist's companions for his St. James excursion included Bernie, Davey, Kenny, John Reid, lensman David Nutter, and David Larkham, the latter of whom personally flew a Christmas turkey over first class.

"We had Christmas dinner out on this patio in our swim trunks," Larkham said. "Totally bizarre. Totally Elton."

The pianist saw in the New Year with a sense of relief that the ceaseless chaos of the last year was finally over with. "I was really quite shattered, physically and mentally," he said. "I'd never really had a long holiday."

"Barbados was magical," David Nutter later recalled. "We would all be woken up in the morning with blasting music." Elton's choice most mornings: a disco-fied cover of "Babyface" by the Wing and a Prayer Fife and Drum Corps. "And then we'd all sit around a huge table for breakfast. Elton and I played endless games of Scrabble and listened to Bob Marley. You've never seen so much alcohol consumption. And one of my favorite memories of that time is sitting with Elton by the sea, rating the incoming waves from one to ten."

After the photographer and his compatriots took their leave each afternoon to go surfing or paragliding, the superstar would continue sitting by himself on the beach, listening to Pink Floyd's *Wish You Were Here* while he contemplated his future. It proved a trying task, for even amongst the aqua tranquility and lush tropical greenery he could never completely escape the populist reality which had so completely come to define him. "You're just lying on the beach and people still come up and prod you, kick sand in your face and go, 'Are *you* Elton John?'"

The new issue of *Playboy*—which included a much-heralded interview with the pianist—hit the stands while Elton was still basking beneath the Caribbean sun. In the interview, conducted by journalists Eugenie Ross-Leming and David Standish, the superstar Brit claimed that—despite the inevitable setbacks and heartache—he actually enjoyed his struggle to remain at the top of his profession. "It's what keeps me going," he said. "I don't begrudge anyone else his success. You have to pay attention to what others are doing, keep listening to what's happening in order to grow. For example, Stevie Wonder can eat me for breakfast as far as musicianship goes, but that doesn't make me angry or jealous or uptight. I'd give anything to have his talent, but I'm not paranoid about it. Perhaps one day I'll be able to write as good as he does."

When queried as to whether attention-shy Bernie Taupin had become a full-on recluse, Elton joked, "If you call staggering out of some place at six-thirty in the morning with a bottle of wine a recluse." He laughed. "No, he's quite busy. He's got a book coming out, he's producing the Hudson Brothers—but he's very loyal, and an integral part of the group. I could never find anyone who could take his place."

Predicting his own future, the Brit claimed that he wouldn't be playing older hits like "Crocodile Rock" in six years' time. "I don't want to become a pathetic rock 'n' roller and take a slow climb down, like a lot of people do. I don't want to be Chuck Berry. When I'm 40, I don't want to be charging around the countryside doing concerts. I'd rather retire gracefully."

The magazine—which also featured fiction offerings from Nabokov and Cheever, as well as a curvaceous centerfold soaking seductively in a stage-lit bubble-bath ("I'm not a women's libber...God forbid!")—disappeared off newsstand shelves in a matter of days. Despite the public approbation, Elton's father was displeased by what his son had to say. "He doesn't seem very happy to me," Stanley Dwight told the Britain's *Daily Mail*. "Last time we saw him I asked him who his friends were, and he said, 'Elvis Presley and Billie Jean King.' But when he was a child, they were his idols. How can someone you've only just met be described as a friend? There are friends, and 'friends'—and I think Reggie has to buy his friendships." Regarding the piano skills of Stanley Jr., a son from his second marriage, Stanley remarked, "He's so much more advanced than Reggie was at that age. I don't think Reggie's all that good even now."

Despite his father's denunciation of his musical talent, Elton's endless vinyl offerings continued apace with the January 9, 1976 U.K. release of "Grow Some Funk of Your Own." Issued as a double A-side, alongside "I Feel Like a Bullet (In the Gun of Robert Ford)," the disc hit American record stores three days later. While English disc jockeys plumped for "Grow Some Funk of Your Own," MCA's initial push was for "I Feel Like a Bullet." When Rick Sklar, program director for influential WABC, declined to add the torrid ballad to the station's Top 40 playlist, it proved problematic. In an effort to win Skylar over, MCA sent him an enormous cake decorated with a fanciful wester six-shooter and inscribed, in blue icing: "'Give Elton a Shot, 'Feel Like a Bullet' is a hit."

"We [still] didn't play it," Sklar said. "We were skeptical."

A week later, MCA sent an even larger cake. This one read: "Disregard previous cake. 'Grow Some Funk' is the A-side."

"Grow Some Funk of Your Own" ultimately gained enough traction in America to peak at a healthy Number 14 on the *Billboard* singles chart. The song failed to chart in the U.K., however—Elton's first misfire in his homeland since the "Friends" single failed to live up to expectations back in 1971.

On Januuary 22, Elton accompanied Princess Margaret to the London movie premiere of Neil Simon's *The Sunshine Boys*. The movie outing came directly after the pianist had given a private performance for the Queen Mother at her royal lodge in Windsor Great Park, during which he changed a key line to "Your Song," telling the Queen Mother, much to her amusement: "I'd buy Windsor Castle, Your Majesty, where we both could live..."

Purchasing Windsor Castle was beyond Elton's means— if just. The Associated Press estimated that the public at large had purchased more than sixty million dollars' worth of Elton John concert tickets and albums, making him the highest-earning performer in entertainment history, easily outdistancing even iconic names like Sinatra, Elvis and the Beatles.

For his peerless efforts, Elton was awarded the honor of becoming the first pop singer since the Beatles to be immortalized at Madame Tussaud's Wax Museum in Baker Street, London on March 7. (Over the coming decades, a proliferation of waxwork likenesses of Elton would appear throughout the world. His grinning visage could be seen beaming out from places as far afield as the Musée Grvin in Paris, the Dreamland Wax Museum Gramado in Brazil, the Wax Museum in Prague, the Museo de Cera in Mexico City, and dozens more as well. Cadbury chocolatier would even go so far as to create a 227-pound milk chocolate statue of the pianist, while Ben & Jerry's devised an ice cream flavor in his honor, "Goodbye Yellow Brickle Road." Non-edible honors bestowed upon the pianist over the coming decades included having three flower species named after him, as well as a crustacean, *Leucothoe eltoni.* "I have always listened to [Elton's] music in my lab during my entire scientific career," explained Dr. James Thomas. "So when this unusual crustacean with a greatly enlarged appendage appeared under my microscope after a day of collecting, an image of the shoes Elton John wore as the Pinball Wizard came to mind.") Elton, who often visited Madame Tussaud's on Saturday mornings while a student at the Royal Academy of Music, was thrilled by the honor.

Dick James attempted to place several congratulatory calls to his one-time golden boy, but Elton resolutely failed to answer the phone. Realizing that his golden goose had well and truly flown, James ordered DJM to raid its vaults; the result was Elton's two-year-old recording of "Pinball Wizard" being released as a single. Backed with the three-year-old "Harmony," the disc quickly soared to Number 7, becoming Elton's first U.K. Top 10 single since "Lucy in the Sky with Diamonds" a year earlier.

While DJM was looking backward, Elton himself had his sights set very firmly on the future. Entering Eastern Sound Studios in Toronto—the first Canadian studio to feature 24-track technology—the pianist began recording his much-anticipated follow-up to *Rock of the Westies* in early March.

"We had to go to Toronto for the next record because of Elton's tax situation," Kenny Passarelli said. "He could only be in America for 180 days a year—and he already had an American tour planned—so he had to be out of the States. And knowing John Reid, he probably got a super deal on the studio, 'cause he was an amazing manager. There was Irving Azoff and then there's John Reid—they were kind of the same, in many ways. They're super loyal to their guys, and they'll just basically beat people up for their guys. I mean, Reid was a bad little fuck. A crazy son of a bitch. But he had vision. He was a brilliant guy, and he really *was* in Elton's corner. It was full-blown, all cylinders going off. He catered to Elton, he would do *anything* to keep him happy."

As far as the new sessions were concerned, the bassist was determined to do whatever was in *his* power to not have to repeat the endless post-session work which had so marred his *Rock of the Westies* experience. To that end, he forewent his trademark fretless style and instead bought the most expensive Olympic bass he could find. "I said, 'Fuck it, I'm *not* gonna deal with overdubbing'. And I didn't have to. The thing is, the band rebelled. *I* didn't, 'cause I was the only American. Well, me and James Newton. But Caleb, he and Davey *did* rebel. They said to Gus, 'Enough of this overdubbing stuff, let's make this new one a very live record.' And they really bullied him to the point where we did it that way. As we laid it down it became a very live record, all those tracks were recorded very much live. Which was good, 'cause I felt like Gus kind of had it in for me. He loved Dee [Murray]. I did, too—I'd met Dee when we were in London for the Wembley gig, and I felt bad, because Dee was really, really hurt that he was out of the picture, but he was really kind to me, and he was a fantastic player, really tasteful—but, y'know, *I* wasn't the one who let him go. Anyway, that's how it happened. That's why those Toronto sessions were all very live."

Realizing that new sessions were imminent, Bernie locked himself away and wrote two-dozen lyrics in three weeks' time. "Basically, I'm a very lazy writer," he said. "Usually I only write when the time approaches to make an album. I don't normally find myself sitting somewhere and finally say, 'Ah, a song has come to me.' I normally write under pressure. I get ideas and I jot them down, but I don't put them together until the time comes to do an album." As for the intricacies of the creative act itself, lyric writing had become a completely straightforward process for the lyricist. "I'll think of something that I like the sound of and work from there," he said. "Then sometimes I'll get a line or something that I particularly like and I'll work around that. But otherwise I never just sit around and say, 'I'd like to write a song about such-and-such or so-and-so.' It's usually the title or a certain line that comes to me first."

"He's a lazy sod, but he comes through in the end, ol' Taupin," Elton agreed. He went on to explain one of the key ingredients to his long-lasting partnership with the lyricist: "If Bernie was musical and I was into writing lyrics, we'd be getting on each other's nerves so much, saying, 'Well, how about doing *this*, then,' and he'd say, 'How about this chord here?' It wouldn't work at all. But since we know nothing about each other's respective field, it *does* work."

The first new lyric which Elton chose to compose to was called "Bite Your Lip (Get Up and Dance!)." He gave the punchy words an urgent musical underpinning that pleased him greatly. A single take was attempted, but—as it was the first of the entire sessions—technical glitches, including an enormous amount of hiss on the master tapes, marred the recording.

The pianist walked into the control room, grinning wildly. "That's it. It's a hit."

Gus genuflected. "Hang on, that's not a final take. I'm still sorting out the sound here."

"Oh, rubbish. Give it a listen."

The producer played the take back, he and Elton sitting stoically side by side as the song came pounding out of enormous wall-mounted monitors.

"*All right!*" Elton shouted gleefully as the song ended. "That's a Number One!"

"Elton was insistent," Caleb said. "He refused to do it again. It was unusual behavior for him. He was always the consummate professional, but the strain he was under was beginning to show itself. It was the beginning of the end, in many ways."

Gus would later bring in the Cornerstone Institutional Baptist and Southern Californian Choir, directed by Reverand James Cleveland, to add soulful backing vocals over Ray's manic congas and Davey's blues-injected slide guitar. Intriguingly, "Bite Your Lip" would prove the only instance during the entire twenty-one-track sessions where a Davey Johnstone solo was featured; Caleb Quaye's lead fret efforts would be chosen in favor of the Scotsman's every other time. "Gus used my solos for whatever reason," Caleb said. "I was at a point where I was just starting to mature in quite a few ways, and it just seemed to work. Gus and everybody seemed to love what I was doing. And Davey at that point was doing a lot of great acoustic work, and mandolin. Davey's a great mandolin player. My style of playing was different from Davey's. I was more from a jazz/funk/rock place, where Davey came from an acoustic folk background. And somehow, between the two of us coming from these polarized differences, it seemed to work."

With the proposed leadoff single in the can, the bulk of recording for the new album began in earnest, with Elton tackling what was to become the session's signature ballad, "Sorry Seems to Be the Hardest Word," on March 22. Recorded largely alone, with only vibraphone, accordion and bass accompaniment, the plaintive track was a rarity in Elton's catalogue, as the majority of the sentiments expressed were provided by the pianist himself. "Most of the lyrics on 'Sorry' are mine," he told *Sounds* magazine. "I was totally infatuated with someone in Los Angeles and it wasn't reciprocal....I was sitting out there in Los Angeles and out it came: What have I got to do to make you love me?" He let out a bittersweet laugh. "I've fallen in love with the wrong people so many times. I used to go to clubs and I'd see people at the bar, and by the time I managed to get to talk to them, I had already planned our entire lives together."

The evocative paean's dramatic, descending-half-tone progression guaranteed that it would become a future standard. Yet the bleak track also hinted at an underlying internal tension, as both Bernie and Elton began feeling that they had nowhere to go but down. "We had done everything," the lyricist said. "There was no mountain to scale or to conquer anymore. We had filled the biggest stadiums. There weren't any places that were bigger. We had seven consecutive Number One albums....You suddenly realize that there's no other place to go but down....For the first time, when we began work I found myself thinking, 'I don't know if I've got it in me. I don't know if I want to do this anymore.'"

Not helping matters, Bernie—caught in the grips of a deep depression over his failed marriage—was abusing alcohol at Olympian levels. "The first thing I'd do [in the morning] would be to reach over to the refrigerator by my bed," he said. "I'd take out a beer, empty half of it away, then fill it up with vodka. I'd drink that every morning before I got up. When I went anywhere in a limo, I'd take a gallon jug full of vodka and orange juice." He also admitted to abusing drugs—especially cocaine, magic mushrooms and heroin. "But not through a needle. Always ingesting it. It was a black-cloud period."

Bernie's latest batch of lyrics clearly reflected his chemical-fueled despondency—from suicidal fantasies to tales of brokenhearted melancholia, his work had turned dark and despairing, even by his own austere standards. The lyricist's desolation reached such a point that Elton—his most steadfast champion over the years—was notably put-off. "I never rejected one of his lyrics before," he said, "but some of the stuff he did for [the new sessions]...I said, 'Taupin, for Christ's sake, I *can't* sing that.' They were just plain hateful, three or four of them."

Much as he had with *Caribou,* Gus brought in a phalanx of top-drawer session musicians to augment Elton's band. Guests this time included the Brecker Brothers horn-section and saxophonist David Sanborn, while background vocals were supplied by Toni Tennille, Beach Boy Bruce Johnstone, and the founding member of the psychedelic supergroup the Millennium, Curt Becher.

The first track to take full advantage of this stellar lineup was the rollicking "Crazy Water." Ostensibly inspired by the 1974 disappearance of the trawler MV Gaul in an artic storm in the North Sea, "Crazy Water" was—beneath it all—

another subtext-veiled look at Bernie and Maxine's broken relationship.

While the dynamic track quickly became one of Gus' favorites, at first the producer was unsure how to proceed with the background vocal arrangement. "Bruce [Johnstone] said, 'You know, Daryl [Dragon, the Captain of the Captain & Tennille] is really good with backing vocals,'" he said. "Daryl came in with this idea that was fucking mad. And I loved it. In the first run-through he was going, 'Hoo-hah-hoodly-doo' and all this stuff....What I do in those situations is I don't say anything. I just sit back...because it might be brilliant or it might be crap, or it might trigger another thought from another direction....Well, we had these guys singing these parts and they were absolutely stunning. Once I understood what he was trying to do and I could remember what it was—because it was so bloody complicated—we then worked on it together."

"We had a fabulous bass singer, Gene Morford, on 'Crazy Water,'" Toni Tennille said. "I love that song."

To further assist the team's efforts, Paul Buckmaster was brought back into the fold for the first time since the '72 sessions for *Don't Shoot Me I'm Only the Piano Player*. The arranger's first task was to provide a pounding orchestral undercurrent on "Crazy Water." "I love it," he said. "Gus did a fabulous job producing [that song]. And those crazy background voices had me in stints of laughter. That reflects [Gus'] sense of humor, which we shared. The same kind of sense of humor—wacked out."

Buckmaster then turned his attention to the darkly atmospheric, tempo-shifting "One Horse Town," for which James Newton Howard received a co-writing credit for his yearning electric piano introduction. The song was a perfect amalgam of delicately nuanced electric keyboard work and adrenaline-pumping rock 'n' roll, which climaxed with Caleb's exuberant guitar solo, introduced by Elton's hectic cry of the seemingly nonsensical "Gonzales!"

"He'd say stuff like that," Caleb said. "He didn't call *me* Gonzalez, but it was at that point in the song where it was time for a ripping solo, so he'd just shout out something like that, it was like Speedy Gonzalez: 'Here we go!'"

When Elton wasn't at work in the studio, he was being squired around Toronto by photographer John Rowlands and MCA promotions manager Scott Richards. "Elton was in the mood in those days to visit radio stations," Rowlands recalled years later. "And he'd go up to local, non-big-league hockey games in suburban arenas. He was a fun guy at those hockey games, buying hot dogs and wearing cowboy hats, it was just like hanging around with a local guy. He was plenty fun. [And] he also went to visit Scott's son Eric, who was in Sick Kids Hospital having some corrective surgery, he had some complications in birth. Elton went there to visit five or six times, and sat and talked with Eric for some time. So much so that the nursing staff became so accustomed to wanting to work around Eric in case Elton came in, so they'd get to see him."

Other points of interest for the superstar included visits to the local radio stations. One trip was particularly memorable. "We were at CHUM Radio, the big AM/FM radio station in Toronto," Rowlands said, "just talking about this, that, and the other thing. Elton knew all about the broadcasting stations we visited, how important they were to his songs airing in the metropolitan Toronto market, and he happened to mention that Patti LaBelle & the Bluebelles were coming in to Massey Hall. And we all knew people at Massey Hall, so we wound up having Elton show up to introduce Patti LaBelle & the Bluebells as a walk-on, and he wowed the audience and gave the girls a hug, and then off we went." The event at that venue sparked a memory Rowlands had from two years earlier. "I was working with Billy Joel at Massey Hall in '74," he said, "they were pushing the album *Piano Man*, I believe, and I said to Billy, 'I'm going up the street to see Elton John perform. If you'd like to come, if we can get backstage you could probably meet the man.' Billy was being managed by his wife Elizabeth at that time, and there was a lot of electricity going on at Massey Hall that night, because Billy and Elizabeth were fighting. So Billy decided to go with me, and he did briefly get to shake Elton's hand, as one piano man to another, as it were. Elton was the top of the mountain and Billy was only halfway up at that time. It was a great moment."

Elton and the band were soon back at work, tackling "Your Starter For...," a brief scale-based tune Caleb had written on acoustic guitar several years earlier as a pre-concert limbering-up exercise. "Elton said that he wanted an instrumental to start the album," the guitarist said. "So I played it for him in the studio and I said, 'What do you think of this?' He said, 'Yeah, that's great, let's do it.'" As for the song's odd title, it was actually a catchphrase from a British quiz show. "We were joking at the time about this guy in England, Bamber Gascoigne, who hosted *University Challenge*," Caleb said. "[Gascoigne] would always say, 'Your starter for...ten points,' for instance. That's where we got the title."

After cutting the tune live in two takes, the band turned their attentions to the angular "Between Seventeen and Twenty," an unblinking study of the strains which the rock 'n' roll lifestyle could take on a marriage—a theme earlier explored on "Love Lies Bleeding." This song, however, proved even more painfully autobiographical, the title directly referencing Maxine and Bernie's respective ages when they'd first met five-and-a-half years prior.

The song was a less-than-subtle commentary on Maxine's tryst with bassist Kenny Passarelli, who had become—ironically—Bernie's closest comrade within the new band. "Bernie's life was not in a good place at the time and it was reflected in that lyric," Roger Pope said. "But Elton was able to spin it into gold. To get the musicians to be so involved and sensitive to the songs was equally amazing. I was playing the song and I'm thinking, 'Cor, Bernie must be seriously fucked-up.' And then I realized that Kenny had gone off with his wife. It was tense."

It was a strain which Kenny felt particularly deeply. "That was a heavy time, playing the bass during that song especially," he said. "I knew how upset Bernie was. He was completely fucked-up about it all. His marriage had fallen apart, and at first he didn't know that I was there on the other side. It was incredibly emotional, just a really heavy time. You can hear it in that song."

Compounding matters, others within Elton's camp secretly expected the pianist to bring the axe down on Kenny's neck. "No one ever talked about it in any kind of direct way," David Larkham said. "One afternoon I tried drawing Elton [out], 'So what do you think of Kenny anyway?'—that sort of thing. He just looked me dead in the eyes, with tremendous seriousness, and he said, 'Kenny is a *great* fucking bass player, and I'm not changing this lineup.' And that was it."

Standing well outside the marital melodrama, Gus was pleased with the way "Between Seventeen and Twenty" had come out, viewing it as proof positive that the initially wrong-footed sessions were finally progressing apace. Thus reassured, his enthusiasm for the entire project blossomed. "There's a lot more instrumental space all the way around," he said. "Loads of long passages, of just music. But they are *arranged* passages. None of that six-minute bullshit, where somebody plays a self-indulgent guitar solo. And I'm talking about proper sections, which have been entirely worked out. Much like what we did with the first [*Elton John*] album. Only much more open and diversified than we did back then. I suppose that you could say we've brought to flower here the promise of much better things to come than one got from *Rock of the Westies*. I really think it comes true on [these new sessions]."

One of the more unusual songs recorded at Eastern Studios began life as a jam in Caleb's hotel room at the Park Hyatt between himself, Davey and James. Caleb had been experimenting with Indian tuning on his twelve-string acoustic when he came up with a pleasingly Hindustani chordal foundation. Davey then added a sitar line, while James pulled it all together with moody modulations on a polyphonic synth.

"We just brought it into the studio the next day," Caleb said, "and [we told Elton], 'We wrote this last night, what do you think of this?'"

"I think I've got some lyrics for that," the pianist said, pulling out a sheet of Bernie's lyrics entitled "The Wide-Eyed and Laughing." He sang a melodic line over the instrumental track and found that it fit perfectly. "We've always been a real band," Davey said, "so if someone had an idea, Elton was keen to try it. And Bernie's lyrics are always so amazing. The whole imagery and passion he delivers on a page is remarkable." Roger agreed. "[Elton had] put us together so we could give him our input as a group. He didn't just want 'yes men', as perhaps he'd had before. He'd always mutter how he was the worst musician of us all, but it wasn't true. He was a bloody fantastic pianist, and a truly great guy. A pain in the arse sometimes, but a great guy."

"The Wide-Eyed and Laughing," accentuated by Ray's rototoms, was laid in a single take. The music came as easily as the lyrics, which were allegedly based on Bernie's brief love affair with Wendy Adler, daughter of famed virtuoso harmonica player Larry Adler, which had begun over a tennis match in Barbados. "I remember thinking that song was amazing," Adler's daughter, Emma Snowdon-Jones, recalled years later. "That's me, I'm the last line in the song. I know my mom broke Bernie's heart, and I know she broke mine. My mother was magical. And when her attention was turned on you, it was like the sun shining on you after being in an air-conditioned room for a long time. Of all my mom's boyfriends, Bernie was the greatest. So shy, so lovely. One time he took me into FAO Schwartz and said, 'You can have anything you want'. I loved him, and I still do."

After the "The Wide-Eyed and Laughing" session had been completed, journalist Paul Gambaccini visited Elton in his hotel room, where a prototype of a *Captain Fantastic* four-player pinball machine sat flashing in a corner.

"Let's have a game," Elton said, adjusting the sleeve of his crimson Canadian hockey jersey. "Come now, Paul."

Though the pianist battled fiercely, Gambaccini proved himself a worthy competitor—after four of the five balls had been played, he found himself well ahead. "I was thinking, 'What do I do now? Dare I win? Dare I beat this guy on his own machine?' It would have been Regicide."

But the journalist needed not worry—Elton's hypercompetitive nature kicked into gear on the final ball. Proving that he truly *was* the undisputed pinball wizard, Elton won the game going away.

"The guy just can't stand to lose," Gambaccini said. (Interestingly, weeks later, the four-flipper *Captain*

Fantastic machine, which featured iconic backglass imagery courtesy of artist David Christensen, would go on sale, quickly eclipsing the sales of the next dozen highest-selling Bally pinball games combined. The machine's success would result in a home-market version, with Alan Aldridge-inspired backglass artwork, to be released the following year.)

The band recorded the hard-hitting revenge fantasy "Shoulder Holster" the next day. The lurching track was notable for featuring a brusquely staccato brass arrangement from the influential Brecker Brothers, as well as solo flourishes from sax guru David Sanborn.

Elton then revisited "Candle in the Wind" territory with "Cage the Songbird," a ruminative, dulcimer-tinged requiem to French chanteuse Edith Piaf—known to fans as "The Little Sparrow"—who died in 1963 at the age of forty-seven. The bewitching acoustic number was a holdover from the *Rock of the Westies* sessions, co-written by Davey Johnstone. "I played [Elton] this little fingerpicking acoustic piece based on the 'Skater's Waltz'," the guitarist said. "We were in need of some fresh air at around six a.m., so we went to the horse corral [at Caribou Ranch] and wrote the song ankle-deep in horse shit....[Elton] went, 'That's beautiful. Wait a minute...' And he pulled out a sheet of lyrics and said, 'Play it again', which I did. He sang the lyrics, and literarily that was it." David Crosby and Graham Nash, founding members of Crosby, Stills & Nash, were later brought in to provide appropriately rustic backing vocals on the track. "David and Graham are wonderful with phrasing and harmonies," Davey said. "So we just let them go for it. It's a lovely little song."

Another older song attempted at these sessions was "Chameleon," the hallucinatory ode rejected by the Beach

579

Boys the summer before. Gus utilized seven background singers on the doleful track, slyly emulating the California band's intricately lush harmonies.

"Better than the real thing?" Elton teased. "Nasty, nasty. Who said that?"

Toward the tail end of the sessions, Elton turned his attention to a set of lyrics which he had asked Bernie to write specifically with a feel similar to those of the American soul quartet the Chi-Lites, whom the superstar had appeared onstage with in London back in '74.

"I love the Chi-Lites," Elton said, "and they had a record called 'There Will Never Be Any Peace On Earth Till God is Seated at the Conference Table'....[So] I said to Taupin, 'Let's do a song like that, with a really tacky lyric, and see if we can get away with it.' It is a ridiculous song, deliberately."

The track featured the Martyn Ford Orchestra, under the leadership of Richard Studt, who would soon go on to lead the London Symphony Orchestra. Ford himself was particularly excited about the Buckmaster-arranged session, having been a huge fan of Elton's since the release of his eponymous LP back in 1970. "I remember walking into a clothes store in the West End of London to buy a pair of jeans, and hearing the *Elton John* album on the sound system in the store," he said, "and I was just rooted to the spot by 'Your Song' and the riffs on that album, all of Paul Buckmaster's extraordinary arrangements. As an arranger who was into pop, *this* was the music I'd heard in my dreams: orchestrations with rock music. I thought, '*This* is what I want to do.' Elton was the talent, and of course Elton wrote the songs, and his vocals were fantastic, and he's the best rock pianist there's ever been, but Paul Buckmaster changed a great album into a milestone album. It's still one of the greatest pop records ever made. It was life-changing. It was industry-changing. It was music-changing. And it certainly changed my life."

Ford was equally as enthusiastic to be working directly with producer Gus Dudgeon. "Gus had an amazing pair of ears," he said. "He was the consummate professional—kind, generous, caring, sympathetic. His professionalism was extraordinary. He's probably the best record producer I've ever worked with, because I've worked with some record producers who couldn't organize a fuck in a brothel. But Gus was just the best. Totally on the ball."

Elton and his musicians next lit into yet another lyrically suspect song, this one entitled "Snow Queen." The acoustic, bongo-laced track was an unabashed critique of what Bernie—who was rumored to have briefly dated Cher back in '73—saw as her superficially self-constructed lifestyle. Fading out on a repeat of Sonny & Cher's "I Got You, Babe"—with snatches of Cher's solo track, "Bang Bang (My Baby Shot Me Down)" thrown in for good measure—Elton hadn't realized who the song was actually about until he'd started recording his vocals. "'Allo, allo', I thought. 'It's Cher,'" he said. "It was so cutting, I had to tell her in advance and apologize in advance." (Elton made his atonements after he and Cher attended a Paul McCartney & Wings concert together at the L.A. Forum that June. "On the way home, [Elton] was saying he wanted to apologize," Cher said. "I've never heard ["Snow Queen"], but I know it's real nasty.")

"Out of the Blue," a Dadaist excursion of repetition and revelation which melded into a heady mix of bluesy jazz and primal garage rock, was tackled next. James Newton Howard's friendship with electronic pioneer Bob Moog paid massive dividends, as the keyboardist was allowed to play one of the first polyphonic Moog synthesizers available at the time on the sinewy, jazz-rock instrumental. ("Out of the Blue" would soon gain fame as the end-credit music for Britain's long-running car show, *Top Gear*.)

"Out of the Blue" then led, in quick succession, to the gospel-infused "Where's the Shoorah?"—an ambient, organ-accented homage to a sultry Argentinian woman—the ennui-drenched ballad "The Man Who Loved to Dance," and the sleek "City of Blue." The former would be covered the next year by Kiki Dee as the B-side to her single "First Thing in the Morning," (credited to the pseudonymous team of "Tripe & Onions"), while the latter was destined to remain forever unreleased. Indeed, from one track to the next, Elton and his band were stretching ever further stylistically, mixing vintage Memphis soul with a plushly aggressive English-music-hall-by-way-of-NYC-jazz-rock sensibility.

With the group's artistic muscles warm and pulsing, attentions were turned to the deep-funk of the choir-drenched "Boogie Pilgrim," which was borne out of an impromptu midnight jam. "The whole point [of the sessions] was that Elton said, 'Let's all perform as much as possible like a band. Let's take ideas into the studio and see what we come up with,'" said Davey, who—along with Caleb—would receive a co-writing credit on the raucous tune. "This was a great opportunity for everyone in the band to throw in their ideas and their tools and see what happened. And 'Boogie Pilgrim' was like that. It was a jam, and it came out great."

A slightly breathless Elton undertook the sorrowful suicide fantasy "Someone's Final Song" next.

"We'd walk to the studio every day, crossing this dual carriageway," Roger said. "I don't know why we didn't just drive—Elton insisted we walk. He was trying to be as incognito as possible, in a tracksuit and with this giant bloody ice hockey mask." The drummer laughed. "It actually worked for a few days, but then one day the kids figured it out and they just chased us down the street. We were all winded off our arses by the time we hit the studio. But I wasn't playing on ["Someone's Final Song"] anyway, so I didn't mind."

A desperate cry for help, the devastating ballad featured one of Bernie's bleakest lyrics yet, with his song's narrator imagining himself succumbing to suicidal thoughts. "Although it was a very bad time," he later said, "I [personally] was never suicidal. There's a fraction of me in the song, but when I'm writing I take my experiences and ideas and stretch them."

A haunting multi-tracked choir consisting of Bruce Johnston, Toni Tennille, Curt Becher, Clark Burroughs and Joe Chemay was later added over Elton's desolate piano line, helping to cement the song's aura of aching remorse. "When we heard the playback," Toni Tennille said, "we just all looked at each other and smiled. It was just a wonderful sound, and really perfect for that song."

Jazz took center stage on "Idol," a seductive number which concerned a blatantly Elvis-like figure who had fallen from grace. Roger traded in his sticks for brushes on the track, providing a sorrowfully sophisticated feel which was further highlighted by a soaring David Sanborn sax solo.

"Yeah, it [eventually] could be me," Elton conceded of the track's doom-laden lyrics. "Will I end up at the Swiss Cottage Holiday Inn when I'm seventy-five in a fishtail coat, a cigarette hanging out of me mouth, singing 'Idol' in cabaret?"

Technical problems reared their ugly head during the concluding days of the sessions. To help kill the downtime, Elton began messing around on a Wurlitzer electric piano; soon enough, he came up with a pleasing F-major/C-major/B-flat chord sequence, as well as a title: "Don't Go Breaking My Heart."

"Listen to this, Gus," Elton said, playing the producer the basic melody while singing the title over and over again.

The producer was confused. "Really? 'Don't Go Breaking My Heart'? I hadn't noticed a lyric with that title."

"That's because Taupin hasn't written it yet," the pianist said with a grin. "Lazy sod, let's ring him up."

Moments later, Elton was speaking to Bernie long-distance. The lyricist, who had elected to remain in Barbados rather than taking direct part in the new sessions ("Maxine was still with Kenny," Caleb explained. "She and Bernie had filed for divorce. As a result, Bernie wasn't with us when we went to Toronto…"), was asked to construct a duet lyric in the Motown mold of Marvin Gaye and Tammi Terrell's "Ain't No Mountain High Enough."

"Something up-tempo, like a disco-soul thing," Elton said. "Our side's counting on you."

Bernie set to work; five minutes later, he was finished.

"It was great," the lyricist said. "It was just one of those things that sparked off immediately. As soon as he played it, I said, 'Well, that's gonna be the next single. That's a hit.'"

The band, who thought that their work on the extended sessions had been completed, balked at having to learn and record yet another track. "'Don't Go Breaking My Heart' was the last thing recorded at the Toronto sessions," Roger said. "Elton told us that he'd just come up with another number. 'Bloody hell, Elton, for fuck's sake,' I said. 'We've been playing for weeks on end here already.' He just stared me down. That fucker's scary when he stares you down."

The band ultimately rose to the occasion, recording the track in a single take.

Elton originally envisioned the song as a duet with Dusty Springfield; due to an illness, however, she wasn't available, and so Kiki Dee was tapped to step in instead. She laid her vocals down weeks later, after the producer had returned to England with the master tapes. "[Elton and I] actually did the song together in London," she later told author Barry Toberman. "But for whatever reason, it was decided to stick with Elton's Canadian vocal track." Recognizing a golden opportunity, Kiki worked extremely hard on her part. "I was secondary [on the song], in the sense that Elton had already stamped the song with his vocal. Which in a way is quite good, 'cause it gives you a groundwork on how you're gonna sing it. The precedent has already been set by him, and [by] the writing and production of the song."

The song's string arrangement, created by James Newton Howard, traced its roots to the airily melodic riffs which graced such soul classics as the Temptations' "My Girl" and "Just My Imagination." "I remember clearly," the producer recalled years later, "Ray [Cooper] just suddenly turned to me one day and he said, 'You know, you really ought to give James a chance to do some orchestral arrangements…he's really good. He knows his stuff.' And a good thing, too…it's a bloody good arrangement."

When Gus played the completed track back to the band, everyone knew instantly that it was a hit. "It gave me a buzz," the producer said, "because you could tell straight away that the song was really commercial. Really vibey and up."

Realizing they had a one-off, pre-album single set to go, the decision was made to have Kiki add prominent backing vocals onto "Snow Queen," so that it could serve as a cohesive B-side.

The sessions concluded with both the shortest song of the entire proceedings. "Theme From a Non-Existent TV Series," a 1:19 electronic minuet, sprang out of a jam that Elton, Caleb and Roger engaged in while reminiscing about "The Dick Barton Theme (The Devil's Gallup)," which they'd all recorded together years before as part of the Bread & Beer Band. The new tune would prove infinitely more successful than its forebear, however, earning Elton a prestigious Ivor Novello Award (Britain's equivalent to the Grammys) for Best Instrumental the following year.

Thirty days after Elton had arrived in Toronto, he found himself preparing to fly out.

"It was interesting," photographer John Rowlands said, "we're at the airport and the same crew that had met him at the airport when he'd first arrived was there now to see him off at the end of it all Elton gave us all little gifts. I got a digital watch from Tiffany's from New York, and in those days that was a pretty scientific gift. And he said to us, while he's waiting there about to go to his aircraft, 'It shows you how sad being on the road is, only six people meet me at the airport, and thirty days later the same six are here to say goodbye, and yet I probably had my picture taken with six-hundred people at all those cocktail parties I went to, and everyone clamors for an eight-by-ten, and they all put them on their wall and say that Elton John in a close personal friend to everybody who goes to their rec rooms, but where are they now?'" Rowlands sighed. "That was such a chilling statement for me to hear from somebody who was absolutely top-of-the-pile. That's the fragility that Elton had. To hear him say that to me, it gave me chills to hear that, that someone who was so popular—I mean, there wasn't anybody in the world who didn't know who he was—was

586

also so alone. All those people who professed to be his best pal, yet where were they?"

Back in Britain, Elton recorded a final track for his upcoming album. "Tonight" would quickly become one of his favorite tracks he'd ever composed, as well as one of his lengthiest—the tortured love song clocked in at a seemingly prohibitive 7:52. "He'd written the whole thing, top to bottom, [as] a complete piece," Gus said. "The first time I heard it, Elton kept going on and on, one movement after another, and I just sat there thinking, 'Well, okay, is he ever going to start singing?' But I shouldn't have worried. He knew what he was on about, he knew what he was doing."

Like many of these latest songs, "Tonight" was again about Bernie's failed marriage. "It's a very personal song," the lyricist admitted. "The line about not fighting again, just going to sleep. It was very difficult for me to listen to."

"'Tonight' was written out of experience," Elton concurred. "It's very moving. I know what Taupin's been through."

The track was recorded live at Abbey Road Studios in London. Elton performed the song live with the London Symphony Orchestra, under the baton of James Newton Howard.

After striking the final low D-1 note which ended the piece, Elton rested his forehead gently upon his piano.

"Okay," he sighed. "Enough."

An exhausted Elton flew back to North America soon after to participate in the Schaeffer Music Festival at the Wollman Rink in New York's Central Park on April 16, alongside Muddy Waters, Bonnie Raitt, bluegrass artist David Bromberg and comedian Martin Mull. The pianist was particularly enthused about Raitt, whom he held in the highest regard. "[Bonnie is] one of the top three…white women vocalists in the world," he said. "One of the nicest guitarists, certainly one of the nicest ladies, and one of the sexiest ladies that I've ever met."

Two weeks on, Elton found himself shepherding in yet another album release. *Here and There* was his thirteenth long-player in six years, and his first live offering since *11/17/70*. A charismatic pocket history of live staples, the disc dropped on April 30 in the U.K., and three days later in America.

Comprised of selections from two 1974 concerts—Elton's Royal Festival Hall show in London and his Madison Square Garden gig in New York City—*Here and There* was issued simply to fulfill the pianist's contractual obligations to DJM. Displeased at having his hand forced, Elton labeled the album "a total fucking disaster." "It was, 'Either release this album or—if you don't—we'll put it out later anyway.' Which would have meant them getting [my next album] as well." He sighed. "It was silly because, unless you're Peter Frampton, you don't sell nearly as many copies of a live album as a studio one. And we'd never gone into live recording properly. [*Here and There*] was a business compromise." Though Dick James had begged Elton to allow the use of John Lennon's historic appearance on the album, he adamantly refused. "I wasn't going to let them use any of that on *Here and There*. No way. It would have been taking advantage of John, who did the gig as a favor."

Melody Maker's Chris Welch was more impressed with the recording than the artist himself had been. "Do not fear a rip-off," he proclaimed, "for this is a worthy selection of live performances from two major concerts which will long serve as a reminder of the extraordinary career of one of modern music's most successful performers….There is a tremendous presence about these recordings. An Elton John concert is one of the few in rock that can be usefully transferred to album, for here is the excitement and emotion that can never be created in a studio. Listening to these concerts, only a couple of years old now, is to be reminded how much has happened already in these baffling Seventies, how much music has been played, and, as Ginger Baker said the other day: 'When's it all gonna end?'"

The taciturn Robert Christgau disagreed with Welch's analysis, however. "I had a syllogism worked out on this one," he wrote. "Went something like a) all boogie concerts rock on out, b) Elton is best when he rocks on out, c) therefore Elton's concert LP will rank with his best. So if this sounds like slop (concert-slop and Elton-slop both), blame Socrates—or find the false premise."

Regardless, *Here and There* easily made its way into the Top 10, reaching Number 6 in Britain and Number 4 in the States. It would soon become Elton's twelfth Gold album, remaining in the U.S. charts for nearly half a year.

Chapter 29:
Louder Than Concorde
(But Not Quite As Pretty)

Elton barely had time to celebrate *Here and There*'s success, for his latest tour—a romp around the British Isles, and, unbelievably, his first major U.K. tour in three years—was slated to kick off on April 29. As with each of his previous outings, the first task at hand was to pull together a proper set list. "It's very important to pace an act," he said. "We could go onstage and do twenty new numbers, but people don't want to hear that. Critics sometimes do, but the audiences don't."

After much deliberation, the pianist decided on a set list which balanced recent rock-heavy tracks with a murderers' row of perennial standards. He and his band then rehearsed solidly for a week and a half before heading out to play thirty dates in thirty-six days. Dubbed *Louder Than Concorde (But Not Quite as Pretty)*, after a tongue-in-cheek remark Princess Margaret had made months earlier. (Referencing the newly minted supersonic airliner, the princess told Elton, "You play piano louder than Concorde." The pianist immediately quipped back, "But I'm not quite as pretty, am I?") The tour was unique for an act of Elton's stature, as it concentrated on smaller towns and halls usually overlooked by the rock star elite. "There were no elegant suites with all-night room service," Bernie said. "No spacious dressing rooms or any of the chauffeured convoys indigenous to American touring. It was back to brown ale and cheese sandwiches, small towns and 3,000-seater halls."

Elton still leapt about the stage as wildly as ever, hurling his piano stool with gusto and using his instrument like a piece of gym equipment, yet his sartorial splendor was noticeably scaled back, his elaborate feather-drenched ensembles replaced by sweatpants, suspenders, and matador jackets. Gone too were his elaborate frames. There were no diamond-studded clouds this time around, no blinking lights, no windshield wipers. Instead, Elton wore the same pair of thick white frames with purple-and-orange-tinted lenses nearly every night.

"He's getting tired," a Rocket Records insider noted. "You can bet the end's in sight."

If Elton's visual excesses were on the wane, however, his musical delivery system proved stronger than ever. Indeed, as technology had advanced throughout the decade, so too did the Brit's state-of-the-art piano. By this tour, his instrument was a high-tech marvel which boasted a Helpinstill pickup, a pair of pressure-zone-sensitive mics, as well as a capacitor mic which had been modified with a Clair Brothers pickup box containing an active mixer. These electronic advances allowed Clive Franks to manipulate the signal at his soundboard through a Lexicon 224 digital reverb unit, creating the fullest-sounding piano to ever grace a concert stage. The rest of the band enjoyed similar sonic verisimilitude; with a consistent 110 decibels of rock 'n' roll pouring forth from endless banks of speakers hanging bat-like above the stage, Elton's latest tour proved to be one of the loudest in history, as well as one of the crispest.

The opening night gig was held at the Grand Theater in Leeds, an Edwardian jewel-box-styled theater that practically had the audience sitting in Elton's lap. The crowd, according to *Sounds'* Vivien Goldman, was "a sea of sheer hysteria and primal, clawing, orgasmatic adulation...decked out in bowler hats with appropriate graffiti around 'em, scarves to be waved in the air like a football match, elaborately constructed facsimiles of the man's old ZOOM glasses, top hats made out of *Capt. Fantastic* posters, the works." Goldman also noted that Elton's fans "knew all the lyrics, mouthing silently all the way through, and they were reverent....I can honestly say that, me excepted, I've never seen a more satisfied audience. All Elton's intense physical and mental activity (that sheen on his face was more than a gentle glow), his extrovert enthusiasm, had all paid off. He's a people's artist, and the people genuinely love him."

That they did. Nothing could seemingly stop Elton's legions of devoted followers from basking in the pure celebratory radiance of his music.

Not even the IRA, who seemed to have a personal vendetta against rock's piano-pounding madman.

Early in his set at Kings Hall in Manchester on May 1, a roadie whispered into Elton's ear that a bomb threat had been phoned in, and that the Chief of Police was shutting down the show.

"Look under your seats, guys," the pianist told the crowd. "And hope nothing's there."

Minutes later, the thousands in attendance were forced to clear out of the arena. "Come back when the all-clear's given," Elton said, "and we'll finish the show, all right? Even if it takes all night. It really doesn't matter what time it is."

The entire audience milled about outside in a chilled rain for over an hour, while local police inspected the arena.

"After the police were through doing their bit," Roger said, "we all went back in, everybody completely soaked through. And it was the same day that Southampton beat Manchester United in the FA Cup Final, so when Elton introduced the band and he got to me and said, 'On drums, Mister Roger Pope from Southampton', well, you never heard an audience boo harder than they did that night. Toilet rolls [were] flying in from every direction. It was fucking brilliant."

Despite the long delay, Elton and his band played the remainder of their pummeling set to unbridled applause. Indeed, the potentially ruinous night turned into a resounding triumph—another feather in the band's cap. "Playing England was amazing," Kenny said, "all those gigs we did where we drove from Leeds to Cardiff, all the way around the island. We played Manchester, Liverpool, all these places that only hold like 2,500 people, and there were *ten* of us onstage. We just tore it *up*. It was insane, it was just incredible. And I gotta give Elton credit, he let his musicians play what they wanted to play, both onstage *and* in the studio. He knew that we were looking out for him, that we weren't showboating. Playing with Elton was just an incredible experience. He's one of the greatest artists I've ever met, and I've met a lot of people, a lot of great artists. I've played with everybody, and I've never seen anybody work so hard as Elton did. He's an incredible person, an incredible artist. Generous as hell, an incredible vibe, and extremely—without a doubt—professional. On every level, that guy was incredible."

During an off night on the tour, Elton had Ringo and his girlfriend, Nancy Lee Andrews, over to his house for a late supper.

"Ringo loved Elton," Nancy recalled years later. "*Loved* him. We went to many of his concerts and ate many a dinner up at his house. And Tony King was so close to Elton, too. It was that 'group of girls, y'know? They all had nicknames for each other—Phyllis, Sharon, Gladys, and so on. Elton called me Easy Grace. And I remember we were up at his house that night and he was lying on his bed and he had this guitar case down on the floor. And I said, "I didn't know you played the guitar'. And he said, 'Hell no, darling, I don't play the guitar. These are my glasses.' And I said, '*What?*' And he started opening up these guitar cases and there were all of his glasses that he wore onstage. It was fantastic. I said, 'Oh my God, you must have one of these for your jewelry as well.' And he said, 'I've gotta show you what I just bought.' And he brought out this black case, and in it were five 1930's Stage-Door-Johnny diamond bracelets, just encrusted with diamonds. And I started putting them on, and Elton's putting them on, and Ritchie—that's what I called Ringo—is sitting at the edge of the bed. And Elton goes, 'God, that looks gorgeous on you. You can have that one.' And it's like a thirty-thousand-dollar bracelet. And I said, '*Really?* Thank you.' And Ritchie says, 'Take it off.' And I went, '*No!*' And he said, 'I can buy you a bracelet like that, you don't need to take his.' And Elton said, 'Oh, don't be silly, Ringo. Let the girl have a bracelet.' And Ritchie said, 'No, *I'll* buy her one.' And I wanted to say, 'Fuck *you!*' After that night I was like a myna bird: 'Get me a bracelet! Get me a bracelet!' And Ritchie *did* get me one—diamonds and emeralds and rubies and sapphires. He bought me one that Christmas. Still, Elton's generosity knew no bounds."

Neither did his self-consciousness.

Throughout the tour, Elton made sure to keep his ever-thinning thatch hidden behind a succession of baseball hats. "[It's] a real drag," he said of his prematurely balding pate.

"It was bad dye. It was when I had my hair pink and green. I used to have it done at Smile [Salon] in London, and it was never a problem. Then I had it done somewhere in New York, and next time I took a shower I glanced down at my feet and it was like the murder scene from *Psycho*—pink water and great tufts of hair everywhere." He grimaced. "So since I've discovered I don't want to be bald, I might have a hair transplant. It's just a matter of going down there with the courage to say, 'I want some more hair, please.'"

The seamless U.K. tour ended on a particularly high note for Elton's sound engineer. The afternoon of the band's second Bristol gig at the Hippodrome, Clive Franks was watching television with Davey Johnstone in his hotel room when their boss stopped by.

"If you could have any car in the world, Clivey, what would it be?" Elton asked.

Clive thought it over. "A Mercedes 350 SL, I guess."

"What color?"

"Silver."

Elton nodded, and left the room.

"A few weeks later, when the tour was over," Clive told author David Buckley, "Elton called me at home and told me to come to his house in a taxi. When I arrived he took me out to his row of garages, opened up one of them, and there was a brand-new silver [Mercedes-Benz] 350 SL, which he said was a present for me. I was totally stunned. I sat in it shaking for about half an hour before I dared reverse it out of the garage and drive it home."

Seventeen days after the tour's conclusion, "Don't Go Breaking My Heart" was released as Elton's summer single. (As with *Rock of the Westies'* "Hard Luck Story," this song was also credited to the songwriting team of Ann

Orson/Carte Blanche.) The superstar was pleased with the release, despite the fact that his original plan of issuing the single under the moniker "Reg & Paulie"—his and Kiki's birth names—had to be abandoned in the mad shuffle of pre-promotion.

The song was an immediate success, easily becoming the most popular song in the U.K.—Elton's first chart-topping single ever in his homeland. "I've had about three Number Twos [in Britain], but never a Number One before," he said. "When I heard it was Number One, I rang everybody I knew to tell them. They were pretty annoyed, but hell, it got me excited again. It really did....I've [now] achieved all my childhood dreams."

"Don't Go Breaking My Heart" proved equally as popular in America. It was exactly the sweet audio tonic that the country needed to help lift itself out of the post-Watergate, gas-crisis-fuelled malaise which it had found itself mired in for so long. The song remained at the top of the *Billboard* charts all summer, becoming the best-selling 45 of the year, as well as Elton's sixth American Number 1 single in less than three years. It would also go on to receive a Grammy nomination for Best Pop Vocal Performance, Duo or Group, and would be named as the Single of the Year. (The honey-soaked trifle, which Elton labeled "an out-and-out pop record," proved equally as popular across the globe, reaching the Top 5 in Switzerland, Holland, Italy and Germany; it would also hit Number 1 in Spain, New Zealand, Australia, Canada and Ireland.)

While preparing to perform the first of twenty-nine-dates for the American leg of his tour, Elton achieved yet another childhood dream when he got to meet Elvis Presley backstage at the Capital Centre in Landover, Maryland on June 27.

Before the concert, Elton, Bernie, Elton's mother and John Reid were taken backstage to meet the bloated, glassy-eyed, 41-year-old singer, who sat wrapped in towels.

"I was introduced to him," Elton said, "and there in front of me was this gross figure staring back at me blankly. I knew immediately that he was going to die. He had destruction written all over him. There were no signs of life. He already seemed like a corpse."

Unsure of what to say to the drugged-out icon whom he'd first glimpsed decades earlier on the cover of *Life* magazine in an English barbershop, Elton joked, "We have the same optician," referring to Optique Boutique's Dennis Roberts.

"Hey, yeah, that's right." Elvis managed a wry smile. "Listen, didn't you write that song, 'Don't Let *Your Son* Go Down On Me'?"

"It's 'Don't Let *the Sun* Go Down On Me," Elvis' stepbrother David Stanley corrected.

The King nodded. "Oh, yeah. Okay."

Elton ignored the feeble mockery. "It's great to finally meet you," he told Elvis earnestly. "I've always admired your music. Maybe I could write a song for us to record together."

"Yeah, sure," Elvis mumbled. "We'll see."

After posing for a photograph with Elvis' daughter, Lisa Marie, the pianist stepped forward and embraced Elvis in a bear hug. Elvis' entourage were stunned. *No* one touched the King—that was the golden rule.

Elton, Bernie, Sheila and Reid were then led out to their seats, stage-right, second row.

Elvis appeared onstage minutes later in a white suit with gold and lavender accents, singing "C.C. Rider" with surprising vigor.

"It was easy to see that Elvis was in a very good mood after meeting Elton," journalist Phil Gelormine reported.

"And he seemed to be putting a bit more of himself into the show, perhaps for the benefit of his guest."

Elvis was *so* pumped by Elton's presence, in fact, that he sang his latest single, "Hurt," twice, even reprising the ending a third time. He also made an impromptu change to his set list, adding in "Heartbreak Hotel," which Elton had personally requested. (Not long after the concert, Elvis would send Elton the golden suit he'd worn on the cover of his *50,000,000 Elvis Fans Can't Be Wrong* album. Moved by the gesture, Elton often wore the suit onstage during his *Breaking Hearts* world tour in 1984.)

Despite the King's benevolence, Bernie was underwhelmed by the brief, seventy-two-minute performance he'd witnessed. "He was so drugged he could hardly sing," the lyricist said. "He just stood there, handing out scarves." (*Washington Star* critic Charlie McCollum seemed to agree, noting in his review of the show that "the lean mean Elvis is long gone, and, in his place, is a William Conrad-figure wearing a Sonny Bono wig. Instead of the lithe movements of a panther, this Elvis moved with the grace of a pregnant water buffalo.")

Elton, however, was more impressed. "Even though [Elvis] was hugely overweight, when he actually sung a couple of lines it was magical. You don't lose that magic, no matter how fucked-up you are....If you're brilliant, snatches of that brilliance will come through."

Elton and Bernie ended the night by catching a Keith Jarrett Trio performance at Georgetown's 9:30 Club. Both men agreed that the Jarrett show was much more to their liking. "Keith Jarrett is, to me, a genius on the keyboard," Elton said. "I mean, I'm not even in the same country as he is, as far as piano playing...not the same planet....He is a genius...so unorthodox....Probably my favorite album still is Keith Jarrett's album, *The Koln Concert.*"

Elton's tenth tour of the States would prove a victory lap of sorts, as it ultimately played to three-quarters of a million raucous, stoned-out fans up and down the East Coast and northern Midwest.

Elton's retinue this time around was mammoth; it included eight musicians, twenty family members, six plane crewmen, five sound technicians, three lighting men, a carpenter, and four truck drivers. Additionally, a piano tuner awaited them in each city where they landed, along with six limo drivers and ninety additional security staff. Eleven roadies and a lighting designer, meanwhile, traveled from city to city a day ahead of the main entourage, setting up an elaborate jukebox-themed stage the night before each show, then tearing it back down in the middle of the night, long after the last notes of music had faded away.

Billy Connolly, who had transitioned from an edgy folk singer to a full-on comic singer in the years since he'd shared a bill with Elton at the ill-fated Krumlin festival back in the summer of 1970, was the support act for the tour. Appearing onstage in giant banana boots, he treated each night's crowd to a series of bawdy songs with flippant titles such as "Her Father Didn't Like Me Anyway" and "Half-Stoned Cowboy."

With near-comic reliability, Connolly was roundly booed each and every night.

"Hearing them announce my name was like someone saying, 'Ready! Aim! *Fire!*'" he said. "In Washington, some guy threw a pipe and it hit me right between my eyes. It wasn't my audience. They made me feel about as welcome as a fart in a spacesuit."

Twenty minutes after Connolly's set, Elton's marathon three-hour-plus shows would begin with four quick clicks of

Roger Pope's drumsticks. The band—sans Elton—would then break into the textural fury of "Grow Some Funk of Your Own." The pianist would appear several moments later twirling an oversized carrot—or strawberry, or banana— around his neck as a manic firestorm of Instamatic flashbulbs lit up whichever darkened cavern Elton found himself in, creating a strobe-lit counterpoint to the glimmering chevron lights which pulsated onstage. After sharing a word with each band member, Elton would make his way over to his carpeted piano—encased for this tour in a crimson-striped, brushed aluminum shell so that it resembled the supersonic jet for which the entire outing was named— and launch into the song proper. Behind him, his three backing vocalists shook their asses enthusiastically. For this outing, Jim Haas was replaced by studio session vocalist Ken Gold. "Cyndi and Jim didn't get along," Jon Joyce said. "And Cyndi kind of threw her weight around with Elton and got Jim fired for that tour. Not *fired*, really—he just wasn't rehired. So Ken came on. I love Ken and we had a great time on tour, the three of us. But the background group on a musical basis always missed Jim Haas. He had the high, piercing, great falsetto rock 'n' roll Beach Boys sound that we all just hooked in with. But we still sounded great. And Cyndi was a force to reckon with. She was often mentioned in reviews, she really made a name for herself. Everybody said: 'Who *is* that up there looking like Mick Jagger?'"

Elton dashed ceaselessly back and forth across the stage every night, causing pandemonium in the stands. The twenty-nine-year-old superstar reveled in the tumult he created. The only downside? "I sometimes think about getting shot," he admitted. "Someone's got to try and do it sometime. But I'm not nervous, ever. There's no point."

After an insurrectionist reading of "Captain Fantastic and the Brown Dirt Cowboy," Elton would don an acoustic guitar to perform his "Crosby, Stills, Nash and John track," Lesley Duncan's elegiac "Love Song" from *Tumbleweed Connection*. "I was laughing so hard, it was hilarious," Caleb said of Elton's attempts to play guitar. "He knew I was laughing, so he would do it and kind of give me a look like, 'What do you think about *this?*' It was hysterical....But he pulled it off."

"He's just not a guitar player," Davey said. "And that's being kind."

Halfway through each show, the synthesized fanfare which opens "Funeral For a Friend" would come blaring through the speakers at maximum volume. The band used the darkness—as well as the billowing clouds of dry ice which were pumped onto stage—as cover to snort copious amounts of cocaine. "While the audience was mesmerized, I would walk back and just fill my face up off the top of my amp," Caleb said. "Then I'd come back and play more raving guitar riffs, and the crowd would go wild."

If the fans in attendance were unaware of the covert drug use, they at least intuitively understood by Elton's soul-crunching stage performance what the radio-listening public at large did not: that their idol was anything but a born balladeer. The pianist himself welcomed this distinction. "'Your Song' was such a fucking misrepresentation of me," he said emphatically, "although it's become almost a trademark. From the first time we went on the road, we were rockers at heart and onstage."

Everywhere the tour stopped, Elton was fêted as a conquering hero. The Mayor of Chicago gave him the key to the city. As did the Mayor of Boston. And the Mayor of Philadelphia. And Atlanta.

Backstage, meanwhile, groups of celebrities—including Patti Smith, Peter Frampton, Frankie Valli, KISS, Queen,

601

Liza Minnelli, Richard Thomas, Clive Davis and Muhammad Ali—would crowd into Elton's dressing room to bask in the reflected glory of the era's brightest star. "Almost every night, in every city, the backstage area was like a 'Who's Who' of the entertainment world," Caleb said. "Movie stars, TV stars, politicians—*everyone* wanted to meet Elton. Elizabeth Taylor, Michael Jackson, Hugh Hefner, you name it. In every town we went to, the ticket to our show was the hottest and hippest in town." Particularly memorable was the night when Leonard Nimoy stopped by to wish the group well. "Lots of us in the band were *Star Trek* fans and we just went crazy," Caleb said. "We were excited to meet him, and here was Mr. Spock excited to meet us."

"Mr. Spock, that was really cool," Roger said. "That whole tour was like a dream, in a way."

Yet another perk of being on the road were, of course, the willing groupies who would slink out of the woodwork to party with the band. "Playing with Elton, who was the biggest artist in the world, women just flocked to us," Caleb said. "After a show, the band would go to the hospitality suite and the roadies would just bring in a whole passel of willing women. Some women hoped to go to bed with Elton, but he'd only be there for a minute, then he'd go off to his own party somewhere else. After a little small talk we'd pair off, then head off to our rooms to get high and have sex. Night after night, city after city, it was the same thing. It became a way of life. Women and drugs. I was high all the time. We were young and we were having fun."

As if the adrenalized rush of a star-flanked, sex- and drug-filled tour wasn't enough of a rush, Elton also found himself inducted into *Playboy*'s prestigious "Jazz and Pop Hall of Fame," alongside such musical luminaries as Louis

Armstrong, Dizzy Gillespie and Frank Sinatra. He was also voted by the magazine's readers as the World's Number One Vocalist and Number One Keyboard Player, while he and Bernie received the nod as the World's Number One Songwriters.

The duo accepted these honors at Hugh Hefner's Playboy Mansion in Chicago on July 29, where they engaged in a heated foosball match with Hef and his current squeeze, Barbi Benton. Afterward, the magazine publisher presented Elton with a stars-and-stripes cape, while the winsome, self-promoting Benton gave the pianist and his songwriting partner T-shirts of herself.

The next day, Elton attended a friend's wedding at the Sheraton-Chicago. After the reception, he enjoyed a special private screening of the horror movie "The Omen," before dining on lobster tails at Zorine's.

"I suppose I'm [one of] the beautiful people now, God help us," he said with a grin.

Later that night, he attended a record company party hosted by WLS, the local FM station. "I think we were at Newbury Plaza," disc jockey Bob Sirott said. "And they had a restaurant downstairs—Arnie's Restaurant. And the rest of the building were condominiums. I was thinking, '*How* do we get Elton John aside to do an interview with him?' We had our portable tape gear with us, and the party is noisy and crazy and it's hard to corner Elton into a quiet area and spend some time with him. But then a salesman from WLS, named Simon, says, 'I live in this building. If we get him upstairs, maybe then you can do an interview with him.' So Simon and I and a couple other guys say, 'C'mon, let's get him.' So we literally kidnapped him. We said, 'Elton, come with us,' and we grabbed him and threw him in the elevator and went up to Simon's apartment." Sirott laughed at the memory. "So I turned on the tape recorder and started interviewing him. And this was before he had come out, so he was much more guarded. During the whole interview, I'm sitting next to him on the couch, I don't know that he looked at me one time. But he was obviously very smart and, you could tell by his answers, a very thoughtful guy who at the time was holding a lot in. He was very guarded and had good reason to be uncomfortable in that situation. About twenty minutes into the interview, he's kind of nervously looking around and wondering when this is going to end, and how it's going to end. Finally we closed up the interview and let him get back to the party."

Though every facet of Elton's frenetic life seemed to be comprised of endlessly surreal moments, nowhere was the lunacy more apparent than onstage. "Even for all the craziness, most of those [*Louder Than*] *Concorde* shows were amazing," Caleb said. "The excitement of the moment and the screaming fans—it always pushed you to give your best."

Having to keep up with his dexterous band mates pushed Elton to become an even more accomplished musician himself. "I've had to play my ass off on this tour," he said, "and that's something I've missed doing before. They've improved my playing, because [the last couple tours] I only used to play block chords. Now I stick my neck out and have a go."

"By the time we got to the U.S., we were smoking hot," Kenny said. "The band was just killing it. Especially with Roger there. I thought he was the best drummer I'd ever worked with. I never even had to look at the guy while we were playing. He was unbelievable. There was just nobody like Roger Pope. He was the funkiest Brit I ever met."

While Elton was musically at ease in stadia packed to overflowing with eighty-thousand maniacal fans, he still found it difficult to walk into an ordinary room without a complete sense of panic sweeping over him.

"My life was desperately trying to keep up with the performer side of me," he admitted. "This will be the last tour in a long while. I feel like stopping for a time. For the last two or three years I've been like a nomad. It's just got so big that it's getting stupid....Sometimes I get a bit depressed playing big places. It's like seeing animals in a cage when you look out towards the audience."

After most shows, Elton would retire alone to his hotel suite, gorge on buckets of extra-crispy Kentucky Fried Chicken—his favorite American "garbage food"—and fall asleep in front of the television.

As the nitro-fueled *Louder Than Concorde* tour rocketed its way across America, a pirated fourteen-track pre-*Empty Sky* compilation entitled *I Get A Little Bit Lonely* hit the underground market. Comprised of a dozen skeletal John/Taupin demos from their late nights at DJM back in the late '60s, along with the Reg Dwight-penned title track, highlights of the LP included the yearning psychedelic-pop of "A Dandelion Dies in the Wind," the wrenching lover's soliloquy "Reminds Me of You," and a solo piano rendition of "The Tide Will Turn for Rebecca" which stripped the song of its overblown, Humperdinck-esque pretentions to reveal an evocative soliloquy of heartbreak and indecision.

Knopf, meanwhile, released a lyrical bootleg of sorts with a hardcover tome called *The One Who Writes the Words for Elton John.* Edited by Alan Aldridge, the book featured 114 lyrics—every one of Bernie's published works from 1968 through *Goodbye Yellow Brick Road*—alongside illustrations by such celebrity friends as Alice Cooper, Peter Blake,

Charlie Watts and Ringo Starr. Joni Mitchell illustrated "Talking Old Soldiers," while John Lennon tackled "Bennie and the Jets."

"I just called them up and said, 'Would you like to do a drawing?'" Bernie said. "And they were all great, they really came through."

Elton himself provided a sardonic introduction to the book ("To be read in a showbiz Las Vegas accent with plenty of drama")—as well as a 'Sideways'. "Having been told that my doodles would not be needed—I felt shunned," he wrote. "How could Taupin put a book together without any mentions of my name!" The pianist switched into third-person to envisage himself performing an onstage tribute to his writing partner—a performance which quickly devolved into anarchy. "The audience starts to rush the exits," Elton imagined. "Sobbing frantically now, John screams at them, and as the last remaining chords of 'Your Song' echo round the now virtually empty room, the last words trickle from this pasty little troll of a man: 'And do you know—the midget can't even spell.' He hurls a copy of Taupin's book at the band and exits shouting, 'Remember "Funeral For a Friend"—huh?'"

The One Who Writes the Words for Elton John sold out its initial print run in a matter of weeks, peaking at Number 2 on the U.K. bestseller list. Bernie was pleased; Elton, perhaps a bit less so. "I was a little sad when he put out the book of the lyrics," he said. "It's all very well—and it's incredibly bold—but I wish he'd just publish some of his children's poems. They're wonderful. But I think he's a bit afraid to take that sort of step."

Perhaps no single concert was more highly anticipated during America's historic Bicentennial year of 1976 than Elton's July 4 show at Schaeffer Stadium in Foxboro,

Massachusetts. The sold-out crowd of sixty-two-thousand—who was more than ready to go ballistic after having sat quietly through dual opening acts John Miles and Dave Mason—rose to their feet in ecstatic anticipation as an enormous firework effigy of Elton began sizzling above the stage.

As "Grow Some Funk of Your Own" came ripping out of ten-story high speakers, Elton made his grand entrance dressed as the Statue of Liberty, standing stock-still atop his candy-striped piano, a flashlight-powered "torch" raised high above.

Grinning at the crowd, Elton whipped off his Liberty garb to reveal a Stars-and-Stripes shirt, tennis shorts and sneakers.

"All right!" he cried, leaping off the piano and pumping his fist as if he'd just hit the winning shot in a Wimbledon final.

A deafening roar rose from the stands.

"The Yanks loved it, got off their asses, and…stayed on their feet all night," noted *Melody Maker*'s Harry Doherty. "The presentation was luxury at its finest, for who else plays on a blue-carpeted 50-grand stage? Gone are the days when such refinery was considered the debasement of rock 'n' roll."

After a pair of shows at the Spectrum in Philadelphia, Elton landed in Detroit for a massive concert at the Pontiac Silverdome on July 11. Running onstage in bionic slow-motion á la *The Six Million Dollar Man*, the stadium exploded at the mere sight of him. Those riotous cheers only increased during "Hercules," when the beloved Brit played the piano while lying atop his instrument; the squeal then reached a crescendo during "Bennie and the Jets," when he played beneath it.

"That was a huge gig," Caleb said. "There was some problem going on down the front with security keeping kids away from the stage. They started getting a bit out of hand, throwing bodies around and this, that and the other. And the next thing I know, I looked over and I happened to see John Reid dive off of one of the trusses into the security and start trying to beat up the security. He was a wild guy. He was turbo-driven at that point. It was crazy."

As always, Elton's performance tempered dazzling brilliance with massive doses of tenderness and soul. Undoubtedly one of the key ingredients to his massive adulation, this addictive admixture caused an orgiastic fervor which lasted throughout the entire show, which went off without a hitch, at least until "Saturday Night's Alright (For Fighting)," when—moments after a bottle came winging out of the darkness, nearly missing Elton's head—a pair of binoculars clocked Kenny Passarelli square in the shoulder.

"Saturday night's alright for fighting, but it's definitely *not* alright for throwing bloody binoculars," Elton warned, tossing a cup of water into the crowd. "*Behave* now, you bastards! What?"

The Silverdome show climaxed with a particularly bruising "Pinball Wizard," which saw a stadium full of fans standing on their seats, arms held high as if to testify before rock 'n' roll's holiest altar. It was another musical frenzy, another spectacle nonpareil.

An equally indelible performance occurred days later at the Charlotte Coliseum in North Carolina, when—halfway through the sweat-soaked show—Elton mockingly read a negative critique from critic Max Bell before setting it on fire to massive cheers.

"That was a highpoint [in my career]," Bell said.

The critique left a sour taste in Elton's mouth which lasted for several songs. "We were doing a tune and our elevated platform was right behind Elton and his piano," background vocalist Jim Joyce recalled years later. "And he was kind of in a state, just kicking ass as a performer, but he was distracted, and the three of us did something background-wise musically he didn't like, and he turned around and scowled at us and flipped us the bird! I'll never forget that. Right there onstage, he flipped us the bird!" Joyce laughed at the memory. "That was probably the lowpoint for me. I'm sure Elton wouldn't remember any of that."

Improbably, the exhausting tour only picked up momentum as it wound its way from Tuscaloosa, Alabama to Louisville, Kentucky.

"I was spoiled after I worked with [Elton]," Kenny Passarelli later admitted to author Tom Stanton. "He really knew how to put together a show. I should have just stopped touring then."

At most shows, the crowds were as energized as the musicians. At the Saint Paul Civic Center on August 24, a crazed blonde leapt onto stage, lassoing Elton around the neck with her bra and yanking him to the floor. A pair of burly bodyguards immediately dispatched her backstage, never to be seen again. The strain of all the madness was slowly wearing on the superstar. "As Elton got so enormous," said longtime friend Linda Lewis, "he got a bit more—what's a good word to say? Out of reach. Not so available. In fact, he seemed quite sad a lot of the time. Sadder than when he was starting out. It seemed like he was always under a cloud of gloom, I think. He went onstage and did his performance, but then he'd come off and he'd be very sad. Still, he was quite a lot of fun at parties, when he'd let his hair down—well, what hair he had at the time. I shouldn't say that." She laughed. "He was fun when he'd had a few drinks and everything else. He'd go from very maudlin—'Oh, I wish I were straight, I wish I could have children'—and then all of a sudden he'd be up and, 'Try my outfits on!' And I remember trying one on once, and it weighed a *ton*. I don't know how he managed to even lift his hands up to play the piano. I was in the wardrobe with him when that happened. Basically he was in the closet, in the closet. But Elton wanted children, and I said, 'I'll have your baby. Just put it in a bottle, we can do it by artificial insemination.' But he never took me up on my offer."

And so the caravan rolled on.

A four-night stand at Chicago Stadium was followed by a pair of highly anticipated gigs at Richfield Coliseum in Ohio. Among the backstage visitors before the first show was Eric Carmen, who'd recently hit it big with the lachrymose ballad "All By Myself." "He introduced himself to Elton," said journalist Chris Charlesworth, "who responded, quick as a flash, with: 'On your own, are you?'"

Elton and his band were riding the thermals, as were his fans—both those lucky enough to have obtained tickets, and the thousands left wanting outside each gig. That frustration came to a head at the Riverfront Coliseum in Cincinnati on August 3. Minutes before Elton was due to take the stage, several dozen rabid souls—frustrated at being locked out of the event—hurled a pair of concrete benches through a glass wall and stormed the building. Security personnel stood by helplessly as a mob hundreds-strong flooded past them. "Those idiots were out of their minds," one guard said. "Lucky no one got hurt." (Indeed, it would only be a single year later before a similar incident at this same venue resulted in the death of eleven people, trampled to death at a Who show.)

The tumultuous feeling at Riverfront only amplified as the concert blasted forth. Fights broke out throughout the arena, causing multiple arrests; when Elton swung like Tarzan from a set of lighting cables during "Love Lies Bleeding," dozens of cherry-bombs exploded from the nosebleed seats.

"They wanted their money's worth," Roger said with a laugh. "And they got it."

After a chilling reading of "Someone Saved My Life Tonight," Elton disappeared offstage for several moments, only to return wearing a Dodgers' baseball cap.

The Cincinnati Reds fans in attendance booed vociferously.

Elton whipped off the cap—beneath it was a St. Louis Cardinals' cap. The boos rained down even harder.

Ripping off *that* cap, the superstar revealed a Cincinnati Reds' cap.

The Coliseum erupted.

"All right then," Elton chuckled, as his band blasted into a slightly altered version of one of his most beloved hits, "Philadelphia Freedom" being rechristened "Cincinnati Freedom" for the night.

Out in the fourteenth row, Pete Rose and Johnny Bench—star members of the Cincinnati Reds' "Big Red Machine"—cheered wildly.

Rain began falling even before John Miles and Boz Scaggs—Elton's opening acts for his August 7 show at Buffalo's Rich Stadium—took to the stage. By the time the superstar himself appeared, the heavens had truly opened up, unleashing iron-gray torrents. Still, the deluge wasn't enough to dampen the enthusiasm of the 84,276 in attendance—or of the man they'd all come to see.

After a luminous "Goodbye Yellow Brick Road," Elton walked to the lip of the rain-slick stage and dumped a cup of water over his own head, in solidarity with the thoroughly soaked fans.

"I'll play for you as long as you're willing to stay and watch," he promised, to massive cheers.

Everyone was impressed with the efforts he and his crack band put forth—none more so than Boz Scaggs, who had stuck around after his opening set to enjoy the main performance. Soon after, he would admit to a touch of professional jealousy. "The perfect band doesn't stay with me," he soon after lamented to *NME*'s Max Bell. "Each musician has new roads to follow. It's difficult and expensive to keep a good group [together]—and only someone like Elton John can afford to retain them."

As successful as the *Louder Than Concorde* outing was proving to be, the entire undertaking was merely a warm-up for the ultimate capstone: a seven-night stand at New York's Madison Square Garden. Elton was more than primed to rock the Big Apple, selling 137,900 tickets in a matter of hours, hauling in 1.25 million dollars and easily shattering the house record set just the year before by the Rolling Stones.

The Garden shows were a homecoming of sorts, with Elton's protégée, Kiki Dee—who'd joined the tour in Chicago—taking to the stage halfway through each night's performance to sing "I've Got the Music In Me" before accompanying Elton on a lively duet on "Don't Go Breaking My Heart." Additionally, Ray Cooper, who had missed the entire tour up to that point due to an undisclosed illness (during his absence, a life-sized dummy stood watch behind his unused timpani, as Elton explained to his audiences that his percussionist was "Ray Cooper-ating from surgery"), also appeared for this final run.

Each show climaxed with a triple encore assault kicked off by a scorching "Saturday Night's Alright (For Fighting)," which Elton would deliver in full-on manic style while surrounded by a revolving cast of guests which included Alice Cooper, drag-queen Divine, Billie Jean King, and the New York Community Choir. By the time he got to his second encore, "Your Song," a good portion of the capacity crowds would have tears in their eyes. The shows then ended with a combustible "Pinball Wizard," which never failed to wring out whatever remaining stores of emotion were left in the spent audience.

"We were the first band to play Dodger Stadium since the Beatles," Caleb said. "One of the first bands to ever play Wembley. We made a lot of firsts. The first band to sell out Madison Square Garden seven nights running. With four-hour shows, mind you, which was unusual. Elvis was only doing sixty-minute shows. The Stones, maybe eighty-five minutes, if you were lucky. Our fans certainly got their money's worth. We always gave them everything we had."

Despite the marathon-like synergetic magic generated within the cement bowels of the Garden, *New York Times'* John Rockwell gave Elton's opening night appearance a derisive review, labeling the event "a smooth show that offered wallpaper music of the most banal sort." While admitting that Elton's music "provokes an indifference in this listener so complete as to preclude any trace of hostility," Rockwell went on to explain that "those of us who write about the arts are used to dealing with popular performers who aren't particularly popular with us. We treat them as fairly as we can, delineating their strengths and weaknesses as we see them, report on the crowd's reaction and call it a day."

Elton appeared on Scott Muni's radio program on WNEW-FM a couple days after the review appeared. Full of righteous indignation and Dom Pérignon, Elton let his displeasure with Rockwell be known.

"If you are listening now, you asshole," he taunted, "come down here and I'll destroy you. I'll rip you to bits on the air."

"I doubt if John Rockwell was even at the concert," Elton later reflected. "It was the most piss-elegant review I've seen: 'Performers come and go but we rock critics have to deal with them.' Who the *fuck* is this John Rockwell?" He grimaced. "I don't mind bad reviews at all. I always get them. In fact, I'm used to them. But [Rockwell's review] was more like an edict: 'You mustn't like Elton John, because I don't think he's very good. Everyone at the concert should have been home listening to Linda Ronstadt's albums.' It was very condescending."

Ken Tucker, in his *Rolling Stone* review, wasn't much kinder than Rockwell. "Elton's a garish, tuneless shuck and decidedly out of fashion since about the time of *Rock of the Westies*," he proclaimed. "His was ultimately a tedious concert: cold-bloodedly entertaining, artless, and other than hopping off the piano, no chances were taken."

"I'm the person rock critics love to hate," Elton said. "You see, there is currently a trend among rock critics: Only if you are genuinely bad will they love you."

On the penultimate night of Elton's Garden stand—mere minutes before hitting the stage—John Reid corralled the band into a hospitality suite behind the stage to make an announcement.

"Tomorrow night's the last [gig]," he told them pointblank. "Elton's taking a year off for tax reasons. He's gonna pay you all for the next year, but tomorrow's gonna be the last show for a bit."

The band members were stunned.

"It was tough," Caleb said. "That was a massive downer. And only twenty minutes before show time: 'Here's your pink slip.' We were at the top of the tree at that time, so that was a tough one. And all of a sudden, it's all over."

"Okay, lads," Reid chortled, clapping his hands while the band stood around him in wordless shock. "Let's have a good show then, eh?"

Roger glared at Elton from behind his drum kit all night long. "Instead of playing all these subtle accents on 'Goodbye Yellow Brick Road' or whatever, like I usually did," he said, "it was just *Bam! Bam! Bam!* [I was] hitting those cymbals as hard as I could. I didn't give a fuck if there was twenty-thousand people in the place or not."

After the show, the drummer headed straight back to the Waldorf Astoria, opened a bottle of Four Roses, and took out his frustrations on his hotel room. "I went a bit mental that night," he confessed. "I wrecked that room like a true rock star. I just couldn't get my head around any of it. It was completely handled the wrong way, if you know what I mean."

Disturbed by the commotion, Ray Cooper poked his head into Roger's room to see what was going on.

"It's okay, Rog," he soothed. "Just relax. It'll be okay."

"Fuck *that!*" Roger screamed, heaving a brass lamp through a television set.

Ray disappeared down the hall and knocked on Elton's door.

"Rog has gone mental," he said. "You might want to sort this out somehow."

To placate the drummer, Elton authorized John Reid to give each band member a bonus royalty point for their upcoming album. Though generous, the gesture meant little to Roger.

"[The whole thing] just fucked me up completely," he said.

"We were all brought down," Kenny later said, "but especially Roger. That was *it* for him. If anything brought Roger down—besides obviously his alcoholism—that was it. It was terrible. Even when he and I and Caleb joined Hall & Oates later, he'd always get hammered and talk about, '*Why* did Elton do that? *Why'd* that fucking happen?'" (After the *Louder Than Concorde* tour ended, Kenny himself would need some time to get over the psychic wounds his time in the band had inflicted on him, but for a decidedly different reason than Roger. "Bernie and Maxine had separated and she moved to Colorado," he said years later. "And gradually the two of us worked that out. It was a really emotional time. Maxine and I were together for seven years, so it was hardly a fling, and we're still really good friends. And Bernie's still so pissed-off at her, even to this day, that he won't acknowledge that 'Tiny Dancer' is about her anymore, when everyone knows that it was. I don't understand that, but—whatever.")

"Poor Roger had flown his mom out for the gig, to witness his success for the first time, and the carpet gets pulled out," Caleb said. "Even though Hall & Oates were hot just then, their music was sort of pseudo-soul to us, and we weren't that excited about it, especially after being with the biggest artist on the planet. Poor Popey never really got over it."

"Kenny and Caleb were right," Roger's widow, Sue, said years later. "Rog never *did* get over it. It destroyed him. It led to him drowning his sorrows in the time-honored rock 'n' roll way."

Elton, for his part, wasn't even entirely sure of his decision to come off the road—or of much else, for that matter. "I was very mentally tired, mentally fed up with myself as a person," he said. "I love performing, but if you go onstage and you suddenly start thinking 'What time's the plane tomorrow?' [or] 'What am I gonna wear [tomorrow]?', and you're halfway through a song and then you panic—'Oh, what's the next word?'—then it's time to stop. Because you can't cheat on a live performance. You can cheat when you make a record, because you can go over and over and over and do it again, but with a live performance, you can't cheat. And I think that's why people like live performances. But I was very bored with playing live. But the ego is such that you think, 'Someone is going to take over my crown.' In fact, my crown had already slipped. You can only have the crown for two years tops, probably. There are always bridges to cross, and as a musician there are always other fields to conquer. But you have to stop and refresh yourself and build up your passion again."

For his part, background vocalist Jon Joyce was unsurprised. "It was a time of cocaine and excess," he said. "And that didn't mix well in the long run. We were all just to-the-wall in terms of all the abuses catching up to us. It was a day of reckoning when all that happened."

During Elton's final concert, a peculiar energy filled Madison Square Garden. "It was a pretty weird night, a very sad occasion," he said. "It came to the point where I sang 'Yellow Brick Road' and I thought, 'I don't have to sing this anymore,' and it made me quite happy inside. Yeah, it could be the last gig forever."

Ray channeled his inner Keith Moon during "Saturday Night's Alright (For Fighting)," attacking his kettle drums with manic relish, slinging his tambourine to the dark recesses and bringing his tubular bells crashing to the floor with an atonal explosion.

"Come *on*, New York!" he roared. "Come *on!*"

Elton attempted to get in on the action by pushing his piano off the stage; fortuitously, the instrument proved too heavy to move more than a few feet.

The crowd cheered the band's efforts madly, compelling the exhausted musicians on. "It was a crazy tour, it was grueling," Cindy Bullens said. "Elton worked his butt off every night, whether he was feeling up to it or not. He was the consummate showman."

To help curb the fatigue, the superstar playfully reneged on a long-held vow. "All the time I'd been back with Elton," Caleb said, "he'd stuck to his promise not to play 'Crocodile Rock'. But at the final gig at Madison Square Garden, he had a meltdown, he was going into retirement, and at the very end of the set he throws in 'Crocodile Rock'. That was his way of giving the finger to me and everybody."

"We were dead in the middle of a number, so there wasn't anything we could do but go along with it," Roger said. "I really hated that bastard. But [I] loved him too. And I still do."

Before launching into his final encore, Elton told the cheering crowd, with an unmistakable note of regret in his ragged voice, "You won't see me for a while, but I'll be back...someday."

True to his word, it would be the last time an American audience got to see Elton perform live with a full band that decade.

Chapter 30:
The Token Queen of Rock

The day after the final Madison Square Garden show, an exhausted Elton granted an interview with *Rolling Stone* reporter Cliff Jahr. The tête-à-tête was held in the Englishman's seven-room faux-Louis XIV suite at the Sherry-Netherland Hotel.

Elton greeted Jahr, and photographer Ron Pownall, with a bone-shattering handshake. Throwing himself onto an enormous white sofa, he glanced out the window at a panoramic view of Fifth Avenue and Central Park while Jahr set up a tape recorder on the coffee table between them.

"My life in the last six years has been a Disney film," the pianist said, "and now I have to have a person in my life."

When Jahr asked about his cynical forebodings, Elton was brutally honest. "I get depressed very easily, very bad moods." His voice dipped low. "I don't think anyone knows the real me. I don't even think *I* do. I don't know what I want to be, exactly."

Did he suffer from a lack of love?

The superstar considered the question thoughtfully.

"I suppose I have a certain amount of love and affection, as far as love and affection go, from friends and stuff," he answered tentatively, hardly making eye contact with Jahr. "But my sexual life...um...I haven't met anybody I would like to have any big scenes with. It's strange that I haven't. I know everyone should have a certain amount of sex, and I do, but that's it, and I desperately would like to have an affair."

Jahr nodded.

"I'd rather fall in love with a woman eventually," Elton continued, "because I think a woman probably lasts longer than a man. But I really don't know. I've never talked about this before, but I'm not going to turn off the tape. I haven't met anybody that I would like to settle down with—of either sex."

"You're bisexual?"

Elton hesitated. "There's nothing wrong with going to bed with someone of the same sex. I think everybody's bisexual to a certain degree. I don't think it's just me....I just think people should be very free with sex. They should draw the line at goats."

Thinking nothing more of the interview, Elton headed back to England the next day to mull over potential projects. The two leading contenders were a feature-length cartoon based on the *Captain Fantastic* album, and the title role in a planned film version of the 1956 Broadway musical *Candide*. He'd soon pass on both.

The pianist hadn't been home a week before David Bowie had a go at him in *Playboy*.

"I consider myself responsible for a whole new school of pretensions," Bowie said coyly. "They know who they are. Don't you, Elton?"

"[Bowie] was obviously a little high when he did [that interview]," Elton countered. "David's one of those people of the moment. I mean, 'What is the fashion this week? What's it going to be next week?' His insults to me go by the board. I think he's a silly boy."

Playboy later followed up with Bowie to ask how his relationship with Elton was faring since his catty pronouncement.

"He sent me a very nice telegram the other day," the Thin White Duke answered.

"Didn't you describe him as 'the Liberace, the token queen of rock'?"

Bowie blushed. "Yes, well, that was before the telegram. I'd much rather listen to him on the radio than talk about him."

While Bowie was walking back his impolitic remarks, "Bennie and the Jets" was stumbling up the U.K. charts. The belated release of the three-year-old track—another vault-raiding release from DJM—only managed a paltry Number 37, as the song, backed with 1970's "Rock 'n' Roll Madonna," had long been in most fans' collections by that point.

Elton hardly gave a toss; his concentration was firmly fixed on his final concert obligation of the year: a long-planned solo gig at the Edinburgh Playhouse in Scotland. The performance, held on September 17, was to be the culmination of Edinburgh's annual arts festival. Organized by John Reid and David Evans, several of the top-tier groups playing during the month-long "Festival of Popular Music" included Queen, Soft Machine and Crosby & Nash.

After an opening set by Billy Barkley, Elton made his entrance from below the theatre, playing a fanfare on the venue's one-of-a-kind house organ. Dressed in a green-and-white-checked suit and heavy white frames, Elton quickly crossed the sheepskin-carpeted stage—which featured a grandfather clock, a stuffed dog and a fully-stocked liquor cabinet—and bowed anxiously.

Visibly nervous—the show was being live-simulcast over radio stations across Europe, and being filmed by ABC-TV for an American special—an already buzzed Elton proceeded to get plastered.

"I don't want the people out there to *think* I'm an alcoholic," he said, pouring himself a Bloody Mary from a pitcher. "I want them to *know* I'm an alcoholic." He downed a healthy swallow. "Tonight I feel a bit lost because I've only ever done one or two of these things before, and it's always been before an absolutely alcoholically pissed audience. So if I forget any of the words, it's absolutely due to the fact that I'm so nervous." He grinned. "Five minutes on TV and I haven't sung anything yet."

With that, he launched into a reflective reading of "Skyline Pigeon."

The pianist nodded gratefully to the 3,200 in attendance as the hymn ended to an enthusiastic round of applause. "There's gonna be a lot of help needed from you tonight, I tell you, in singing and things like that," he confided. "I'd like to extend a warm welcome to everybody listening on the radio, because it's the first time that Radio Forth and Radio Clyde have linked up, and I think that should happen a lot more often. More live concerts, y'know? If people did some concerts broadcast live—like they do in America—I think it'd be a lot better for British radio. It couldn't be any worse, could it?"

"What was very special about this is this was the first pan-global satellite solo concert to go right around the world," video archivist Henry Scott-Irvine later told journalist John F. Higgins. "I mean, the Beatles did it famously in 1967 with 'All You Need is Love' from Abbey Road studios, but this was the first color, live, solo concert to go around the world as it happened....It was a big thing."

After performing particularly heartfelt renditions of "I Need You to Turn To" and "Sixty Years On," Elton premiered a new composition. "This is a song which we wrote about a year ago in Colorado," he said, "and it's a song called 'Tonight'. And I'm playing it tonight. And this is the first time I've played it. And it has a very long piano intro."

"I like it!" someone called from the rafters before a note had been struck.

Elton flashed an electric smile. "You like it already? I'm onto a winning thing. Actually, it resembles 'Save Your Kisses for Me' by the Brotherhood of Man. Do you know that?" The audience jeered blithely. "Now, now, now—it *did* win the Eurovision Song Contest. And it *is* rubbish, but never mind."

Despite his reckless imbibing, the pianist gave a commanding performance.

"This is a song you'll have to help me out on," he said after his third standing ovation of the night, "because I usually play it with the band and it needs a lot of rhythmic accompaniment. Anyway, I'm gonna try it, 'cause you can only sing so many down songs, otherwise people nod off. You know what I mean?" A moment later, a familiar B-minor-over-G-major-7 chord sounded.

The audience reacted with a deluge of unchecked emotion.

"Al-right Ed-in-burgh, get it *on!*" Elton cried out rhythmically as "Bennie and the Jets" swung into an extended call-and-response coda.

"Where's Kiki?" someone yelled afterward.

Elton shrugged. "Kiki Dee is not here tonight, let me say. She's in Hyde Park. Well, she's not in Hyde Park at the *moment*. If she was, I'd want to know what she's doing—

and who she's doing it with. I've got a fair idea who she's doing it with—and let's face it, it's *not* Freddie Mercury."

Before launching into the musical triumvirate of "I Think I'm Gonna Kill Myself," "Don't Let the Sun Go Down On Me" and "Better Off Dead," the pianist noted with a self-deprecating grin that, "on reflection, the next three numbers are very suicidal, so all you manic-depressives better take your uppers now."

A storm of applause greeted Elton as he shook out his cramping hands after a tautly angular "Better Off Dead" ended.

"Cor! Me fingers caught fire on that one, tell you what." He laughed. "We're gonna do a song—'*We're* gonna do…' See? That's habit—me and the *piano* are gonna do a song for a lady who came all the way up from London. She's a blind lady called Catherine, and I'd like to dedicate this next song to her because I think that's incredible to come all the way up from London and be so loyal. Well done." He grimaced. "I made a statement in the press—or in the *Melody Maker*, ha, sorry about that—saying about [how] you *do* lose touch about things. And for someone to come up from London— when you think about it, to take all that trouble—is incredible. And you sometimes take it for granted…and that's one of the reasons why I think a lot of us need bringing down to earth and coming back off the road, as it were, to reevaluate things. I said in the *Melody Maker* this week, 'It needs four phone calls to get even close to me.' And that's sort of infuriating sometimes. So Catherine, you did a really nice job for coming up for me, and that's very important. I'm not bloody well giving you the fare to go back, though. No, seriously, this is a new song from the new album, and it's called 'Sorry Seems to Be the Hardest Word'. All right." He began the delicate, descending-chord intro with a knowing smirk, before jokingly adding: "It's not a twist number."

The program proper ended with "Your Song." Before performing the emotional serenade, Elton told his audience, "I got interviewed on the news tonight, and I looked like a pregnant coalminer—in fact, I *am* a pregnant coalminer— and I said I was petrified, and that's not too far off from the truth. Because it's very rarely that I get the chance to do one of these things, and usually, as I said, most people are drunk, so it doesn't matter, but tonight was a rare occasion....But it's good to get the jitters, 'cause sometimes you can take things for granted. And I never took you for granted tonight, and I want to thank you very much."

As "Your Song's" final E-flat chord rang throughout the hall, the pianist bowed modestly and left the stage, only to be brought back for an inevitable suite of encores. Shaking hands with fans at the front of the stage, he handed out bottles of Coca-Cola and tomato juice from the antique drinks cabinet onstage.

As he prepared to launch into his first encore, he spilled a splash of Bloody Mary on his keyboard.

"Oh shit, hang on." He ran a hand up the keys to clean them off, before remembering that his performance was being beamed out live. "Oh, I beg your pardon, radio listeners." He laughed. "Never mind, I'm sure you've heard worse than that. Give me another drink and *I'll* say worse myself. I'm gonna try to do something, [but] it's very hard, y'know—as the Bishop said to the actress."

With that, he tore into a blistering "Island Girl," which incorporated generous passages from "The Bitch is Back."

After taking his leave, Elton was soon called back for more. He was truly moved, and truly at a loss.

"I was there at the show," Henry Scott-Irvine said. "It was an incredible concert to be at, and...a good Edinburgh crowd really gets into it. So they were standing for quite a lot of the show, and when he played a song they really liked, everyone would stamp their feet as well as applaud. You could hear the whole theater literally resounding with applause that night. It was overwhelming."

"Now I don't know what to do," Elton admitted to the enthusiastic crowd, "'cause I've only rehearsed that much." He thought for a moment. "I'm gonna try something that's gonna be quite out of the ordinary and mad and totally ridiculous. I haven't rehearsed it, so you'll have to help."

"Don't Go Breaking My Heart" came rolling breezily off his piano keys, the audience gleefully singing counterpoint.

"All right," the pianist huffed afterward. "Lunacy prevails on this evening." He stared out into the darkened recesses of the wrung-out crowd. "I've had an effing great time. Thank you very much....But most of all, I'd like to say how pissed I am. How pissed I am to be on the stage." He held up his glass. "No, really, this is pure tomato juice. I'm willing to go to the lab. I'm willing to be given the green breathalyzer test..."

Launching into a turbulent "Saturday Night's Alright (For Fighting)," Elton ended up atop his piano, the entire hall clapping along to an imaginary beat. A tartan scarf landed at the pianist's feet; he tied it bandana-style around his head, leapt off the piano, and fell to his knees before his keyboard, finishing the song in grand style.

The crowd rose for one final standing ovation as Elton handed his piano bench to a star-struck girl in the front row.

"I like to share things," he'd later explain of the unique gesture. "It's not easy when you're that big a megastar. When you look at seventy-thousand people, how the fuck can you share things? That's another thing that depressed me on the last tour. It suddenly struck me it was like a Nuremburg rally."

Despite surviving the evening unscathed, Elton couldn't foresee many more solo shows in his future. "One-man shows are boring," he declared. "I'll never do that again. I mean, who wants to see one guy up there for two-and-a-half hours?"

The *Rolling Stone* issue featuring Elton's interview with Cliff Jahr hit the newsstands weeks later. While the cover showed the pianist in a wholesome pose, reclining on a pillow-filled bed while dressed boyishly in a striped sweater which featured soccer players battling it out on the pitch, the headline luridly promised: "Elton's Frank Talk: The Lonely Life of a Superstar."

The publication of the interview had tectonic ramifications. In the socially conservative United States of 1976—where the Center for Disease Control still listed homosexuality as an aberrant mental disorder—Elton's admission of bisexuality had an immediately chilling effect on his career. Overnight, his records stopped selling in the massive quantities they'd always had before; the near-saturation-level radio-play which his music routinely enjoyed also came to an abrupt halt. In a matter of days, Elton went from celebrated media darling to a foreigner with dubious leanings. Someone to be suspected. Somebody *different*.

16 Magazine, a glossy publication filled with soft-focus "exposés" on teen heartthrobs like Leif Garret, David Cassidy and the Bay City Rollers, had long made Elton their favored point of focus. As often as not, he could be seen gracing their covers beside such overheated headlines as "The Truth About Elton!" and "Elton—Hot Secrets!" Once his admission of bisexuality became public fodder, the magazine decisively dropped him from their pages without a word of explanation.

More ominously, Elton's records were ritualistically burned in public bonfires throughout the culturally-conservative American South. This overheated reaction was perhaps best summed up by a letter-to-the-editor which appeared in a follow-up issue of *Rolling Stone*, where a young girl from Provo, Utah wrote: "As a highly devoted Elton John fan, I regret being needlessly informed that my 'hero' is bisexual. The effect is shattering. He needn't have revealed his moral midgetness. I regret facing the fact that he is a gross perverter of the sacred (ignorance was bliss). Luckily, his decrepit morality hasn't affected his musical abilities, although it may take an exercise in "separating the man from the music" to enjoy him again. My disgust is matched only by my disappointment, while both are overshadowed by pity; I pity him for his sexual illusions and perversions."

Elton could only laugh.

"America's supposed to be the great liberated free-minded society—which, of course, it isn't," he said. "Everyone goes: 'Peace and love, man,' but it'll never happen because hatred is rammed into kids by their parents, and hate makes much more money....People burnt my records. But you know what? It was a very small price to pay for the freedom that it gave me....[And] to be honest, I don't believe that I'm one-hundred percent gay [anyway], because I'm attracted to older women, and I can't dismiss that side of my character."

The day after the *Rolling Stone* issue hit the stands, Elton was due to fly up to Manchester to attend Watford's game at Rochdale. "My mother was up with me," he said, "and she came into the hotel bedroom with all the Saturday papers:

'Bisexual Elton Said…' She said, 'Have a look at this then!' I thought, 'Oh my God'….I'd expected it to come out, but on a Saturday morning when I'm going to meet the team? And I walked into the hotel in Manchester, and the then-manager, Mike King, came out and said, 'Listen, we've seen the papers. What you do with your life is your own business'…They handled it superbly. British people do."

Some British people did. That afternoon, a frigid, gray Saturday, saw thousands of Rochdale supporters taunting the singer with a rousing chorus of: "Don't sit down while Elton's around, or you'll get a penis up your arse!" to the old Cockney tune "My Old Man (Said Follow the Van)." Later, with the match well underway, they began chanting: "Elton John's a homosexual!" to the tune of "Glory, Glory, Hallelujah."

Elton simply nodded.

"They're doing it to test you out," he said. "And if you get uptight about it, that's the wrong thing to do. It's been very hard for me, but I've sat there and grinned and borne it, and it's taught me a lot about dignity."

Despite the taunts of rival soccer fans, the fallout over Elton's admission in Britain was, in general, noticeably less severe than it had been in the States. "I found that when I was driving around London, I got far more waves from taxi drivers and lorry drivers than I ever had before," he joked.

Despite the career-shifting power the interview exerted, the pianist harbored no ill feelings toward Cliff Jahr. "It was a great interview. [Jahr] was one-hundred percent fair….Nobody's had the balls to ask me about it before. I would have said something all along if someone had asked me, but I'm not going to come out and say something just to be [outrageous]. I don't want to shove it all over the front pages like some people I could mention."

While glam rockers like Mick Jagger and David Bowie had playfully toyed with their images—leveraging androgynously bisexual mystiques in a bid to increase their artistic credibility—no personality as universally adored as Elton had ever dared make such a blunt disclosure of their sexuality. It was, at the time, a monumental revelation. (Interestingly, years later, Bowie would recant his claims of bisexuality to *Rolling Stone,* insisting that it was the biggest mistake he'd ever made, and that he "was always a closet heterosexual.")

Recognizing the daring nature of his confession, Elton's friends rallied around him for support. "I'm sure it was a great relief to him once the article was printed," Kiki Dee said. "It was typical of him to follow his instincts, even if what he said was potentially risky." Rod Stewart, however, was less certain. "I saw him at his lowest ebb after he did [that] interview. I think that was probably a turning point in his career, too, but he won't admit that. I still can't see why he said that."

Amidst all the controversy, Gus was as busy as ever, recording overdubs and creating final mixes for Elton's upcoming album at Marquee Studios in Soho. "The plan was to mix the Canadian tracks into a solid single [album]," he said. "But then I made the mistake of letting it slip at this luncheon I was attending with some of the MCA brass that we'd actually recorded enough material for a double album. They immediately rang up John Reid, and next thing I knew I was back in England mixing a double album instead of a single. It was a great shame."

Many of the songs which Gus had already planned on scrapping—"Shoulder Holster," "Boogie Pilgrim" and "Where's the Shoorah?" amongst them—were suddenly reinstated. Particularly painful for the producer was the restoration of "The Wide-Eyed and Laughing," a track he openly loathed. "Sitars for bloody years, that one" he said. "Crosby and Nash [sang] backup on it. Crosby was such an unbelievable asshole, so, yeah—not my favorite [song]."

Gus purposefully sequenced "Bite Your Lip (Get Up and Dance!)" as the album's final track, as a subtle protest to its "ninety-five-year fadeout."

"One does what one can," he said. "End of [the] bloody story."

The producer invited the Captain & Tennille to the studio one day to show them his work process as he created final mixes. "We were in England, Daryl and I, doing this special for the BBC," Toni Tennille said. "So we went into the studio and it was *so loud* that my chest was rattling, my ears were burning. I went, 'Oh my God, how can this man still *hear?*' [Gus] told me later on that same day that his theory for getting the best mix was to listen to it so loud that it would start to hurt his ears, and then he would turn it down just until it was sort of comfortable, and that's how he would mix, at that level."

Assisting Gus at Marquee was lead engineer Phil Dunne, as well as a trainee engineer named Gary Bremner. It was Bremner's job to set up the studio pre-session, and then de-rig it all afterward. "It was a tough job at times, with little financial reward or thanks," he said, "but you knew that a queue would quickly form to take your place if you left, as you were right in the center of the heartbeat of the music industry, working and meeting with some of the biggest stars in the business—both behind and in front of the microphone."

It was particularly rewarding to the novice engineer that he was able to observe one of the most highly-respected producers in the industry up close. "Gus was a larger-than-life character that would arrive at the studio in his chauffeur-driven Rolls-Royce, and he wore a long floor-length fur coat," Bremner said. "He had this amazing presence and energy that was infectious, and he brought such an enthusiasm to his work. He had a clear idea of what he wanted, and was an absolute perfectionist. With Gus, there was no second best—he strove for the highest standards. He was charming and daunting at the same time, and he'd play the mixing desk like it was a collection of instruments and he was the conductor. The faders were manually operated, and it would not be long before the mixing desk was a myriad of [hieroglyphic-like] level marks and masking tape, each marker delicately inscribed and notated. Each had its own special role to play in the overall produced sound that Gus wanted, and that he created."

The track which left the most indelible impression upon Bremner was "One Horse Town." "The studio control room was rocking on that one," he said. "It took forever to mix, but it was a roller coaster ride of adrenalin and emotion. Gus spent hours setting up the sound balances for the drums, building his music up from the foundations of his drum sound, bass, and rhythm guitars. Those were the building blocks. If they were all in sync, then he would add vocals and other instruments, like he was an artist adding colors to a painting. And Elton's band was so tight—so on-point—that no one could afford to miss anything the guys were playing. The drum sound on 'One Horse Town' in particular was sensational. Roger Pope was on fire when it was recorded. [There was] no digital tech then, it was all [done] on magnetic tapes and an MCI Desk, and—I can tell you—when we mixed this track the studio monitors were rocking their socks off. Hearing Roger Popes drum patterns pan from left to right across the studio was just incredible, because—even with all the other instruments and vocals in perfect balance with each other—his drum sound still came through so clearly and so defined. I've never heard a better drum sound before or since. In fact, 'One Horse Town' is still my all-time favorite track of Elton's. It has such energy and build to it, and Roger's drumming was world-class throughout. It's timeless, and—in my opinion—it will never age."

Bremner was equally impressed with the talent and gentlemanliness of percussionist Ray Cooper, who turned up at the studio one day to overdub bongo drums on "Crazy Water." "Gus asked him to go listen to the track and fill in where he felt. Within minutes, he was playing these amazing patterns that just brought the whole track to life. He was an incredible percussionist. What I remember most about him, however, was the fact that he was so down-to-earth and such a nice guy. One lunchtime, Gus and everybody disappeared for a meal, and I was left on my own in the studio. Ray came into the control room and I told him everyone had gone out to a certain restaurant. He asked why I hadn't gone, and I said I had not been invited. He then said, 'Well, in that case, we will both go out and have a pint and a sandwich together, if you are up for it.' So I spent the next hour in the corner of this small pub in Soho sipping a pint and chatting away with one of the world's most talented percussionists. No one had a clue who he was, and he didn't care a jot."

Forty-eight hours after the Sex Pistols signed a record contract with EMI—the deal portending a seismic shift in the landscape of popular music—"Sorry Seems to Be the Hardest Word," was released as the leadoff single from Elton's upcoming LP, *Blue Moves*. Backed with "Shoulder Holster," the disc peaked at Number 11 in the U.K., and—on Christmas Day—at Number 6 in America. It was another hit for Elton, his fourteenth *Billboard* Top 10 single in four years. "Sorry Seems to Be the Hardest Word" would eventually go on to sell over a million units in its three-month residency in *Billboard*'s Hot 100, technically becoming Elton's first Platinum single, as the Platinum certification had only recently been instated by the RIAA.

As *Blue Moves* was being readied for the shops, Bernie promised "up-tempo disco stompers, Bob Marley-type tracks, Spinners-type tracks, [and] a few instrumentals. There's a lot of very downer songs, too—suicide material—but good at the same time."

Days later, on October 22, a *Blue Moves* launch party was held at a Savile Row art gallery to herald the disc's release. Elton's debut on his own Rocket Records label (which now featured a sleeker corporate logo of an angular train slicing determinedly through a darkened countryside), the album's title had been amended at the last minute from the bleaker *Black Moves*. The LP would go Gold in less than a month, though it would only manage to secure a Number Three showing on either side of the Atlantic. Elton's first collection of new material since 1971's *Madman Across the Water* to stall out before reaching the top spot in the States, the sepulchral song cycle was—at 84:47—the longest studio album the pianist had ever delivered, besting *Goodbye Yellow Brick Road* by a good eight-and-a-half minutes.

Though Gus was displeased at having been forced to artificially extend the album's length for commercial considerations, he was at least content that the recording had been officially finalized in vinyl. "There's something very strange about making records," he said. "It isn't until you get a bit of black plastic in your hand and you hear it on the radio that you actually believe you've made a record. While it's still a tape and it goes around [in the studio], it doesn't really appear to be what it is."

Blue Moves proved to be a unique album in nearly every way. Gone was the accessible iconography which helped delineate *Don't Shoot Me I'm Only the Piano Player* and *Captain Fantastic and the Brown Dirt Cowboy*. Gone too were the pinup portraits featured so heavily on *Caribou* and *Rock of the Westies*. Instead, *Blue Moves'* cover featured a reproduction of Irish artist Patrick Procktor's "The Guardian Readers," an impressionistic blue-on-blue enamel which showed a group of men lounging in a park in various stages of undress.

"I bought [the canvas] without realizing it was all blokes," Elton said. "It fitted the mood of the album exactly. People said I should have a picture of me on the front, but I've had enough of those. I put me little food down. And then *The Sun* were going to use the album as contest prizes and they rang us up to say they couldn't do it because of the painting. Silly, isn't it?" Even with this slight dust-up, the pianist was decidedly pleased with his efforts. "We had tried to change with every album up to that point, but *Blue Moves* was the most drastic. I was aware that we had been at the peak of our careers, and that that was going to level off. And we just did a blatantly uncommercial album. It wasn't on purpose—it's full of fine songs and has a great band. I think *Blue Moves* is a very poignant album. We were all weary, feeling the pressure, and needed a break. Out of those situations comes rawness, and some of the lyrics are desperate...[but] musically I attribute it to the *Elton John* album—lots of slow, romantic songs and jazzy-type tinges in them. Three instrumentals. But who knows?"

Unable to appreciate the more subtle charms the collection had to offer, Robert Christgau lamented that "none of the few rockers on this impossibly weepy and excessive double-LP match anything on *Rock of the Westies*," while *Rolling Stone's* Ariel Swartley condemned the work as "one of the most desperately pretentious albums around. It's a two-record catalog of musical excess."

Sounds' Mick Brown dissented. "Even before I'd heard one note of *Blue Moves*, I had divined that this album was going to be the Big One," he wrote. "This is an album that's going to slowly insinuate its way into your bloodstream, pump round your body for a few days and finally end up lodging in your brain, rather than grabbing you by the throat and *demanding* you to take notice. It couldn't be otherwise." Much in the same vein, *ZigZag's* John Tobler declared the work "absolutely essential listening....In fact, this is the album for which 1976 will be remembered. Forget Frampton, Stevie Wonder and all the rest—they're by no means bad records, but they just don't live next to this one."

"Elton has given us a more-than-generous supply of often-breathtaking, often moving rock 'n' roll to sing along with," *Phonograph Record's* Bud Scoppa noted days later in his review. "Theme music for all of us, like we haven't had in ages. Because of the hours, days and dawns we've spent together, I've come to think of this now-scratchy album as a buddy."

"It's a different album," Caleb said. "I think it was ahead of its time. There was some great musical stuff on there. That band was very tight, and we had already toured from the previous album, so we got very tight on the road. Ninety percent of the *Blue Moves* album was done live in the studio, very few overdubs. A lot of the solos were done live. Roger Pope's drumming, with Ray Cooper's percussion, that was all done live. It was a great album, great musicians. There wasn't a weak link in the band at all."

The broodingly contemplative LP was destined to become Elton's personal favorite. Bernie's, as well. "*Blue Moves* was like our Mount Everest in many ways," the lyricist said. "Elton had filled every major stadium in the world. We'd written strings of Number One records. You couldn't fart without hearing Elton John....It felt like there was no way we could go any further. There was only one way to go from here."

"[*Blue Moves*] was a steel curtain for me," Elton was to later reflect. "It slammed down, and things weren't quite the same after."

The first order of change occurred the very night *Blue Moves* was released, at Rocket Records' Annual General Meeting.

"That evening there was a press reception," Gus told journalist David Wright. "Everyone was going to be in [England] at last—Bernie, John, Elton, all the directors of the company. There were a lot of things about Rocket that I really didn't like, so I let one particular person know a good month before the meeting that there were a lot of things I was very upset about. And that unless they were taken care of, I was going to have to quit."

During the meeting, Gus noticed that Elton seemed particularly restless.

"Someone turned to me and said, 'Gus, we understand that you've got some particular things you want to discuss.' I said, 'Yeah, I do. The things I think need to be taken care of are as follows...'" The producer listed a half-dozen items which he felt had to be addressed, from signing Dave Edmunds to instituting tighter accounting protocols. "Everyone sat there and listened, and Elton was shuffling about more and more. When I finished, there was a long silence."

"Well, quite honestly, Gus," John Reid said, "we don't agree with you."

"So what you're saying is that you don't agree with anything I've proposed, and you understand that if these things aren't sorted out, I'm going to have to go?"

"Yes."

The producer stood. "Well, okay. Looks like we have nothing more to discuss."

Stepping out of the office, Gus stayed by the door for a good ten seconds. "[I was] waiting for someone to go, 'Hang on, Gus. Hold it. Let's talk about this.' And no one did. So I thought, 'Right. Well, I've obviously made the right decision.' And off I went."

The producer fully understood that severing ties with Rocket meant severing ties with Elton as his producer as well, but it didn't matter—they'd already accomplished everything they'd originally set out to do, and much more. "I felt I needed to quit, and I was very glad I did," Gus later told *East End Lights'* John F. Higgins. "I mean, okay, yes, of course my income altered very radically. But so what? I've got to live with myself, and you have to have some pride. That's what it really comes down to—pride." (In future years, Gus—whom Elton would call "the greatest producer of his generation"—would go on to helm albums for a wide variety of artists, from husky-voiced guitarist/singer Chris Rea [including his hit, "Fool (If You Think It's Over)"], to Irish alt-rock duo the Frank and Walters, to new-wave pioneers XTC [on their seminal *Nonsuch* LP].)

Elton was nonplussed about the separation. "I haven't fallen out with Gus," he said. "But I honestly believe that after fourteen albums we needed a break from each other. Also, by now I know exactly what I want."

Blue Moves' relative chart failure ("We thought we were finished," Bernie admitted)—combined with Gus' unceremonious exit—forced Elton and his lyricist to reevaluate their nearly decade-long partnership.

"I didn't think we had any choice but to take a break," Bernie said. "I had to run away from it, because I was frightened to keep going. I was frightened of failure. I'm sure drugs, alcohol, the geographical thing, it all contributed. But the base core of it was, I don't know if we knew what we wanted to do next. Or if we *could* do it. But we never argued about it."

The amicable break was, seemingly, a minor hiccup, as—for the fourth year in a row—Elton topped the list of the world's most successful entertainers, earning the first Platinum double album ever to be awarded, as well as laying claim to the top-selling single of the year. His concert gross receipts topped those of Elvis Presley, Led Zeppelin, Paul McCartney & Wings, the Who, Bob Dylan and everybody else. He was still, ostensibly, at the very top of the heap.

But that was about to change.

Part Five:
A Single Man

Chapter 31:
'Get Me a Grand Piano and You're On'

1977 began in relative calm. Declaring to *Daily Express'* David Wigg on January 27 that he'd "had five or six great years, but I have to say goodbye to that era, I have to start from the word go again," Elton claimed that he "would rather have a wife and children [than a full-time career], because I adore children. That's one of the things I would really like to do." When asked about his enormous salary as the world's top-earning entertainer, the singer was forthright. "Sure, I'm earning more than a doctor or a nurse, but then I'm paying more to help bail out this country. I think people tend to forget that a lot of the time."

The interview served as modest damage control for the continued fallout generated by Elton's *Rolling Stone* admission. Also helping mitigate matters—to some lesser degree—was the February 4 release of his latest U.K. single, "Crazy Water." Backed with "Chameleon," the single quickly broke into the Top 40, ultimately managing a modest Number 27 placement.

Though the cracks were clearly beginning to show, that didn't stop the pianist from still proving popular in America as well, taking the Favorite Rock or Pop Vocalist nod on *The People's Choice Awards*.

Unable to accept the award himself, Elton sent Ronnie Wood and Keith Moon on his behalf.

"Elton gave me a special message to say tonight," a visibly confused Moon said, fumbling with a handwritten scroll.

"Which, in fact, he can't remember," Wood teased. "But I know [Elton] would love to say, 'Thank you,' wouldn't he?"

Moon blinked. "Yeah, he'd love to say thank you."

"Stupid boy."

"Stupid boy," Moon repeated amiably. Sadly, the affable drummer would be found dead a little over a year later, a victim of his own extravagant excesses.

Though Elton and Bernie's professional sabbatical was by now in full effect, their personal friendship was still very much alive and kicking, as evidenced by their joint attendance at Frank Sinatra's March 1 concert at the Royal Albert Hall.

"Here's an interesting song, fairly new, by Elton John," Ol' Blue Eyes announced before breaking into a tenderly nuanced rendition of "Sorry Seems to Be the Hardest Word" as the John/Taupin team sat in stunned silence.

After the song ended to enthusiastic applause, Sinatra asked the songwriters to stand up and take a bow. "I nearly died," Elton said. "[Sinatra's] someone I admire because he always credits the writer, the arranger, and he tries not just to do his old songs, he tries to do obscure things. As an artist, he's remarkable."

So flattered by Sinatra's attentions was Elton, he decided to suspend the recently self-imposed hiatus he and Bernie had implemented long enough to write one final song together. The result was "Remember (I'm Still in Love with You)," a ballad specifically tailored to the iconic crooner's barroom style. Sinatra would go on to record the song the following July, at TBS Studios in Burbank, California.

Mysteriously, his version of the lonesome plaint would remain forever locked in the vaults, though singer Donatella Rettore would score a Top 10 hit in 1981 with her rendition of the wistful serenade.)

Weeks later, Elton turned thirty. He wasn't alone in hitting a major milestone, however—the music industry of which he was very much a part was feeling its age, as punk rock exploded onto the scene and threatened to shove established stars like Elton off to the sidelines.

"The first time I saw punk," he said, "was on the Janet Street-Porter Saturday morning show, when she did an interview with the Sex Pistols, Siouxsie and the Banshees and the Clash. I sat there in my bed in Windsor watching it, and I got slagged off by one of them. But it was kind of endearing. 'God,' I thought, 'you cheeky buggers.'" Recognizing the protean nature of musical fashions, the pianist remained equanimous about the entire situation. "Five years ago it was high-heeled shoes. Now it's safety pins through the nose. The funny thing is, they have all the same things as we have. There's no way they can avoid having their Rolls-Royces, their accountants. They'll end up the same as we do."

As punk gained a safety-pin-pierced toehold in the music industry, eventless days turned into restless weeks and months for the world's biggest star. Finding himself alone in his Windsor manse with no commitments in front of him for the first time ever in his adult life, Elton became despondent. "I thought, 'What am I going to do? *Sit* here for two years?'"

Salvation came, as it had so many times before, in the form of the Watford Football Club, which offered the pianist their chairmanship, following the resignation of sixty-nine-year-old Jim Bonser. "If I didn't have [the chairmanship], I don't know what would have happened to me," Elton would later admit to Chris Charlesworth. "I owe a great deal to Watford. They gave me a sense of balance. They were the sanity to the pop side of it all. They say they owe a lot to me, but I owe far more. I dream about standing there in the Directors' Box the night that Watford wins promotion. All the time, that's my one dream."

While sipping a scotch and soda in Watford's VIP box during a Saturday afternoon match against Sunderland AFC, Elton noticed a familiar face from his past—George Hill, owner of the Northwood Hills Hotel pub where he'd gotten his professional start years before. The two men got to talking, and, after the soccer match had ended, George invited Elton back to the pub to look around his old stamping grounds. The pianist was greeted there by George's wife, Ann, and their eighteen-year-old son, Andrew, who was preparing to head off to university that fall.

"You shouldn't go straight from A-levels to college," Elton told Andrew. "Take some time off first. See the world, broaden your horizons."

The pianist offered to take him on as his personal assistant for a year, as a way of thanking George and Ann for their kindness to him years before. Paid £420 per month, Andrew's first duty was to follow the superstar on a trip to the United States. "Elton turned up for the Concorde flight trip in white shorts," Hill later recalled to author Philip Norman. "And each of his socks was a different color, and each of his shoes was a different pattern." It didn't take long for Hill to notice how lonely the pianist's life truly was. "Everyone else in [Elton's] organization had a circle of friends that they could call on at the end of the day. Elton had good friends, but they didn't make any kind of structure around him. I couldn't believe how this incredible figure, who was the envy of millions, used to go back to an empty house most nights, and just be there on his own."

Left to his own lonesome devices, Elton had more than enough time to ponder his life and career. Yet foremost in his thoughts was the fate of his football club. Eager to help lift Watford out of their extended slump, he attempted to secure the services of Lincoln City FC's manager Graham Taylor.

"I thought it was the last thing I wanted, to go back into the Fourth Division," Taylor said, "managing some southern club with an outrageous pop star messing around as chairman." Yet the coach eventually succumbed to Elton's persistence. "What impressed me was Elton's reaction when I rang him to say no. I expected him to try to hustle me with big talk about money and potential. But he didn't argue, didn't try to change my mind. Just wished me all the best at Lincoln and said he hoped he might see me one day. By the time I rang off, I wanted to meet him."

Within weeks, Taylor had signed a five-year deal with Watford, officially taking over the club's reins for the upcoming 1977-78 season. Elton's vision for Watford proved the deciding factor. "I asked Elton what was his ambition for the club," Taylor said. "I thought he would say promotion, perhaps Second Division football. [But] he replied that he wanted the club to get into Europe. I thought, 'You will do for me, pal!'"

Elton's optimism seemed to grow boundless after the success of securing Taylor's talents. Yet beyond any eventual win/loss statistics on the pitch, he was well aware that Watford's true and lasting value was in allowing him to shake free of the coddled superstar lifestyle which had kept him in a state of suspended animation for so many years. For the first time in his life, he was beginning to live an existence of true adult independence. "At the start [of my career] I was glad to be protected, because I was frightened of something," he conceded to *Sounds'* Phil Sutcliffe. "I don't know what of. But then it got so that everything was done for me. The only thing I did for myself was get in the shower and wash. Royalty probably weren't treated as well....I was being completely locked away, like a prize tiger....I know it's boring, but being involved in the soccer club has brought me down to earth, mixing with the same people who used to go to the pub I played in when I was seventeen or eighteen."

When not in Watford's Director's Box, Elton's days were taken up with endless tennis matches against fellow enthusiasts like Rod Stewart and Roxy Music's Bryan Ferry. He also began dating Melanie Green, the stunning seventeen-year-old daughter of an international banker whom he'd met at a Prince Charles-attended charity dinner at the Ritz Hotel the year before.

"[Melanie] came to post-gig parties but was not a regular companion in the sense of being a steady girlfriend," a Rocket Records associate said. "Still, she *was* pretty wild for him there for a time. And he [was] too, or so it seemed."

The romance with Green would prove short-lived, as Elton decided that the disparity in their ages was too prohibitive for any kind of sustained relationship. Thereafter, his love life fell "a bit off the rails"—as did that of old friend Kiki Dee, whose relationship with Davey Johnstone had recently ended. ("I thought [Davey] was 'The One'," Kiki later admitted. "It took me a long time to get over the end of our relationship.") Evidence came in a pair of cryptic ads which appeared in *The Time*'s Personal Column weeks later. One read: *Pauline from Sheffield would like to announce it is a year since she last had a man*, while the other simply stated: *Lord Choc Ice would like to announce it is 10 years since he travelled on a bus.*

Elton attempted to soothe the wounds caused by his unfulfilled love life by turning to the one great constant in his life: music. Together with Clive Franks, he produced an album for Rocket Records' latest signees, China. The group, whose seemingly random name actually derived from Cockney rhyming slang, 'china plate' meaning mates, featured ex-band members Davey Johnstone and James Newton Howard, who had formed a songwriting partnership during the *Louder Than Concorde* tour. Filling out the roster was drummer Roger Pope, guitarist Jo Partridge, and bassist Cooker Lo Presti.

The process of producing a full-length LP's worth of material for an up-and-coming band might have proved both cathartic and fulfilling—unless, of course, you were the brightest star in the entirety of the rock firmament. Sure enough, it wasn't long before the inevitable siren song of the stage came calling yet again. Elton found himself missing the chaos, the adrenalized waves of affection which rolled in nightly from shriek-filled chasms. Yet thoughts of pulling a band together and heading out on another lengthy world tour left him enervated.

It seemed an unresolvable quandary. Until one gray-skied Saturday afternoon, when—sitting alone at his piano, half-heartedly playing Chopin's Piano Sonata No. 2, Op. 35—inspiration struck Elton hard. Why not perform a two-man show at an intimate theater? It would afford the pleasures of performing before a live audience without the extended tour commitments and byzantine machinations which inevitably drained all the joy out of the whole enterprise.

The pianist rang up Ray Cooper, deciding that he would be the perfect foil, adding percussive depth without ruining the stark nature of the presentation he envisioned. Ray was intrigued by the idea—for reasons as much financial as artistic. "Suddenly the touring and the pay-packets stopped," he noted of Elton's dismissal of the band the year before, "and I had to go back to work. Everybody thinks you're a millionaire because of your associations, but your bank balances are vastly different."

With Ray onboard, Elton booked the three-thousand-seat Rainbow Theatre in Finsbury Park, North London, for a string of shows that first week of May. Writing out a list of songs he wanted to perform, the pianist decided that lesser-known tracks such as "Ticking," "Solar Prestige a Gammon" and "Crazy Water" should finally get their day in court, while more familiar fare would be performed in largely altered states. "Funeral For a Friend" would be given a dramatically sparse reading which would segue not into "Love Lies Bleeding," as it always had before, but rather into *Blue Moves'* towering ballad, "Tonight." The rollicking band romp "Dan Dare (Pilot of the Future)," meanwhile, would be recast as an exuberant solo piano boogie, while "Where to Now, St. Peter?" metamorphosized from a broodingly melodic rocker into an effervescent, Rhodes-soaked moondream.

Rehearsals began in earnest in late April.

"The satisfaction of hearing our songs stripped down in their rawest state was very exciting," the pianist admitted.

Ray grinned at Elton over an assemblage of timpani as they routined an inventively galvanizing rendition of *Captain Fantastic's* "Better Off Dead."

"Rock on, Mr. John," the flamboyant percussionist urged. "Rock *on*."

650

Elton took to the Rainbow's stage for the first of six sold-out shows just after eight p.m., May 2, in a checkered jacket, green football jersey and dark blue sweatpants. As this opening night performance, billed as *The Elton John and Ray Cooper Charity Gala,* was in support of the Queen's Silver Jubilee Appeal, Princess Alexandra and Angus Ogilvy could be found perched rigidly in the Royal Box. Below them, meanwhile, sitting expectantly in the cheap seats, mixed members of Queen and the Eagles, as well as singers Lorna Luft and Lynsey De Paul.

"Your Royal Highnesses, ladies and gentlemen, and Moss Brothers...good evening," Elton said, teasing the well-heeled crowd with a playful reference to the high-end tuxedo rental shop. "Thank you for splashing out an awful lot of money to see a receding-hair-lined player in a ridiculous jacket. I hope you've brought your choc ices with you, it's a long program."

The show then commenced with Elton alone at the piano, singing ethereal ballads such as "Candle in the Wind" and "Cage the Songbird" to maximum effect.

An hour and twenty minutes into the performance, Ray Cooper shattered the calm, bashing away like a lunatic on a litany of tuned percussive instruments during "Funeral For a Friend/Tonight." After a vaporously romantic "I Feel Like a Bullet (In the Gun of Robert Ford)"—which featured Ray's melodic accompaniment on the vibraphone—Elton wiped at his nose and gave a sly grin to the front row. "This one's for Charlie. He's doing well tonight." Moments later he launched into an energetic, marimba-suffused "I Think I'm Gonna Kill Myself," which had the thousands in attendance on their feet.

The evening then ended much as it began, with Elton alone at the piano.

"Thank you, you're incredible. Amazing," he told the cheering audience. "Gonna leave you with a song, very appropriate...from the *Madman Across the Water* album. It's called 'Goodbye'."

With bootleggers already busy pressing recordings of the performance (pirated discs would appear days later under the titles *Rocket Man Over the Rainbow* and *Rainbow Rock*), Princess Alexandra asked Elton at an after-show party if he had self-medicated before taking to the stage.

"You mentioned 'Charlie'," the forty-seven-year-old first cousin to the Queen said. "Surely, you meant cocaine."

"I was so stunned," the singer confided to a reporter from *The Sun*. "I'm not sure what I replied. She asked me how I could play for two-and-a-half hours at a stretch. Did I take some sort of drug? Did I take cocaine? I couldn't believe it."

The next day, Britain's myriad daily papers splashed the story across their front pages. The Royals were decidedly not amused. Word of their displeasure quickly reached Elton, who held a makeshift press conference to handle damage control.

"I very much hope I have not embarrassed the Princess," he said contritely. "I thought [her story] was very amusing, and this is why I repeated it. Of course I do not take cocaine. It was only meant as a light-hearted comment."

Elton turned to John Reid.

"Get me the fuck out of here," he whispered.

Elton's *mea culpa* was apparently enough to satisfy any ruffled feathers, for on May 28 Britain's First Family invited him to take part in the *Royal Windsor Big Top Show*, held at Billy Smart's Circus at Home Park, Windsor. Her Majesty and Prince Philip were the guests of honor for the in-the-round performance, which offered such diverse acts as Olivia Newton-John, Leo Sayer, trapeze artists and tightrope walkers. Elton's set was widely agreed to be the highlight of the show, which aired on BBC-TV the next night to a record audience.

The broadcast was perfectly timed, allowing Elton to maximize promotional efforts for his latest single, "Bite Your Lip (Get Up and Dance!)," which—backed by a jazz-ballad double A-side offering from Kiki Dee entitled "Chicago"—was released on June 3. Despite a punchy remix by famed New York producer Tom Moulton, who brought the 6:37-long album track down to a more palatable 3:38, "Bite Your Lip" only managed to reach Number 28 in both England and America. For almost any other artist, a Top 40 showing have been considered a smashing success, and possibly even a career-defining apex. For Elton, however, it was seen as an abject failure portending even more ominous things to come.

With the pianist holed up in rain-swept London fretting over his latest single's chart performance, his erstwhile lyricist was standing beneath the sharp Los Angeles sunshine, fighting lethargy and desolation.

"There was nothing to do," Bernie lamented. "I was bored and depressed." A hastily arranged trip to Albuquerque didn't help matters, as he found himself drunkenly wrecking his hotel room and firing a .45 magnum at John Wayne as *The Barbarian and the Geisha* played across the television screen. Despite his reckless behavior, however, no amount of vodka or beer could provoke Bernie beyond a certain point of carelessness. "It takes flair to drive a car into a swimming pool," he conceded. With the songwriting duo orbiting in such vastly different—yet equally ponderous—universes, it didn't seem beyond the realm of possibility that "Bite Your Lip" might be the final John/Taupin platter ever released.

"Continental drift had set in," Bernie said. "I wasn't holding my breath."

Any hope for an immediate reconciliation of the star songwriting duo's old work habits was squashed when Bernie—fresh from an appearance on *The Hardy Boys*, where he made his acting debut as guitar-strumming pop singer Tim Carstairs—accepted an offer from drinking buddy Alice Cooper to help write his next album, tentatively titled *From the Inside*.

"Alice and I were inseparable," the lyricist said. "Alice was my best friend. After the Elton thing, Alice and I were basically living together up in his house. It was a messed-up, fucked-up time." The two often watched Monday Night Football together while playing pool and trying to out-drink each other. One night, after the Washington Redskins had bested the Green Bay Packers 10 to 9, Bernie and Alice wound up at the On the Rox club, both so obliterated that they ended up filling each other's cowboy boots with tequila. "We spent so much time together that making [*From the Inside*] was just a natural extension of our relationship," Bernie said.

"I think I may be one of the only lyricists that ever collaborated with Bernie," Alice later noted. "He was one of my blood brothers during the L.A. years....*From the Inside* [was] about an insane asylum. We were certainly qualified for that."

Feeling secretly betrayed by Bernie's creative philandering, Elton would only later admit to feeling hurt. "We were doing a lot of drugs and drinking heavily," he said, "and [Bernie] was beginning to write with other people, which made me a little jealous, but I decided I'd write with some other people [too]....We both had the resilience and the intelligence to know that if we didn't let each other write with other people, it would be the end of our relationship."

The pianist attempted to fill the artistic void in his life by turning to Gary Osborne, a jingle writer and lyricist who had composed the English words for Kiki Dee's 1973 hit "Amoureuse," which Elton had co-produced with Clive Franks. (Osborne would also soon score a major success writing the lyrics for Jeff Wayne's *War of the Worlds*, a symphonic rock retelling of H.G. Wells' classic novel; *War of the Worlds* would, in fact, go on to become one of the biggest-selling albums in the history of the British charts.)

Their association blossomed over nightly games of poker. "I was a unique friend in the respect that I was neither a colleague nor was I gay," Osborne said. "A lot of his friends didn't understand that. We just liked each other's company."

Elton became particularly close to Osborne's wife, Jen. He thus soon found himself spending more and more time over at their modest Tudor in Hampstead—sipping tea with Jen in the living room, or chugging scotch with Gary in the basement, which had been turned into a mock beach, complete with sand-covered floor, sky-blue ceilings, and a fully-stocked tiki bar.

Other times, the Osbornes would head over to Elton's manse. The three got on incredibly well.

"We just hung out as mates," the lyricist told the BBC years later. "We would go to his house, we'd play cards, we'd play backgammon, we'd watch the telly. He seemed very happy. He was optimistic. We did just all the kind of things that regular mates do. And having a good time. Because he had been on a treadmill. He'd disbanded the band, he had no plans for recording. He said, 'I'm just going to concentrate on Watford Football Club and Rocket

Records. I'm going to produce Kiki, and I'm going to take a break.'"

Elton's professional involvement with Gary Osborne began one humid day in early June, 1977, at *Chez Osborne*. "[Jen and I] had some beautiful red wine," Osborne said, "the most expensive wine I'd ever seen, *Mouteau* something-or-other, and I had a great big grand piano that was left over from when my father had the house, and [Elton] was playing around and he said, 'Listen to this.'" A somber new melody bled forth from the piano, a heartrending E-flat ballad cut from the same cloth as "Your Song."

"Well, that's lovely, that's gorgeous," Osborne said.

"Fancy writing a lyric to it?"

"Hold on—what would Bernie say about that?"

Elton shrugged. "I've played it to Bernie. He's over in L.A., working with Alice Cooper. He's already had a go at it, and hasn't come up with anything."

Osborne did his best to hide his excitement.

"If you insist," he said mildly, grabbing a cassette recorder and placing it by the piano. "Play it again."

Elton ran through the song a second time before turning back to the wine.

"And when he left," Osborne said, "at about two in the morning, I immediately got my notebook out and got the cassette back out and started to see if I could get a few ideas going on it."

Osborne spent two full days working on the song. Refining it, trying to make it as perfect as possible. That next weekend, he invited Elton back to the house.

"I've got a lyric for that tune of yours," he said as nonchalantly as possible. Presenting him with a set of words called "Smile That Smile," Elton was impressed. After providing a few suggestions, Osborne reworked the lyric, rechristening it "Shine on Through." "And I actually kind of expected that that would be the end of my writing with Elton," he told the *Times'* Peter Paphides. "I mean, what a wonderful thing to have on my CV: 'I wrote a song with Elton John.'"

Briefly setting "Shine on Through" aside, Elton jammed onstage with the Eagles on the final night of their four-night stand at the Empire Pool. Days later, on Friday, June 17, the pianist performed a more intimate show, and one of the more unique gigs of his entire career, at Shoreditch College Chapel in Egham, South London. As fate would have it, the scheduled musical performer for the school's Valedictory Ball—American soul singer Jimmy Helms—had canceled out at the last minute. "A bunch of us were sitting around and somebody mentioned that Elton John lived nearby," former student Paul Davies recounted to *Q* magazine decades later. "We didn't really think he'd play, but it was worth a try."

Davies and a handful of students headed over to Elton's house, only to find his massive iron gates locked. At a loss, one of the more enterprising members of their group got on the intercom and was soon chatting with the pianist's housekeeper. "Elton was apparently lying on his bed watching the tennis," Davies said. "It was Wimbledon week."

"What time will he have to appear?" Elton's housekeeper inquired.

"9:30."

There was a long pause as the pianist mulled it over.

"I wasn't doing anything that night," Elton said. "So I thought, 'Why not?' I admired their nerve."

The housekeeper got back on the intercom.

"Elton will do it," she told the students. "But make sure you have a decent grand piano available."

"That's tremendous."

"And please don't tell the press."

"Absolutely."

True to his word, Elton arrived at the school's chapel in a green-and-black striped jacket, blue sweats, and a pale green cap, a set list hastily scribbled on the back of a Barclays Bank checkbook. After rehearsing for twenty minutes in an antechamber, he was taken into the sacristy and announced to the crowd through a Marshall 100 watt PA borrowed from the local Birdcage disco down the lane.

"Even then, we still thought it must be a joke," said Tom Watson, another former student. "I really expected somebody to come in dressed up as Elton John. But then he came in through the side door. We were no more than ten feet from him....He didn't ask for a penny, although I gather he could get about £70,000 for Madison Square Garden at the time."

Elton played an enthusiastic, nearly two-hour-long solo set—a decade to the day after having first spied the Liberty advertisement in *NME* which had, in so many ways, helped change his life forever.

The superstar accepted an invitation for a few post-show drams of scotch with a dozen students in one of their rooms. As he amused the students with a comical account of his meeting with Elvis the summer before, he noticed a poster of himself hanging on the far wall. Grabbing a magic marker, he scribbled across the top of the poster: *Watch out! Ol' four eyes is back!*

The next afternoon, a group of students brought Elton a cut-glass goblet featuring the school's colors, along with a couple bottles of wine.

"We could see him over the other side of the garden, fiddling with the lawnmower," Davies said. "The housekeeper thanked us and took [the gifts] in for him."

Things went less fortuitously for Rocket Records' signee Maldwyn Pope; with Gus having departed the label, his half-completed album was left in limbo.

"My career was completely on hold [at that point]," he said. "So I wrote to Elton directly and I said, 'I feel like I'm a sixteen-year-old failure.' And it was funny, it was Christmas time, I was in a school production of Charles Dickens' *Christmas Carol*, and I was waiting for a bus to go home—it's nine o'clock at night—and suddenly my dad and my brother arrive in a car, and they said, 'Quick! Get in!' And I'm thinking, 'My grandmother's dead, my mother's dead.' But they said, 'Hurry! Elton's rung and he's going to ring back in twenty minutes!' And he did. He spent half an hour on the phone saying, 'I'm going to take control of your career, we're going to do this, we're going to do that.' That was in January, but we didn't get to the sessions till July, because he was so incredibly busy."

Arriving early for the first session, which was being held at Abbey Road, Pope witnessed Elton—dressed in full Watford regalia—recording an infectious, piano-driven charity single entitled "The Goaldiggers Song," to help raise funds for the construction of soccer pitches for underprivileged children across the U.K. "And as I walked into the room," Pope said, "there was Brian Moore and Eric Morecambe—Morecambe and Wise were enormous, they were the Martin and Lewis of Britain—so it was just incredible."

After recording the track, Elton listened back to what he'd done.

"I don't know if I really like it," he said, shaking his head dubiously.

"But it's really catchy," Brian Moore said.

Elton shrugged. "Well, so is chicken pox." (Only five-hundred copies of "The Goaldiggers Song"—half of them personally autographed by Elton—would ever be released, in a special limited-edition mail-order run which ensured that the platter would become a highly sought-after collector's piece. Adding to the value of the obscure disc, the B-side was a humorous spoken-word message from Elton, TV sportscasters Jimmy Hill and Brian Moore, and comedian Eric Morecambe, entitled, appropriately enough, "Jimmy, Brian, Elton & Eric." The charity single would end up raising over £2,500 for the cause.)

Bidding Brian Moore and Eric Morecambe a fond adieu, Elton arched a bemused eyebrow in Maldwyn Pope's direction.

"All right then," he said. "Shall we start with 'How It Hurts'?"

Nodding his ascent, the teenager situated himself behind the studio's grand piano. "So I'm playing the piano and I'm singing my song at the same time as well," he said, "and obviously my voice is starting to spill over on the piano tracks, so Elton said, '*You* concentrate on playing the piano and *I'll* sing.' That's just bizarre, isn't it? So he's singing my song as a guide vocal. The next day we started doing backing vocals, and I kept on saying, 'I can't do this, can *you* do it?' 'Cause I just wanted him on the record. Even at whatever age I was then—sixteen, I think—I knew that I had to somewhere put Elton on one of my records. And he did the backing vocals, and it's there for all time. He was my hero. And he still is."

Elton next turned his hyper-attuned attentions to the Glasgow-based pop band Blue, who had recently been signed to Rocket Records.

"They're very raw," he enthused. "It's like working with the early Beatles, in a way."

Elton again enlisted Clive Franks to help co-produce an album's worth of material. "Me and Elton had a great time producing them," Clive said. "The recording was open, very basic, organic." As none of the band members could play piano, Elton decided to lend a hand on several tracks. "Elton didn't want to be credited as Elton John," the engineer/producer said. "The band had a Budget Rent-a-van outside the studio, [so] he decided to be called Redget Buntavan—as opposed to Budget Rent-a-van."

After the band sessions were complete, Elton brought Martyn Ford in to arrange string charts for several tracks. "He'd had a falling out by then with Paul [Buckmaster], who was very untogether," Ford said. "I'm not in Paul's league, I make no bones about it, but I'm reliable. So Elton asked me, because he knew I'd turn up with an arrangement. And that was the first time I really got to spend time with him. Because he wasn't surrounded by a great entourage like before. So we just hung out together and did the job. He was very professional. He was charming, he knew exactly what was going on, and he seemed like he was totally under control."

Blue's completed album, entitled *Another Night Time Flight*, would produce one moderate hit for the group, "Capture Your Heart." Despite Elton and Clive's best efforts, however, Blue soon found themselves relegated to the musical sidelines. "They had one album and it was over," album designer Hogie McMurtrie said. "It must have been nepotism, or friends of the band, and it wasn't marketed....Rocket Records really wasn't in the business of promotion, they just put the stuff out and it would go through regular channels of promotion, to the radio stations, and typical marketing channels. But Rocket never had what you might call a real go-getting PR person, or even an A&R person. They didn't have the machine set up, and they didn't have the mentality for marketing. I just think maybe it was there for Elton's enjoyment."

Bored producing music for others, Elton escaped into the Hawaiian sun for a week-long vacation in mid-July. Landing in Lahaina, the chic playground for movie stars and rock stars like Peter Fonda, Boz Scaggs, Jack Nicholson and Walter Becker, Elton spent most of his time at the Blue Max, a stylish seaside restaurant at 730 Front Street.

"I should play here," he told the establishment's manager, Bobby Lozoff—creator of the Tequila Sunrise—late one night, after the two had shared an in-depth discussion about the 'Save the Whale' campaign over countless Sea Breezes. "I haven't done much in a while. Let's do a gig for 'Save the Whale'. It'd be fun."

Lozoff laughed in disbelief. "Sure."

"Get me a grand piano and you're on."

The next afternoon, July 17, a Steinway grand could be seen being transported across town and up the Blue Max's double staircase.

The island was abuzz with excitement as word quickly spread that Elton was going to give a one-man concert. By the time he sat down to play at seven-thirty sharp, the restaurant was overflowing with excited patrons. "The stairway was full out onto the street," Coco Souza, a Blue Max waitress, told *Lahaina News'* journalist Louise Rockett. "They were starting to crawl in from the balcony of the store next door. When [Elton] started playing, the town just stopped. You couldn't move on the sidewalk. It was packed.

662

And, as far as I could see, when I looked up and down the street, there were people. The cars could not move anymore. They were either parked or stuck where they were."

Those fortunate enough to be inside the restaurant that night were treated to a uniquely one-off performance.

"Everybody knew the words to all of his hits," Souza said. "They were dancing, rock 'n' rolling, yelling, singing, hugging and carrying on. The people outside were having as much fun as the people inside. The music was fabulous. [Elton] had a fabulous time. I remember him standing up on top of the piano. He got close enough to the ceiling fan that I think it knocked his hat off."

As the performance grew in raw intensity, the Blue Max staff were unable to hold back the crowds amassed on the street. "People poured in, and then there was no movement," Souza said. "You *couldn't* move in there, because the place was packed. At that point, you realized you were participating in something fantastic."

"The piano was just thumping," said Anne Haley, another waitress, who watched the impromptu exhibition from atop the hostess station. "And we were just wild-eyed kids jumping up and down. Oh my Lord, it was just magical."

Chapter 32:

Mama Can't Buy You Love

Elton flew off to America to duet with Kiki Dee in Central Park on August 2. Soon after, he was back in England, pacing his Gold-record-lined halls and reading J.R.R. Tolkien's "The Lord of the Rings," which Bernie had given him as a birthday gift the year before.

His idyll was shattered on August 16, when news broke that Elvis Presley had died.

"Elvis changed everyone's life," a saddened but not stunned Elton said. "There would be no Beatles, there would be no Hendrix, there would be no Dylan [without Elvis]. He just was the man who changed music without question. He *was* 'The King', and he was the one that started it all."

Reverberations were felt far across the globe. "I certainly hope I don't pop off in the next few weeks, as I'll only get page-three coverage," Marc Bolan joked.

Elton shuttered his windows, grabbed a bottle of Glenlivet, put "Heartbreak Hotel" on the stereo, and retreated into the darkness.

The pianist's only album release of the year—*Elton John's Greatest Hits Vol. II*—hit the streets on September 13. The LP was important to Elton, as it finally fulfilled his commitment to DJM. (After a legal dispute had arisen as to whether *Here and There* truly settled Elton's contractual obligations, his *Greatest Hits Vol. II* was given to DJM in final settlement of his contract.) Not wishing to put out a substandard collection, Elton leased two Rocket-owned hits—"Don't Go Breaking My Heart" and "Sorry Seems to Be the Hardest Word"—for inclusion in the set. Even with their addition, the U.S. and U.K. pressings differed slightly, with the English version including "Bennie and the Jets"— which had not been part of the original British pressing of Elton's first *Greatest Hits* package—while "Levon" appeared on the American release.

Reviews for the album, which featured a cover shot of the bespectacled superstar posing in white linen—a determined batsman smiling confidently before the wickets—were generally positive. "The two previously-unavailable-on-LP originals here are peaks," critic Robert Christgau noted. "Plus [the listener receives] the lead cut from *Caribou* and two hits from *Rock of the Westies* and leftovers from 1971 and 1976 and the climax of *Captain Fantastic*. Is this product necessary? Depends on who's doing the needing. B+."

The album, supplemented by a 12-page, fully illustrated lyric booklet, shipped Gold on both sides of the Atlantic. It would ultimately reach Number 21 in the U.S. and Number 6 in the U.K. Six weeks later, it quietly went Platinum.

Elton awoke days later to learn that his good friend, Marc Bolan, had died tragically the night before. On September 16, two weeks shy of his thirtieth birthday, Bolan had become the latest rock 'n' roll casualty, when his girlfriend, Gloria Jones, lost control of their purple Mini Clubman GT as they were on their way home from Morton's Club, and wrapped it around a sycamore tree.

Elton attended Bolan's funeral at Golders Green Crematorium alongside Rod Stewart, David Bowie and Linda Lewis.

"I was distraught after Marc died," Lewis later recalled. "Gloria had been driving and had broken her arm and jaw. She had her mouth wired shut in hospital and wrote me a handwritten note: 'Did you ever sleep with Marc?' I told her, 'No.' She was very near death herself, so I told her what she wanted to hear. You have to remember, in those days, everyone slept with everyone. But I'd always feel guilty later and go to confession." She laughed grimly. "The priest was always really keen to hear all the details of my life."

For Elton, Bolan's loss was one he would feel for years to come.

"Marc was a larger-than-life figure," the pianist said solemnly. "He lived in this fantasy land, but he was sweet, and loveable, and very, very clever....It was like he was from another planet, but with not a bad bone in his body. And it's very rare that you find that amongst people."

After a brief ceremony, a shattered Elton fell into the backseat of his Rolls-Royce and wept. First Elvis, now Marc. Death was seemingly everywhere, all at once.

Life's transient nature spurred Elton into making good on a long-held promise to himself: to finally solve the maddening riddle of his prematurely thinning thatch. Life was far too short to be so fundamentally displeased with yourself, he decided. He was already more than self-conscious enough as it was. The time was nigh.

Having made up his mind, the pianist flew to Paris weeks later for the first of six square-grafting procedures. Performed by Dr. Pierre Pouteaux, the world's leading hair transplant surgeon, the painful five-hour procedure involved harvesting hair follicles from the back of Elton's head and surgically implanting them into the top of his scalp. While the initial surgery went well, he smashed his tender, gauze-wrapped head against the metal doorframe of his car as he was ducking into the backseat, causing agonizing pain and knocking out a good portion of the newly embedded hair plugs.

Nearly as unpleasant, Elton would be forced to wait a full six months to learn if the transplant had successfully taken hold. In the meantime, he began hiding his much-speculated-upon scalp beneath a rotating succession of berets, floppy caps and boaters—despite Dr. Pouteaux's insistence that he leave his head exposed to fresh air as much as possible to help the recently transplanted follicles take root.

Despite all the hardship, the pianist was enthusiastic. "It's all one-hundred-percent vanity," he admitted. "But I'm thrilled with the result."

On October 1, a be-capped Elton was inducted into Madison Square Garden's Walk of Fame, alongside such sporting greats as Muhammad Ali and Sugar Ray Robinson. "I've got a great ego as far as sports goes," he admitted. "I'm a great fan. I'll go anywhere to meet anybody who's got anything to do with sports, 'cause I love it. And when MSG came up with this honor—which it is for me, to be indoctrinated into the Hall of Fame—and be the first non-sportsman or someone not connected with sports to be indoctrinated in it, I was so pleased, I said 'Of *course* I'll do it.'" He smiled. "I was just knocked out to be on the walls with all those great boxers and athletes. Wonderful. I'll go anywhere to get a Gold record, and I mean that most sincerely, and I'll go anywhere to meet sports people."

While in New York, Elton sat for a rare television interview with talk show host Mike Douglas. The appearance was ostensibly to promote the release of a new book, *It's a Little Bit Funny*. A visual essay of Elton's 1976 tour, the tome featured photographs by David Nutter (whose brother, Tommy, had designed Elton's jackets for the tour after having similarly outfitted John Lennon, Paul McCartney, David Hockney, and many others), and text by Bernie Taupin.

After briefly discussing the photo book, Elton's discussion with Douglas turned to his dissatisfaction with his last U.S. campaign. "I got fed-up during my concert at Pontiac Stadium in Detroit," he said with a wince. "I saw all these faces squashed up against the barriers and I thought, 'This isn't what I started out wanting to do.' It's a great ego trip seeing sixty- [or] seventy-thousand people there to see you, and it's great fun, I don't deny it. But somewhere along the way I think rock 'n' roll has lost its path in the fact that it's become so big, it's become such a big machine, the record companies have taken over, and I helped contribute to that, so now I have to really go back and do what I feel artistically is best for me....I don't want to play too big a place again. I'd rather reach and touch the audience rather than see them squashed against a fence."

As for his personal life, Elton quickly dismissed the possibility of living with someone on a permanent basis. "I'm so selfish and self-centered," he admitted. "For the moment, I've accepted that I'm a loner. I don't mind, I'm beginning to enjoy it. There was a period for two or three years where it made me really miserable, but I think I've come to grips with it. But if that's the way it is, that's the way it is."

The pianist brought that *laissez-faire* attitude with him to the Sam Goody's record store at Rockefeller Center that same afternoon, where he and Bernie briefly reunited to sign copies of *It's a Little Bit Funny* and *Greatest Hits Vol. II* while a hysterical throng twelve-deep wept and screamed around them.

Later that evening, John Reid placed an international call to inform Elton that he and the group Queen had begun the process of severing ties with each other. "Freddie [Mercury] and Elton got on very well, but you couldn't manage Freddie *and* Elton," publicist Caroline Bouncher succinctly told author Mark Blake. It was a position Queen's drummer, Roger Taylor, readily agreed with. "[Reid] was put under a tremendous amount of pressure from his other artist, Elton John, who naturally felt we were being very successful—and I think Elton felt a bit threatened. Elton was absolutely massive at the time. So I think we came to the conclusion mutually it would be a good idea to split."

"John promised [Queen] the world, but when they signed he was difficult to get hold of," EMI song-plugger Eric Hall said. "He was so busy with Elton John that he didn't really have the time to spend with anyone else."

For Reid's part, he harbored no ill feelings toward Queen. "Jim Beach came to me and said, 'Look, you know, the band is not unhappy with what you've done,'" he'd later recall in the documentary *Days of Our Lives*. "'The contract is coming up [and] going forward they think they would like to manage themselves.' And I thought that was a very nice way to tell me, and it was the correct way to tell me, and I've never had any difficulty with them at all. It was one of the gentlest parting of the ways of anybody I'd ever worked with."

With his stable of superstars now back down to one, the Scotsman strongly suggested to Elton that he might think about considering a new recording project; the noncommittal artist mulled the idea over while attending a party held in his honor at Studio 54 that night. The recently opened hot-spot for New York's glamorati at 254 West 54th Street was packed that night with some of Elton's biggest supporters, including ex-New York Doll David Johanssen, *Saturday*

Night Live's Gilda Radner and Laraine Newman, actress Ellen Burstyn, journalist Geraldo Rivera, Ashford & Simpson, several members of Monty Python, and a nineteen-year-old Michael Jackson. After a brief appearance which saw him being engulfed by photographers, the velvet-suited pianist disappeared into a back room and sat for a while alone in the semi-dark.

While in America, Elton found himself listening incessantly to a demo he'd made of "Shine on Through" weeks before. The urge to record was slowly coming back to him—organically, as he knew it should, and not through his manager's business-minded pleading. By the same token, Elton knew that if he ever *did* make his way back into a studio, it would have to be with a brand-new team. He needed a fresh start, a unique challenge.

After considering various big-name producers, the pianist decided that Thom Bell, who had produced innumerable hits for the Stylistics, the Spinners and the Delfonics, amongst countless others, would be the perfect collaborator.

"I'm a big soul fan, and that led me to Thom Bell," Elton said. "I just loved the way his records sounded. Very dry-sounding records."

Elton met with the architect of the popular "Philly Soul" sound days later in Los Angeles. After a competitive game of Ping-Pong, Elton set down his paddle and grinned across the table.

"I want to do something I haven't done before, Thom."

"And what's that?"

"I don't want to do anything."

Bell smiled patiently. "Okay. What is it that you don't want to do?"

"*Anything.*" Elton grinned. "Not a single thing."

"Well, how do *I* fit into this picture then?" the producer asked, confused.

"I want to record with you, and I want you to be the boss of the whole thing. For the first time, I just want someone to tell *me* what to do."

Bell couldn't believe what he was hearing. "I kept saying, 'Man, are you *sure* that you want to do this? Are you *positive?* Because we don't want to get into midstream and all of a sudden [we have] these great ideas and I hear it one way and you hear it the other way, then we're going to have problems.' And I kept asking him to make sure."

Elton was sure; the two shook hands on it.

Several weeks later, the two men reconvened at Kaye-Smith Studios in Seattle. Even after the contracts had been signed and the sessions got under way, Bell kept waiting for the temperamentally quicksilver superstar to renege on his promise to give up the reins of power. But it never happened. "[Elton] did not change, he stuck to the plan," Bell said. "It's unbelievable that he will work for you as hard, or harder, than he works for himself."

The producer's first challenge was to come up with the correct material for the world's biggest star to record. "The artist and their voice is what tells me what to do," Bell said. "And I heard melodies in my mind, the way [Elton] phrases. And also, being English, he says words differently....His voice—it gives you the secret." In the end, the soul maven decided to move in the direction suggested by "Philadelphia Freedom." "I think he was emulating the Thom Bell sound at that point, which he did a nice job with," the producer said. "'Philadelphia Freedom' was one of my favorite ones that he did, actually."

Bernie Taupin flew up from California to join Elton at the sessions. "Elton John and Bernie Taupin were frozen," session drummer Charles Collins later told author Randy Alexander. "As if they were mentally recording every reaction. I just felt they were totally in awe of Thom Bell."

Before laying down a single vocal track, Bell taught Elton how to breathe properly. "You sing too high and you don't use your lower register properly," he told his new charge. "I've listened to a lot of your stuff, and you hardly ever use the lower range of your voice anymore."

"He was right," Elton conceded. "I thought, 'Oh fabulous, we're going to get on really well.' Well, he was right."

Elton contributed two songs to the six-song project: "Shine on Through," and an older Bernie Taupin lyric leftover from the *Rock of the Westies* sessions which he'd recently set to music called "Nice and Slow." A third song, "Country Love Song," sprang from the pen of Joseph B. Jefferson, who had written hits for the Spinners and the O'Jays, while the remaining three tracks were composed by Thom Bell's nephew—LeRoy M. Bell—and Casey James.

"[Elton] was a superstar," LeRoy said, "so I was expecting a little more of an attitude, [but] he was a very pleasant guy to be around. I think everybody was excited to work on the project. Everybody got along really well. It was kind of an emergence of two worlds kind of colliding, but with a lot of excitement."

In only a day and a half, Elton laid down lead vocals on all six tracks. ("When it was time for him to sing," Thom Bell said, "he just nailed it.") The consensus favorite of the session was "Three Way Love Affair," a deftly understated funk spasm which—powered by Bob Babbit's sinewy bass—perhaps best fulfilled the promise of the project. "I remember liking that song a lot when [Casey and I] wrote it," LeRoy said. "We wanted something real pop and danceable at the same time. So, as writers, we just tried to come up with a melody and lyrics that you imagine Elton's voice on, and coming up with a lyric."

After Elton took his leave, Thom Bell held additional overdub sessions to add strings and horns from M.F.S.B.— as well as backing vocals from the Spinners—at Sigma Sound Studios in Philadelphia.

Back in England, Gary Osborne was pleased when he heard what Bell had done with "Shine on Through." "Actually, I love it," the lyricist said. "[Bell] made it looser, he made it funkier. And it's not a funky song, it's an Elton John ballad. It's not born to be funky. But Thom Bell is born to be funky, and he doesn't know it any other way."

Elton was less impressed, however, deeming the mixes to all six songs "too sweet." Not helping matters: the Spinners' backing vocals ended up taking over nearly the entirety of the planned single, "Are You Ready for Love." "When his mix came through, I only sang one verse and they did the whole lot," the pianist grumbled. Consequently, instead of releasing the song for the upcoming Christmas season—and then reconvening in early '78 for further sessions to complete an entire album's worth of material, as had originally been planned—the miffed Brit shelved the entire project indefinitely.

While mulling over how best to proceed with the Thom Bell recordings, Elton pulled a few of his more flamboyant costumes out of mothballs for a guest appearance on *The Muppet Show*, which was filmed at Elstree Studios in London on October 25-27.

"The idea of having Elton on the show doing all that crazy stuff with those flamboyant costumes, the big crazy glasses and feathers everywhere, particularly excited the Muppets," said Brian Henson, son of Muppets' creator Jim

Henson. "So this whole episode is about the Muppets really wanting him to do that flamboyant crazy look, and him not wanting to. But as always, the Muppets always sort of win out in the end."

Highlights of the program included a rousing performance of "Crocodile Rock," which saw Elton singing alongside Dr. Teeth and the Electric Mayhem Band while sitting in a swamp full of colorfully be-furred reptiles, and a comic duet with Miss Piggy on "Don't Go Breaking My Heart."

"I had to do eleven takes before I could even stop laughing," Elton said. "At one point I broke down again and [Miss Piggy] looked at me and said, 'I am *not* used to working with amateurs,' and stormed off, and it was wonderful."

The show ended with Elton arriving onstage in a conservative tweed suit, while the Muppets surrounded him decked out much like the superstar had been during his mid-70s outrageous peak.

"Boy, Elton," Scooter exclaimed, "you look *weird!*"

The pianist grinned. "Well, *you* guys are all dressed like stolen cars."

Airing the following January 8 in the U.K., and February 6 in America, the episode would become the highest-rated program of the entire series, earning an Emmy nomination— a first for the show—for "Outstanding Directing for a Comedy-Variety of Music Series."

Elton next turned his mercurial focus toward a one-off band gig scheduled for November 3 at Wembley's Empire Pool arena, a charity performance for the Royal Variety Club and the Goaldiggers' Association.

Feeling that his decision the year prior to come off the road may have been premature, Elton planned on using the show as a bellwether of sorts. If he enjoyed it as much as he was hoping he might, then he would hit the road the following February with a slightly reconfigured China—Dennis Conway had recently taken over drumming duties from Roger Pope—as his backup band. Elton rehearsed the group, augmented by Ray Cooper, for three weeks at Shepperton Studios. Though run-throughs went well, the night of the actual show found a coked-up Elton in a bleak mood. When a requested collection of hats failed to turn up in time for his stage entrance, the storm clouds erupted.

"I'm *not* bloody well going on!" he snarled, his nerves getting the better of him. "I'm *not* bloody well doing it!"

His musicians glanced warily at each other. Davey rubbed his face. Ray checked his watch. No one said a word.

"On drugs I was divine, lovely and fabulous," Elton later reflected. "Coming off drugs, I was a nightmare. I used to fly over anger and land in rage."

Elton walked onstage twenty minutes late in a black leather jacket and black beret, looking pale and distracted.

"Right," he sighed, sitting at the piano and playing the first jagged chords of "Better Off Dead." Abruptly, he stopped. "That's a good start. Hang on." He stood, walked in a circle, and sat back down. "We're just testing you, that's all," he said, grimly launching into the song proper.

After a brief solo set which included rarities like "Roy Rogers" and "The Goaldiggers Song," Elton was joined by Ray for a particularly passionate reading of "Tonight." China then seamlessly merged behind the pair for an enthusiastic version of "I Heard It Through the Grapevine," while spirited backing vocals were provided by Gary Osborne, Chris Thompson and Stevie Lange. "Gary Osborne had booked myself and Chris Thompson to sing," Lange said. "We were thrilled. Our first gig was Wembley. [It was] incredible."

"Bennie and the Jets" followed "One Horse Town," which followed "Island Girl." Everything was rocking along smoothly. Even so, Elton seemed to grow more and more tense with each successive song. Deep down he understood what the problem was: he'd come back too soon. "I suddenly saw all the machinery and all the reasons that I wanted to stop," he admitted. "I was doing things that I'd promised myself I'd never do again. I was angry with myself."

As the set swung into its electrifying homestretch, Elton came to a rash—yet seemingly inevitable—decision.

"I'd just like to say something," he told the crowd. "It's very hard to put it in words, really, but I haven't been touring for a long time, and it's been a painful decision whether to come back on the road or not, and I've really enjoyed tonight—thank you very much—but I've made a decision tonight that this is going to be the last show tonight. All right? There's a lot more to me than playing on the road, and this is the last one I'm gonna do."

The crowd cried out their displeasure as the pianist broke into the sorrowful opening chords of "Sorry Seems to Be the Hardest Word." Sitting behind the soundboard, Clive Franks was shattered by Elton's impromptu announcement. "My last five years had been on the road with him," he said. "I was having trouble mixing [his sound] that night, because everything was so emotional. I was shaking."

After a final megablast of hits—from "Funeral For a Friend" to "Rocket Man" to "Your Song"—Kiki Dee led Stevie Wonder onto stage to join Elton on the finale, an eighteen-minute rave-up of "Bite Your Lip (Get Up and Dance!)."

The two piano men embraced near Elton's piano.

"Please don't do it," Wonder told his English counterpart. "You may think you mean it, but it's hard to retire in this game."

"I thought, 'Fuck, *this* is the reason I stopped, and I'm doing it again,'" Elton later told *Musician*'s Chris Salewicz. "The whole night was a nightmare. I knew I shouldn't be up there....I felt like something out of Las Vegas."

Daily Telegraph's John Coldstream was considerably less desolate about the whole affair. "If this was a wake," he wrote, "it will not be forgotten by any of the 8,000 present. It was a glorious way to go, but the concert stage will be a less colorful place even if Watford FC is the richer."

"I've got to discuss this whole thing with him," a flustered John Reid told reporters backstage as Elton's limousine tore off into the chilled British night.

Confused and distressed, Elton spent the holidays locked behind the gates of his mansion, mulling over his future. He would step out only once that December, appearing on *The Morecambe & Wise Christmas Special* on BBC-TV. The British Commonwealth came to a near-standstill that evening, as more than two-thirds of all U.K. television sets were tuned in to the highly anticipated program, which had promised the airing of Elton's newest composition.

The special was built around a running gag which posited that the pianist—demure in a blue piano-key-striped suit—was incapable of finding the studio where the special was being filmed. And indeed, he spent the entire show hopelessly lost, following misguided directions from one incorrect locale to the next. By the time the end credits began to roll, Elton was still yet to find either Morecambe or Wise.

Watching the broadcast at home with his wife and friends, Gary Osborne was mortified. "I thought that the ground might as well open up and swallow me," he said, "because everybody in the entire world had been told that my song was on this show, and it wasn't. Most disappointing moment of my entire life."

As the credits finished rolling, the show cut to Elton as he stumbled upon a pair of cleaning ladies tidying up an empty studio while listening to a Muzak rendition of "The Long and Winding Road." In reality, the women were Morecambe and Wise in drag. Telling a despairing Elton that he was too late, that the show was in fact over, the pianist hung his head in defeat.

"Well, I don't know what to say," the pianist lamented. "I might as well do it. Do you wanna hear a new song? I've been all over the place."

Elton sat forlornly at a grand piano which conveniently enough just happened to be sitting there, and began playing a particularly anguished rendition of "Shine on Through."

"That was what I was gonna sing on the *Morecambe and Wise Show*," he said as the final chord rang out plaintively.

Morecambe nodded. "It's a good job you didn't."

Chapter 33:
Ego

Members of the Elton John Fan Club rang in 1978 with a unique curio: an oversized, twelve-month calendar which featured photographs of their favorite piano thumper as he made his way around central Watford in a red beret, pink jacket and dark blue sweat pants. Taken the year before (and from which the front and back covers of *Elton John's Greatest Hits Vol. II* derived), the images showed Elton striking a variety of mundane poses: smiling in his Silver Rolls, driving a boat down the Grand Union Canal, kneeling proudly before the Watford football club, mischievously mourning a missed putt on the Moor Park golf course, standing triumphantly on a concrete landing above the fountains before the Town Hall, and on and on.

Each image came with a typically cheeky note from Elton himself, as exemplified by the caption which accompanied the image before the fountains: "No, I'm not taking the waters of Watford or practising [sic] for another live outside broadcast....I've only done one outside broadcast in Watford and that was at Vicarage Road, on the pitch. We won't be doing that again in a hurry...the groundman didn't speak to me for weeks." For June's photograph, which showed Elton standing on an overpass with the seven hills of Croxley Green behind him, his glasses notably removed, he wrote: "This is the real me, as nature, or my mother, intended. It's just too much, I know."

On January 14, two days after the Sex Pistols stumbled through the final show of their highly abbreviated career, at San Francisco's Winterland Ballroom, a new-look Elton was appearing on the cover of *People* magazine, sans his trademark glasses. "The New Elton John: He's given up touring and those nutty glasses—but not lasses," the magazine's headline provocatively promised.

In the accompanying article, the pianist confessed that while the recent punk rock phenomenon made him feel old, he still held a bright outlook for his own future plans. "I know I have more talent than most of them," he told journalist Fred Hauptfuhrer. "I do believe that I could come back anytime I want to. I'm fortunate I'm only 30. There's so much time still." As for the songs he'd already created throughout his unparalleled career, Elton was as unfailingly forthright as ever. "What I have done is musically of no great importance next to what's been done down the centuries....You can't produce a major work between climbing off the stage and getting onto a plane. There's so much inside me that still has to come out."

Toward the end of the article, Hauptfuhrer switched gears, noting blithely that, for all his trials and tribulations, the superstar's sex life didn't seem to be suffering. Elton begged to differ. "I mean, not once a day. Say three times a week, at best. And more female than male....I like pretty people, but I don't have a rampant sex life. I can get off on my work just as well."

As if to prove his point, on March 10, a rejuvenated Elton stepped into Gus Dudgeon's Mill Studio—a quadraphonic facility in Cookham on the River Thames—to work on a new single. Though he and Gus hadn't professionally reconciled, the pianist had chosen the Mill to soften the financial impact their split had caused the producer, and to generate positive press for his new facility. (Despite the consideration, Gus Dudgeon wouldn't helm another Elton John project until the middle of the next decade, when he produced three LPs in succession: 1985's *Ice on Fire,* 1986's *Leather Jackets,* and 1987's *Live in Australia with the Melbourne Symphony Orchestra.*) It was an easy decision for Elton, given that the Mill was a state-of-the-art facility. "The Mill was the most technologically advanced studio for its time," said Stuart Epps. "When Gus decided to build the Mill, he wanted it to his own specifications. He went over to Miami, and he met with sound guys and soundboard builders and said, 'I want this and I'd like that.' All the things that he'd been frustrated with in other studios, he wanted to put right for his. Any bit of technical advancement, he would always be straight on it. He would go to the most extreme lengths. John Reid used to say that Gus' theme song should have been, 'I'm Forever Blowing Budgets.'"

The producer hardly recognized his old partner when he first stepped into the studio without a pair of glittering specs hiding half his face. Why the change, he wondered? "I actually went scuba diving in 1976 and I couldn't see without my glasses," Elton explained, "and I thought, 'Well, this is ridiculous.' I'd tried contact lenses before, hard ones, and I went scuba diving and I loved it, and I thought, 'If I'm gonna improve at this, I've gotta get soft contact lenses,' so I did."

As for these latest sessions, Elton's plan was simply to record a song he'd written with Bernie during the *Blue Moves* sessions called "Ego." "It's dedicated to the Jaggers and Bowies of the world," he said. "And especially Mr. McCartney. I like most of the stuff the Stones have done, but they're one of the worst live bands I've ever seen. David Bowie is a pseudointellectual, and I can't bear pseudointellectuals. 'What clothes shall I wear for the next album?' Coming to London in a train and giving the Hitler salute. And McCartney's music has gone so far down the tubes, I can't believe it....They all just annoy me." Elton paused thoughtfully. "There's a lot of me in [the song] as well. Music is still important, but selling oneself at a price isn't. Once you've attained success, you reach a crossroad and you have to be totally honest, and I feel that's what 'Ego' [is] all about."

Elton produced the song along with Clive Franks. When the sound engineer was informed that Gus wouldn't be involved in the recording process, he was floored. "I really didn't consider myself a producer, per se. I was always an engineer," Clive said. "I didn't have [Gus'] perspective or attention to detail, at least not in a studio setting. I had no master vision, and couldn't see beyond the moment until I went back later and listened to what we'd done."

On the first day of recording, Elton sat behind a gleaming nine-foot grand and broke into the demonic broken-chord triplets which opened "Ego."

"What do you think of this?" he asked with a malevolent grin.

"I've no idea," Clive confessed. "Sounds like a silent movie."

Elton laughed. "Good. Let's put it down."

After recording a detailed piano demo, the two men quickly went about the process of recruiting a group of top session men to help flesh out the tune. Those musicians included Tim Renwick—who had played lead guitar for the Sutherland Brothers & Quiver when they'd opened for Elton on his fall '73 tour—and Steve Holley, who was soon to be recruited as Wings' final drummer. "I was slightly stunned, being in Elton's orbit," Holley said. "I had youth on my side,

I had a lot of gusto. I was very hot-headed and was very full of myself. And I felt really at home with Elton. He's such an ingratiating character, I actually really adored being in his company. We shared a love of backgammon, amongst other things, and we'd play endless games [between sessions]. I was a huge fan to begin with. I remember clearly the first time I listened to *Empty Sky,* and I was blown away with that record. I was just blown away to be in the same room as him, yet at the same time you're trying not to be too over-the-top about it, so I was acting as cool as I could be."

As Elton's first choice for a bassist—Yes' Chris Squire—was unavailable, the pianist turned to Clive instead.

"You play bass, Clivey. Don't you?'

His co-producer shrugged. "Not for years. Not seriously."

"You can do it."

So it was decided. Though petrified ("I was seriously shitting myself that first day!"), Clive played bass live on "Ego," sitting in the control room with a direct line plugged into the console. "It was a real challenge," he said. "That song in particular has so many chord changes to it, it's ridiculous. I kept thinking, 'If only Dee Murray were here.' But he wasn't."

With its calliope rock soundscape—the song contains everything from castanets to triangles to train whistles—and ever-shifting time signatures, "Ego" possessed an oddly flinty beauty. Even so, Clive was dissatisfied with his steady yet unadventurous performance. "I kept bringing my bass down [in the mix], so I didn't have to hear it. But Elton kept pushing it back up. 'It's fine,' he'd say. Ultimately, he knew better than I did."

As he sat at the studio's grand, Elton found a host of melodies coming to him unbidden. "Because I hadn't written for so long, I sort of got 'writer's diarrhea' as I call it, and suddenly I began to write melodies first—after all these years of lyrics coming first and then melodies."

"Those sessions were just tremendous fun, there was nothing difficult about it, nothing strange," Steve Holley said. "At the end of the session for 'Ego', Elton said, 'Do you have any plans for the next five to ten days?' And I said, 'No. Why?' And he goes, 'Well, I don't have anything else written, but I'll start working on some stuff now, and if you can come back for a few days, we'll see what we can do.' I just remember him going home and coming back the next day and he had three more songs, four more songs, six, eight, ten, twelve more songs. I don't think we recorded anywhere near as many songs as he wrote during that time period. And I was astounded by the wealth of material. For me, it was the turning point. There was something about him and his musicianship, I was just completely blown away by it."

Elton called Gary Osborne into Mill Studio and had him craft lyrics around his new melodies. "[Osborne] fills a creative need right now," the pianist said. "Sometimes I'd have one line in a song that I wanted to keep, and he would say, 'That's all right, I'll try and work around it,' and he did that admirably, which helped me a lot, and I'm very grateful for that."

The pair quickly came up with the mesmerizing, vibe-soaked "It Ain't Gonna Be Easy"—initially a twelve-minute-long take, Elton felt he'd given his single best vocal performance to date on the track—and the never-issued "I'll Try," a piano ballad which, like "Sorry Seems to Be the Hardest Word" before it, quivered with shadowy angst. "I can write that sort of melody every day," Elton said. "I find it harder, because I'm a pianist, to write a good up-tempo song. When you play piano, the chord structures of songs are so much different. You tend to put in more chords, whereas when you're on a guitar, a three-chord song on a guitar always sounds better than a three-chord song on a piano for some reason." He shrugged. "It's ludicrous. It has to do with the structure of the instrument."

Elton then wrote both the words and music for "Flintstone Boy," a slyly subversive track about a failed love affair. Pleased with the way the song turned out, he briefly contemplated writing an entire album's worth of lyrics, before finally deciding against the idea. "[My lyrics] might come out very raw and very crude," he reasoned. "Also, I'm quite positive it would be extremely bitter. There have been periods in my life where, if I'd had the ability to write good lyrics and write them down, they would have been quite heavy statements for me to make, but I just couldn't do it so I didn't even bother to try. If I had, I would've probably ended up in jail with libel suits."

Elton's burgeoning partnership with Gary Osborne proved not only productive, but it also gave him cause to rethink many of his long-held work patterns. "I've made the mistake of writing too many albums in the same key," he said. "The wrong key for my 'poofy little voice', as Rod Stewart calls it. You spend half an hour on a song, then sing it in the key you wrote it in. It's very easy to get into a rut." With that in mind, he recorded his own version of "Shine on Through"— much more faithful to the tenor of the original composition than the Thom Bell-produced version had been—lying prone on the studio floor as he sang the lyrics, to add a guttural depth to his vocals.

"I remember sitting behind a drum kit with a pair of headphones on and Elton started to sing, and I couldn't play," Steve Holley said. "On 'Shine on Through', I started to play, and then I fumbled immediately, just because the sound of his voice and his piano just blew me away. I was like, 'Oh Lord.' I said, 'I'm sorry, let me try that again.' It was just mind-blowing. I was just listening to him and I just blew my intro completely. Recording with Elton was a fantastic experience. It's way up there on life's spectrum of fun and frivolity."

After tracking the fist-pumping pop-rocker "Part-Time Love"—the only song of these new sessions which would feature Davey Johnstone—Elton interrupted his studio efforts to film a £40,000 promotional film for "Ego." Premiering soon after at the National Theater in Westwood, L.A. and the West End cinema in London, the mini-film would also be shown theatrically across Europe and America as a "short" before such major motion picture offerings as *F.I.S.T* and *Pretty Baby.*

The clip, directed by Michael Lindsay-Hogg, who had helmed both the Beatles' *Let It Be* and the Rolling Stones' *Rock and Roll Circus,* featured a child actor posing as a youthful Elton trapped alone on the Circle Line subway, cleaning his National Health specs and scrawling *Watford* on the train wall. The film then cut to random vignettes of a sneering, gaunt-faced, fedora-wearing Elton as he held court in some otherworldly pop empire, his right ear pierced by a sapphire stud. The effect was jarring—Elton looked like a darker, almost wholly unfamiliar personality. (And on a historical level, "Ego" would, in many ways, help pioneer the high-budget, high-concept video craze which would soon lead to the inception of MTV, causing a fundamental shift in the way pop music was thereafter consumed.)

"["Ego" is] slightly weird and spooky," the pianist reckoned. "It was [certinaly] a new experience. That was the first time I'd ever consciously done any camera work. But what was really strange was performing without glasses on. I used to hide behind them so much. They were a real safeguard for me, so all of a sudden there was a brave new world out there, and I had to look it straight in the face with contact lenses on. That was very hard to do after hiding behind my defenses for so long."

The moment filming wrapped, Elton headed back to Mill Studio to continue work on his new songs. One brandy-and-cocaine-fueled session saw both the writing and recording of a chaotic, timpani-laced rocker called "Madness." An incandescent account of the London terrorism offensive waged by the IRA throughout the '70s, the frantically appregiated piano-line Elton devised for the track perfectly underscored the unrequited rage seething between each line of the fervent lyrics. "I got a letter from a policeman from Dundee saying the song meant a lot to him, because he had attended the aftermath of a bomb blast," Osborne later told author David Buckley, "The song meant a lot to him, and the letter meant a lot to me."

Elton laid "Shooting Star" the next day. A personal favorite of the pianist's, the evanescent, sax-and-upright-bass-perfumed ballad had been inspired by a trip he'd recently taken that February, with Rod Stewart, to Rio de Janeiro for Carnivàle. A fifty-two-second-long piano-and-ARP-synth instrumental called "Reverie," which he labeled "a very wistful death thing," followed. Elton smiled after the song was completed. Suddenly, and quite unintentionally, an album's worth of material was beginning to form.

Far across the heaving Atlantic, Elton's old partner Bernie was busy attending the Science Fiction Film Awards in Los Angeles. Introduced onto stage by actress Karen Black, the lyricist—in dark aviator shades and a frilly black tux—told those amassed before him: "I'm truly pleased...to present my 'Rocket Man' as interpreted by our host, William Shatner."

The camera cut to *Star Trek*'s Captain Kirk seated on a stool center stage, dragging on a cigarette and portentously intoning the lyrics to the classic track. Utilizing crude '70s-era chroma-key video technology, Shatner was soon joined onstage by a second, more gleeful Shatner, who tunelessly warbled out the song's chorus before a third Shatner joined in, dancing like a demon possessed. It was performance art on an epically loony scale, an indelible act which would be satirized for decades to come—from singer Beck's video for "Where It's At," to Stewie's pitch-perfect rendition on the animated show *Family Guy*.

At the same time, Elton and Gary Osborne were coming up with a playful New Orleans-accented romp entitled "Big Dipper" (British slang for a rollercoaster). "I said to Elton, 'I am going to write you a poofy song about a sexual encounter on a Big Dipper'," Gary later recalled. "And he said, 'Oh that's good, I'll get the Watford football team to sing on it'....They loved it, because they loved him."

"Twenty-five players were at the session, including one or two excellent singers," Clive said. "There was only one atrocious voice, but he was kept well away from a mic. Anyway, one out of twenty-five isn't bad." The song would also feature the vocal talents of the female staff from Rocket Records, who were billed as the South Audley Street Girls' Choir.

A rare story-song, "Big Dipper" followed the fortunes of a lonely, fairground-bound man who takes a ride on a Big Dipper and receives head from a sailor while at the top of the tracks. "It had to be slightly disguised," Osborne said of the obtuse lyrics. "Because, firstly, it was 1978. And secondly, we wanted the Watford football team to sing on it and we couldn't have them singing words that were...too poofy. I was trying to put a bit of Elton's wicked sense of humor into his songs."

"Ego" was released as a single on March 21. Backed with "Flintstone Boy," the disc charted at a disappointing Number 34 in both the U.S. and the U.K. Elton was stoic about its performance. "Ego was just something I had lying around and I wanted to release it for a long time," he said. "Unfortunately, the time wasn't right. It's been disappointing. I really had hoped it would do well because I really liked it....There's no getting away from it—my popularity has slumped, record-wise. But I realize it." (Not merely an exemplar of the singer's waning popularity, "Ego" would also prove to be the final John/Taupin song released during the '70s, and their final A-side single together until 1982's moving John Lennon tribute, "Empty Garden [Hey Hey Johnny]," which May Pang would call "a beautiful song, because I know how much Elton treasured John's friendship.")

Ironically enough, the more he reflected on the relative failure of his new single, the more Elton's own ego got bruised. He publicly questioned the legitimacy of the BBC's chart, which was compiled by the British Market Research Bureau, and which had been subject to rumors of payoffs and bribes for the last couple years. "It's highly inaccurate...[and] everybody knows it's ridiculous," the frustrated pianist told *The Sun* newspaper. "But far too few people have had the courage to say so. Until something is done about it, I've decided to withdraw my record company's advertising from any publication printing the BMRB chart."

John Reid had a predictably more overt reaction—he sacked the entire Rocket Record staff at their new Grosvenor Square offices. "It was all done in a fit of anger," he said soon after. Once his rage had passed, everyone was rehired. "I have apologized for screaming so loudly."

Not allowing 'Ego's relative failure to dampen his enthusiasm for long, Elton was soon hard at work on "Love Sick," a breezy track which switched from a steady 4/4 beat on the verses to a slinkier 5/4 time during the choruses. Originally composed during the *Blue Moves* sessions, Bernie's dour lyric referred, not surprisingly, to his split from Maxine.

Though the song was completed in only two takes, the remaining sessions would stretch out, in fits and starts, over a period of months. That was fine with Elton—he was determined to take his time and truly get things right. "You can have a really good song," he told *Billboard*'s Timothy White, "but it sometimes loses it between the demo and the recording. Sometimes the way you record a song is not the best way a song should be recorded. And you find that that is a very frustrating thing. There are lots of songs that I've written that I think are as good as 'Don't Let the Sun Go Down On Me', but they haven't come out as well on record. It's so important, the way you approach recording a thing, and fifty percent or sixty percent of the time you get it wrong."

The pianist next recorded the marimba-accented "Return to Paradise," an ironic account of forever-displeased British vacationers. "They go abroad every year to find the sunshine, and a lot of them go to Spain," he said. "When they get there [they're unhappy]; they expect to eat English food, English beer."

As preparations were being made to record lead vocals on the track, Gary Osborne realized that the chorus melody Elton had devised bore an uncanny resemblance to Harry

Belafonte's 1957 hit, "Jamaica Farewell." Quickly composing a different melody, the lyricist played it for Elton, who listened intently, headed into the vocal booth, and sang it perfectly. "So on that song," he said, "I wrote the chorus melody as well as the actual [lyrics], which is fair enough, because quite a lot of the words I am credited with [on other songs] are [Elton's] words, so it works both ways."

Jazz trumpeter Henry Lowther, who had worked with Bryan Ferry and Richard Thompson, amongst many others in his storied career, completed the recording with a forlorn solo.

Elton turned thirty-one at Vicarage Road, watching with bated breath as Watford FC posted a win which would put the club on the brink of league promotion. After the game, Graham Taylor's wife presented the pianist with a cake in the shape of the Rocket Records train logo.

"Tremendous," a visibly pleased Elton grinned.

The next day, in a particularly productive sugar-rush-fueled afternoon, he knocked out the sparsely wrenching "I Cry at Night"—another older Bernie Taupin lyric from the *Blue Moves* sessions—a bouncy bit of throwaway fluff entitled "Hello Campers" ("Luckily it didn't make it on the album," said Stuart Epps with a sigh), "Dreamboat" (co-written with guitarist Tim Renwick), and "I Don't Care," a vehement, piano-driven rocker powered by Paul Buckmaster's sweeping strings. "I'm amazed at the playing, at the precision of those very fast passages," the arranger later reflected. "All these rapid flurries of machine-gun sixteenth-notes from the strings. Such precision. So in-the-pocket. It made me step back and say, 'Wow, did I write *that?*'"

The team then turned their sites on "Georgia," a Southern-gospel piece which saw Elton pulling triple duty on piano, harmonium and church organ. Pedal steel guitar for the track was provided by B.J. Cole, who was making his first appearance on an Elton John recording since 1971's "Tiny Dancer." While duly impressed with Mill Studio, its opulence also proved a bit problematic for Cole. "The studio had a thick shag-pile carpet that—when I set my pedal steel upon it—the pedals disappeared down into the shag-pile," he said. "So I had to set up on a piece of plywood. Total excess, you know. It wasn't a big studio, but it was very nice." As for Elton himself, Cole noted that "he had changed out of all recognition by that point. He'd just gone through all the excess of super-fame, and was a different person to me. Not unpleasant. Just a totally different person."

That same night, Elton would track a mournfully melodic meditation on the deterioration of a broken love affair called "Strangers." Though the track was ultimately destined for B-side status, both Heart's Ann Wilson and ex-Eagle Randy Meisner would release successful cover versions of the heart-rending tune in the coming years.

Elton took a break from recording to attend Britain's prestigious Capital Radio Awards, where he created a bit of a stir after winning for Best Male Singer, claiming that the award more rightfully belonged to newcomer Elvis Costello instead. "I really hadn't done anything during that year to warrant it," he said, "hadn't put out any new product. I honestly felt that of all the people who had emerged, Elvis Costello was the most important—by far the best songwriter and the best record maker. It seemed a bit farcical for me to pick up the award. I was genuinely shocked."

The pianist would also win for Best Concert of 1977, for his "farewell" gig at the Empire Pool. The irony was hardly lost on him.

"I ought to retire more often," he said.

"Most people have completely the wrong idea of me," Elton told the *Sunday Times* on April 16. "They think I'm going to go on doing the same things in glittering clothes, going to Las Vegas till I'm 55. I turned down one offer of a million dollars to do a week in Vegas. I didn't even think about it. No, I'm looked upon as one of the artists in this country who has the least credibility, and I think I have the most credibility."

While his validity was consistently undermined by the more studiously hip and politically reactionary corners of the music press, the pianist was at least able to find continued refuge within the familiar confines of Watford FC, which had quickly amassed a record seventy-one league points under Graham Taylor's direction. The club's crowning glory came when the team knocked Manchester United out of the League Cup to earn promotion to Division Three.

Elton was ecstatic.

"The feeling of promotion was better than having a record at Number One," he said. "The last forty-five minutes [of the game against Manchester United] aged me by three or four years. Incredible." Could he foresee a Cup Final for Watford? "I don't think I'd make it. I'd have to be sedated."

In a jubilant mood, Elton flew off to America. On June 12, the flamboyant star found himself at the Xenon Disco in New York City, at a party in honor of singer Roberta Flack. Other guests included Andy Warhol, David Frost, Jerry Hall, Peter Frampton, and *Penthouse* Pet Cheryl Rixon. The next night, Elton attended the world premiere of the film *Grease*, for which his ex-backing vocalist, Cindy Bullens, had contributed lead vocals on several songs. After the screening, the pianist partied the night away at Studio 54, along with clothes designer Fleur Thiemeyer, actress Stockard Channing, and Olivia Newton-John.

Days later, the jet-setting Brit found himself on a Concorde bound for France, for yet another hair transplant operation. With the pianist's career in a state of flux, his beleaguered scalp became a major focus of discussion in the media. So much so that a rare photograph of the superstar sans headgear would make headline news on the same July day that Bob Dylan's much-hyped return to the U.K. concert stage at Blackbushe Aerodrome—alongside Eric Clapton and Graham Parsons—was relegated to a few lines buried on the back page. It was karmic payback, perhaps, for the critical crossfire Elton had continuously found himself in with London's punk rock scene. "I get all the shit slung at me," he said. "When people like Generation X or Sham 69 have a go at me, they don't stop to think that maybe I've bought their records, enjoyed them, and have gone around telling other people how good they are."

With his Mill sessions on extended hiatus—Clive Franks having gone away on holiday by the time Elton re-entered Britain—and without the strictures of a firm work schedule to provide much-needed structure, the pianist found himself spending a significant portion of the summer of '78 alone in his house, working through a pint of scotch a day. There was also an ever-growing dependence on cocaine—which roused the truculent star's darker impulses—and loads of spliffs, though, as he would later explain, "I only ever used dope to come down off coke."

Those around him began to worry about Elton's increasingly compulsive behavior. "I honestly began to think he was in danger of turning into a recluse," John Reid said. Yet no one dared say a word.

Elton composed an eerie, largely instrumental samba in mid-August. "It's about death," he said of the cathartic requiem. "An optimistic death song, sort of like *Close Encounters* being an optimistic space movie....I like death music, I don't know why....*The Enigma Variations,* for example. You've only got to start playing [it] and I'm in floods of tears."

The next day, an overcast Sunday, the pianist headed to Mill Studio to record the song.

"Roll the tape," he told Clive Franks as his fingers struck a C-major chord, a Roland rhythm box keeping tempo as he played.

Halfway through the take, Elton broke down in tears.

Collecting himself, he began the song anew. When Clive went to rewind the recording tape, Elton stopped him. "Just keep going," he instructed, launching into the song again. Near the end, he made a mistake; he immediately started over.

This third attempt was flawless.

Clive glanced nervously at Stuart Epps, who was engineering the session. Together they stared anxiously at the reel-to-reel console—the master tape was about to run out, just as Elton was finishing up the pivotal track.

"The tape is getting thinner and thinner," Clive recounted to *East End Lights'* Tom Stanton and James Turano. "I'm thinking, 'Oh please, *please*...'"

"[Clive and I] were nearly dying, we're having heart attacks all over the place," Stuart said. "And it's no word of a lie, as Elton finished the last chord—as the last chord died away—the tape ran out. And Clive and I sort of collapsed on the floor, thanking God and everything else for what had happened. And then Clive said, 'Oh yeah, we got it Elton, come in and have a listen.' And we never told him what murders we'd been through, because by then he was relieved to have got through the song. So we didn't bother telling him that we nearly lost it." (Decades later, Stuart Epps would again find himself in the same studio with Clive Franks and Elton. "They were rehearsing," he said, "and I went over there and Elton was in a good mood, so I thought, "I don't know, I just fancy telling him." So I told him the story about the tape running out....But he couldn't give a shit. He was completely uninterested. It was quite funny, really.")

Ray Cooper added a wind chime and shaker to the swirling elegy the next day, and Clive added bass. "Then I had this idea for doubling the bass," he said, "putting it marginally out-of-tune for this odd effect. It's hard to hear. If you play it in headphones, you can hear that there are two basses. Over stereo [speakers], it gels into one."

Elton completed the recording by laying a minimal vocal line over the coda, huskily singing how life wasn't everything in a mesmeric death chant.

"I want that mixed so far down that no one's going to really know what I'm saying," he told Clive as Gus Dudgeon walked into the studio.

"What's all this, then?" Gus asked.

"Just a track," Elton said.

Clive played a rough mix of the song back for the master producer.

"That's a smash," Gus said.

Elton looked at him, astonished. "Sorry? What do you mean? It's a piano instrumental."

Gus simply nodded. "Elton never knows which songs are his best," he later noted. "Yet [that instrumental] was just so obvious to me. It was perfect."

Unsure of what to name his new song, Elton soon learned that Guy Burchett, a Rocket Records employee, had died mere hours before. "As I was writing," he said, "I imagined myself floating into space and looking down at my own body. I was imagining myself dying. Morbidly obsessed with these thoughts, I wrote this song about death. The next day I was told that Guy, our seventeen-year-old messenger boy, had been tragically killed on his motorcycle the day before. Guy died on the day I was writing this song."

Thus it was decided: the spectral instrumental would be called "Song for Guy."

"I remember trying to persuade Elton to let me overdub some guitar on 'Song for Guy' without success," Tim Renwick would later recall. "Shame, as it was such a big hit."

With "Song for Guy" in the can, Elton and Clive were ready to mix down the eighteen tracks they'd recorded. Each song became a mini-battle between the two men, with Elton inevitably pushing his voice down in the mix and Clive then pushing it back up again, arguing, "*That's* what people want to hear."

Elton always acquiesced with the utmost reluctance, understanding that he perhaps lacked the critical distance necessary to make the best decisions. "I've never liked some of the mixes on my albums," he said, "but everybody else thought they were great, so as a musician you can sometimes be wrong. You might look for a certain bass part or rhythm guitar part, or an electric piano thing you like, to lift in the mix, to the detriment of your own vocal performance. Knowing the best road to take is very hard."

After the final mixes were locked in, it came time to decide which tracks would make the final cut for an album release. To aid in the decision, Elton enlisted a cadre of music-minded friends, including Gus Dudgeon, disc jockey Kenny Everett, and journalist Paul Gambaccini. A playback was then arranged, with each person marking off a list of songs, rating them from their favorite to least favorite. Purposefully or not, the few tracks which bore Bernie's imprimatur were all relegated to B-side status. The pianist was quite aware that Bernie might be upset that the new LP wouldn't feature even a single track which had sprung from his pen, but that didn't change his decision-making process one iota.

"He'll probably feel extremely hurt," Elton conceded, "but it'll give him a much-needed kick up the arse."

Chapter 34:
Benedict Canyon Boogie

After final track selections for his new album—and a proper running order—had been sorted, Elton headed off to New York to host a party at the tony One Fifth Avenue restaurant. The event was, at least in part, an attempt to revitalize the fortunes of Rocket Records. Joining Kiki Dee for a spiritedly sassy rendition of "Don't Go Breaking My Heart," Elton's never-flagging energy ensured that the party was a wild success, even if its ultimate aim would fall well short of the mark.

The restless Brit then turned his attention to fleshing out an idea he'd recently had for a Hope/Crosby-styled "road picture" entitled *Jet Lag,* which he envisioned starring in alongside Rod Stewart, as a pair of competitive rock stars jetting compulsively around the world. "It will be a film about the rock business that leans towards the funny side of it, and some of the incredible things which go on," Elton said. "My idea for the opening is to have two superstars landing in their private jets in L.A., and jamming up the runway because neither of them wants to get out first. I could name two or three people who would do that."

Rod found *Jet Lag* to be a "totally barking idea," and agreed at once to costar in the vehicle. Unfortunately, the motion picture, which was slated to go into production in the summer of '79, would ultimately never materialize. In an ironic, life-imitating-art twist, Elton and Rod were both unable to sync-up their hectic schedules and agree upon a proper filming schedule; the project was thus put on indefinite hold.

Elton received the Golden Note Award from the American Society of Composers, Authors, and Publishers days later. He was particularly moved, being only the third performer to ever secure the prestigious honor. In the wake of that accomplishment, he released "Part-Time Love," the leadoff single from his forthcoming album, which he'd decided to call *A Single Man*. Backed with "I Cry at Night," and powered by a video featuring '60s icon Cathy McGowan which had been shot at Ladbroke Grove, the song reached Number 22 on the U.S. charts and Number 15 in England—giving Elton his first U.K. Top 20 single since "Sorry Seems to Be the Hardest Word" two years earlier.

Besides rejuvenating his fortunes in the charts, "Part-Time Love"—and the long-player from whence it came—would also prove instrumental in reaffirming Elton's belief in his vocal abilities. "In the past, I've often neglected my singing," he told journalist Rick Carr. "On this new album...I've sung far better than I've ever sung in my entire life. If [*A Single Man*] *does* flop, I'll be very disappointed, but I won't be destroyed. In the past, if something failed I could put it down to other things, to other people. This time it's really all down to me."

All down to him on record, though not on stage—at least for the time being. 1978 would, in fact, prove to be Elton's least active year on the road since his early teens. With no tours planned, foreign or domestic, his only full-length live performances—three in total, and all solo outings—would come in relatively quick succession that fall.

The first, and perhaps most memorable, took place on October 14 in L.A. Performing an impromptu ninety-minute set in front of two-hundred-and-fifty MCA executives in the Westside Room at Century Plaza. "I'm so nervous," he admitted before the show, his first Los Angeles-area appearance since his massive Dodger Stadium triumphs three years earlier. "I just hope I can remember all the words."

Elton's adrenaline was pumping so hard, he was forced to press down on the sustain pedal just to keep his right leg from shaking.

"How wonderful to play this room," the frightened artist told the relatively small crowd gathered before him. "I came in with Bob Hilburn, he's an old friend and a good friend, and he said, 'No need to worry. Dusty Springfield's played here, Sergio Franchi's played here…' And I said, 'Yes, but what's fucking happened to *them?*'" Everyone laughed. "But if you're gonna go out, go out in a blaze of glory. Which I intend to do."

Elton served up a heavy dose of older material, alongside such newer titles as "I Don't Care," "Shooting Star," "Part-Time Love" and "Return to Paradise." After performing a beautifully ragged "Ego," Elton noted that "those expert lyrics were by Mr. Taupin. And they *are* expert lyrics, they're exactly what I wanted. All power to his elbow, if not any other part of his anatomy."

Twenty-five minutes into his performance, a drunken woman in a gold silk dress shouted, "Do the Benedict Canyon Boogie!"

"Another drink for that lady," Elton said, launching into an improvised 12-bar blues.

Halfway through "Sixty Years On," the Brit forgot the lyrics and was forced to hum his way through the entire third verse. "Sorry, sorry," he said afterward, blushing. "Nerves, you see. It's just a new era for me. And an important era, 'cause I'm nervous as hell about [*A Single Man*], I'm nervous as hell coming on tonight. But that's the best thing about it, because in this business, unless you've got a bit of adrenaline, it becomes too easy. And perhaps I got a little too cozy in what I was doing, and too safe, and it's a good thing we had a two-year layoff, 'cause I'm excited again, and that really *is* important."

By the end of Elton's set, everyone was on their feet, shouting out his name and asking for more. It was another standing ovation, another satisfied audience.

"Tonight it was more like it should be out there," the pianist said. "The adrenaline was really pumping....If I *do* come back, that's what I want to do, just me and the piano."

He took a sip of Perrier, shut his eyes, and laughed at nothing at all.

A Single Man was released two days later, on October 16. Critics immediately took note of the title, which made specific reference not only to Elton's status as the world's most infamous bachelor, but which also stood as a clear indication that this would be his first LP not to feature Bernie Taupin, Gus Dudgeon, or either incarnation of his previous bands.

"It's an album that's marked by change in a lot of ways," Elton said of the disc, which he'd dedicated to Graham Taylor in recognition of the sweeping changes the coach had instituted at Watford. "The album is a very sensitive one, simpler than the stuff I've done before, reflecting the time that I took to take stock of my situation."

Change was evident from the album cover itself, which featured Elton in a black greatcoat, black judo trousers, patent leather jackboots, top hat and cane, standing grimly on the Long Walk drive which led to Windsor Castle, which sat forebodingly in the background. Though the superstar looked positively funereal, the shoot itself wasn't without its lighter side. "I was in a lazy mood," Elton said, "and we just went up the road to Windsor Castle. And so many people think that's the house in which I live." He smirked. "[The photo shoot] was terribly embarrassing because there were picnickers and everything, we had to get them out of the way. Terry O'Neill was like a used-car salesman: ''Scuse me, Luv, get outta the way...'"

The iconic photograph O'Neill took that wet afternoon, so reminiscent of a classic image Henri Cartier-Bresson had crafted of a caped gentleman decades earlier, sent a clear signal that the glamor and excess Elton had once worn like a second skin was very much a thing of the past. Moreover, the pianist truly *was* on his own now—a single man in every way. This idea would be further driven home with the release of Alice Cooper's *From the Inside* weeks later—an album that was not only co-written by Bernie Taupin, but which also featured the talents of such Elton stalwarts as Davey Johnstone, Dee Murray, Kenny Passarelli and Kiki Dee.

In a scalding review of *A Single Man* presented under the title, "Elton John: No Future? Apathy in the U.K.," *Rolling Stone*'s Stephen Holden didn't mince words: "John's coproduced himself and used studio musicians to turn out his sparest LP since *Honky Château.* But this move towards simplicity is a step into emptiness, since *A Single Man* is nothing more than a collection of trivial hooks performed about as perfunctorily as possible. Even the best tune, 'Shine on Through,' is marred by hopelessly trite words and a dull slogging arrangement." Holden went on to claim that the album "demonstrates just how thin the line really is between disposable radio pop and elevator music....If John and Taupin's final collaboration, *Blue Moves,* was a disastrous exercise in inflated pop rhetoric, *A Single Man* is an equally disastrous exercise in smug vapidity."

The New Orleans Times-Picayune disagreed with Holden, calling the LP one of Elton's "most brilliant efforts." The *Village Voice*'s Robert Christgau, meanwhile, wrote, "Like the homophilophile I am, I'm rooting for Elton, but though it [*A Single Man*] isn't as lugubrious as *Blue Moves,* it comes close, and the flat banalities of new lyricist Gary Osborne make Bernie Taupin's intricate ones sound like Cole Porter. Personal to Reg Dwight: Rock 'n' roll those blues away."

Many other reviewers would also compare Osborne unfavorably with Mssr. Taupin. Elton's new lyricist adopted a Zen-like attitude toward the inevitable situation. "In the real world, it doesn't matter to me whether I'm being known for not being as good as Bernie," he told journalist Randy Alexander. "I just thank God that somebody, somewhere, recognizes me. I'm just a songwriter, for God's sake."

Despite the lackluster reviews—and in the face of DJM having flooded the market with newly repackaged collections of older Elton John material (*Here and There* became *London & New York, 17/11/70* became *Elton Live,* and so on) in a seemingly purposeful act of sabotage—*A Single Man* easily managed to secure the Number 8 spot in Britain. The album would remain in the U.K. charts for well over six months, longer than any of his other LPs since his first *Greatest Hits* package back in 1974. (*A Single Man* would also win the Capital Radio Award for Best Album, beating out offerings by Kate Bush, Ian Dury and Elvis Costello.)

The disc would also prove popular in the U.S., going Gold eight days after its release, and Platinum three weeks later. (*A Single Man* hit many Top 20 charts around the world as well, going Gold or Platinum in Canada, France,

Italy, New Zealand, Australia, Spain, Norway, Germany and the Netherlands.)

With the French-only release of "Return to Paradise" nestled comfortably in the Number 2 spot on the Continental charts, Elton played a one-off solo show at RTL Studios in Paris on October 20 in front of a select group of fifty. It was a significant performance, his first on French soil since his self-imposed exile after the MIDEM disaster of '71.

Wearing a brown tweed jacket and beret, and with a small gold hoop earring gleaming in his right ear, Elton sat at a black baby grand and performed an enthusiastic which was set nearly identical to his L.A. show. (The pianist's impassioned performance would soon be released by French bootleggers as *A Single Man in France*; the disc would sell out in a matter of days.) As far as the Briton was concerned, he was happy just to play the occasional promotional gig. "I enjoy making records, but I don't particularly want to go back out on the road again," he said. "If you're half-hearted when you go on the road, you're cheating the public. Let's own up—half the bands who go out on tour hate each other's guts, and [they] channel the aggression into their music. I couldn't exist under such conditions."

Elton revisited the familiar environs of *The Old Grey Whistle Test* studios to deliver a delicate reading of both "Shooting Star" and "Song for Guy" on October 31, before performing a final promotional gig three nights later, at the British Phonographic Industry's Annual Ball at the Hilton Hotel in London.

The Hilton show marked the end of his official stage commitments for the year, such as they were. Yet that wouldn't slow the restless artist down. He immediately launched into a heavy round of press interviews for *A Single*

Man, before participating in a grueling five-a-side charity soccer game at Wembley that Saturday, with Rod Stewart and Billy Connolly making up his backfield. A three-hour tennis exhibition match with Billie Jean King followed that Sunday.

The bill for this non-stop energy expenditure came due less than forty-eight hours later, when, on November 9, while preparing to fly to Paris for a final hair transplant procedure, a searing pain shot up Elton's left shoulder blade and drove him to his knees. Moments later, he collapsed in his front hall, debilitating spasms tearing through his chest, arms and legs. Personal assistant Bob Halley phoned an ambulance; minutes later, the superstar was being rushed to Harley Street Clinic's coronary care unit.

"I could hardly move for the pain," Elton said. "As I went down I said to myself, 'Hello, this is it. The Grand Heart, then out you go.'"

Initially thought to be a case of cardiac arrest (the BBC had breathlessly reported: "Pop star Elton John has been rushed to hospital after suffering a heart attack!"), the doctors—at John Reid's urging—officially ruled the episode a severe panic attack brought on by nervous exhaustion.

"This has really shaken me," the pianist admitted. "When you are used to nonstop tours across the States and so on, you start to think you are superhuman. Then something like this happens and you realize you're not. Sometimes you've got to slow down like everyone else."

Despite the grave health scare, Elton's priorities remained unchanged. Upon regaining consciousness, his first request was to have a special telephone line set up in his hospital room so he could keep abreast of Watford's game against Exeter. His team ultimately prevailed by a score of 2-0, which pleased their ailing chairman no end. "There's no way

I'm leaving this earth before Watford have gone the First Division," he declared.

Tellingly, news of Elton's collapse caused sales for "Part-Time Love" to spike. Instead of moving three-thousand units a day, it was now shifting over twenty-thousand. "If any of you artists want to sell more records," Elton said, "just have a heart attack scare and go into hospital, because your sales go up immediately."

With the specter of oblivion looming large, it struck some as ironic that the death-centric "Song for Guy" should be chosen as Elton's first post-collapse offering. Released in the U.K. on November 28, and backed with a slice of chiming pop-rock whimsy entitled "Lovesick," the single quickly reached Number 4 on the BBC charts. "Song for Guy" would also prove a major success around the globe, rising into the Top 10 in Portugal, Scandinavia, East German, Italy, Belgium and Spain. Called "the most elegant piece of music that Elton has ever recorded" by *Melody Maker,* the mournfully melodic song would soon earn the composer another prestigious Ivor Novello Award.

While reviews for the single were overwhelmingly positive, one brash critic likened the piquant track to something by Ferrante & Teicher, American pianists popular in the late '50s for light treatments of classical pieces. But Elton didn't mind the comparison. "I take that as a compliment," he said.

Despite the single's overwhelming success, MCA was reluctant to release "Song for Guy" in the States, fearing that Frank Mills' recent hit, "Music-Box Dancer," had sucked all the air out of the charts for another piano-based instrumental. Elton was insistent, however, and the song was belatedly released the following March. Displeased with having their hand forced, MCA refused to expend any promotional effort on the track, allowing it to die a quiet death outside the Hot 100.

Elton was hardly surprised by MCA's cold shoulder; he'd been too often burnt by the capricious devotions of various record labels throughout his career to ever invest any real or lasting faith in them. Musicians, however, were a different story. They were comrades, trusted allies. Thus the pianist soon found himself jamming with rockers both old and new. First he stepped onto stage with Wreckless Eric, Lene Lovich, Jona Lewie, Mickey Jupp and Rachel Sweet, to add his vocal chops to "Sex & Drugs & Rock & Roll" during a *Live Stiffs/Be-Stiff Tour* gig at Hemel Hempstead.

"I like Wreckless Eric a lot, I like all that Stiff catalogue," Elton said. "They're tremendous."

The superstar followed up this performance with a show at the Civic Hall in Guildford with fellow rock dinosaurs Eric Clapton and George Harrison, and blues great Muddy Waters. Together, the four aging icons joined forces on a convivial rendition of "Further On Up the Road," which proved to be the clear highlight of the evening.

Appearing on a special anniversary edition of Michael Parkinson's self-titled television program on December 2, Elton shared the stage with *Sunset Boulevard* actress Gloria Swanson, Olivia Newton-John, and Australian comedian Barry Humphries, who appeared under the guise of his alter-ego, wisteria-wigged Dame Edna Everage.

The highpoint of the broadcast came when Everage sang her recent hit, a bouncy comic trifle called "Every Mother Wants a Boy Like Elton."

"Do you think Dame Edna has a career, Elton, as a pop singer?" Parkinson asked the pianist after the performance. "What would you advise her to do now?"

"Ummm...shall we skip that question?"

Parkinson nodded. "Well, how did she do today?"

Elton raised an eyebrow. "Let's skip that one as well."

The pianist had a giant banner placed above the entrance to Olympia Hall days later, where Rod Stewart was to give a concert in promotion of his latest album, *Blondes Have More Fun*:

Blondes have more fun, but brunettes have lots more money. Happy Christmas.

Rod had the banner torn down, and a new one hung in its place:

Blondes may have more fun, but brunettes have more transplants.

Elton himself took to the concert stage briefly on Christmas Eve, appearing at the Hammersmith Odeon for a charity show alongside Peter Gabriel and Tom Robinson. Pleased that he'd survived an unusually trying year, the pianist then flew down to Australia to assist Ian "Molly" Meldrum—a leading music journalist whom the pianist had befriended during his first tour of Oz back in '71—in his review the top songs of the year on the December 10 episode of Meldrum's *Countdown* show. After airing the third most popular song of the year—the Bee Gees' "Staying Alive"—Meldrum queried Elton as to why he had yet to 'go disco'. "I like disco music," the pianist allowed, "but I never consciously wanted to write disco music. I'd not be very good at it, I would think."

"Did you like the Stones' *Some Girls*?"

"I liked 'Miss You', I thought it was brilliant. I thought the rest of the album was abysmal, I thought they should

709

give up. I mean, 'Respectable'—really crass rubbish. I liked Charlie Watts on it, though."

Meldrum changed the subject to Billy Joel's latest album, *52nd Street*.

Elton sighed. "Billy Joel, yeah. He's pinched me like mad. 'My *life…*' Before, I always felt sorry for the bloke, 'cause everyone always said, 'Poor man's Elton John,' and I always thought that's really rubbish, 'cause the guy writes really great songs, and he's made four or five good albums. This album—and it's very weird how I heard it, because Billie Jean King came up to my hotel while I was doing interviews and said, 'You've *gotta* listen to this album,' and I said, 'Well, it's Billy Joel, I've heard a couple tracks.' She said, 'Well, listen to this whole album.' I've never heard such blatant copying of my vocal style ever. 'My *life…*' You go back and listen to the way I pronounce 'life' in any of my songs. *Life.* And you listen to 'Big Shot'—it's 'Bennie and the Jets' backwards."

Meldrum nodded. "What do you think about Linda Ronstadt? Do you like her?"

Elton hesitated.

"She's very pretty," he said with the slyest of grins.

Chapter 35:
To Russia…With Elton

As the clangorous cacophony of the punk revolution was mutating into the more copacetic tunefulness of New Wave bands like Blondie, Talking Heads and the Police, Elton decided to dip his toe back into the touring waters. An ambitious 73-date two-man show was quickly set up. It would be a unique outing—no band, no extended entourage. Just Elton and his piano, and his longtime percussionist.

"I determined the only way to come back was just on my own, or at least only with Ray Cooper," he said. "To play on my own and get my fear back, because I wasn't afraid any more. I'd lost the whole fear thing. It was just routine. I'd lost my edge completely. It was too comfortable, I could've gone onstage and read poetry for an hour and they'd have applauded."

The massive twelve-country tour, billed as *Elton John: A Single Man in Concert with Ray Cooper*, kicked off at the Concerthaus Hall in Stockholm, Sweden on February 5. Eventually it would wind its ways from Antwerp, Belgium to Wiesbaden, Berlin. The shows followed the same general pattern set by the two musicians' weeklong stand at the Rainbow back in '77. Elton would begin each night alone at the piano, reaching deep into his back catalogue to air out hidden treasures like "Come Down in Time" and "The Greatest Discovery." The emotional intimacy proved a real challenge for the pianist, who admitted: "I never was nervous in the past with the band, but now I get physically sick with nerves every night." Still, performing alone—or nearly alone—had a very definite upside, as it allowed Elton to appreciate the depth of his oeuvre more than ever before. "That's when I realized that Bernie is one of the great lyric writers, because I suddenly got into those songs all over again. Some of the lyrics are timeless."

Halfway through the shows, Elton would amble from his somber midnight black nine-foot grand over to an electric CP-80 piano set up on the other side of the stage, where he'd perform *Tumbleweed Connection*'s haunting "Where to Now, St. Peter?," as well as a pair of covers: Jim Reeves' "He'll Have to Go"—the song he'd performed at his failed audition for Liberty Records back in '67—and a raging ten-minute-plus version of the R&B classic, "I Heard It Through the Grapevine."

Heading back to his grand piano, Elton would begin the second half of each night's show by launching into the familiar opening chords of "Funeral For a Friend" as a shell-like backdrop—glowing an ethereal orange—slowly rose to reveal a statue-like Ray Cooper standing behind a row of timpani, dry ice swirling about him.

"I come on in a very strange part of the show," the percussionist said, "where everybody's already had an hour and fifteen minutes, an hour and twenty minutes, of very much Elton and his piano, and Bernie's lyrics, and the songs and everything else, which is wonderful, and there's almost a feeling—perhaps one senses it backstage, and certainly I think if one's in the audience one certainly feels it—that it's either time to go home, having been totally fulfilled as an evening's entertainment, or to switch over channels virtually to the next [level]. So I come on in a poof of smoke and produce what is perhaps a little bit extra, and it should be [experienced as something] totally different."

Like some freshly animated creature out of Madame Tussaud's Chamber of Horrors, Ray would prowl the stage like a demented civil servant each night, easily upstaging his superstar boss. "It could be Rubenstein playing the piano," Ray noted philosophically. "Everybody will still be looking at the drummer."

For his part, Elton appreciated touring with someone who was not only attuned to him musically, but who was also an intelligent and sympathetic traveling companion. "Ray and I work very well," he said. "It's really just like going on holiday when we go out on the road."

Though their shows offered a seemingly effortless blend of hard-edged rock 'n' roll and old school theatricality, Elton and Ray in fact worked ceaselessly to choreograph their performances.

"We have to," Ray said. "Although within the songs [Elton] can do what he wants, and I'll just float with him. If he wants to make 'Rocket Man' twenty minutes long, that's fine. I'll play a bit, wander off for a cup of tea, whatever." Elton agreed, noting that "without a band you're free to extemporize whenever you want, and within certain limits when you've got Ray onstage with you. But there was no real framework [on this tour], and it was quite exciting. It also gave me my confidence back as a musician."

That feeling of newfound liberation extended to Clive Franks, who was given a free artistic hand to mix the sound whichever way he thought best each night. "I could [finally] do my effects," the sound engineer said, "which you could never hear in the past because the band covered it. My little reverbs and subtle effects and delays."

The enthusiastic response which Elton's two-man outings drew provided him with the confidence to take his show to countries he'd never toured before, including France, Spain, Belgium, Israel, Northern Ireland and Southern Ireland. These virgin audiences provided unpredictable, and thus inherently valuable, reactions for the jaded star. In return, Elton began adding impromptu flourishes to his performances, as at his shows at the Theatre De Champs Elysées, where he seamlessly folded "*Iles Amore*" and "I Love Paris in the Springtime" into the set list. Appreciative Parisians gave him standing ovations every night—a far cry from the hot-dog-throwing reception he'd received as a lowly opening act at the start of the decade.

"Things are looking up," Elton chuckled. "Sérgio who, you say?"

Elton and Ray took their largest artistic gamble yet on February 18, heading behind the Iron Curtain to play the Kongresshalle in East Berlin, a city the pianist found depressing and dark. "It seemed to have been left just as it was after the war," he said. "Really dire."

Billy Joel and his band caught Elton's show in the Netherlands days later. "The first time I saw Elton was in the lobby of a hotel in Amsterdam," drummer Liberty DeVitto said. "He went walking by in a flowing cape, and I thought, 'Wow!' Our lighting designer knew his manager, John Reid, but Elton rushed by so fast I only got to meet John Reid. We—the band and Billy and I—went to see him at the Hague. He was great."

As the tour rolled through cities both bleak and beautiful, London's Capital Radio named Elton the Top British Singer for the third consecutive year, while a three-song EP of his transitional Seattle recordings, entitled *The Thom Bell Sessions '77,* was finally released—eighteen months after the sessions had transpired, and two months after Elton and Clive Franks had remixed the master tapes in London. (In the main, Elton and Clive lowered the swirling strings, while making a wholesale edit of the Spinners' dominant backing vocals.) "Are You Ready for Love" was concurrently issued as a single in the U.K. Backed by an extended, largely instrumental coda entitled "Are You Ready for Love (Part 2)," the song rose no higher than 42, becoming Elton's worst-performing single ever in his homeland. (In a true case of poor timing, "Are You Ready for Love" was destined to languish in relative obscurity for decades, until it was finally resurrected by Fat Boy Slim nearly a quarter-century later. The enterprising English disc jockey released an Ashley Beedle remix of the tune on his Southern Friend label in August, 2003, after realizing that English DJs were paying upward of £100 each for rare copies of the 1979 12-inch. In its first week of release in the U.K., "Are You Ready for Love" would shoot to the top of the British charts, easily displacing Beyonce's "Crazy in Love" and giving Elton his fifth British Number One. The song would then be issued in America, where it would claim the Number 1 spot on *Billboard*'s dance chart. "We were ahead of our time," Thom Bell said with a laugh.)

Success arrived in a much more timely manner on the pitch, with Watford winning promotion and advancing from the Third Division to the Second. An ecstatic Elton presented the club's manager, Graham Taylor, with the Gold disc for *A Single Man* as a thank you gift before boarding a plane to Israel, where he was to become the first major pop star to ever perform in Jerusalem and Tel Aviv.

Critical reception for the gigs was overwhelming.

"At Elton John's opening concert in Jerusalem," the *Jerusalem Post*'s Natan Y. Shaw reported, "the atmosphere was electric and expectant, as before a cup-final. The lights went out and a tremendous roar rose up in the hall....For two-and-a-half hours, [Elton] played his brains out, paralyzing the audience. His voice was in tremendous form, the piano never sounded more percussive, and there was an all-around aura of celebration."

"I know I must be getting old because I now think pop groups with red-dyed hair look ridiculous—and only five years ago I thought nothing of appearing with pink hair, fur stoles and eight-inch heels," Elton said at a press conference held days later at the Tel Aviv Sheraton. "I was in a state of limbo before the opening night [in Jerusalem], didn't know what to expect of an Israeli audience....I can honestly say I have never heard any audience at any concert I've ever given sing along with me so much. I couldn't even see them— there were spotlights shining straight into my eyes—it was like playing to a vast black hole. But the audience participation was something absolutely incredible."

Though the tour was met by an ecstatic response everywhere it touched down, the campaign wasn't without the occasional mishap. During the March 4 show in Lausanne, Switzerland at the Theatre Di Beaulieu, Ray tripped and fell onto Elton's piano during an encore of "Pinball Wizard," breaking a rib. Weeks later, in the U.K., the unlucky percussionist came down with pneumonia. "I was wearing a three-piece suit and a tie onstage every performance," he said. "I must have been crazy."

Before his Edinburgh concert at the Odeon on March 19, Elton was introduced to members of the bubblegum-pop boy band the Bay City Rollers—recently rechristened the Rollers—who had scored chart successes with such sleekly prefab offerings as "Saturday Night" and "Rock 'n' Roll Love Letter."

"We were taken backstage, and there stood Elton," said Rollers bassist Duncan Faure. "And my girlfriend, Francine, she said, 'He's like a cartoon caricature coming to life.' And he was one of the funniest blokes I've ever met. It was incredible. I mean, it's *Elton John,* you know? It's like the Beatles—there can never be another Elton." (Elton and Faure would soon became good friends, with the Roller being invited to stay at the pianist's home. "His house looks like a small Buckinghma Palace, and I stayed in the Rod Stewart Suite," Faure said. "And a few years later, Elton told me that he saw Yoko [Ono] after John Lennon was murdered. And he said that Lennon's last words to Yoko were, 'You're beautiful.'")

As the tour progressed, Elton decided that he was ready to take the biggest artistic gamble of his entire career and play inside the Soviet Union. Given the bleak political climate, frosted over by a decades-old Cold War, a flamboyant—not to mention openly bisexual—rock star playing within the confines of the socially austere U.S.S.R. seemed an impossibility, however.

Still, an attempt was made.

John Reid invited Vladimir Kokonin, an official from the Soviet Ministry of Culture, to Elton's April 17 show at the Oxford Theatre, to gauge the Russian's impressions of the presentation.

Kokonin was dazzled.

"Is that the concert we will see?" he asked.

"Yes, that's it," Elton told him.

"Very well, then. Please come."

Kokonin set into motion the official paperwork which would allow Elton and Ray entry into the Soviet Union. Initially, the Soviets asked for twenty concerts—ten each in Leningrad and Moscow. Reid made a counter-offer: four shows in each city. The pre-Glasnost Russians, starved for even the slightest taste of Western decadence, agreed without hesitation.

"Even so," the pianist admitted, "I think we all felt that someone somewhere would give us a 'no'—or a *nyet,* as they say. Bennie and the *Nyets.*"

Bags packed and visas stamped, Elton boarded an Aeroflot plane bound for the Soviet Union on May 20. "I don't know if they've heard of Watford in Russia, but they soon will," he said. "Mind you, this could be the last time you see me. If they don't like you in Moscow, you end up down a salt mine."

Arriving in Moscow in a blue satin shirt and baggy Cossack pants tucked into patent leather boots, his hair and sideburns longer than ever, Elton and his entourage were taken directly from the airport to a train station, where they boarded the midnight Red Arrow for the 500-mile trek to Leningrad. As to why they weren't simply allowed to fly directly to the once and future St. Petersburg, Elton surmised, "We presume there was something they didn't want us to see."

Anticipation for the eight shows ran high. With ninety-five percent of the tickets going to military officers, city bureaucrats and top-ranking Communist Party members, nosebleed seats—priced at eight rubles, more than the average Soviet earned in two weeks—were trading on the black market for up to twenty-five times their face value.

As Elton's group—which included his mother and step-father, John Reid, and assistant Bob Halley—settled into their muggy, un-air-conditioned hotel rooms, two eighteen-wheelers packed with thirteen tons of equipment—musical instruments, lighting systems, sound systems, carpets, drapes and wardrobe—were winding their way through Eastern Europe and into the barren Russian hinterlands. The trucks arrived the day before the first performance. Practiced

English roadies set to work posthaste, stopping only for the occasional tea break; they had the entire stage set—drapes hung, lighting rig operational, Elton's piano tuned—by the early afternoon of May 21.

The aura inside the 3,800-seat Bolshoi Oktyabrsky Concert Hall that night was unlike any in a Western arena. No Frisbees flew from the balconies, no beach balls bounced across the floor seats. Not even the minutest trace of marijuana could be detected wafting through the non-proletariat air. Instead, stolid Politburo wives of a certain age sat waiting grimly, hands folded impatiently on graying laps.

Backstage, Elton was unusually pensive. "*Spaseeba* is 'thank you'. *Dobriy vecher*, somehow I'll remember that....*Nasdarovje* is 'cheers'. And *Spakona noche—"No, spakona noche!"*—that's 'goodnight'. Yeah, that's all right." He glanced furtively around his dressing room. "What is 'help'?"

An announcer began reading brief biographies of Elton and Ray over the loudspeaker system at eight-twenty-five p.m., and at eight-thirty precisely, the house lights cut off and a pair of white spotlights picked out Elton as he entered from stage-left.

After a nervous bow, the pianist—dressed in an emerald shirt, sapphire velvet trousers, and a flat cap—began the show with a solemn reading of "Your Song."

"*Dobriy vecher*," he said afterward to polite applause.

A barrier of wary culture shock clearly separated artist and audience, the barometric pressure in the hall dropping only after a fan came to the lip of the stage and asked for an autograph.

"*Spasibo*," a visibly relieved Elton said, launching into a poignant rendition of *Empty Sky*'s signal ballad, "Skyline Pigeon."

As usual, the performance truly caught fire with Ray Cooper's emergence at the midway point. Dressed like an undertaker's assistant in a dour pin-striped suit, the unsmiling percussionist cut a commanding figure which the Soviets responded to with understated awe. "The concerts in Russia, unlike those in the United States, would not start with the audience screaming and shouting," Ray noted. "They wanted to see us, listen to us, and experience the music. I had experienced this response in the theater as an actor, but never at a rock 'n' roll concert. It was an exhilarating experience."

After a stormy, snare-drum-laced "Better Off Dead," a jubilant "Merry Month of May" suddenly burst into an eviscerating rendition of "Bennie and the Jets." Aided by Ray's fiercely rhythmic tambourine, the Muscovites clapped along enthusiastically. Sparks flew, and the song was met by deafening applause.

"All right," Elton sighed. "Well done."

After the show proper ended with a stridently convulsive "Crazy Water"—Elton and Ray rocking back-to-back on the piano bench—the stage lights kicked on and the official guests in the front of the hall got up to leave. For these creatures of structured protocol, the show was over. At the same time, the younger crowd in back—the true fans—surged toward the stage. "I was watching the official guests' faces," Robert Hilburn said. "And there was that registering of, '*Why* is this all going on?' And you see this dawning, and this expression and so forth, and it's a dangerous thing, it's a real powerful force. You saw what happened in the West in the '50s and '60s with this music."

Elton and Ray were called back for multiple encores, as renegade fans leaped maniacally atop their seats, crooning and shimmying and flashing peace signs in security guards' faces in an extraordinary display of defiance. The four-dozen-strong police force within the hall watched on with stony gazes, making no move to break up the riotous party. In the lockdown world of Brezhnev's Soviet Union, it was a truly historic moment—a notable fissure in Communism's iron grasp.

"Fantastic," Ray called gruffly from the stage. "Really amazing."

Elton finished the show alone, in spectacular fashion, on his Fender Rhodes. After toasting the crowd with a healthy swig of Stoli, he launched into an adrenaline-pumping "Back in the U.S.S.R." His breakneck rendition of the Beatles' classic dissolved any last pockets of restraint which may have existed within the already frantic audience. "I didn't mean to do that song," he said after the show. "It just came to me, and I was singing it before I realized I didn't know any of the words. So I just sang 'Back in the U.S.S.R.' over and over again." He smiled. "They went apeshit. It was like playing 'Philadelphia Freedom' in Philadelphia."

After the concert, thousands of desperate fans—many of whom had traveled up to a thousand miles without any hope of obtaining a ticket—stormed police barriers outside the hall to beg of concertgoers, "*What* was he like? Tell us what he was *like!*"

"El-*tone!* El-*tone!*" they chanted below the singer's third-floor dressing room window, blocking tram lines and refusing to disperse as the pianist tossed tulips down to them, tears in his eyes.

"As I watched [Elton] wave to the fans below," Robert Hilburn said, "I remembered Janis Joplin and what she had said about how hard it is to be loved by thousands on stage and then face the world alone. I stood next to him as he listened to the continuing chants of 'Elton, Elton.' Even on this night of triumph, there was something about Elton that made it obvious he felt terribly alone."

"Audiences are specially attracted to the lyrical ballads and folk songs performed by R. Dwight," read the staid, Soviet-penned program. Across the globe, headlines screamed out a more accurate picture of the event. "Elton John Stuns Soviet Rock Fans," proclaimed the *Daily Telegraph.* "Elton John, Super-Czar, Rocks Them Back In The U.S.S.R.," shouted the London *Daily Mail* ("[Elton] won the acclamation of an audience that almost deafened itself in its own applause…"), while the *Los Angeles Times* simply declared: "Rock Star Rises Over Russia."

"The first concert in the Soviet Union by the British rock star Elton John erupted into a frenzy last night," *The New York Times* noted, "with nearly 4,000 Russian fans dancing on their seats and in the aisles. Uniformed policemen and other Soviet officials were helpless to control the screaming, clapping mob in the Bolshoi Oktyabrsky Concert Hall here." Critic John Rockwell, possibly still stinging over his battle-of-words with Elton back in '76, did his best to downplay the pianist's specific role in the historic concert. "[Elton] is the best-known rock star ever to be allowed to perform in the Soviet Union," he wrote. "Thus the fanatic enthusiasm of the Russians may be as much an attestation of his symbolic status and a sign of their longing for Western popular music as it is a response to his considerable performing talents."

"Ol' Rockwell," Elton laughed. "Never lets our side down. Blimey."

Elton and Ray's victory was short-lived, as they began receiving warnings to tone down their show the very next day.

"Everyone's very aware and frightened of a normal show, bringing people to their feet too much," Ray said from his hotel room. "It's sad, because the warnings are coming from people that I don't really consider to understand what crowd-control is about. It's up to Elton and myself, who are, after all, supposedly the artists." He stared forlornly out the window. "When the lights go down, it's *our* show."

Soviet officials asked that Elton not kick his piano stool away during future performances, as he was damaging official Soviet property. Nor was he to pound his piano in quite so vigorous a manner. Most especially, they banned him from ever singing "Back in the U.S.S.R." again.

Elton summarily ignored all their requests. Yet even with the uncompromised, full-tilt performance the second night, proceedings *were* noticeably more subdued. During "Bennie and the Jets," not a single person got up to dance.

"Come *on!*" Ray exhorted, clapping his beefy hands forcefully above his head. "Come *on!*"

Nothing.

Elton and Ray were confused.

"It was funny," the pianist said, "'cause we really couldn't tell onstage what was different from the first night. I mean, they all seemed to be enjoying it, and you could see it. But I kept looking over at Ray, and he was working his nuts off, and people weren't getting up at all. And we found out later that if the kids *did* get up, then there were men in navy blue suits who'd push them down again."

Despite the uphill battle, Elton finally got the crowd to display a measure of enthusiasm by working a chorus of "Midnight in Moscow" into the coda of "Bennie and the Jets." (On other nights, he'd fold in snippets from the Russian banquet song "Podmoskovnye Vechera" into his set, along with fragmentary motifs from Tchaikovsky's Piano Concerto No 1.)

"Bloody commies," a bearded roadie in a faded red *Midnight Special* T-shirt chuckled from the wings. "No thanks, mate."

Back at his hotel that night, Elton was asked to perform in the dining hall. He was initially less than enthusiastic about the idea. "When I was first trying to make it as a musician, as Elton John, I always said that I would try and avoid playing to people who were eating, 'cause I'd had enough of that in cabaret when I was playing piano for Long John Baldry," he said. "So when I got to the hotel and people were saying, 'Go on, get up onstage,' I was very reluctant. But the first bottle of vodka sort of took my mind off it, really."

To the delight of the hundreds in the room, Elton performed a driving "I Heard It Through the Grapevine," with Ray Cooper on drums and Clive Franks on bass. Thereafter, it was back to the Stoli, before meeting one of his Soviet handlers, a lanky young KGB agent named Sacha, for a rooftop assignation.

The superstar was so hungover the next morning, he had to cut short a visit to the Winter Palace after only ten minutes, leaving it to Ray Cooper to hold up their end. *Elton Snubs Russians In Winter Palace Revolt,* one British tabloid declared with their usual understated aplomb.

After two more Leningrad performances, Elton and his retinue boarded the Red Arrow bound for Moscow, as dozens of poverty-stricken Soviets tossed flowers and boxes of candy and stuffed teddy bears at them. Elton was touched—they were sharing items purchased at hugely inflated prices on the black market, items they most likely couldn't even afford for themselves. Their selfless largesse brought the cultural iconoclast to tears.

"They're such a generous people," he said quietly.

The pianist was equally impressed with how polite and reserved the Soviets proved to be whenever he'd encounter them on the streets. "They gather around in crowds but they don't gawk, and they're not rude like other people out of other places," he noted in the documentary *To Russia...With Elton*, shot by Ian La Frenais and Dick Clement. "Although I've noticed that when they ask you for your autograph, you just get halfway through signing it and they think that's it. And I'm saying, 'No no no, there's more to come yet,' as I start on the 'John'. And they just run away halfway through."

While in Moscow, Elton visited the Olympic Stadium, which was still under construction. This was followed by a soccer match between Dynamo Moscow and a team made up of Red Army members. Appearing on a Russian talkshow, the pianist claimed that he'd "gleaned something from the [Soviet] atmosphere to write something." The next day, after taking in the changing of the guard outside Lenin's tomb, Elton held a press conference before his first show at Moscow's 2,500-seat Rossiya Concert Hall.

"Are you against apartheid in sport?" one Soviet journalist asked.

"I object to apartheid, whether it's because of color, class or sexual preference," Elton firmly replied. His answer was translated into Russian sans any mention of sexual preferences—at the time, homosexuality in the U.S.S.R. was punishable by a five-year prison sentence.

Elton's first Moscow concert was another triumph; diplomats from Britain's embassy hailed the tour as the single most important step forward in East-West relationships since Khrushchev had visited Hollywood back in '59.

Fully understanding the political implications of his visit, a celebratory Elton struck a playful, Cossack-like pose for the press outside the Kremlin. Wearing a magenta jacket, bright yellow trousers and a four-foot rope of pearls, he told his Russian guides that Paul McCartney should be allowed to play in Red Square. His suggestion was met with pointed silence.

The next show went as well as the ones before it, the Soviets lapping up the Brit's magnetic live performances as much as the rest of the world.

After Elton's penultimate show, he was shocked when Sacha, the KGB agent he'd shared an intimate encounter with on a Leningrad hotel rooftop, brought his wife and children backstage to meet him.

Elton and Ray's final show, on May 28, created another bit of history when it was beamed live throughout Europe on the BBC, thus becoming the first satellite broadcast ever between the Soviet Union and the Western world. (The show itself would soon be bootlegged under a preponderance of titles, from *Russian Bullet* to *A Single Man in Moscow*.)

   BBC Radio 1 producer Jeff Griffin was in charge of making sure that the broadcast went off without a hitch. With exactly two-and-a-half hours of signal time allotted to bounce the show from Moscow to the Ukraine to London, the margin for error was slim. "Elton had promised me if I gave him signals all the way through, especially the last half hour, he would come out on time," Griffin said. "On the last but one encore, we were running very tight on time. So instead of staying off the stage for about a couple of minutes like an artist usually does while the applause builds and builds, I had [a roadie inform Elton], 'You've got to go straight back on!'" The pianist complied, making a mad dash behind the curtains before appearing on the other side of the stage seconds later. He finished his final song with only moments to spare before the satellite feed went dark."

As always, the performance was met with a fanatical response, leaving Elton beside himself with joy. "The last show was probably the best I've ever given in my life," he said. "This has to be my biggest achievement as an artist. I'm at a loss for words."

Landing back at Heathrow on May 31 to a hero's welcome, promoter Harvey Goldsmith stood beside Elton with a satchel full of pound notes—the pianist's payment for the eight shows. Even with the remittance (the bills were so old and worn, they had to be exchanged for newer ones at the Bank of England), Elton ended up losing over £25,000 on the tour. But he hardly cared. For him, the artistic benefits far outweighed any financial considerations.

"I had the most fantastic time [musically]—culturally as well—seeing the most beautiful things," he said. "I came back and the first questions that were asked were negative. At London Airport: 'What do you think of Communism?' First typical English quote." He shrugged. "You hear a lot about the U.S.S.R. at home, but you've got to see things for yourself. I thought Leningrad was easily one of the most beautiful cities I've ever been to....The country is not dark, gray, grim or drab. It's beautiful, and the people are very warm."

Did Elton feel any qualms playing for such an aggressively oppressive regime? "I'm against bigotry and prejudice and persecution," he said. "But if that stopped me from playing my music, I wouldn't play [in Britain], because of the National Front or the campaign against homosexuality. You don't go in with guns blazing, saying, 'I want this and that.' You've got to approach things gently. I'd be very presumptuous to consider myself an ambassador of any sort, but I'm glad to do my bit."

In actuality, Elton had built a vinyl bridge between East and West—soon after the conclusion of his brief tour, *A Single Man* became the first Western rock album to enjoy official distribution within the U.S.S.R. Released on Melodiya, the Soviet record label, the album was given the green light only after a pair of caveats were met: that the LP's title be changed to *Poyot Elton John* ("Elton John Sings"), and that two of the lyrically more questionable tracks—"Part-Time Love" and "Big Dipper"—be excised, both having been deemed too morally suspect for pristine Russian ears.

Back in England, a full-length film documenting Elton's Russian trip was issued under the title *From Russia...With Elton*. "It was one of the most memorable and happy tours I've been on," Elton reflected at the premiere, despite his having received only $1,000 per performance—his lowest wage since his days back at the Troubadour. "The hospitality was tremendous. The only negative experience [were] two or three vodka hangovers. Plus Russians are lousy lays."

Elton was impressed enough with the U.S.S.R. that he promised to write a song specifically for the upcoming 1980 Olympics, which were being hosted in Moscow. Entitled "Tactics," the fragile instrumental would never reach Soviet ears, as the U.K.—along with sixty-five other countries—soon joined together in an international boycott against the Soviet Union, after their unwarranted invasion of Afghanistan.

"I was very disappointed in fact when they invaded Afghanistan," Elton told Johnny Carson soon after on *The Tonight Show*. "I was growing some of my best pot there."

Chapter 36:
Back in the U.S.S.A.

"Loneliness—that's what I worry about for him more than anything else," Elton's mother confided to David Wigg of the *Daily Express* soon after her son's Soviet foray. "I think he's desperate. He's got all the possessions you could wish for, but that doesn't make him happy. He hasn't anyone to share it with, and that's what he needs. He said he'd like to have a family. Unfortunately, his lifestyle doesn't allow him to meet anybody. And he won't allow himself. It's as if he holds back all the time. I feel that he's got everything—but nothing."

While her maternal concerns held more merit than Elton perhaps cared to admit, he had more immediate matters to attend to, such as the American release of *The Thom Bell Sessions '77* that June. The release proved problematic, as *Billboard* insisted on treating the disc as a full-fledged LP, despite the fact that its three tracks combined totaled for a running length of just over eighteen minutes. Had it been properly reported as a maxi-single, it would have easily made Number 1 on the EP charts. As a long-playing "album," however, the disc faltered at an anemic Number 51.

"It was the first time a twelve-inch EP ever got on the album charts," Elton said. "I couldn't believe it. It looked as if I were making a desperate attempt to get back on the charts."

The 45 release of "Mama Can't Buy You Love" fared considerably better. Backed with the contemplative soul-jam "Three Way Love Affair," the single reached Number 9 in the U.S. charts that August. Elton's first Top 10 single in three years, the song also hit Number 1 on *Billboard*'s Adult Contemporary chart. "Mama Can't Buy You Love" would also give the artist a hit on the black charts, earning him a Grammy nomination for Best R&B Vocal Performance, Male. "With 'Philadelphia Freedom,' 'Bennie and the Jets' and then 'Mama Can't Buy You Love', I had three Number One R&B records," Elton said, "which meant a huge deal to a white guy from Pinner."

Elton headed to Grasse in the south of France that same month to begin composing material for a proposed double album. Though the eventual LP, *21 at 33,* would only be released as a single album, many of the other songs written and recorded at the new sessions would make up more than half of his 1981 offering, *The Fox*—as well as providing enough B-sides to see him through 1984.

Five days into the proceedings, he jetted over to Musicland Studio in Munich for a session with producer Pete Bellotte, who had successfully collaborated with disco kingpin Giorgio Moroder on such Donna Summers hits as "Hot Stuff" and "Last Dance." Having known Bellotte since his days with Bluesology, Elton had recently reconnected with the producer backstage at his two-man show at the Theatre Royal Drury Lane in London.

"Would you fancy doing an album?" Bellotte had asked. "It's gonna be called *Thunder in the Night.*"

Elton immediately agreed to the project. "Because I *do* like disco music if it's good," he explained. "I like *any* sort of music, if it's good."

Elton's proviso—much as it had been with Thom Bell two years before—was that Bellotte oversee the entirety of the project. "I said, 'I don't have to play on it,' which is more fun for me," the superstar said. "The keyboard parts are played by two other musicians. I know I'm going to get knocked for the album, but so what?"

Bellotte presented Elton with seven dance tracks—a fascinating amalgam of guitar-based rock and thumping Eurodisco. Keith Forsey, who would garner acclaim for his production work on Billy Idol's records in the coming decade, played drums, while future Miles Davis virtuoso Marcus Miller added a molten bass line to each song. Celebrated Brazilian musician Paulinho da Costa was then brought in at the eleventh hour to add dynamic percussive flourishes to the project.

Elton recorded his lead vocals in one eight-hour session at Musicland. The basic tracks were then flown to Los Angeles for overdubs at Rusk Sound Studios, where Tower of Power saxophonist Lenny Pickett—author of the fearsome solo on "The Bitch is Back"—was recruited for a fiery turn on the session's key track, a trance-inducing cover of Chucky Berry's immortal "Johnny B. Goode." Additional help came from the Doobie Brothers' Patrick Simmons and Michael McDonald, who contributed backing vocals to the luminous title track, and Toto's guitar ace Steve Lukather, who who add stinging solos to such Möbius-strip exercises as "Warm Love in a Cold World" and "Born Bad."

Soon back in Grasse, Elton began composing and recording tracks for his new album in earnest. As with *A Single Man,* he decided to utilize Gary Osborne as a lyricist. More intriguingly, he also turned to his old writing partner, Bernie Taupin. Though their professional reunion was heralded as a major event within the music press, the men themselves remained stoic about the whole affair.

"There was never any feud," Elton insisted. "It's the typical thing you read in the papers—just because he lived in America and I had an album out and he had an album out with different people, the tongues started to wag."

"We just needed a little freedom from each other," Bernie said. "It was never intended to be permanent. What had caused some tension was that [Elton] was in England, and I had moved to America. When Elton wanted to write, I wasn't there to work....Everybody seems to think that we fell out and we weren't going to ever work together again. It wasn't that. We never fell out. I think we just needed to get away from it for a while."

The break not only rejuvenated the team's creative juices, it also gave Bernie the necessary space to secure a new outlook on life—a necessity, given how tumultuous his post-Maxine existence had become. The introspective lyricist had bounced around aimlessly for several years, indulging in several half-hearted affairs—one of which ultimately broke the heart of twenty-two-year-old model Loree Rodkin. Rodkin, in turn, shattered the romantic illusions of the Eagles' Don Henley. When she ended their brief tryst, Henley took it hard, funneling his rage into the biting lyrics of "Hotel California."

"Some of the more derogatory parts of 'Hotel California' are definitely about Loree Rodkin," Henley said. "'Her mind is Tiffany twisted/She got the Mercedes bends/She got a lot of pretty boys that she calls friends'—that's about her, and I wouldn't be crowing if I were Ms. Rodkin."

After writing "Wasted Time" about their failed romance, a venom-drained Henley called Rodkin and begged her to get back together.

"It can't happen," Rodkin said. "I'm involved with someone else."

"Already? *Who?*"

"Let's just say he's a very successful man."

"Goddammit," Henley fumed. "Who the hell *is* it?"

"I'm back with Bernie, Don."

Henley slammed the receiver down.

Taking the conflict to heart only served to accelerate Bernie's already redlining alcoholic tendencies. It was, indeed, a black-cloud period unlike any he had ever experienced before. "I did some heavy, heavy drinking," he said. "So bad, I had to dry out....I became a recluse. I just wanted to forget rock 'n' roll because it made me a drunk, and it made me lose my wife. I felt like a part of my life was missing."

After publishing a coffee table book with photographer Gary Bernstein called *Burning Cold* (Bernie authored melancholy lines to accompanied erotic images of model Kay Sutton York)*,* the lyricist sequestered himself at Horseshoe Bay, Acapulco. Spending several months detoxing both body and soul, he emerged with a renewed sense of self. "I kept a diary [while at Horseshoe Bay]," he said, "and as I wrote it, gradually I could feel my mind unfogging and clearing, and it was beautiful. There's nothing heroic in being a fall-down drunk. It's pathetic, and *I* was pathetic."

Now sober and refreshed, Bernie was ready to tackle new creative challenges once again. The sessions at Superbear Studios would, in fact, mark the first time Elton and Bernie had sustained a working relationship in over three years. Many industry insiders breathed a sigh of relief that the John/Taupin partnership was finally back on the rails. As Billy Joel later related, "Their work has had a profound impact on an entire generation of popular music and musicians. To me, they are the Gilbert & Sullivan of our generation."

Elton invited Bernie and his new wife, fashion model Toni Russo—sister of movie actress Rene Lynn Russo—to join him at his rented house on the Côte d'Azur during the new album's gestation. Bernie appreciated the gesture; from day one of the project, he was one-hundred-percent onboard. "I'll write songs for Elton as long as he breathes and wants me," he swore.

The first song the Brits attempted was the highly autobiographical "Two Rooms at the End of the World." Playing off the *Captain Fantastic* tagline, the track's steely cadences provided a telling look at the Captain and the Kid's symbiotic ties five years down the line. "It's a song saying, 'You can judge us individually, but together this is what we do,'" Bernie said. "Accept it or get out of the way."

Other new compositions the duo concocted included the meticulously sculpted love lament "Tortured," a broiling "Sympathy for the Devil" update entitled "Chasing the Crown," a wistful midtempo piano ballad called "Indian Maiden," and the vital cocaine kiss-off, "White Lady White Powder," which would feature Eagles Glenn Frey, Timothy B. Schmit, and (a forgiving) Don Henley on backing vocals.

"They were all exorcism songs," Bernie said. "They were songs saying, 'Yeah, we've been there, now let's get it back together.'"

For these sessions, Elton composed exclusively on a Yamaha CP-80 electric piano, while a four-track recorder ran in the background to capture his musical ideas. Though he hadn't written in earnest in nearly a year, he found that music still flowed as readily as ever from his calloused fingertips. On just his first day of composing, he came up with six songs, including what would become his new LP's leadoff single, "Little Jeannie." "There are times I want to cry after I've finished composing," Elton admitted soon after writing the song. "Because when I've created a song it becomes almost like my child....You want to hold onto the miracle for as long as possible." Though he was to come up with the most memorable line of that sweetly intimate track—wanting a lover to be his acrobat—Gary Osborne wrote the lion's share of the lyrics. The two also collaborated on "Dear God," the countrified "Can't Get Over Getting Over Losing You," "Chloe," "Take Me Back," "Sweetheart on Parade" (which would soon appear on Judy Collins' album, *Home Again*), "Conquer the Sun," and the aching lullaby, "Steal Away Child."

Pleased with his work on *Victim of Love,* Elton invited twenty-one-year-old guitar ace Steve Lukather to participate in the sessions. "Toto was in the middle of our second album, *Hydra,*" Lukather said years later, "and I asked the guys in my band if they minded I go play hookey and go to do an album with Elton for two weeks. All the guys were very jealous, as *all* of us were, and still are, massive Elton fans. [Elton and his musicians] lived in a house in the mountains away from everything and everyone. We were the next band in after Pink Floyd had cut tracks for *The Wall.* There was magic in that room, but also it kept blowing up, so we laughed through all that as well." As for meeting the iconic pianist in person, Lukather was full of praise. "He welcomed me with open arms, and after a few days of cutting tracks he really warmed up to me and we had a fucking blast waking up and going into the studio to hear Elton's next new song and help arrange and interpret his new music. [And] watching Elton work and write was something else. The man is a genius. I watched him write a song from scratch with lyrics he had never seen. The music flowed from him." The memories would remain some of Lukather's fondest, even in an incredibly successful forty-year career. "We were cutting and overdubbing on at least two tracks a day—Elton let me play whatever I liked and heard on his new music—and then we would hang out at night and drink too much, and Elton told us stories and played for us. It was magic."

Elton would also expand his roster of lyricists this time around to include "2-4-6-8 Motorway" rocker Tom Robinson, whom he'd met the fall before at a photo shoot for the Guinness Book of Pop Singles the day before his heart scare had sent him into the hospital. The first song they created together was "Elton's Song," a sorrowful hymn of unrequited love. "This was the first heartbroken love song I had written really deep from the heart," Robinson later confessed to author Tom Stanton. "I sent off the lyric and went off on tour and came back and heard nothing from Elton. And apparently, he told me later, he had actually looked at it and put it aside because the lyrics didn't conform to any of the suggestions he had made at the time of recording the tune. He came back to it a few months later at the piano and said, 'Oh, let's give it a go anyway', and suddenly said, 'Oh yeah, I rather like that.'"

Reminding the pianist of the film *if...* by Lindsay Anderson, the track held a tremendous amount of meaning for the composer. "'Elton's Song' is so beautiful," he said, "and Tom Robinson's lyric is so beautiful. It was the first gay song that I actually recorded as a homosexual song. Rather than 'All the Girls Love Alice', it was the first boy-on-boy song I wrote—because Tom, of course, is a gay man, and we became great friends."

Interestingly, the track's oddly meta title derived from what may have been a misunderstanding—Robinson had provisionally scrawled "Elton's Song" at the top of the lyrics simply to remind himself that that particular effort was intended for Elton, and not for his own upcoming album. "Rather than choose a title for the song," Robinson said, "[Elton] figured he'd call it ["Elton's Song"]. And he did. Maybe he identified with the sentiment of the lyric. Or maybe he thought I meant that to be the title."

The two sophisticates also collaborated on the evocative "Never Gonna Fall in Love Again," as well as a cosmopolitan serenade to broken expectations entitled "Sartorial Eloquence." (The song would be released in the States in mid-1980 under the more prosaic title, "Don't Ya Wanna Play This Game No More?") "I spent a lot of time thinking about past relationships and put them into songs," Robinson said. "I remember that the line [about being lonely but trying to keep it all under control] was one that Elton particularly liked. It was a kind of similarity in our personalities, the way we felt about breakups and things."

For these final band sessions of the decade, Elton also wrote with Judie Tzuke, a British pop singer signed to his Rocket label who'd recently scored a Top 20 U.K. hit with the love ballad "Stay with Me Till Dawn." "She's got the biggest tits in the world," the pianist said with a jovial laugh. "She's just lovely." For her part, Tzuke was grateful for the guidance Elton provided. "It used to be a real challenge in the '70s to not get saddled with the whole 'pretty girl at the piano' mold that women songwriters were often stuck with, especially if they'd had any real commercial success," she said. "[But] Elton had total faith. He was a godsend that way."

Their combined effort resulted in a lacquered jazz-pop piece called "Give Me the Love." "He asked me if I'd like to write together," Tzuke later recalled, "and I said, 'I really would.' So he sent me a track with some words on [it], and he wanted some of them used, but he gave me freedom to write the rest. I wrote tons of lines, some of which I was sort of quite proud of, and some of which I wasn't really sure of. And I just said to him, 'Use whichever ones you like.' And he did. But he threw away some of the ones I liked. I would have loved to have actually sat down with him and written a song [from scratch], but I don't think he does that very often. But I was very flattered and honored to have written a song with him."

Elton would also compose several instrumentals during these sessions, including the atmospheric "Basque," which—as later recorded by flutist James Galway—would earn the composer a Grammy for Best Instrumental.

Other music-only tracks included the pyrotechnic jam "Earn While You Learn," and the classically stained "Carla/Etude," which Elton wrote in honor of Clive Franks' wife, who had served as makeup artist on his most recent tour. "He played it to us, and it was lovely," Clive later told journalist George Matlock. "I asked him what it was called, and Elton said he was trying to title it in an anagram of our names....Elton is very clever with words, even though he doesn't write lyrics. [But] after ten minutes, he came back into the control room where me and my wife, Carla, were sitting and said, 'I can't get an anagram of your names, so sod you, I'm just calling it ['Carla/Etude']."

Their final week in France, Elton and Bernie worked on a final batch of songs together, including the brass-tinged "Hey Papa Legba," "White Man Danger," the cynical, harmonica-accented "Fools in Fashion" [sic], and a tenderly bittersweet tale of weary Civil War soldiers called "The Retreat."

Both men had to laugh—despite their many trials and tribulations, the rapidity of their songwriting magic was still very much intact. "Don't ever let anybody tell you that if it takes you a long time to write a song it's going to be any better than if you write it in ten minutes," Bernie told journalist Steven P. Wheeler. "Certain people, like Don Henley or Robbie Robertson, are great writers, but they slave over the songs and it takes them three years to make an album because they're meticulous in the sense that they go over and over and over things. I'm the sort of writer to where if it's not working for me in like ten minutes, I know it's going nowhere. My best stuff comes straight out and pours out, and the same with Elton."

Another new John/Taupin composition, "Love So Cold," dealt intriguingly with the sexual politics of aging. Elton spent three hours attempting to record a steel drum solo on the track, all to no avail. Frustrated with his crew's inability to properly mic the island instrument, he whipped off a harmonized piano solo in ten minutes instead. "One of the best piano solos I've ever done," he said. "It's not a jazz solo, it's just a solo melody line which was done off the top of my head out of the frustration of trying to get some steel drums onto the record." Despite the superior piano line, the song would be relegated to B-side status—except in France, where it was released as a single.

Elton and Bernie then completed their efforts for the new sessions—and for the '70s as a whole—with "Bobby Goes Electric," a taut rocker about an expat drug smuggler who recounts the day Bob Dylan traded in his acoustic guitar for an electric one at the Newport Folk Festival in '65.

The song would remain forever unreleased.

The sessions thus completed, Elton oversaw the release of his latest single. "Victim of Love." Backed with the *Single Man* holdover "Strangers," the disc was issued in Britain on September 14. A heady mix of hard beats and unabashedly inventive dance-pop melodicism, "Victim of Love" failed to chart. In America, the single would fare better; though Stateside radio stations were initially loathe to play such a blatantly discofied track, the song would enter heavy rotation once word leaked that the Doobie Brothers were singing backup.

"Typical," Elton laughed.

"Victim of Love" ultimately climbed deep into the *Billboard* charts, giving the Brit his twenty-fourth, and final, Top 40 single of the decade—nine years to the day that his historic WABC radio concert which resulted in *11/17/70*, had taken place. ("Victim of Love" would also chart worldwide, reaching Number 28 in Canada and Number 19 in Italy.)

Elton set vinyl matters temporarily behind him so that he could gear up for his final America tour of the '70s, another two-man outing with Ray Cooper. Dubbed *Back in the U.S.S.A.*, the campaign was a mammoth undertaking—forty-two concerts across seventeen cities, anchored by a ten-night run at L.A.'s Universal Amphitheater, and an eight-night stand at New York's Palladium on 14th Street. The pianist was characteristically enthusiastic about stepping back onto the American stage. "Returning to America has been the most important thing," he said. "I have my enthusiasm for concerts back, and am already thinking about putting a band together next year."

For this tour, Elton had his ever-faithful Steinway painted fire-engine-red, with canary yellow legs. His instrument would prove the sole bit of flash, however. Gone were the wild costumes of the mid-70s. Gone, too, was his recent Cossack look. In their stead were shiny silk suits of pink and gold and silver. With his hair transplant finally sprouting wispy dividends, Elton would step onstage bareheaded for the first time since '76, as vulnerable as he'd ever been. Equally as shocking to American audiences was the fact that the man who had single-handedly made glasses cool was now taking the stage wearing contact lenses. "The big glasses and the weird clothes were a way of hiding my shyness," the pianist admitted. "Since I started wearing contact lenses, I've had to overcome that. I was forced to look people in the face, and you have to find confidence from somewhere to do that."

The bicoastal outing was nearly identical to its European and Russian counterparts, the main alteration being the addition of a rhythmic "Mama Can't Buy You Love," and a classic rock encore medley consisting of "Whole Lotta Shakin' Going On," "I Saw Her Standing There" and "Twist and Shout."

As ever, Ray Cooper proved as much of an attraction as Elton. But the reality was a hard truth the percussionist understood all too well. "My tragedy," he said, "is that I know I'm totally dispensable. Hopefully I give audiences something to laugh at and look at, but I'm only allowed to do what I do because there's such a strong structure around me."

The three-hour shows that Elton and Ray gave were ubiquitously hailed as the apex of the Englishman's stage life. Indeed, the atmosphere from coast-to-coast was intimate and electric as Elton rocked with abandon, a jackknife marionette pounding the keys as relentlessly as he had back in his Bluesology days.

Kicking off with a two-night run at Gammage Auditorium in Tempe, Arizona, the tour soon moved on to Berkley for a three-night run at the city's Community Theatre. In the crowd for the second show, on September 23, sat none other than Davey Johnstone. The guitarist was duly impressed by his once and future boss.

"I loved watching from the audience," he said. "It was a first for me."

Elton and Ray next set up camp at the Universal Amphitheatre for a ten-night stand beginning on September 26.

"It's only taken me fifteen grams of coke and twelve Quaaludes tonight," the pianist cheekily told the sea of faces before him. "*There's* self-confidence for you."

An early highlight of the performance came during an extended "Rocket Man"—Elton crying out a desperate "I'm *burning* out, I'm *burning* out," while the crowd yelled back in chorale counterpoint: "No! No!" Perhaps the most dramatic moment of the evening, however, came halfway through "I Think I'm Gonna Kill Myself," when Elton— suffering from a stomach bug—took a couple woozy steps backward and collapsed unconscious into the arms of a roadie. Ten minutes after being dragged offstage and being made to be sick, he reemerged from the wings to perform the final hour-and-a-half of the show as if nothing had happened.

Several weeks into the tour, the Pete Bellotte-produced album *Victim of Love*—its title having been changed at the last minute from *Thunder in the Night*—was issued. Featuring a stark black-and-white portrait of an aloof-looking Elton in oversized glasses—the image taken by photographer David Bailey in his tiny studio in Primrose

Hill—the album hit the racks on October 13. Elton had high hopes for the disc, as its core tracks—"Warm Love in a Cold World," "Born Bad," "Street Boogie," "Thunder in the Night" and "Spotlight"—were a taut maelstrom of melodic momentum and urgent white gospel vocals which belied an emotional gravity usually not found in the disco landscape. But the timing of the release would prove inauspicious, as only three short months earlier a riot-like disco-record-burning demonstration, known as "The Day Disco Died," had been held at Chicago's Comisky Park. Even so, remixes of the title track and "Johnny B. Goode," would prove popular throughout U.S. dance clubs, with a special promo-only boxed set of extended 12-inch singles being released exclusively to club disc jockeys, who appreciated the exclusionary grooves.

Not unexpectedly, music critics weren't as appreciative as the DJs had been. Indeed, rock's self-appointed tastemakers wasted no time pilloring the superstar. Disco was the natural nemesis of any self-respecting, head-banging malcontent, and the fact that the genre was currently in free-fall only provided additional ammunition. *Rolling Stone*'s Stephen Holden took the lead, summing up the general critical reception to Elton's thrumming valedictorian statement thusly: "Elton John's entry into the rock-disco sweepstakes comes a year too late.…It's Munich pop disco with no climaxes. Only two of the new numbers, the title tune and 'Thunder in the Night', have catchy melodies. Otherwise, the album is empty of ideas." *US* magazine was in vitriolic lockstep. "He should have called it *Victim of Boredom,*" reviewer Martha Hume sniped. "If *Victim of Love* is the best Elton John has to offer these days, he ought to retire." Colin Irwin, writing in *Melody Maker,* similarly opined, "This album can't even be blithely dismissed as a bore. There are moments when it's thoroughly objectionable." Robert Christgau felt much the same: "What's most depressing about this incredibly drab disc is that Elton's flirtation with Eurodisco comes a year too late. Even at his smarmiest, the man always used to be on top of the zeitgeist. C-."

Stalling in the outer reaches of *Billboard*'s Top 40, Elton's seventeenth album of the decade proved more successful globally, reaching Number 28 in Canada, Number 23 in France, Number 20 in Australia and Number 18 in Norway. Though ultimately being certified Gold—and remaining in the U.S. charts for more than two months— *Victim of Love* would prove to be the unquestionable nadir of his commercial fortunes. Elton, however, had no regrets. "I wanted to make a record that people could dance to in Rochdale or somewhere like that without sort of taking the needle off," he said. "I like to go off sometimes and do something a little different. This one was disastrously timed, but I enjoyed doing it."

As the decade drew to a close, Elton's sexuality seemed to again become a major point of focus in the media. "I realize it's not everyone's cup of tea, and I try not to dwell on it too much," he told Alasdair Buchan of the *Daily Mirror.* "I didn't ask to be this way, but it just came out like that…and it's no good hiding it."

Elton found himself flooded by letters from gay people who lived in small towns throughout Europe and America, folks too afraid to reveal their true identities to those around them. The pianist had the utmost respect for those who took the time to write him, people in less artistic walks of life who had no choice but to grapple with their sexuality in private. "I know it was far easier for me to come out than for many others," he said. "They go through a hell of a lot of pain, and I would support anyone who was totally frank, because it's never easy. I've had a lot of letters from people who think they're gay but live in small communities where it would be very hard to say so. I rarely write back to anyone, but I wrote back to every one of those people and said, 'If you ever get down in the dumps, write again.'"

After his final American date on November 11 in Houston, Elton flew to Maui for a brief respite before heading to Australia for the final leg of his global campaign. He arrived in Oz for his *Down Under '79* tour in a wheelchair propelled by John Reid, his injury the result of a pinched nerve in his back suffered while competing in a drunken arm-wrestling contest. Even with this limitation, however, the pianist played two shows at Sydney's Hordern Pavilion with his usual physical abandon.

"A Genius with Guts," the Melbourne *Herald* declared.

Elton's final Australian concert—his one-hundred-and-twenty-fifth of the year—occurred at Perth's Entertainment Center on December 7. Having consumed nearly an entire bottle of Lagavulin before the show, Elton arrived onstage nearly legless. His performance that night was particularly notable for a twenty-five-minute rendition of "Rocket Man," during which he railed against the Ayatollah Khomeini. (Iranian students had seized more than sixty Americans from the U.S. Embassy in Tehran just weeks before, on November 4, while Elton was busy playing what he soon after called "the most satisfying gig of my life," at Constitution Hall in Washington, D.C.)

"To hell with dissidence," he sang passionately. "To hell with hate…"

Giving his final interview of the '70s to *Countdown*'s Molly Meldrum on December 16, Elton admitted that "when

Captain Fantastic came in at Number One, then I wanted the next one to come in at Number One, and it did. But then you tend to want *everything* to be Number One, and you suddenly realize you can't. I *did* become a bit obsessed about being Number One, but I'm certainly not obsessed anymore."

Things grew a bit terse between the singer and the genial Meldrum when the latter showed the Brit a brief video Rod Stewart had shot ten days earlier in an English pool hall. "[Elton] phoned up," Rod noted in the clip, "and he said, 'I've made a disco album,' and I said, 'You're a bit late dear, aren't you?' And I haven't heard from him since."

"He could not understand why you'd done a disco record," Meldrum said to Elton. "Which he said he hated, incidentally, because he felt that you were too late doing that, and he was looking forward to a rock 'n' roll album."

Elton's countenance darkened. "I don't think it's just a disco album, I think there's a lot of rock 'n' roll on it," he said through gritted teeth. "And [Rod] made a very big disco record, which he stole the tune of—from Brazil—and had to settle out of court and pay money. 'Do Ya Think I'm Sexy' was stolen. We went to Rio together to the Carnivàle, and he bought a record in Rio, 'Ole, Ole...' No, that's the wrong cut—which he also stole. Not many people know it, but I have the record, it's by a guy called Jorge Ben. So I'd rather make a not-so-big-selling record and actually give the writers the right amount of money. If Mr. Stewart's gonna have a go at [*Victim of Love*], then why did he steal a tune and try and hush it up?"

Elton's final single of the decade, a 3:47 edit of his propulsive four-on-the-floor rendition of "Johnny B. Goode," was released that same week to overwhelming indifference. The 45 failed to gain a toehold in the charts on either side of the Atlantic—a dismal fate which hadn't befallen an Elton John single since "Rock 'n' Roll Madonna" back in June, 1970.

Billboard helped soften the blow, to a certain moderate degree, by listing the pianist in its December 22 issue—the venerable music magazine's final publication of the decade—as the nineteenth most popular male album artist of the year, and fifth most popular male singles artist. But Elton hardly took much notice. His lonely private life, made bleaker still by the holidays, had him in a particularly black state. After spending Christmas night partying nonstop, his own "Step Into Christmas" blaring incessantly from an antique radio tuned to BBC 1, he attended Watford's game against Luton on Boxing Day looking quite a bit worse for wear.

"I was drinking very heavily, I wasn't particularly very happy," he said. "Graham Taylor said, 'I'm gonna see you for lunch.' And I thought, 'I know what he's gonna say, he's gonna give me a lecture.'"

Elton went to Taylor's house at noon the next day. As they sat together around an ornate dining table, Taylor produced a large bottle of brandy and slammed it down hard.

"*Here* you are, Elton. Fucking drink *this*. It's what you want, isn't it?" Taylor smashed his fist against the table. "For fuck's sake, what's *wrong* with you? Stop *doing* this to yourself, you fool."

"He frightened the fucking life out of me," Elton confessed.

The emotionally bruised pianist was thus painfully sober as he entered EMI Studios at Abbey Road on New Year's Eve to record "Carla/Etude" with the London Symphony Orchestra. Playing under the baton of James Newton

Howard, Elton gave the performance every drop of artistic nuance he possessed.

Pleased with the way the session turned out, he returned to Woodside and reflectively paced through his silent halls.

Alone, seemingly always alone.

Finally, he stopped by his grand piano and sat down. His fingers found an E-major chord, and the first few notes of "Skyline Pigeon" reverberated achingly throughout the empty rooms.

Elton breathed in the melody, letting it flood through the darker recesses of his soul.

Music was his greatest passion.

His strongest addiction.

His saving grace.

"Never give up, there's always hope," he once said. "There's so much more to do. But you have to be true to yourself, because you're creating your own future."

Epilogue:
CENTRAL PARK

(September 13, 1980)

Time has a way of bending the truth.

Memories have been known to lie. Calendars, too.

As often as not, a decade's defining parameters aren't what they may first appear to be. Did the '50s really begin on January 1, 1950—or did they in fact truly blossom on September 2, 1945, the day World War II ended? And were the '60s forged into being on January 1, 1960? Or did their true inception lie three years later, on that bright and windless afternoon when Kennedy visited Dallas?

In much the same manner, the 1970s—*Elton John's '70s*—hadn't ended on December 31, 1979, but rather on a glorious Indian summer day in mid-September, 1980. Inside that gleaming emerald slab deep in the heart of Manhattan known as Central Park, nearly half a million aging hippies amassed for one last communal bacchanal, to hear the soundtrack of their lives blasted back at them through massive stacks of thousand-amp speakers. The open-air concert, a charity event held in partnership with designer Calvin Klein, wasn't merely the anchor gig of a tour which would see Elton spinning ceaselessly around the globe yet again—it would also be the largest single audience the Brit had ever played to before. It was Woodstock for the Me Generation; one last salute to dreams long forgotten and future hopes as yet unwritten.

The historic concert's subtext seemed entirely appropriate, for Elton had somehow managed to survive the emotional and physical consumption of the last ten years relatively unscathed. The performance was therefore both a summation and a new beginning; Central Park was *his* celebration as much as it was anyone else's.

Even better, the new decade had already started out well for Elton. He'd enjoyed his first Number 1 in the French charts with "Les Aveux," a melodic curio recorded that April—based on Tom Robinson's English-language lyrics, "Reach Out to Me"—with French pop icon (and inspiration for the music behind Frank Sinatra's classic "My Way") France Gall. Even more promising, his latest album, *21 at 33*—the cryptic title denoting the fact that it was Elton's twenty-first album (with double albums counting as two releases, and hits compilations and live discs also included) released at the age of thirty-three—had charted at a healthy Number 13 in the U.S., and at Number 12 in the U.K., giving him his highest ranking long-player since 1976's *Blue Moves*. (The disc would prove equally as successful internationally, reaching Number 16 in Sweden, Number 10 in Canada, Number 7 in Australia, Number 6 in Norway, and Number 3 in both France and New Zealand.) Moreover, the LP would spawn a pair of Top 40 hits—"Sartorial Eloquence" and "Little Jeannie"—the latter making it all the way up to the Number 3 spot on the *Billboard* charts, becoming Elton's best-performing American single since "Don't Go Breaking My Heart" back in the heady summer of 1976. ("Little Jeannie" would also provide Elton with his longest residency to date within *Billboard*'s Top 10 singles charts.)

People began arriving days in advance of the Central Park show, roping off valuable turf near the stage as if they were settlers claiming their children's birthrights in some mad Old West scramble.

As the day of the concert dawned, greedy territorialism transmuted into intermutual celebration. Across the Great Lawn, Frisbees soared and joints flamed as fans reminisced about Elton's past triumphs which they'd borne witness to. Backstage, meanwhile, champagne frothed over crystal flutes as John McEnroe rubbed shoulders with Carly Simon, Dudley Moore and Susan Anton.

Elton arrived just past noon, in an unmarked van. He was, as always, the calm eye of a frenetic storm.

"Nice crowd," he said with a laugh. "Who's on, then?"

Others around him weren't quite as calm.

"I've always been absolutely terrified of performing," said Judie Tzuke, who had been chosen as the tour's opening act, "but Central Park was probably the pinnacle of my nerves. When I was on tour with Elton, most of the nights were like twenty-thousand people and thirty-thousand people. But when you're onstage—with the lights and everything—you can only see the first few rows anyway. So it doesn't really make any difference if it's one-thousand or ten-thousand [people], 'cause you can only see the first few rows. Of course, Central Park was in the daytime, so there was no hiding from anything. You could see *everybody*. And so Elton and I ended up backstage drinking hard. I think we cleaned up most of a bottle of whiskey between us. I'm sure he wasn't anywhere near as nervous as me. I think he was just being very kind and sort of keeping me from internally combusting backstage beforehand."

Stepping out before nearly half-a-million people, Tzuke found herself in a near-catatonic state. "I don't remember much about going onstage," she said. "All I know is that we did it in twenty minutes. It was supposed to be a thirty-minute set, but we were so scared that we played everything fast, and just got through it really quickly. I'm very proud of the fact that I played to that many people, even though, unfortunately, nobody knew who I was."

Elton cheered Judie's efforts from the side of the stage, alongside his oldest friend and closes collaborator, Bernie Taupin. When her set was over, the pianist gave his lyricist a warm embrace before stepping onto the sleek, high-tech stage. Dressed in a mirrored cowboy suit, and hidden from view by a massive curtain, Elton took a seat at his nine-foot grand (painted virgin white for this outing) and slowly closed his eyes. He was about to embark upon the biggest challenge of his entire career, with only the vaguest inkling of what lay ahead. So many future classics—"I'm Still Standing," "Blue Eyes," "Empty Garden (Hey Hey Johnny)," "I Want Love," "Sad Songs (Say So Much)," "Circle of Life," "I Guess That's Why They Call it the Blues," "The One," "Something About the Way You Look Tonight," "I Don't Wanna Go On With You Like That," "Believe," "Can You Feel the Love Tonight," "Sacrifice," "Kiss the Bride," "Nikita," and countless others—were mere vapors on the breeze that humid afternoon.

Indeed, Elton could have hardly foreseen that his already storied career would remain vital for decades to come, his consecutive streak of Top 40 hits extending straight through the '80s and well into the '90s, easily besting Elvis Presley's long-standing, and seemingly impenetrable, record of having scored a Top 40 hit twenty-three years in a row. Ultimately, the pianist would place a staggering seventy-one singles in the *Billboard* Hot 100 singles chart.

These feats would be just a couple of the many which Elton would achieve throughout the coming years. Inducted into the Rock 'n' Roll Hall of Fame—as well as the Songwriters Hall of Fame—he would not only help revive the career of his idol, Leon Russell, he'd also successfully diversify his musical palette, composing multiple long-running Broadway musicals which would earn him a Tony (for *Aida*), a Disney Legend Award (for *The Lion King*), and an Olivier (for *Billy Elliot*). His mantle would also boast an Oscar, a handful of Grammys, and multiple Golden Globes. He would be selected for a Kennedy Center Honor, a *Billboard* Magazine Legend of Live Award, twelve Ivor Novello statuettes, a Rockefeller Foundations Lifetime Achievement Award, a Kennedy Center Honor, a Grammy Legend Award, and five Brits Awards. He would also receive a special Brits Icon honor for his "lasting impact on British culture," presented to him by longtime friend and musical rival, Rod Stewart.

The RIAA would name Elton one of the "Artists of the Century," alongside Elvis Presley, the Beatles, Barbara Streisand, and the Eagles. He'd receive an honorary doctorate from the Royal Academy of Music, and would become a Fellow of the British Academy of Songwriters and Composers, even as *Billboard* ranked him as the most successful solo male artist of all-time on their "Hot 100 All-Time Artists" list. Other accolades Elton would garner included the Society of Singers' Lifetime Achievement Award, and the PRS for Music Limited Heritage Award. The French government would bestow one of their greatest honors upon him, naming the pianist an Officer of Arts and Letters, while the King of Sweden would present him with the prestigious Polar Music Prize, along with cellist/conductor Mstislav Rostropovich.

Perhaps most meaningfully, Queen Elizabeth II would name Elton a Commander of the Order of the British Empire (CBE) for "services to music and charitable services."

Sir Elton's final sales tallies would prove every bit as remarkable as his career-spanning awards, including as they did more than thirty-eight Gold albums, twenty-seven Platinum LPs, twelve Multiplatinum discs, and a staggering *fifty-eight* Top 40 hits, made up of twenty-seven Top 10 singles, four Number 2s, and nine Number 1s. He would also hold the record for the most Adult Contemporary hits, besting the likes of Elvis Presley, Neil Diamond and Barbara Streisand, with a staggering *seventy-two* separate hits—as well as having the most Top 10s *and* the most Number 1s.

300 million records and counting, Elton would become the third most successful artist in the history of recorded music, behind only Elvis and the Beatles. Unlike his progenitors, however, the pianist's creative impulses would never wane, with some of the highest-charting and best-reviewed albums of his unparalleled career—including 1983's *Too Low For Zero,* 1995's *Made in England,* 2006's *The Captain and the Kid,* 2012's *Good Morning to the Night* (a U.K. Number 1 collaboration with Australian electronica duo Pnau), and 2016's sterling, T-Bone Burnett-produced effort, *Wonderful Crazy Night*—still well ahead of him.

Gracefully growing into an elder musical statesman—a true and literal Knight of the Realm—Elton would become nearly as well-known for his tireless humanitarian efforts as he was for his timeless melodies. Founding the hugely influential Elton John AIDS Foundation in 1992, the Brit would help raise hundreds of millions of dollars for patient care services and prevention education—for a disease which was as yet unnamed on that celebratory September afternoon in 1980.

The pianist would also give voice to global grief at Princess Diana's funeral with "Candle in the Wind 1997 (Goodbye England's Rose)," a reworking of his 1973 classic. The first single to ever be certified Diamond in the United States by the RIAA, "Candle in the Wind 1997" would quickly become the biggest-selling release since U.S.

and U.K. singles charts began keeping tally back in the 1950s, shifting over 33 million copies worldwide in a matter of days while also raising over £55 million for the Diana, Princess of Wales Memorial Fund.

"Right," Elton said, nodding at his band as the anticipatory screams on the other side of the stage curtain grew to a fevered pitch.

Original sidemen Nigel Olsson and Dee Murray—finally back in the fold after years in the musical wilderness—nodded back. As did keyboardist James Newton Howard and guitarists Tim Renwick and Richie Zito. A hometown boy, Zito was particularly enthused about the Central Park gig. "Playing in front of 500,000 people felt like the culmination of my guitar-playing career," he said. "It was absolutely amazing. Working with Elton was truly the highlight of my career. What an incredible experience, and an honor."

At exactly 3:00, the curtains pulled back as a massive barrage of red, white and blue balloons were released into the hazy New York sky. The magisterial strains of "Funeral For a Friend" blasted forth at maximum volume as Elton calmly surveyed the endless sea of humanity before him. A decade after playing his first American show to two-hundred-and-fifty people in a smoky West Hollywood club, he had to smile as his vision swept over the untold legion of admirers that spread out as far as the eye could see.

Twirling a drumstick in one gloved hand, Nigel anxiously awaited his cue. "Central Park was the most nervous I was of any show in my life," he later confessed. "It was so overwhelming, really….It was like an ocean of people, of all races and denominations….Everybody was on the same wavelength."

Elton morphed into a human jukebox that afternoon, running through a twenty-two-song set which included a generous helping of classics from every phase of his career, from "Your Song" to "Tiny Dancer" to "Goodbye Yellow Brick Road." He also provided acidic readings of lesser-known gems such as "All the Girls Love Alice" and "Have Mercy on the Criminal," as well as a gorgeously anthemic reading of "Philadelphia Freedom."

"Elton played ravingly," Judie Tzuke said of the frisson-soaked show, "as he always does."

"There was a certain magic," Nigel agreed. "It was like never having been away."

Halfway through the afternoon, Elton told the enthralled crowd, "We're gonna do a song written by a friend of mine, who I haven't seen for a long time. He only lives just over the road, and he hasn't made a record for ages, but he's doing one at the moment."

The friend was John Lennon, and the record was to become *Double Fantasy*.

Lennon was listening intently, his Dakota windows thrown wide as Elton's moving rendition of "Imagine" swept past the oak trees and floated out into the deep summer gloaming.

"John Lennon," Elton said with an appreciative nod as the song ended to a tsunami of fanatical screams.

Beyond its import as a cultural touchstone, the Central Park show was definitive proof that Elton's self-imposed exile was well and truly over. His experimental flirtations with Philly soul and Eurodisco behind him, he was free to fire off one perfect pop gem after another into the jagged Manhattan skyline: "Harmony," "Ego," "Sorry Seems to Be the Hardest Word," "Little Jeannie," "Rocket Man"—each one better received than the last.

"[The concert] was a welcome gift from the reigning King of pop-rock," journalist Roy Trakin noted in his *Musician* review days later. "[Elton] mesmerized what seemed to be an entire city with his music, which long ago became our songs."

While the musical highlight of the day was undoubtedly a bravura ten-minute rendition of "Bennie and the Jets"—which featured an inventively syncopated boogie-woogie piano solo which Elton would more fully explore with each successive tour throughout the coming decade—the key moment actually came during "Someone Saved My Life Tonight," when a dark-haired fan darted across the stage to hug Elton as he pounded away on his piano.

After a quick embrace, she turned to run offstage before a burly bodyguard could dispatch her.

But Elton had other plans.

Taking her by the arm, he guided her to sit beside him as the song surged toward its emotional climax.

"I made it!" she told him ecstatically.

The pianist nodded—they'd *both* made it.

Elton was reenergized. Back on top of his game and looking boldly toward the future.

The bitch was back.

He'd never left at all.

∞

AFTERWORD

Elton John has influenced me in every way. Ray Charles was
a direct influence, and Little Richard, Fats Waller, people
like that—stride piano players. And in the '70s, Elton was
inescapable. He was everywhere. I had a transistor radio and
I used to play along with whatever played on the radio. I dug
the soulful artists—Otis Redding, Sam Cooke, James Brown,
all those things—and Elton really tapped into that. He tapped
into the gospel thing, into the same things that Leon Russell
tapped into. And of course, pop music, too. It was really
amazing. Elton incorporated all these different elements and
genres of music and made them uniquely his own. And he's
done that for many years. He's really created his own thing,
with Bernie Taupin, especially. This really unique
combination of pop music and poetic conceptual ideas and
rock 'n' roll and gospel and roots music of all kinds. He's so
soulful. Elton's a really soulful dude.

And when I was a kid, Elton John was also around in my
life in a different way. My mom had a mutual friend, and
Elton and Rod Stewart lived next door to each other on
Doheny Drive in Los Angeles. It was a regular party. When
Elton was in town, it was a bigger party. And when he
wasn't in town, it was still a party. Same thing with Rod
Stewart. It was like a totally crazy party at that time in the
'70s. There were a lot of drugs, a lot of everything. And once
that ended in the early '80s—maybe even 1980—it was a
totally different scene, and I never connected with that.

In the early 2000s I started covering "Take Me to the
Pilot" in my live set, because I thought it was such a fun
song. And it really captured this particular facet, this

connection of gospel chords, R&B, soul music, and really interesting lyrics. Even to this day I don't know that I fully understand that song. There's a lot of Bernie Taupin songs that I don't really understand, but that's all right. Sometimes you don't need to understand something to love it. So "Pilot" is one of my favorites. And "Burn Down the Mission," "Border Song"—there's a lot of good ones. I love the tone of his music. It's funny, there's a whole fan base of Elton's that are like Deadheads, they go to every show. And there are all these bootlegs, like the night he opened for Leon Russell back in '70. I was given these two bootlegs of Elton's, one from the show before *11/17/70*. It's very cool. I even have a recording of my dad [Jim Croce] playing "Your Song" on guitar in the kitchen, back in 1970. It's really sweet.

I was having dinner one time with a great jazz musician, and we had this really interesting conversation about musicianship. The idea that he had, which I feel is absolutely true, is that there are certain players who are otherworldly, like Oscar Peterson and Vladimir Horowitz—they're playing at such a high conceptual level. John Coltrane, Thelonius Monk. These guys are playing at a kind of level that is so unique and special and rare. But when people play to their fullest potential, regardless of what natural gifts they have, when they pursue music with all their heart, it sometimes lifts them far above anything that should be there. To me, Bob Dylan is in that category. And John Lennon. These are people that are not musical geniuses on one level—they were good players, but there was nothing genius in their playing, it wasn't at the same level as an Art Tatum or something like that. But when they played to their full potential, it changed the world, and it changed the way people felt about themselves and about other people. And Elton John is like that. He's a really gifted musician, he's a really gifted player, and when you see footage of him playing in the '70s, or hear live recordings of him playing in the '70s—and playing to his full potential—you're just like, 'Wow, he is playing as well as he can play!' And when you hear that, it's life-changing. It's not because he's playing a million notes, or because he's deconstructing a song in a way that no one's ever done before. It's because he's playing his heart out. And that is just completely magic.

So I've loved Elton's music my whole life. And still to this day, when my wife and I are driving into the sunset, we have this ritual—especially on a long drive, if we're in the desert or the country, it doesn't matter where we are—if we're driving and the sun is setting, we have this ritual of playing an Elton John song. And I don't know why, but every single time, it's magic. I've got three different songs of Elton's stuck in my head now. "Rocket Man," for one. That's one of my favorite Elton hits ever. And if the sun's going down and you're listening to "Rocket Man," it's an amazing thing. And if you're on the West Coast as you're driving through the desert to the beach, and you see that green flash from the sun refracting through the atmosphere, it's an awesome kind of moment. I'm telling you—try it out sometime and see what you think.

A.J. Croce, June, 2016

ACKNOWLEDGEMENTS

Elton John's story would have been impossible to properly tell without the kind assistance of Gus Dudgeon, producer extraordinaire. Gus was always unfailingly witty and forthcoming during our extensive discussions together, and for that I'm eternally grateful. Thank you also to his wonderful wife Sheila, for her generosity of spirit. They are both missed.

I am further indebted to Nigel Olsson and Davey Johnstone, both of whom graciously shared their insights with me at an Elton John Expo in Atlanta, Georgia; thank you also to Clive Franks, who took the time to let me interview him before an Elton John concert in Phoenix, Arizona.

My sincere thanks also extend to the many others who were kind enough to open their memory banks to me for this years-long project. They include Sir Tim Rice, Spencer Davis, Rick Wakeman, Paul Buckmaster, Caleb Quaye, Steve Lukather, May Pang, Eric Van Lustbader, José Feliciano, Robert Lamm, Fred Mandel, Linda Lewis, Stuart Epps, Ian Anderson, Dee Murray, David Larkham, Russ Regan, Kenny Passarelli, Sherlie Matthews, Clydie King, Richie Zito, Tim Renwick, Evel Knievel, Jean-Luc Ponty, Ray Williams, Uri Geller, B.J. Cole, Gene Page, Chris Charlesworth, Roger Pope, Sue Pope, Andrea Grasso, Gavin Sutherland, Angela Bowie, Ian Beck, David Nutter, Ross Wilson, Phil Ramone, Liberty DeVitto, James Fortune, Martyn Ford, Maldwyn Pope, Leon Russell, Judie Tzuke, Pete Gavin-Rowney, Helen Piena, John Carsello, Stevie Lange, Leo Lyons, Valerie Tucker, Linda Hannon (née Woodrow), Sue Ayton, Norm Winter, Steve Holley, Alzi Clanton, Madeline Bell, Ross 'Fergie' Ferguson, Jon Scott, Joe Boyd, Guy Babylon, Simon Nicol, Dave Pegg, Bob Birch, Michele Birch, Bill Cameron, John Baldry, Van Dyke Parks, Gerry Bremner, Duncan Faure, Barry Morgan, Bob Sirott, Barbara Moore, Jerry Hey, Bill Reichenbach, Alvin Taylor, A.J.

Croce, Michael Chapman, Paul Linehan, Rick Kemp, Richard Barnes, Harry Casey, Nancy Lee Andrews, David Dills, Dave Mattacks, Emma Snowdon-Jones, John "Fee" Waybill, Brenda Russell, The Overtures' Steve Phypers and Den Pugsley, Charlie Morgan, Jon Joyce, John Rowlands, Geoffrey Ellis, Bill Martin and Cidny Bullens—who performed and recorded as Cindy Bullens in the '70s. I also wish to thank a certain key insider who has asked to remain anonymous ("Deep Throat II, if you like…"), as well as the amazing Mr. Robert Hilburn, a musical scribe of Gandalf-like stature, for his kind words of encouragement.

To live a life as kaleidoscopic as Elton's is, undoubtedly, to live inside an alien funhouse. Fortuitously, few members of that rarest of fraternities, the über-famous, have ever managed (or dared) to provide such consistently penetrating, honest and self-aware insight as Britain's favorite son. Thus I've relied to a great extent on the many contemporaneous interviews which Elton—as well as Bernie, and others within their small circle of intimates—gave during the '70s. In real time, as it were, when insights were at their most agenda-free and memories were at their sharpest.

Further detail was gleaned through multiple online resources, including *eltonography.com, eltondaily.com, eltonjohnworld.com* and *eltonjohn.com*—the latter Elton's official website and a tremendous source of up-to-the-minute news and tour-date information. I also wish to thank Kevin Bell, editor/owner of *East End Lights* (*eastendlights.com*), a trailblazing fanzine that has been holding the Elton flag high since the early '90s, for allowing me full access to the *EEL* archives.

Allow me to extend a grateful nod of the cap to the biographers who have come before me, chief amongst them Philip Norman, David Buckley, Mark Bego, Keith Hayward and Elizabeth Rosenthal. I humbly thank each and every one of them for their efforts, often undertaken not for monetary gain—for compensation in this particular realm is negligible, if it exists at all—but rather out of a shared passion to celebrate the music which helped lend meaning and depth to so many of our lives.

A heartfelt kiss on the head to Cooper, the best Golden Retriever in three counties, for loyally keeping my feet warm during endless hours of research and rewrites; let it be known that he never once complained, not even after sitting through "Billy Bones and the White Bird" for the six-hundredth time. *Muchas gracias* to Jeff Singer, the only person I know who can see the philosophical value in walking endlessly around Greenbelt Lake while discussing the merits of "Sick City" vs. "Cold Highway." Wheat-wheat, Jeff. And finally, a very special thank you to David Provini, who kept me on the straight and narrow throughout the arduous and seemingly never-ending journey I found myself on during the writing of this book. Without him, this book wouldn't be what it finally became.

A portion of the proceeds from this book will go to the Elton John AIDS Foundation. EJAF is an amazing organization, one which I highly recommend you investigate and support, if you're so inclined. They do important work.

Finally, please feel free to contact me directly at: DavidJohn2007@gmail.com if you have noticed any inconsistencies or incorrect information within the text of this book, or if you played a part in Elton's journey through the '70s and would like to add your voice to the choir, as it were. I intend for this book to be a 'living document', as it were, periodically updated and expanded as new information, and new interviews, come available to me, so future generations may fully appreciate the rich musical and cultural legacy which Sir Elton Hercules John has left us all. Thank you.

David John DeCouto

Discography

1970-1979

Singles

	U.S.	U.K.
Border Song (3:20)/Bad Side of the Moon (3:11) DJM DJS 217 (U.K.), Congress C6022 (U.S.), March, 1970	92	--
Rock 'n' Roll Madonna (4:15)/Grey Seal (4:00) DJM DJ S222 (U.K.), June, 1970	--	--
From Denver to L.A. (2:21)/Warm Summer Rain [The Barbara Moore Singers](2:18) Viking VIK 1010 (U.S.), July, 1970	--	--
Your Song (3:57)/Take Me to the Pilot (3:47) DJM DJS 233 (U.K.), UNI 55265 (U.S.) October, 1970	8	7
Friends (2:22)/Honey Roll (2:57) DJM DJS 244 (U.K.), UNI 55227 (U.S.), April, 1971	34	--
Levon (5:22)/Goodbye (1:45) UNI 55314 (U.S.), November, 1971	24	--
Tiny Dancer (3:38)/Razor Face (4:44) UNI 55318 (U.S.), February, 1972	41	--
Rocket Man (4:35)/Susie (Dramas) (3:25) DJM DJX 501 (U.K.), UNI 55328, April, 1972	6	2
Honky Cat (5:12)/Slave (4:22) DJM DJS 269 (U.K.), UNI 55343 (U.S.), July, 1972	8	31
Crocodile Rock (3:56)/Elderberry Wine (3:34) DJM DJS 271 (U.K.), MCA 40000 (U.S.), November, 1972	1	5
Daniel (3:52)/Skyline Pigeon (3:45) DJM DJS 275, March, 1973	2	4
Saturday Night's Alright (For Fighting) (4:55)/Jack Rabbit (1:50)/ Whenever You're Ready (We'll Go Steady Again) (2:50) DJM DJX 502 (U.K.), MCA 40105, June, 1973	12	7
Goodbye Yellow Brick Road (3:13)/Screw You (aka Young Man's Blues) (4:41) DJM DJS 285 (U.K.), MCA 40148, September, 1973	2	6
Step Into Christmas (4:30)/ Ho! Ho! Ho! (Who'd Be a Turkey at Christmas?) (4:04) DJM DJS 290 (U.K.), November, 1973	--	24
Candle in the Wind (3:50)/Bennie and the Jets (5:10) DJM DJS 297 (U.K.), February, 1974	--	11
Bennie and the Jets (5:10)/Harmony (2:46) MCA 40198 (U.S.), February, 1974	1	--
Don't Let the Sun Go Down On Me (5:33)/Sick City (5:22) DJM DJS 302 (U.K.), MCA 40259 (U.S.), May, 1974	2	16
The Bitch is Back (3:40)/Cold Highway (3:20) DJM DJS 322 (U.K.), MCA 40297 (U.S.), September, 1974	4	15

Lucy in the Sky with Diamonds (5:58)/One Day at a Time (3:47) | 1 | 10
DJM DJS 340 (U.K.), MCA 40344 (U.S.), November, 1974

Philadelphia Freedom (5:38)/I Saw Her Standing There (3:53) | 1 | 12
DJM DJS 354 (U.K.), MCA 40364 (U.S.), February, 1975

Someone Saved My Life Tonight (6:45)/House of Cards (3:09) | 4 | 22
DJM DJS 385 (U.K.), MCA 40421 (U.S.), June, 1975

Island Girl (3:46)/Sugar on the Floor (4:31) | 1 | 14
DJM DJS 610 (U.K.), MCA 40461 (U.S.), September, 1975

Grow Some Funk of Your Own (4:45)/I Feel Like a Bullet
    (In the Gun of Robert Ford) (5:30) | 14 | --
DJM DJS 629 (U.K.), MCA 40505 (U.S.), January, 1976

Pinball Wizard (5:14)/Harmony (2:46) | -- | 1
DJM DJS 652 (U.K.), March, 1976

Don't Go Breaking My Heart (4:23)/Snow Queen (5:54) | 1 | 1
Rocket ROKN 512 (U.K.), MCA PIG40585 (U.S.), June, 1976

Sorry Seems to Be the Hardest Word (3:48)/Shoulder Holster (5:05) | 6 | 11
Rocket ROKN 517 (U.K.), MCA 40645, October, 1976

Crazy Water (5:40)/Chameleon (5:25) | -- | 27
Rocket ROKN 521 (U.K.), February, 1977

The Goaldiggers Song (2:48)/Jimmy, Brian, Elton, Eric [Jimmy Hall, | -- | --
    Brian Moore, Elton John and Eric Morecambe] (6:47)
Rocket GOALD 1 (U.K.), April, 1977

Bite Your Lip (Get Up and Dance) (3:38)/Chicago [Kiki Dee](4:18) | 28 | 28
Rocket ROKN 526 (U.K.), June, 1977

Ego (3:57)/Flintstone Boy (4:07) | 34 | 34
Rocket ROKN 538 (U.K.), MCA 40892 (U.S.), March, 1978

Part-Time Love (3:12)/I Cry at Night (3:10) | 22 | 15
Rocket XPRESS 1 (U.K.), MCA 40973 (U.S.), October, 1978

Song for Guy (5:01)/Lovesick (3:55) | 110 | 4
Rocket XPRESS 5 (U.K.), MCA 40993 (U.S.), November, 1978

Are You Ready for Love (Part I) (5:05)/Are You | -- | 42
    Ready for Love (Part II) (3:26)
Rocket XPRESS 13 (U.K.), April, 1979

Mama Can't Buy You Love (4:03)/Strangers (4:40) | 9 | --
Rocket XPRESS 20 (U.K.), MCA 41042 (U.S.), June, 1979

Victim of Love (3:18)/Strangers (4:40) | 31 | --
Rocket XPRESS 21 (U.K.), MCA 41126 (U.S.), September, 1979

Johnny B. Goode (3:12)/Thunder in the Night (4:40) | -- | --
Rocket XPRESS 24 (U.K.), MCA 41159 (U.S.), December, 1979

Studio Albums

	U.S.	U.K.

Elton John

4   5

DJM DJLPS406 (U.K.), April 10, 1970/UNI 73090 (U.S.), May 22, 1970
Your Song (4:00)/I Need You to Turn To (2:30)/Take Me to the
Pilot (3:48)/No Shoestrings on Louise (3:30)/First Episode at
Hienton (4:52)/Sixty Years On (4:33)/Border Song (3:19)/
The Greatest Discovery (4:11)/The Cage (3:28)/The King Must
Die (5:09)

ADDITIONAL CHART POSITIONS: AUSTRALIA 2, CANADA 4, NETHERLANDS 2, JAPAN 40

Tumbleweed Connection

5   2

DJM DJLPS410 (U.K.), UNI 73096 (U.S.), October, 1970
Ballad of a Well-Known Gun (4:59)/Come Down in Time (3:24)/
Country Comfort (5:07)/Son of Your Father (3:46)/My Father's
Gun (6:19)/Where to Now, St. Peter? (4:12)/Love Song (3:39)/
Amoreena (5:02)/Talking Old Soldiers (4:02)/Burn Down the
Mission (6:20)

ADDITIONAL CHART POSITIONS: AUSTRALIA 4, CANADA 4, NETHERLANDS 4, JAPAN 30, SPAIN 7

Madman Across the Water

8   41

DJM DJLPS414 (U.K.), UNI 93120 (U.S.), November, 1971
Tiny Dancer (6:12)/Levon (5:37)/Razor Face (4:46)/Madman Across
The Water (5:22)/Indian Sunset (6:45)/Holiday Inn (4:22)/Rotten
Peaches (5:14)/All the Nasties (5:08)/Goodbye (1:48)

ADDITIONAL CHART POSITIONS: AUSTRALIA 8, CANADA 9, ITALY 14, JAPAN 13, SPAIN 11

Honky Chateau

1   2

DJM DJLPH423 (U.K.), UNI 93135 (U.S.), May, 1972
Honky Cat (5:12)/Mellow (5:30)/I Think I'm Going to Kill
Myself (3:32)/Susie (Dramas) (3:24)/Rocket Man (I Think It's
Going to Be a Long, Long Time) (4:40)/Salvation (3:26)/Slave (4:20)/
Amy (4:02)/Mona Lisas and Mad Hatters (5:00)/Hercules (5:20)

ADDITIONAL CHART POSITIONS: AUSTRALIA 4, CANADA 3, NETHERLANDS 9, ITALY 5, JAPAN 21, NORWAY 8,
WEST GERMANY 43, SPAIN 1

Don't Shoot Me I'm Only the Piano Player

1   1

DJM DJLPH427 (U.K.), MCA 2100 (U.S.), January, 1973
Daniel (3:52)/Teacher I Need You (4:08)/Elderberry Wine (3:34)/
Blues for Baby and Me (5:38)/Midnight Creeper (3:53)/Have Mercy
on the Criminal (5:55)/I'm Gonna Be A Teenage Idol (3:55)/
Texan Love Song (3:33)/Crocodile Rock (3:56)/High Flying Bird (3:56)

ADDITIONAL CHART POSITIONS: AUSTRALIA 1, CANADA 1, CANADA 1, NETHERLANDS 2, FINLAND 2, ITALY 1,
WEST GERMANY 16, JAPAN 4, NORWAY 1, SPAIN 1

Goodbye Yellow Brick Road

1   1

DJM DJLPH10012 (U.K.), MCA 210003 (U.S.), October, 1973
Funeral For a Friend/Love Lies Bleeding (11:05)/Candle in
the Wind (3:41)/Bennie and the Jets (5:10)/Goodbye Yellow Brick
Road (3:13)/This Song Has No Title (2:18)/Grey Seal (4:03)/
Jamaica Jerk-Off (3:36)/I've Seen That Movie Too (5:59)/Sweet
Painted Lady (3:52)/The Ballad of Danny Bailey (1909-34) (4:24)/
Dirty Little Girl (5:03)/All the Girls Love Alice (5:13)/Your Sister
Can't Twist (But She Can Rock 'n' Roll) (2:41)/Saturday Night's
Alright (For Fighting) (4:50)/Roy Rogers (4:10)/Social Disease (3:45)/
Harmony (2:49)

ADDITIONAL CHART POSITIONS: AUSTRALIA 1, CANADA 1, DENMARK 4, FINLAND 26, ITALY 5, JAPAN 22,
NORWAY 5, WEST GERMANY 41, SPAIN 8, SWEDEN 7

Caribou

1   1

DJM DJLPH439 (U.K.), MCA 2116 (U.S.), June, 1974
The Bitch is Back (3:42)/Pinky (3:53)/Grimsby (3:47)/Dixie
Lily (2:48)/Solar Prestige a Gammon (2:50)/You're So Static (4:49)/
I've Seen the Saucers (4:45)/Stinker (5:16)/Don't Let the Sun Go
Down on Me (5:33)/Ticking (7:34)

ADDITIONAL CHART POSITIONS: AUSTRALIA 1, CANADA 1, DENMARK 1, FINLAND 21, ITALY 8, JAPAN 20,
NEW ZEALAND 20, NORWAY 6, SPAIN 4, WEST GERMANY 33, SWEDEN 3, YUGOSLAVIA 5

Captain Fantastic and the Brown Dirt Cowboy

1   2

DJM DJLPX1 (U.K.), MCA 2142 (U.S.), May, 1975
Captain Fantastic and the Brown Dirt Cowboy (5:45)/Tower of
Babel (4:28)/Bitter Fingers (4:32)/Tell Me When the Whistle
Blows (4:20)/Someone Saved My Life Tonight (6:45)/(Gotta Get A)
Meal Ticket (4:00)/Better Off Dead (2:35)/Writing (3:38)/We All Fall
in Love Sometimes (4:15)/Curtains (6:12)

ADDITIONAL CHART POSITIONS: AUSTRALIA 1, AUSTRIA 7, CANADA 1, FINLAND 10, FRANCE 1, ITALY 12,
JAPAN 20, WEST GERMANY 22, NEW ZEALAND 1, NORWAY 2, SPAIN 3

Rock of the Westies

1   5

DJM DJLPH464 (U.K.), MCA 2163 (U.S.), October, 1975
Medley (Yell Help/Wednesday Night/Ugly)(6:30)/Dan Dare (Pilot
of the Future)(3:25)/Island Girl (2:45)/Grow Some Funk of Your
Own (4:45)/I Feel Like a Bullet (In the Gun of Robert Ford)(5:30)/
Street Kids (6:30)/Hard Luck Story (5:05)/Feed Me (4:00)/Billy
Bones and the White Bird (4:25)

ADDITIONAL CHART POSITIONS: AUSTRALIA 4, CANADA 1, FINLAND 25, FRANCE 5, ITALY 16, JAPAN 47,
WEST GERMANY 33, NEW ZEALAND 4, NORWAY 6, SPAIN 8, SWEDEN 6

Blue Moves

3   3

Rocket ROSP1 (U.K.), MCA/Rocket 211004 (U.S.), October, 1976
Your Starter For… (1:25)/Tonight (8:02)/One Horse Town (5:47)/
Chameleon (5:27)/Boogie Pilgrim (6:03)/Cage the Songbird (3:28)/
Crazy Water (5:42)/Shoulder Holster (4:20)/Sorry Seems to Be the Hardest
Word (3:43)/Out of the Blue (6:10)/Between Seventeen and Twenty (5:10)/
The Wide-Eyed and Laughing (3:20)/Someone's Final Song (4:00)/Where's
the Shoorah (4:10)/If There's a God in Heaven (What's He Waiting For?)(4:20)/
Idol (4:10)/Theme From a Non-Existent TV Series (1:20)/Bite Your Lip (Get Up and Dance!)(6:37)

ADDITIONAL CHART POSITIONS: AUSTRALIA 8, CANADA 4, NETHERLANDS 7, FINLAND 22, FRANCE 6,
WEST GERMANY 39, ITALY 9, JAPAN 53, NEW ZEALAND 7, NORWAY 5, SPAIN 10, SWEDEN 12

A Single Man

Rocket TRAIN1 (U.K.), MCA 3065 (U.S.), October, 1978
Shine on Through (3:40)/Return to Paradise (4:12)/I Don't
Care (4:23)/Big Dipper (4:04)/It Ain't Gonna Be Easy (8:23)/
Part-Time Love (3:12)/Georgia (4:47)/Shooting Star (2:43)/
Madness (6:07)/Reverie (0:52)/Song for Guy (6:34)

ADDITIONAL CHART POSITIONS: AUSTRALIA 8, CANADA 12, NETHERLANDS, FRANCE 2, ITALY 13,
JAPAN 74, NEW ZEALAND 5, NORWAY 4, SPAIN 12, SWEDEN 26, WEST GERMANY 17

Victim of Love

35   41

Rocket HSPD125 (U.K.), MCA 5104 (U.S.), October, 1979
Johnny B. Goode (8:06)/Warm Love in a Cold World (3:22)/
Born Bad (6:20)/Thunder in the Night (4:40)/Spotlight (4:22)/
Street Boogie (3:53)/Victim of Love (5:02)

ADDITIONAL CHART POSITIONS: AUSTRALIA 20, CANADA 28, NEW ZEALAND 44, NORWAY 18

Soundtrack Albums

Friends (Original Soundtrack Recording)

36   –

Paramount SPFL269 (U.K.), Paramount PAS6004 (U.S.), May, 1971
Friends (2:20)/Honey Roll (3:00)/Variations on Friends (1:45)/
Theme (First Kiss) Seasons (3:52)/Variations on Michelle's Song (2:44)/
Can I Put You On (5:52)/Michelle's Song (4:16)/I Meant to Do My
Work Today (A Day in the Country) (1:33)/Four Moods (10:56)/
Seasons (Reprise) (1:33)

ADDITIONAL CHART POSITIONS: N/A

Live Albums

11/17/70 (17/11/17)

11   20

DJM DJLPS414 (U.K.), UNI 93105 (U.S.), April, 1971
Take Me to the Pilot (6:43)/Honky Tonk Woman (4:09)/Sixty Years
On (8:05)/Can I Put You On (6:38)/Bade Side of the Moon (4:30)/
Burn Down the Mission (includes My Baby Left Me and
Get Back) (18:20)

ADDITIONAL CHART POSITIONS: CANADA 20

Here and There

4   7

DJM DJLPH473 (U.K.), MCA 2197 (U.S.), April, 1976
Skyline Pigeon (4:44)/Border Song (3:23)/Honky Cat (7:32)/Love
Song (5:41)/Crocodile Rock (4:04)/Funeral For a Friend/Love Lies
Bleeding (11:47)/Rocket Man (I Think It's Going to Be a Long,
Long Time)(4:48)/Take Me to the Pilot (5:55)

ADDITIONAL CHART POSITIONS: N/A

Compilation Albums

Greatest Hits

MCA 2128 (U.S.), November, 1974
Your Song (4:00)/Daniel (3:52)/Honky Cat (5:12)/Goodbye Yellow
Brick Road (3:13)/Saturday Night's Alright (For Fighting)(4:55)/
Rocket Man (I Think It's Going to Be a Long, Long Time)(4:40)/
Bennie and the Jets (5:10)/Don't Let the Sun Go Down on Me (5:33)/
Border Song (3:19)/Crocodile Rock (3:56) [NOTE: Releases outside
the U.S. replaced Candle in the Wind with Bennie and the Jets.]

ADDITIONAL CHART POSITIONS: AUSTRALIA 1, CANADA 1, NETHERLANDS 16, FINLAND 6, FRANCE 8,
JAPAN 67, WEST GERMANY 43, NEW ZEALAND 2, NORWAY 3

Greatest Hits Volume II

MCA 3027 (U.S.), October, 1977
The Bitch is Back (3:42)/Lucy in the Sky with Diamonds (5:58)/
Sorry Seems to Be the Hardest Word (3:43)/Don't Go Breaking
My Heart (4:23)/Someone Saved My Life Tonight (6:45)/
Philadelphia Freedom (5:38)/Island Girl (3:45)/Grow Some Funk
of Your Own (4:45)/Levon (4:59)/Pinball Wizard (5:08)
[NOTE: Releases outside the U.S. replaced Bennie and the Jets
with Grow Some Funk of Your Own.]

ADDITIONAL CHART POSITIONS: N/A

Extended Play (EP) Discs

The Thom Bell Sessions (U.S.)* -- --

MCA 13921, June, 1979
Three Way Love Affair (4:03), Mama Can't Buy You Love (5:31),
Are You Ready for Love (8:31)

ADDITIONAL CHART POSITIONS: [N/A]

The Thom Bell Sessions '77 (U.K.)* -- --

Rocket XPRESS 13-12, April, 1979
Three Way Love Affair (4:03), Mama Can't Buy You Love (5:31),
Are You Ready for Love (8:31)

ADDITIONAL CHART POSITIONS: [N/A]

*A more complete and truly album-length reworking of this title would be released in 1989 under the title, *The Complete Thom Bell Sessions,* featuring the tracks Nice and Slow (4:43), Country Love Song (5:05) and Shine On Through (7:46). Are You Ready for Love would also be re-leased as a single in 2003, topping the dance charts in both the U.S. and the UK.

Bootleg Albums

First Visit 1971

M-9501/2 / Tokyo, Japan, October 11, 1971
It's Me That You Need/Your Song/Rock Me When He's Gone/Come
Down in Time/Skyline Pigeon/Rotten Peaches/Indian Sunset/Ballad of a
Well-Known Gun/Friends/The King Must Die/Holiday Inn/Can I Put You
On/Country Comfort/Honky Tonk Woman/Border Song/Madman Across
the Water/Amoreena/Take Me to the Pilot/My Baby Left Me/Whole Lotta
Shakin' Going On

Live Anaheim 12/4/70

70010 RD / Anaheim Convention Centre, California, December 5, 1970
Your Song/Bad Side of the Moon/Can I Put You On/Honky Tonk
Woman/Burn Down the Mission/Get Back/My Baby Left Me

Madman Shakes Tokyo!

Gates of Paradise XS004/5 / Tokyo, Japan, October 11, 1971
It's Me That You Need/Your Song/Rock Me When He's Gone/Come
Down in Time/Skyline Pigeon/Rotten Peaches/Indian Sunset/Ballad of a
Well-Known Gun/Friends/The King Must Die/Holiday Inn/Can I Put You
On/Country Comfort/Honky Tonk Woman/Border Song/Madman Across
the Water/Amoreena/Take Me to the Pilot/My Baby Left Me/Whole Lotta
Shakin' Going On

Honky Chateau Tour 1972

Bell Bottom BB058/059 / Frankfurt, Germany, March 12, 1972
Tiny Dancer/Rock Me When He's Gone/Suzie (Dramas)/Levon/Border
Song/Can I Put You On/Your Song/Holiday Inn/Mona Lisas and Mad
Hatters/Rocket Man/Honky Cat/Country Comfort/Madman Across the
Water/Take Me to the Pilot

Rudolph the Red Nosed Reindeer

Wild Street Ws005A/B, December 22, 1973
Funeral For a Friend/Love Lies Bleeding/Candle in the
Wind/Hercules/Rocket Man/Bennie and the Jets/Daniel/This Song as No
Title/Honky Cat/Goodbye Yellow Brick Road/The Ballad of Danny Bailey
(1909-34)/Elderberry Wine/Rudolph the Red-Nosed Reindeer/I've Seen
That Movie Too/All the Girls Love Alice/Crocodile Rock/Your
Song/Saturday Night's Alright (For Fighting)

Seattle Night's Alright for Playing

Midnight Dreamer MD-486A/B, Seattle Center Coliseum, October 13, 1974
Funeral For a Friend/Love Lies Bleeding/Candle in the Wind/Grimsby/Rocket
Man/Take Me to the Pilot/Bennie and the Jets/Daniel/Grey Seal/Goodbye Yellow Brick
Road/Lucy in the Sky with Diamonds/Don't Let the Sun Go Down On Me/Honky
Cat/All the Girls Love Alice/Saturday Night's Alright (For Fighting)/Your Song

Lonely Mansion

Dasaye/Odeon 19741013 / Seattle Center Arena, Seattle, WA, October 13, 1974
Funeral For a Friend/Love Lies Bleeding/Candle in the Wind/Grimsby/Rocket
Man/Take Me to the Pilot/Bennie and the Jets/Daniel/Grey Seal/Goodbye Yellow Brick
Road/Lucy in the Sky with Diamonds/Don't Let the Sun Go Down on Me/Honky
Cat/All the Girls Love Alice/Saturday Night's Alright (For Fighting)/Your
Song/Harmony/Dixie Lily/Captain Fantastic and the Brown Dirt Cowboy/Philadelphia
Freedom/Island Girl/We All Fall in Love Sometimes

Live in London

Super Golden Radio Shows SGRS009 / Multiple venues & dates
Skyline Pigeon/I Need You to Turn To/Border Song/Take Me to the Pilot/Country
Comfort/Holiday Inn/High Flying Bird/Burn Down the Mission/Funeral For a
Friend/Love Lies Bleeding/Candle in the Wind

All Across the Havens

TAKRL 1946 / Hammersmith Odeon, London, December 24, 1974
Funeral For a Friend/Love Lies Bleeding/Candle in the Wind/Grimsby/Crocodile
Rock/Goodbye Yellow Brick Road/Grey Seal/Don't Let the Sun Go Down on
Me/Saturday Night's Alright (For Fighting)/Your Song

Just Like Strange Rain

TAKRL 1947/ Hammersmith Odeon, London, December 24, 1974
Rocket Man/High Flying Bird/Burn Down the Mission/The Bitch is Back/Daniel/Bennie
and the Jets/Lucy in the Sky with Diamonds/I Saw Her Standing There/Honky Cat

West of the Rockies

Bell Bottom BB041/42/43, Portland Memorial Coliseum, Oregon, October 14, 1975
Your Song/I Need You to Turn To/Border Song/Take Me to the Pilot/Dan Dare (Pilot
of the Future)/Country Comfort/Levon/Rocket Man/Hercules/Have Mercy on the
Criminal/Empty Sky/Funeral For a Friend/Love Lies Bleeding/Goodbye Yellow Brick
Road/Bennie and the Jets/Harmony/Dixie Lily/Captain Fantastic and the Brown Dirt
Cowboy/Bitter Fingers/Someone Saved My Life Tonight/The Bitch is Back/Don't Let the
Sun Go Down On Me/(Gotta Get A) Meal Ticket/Lucy in the Sky with Diamonds/I Saw
Her Standing There/Island Girl/We All Fall in Love Sometimes/Curtains/Pinball Wizard

RAINBOW ROCK

Silver Rarities SIRA56/56 / Rainbow Theatre, London, May 13, 1977
Your Song/The Greatest Discovery/Border Song/Daniel/Sweet Painted
Lady/Rocket Man/I Heart it Through the Grapevine/Candle in the Wind/Roy
Rogers/Dan Dare (Pilot of the Future)/Cage the Songbird/Where to Now, St.
Peter?/Ticking/Don't Let the Sun Go Down on Me/Take Me to the Pilot/Funeral
For a Friend/Tonight/Better Off Dead/Idol/I Feel Like a Bullet (In the Gun of
Robert Ford)/I Think I'm Gonna Kill Myself/Sorry Seems to Be the Hardest
Word/Crazy Water/Bennie and the Jets/Saturday Night's Alright (For
Fighting)/Goodbye

I GET A LITTLE BIT LONELY

APPY 1 / 2, DJM Studio Demos ('68-'70)
I Get a Little Bit Lonely/The Flowers Will Never Die/Rock Me When I'm
Gone/Tartan Coloured Lady/I've Been Loving You/Sitting Doing Nothing/Sing Me
No Sad Songs/I Love You & That's All That Matters/The Tide Will Turn for
Rebecca/A Dandelion Dies in the Wind/Hourglass/Baby I Miss You/Reminds Me of
You/When the First Tear Shows

FINE CHINA

Big Music BIG092 / Wembley Pool, London, November 3, 1977
I Heard It Through the Grapevine/Daniel/Island Girl/Candle in the Wind/
Rocket Man/Sorry Seems to Be the Hardest Word/Philadelphia Freedom/
Funeral For a Friend/Love Lies Bleeding/Your Song

RETURN TO THE CENTURY

Shout To The Top STTP125 / Century Plaza, L.A., October 14, 1978
Bennie and the Jets/Sixty Years On/Rocket Man/Benedict Canyon
Boogie/Daniel/Ego/Shine on Through/Return to Paradise/Candle in the Wind/Roy
Rogers/I Think I'm Gonna Killy Myself/Shooting Star/Song for Guy/Your Song

A SINGLE MAN IN MOSCOW

Octopus Records OCTO 013-014, Rossya Hall, Moscow, May 28, 1979
Your Song/Sixty Years On/Daniel/Skyline Pigeon/Take Me to the Pilot/Rocket
Man/Don't Let the Sun Go Down On Me/Goodbye Yellow Brick Road/Roy
Rogers/Candle in the Wind/Ego/Where to Now, St. Peter?/He'll Have to Go/I
Heard it Through the Grapevine/Funeral For a Friend/Tonight/Better Off
Dead/Idol/I Think I'm Going to Kill Myself/I Feel Like a Bullet (In the Gun of
Robert Ford)/Bennie and the Jets/Sorry Seems to Be the Hardest Word/Part-Time
Love/Crazy Water/Song For Guy/Saturday Night's Alright (For Fighting)/Pinball
Wizard/Crocodile Rock/Get Back/Back in the U.S.S.R.

Unique International Singles

The following are a sampling of international singles released throughout the '70s
that vary from standard releases.

SPAIN
Your Song (3:56)/Into the Old Man's Shoes (4:02)
DJM 1J00692340

BELGIUM
Your Song (3:56)/Into the Old Man's Shoes (4:02)
DJM/Suprema S301

MALAYSIA
Puppet Man (3:23) [Tom Jones]/Friends (2:24)/Rainy Days and Mondays
(3:32) [The Carpenters]/My Name is the Wind (3:21) [Frankie]
Apache AEP9026

FRANCE
Levon (5:20)/Goodbye (1:45)
DJM 17599

JAPAN
Levon (5:20)/Madman Across the Water (5:57)
DJM FR2952

ANGOLA
Tiny Dancer (6:16)/Indian Sunset (6:46)
DJM 81:00693099

PORTUGAL
Honky Cat (5:18)/Lady Samantha (3:06)/It's Me That You Need (4:06)
DJM 81:00693860

ARGENTINA
Rocket Man (4:41)/Holiday Inn (4:17)
Fermata 3F-0420

FRANCE
Daniel (3:51)/Midnight Creeper (3:53)
DJM 17612

MEXICO
Daniel (3:51)/Midnight Creeper (3:53)/Teacher I Need You (4:09)/Come Down
in Time (3:25)
DJM/Musart EXI40039

GERMANY
Daniel (3:51)/Skyline Pigeon (3:51)
DJM 12530AT

BRAZIL
Candle in the Wind (3:48)/Jamaica Jerk Off (3:38)
Young 301.1147

GREECE
Bennie and the Jets (5:22)/Candle in the Wind (3:48)
Columbia SCMG541

ITALY
Bennie and the Jets (5:22)/Candle in the Wind (3:48)
DJM SIR20176

HOLLAND
Saturday Night's Alright (For Fighting) (4:12)/Whenever You're Ready
(We'll Go Steady Again) (2:51)
DJM 6102322

AUSTRIA
Saturday Night's Alright (For Fighting) (4:12)/Jack Rabbit (1:49)
DJM 12901AT

BRAZIL
Goodbye Yellow Brick Road (3:12)/Screw You (4:43)
BZ 301.1056

TAIWAN
Goodbye Yellow Brick Road (3:12)/Be (6:33) [Neil Diamond]/All I Know (3:49)
[Art Garfunkel]/Lifestream (2:39) [Rick Nelson and the Stone Canyon Band]
Royalsound TKR-122

PHILIPPINES
Don't Let the Sun Go Down On Me (5:34)/Sick City (5:22)
PAL-61093

JAPAN
Don't Let the Sun Go Down On Me (5:34)/Sick City (5:22)
DJM IFR10563

SCANDINAVIA
The Bitch is Back (3:45)/Harmony (2:47)
DJM DJX322

ITALY
Lucy in the Sky with Diamonds (6:14)/One Day at a Time (3:48)
DJM SIR2018

CANADA
Pinball Wizard (5:09)/Acid Queen (3:53) [Tina Turner]
Polydor DJ7

CHILE
Someone Saved My Life Tonight (6:48)/House of Cards (3:05)
Bangland DJ-111-5

TAIWAN
Only One Woman (3:11) [Nigel Olsson]/Hush—I'm Alive (3:29) [Blue
Suede]/The House on Telegraph Hill (3:40) [Bo Donaldson and the
Heywoods]/Philadelphia Freedom (5:24)
FT208

AUSTRALIA
Island Girl (3:48)/Sugar on the Floor (4:25)
DJM K-6109

TAIWAN
You [George Harrison] (3:41)/Out of Time (5:37) [The Rolling
Stones]/Island Girl (3:48)/Sky High (2:56) [Jigsaw]
FT272

GERMANY
Grow Some Funk of Your Own (4:26)/I Feel Like a Bullet (In the Gun of
Robert Ford) (5:27)
DJM 2043007

BRAZIL
Don't Go Breaking My Heart (4:27)/Snow Queen (5:56)/Sorry (3:43) [Kiki
Dee]/I've Got the Music in Me (5:05) [Kiki Dee]

CANADA
Pinball Wizard (5:09)/Acid Queen (3:53) [Tina Turner]
Polydor DJ7

HOLLAND
Bite Your Lip (Get Up and Dance) (3:39)/Chicago (4:20) [Kiki Dee]
Rocket C00699242

PORTUGAL
Crazy Water (5:42)/Chameleon (5:27)
Rocket 8E00698717

BRAZIL
Ego (4:00)/Flintstone Boy (4:13)
Rocket 31C0060738

PORTUGAL
Song for Guy (5:00)/Return to Paradise (4:12)
Rocket 6079655

ARGENTINA
Part-Time Love (3:16)/Dame Algo De Amor (3:40) [Kongas]
Rocket/Polydor 0000135

GERMANY
Return to Paradise (4:12)/Song for Guy (5:00)
Rocket 6299038

BELGIUM
Song for Guy (5:00)/Lovesick (3:40)
Rocket 6079655

VENEZUELA
Mama Can't Buy You Love (4:03)/Three Way Love Affair (5:00)/Are You
Ready for Love (7:47)
Rocket 5001

BRAZIL
Mama Can't Buy You Love (4:03)/Return to Paradise (4:12)
BZ 6079689

HOLLAND
Are You Ready for Love [Part 1] (5:05)/Are You Ready for
Love [Part 2] (3:26)
Rocket 6079678

CANADA
Victim of Love (3:18)/Strangers (4:40)
MCA 41126

FRANCE
Thunder in the Night (3:47)/Johnny B. Goode (3:22)
Rocket 6079692

Unique International Albums

The following are a sampling of international albums released throughout the '70s
that vary from standard releases.

URUGUAY
Adios Camino De Ladrillo Amarillo
DJM SDJM700.502

PORTUGAL
Elton John
DJM/Wheat121365

GERMANY
Your Song
SR International/Hansa 92884

NORWAY
The King Must Die
DJM6491132

VENEZUELA
Lo Mejor De Elton John
Promus LPPS-2058

PERU
Ballad of a Well-Known Gun
Fermata SE-F-504

JAPAN
A Very Special Collection
DJM FP-80329

GERMANY
Pop Chronik
DJM 87-571-XCT

ARGENTINA
Rock Del Cocodrilo
Parnaso PNE-10003

SPAIN
Canciones De Oro
K-TEL SL-1012

NORWAY
From My Song Book
DJM 6499882

HOLLAND
From My Song Book
DJM 6376457

MALAYSIA
Afire!
Peace NTLP262

GREECE
Don't Shoot Me I'm Only the Piano Player
Columbia/EMI SCXG1030

TURKEY
Greatest Hits
S&S 11047

TAIWAN
The Best of Elton John
Holy Hawk HH-581

KOREA
The Very Best of Elton John
Tower AJR0017

CHILE
Cancion A Michell
DJM/Banglad LPDJ-55

ITALY
La Grande Storia Del Rock
Armando Curcio Editore GSR-37

CHILE
Amigos
DJM/Banglad LPXXXDJ-33

U.K.
Candle in the Wind
St. Michael 2094/0102

GERMANY
Limitierte Auflage
DJM 0900.187

CHILE
A Traves Del Agua
DJM/Banglad LPXXXDJ-56

CHILE
Sus Mas Grandes Exitos
DJM/Banglad LPXXXDJ-52

BRAZIL
One Day at a Time
Young 304.1077

VENEZUELA
Concierto Grabado En Vivo
Promus LPPS-20128

U.K.
Elton John Box Set
DJM LSP13833/34/35/36/37

CHILE
Lucy En El Cielo Con Diamantes
DJM/Banglad LPXXXDJ-34

FRANCE
Portrait
Carrere CA681

TAIWAN
Greatest Hits
First Records FL-2133

AUSTRALIA
The Very Best of Elton John
DJM RML52002

MEXICO
Coleccion Definitiva
DJM/Musart 60512

SOUTH AFRICA
Goodbye Norma Jean
DJM DLPL457/8

TAIWAN
Greatest Hits Volume 2
First Records FL-2831

EAST GERMANY
Greatest Hits
Amiga 855563

ITALY
Lady Samantha
DJM/Record Bazaar RB219

FRANCE
Recital
K-TEL BLP7904/7905

HOLLAND
Greatest Hits
BRMusic BRLP14

CHINA
Elton John Band Greatest Hits
HV 3131

RUSSIA
Poyot Elton John
Philips C60-15147-8

Czechoslovakia
Elton John
Supraphon 11132530ZN

GERMANY
Seine Schonsten Lieder
DJM 0064.235

Guest Appearances

Following is information on other artists' sessions that Elton sat in on throughout the 1970s,
and how he contributed to each recording.

Argosy single
Mr. Boyd/Imagine
Elton played piano on both tracks

The Hollies single
I Can't Tell the Bottom From the Top
Elton played piano

Fairfield Parlour single
Just Another Day
Elton played piano and sang backing vocals

My Dear Watson single
Have You Seen Your Saviour/White Line Road
Elton played piano on both tracks

The Games Soundtrack LP
From Denver to L.A.
Elton sang lead vocals

Birds of a Feather LP by the Chanter Sisters
Bad Side of the Moon
Elton played piano and sang backing vocals

I Who Have Nothing LP by Tom Jones
Daughter of Darkness
Elton sang backing vocals

Climb Ev'ry Mountain LP by Judith Durham
Skyline Pigeon
Elton played piano

It Ain't Easy LP by Long John Baldry
Let's Burn Down the Cornfield/Mr. Rubin/Rock Me When He's Gone/Flying
Elton played piano on all tracks and produced all tracks as well

Sing Children Sing LP by Lesley Duncan
Help Me Jesus/Mr. Rubin
Elton played piano on both tracks

Everything Stops for Tea LP by Long John Baldry
Come Back Again/Wild Mountain Thyme/Iko Iko/Jubilee Cloud
Elton sang backing vocals on all tracks and produced all tracks as well

Born To Boogie Soundtrack LP
Children of the Revolution
Elton played piano

For Everyman LP by Jackson Browne
Redneck Friend
Elton played piano

Kiki Dee single
The Last Good Man in My Life
Elton played piano

Smiling Face LP by Davey Johnstone
Keep Right On
Elton played piano

Smiler LP by Rod Stewart
Let Me Be Your Car
Elton played piano and sang backing vocals

Ebenezer moon single
God Rest Ye Merry Gentlemen/Silent Night
Elton played the Moog synth on both tracks

Goodnight Vienna LP by Ringo Starr
Snookeroo
Elton played piano

Walls and Bridges LP by John Lennon
Whatever Gets You Through the Night/Surprise Surprise
Elton sang backing vocals on both tracks

Nigel Olsson single
Only One Woman
Elton played piano

Nigel Olsson single
In Good Time
Elton sang backing vocals

Tommy Soundtrack LP
Pinball Wizard
Elton played piano and sang lead vocals

Overnight Success LP by Neil Sedaka
Bad Blood
Elton sang backing vocals

Sweet Deceiver LP by Kevin Ayers
Toujours La Voyage/Circular Letter/Guru Banana
Elton played piano on these tracks

Word Called Love LP by Brian and Brenda Russell
Tell Me When the Whistle Blows
Elton played piano

Steppin' Out LP by Neil Sedaka
Steppin' Out
Elton played piano and sang backing vocals

Another Night Time Flight LP by Blue
Elton played piano on multiple tracks

China LP by China
Shameful Disgrace
Elton played piano

Puttin' on the Style LP by Lonnie Donegan
Diggin' My Potatoes/Puttin' on the Style
Elton played piano and both tracks

Fools Party LP by Blue
Victim/Love Stings
Elton played piano on both tracks

Sound-a-Like Recordings

As a working musician, one of Elton's steady gigs was to record budget "sound-a-like" songs, which were sold in compilation LPs throughout England. Beginning in late 1968 and lasting through August, 1970, Elton appeared on many such recordings. The tracks listed below are from his 1970 output, and are listed along with the each song's original artist.

Elton sang lead vocals on the following tracks:

Come and Get It / Badfinger
Bridge Over Troubled Water / Simon & Garfunkel
August October / Robin Gibb
Ma Belle Amie / Tee Set
United We Stand / Brotherhood of Man
Young Gifted and Black / Bob and Marcia
Good Morning Freedom / Blue Mink
I Can't Tell the Bottom From the Top / The Hollies
Travellin' Band / Creedence Clearwater Revival
Question / The Moody Blues
Yellow River / Christie

Spirit in the Sky / Norman Greenbaum
Cottonfields / The Beach Boys
In the Summertime / Mungo Jerry
Up Around the Bend / Creedence Clearwater Revival
Lady D'Arbanville / Cat Stevens
Love of the Common People / Nicky Thomas
Neanderthal Man / Hotlegs
Natural Sinner / Fairweather
Singed Sealed Delivered (I'm Yours) / Stevie Wonder
Let's Work Together / Canned Heat

Elton sang backing and/or harmony vocals on the following tracks:

Get Together / The Dave Clark Five
Wand'rin' Star / Lee Marvin
Down the Dustpipe / Status Quo
Knock Knock (Who's There) / Mary Hopkin
Back Home / England World Cup Squad
All Right Now / Free
It's All in the Game / The Four Tops
I Will Survive / Arrival
Goodbye Sam, Hello Samantha / Cliff Richard
Lola / The Kinks
I'll Say Forever My Love / Jimmy Ruffin
The Wonder of You / Elvis Presley

Unreleased Demos of Other Songwriters' Work

Elton sang lead vocals for the following songwriters in 1970:

Nat Kipner & Mike Bradley: Green is the Colour/If You Say Goodbye/Only Love/That Old Fashioned Game/Words and Music

Bryce Bradley: Life is What You Make It

Nick Drake: Day is Done/Saturday Sun/Time Has Told Me/Way to Blue

John Martyn: Go Out and Get It/Stormbringer

Beverly Martyn: Sweet Honesty

Concerts

1970

UNITED KINGDOM/EUROPEAN TOUR
March 24 / Revolution Club, London, UK
April 21 / Roundhouse, Chalk Farm, London, UK
May 7 / Roundhouse, Chalk Farm, London, UK
May 9 / Slough College, Slough, UK
June 5 / Marquee Club, London, UK
June 17 / Lyceum Ballroom, London, UK
June 21 / Roundhouse, Chalk Farm, London, UK
June 25 / Playhouse Theatre, London, UK
June 26 / St. Mary's College, Twickenham, UK
July 3 / Haverstock Hill, Hampstead, London, UK
July 4 / Speakeasy, London, UK
July 11 / Knokke Festival, Knokke, Belgium
July 28 / Champs Elysee Theatre, Paris, France
August 13 / Playhouse Theatre, London, UK
August 15 / Krumlin Barkisland, Halifax, UK

NORTH AMERICAN TOUR
August 25 / Troubadour Club, Los Angeles, California, US
August 26 / Troubadour Club, Los Angeles, California, US
August 27 / Troubadour Club, Los Angeles, California, US
August 28 / Troubadour Club, Los Angeles, California, US
August 29 / Troubadour Club, Los Angeles, California, US
August 30 / Troubadour Club, Los Angeles, California, US
September 8 / Troubadour Club, San Francisco, California, US
September 9 / The Playboy Club, New York, New York, US
September 11 / Electric Factory, Philadelphia, Pennsylvania, US
September 12 / Electric Factory, Philadelphia, Pennsylvania, US

October 2 / Royal Albert Hall, London, UK

NORTH AMERICAN TOUR
October 29 / Boston Tea Party, Boston, Massachusetts, US
October 30 / Boston Tea Party, Boston, Massachusetts, US
October 31 / Boston Tea Party, Boston, Massachusetts, US
November 6 / The Electric Factory, Philadelphia, Pennsylvania, US
November 7 / The Electric Factory, Philadelphia, Pennsylvania, US
November 8 / The Mill Run Theatre, Baltimore, Maryland, US
November 12 / Fillmore West, San Francisco, California, US
November 13 / Fillmore West, San Francisco, California, US
November 14 / Fillmore West, San Francisco, California, US

November 15 / Santa Monica Civic Auditorium, L.A., California, US
November 17 / A&R Studios, New York, New York, US
November 20 / Fillmore East, New York, New York, US
November 21 / Fillmore East, New York, New York, US
November 22 / University of Bridgeport, Bridgeport, Connecticut, US
November 23 / Glassboro State College, Glassboro, New Jersey, US
November 25 / Auditorium Theatre, Chicago, Illinois, US
November 26 / Music Hall, Cleveland, Ohio, US
November 27 / East Town Theatre, Detroit, Michigan, US
November 28 / East Town Theatre, Detroit, Michigan, US
November 29 / Guthrie Theatre, Minneapolis, Minnesota, US
December 1 / Champ Auditorium, Fulton, Missouri, US
December 2 / War Memorial Coliseum, Syracuse, New York, US
December 4 / Anaheim Convention Centre, Anaheim, California, US
December 5 / Swing Auditorium, San Bernadino, California, US
December 6 / Royce Hall, Los Angeles, California, US

December 20 / The Roundhouse, Chalk Farm, London, UK

1971

UNITED KINGDOM TOUR
January 2 / Mothers, Birmingham, UK
January 3 / Pavilion, Hemel, Hempstead, UK
January 8 / Haverstock Hill Country Club, Hampstead, UK
January 10 / Guildford Civic Hall, Guildford, UK
January 11 / Winter Gardens, Cleethorpes, UK
January 13 / City Hall, Hull, UK
January 15 / Southampton University, Southampton, UK
January 16 / Loughborough University, Loughborough, UK
January 27 / Philharmonic Hall, Liverpool, UK
January 29 / University of Lancaster, Lancaster, UK
January 30 / Regent Theatre Concert Hall, Brighton, UK
January 31 / The Fox, Croydon, UK
February 1 / Cooks Ferry Inn, Edmonton, London, UK
February 5 / Students Union Main Hall, Coventry, UK
February 6 / Leeds University, Leeds, UK
February 9 / Bumpers Nightclub, London, UK
February 12 / Stirling University, Stirling UK
February 13 / Stratchclyde University, Glasgow, UK
February14 / Kinema Ballroom, Dunfermline, UK
February 20 / Newcastle City Hall, Newcastle, UK
February 24 / Imperial College, London, UK

February 26 / Brunel University, Uxbridge, UK
February 27 / Bradford University, Bradford, UK
March 1 / Tivoli Gardens, Copenhagen, Denmark
March 3 / Royal Festival Hall, London, UK
March 6 / Leicester University, Leicester, UK
March 13 / Kingston Polytechnic, Kingston Upon Thames, London, UK
March 14 / Colston Hall, Bristol, UK
March 20 / University College, London, UK
March 21 / Dagenham Roundhouse, Dagenham, UK
March 28 / Fairfield Hall, Croydon, UK

NORTH AMERICAN TOUR
April 2 / Loews Theatre, Providence, Rhode Island, US
April 3 / Boston Music Hall, Boston, Massachusetts, US
April 7 / The Spectrum, Philadelphia, Pennsylvania, US
April 8 / Fillmore East, New York, New York, US
April 9 / Fillmore East, New York, New York, US
April 10 / Fillmore East, New York, New York, US
April 11 / Painters Mill Music Fair, Owings Mills, Maryland, US
April 13 / Auditorium Theatre, Chicago, Illinois, US
April 14 / Auditorium Theatre, Chicago, Illinois, US
April 15 / Auditorium Theatre, Chicago, Illinois, US
April 16 / University of Detroit Fieldhouse, Detroit, Michigan, US
April 17 / Veterans Memorial Auditorium, Columbus, Ohio, US
April 18 / Cincinnati Music Hall, Cincinnati, Ohio, US
April 20 / Civic Auditorium, Omaha, Nebraska, US
April 21 / Memorial Coliseum, Portland, Oregon, US
April 23 / Agrodome Theatre, Vancouver, British Columbia, Canada
April 24 / Centre Coliseum, Seattle, Washington, US
May 1 / Hawaii International Centre, Honolulu, Hawaii, US
May 9 / Civic Auditorium, San Francisco, California, US
May 11 / Memorial Auditorium, Sacramento, California, US
May 12 / Convention Centre, Fresno, California, US
May 14 / Convention, Centre, Fresno, California, US
May 15 / Arizona Veterans Memorial Coliseum, Phoenix, Arizona, US
May 16 / Denver Municipal Auditorium, Denver, Colorado, US
May 17 / University of Colorado, Boulder, Colorado, US
May 19 / Civic Centre Music Hall, Oklahoma City, Oklahoma, US
May 20 / Sam Houston Coliseum, Houston, Texas, US
May 21 / Municipal Auditorium, Antonio, Texas, US
May 22 / Fair Park Music Hall, Dallas, Texas, US
May 23 / Fair Park Music Hall, Dallas, Texas, US
May 24 / Tarrant County Theatre, Fort Worth, Texas, US
May 26 / The Warehouse, New Orleans, Louisiana, US
May 28 / Curtis Hixon Auditorium, Tampa, Florida, US

May 29 / Hollywood Sportatorium, Hollywood, Florida, US
May 30 / Coliseum, Jacksonville, Florida, US
June 4 / Kiel Auditorium, St. Louis, Missouri, US
June 5 / Ellis Auditorium, Memphis, Tennessee, US
June 6 / Convention Centre, Louisville, Kentucky, US
June 8 / Municipal Auditorium, Atlanta, Georgia, US
June 10 / Carnegie Hall, New York, New York, US
June 11 / Carnegie Hall, New York, New York, US
June 12 / Cleveland Arena, Cleveland, Ohio, US
June 13 / Rhode Island Auditorium, Providence, Rhode Island, US
June 16 / Merriweather Post Pavilion, Columbia, Maryland, US
June 18 / Farm Show Arena, Harrisburg, Pennsylvania, US

July 8 / Liseberg Park, Liseberg, Sweden

July 31 / Crystal Palace Bowl, London, UK

August 9 / Vilar De Mouros, Caminha, Portugal

NORTH AMERICAN TOUR
August 26 / Onondaga War Memorial, Syracuse, New York, US
August 27 / Wildwood Convention Hall, Wildwood, New Jersey, US
August 28 / Convention Hall, Asbury Park, New Jersey, US
August 30 / Marcus Amphitheatre, Milwaukee, Wisconsin, US
September 2 / Performing Arts Centre, Saratoga Springs, New York, US
September 3 / Onondaga War Memorial, Syracuse, New York, US
September 4 / Rochester War Memorial, Rochester, New York, US
September 6 / Greek Theatre, Los Angeles, California, US
September 7 / Greek Theatre, Los Angeles, California, US
September 8 / Greek Theatre, Los Angeles, California, US
September 9 / Greek Theatre, Los Angeles, California, US
September 11 / Greek Theatre, Los Angeles, California, US
September 12 / Greek Theatre, Los Angeles, California, US
September 15 / Convention Centre, Las Vegas, Nevada, US
September 16 / Fairgrounds Pavilion, Reno, Nevada, US

JAPANESE TOUR
October 5 / Shibuya Kohkaido, Tokyo, Japan
October 6 / Shibuya Kohkaido, Tokyo, Japan
October 7 / Kosei Nenkin Hall, Osaka, Japan
October 8 / Kosei Nenkin Hall, Osaka, Japan
October 10 / Shinjuku Kohsei Nenkin Hall, Tokyo, Japan
October 11 / Shinjuku Kohsei Nenkin Hall, Tokyo, Japan

AUSTRALIAN/NEW ZEALAND TOUR

October 16 / Subiaco Stadium, Perth, Australia
October 24 / Kooyong Stadium, Melbourne, Victoria, Australia
October 26 / QLD Tennis Courts, Brisbane, Australia
October 29 / Western Springs Stadium, Auckland, New Zealand
October 31 / Sydney Festival, Sydney, New South Wales, Australia

UNITED KINGDOM TOUR

November 21 / Coventry Theatre, Coventry, UK
November 22 / Free Trade Hall, Manchester, UK
November 24 / De Montfort Hall, Leicester, UK
November 26 / Winter Gardens, Bournemouth, UK
November 27 / ABC Theatre, Plymouth, UK
November 28 / Colston Hall, Bristol, UK
December 3 / Town Hall, Birmingham, UK
December 4 / Dome, Brighton, UK
December 5 / Fairfield Hall, Croydon, UK
December 10 / City Hall, Newcastle, UK
December 11 / ABC Theatre, Stockton On Tees, UK
December 16 / Town Hall, Leeds, UK
December 17 / City Hall, Sheffield, UK
December 24 / City Hall, Sheffield, UK

1972

UNITED KINGDOM TOUR

February 5 / Royal Festival Hall, London, UK
February 19 / University of Lancaster, Lancaster, UK
February 20 / Shaw Theatre, National Youth Theatre, London, UK
February 23 / Exeter University, Exeter, UK
February 24 / Town Hall, Watford, UK
February 26 / Waltham Forest Technical College, Waltham Forest, UK
February 27 / Shaw Theatre, National Youth Theatre, London, UK
March 1 / The Music Hall, Aberdeen, UK
March 2 / Caird Hall, Dundee, UK
March 3 / Kelvin Hall, Glasgow, UK
March 4 / Empire Theatre, Edinburgh, UK

GERMAN/MONACOAN TOUR

March 12 / Frankfurt Theatre, Frankfurt, Germany
March 14 / Sporting Club, Monte Carlo, Monaco
March 15 / Sporting Club, Monte Carlo, Monaco
March 17 / Ernst-Mercke Halle, Hamburg, Germany

March 19 / Deutschland Halle, Berlin, Germany
Marcy 20 / Frankfurt Theatre, Frankfurt, Germany

NORTH AMERICAN TOUR
April 27 / Convention Centre, Baylon Uni, Waco, Texas, US
April 28 / Sam Houston Coliseum, Houston, Texas, US
April 29 / Sun Bowl, El Paso, Texas, US
April 30 / Austin College, Austin, Texas, US
May 2 / Merriweather Post Pavilion, Columbia, Maryland, US
May 3 / Notre Dame, South Bend, Indiana, US
May 4 / Jenison Field House, East Lansing, Michigan, US
May 5 / Memorial Gym, Kent State University, Cleveland, Ohio, US
May 6 / St. John Arena, Ohio State University, Columbus, Ohio, US
May 7 / Millett Hall, Oxford, Ohio, US
May 8 / Aire Crown Theatre, Chicago, Illinois, US
May 9 / Aire Crown Theatre, Chicago, Illinois, US
May 10 / Assembly Hall, Urbana, Illinois, US
May 12 / Southern Illinois University, Illinois, US
May 13 / Northern Illinois University, Illinois, US
May 14 / University of Wisconsin, Madison, Wisconsin, US
May 15 / St. Cloud University, Minneapolis, Minnesota, US
May 16 / University of Texas, Austin, Texas, US

UNITED KINGDOM TOUR
June 3 / Crystal Palace Bowl, London, UK
August 26 / The Guildhall, Portsmouth, UK
August 27 / Shaw Theatre, London, UK
August 31 / City Hall, Newcastle, UK
September 1 / Free Trade Hall, Manchester, UK
September 3 / Fairfield Hall, Croydon, UK
September 8 / Green's Playhouse, Glasgow, UK
September 10 / New Theatre, Oxford, UK
September 17 / Shaw Theatre, London, UK

NORTH AMERICAN TOUR
September 26 / Cornell University, Ithaca, New York, US
September 27 / Music Hall, Boston, Massachusetts, US
September 28 / Music Hall, Boston, Massachusetts, US
September 29 / New Haven Arena, New Haven, Connecticut, US
September 30 / The Spectrum, Philadelphia, Pennsylvania, US
October 1 / Memorial Auditorium, Rochester, New York, US
October 2 / The Forum, Montreal, Quebec, Canada
October 5 / Maple Leaf Gardens, Toronto, Ontario, Canada
October 6 / Cobo Hall, Detroit, Michigan, US
October 7 / Memorial Auditorium, Buffalo, New York, US

October 9 / Nassau Coliseum, Uniondale, New York, US
October 11 / Illinois State University, Horton Fieldhouse, Normal, Illinois, US
October 12 / Cultural Centre, Wichita, Kansas, US
October 14 / Iowa State University, Ames, Iowa, US
October 15 / Municipal Auditorium, Denver, Colorado, US
October 17 / Anaheim Convention Centre, Anaheim, California, US
October 18 / Hawaii International Centre, Honolulu, Hawaii, US
October 20 / Seattle Centre Coliseum, Seattle, Washington, US
October 21 / Community Theatre, Berkeley, California, US
October 22 / Convention Centre, Anaheim, California, US
October 23 / The Forum, Los Angeles, California, US
October 24 / The Forum, Los Angeles, California, US
October 25 / Berkeley Community Theatre, Berkeley, California, US
October 26 / Civic Plaza, Tucson, Arizona, US
October 27 / Sports Arena, San Diego, California, US
October 30 / Palladium, London, UK
November 1 / Oklahoma State University, Stillwater, Oklahoma, US
November 2 / Assembly Centre, Tulsa, Oklahoma, US
November 3 / Fairgrounds Arena, Oklahoma City, Oklahoma, US
November 4 / Municipal Auditorium, Kansas City, Missouri, US
November 4 / Memorial Auditorium, Dallas, Texas, US
November 8 / Texas A&M, College Station, Texas, US
November 9 / Municipal Auditorium, San Antonio, Texas, US
November 10 / Louisiana State University, Baton Rouge, Louisiana, US
November 11 / Mid-South Coliseum, Memphis, Tennessee, US
November 12 / Memorial Auditorium, Nashville, Tennessee, US
November 13 / Scope Auditorium, Norfolk, Virginia, US
November 14 / University of Alabama, Tuscaloosa, Alabama, US
November 15 / Atlanta Coliseum, Atlanta, Georgia, US
November 16 / Charlotte Coliseum, Charlotte, North Carolina, US
November 17 / Civic Centre, Charleston, West Virginia, US
November 18 / Hampton Roads Coliseum, Hampton, Virginia, US
November 19 / Carnegie Hall, New York, New York, US
November 20 / Carnegie Hall, New York, New York, US
November 21 / Civic Centre, Baltimore, Maryland, US
November 22 / State Farm Arena, Harrisburg, Pennsylvania, US
November 24 / Jacksonville Coliseum, Jacksonville, Florida, US
November 25 / Hollywood Sportatorium, Hollywood, Florida, US
November 26 / Bay Front Centre, St. Petersburg, Florida, US

1973

January 20 / Carnegie Hall, New York, New York, US

UNITED KINGDOM TOUR
February 24 / Starlight Rooms, Boston, UK
February 25 / Green's Playhouse, Glasgow, UK
February 28 / Town Hall, Birmingham, UK
March 1 / De Montfort Hall, Leicester, UK
March 2 / Empire Theatre, Liverpool, UK
March 3 / Empire Theatre, Liverpool, UK
March 6 / Guildhall, Preston, UK
March 7 / City Hall, Newcastle, UK
March 9 / City Hall, Sheffield, UK
March 10 / Leeds University, Leeds, UK
March 11 / Leeds University, Leeds, UK
March 12 / Imperial College, London, UK
March 15 / Colston Hall, Bristol, UK
March 16 / Dome, Brighton, UK
March 17 / Winter Gardens, Bournemouth, UK
March 18 / Guildhall, Southampton, UK
March 22 / Sundown, Edmonton, East London, UK
March 23 / Sundown, Edmonton, East London, UK
March 24 / Sundown, Brixton, South London, UK
March 25 / Coventry Theatre, Coventry, UK
March 26 / Hard Rock, Manchester, UK
March 27 / Hard Rock, Manchester, UK

ITALIAN TOUR
April 11 / Palasport, Napoli, Italy
April 12 / Palazzo Dello Sport, Rome, Italy
April 13 / Vigorelli Velodrome, Milan, Italy
April 14 / Palazzo Azzarita, Firenze, Italy
April 15 / Bologna Stadium, Bologna, Italy
April 18 / Palazzo Dello Sport, Torino, Italy
April 19 / Palasport, Genova, Italy
April 24 / Marquee Club, London, UK
April 25 / Marquee Club, London, UK

NORTH AMERICAN TOUR
August 15 / Municipal Auditorium, Mobile, Alabama, US
August 16 / Sam Houston Coliseum, Houston, Texas, US
August 17 / Hemisphere Arena, San Antonio, Texas, US

August 18 / The Cotton Bowl, Dallas, Texas, USA
August 19 / Arrowhead Stadium, Kansas City, Missouri, US
August 23 / Metropolitan Sports Centre, Minneapolis, Minnesota, US
August 24 / Chicago Amphitheatre, Chicago, Illinois, US
August 25 / Chicago Amphitheatre, Chicago, Illinois, US
August 26 / Iowa State Fairgrounds, Des Moines, Iowa, US
August 28 / University of Special Events Centre, Salt Lake City, Utah, US
August 30 / Portland Memorial Coliseum, Portland, Oregon, US
August 31 / Seattle Centre Coliseum, Seattle, Washington, US
September 1 / Balboa Stadium, San Diego, California, US
September 2 / The Coliseum, Denver, Colorado, US
September 3 / University Arena, Albuquerque, New Mexico, US
September 4 / Big Surf, Phoenix, Arizona, US
September 7 / The Hollywood Bowl, Los Angeles, California, US
September 8 / Long Beach Arena, Long Beach, California, US
September 9 / Oakland Coliseum, Oakland, California, US
September 10 / The Coliseum, Vancouver, British Columbia, Canada
September 17 / International Centre, Honolulu, Hawaii, US
September 21 / Greensboro Coliseum, Greensboro, North Carolina, US
September 22 / Braves Stadium, Atlanta, Georgia, US
September 23 / Madison Square Garden, New York, US
September 24 / Nassau Coliseum, New York, New York, US
September 25 / Boston Gardens, Boston, Massachusetts, US
September 28 / The Spectrum, Philadelphia, Pennsylvania, US
September 29 / Richmond Coliseum, Richmond, Virginia, US
September 30 / Civic Centre, Baltimore, Maryland, US
October 3 / University of Dayton Arena, Dayton, Ohio, US
October 4 / Kiel Auditorium, St. Louis, Missouri, US
October 5 / Cobo Hall, Detroit, Michigan, US
October 6 / St. John Arena, Ohio State University, Columbus, Ohio, US
October 7 / Indiana University Assembly Hall, Bloomington, Indiana, US
October 9 / Civic Arena, Pittsburgh, Pennsylvania, US
October 11 / Mid-South Coliseum, Memphis, Tennessee, US
October 12 / Mid-Tennessee State University, Murfreesboro, Tennessee, US
October 13 / Stokely Athletic Centre, Knoxville, Tennessee, US
October 14 / Hampton Coliseum, Hampton, Virginia US
October 18 / Memorial Stadium, Auburn, Alabama, US
October 19 / University of Georgia, Athens, Georgia, US
October 20 / Hollywood Sportatorium, Hollywood, Florida, US
October 21 / Ben Hill Griffin Stadium, Gainesville, Florida, US
October 25 / U.G.A. Coliseum, Atlanta, Georgia, US

UNITED KINGDOM TOUR
November 27 / Colston Hall, Bristol, UK
November 29 / Belle Vue, Manchester, UK

December 8 / Empire Theatre, Liverpool, UK
December 10 / Apollo Theatre, Glasgow, UK
December 11 / Apollo Theatre, Glasgow, UK
December 12 / City Hall, Newcastle, UK
December 15 / American School, London, UK
December 16 / Town Hall, Birmingham, UK
December 17 / Town Hall, Birmingham, UK

UK CHRISTMAS SHOWS
December 20 / Hammersmith Odeon, London, UK
December 21 / Hammersmith Odeon, London, UK
December 22 / Hammersmith Odeon, London, UK
December 23 / Hammersmith Odeon, London, UK
December 24 / Hammersmith Odeon, London, UK

1974

JAPANESE TOUR
February 1 / Budokan, Tokyo, Japan
February 2 / Budokan, Tokyo, Japan
February 3 / Kosei Nenkin Hall, Osaka, Japan
February 4 / Kosei Nenkin Hall, Osaka, Japan
February 5 / Kosei Nenkin Hall, Osaka, Japan
February 7 / Kyuden Kinen Tallkukan, Fukuoka, Japan
February 8 / Yubin Chokin Hall, Hiroshima, Japan
February 9 / Kyoto Kaikan, Kyoto, Japan
February 10 / Festival Hall, Osaka, Japan
February 11 / Nagoya Civic Hall, Hagoya, Japan
February 13 / Shinjuku Kohsei Nenkin Hall, Tokyo, Japan

AUSTRALIAN/NEW ZEALAND TOUR
February 21 / South Melbourne Football Ground, Melbourne, Australia
February 28 / Western Springs Stadium, Auckland, New Zealand
March 14 / Randwick Racecourse, Randwick, Australia
March 18 / WACA Grounds, Perth, Australia

UNITED KINGDOM TOUR
May 5 / Watford Football Club, Watford, UK
May 18 / Royal Festival Hall, London, UK
May 27 / Empire Pool Wembley, London, UK

NORTH AMERICAN TOUR
September 25 / Dallas Convention Centre, Dallas, Texas, US

September 26 / Hofheinz Pavilion, Houston, Texas, US
September 27 / Municipal Auditorium, Mobile, Alabama, US
September 28 / Memorial Coliseum, Tuscaloosa, Alabama, US
September 29 / Louisiana State University, Baton Rouge, Louisiana, US
October 3 / The Forum, Los Angeles, California, US
October 4 / The Forum, Los Angeles, California, US
October 5 / The Forum, Los Angeles, California, US
October 8 / The Forum, Los Angeles, California, US
October 9 / Cow Palace, Daly City, California, US
October 10 / Oakland Coliseum, Oakland, California, US
October 12 / Seattle Centre Coliseum, Seattle, Washington, US
October 13 / Seattle Centre Coliseum, Seattle, Washington, US
October 14 / Pacific Coliseum, Vancouver, British Columbia, Canada
October 15 / Memorial Coliseum, Portland, Oregon, US
October 26 / Hawaii International Centre, Honolulu, Hawaii, US
October 27 / Hawaii International Centre, Honolulu, Hawaii, US
October 30 / St. Louis Arena, St. Louis, Missouri, US
October 31 / Civic Centre, St. Paul, Minnesota, US
November 1 / Chicago Stadium, Chicago, Illinois, US
November 2 / Chicago Stadium, Chicago, Illinois, US
November 3 / Ohio State University, Columbus, Ohio, US
November 4 / Cleveland Coliseum, Cleveland, Ohio, US
November 8 / Greensboro Coliseum, Greensboro, North Carolina, US
November 9 / Stokely Athletic Centre, Knoxville, Tennessee, US
November 10 / The Omni, Atlanta, Georgia, US
November 12 / Civic Arena, Pittsburgh, Pennsylvania, US
November 13 / Cincinnati Gardens, Cincinnati, Ohio, US
November 14 / Olympia Stadium, Detroit, Michigan, US
November 15 / Olympia Stadium, Detroit, Michigan, US
November 17 / The Forum, Quebec, Montreal, Canada
November 18 / Boston Garden, Boston, Massachusetts, US
November 20 / Capital Centre, Largo, Maryland, US
November 21 / Capital Centre, Largo, Maryland, US
November 23 / Veterans Memorial Coliseum, New Haven, Connecticut, US
November 28 / Madison Square Garden, New York, New York, US
November 29 / Madison Square Garden, New York, New York, US
November 30 / Nassau Coliseum, Uniondale, New York, US
December 1 / Nassau Coliseum, Uniondale, New York, US
December 2 / The Spectrum, Philadelphia, Pennsylvania, US
December 3 / The Spectrum, Philadelphia, Pennsylvania, US

UK CHRISTMAS SHOWS
December 20 / Hammersmith Odeon, London, UK
December 21 / Hammersmith Odeon, London, UK
December 22 / Hammersmith Odeon, London, UK

December 23 / Hammersmith Odeon, London, UK
December 24 / Hammersmith Odeon, London, UK

1975

February 18 / Bailey's, Watford, UK

June 21 / Wembley Stadium, London, UK

June 29 / Oakland Coliseum, Oakland, California, US

July 20 / Hughes Stadium, Fort Collins, Colorado, US

August 9 / Civic Auditorium, Santa Monica, California, US

TROUBADOUR 5-YEAR ANNIVERSARY SHOWS
August 25 / Troubadour Club, Los Angeles, California, US
August 26 / Troubadour Club, Los Angeles, California, US
August 27 / Troubadour Club, Los Angeles, California, US

NORTH AMERICAN TOUR
September 29 / Sports Arena, San Diego, California, US
October 1 / Community Centre Arena, Tucson, Arizona, US
October 2 / Convention Centre, Las Vegas, Nevada, US
October 3 / Arizona State University, Tempe, Arizona, US
October 5 / McNichols Arena, Denver, Colorado, US
October 6 / McNichols Arena, Denver, Colorado, US
October 7 / Special Events Centre, University of Utah, Salt Lake City, Utah, US
October 12 / Pacific Coliseum, Vancouver, British Columbia, Canada
October 13 / Pacific Coliseum, Vancouver, British Columbia, Canada
October 14 / Memorial Coliseum, Portland, Oregon, US
October 16 / Centre Coliseum, Seattle, Washington, US
October 17 / Centre Coliseum, Seattle, Washington, US
October 19 / Coliseum, Oakland, California, US
October 20 / Coliseum, Oakland, California, US
October 21 / Coliseum, Oakland, California, US
October 25 / Dodgers Stadium, Los Angeles, California, US
October 26 / Dodgers Stadium, Los Angeles, California, US

1976

UNITED KINGDOM TOUR

April 29 / Grand Theatre, Leeds, UK
April 30 / Grand Theatre, Leeds, UK
May 1 / Belle Vue, Manchester, UK
May 2 / Guildhall, Preston, UK
May 3 / Empire Theatre, Liverpool, UK
May 4 / Empire Theatre, Liverpool, UK
May 5 / De Montfort Hall, Leicester, UK
May 6 / Victoria Hall, Hanley, UK
May 7 / Civic Hall, Wolverhampton, UK
May 9 / Fairfield Hall, Croydon, UK
May 11 / Earls Court, London, UK
May 12 / Earls Court, London, UK
May 13 / Earls Court, London, UK
May 14 / Bailey's, Watford, UK
May 16 / Odeon, Birmingham, UK
May 17 / Odeon, Birmingham, UK
May 18 / City Hall, Sheffield, UK
May 20 / City Hall, Sheffield, UK
May 21 / Usher Hall, Edinburgh, UK
May 22 / Caird Hall, Dundee, UK
May 24 / Apollo Theatre, Glasgow, UK
May 25 / Apollo Theatre, Glasgow, UK
May 27 / New Theatre, Coventry, UK
May 28 / New Theatre, Coventry, UK
May 29 / Gaumont Theatre, Southampton, UK
May 30 / Odeon, Taunton, UK
May 31 / Hippodrome, Bristol, UK
June 1 / Hippodrome, Bristol, UK
June 3 / Cardiff Capitol, Cardiff, UK
June 4 / Cardiff Capital, Cardiff, UK

NORTH AMERICAN TOUR

June 29 / Capital Centre, Largo, Maryland, US
June 30 / Capital Centre, Largo, Maryland, US
July 1 / Capital Centre, Largo, Maryland, US
July 4 / Schaefer Stadium, Foxboro, Massachusetts, US
July 6 / The Spectrum, Philadelphia, Pennsylvania, US
July 7 / The Spectrum, Philadelphia, Pennsylvania, US
July 8 / The Spectrum, Philadelphia, Pennsylvania, US
July 11 / Pontiac Silverdome, Detroit, Michigan, US

July 13 / Greensboro Coliseum, Greensboro, North Carolina, US
July 14 / Charlotte Coliseum, Charlotte, North Carolina, US
July 16 / The Omni, Atlanta, Georgia, US
July 18 / Memorial Coliseum, Tuscaloosa, Alabama, US
July 20 / Freedom Hall, Louisville, Kentucky, US
July 21 / Market Square Arena, Indianapolis, Indiana, US
July 24 / Civic Centre, St. Paul, Minnesota, US
July 26 / Chicago Stadium, Chicago, Illinois, US
July 27 / Chicago Stadium, Chicago, Illinois, US
July 28 / Chicago Stadium, Chicago, Illinois, US
August 1 / Richfield Coliseum, Richfield, Ohio, US
August 2 / Richfield Coliseum, Richfield, Ohio, US
August 3 / Cincinnati Gardens, Cincinnati, Ohio, US
August 7 / Rich Stadium, Buffalo, New York, US
August 10 / Madison Square Garden, New York, New York, US
August 11 / Madison Square Garden, New York, New York, US
August 12 / Madison Square Garden, New York, New York, US
August 13 / Madison Square Garden, New York, New York, US
August 15 / Madison Square Garden, New York, New York, US
August 16 / Madison Square Garden, New York, New York, US
August 17 / Madison Square Garden, New York, New York, US

September 17 / Edinburgh Playhouse Theatre, Edinburgh, UK

1977

UNITED KINGDOM TOUR
May 2 / Rainbow Theatre, London, UK
May 3 / Rainbow Theatre, London, UK
May 4 / Rainbow Theatre, London, UK
May 5 / Rainbow Theatre, London, UK
May 6 / Rainbow Theatre, London, UK
May 7 / Rainbow Theatre, London, UK
June 17 / Shoreditch College Chapel, Egham, UK

July 17 / The Blue Max, Lahaina, Maui, Hawaii, US

August 1 / Central Park, New York, New York, US

November 3 / Empire Pool, Wembley, London, UK

1978

October 14 / Century Plaza, Los Angeles, California, US

October 20 / RTL Studios, Paris, France

November 2 / Hilton Hotel, London, UK

1979

EUROPEAN TOUR
February 5 / Concerthaus, Stockholm, Sweden
February 6 / Concerthaus, Stockholm, Sweden
February 7 / Tivoli, Copenhagen, Denmark
February 8 / Tivoli, Copenhagen, Denmark
February 10 / Musikhalle, Hamburg, Germany
February 11 / Congressgebau, The Hague, Netherlands
February 12 / Doelen, Rotterdam, Netherlands
February 14 / Concertgebau, Amsterdam, Netherlands
February 15 / Mozartsaal, Mannheim, Germany
February 16 / Deutschen Museum, Munich, Germany
February 18 / Kongresshalle, Berlin, Germany
February 19 / Opera House, Cologne, Germany
February 20 / Theatre De Champs Elysees, Paris, France
February 21 / Theatre De Champs Elysees, Paris, France
February 22 / Theatre De Champs Elysees, Paris, France
February 23 / Theatre De Champs Elysees, Paris, France
February 24 / Theatre De Champs Elysees, Paris, France
February 25 / Theatre De Champs Elysees, Paris, France
February 26 / Queen Elizabeth Hall, Antwerp, Belgium
February 27 / Queen Elizabeth Hall, Antwerp, Belgium
March 1 / Philipshalle, Dusseldorf, Germany
March 2 / Rhein Main Halle, Wiesbaden, Germany
March 3 / Theatre Di Beaulieu, Lausanne, Switzerland
March 4 / Theatre Di Beaulieu, Lausanne, Switzerland
March 6 / Theatre De Verdure, Nice, France
March 7 / Theatre De Verdure, Nice, France
March 9 / Pavello Del Joventud De Badalona, Barcelona, Spain
March 10 / Pabellon Del Club Juventud, Barcelona, Spain
March 11 / Pabellon Real Madrid Pavilion, Madrid, Spain

UNITED KINGDOM TOUR

March 17 / Apollo Theatre, Glasgow, UK
March 18 / Apollo Theatre, Glasgow, UK
March 19 / Odeon Theatre, Edinburgh, UK
March 21 / City Hall, Newcastle, UK
March 22 / City Hall, Newcastle, UK
March 23 / Guild Hall, Preston, UK
March 26 / Whitla Hall, Belfast, UK
March 27 / Whitla Hall, Belfast, UK
March 29 / National Stadium, Dublin, Ireland
March 30 / National Stadium, Dublin, Ireland
April 2 / Theatre Royal Drury Lane, London, UK
April 3 / Theatre Royal Drury Lane, London, UK
April 4 / Theatre Royal Drury Lane, London, UK
April 5 / Theatre Royal Drury Lane, London, UK
April 6 / Theatre Royal Drury Lane, London, UK
April 7 / Theatre Royal Drury Lane, London, UK
April 9 / Dome, Brighton, UK
April 10 / Dome, Brighton, UK
April 11 / Gaumont Theatre, Southampton, UK
April 12 / Gaumon Theatre, Southampton, UK
April 14 / Hippodrome, Bristol, UK
April 15 / Hippodrome, Bristol, UK
April 17 / Oxford Theatre, Oxford, UK
April 18 / Coventry Theatre, Coventry, UK
April 19 / Assembly Rooms, Derby, UK
April 21 / Hippodrome, Birmingham, UK
April 22 / Hippodrome, Birmingham, UK
April 24 / Apollo, Manchester, UK
April 25 / Apollo, Manchester, UK
April 26 / Apollo, Manchester, UK

ISRAELI TOUR

May 1 / Philharmonic Hall, Jerusalem, Israel
May 2 / Philharmonic Hall, Jerusalem, Israel
May 3 / Philharmonic Hall, Jerusalem, Israel
May 5 / Mann Auditorium, Tel Aviv, Israel
May 6 / Mann Auditorium, Tel Aviv, Israel

SOVIET TOUR

May 21 / Bolshoi Oktyabrsky Concert Hall, Leningrad, USSR
May 22 / Bolshoi Oktyabrsky Concert Hall, Leningrad, USSR
May 23 / Bolshoi Oktyabrsky Concert Hall, Leningrad, USSR
May 24 / Bolshoi Oktyabrsky Concert Hall, Leningrad, USSR
May 25 / Rossya Hall, Moscow, USSR

May 26 / Rossya Hall, Moscow, USSR
May 27 / Rossya Hall, Moscow, USSR
May 28 / Rossya Hall, Moscow, USSR

NORTH AMERICAN TOUR

September 19 / Gammage Auditorium, Tempe, Arizona, US
September 20 / Gammage Auditorium, Tempe, Arizona, US
September 22 / Community Theatre, Berkeley, California, US
September 23 / Community Theatre, Berkeley, California, US
September 24 / Community Theatre, Berkeley, California, US
September 26 / Universal Amphitheatre, Los Angeles, California, US
September 27 / Universal Amphitheatre, Los Angeles, California, US
September 28 / Universal Amphitheatre, Los Angeles, California, US
September 29 / Universal Amphitheatre, Los Angeles, California, US
September 30 / Universal Amphitheatre, Los Angeles, California, US
October 2 / Universal Amphitheatre, Los Angeles, California, US
October 3 / Universal Amphitheatre, Los Angeles, California, US
October 4 / Universal Amphitheatre, Los Angeles, California, US
October 5 / Universal Amphitheatre, Los Angeles, California, US
October 6 / Universal Amphitheatre, Los Angeles, California, US
October 9 / Northrop Auditorium, Minneapolis, Minnesota, US
October 10 / Northrop Auditorium, Minneapolis, Minnesota, US
October 11 / Auditorium Theatre, Chicago, Illinois, US
October 12 / Auditorium Theatre, Chicago, Illinois, US
October 13 / Elliott Hall of Music, West Lafayette, Indiana, US
October 15 / Music Hall, Boston, Massachusetts, US
October 16 / Music Hall, Boston, Massachusetts, US
October 18 / Palladium, New York, New York, US
October 19 / Palladium, New York, New York, US
October 20 / Palladium, New York, New York, US
October 21 / Palladium, New York, New York, US
October 23 / Palladium, New York, New York, US
October 24 / Palladium, New York, New York, US
October 25 / Palladium, New York, New York, US
October 26 / Palladium, New York, New York, US
October 27 / Eisenhower Hall, West Point, New York, US
October 29 / Hill Auditorium, Ann Arbor, Michigan, US
October 30 / O'Keffe Centre, Toronto, Ontario, Canada
October 31 / O'Keffe Centre, Toronto, Ontario, Canada
November 2 / Tower Theatre, Philadelphia, Pennsylvania, US
November 3 / Tower Theatre, Philadelphia, Pennsylvania, US
November 4 / Constitution Hall, Washington, D.C., US
November 5 / Constitution Hall, Washington, D.C., US
November 7 / Grand Ole Opry House, Nashville, Tennessee, US
November 8 / Civic Centre, Atlanta, Georgia, US

November 10 / Moody Coliseum, Dallas, Texas, US
November 11 / Hofheinz Pavilion, Houston, Texas, US

AUSTRALIAN TOUR
November 25 / Hordern Pavilion, Sydney, New South Wales, Australia
November 26 / Hordern Pavilion, Sydney, New South Wales, Australia
November 27 / Hordern Pavilion, Sydney, New South Wales, Australia
November 28 / Hordern Pavilion, Sydney, New South Wales, Australia
November 30 / Festival Hall, Melbourne, Victoria, Australia
December 1 / Festival Hall, Melbourne, Victoria, Australia
December 2 / Festival Hall, Melbourne, Victoria, Australia
December 3 / Festival Hall, Melbourne, Victoria, Australia
December 6 / Entertainment Centre, Perth, Australia
December 7 / Entertainment Centre, Perth, Australia

Bibliography

Alexander, Randy, "Dee Murray Yearns for Taste of Past Glories," *East End Lights,* No. 1, 1990.

Alexander, Randy, "Search for Philly Sound Led EJ to Thom Bell," *East End Lights,* No. 2, 1991.

Bailey, Steve, "I Felt I Was Dying," *Mail on Sunday* (London), December 10, 1978.

Balmer, Elizabeth, *Elton John: The Illustrated Biography,* Transatlantic Press, 2010.

Bangs, Lester, "Bernie Taupin: *Bernie Taupin* (Elektra)," *Phonograph Record,* March, 1972.

Barber, Richard, "'I've Still Got the Music In Me'" *Daily Mail,* August 21, 2008.

Bego, Mark, *Elton John: The Bitch is Back,* Phoenix Books, Inc., 2009.

Bell, David (dir.), *Elton John, Aquarius,* documentary, BBC-TV, 1971.

Bell, Kevin, "Interview with Hoagie McMurtrie, Part One," *East End Lights,* issue 53.

Bell, Kevin, "Neil Sedaka: Bad Blood—Absolutely Not!," *East End Lights,* issue 59.

Bell, Kevin, "Rocket Records—Back in the Day/Interview with Hogie McMurtrie, Art Director, Rocket Records, Part 2," *East End Lights*

Bell, Max, "Bar-Room Brawls Are Out Man," *New Musical Express,* November 13, 1976.

Bell, Max, "Introducing Max Bell," *Rock's Back Pages*, 2010.

Bender, William, "Handstands and Fluent Fusion," *Time,* December 14, 1970.

Bennetts, Leslie, "Still Captain Fantastic," *Vanity Fair,* November, 1997.

Bernardin and Stanton, Tom, *Rocket Man: Elton John From A—Z*, Greenwood Press, 1995.

Bessman, Jim, "Three Decades of "Their Songs," *Billboard,* October 4, 1997.

Billboard, "Dick James in Scandinavia," September 18, 1971.

Billboard, "John at Troubadour Brings $150,000 Net," September 6, 1975.

Beviglia, Joe, "Behind the Song: 'Tiny Dancer'," *American Songwriter,* December 23, 2013.

Binyon, Michael, "Elton John: In Russia with Love," *Washington Post,* May 29, 1979.

Black, Johnny, "Eyewitness," *Q,* February, 1995.

Black, Susan, *Elton John in His Own Words,* Omnibus Press, 1993.

Blake, Mark, *Is This the Real Life? The Untold Story of Queen,* First Da Capo Press, 2011.

Bosso, Joe, "Davey Johnstone: My Career with Elton," *MusicRadar.com,* April 4, 2011.

Bowie, Angela with Carr, Patrick, *Backstage Passes,* Cooper Square Press, 2000.

Bowie, David and Rock, Mick, *Moonage Daydream,* Cassell Illustrated, 2005.

Brompton, Sally, "Problems of a Superstar's Father," *London Daily Mail,* May 20, 1976.

Bronson, Fred, "Charting History," *Billboard,* October 4, 1997.

Bronson, Fred, *The Billboard Book of Number One Hits,* Billboard Publications, 1988.

Bronson, Harold, "What Do Bowie, Elton, and Mantovani Have in Common? [Gus Dudgeon]," *Music World,* June 1, 1973.

Brown, Mick, "Elton John: *Blue Moves* (Rocket), *Sounds,* October 23, 1976.

Buchan, Alisdair, "Elton!" *London Daily Mirror,* November 5, 1979.

Buckley, David, *Elton: The Biography,* Chicago Review Press, 2007.

Buckley, Peter, "Is Elton John Obsolete?" *Circus,* 1972.

Burros, Marian, "Elton, Mum...and Yum," *The Washington Post,* June 30, 1976.

Byrom, Sue, "Captain Fantastic Marshals His Troops," *Record Mirror,* June 21, 1975.

Cant, Holly, "Pictures: Elton John performs at Baileys nightclub," *Watford Observer,* February 11, 2017.

Carlo, Darius (dir.), *A Voice Louder Than Rock,* documentary, 2016.

Carr, Roy and Murray, Charles Shaar, "The Life and Times of Elton John," *Rock Australia Magazine*, April, 1975.

Cass, Caroline, photographs by Twort, Andrew, *Elton John: Flower Fantasies,* Weidenfeld & Nicolson, 1997.

Cassata, Mary Ann, *The Elton John Scrapbook,* Citadel Press, Kensington Books, 2002.

Charlesworth, Charles, "Elton John: He's Got the Whole World in His Hands," *Melody Maker,* August 14, 1976.

Charlesworth, Chris, "Elton John: Elton's Bitter Sweet Album," *Melody Maker,* May 10, 1975.

Charlesworth, Chris, "Elton's Finest Hour!" *Melody Maker,* September 15, 1973.

Charlesworth, Chris, *Elton John,* Bobcat Books, 1986.

Christgau, Robert, "Elton John: The Little Hooker That Could," *The Village Voice,* November 24, 1975.

Christgau, Robert, "The Christgau Consumer Guide," *Creem,* February, 1974.

Circus Raves, "Elton Braves Arrest to Save Fans," winter, 1975.

Coburn, Bob, *Rockline* radio interview, WNEW-NY, August 20, 1984.

Cohn, Nik, "I'm a Mess But I'm Having Fun," *The New York Times,* August 22, 1971.

Colclough, Beechy, "My Pal's Been to El and Back," *Sun TV,* July 8, 1996.

Coleman, John radio interview with Elton John, "The Radio One Hype," *Friends,* October 2, 1970

Coleman, Ray, *Brian Epstein: The Man Who Made the Beatles,* Penguin Books, 1990.

Conconi, Chuck, "Personalities," *Washington Post,* May 30, 1990.

Conley, Jim radio interview with Elton John, *Startrak,* Westwood One, 1983.

Coon, Caroline, "Elton John: I want to Chug, Not Race," *Melody Maker,* June 21, 1975.

Cowton, Mike, "Don't Shoot Me I'm Only the Lyricist," *New Musical Express,* March 10, 1973.

Crane, Lisa, "Correspondence, Love Letters, and Advice," *Rolling Stone,* November 4, 1976.

Crespo, Charley, "P.T. Barnum, Muhammad Ali and Elton John?" *Circus,* December 8, 1977.

Crimp, Susan and Burstein, Patricia, *The Many Lives of Elton John,* Birch Lane Press, 1992.

Cromelin, Richard, "The Elton John Career," *Phonograph Record,* November, 1973.

Crowe, Cameron, "My Life in 20 Songs," *Rolling Stone,* October 10, 2013.

Crowe, Cameron (dir.), *Elton John and Leon Russell—The Union Documentary,* 2010.

Cunniff, Al, "The Beatin' Path: How Elton Spent His Days in D.C.," *The News American,* July 11, 1976.

Dahl, Bill, "Fats Domino: The King of Blueberry Hill," *Goldmine,* June 29, 2001.

Dallas, Karl, "Fotheringay: Albert Hall," *The Times* (London), October 3, 1970.

Dan, Uri and Standora, Leo, "Elton's Going Back to Israel," *New York Post,* June 17, 1993.

Darling, Cary, "John's *Visions,* Tells a Story," *Billboard,* October 30, 1982.

Davis, Stephen, review, *Goodbye Yellow Brick Road,* *Rolling Stone,* November 22, 1973.

Dee, Kiki, "My Mate Elton," *Rock World,* December, 1993.

Delacorte, Peter, "Sound Track," *Modern Screen,* December, 1975.

Demorest, Steve, "Elton John Rockets Over the Rainbow," *Circus,* December, 1973.

DeVoss, David, "Elton John, Rock's Captain Fantastic," *Time,* July 7, 1975.

DeYoanna, Michael, "As Auction Nears, Jim Guercio and Kenny Passarelli Share Caribou Rock Star Tales," Colorado Public Radio, 2014.

Dickinson, Lorna and Rosencrantz, Claudia, *Two Rooms: Elton John and Bernie Taupin in Their Own Words,* Boxtree Limited, 1991.

DiStefano, John, with additional research by Dobbins, Peter, *The Complete Elton John Discography,* 1993.

Ditlea, Steve, "Offstage with Elton John," *New Ingénue,* March, 1974.

Doerschuk, Bob, "Elton John's Multi-Keyboard Sideman: James Newton Howard," *Contemporary Keyboard,* February, 1981.

Doherty, Harry, "Elton John, Dave Mason, John Miles: Schaeffer Stadium, Boston," *Melody Maker,* July 17, 1976.

Dolce, Joe, "David Geffen Q&A," *Details,* July, 1996.

Donovan, Paul, "Elton John Superczar Rocks Them Back in the U.S.S.R.," *London Daily Mail,* May 29, 1979.

Dream Ticket: Elton John Across Four Decades, HST Management Press, 2004.

Droganes, Constance, "Captains Courageous," *Images,* spring, 1996.

Dubro, Alec, review, *Madman Across the Water, Rolling Stone,* January 20, 1972.

Dudgeon, Gus, "Introduction," *Rock of the Westies: Songs from the Album by Elton John and Bernie Taupin,* Melville, NY: Big Pig Music Ltd., 1975.

Duncan, Kirk, "Elton: The Apprentice," *Record Collector,* February, 1998.

Dunn, Andrew (producer) and Cooper, Mark (executive producer), *The Making of Elton John: Madman Across the Water,* documentary, BBC-TV, 2011.

Edmonds, Ben, "Elton John, Prisoner of Wax," *Creem,* February, 1974.

Edmonds, Ben, "Elton John: *Rock of the Westies* (MCA)," *Phonograph Record,* November 1975.

Edwards, Henry, "The Rise of Ziggy Stardust: David Bc October, 1972.

Edwards, Henry, "Tripping on the Traces of Elton John," *After Dark,* March, 1976.

Ellis, Geoffrey, *I Should Have Known Better,* Thorogood, 2004.

Elsus, Dennis radio interview with Elton John, WNEW-NY New York, November 29, 1974.

English, Margaret, "Elton John," *Look,* July 27, 1971.

Epand, Len, "Madman Across the Net," *Zoo World,* November 21, 1974.

Epps, Stuart, "Elton John: The Early Years," online essay, stuartepps.co.uk, 2010.

Epps, Stuart, "Tributes to Gus from Friends and Colleagues," *eltonjohn.com*, 2002.

Ewbank, Tim and Hildred, Stafford, *Rod Stewart: The New Biography,* Portrait, 2003.

Ewbank, Time, "Sitting Pretty," *London Daily Mail,* April 8, 1976.

Felton, David, "Elton John One Year Out," *Rolling Stone,* June 10, 1971.

Fields, Danny and Reisfeld, Randi and Wadsley, Pat, "The Story of Elton's Life," 1975.

Finch, Alan, *'Only the Piano Player': An Illustrated Discography,* Omnibus Press, 1983.

Finke, Nikki, "Leningrad, U.S.S.R.," Associated Press, May 21, 1979.

Flynn, Darryl, "Why Elton Didn't Commit Suicide," *Pageant,* November, 1975.

Fong-Torres, Ben, "The Four-Eyed Bitch is Back," *Rolling Stone,* November 21, 1974.

Forbes, Bryan, television documentary, *Elton John and Bernie Taupin Say Goodbye Norma Jean and Other Things,* ABC-TV, May 12, 1974.

Fornatale, Pete, radio interview, WNEW-FM, November 10, 1970.

Foster, Alex, "I Knew Him Better Than His Mother," *Mail on Sunday,* November 23, 1980.

Fountain, Nigel, "Elton John: A Matter of Numbers," *Street Life,* May 19-June 11, 1976.

Freedland, Nat, "Talent in Action: Elton John, Family," *Billboard,* December 23, 1972.

Frith, Simon, "Elton John: *Greatest Hits*; Randy Newman: *Good Old Boys*; Pete Atkin: *Secret Drinker*," *Let It Rock,* January, 1975.

Frost, David television interview with Elton John, PBS-TV, November 22, 1991.

Furnish, David, *Tantrums and Tiaras* documentary, Cinemax, September 21, 1997.

Gaines, Steven, "The Flip Side of Elton John," *New York Daily News,* June 23, 1974.

Gallagher, Jim, "Elton John Wows 'Em—to Put it Mildly—Back in the U.S.S.R.," *The Chicago Tribune,* May, 1979.

Gambaccini, Paul, radio interview with Elton John, Bernie Taupin, Gus Dudgeon and others, fall, 1976.

Gambaccini, Paul, "The Rolling Stone Interview: Elton John," *Rolling Stone,* August 16, 1973.

Gambaccini, Paul, *A Conversation with Elton John and Bernie Taupin,* Flash Books, 1975.

Gardella, Kay, "Will Cher Be a Long Playing Single?" *The New York Daily News,* February 9, 1975.

Garfield, Kim, "Bernie Taupin, The One Who Writes the Lyrics For Elton, Really Wants To Be An Actor," *In the Know,* September, 1976.

Garner, Ken, *In Session Tonight: The Complete Radio I Recordings,* BBC Books, 1993.

Garrett, Susanne, "Bernie Taupin in Words and Pix," *Melody Maker,* April 17, 1976.

Gaskell, Jane, "Listen to a Superstar's Mother Talking Frankly About Her Son," *London Mail,* May 20, 1972.

Gilbert, Jerry, "The Bernie Taupin Talk-In," *Sounds,* November 10, 1973.

Gilchrist, Roderick, "King John," *London Daily Mail,* June 29, 1973.

Glanville, Brian, "The Thoughts of Chairman Elton," *The Times* (London), April 16, 1978.

Goldberg, Michael, "Elton John: A Commercial Success," *Rolling Stone,* October 11, 1984.

Goldman, Albert, "Copycat in Wild Threads," *Life,* February 5, 1971.

Goldman, Vivien, "Elton John: Ol' Four Eyes is Back," *Sounds,* May 8, 1976.

Goldstein, Mike, "Interview with David Larkham," *albumcoverhalloffame.com,* April 18, 2014.

Goldstruck, Arthur, "The British Abroad: Elton John," *Billboard,* February 12, 1994.

Gomez, Lisa, "Number 29 for Elton John," *QC Quad,* September 19, 1989.

Goodall, Nigel, *Elton John: A Visual Documentary,* Omnibus Press, 1993.

Goodman, Mark, "Trimmed Down Megamillionaire," *People,* August 8, 1975.

Graustark, Barbara, "Elton Shoots Back with 'Piano Player'," *Circus,* April, 1973.

Greenblatt, "Elton John is Back," *Aquarian Weekly,* October 18-25, 1978.

Greenfield, Robert, "Elton John Steams 'Em Up," *Rolling Stone,* November 12, 1970.

Gregutt, Paul, "Elton's Next Album," *The Weekly of Metropolitan Seattle,* October 26-November 1, 1977.

Griffin, Sid, album liner notes, *It Ain't Easy* by John Baldry, Warner Brothers Records, 2005.

Griggs, Barbara, "Restyled Superstar," *London Daily Mail,* December 15, 1977.

Gross, Terry, "Thom Bell Interview," radio interview, December, 2008.

Guthrie, Bruce, "Extravaganza of Sight and Sound," unknown publication, February, 1974.

Haber, Joyce, "Million-Dollar Mansion for Elton," *Los Angeles Times,* April 22, 1975.

Hagerty, Bill, "King John Sleeps Here," *London Daily Mail,* January 21, 1976.

Hamshire, John, "Elton...Escort to a Princess," *London Daily Express,* January 23, 1976.

Harper, Leah, "Elton John: Soundtrack of My Life," *The Guardian,* August 31, 2013.

Harris, Bob, *The Whispering Years,* BBC, 2001.

Harris, Mike, "Kiki Dee: He Put the Music in Me," *Record World,* January 31, 1976.

Harty, Russell (dir.), *Elton at Dodgers,* documentary, *Russell Harty Plus,* 1975.

Hasted, Nick, "Hello, Yellow Brick Road," *Record Collector,* May, 2018.

Hatlestad, Luc, "Life According To...Kenny Passarelli," *52901—The Denver Magazine,* May, 2010.

Hauptfuhrer, Fred, "Through Crazy Glasses, Darkly," *People,* January 16, 1978.

Hayward, Keith, *Elton John: From Tin Pan Alley to the Yellow Brick Road,* Wymer Publishing, 2015.

Hayward, Keith, *Tin Pan Alley: The Rise of Elton John*, Soundcheck Books LLP, 2013.

Henderson, Richard, "The Little Label That Could," *Billboard,* October 4, 1997.

Herman, Cheryl, "A 'GBYBR' Oldie But Goodie," *eltonjohnworld*.com, March 21, 2007.

Herman, Cheryl, "An Interview with One of Elton's Early Publicists," *eltonjohnworld.com*, August 9, 2013.

Herman, Cheryl, "One Night on the Yellow Brick Road, As Experienced by Leroy Gomez," *eltonjohnworld.com,* February 23, 2007

Higgins, John F., "Dudgeon on the Record," *East End Lights,* winter, 1993.

Higgins, John F., "The Amazing Mr. Buckmaster," *East End Lights,* No. 18, spring, 1995.

Higgins, John F., "Out from Behind the Kit: Rapping with Charlie Morgan," *East End Lights,* spring, 1995.

Hilburn, Robert, "Christmas Comes Early for Elton John," *Los Angeles Times,* October 6, 1974.

Hilburn, Robert, "Elton John New Rock Talent," *Los Angeles Times,* August 27, 1970.

Hilburn, Robert, "Elton John Returns to Troubadour," *Los Angeles Times,* August 27, 1975.

Hilburn, Robert, "Elton John—The $8 Million Man," *Los Angeles Times,* June 25, 1974.

Hilburn, Robert, *Five Years of Fun,* Boutwell Enterprises, Inc., 1975.

Hilburn, Robert, *Corn Flakes with John Lennon,* Rodale, 2009.

Holden, Stephen, "Elton John: No Future? Apathy in the U.K." *Rolling Stone,* January 25, 1979.

Holden, Stephen, review, *Victim of Love, Rolling Stone,* December 13, 1979.

Holloway, Danny, "The Fightin' Side of Elton John," *New Musical Express,* February 17, 1973.

Hope, Adrian, "Honky Château," *Studio Sound,* May, 1975.

Hume, Martha, "Elton's Comeback Ignites On-Stage but Not on Record," *US,* November 27, 1979.

Humphries, Patrick, *A Little Bit Funny: The Elton John Story,* autumn, 1998.

Inglis, Sam, "High Dudgeon," *Sound on Sound,* July, 2001.

Irwin, Colin, "Elton Quits—and Wembley Weeps," *Melody Maker,* November 12, 1977.

Jackie, "His Hobby's a Prickly Subject," 1969.

Jackson, John, "My Hell," *Daily Mirror,* May 19, 1987.

Jahn, Mike, "Solo or With Group, Elton John Thrills Carnegie Audiences," *New York Times,* June 12, 1971.

Jahr, Cliff, "Elton's Frank Talk: The Lonely Love Life of a Superstar," *Rolling Stone,* October 7, 1976.

John, Elton and Taupin, Bernie, *Elton John/Bernie Taupin: The Complete Lyrics*, Hyperion, 1994.

Johnston, Jenny, "A Very Curious Bond," *DailyMail.com,* July 31, 2015.

Jones, Ashley, *Dee Murray: An Extraordinary Life Cut Too Short,* 2015.

Jones, Cliff, "Sound Your Funky Horn: Elton John," *Mojo,* October, 1997.

Jones, Edward, "Welder's Son Who Built a Pop Empire," *London Sunday Times,* May 8, 1977.

Jones, Lesley-Ann, *Freddie Mercury: The Definitive Biography,* Hodder & Stoughton, 1997.

Juke, "Elton John: The Elton John Mystique" September 4, 1976.

Karger, Dave, "The Rocket Man Blasts Off," *Entertainment Weekly,* November 5, 2004.

Kaye, Lenny, "Live on Stage in New York: Elton John Lennon," *Disc,* December 14, 1974.

Keane, Trace, "Kenny Passarelli Interview," *Hush Magazine,* 2010

Kemble, Kimberlee, "Ladies and Gentlemen...Stuart Epps," EltonJohnAllSongsList blog, October 15, 2010.

King, Tony, "Tony King Salutes 'A Competent Piano Player,'" *Record World,* January 31, 1976.

Kirby, Fred, "Talent in Action: Leon Russell/Elton John," *Billboard,* December 5, 1970.

Kirkeby, Marc, "Bill Martin Recalls an Early Elton Tune," *Record World,* January 31, 1976.

LaBelle, Patti with Randolph, Laura B., *Don't Block the Blessings: Revelations of a Lifetime,* Riverhead Books, 1996.

Landau, John, "Elton John Gets into Fantasy on '*Chateau*', '*Blue River*' is Eric's Finest Hour," *Rolling Stone,* August 17, 1972.

Landau, Jon, "*Tumbleweed Connection*: Elton John," *Rolling Stone,* February 18, 1971.

Lannert, John, "Elton, Soda Play Chile," *Billboard,* December 16, 1995.

Lappen, John, "Where It All Began," *East End Lights,* Premier Issue, autumn, 1990.

Larkham, David, U.S. Elton John Tour Book, *Louder Than Concorde But Not Quite As Pretty,* 1976.

Ledgerwood, Mike, "Everything Stops for Baldry," *Disc,* June 3, 1972.

Lehecka, Mike, "Geezers," *Request,* March, 1994.

Letter from Stanley Dwight to Edna Clough, dated December 2, 1962, personal collection of Edna Clough Dwight.

Levy, Arthur, "Elton John: The Leaving of America; Beau Brummel Meets Yogi Berra," *Zoo World,* December 6, 1973.

Lewis, Barbara, "What Does Elton Do With His Money?," *In the Know,* September, 1976.

Lewis, Linda, "The Night I Asked My Boyfriend 'Do You Mind If I Sleep With Cat Stevens?'" *DailyMail.com,* June, 2009.

Lewis, Vic, "Vic Lewis: Aiding Elton's Breakout," *Record World,* January, 1976.

Lewisohn, Mark, discography, *Sir Elton,* Sidgwick & Jackson, 2001.

Life, "The Rock Family Affair," September 24, 1971.

Longmore, Andrew, "Watford's Greatest Hits Back in Harmony," *The Times* (London), February 23, 1996.

Los Angeles Times, "Elton John Honored by 'The Rock Music Awards,'" August 12, 1975.

Lustbader, Eric Van, "The Songs of Elton and Bernie: A Musical Monument to the '70s," *Record World,* January 31, 1976.

Lustbader, Eric Van, liner notes, *To Be Continued...* box set (U.S.), MCA Records, 1990.

Lyric Financial, "Q&A With Kenny Passarelli," December 19, 2013.

MacDonald, Patrick, "Elton John Begins New Album Here," *Seattle Times,* October 22, 1977.

Madley, Brian, "Lazy Bones! Pop-Star Elton John Sounds Off...With a Brand-New Theme," *London Daily Mail,* March 16, 1975.

Mandell, Ellen, "The Many Faces of Elton John," *Good Times,* originally printed winter, 1971, reprinted June 21, 1988.

Mann, William, "Elton John: Festival Hall," *The Times* (London), February 7, 1972.

Marcus, Greil, "Elton John Superfan," *Village Voice,* June 16, 1975.

Marks, J., "So You Wanna Be a Rock 'n' Roll Star," *Gallery,* January, 1973.

Marsh, Dave, "Captain's Latest Feat Is Not So Fantastic," *New Orleans Times-Picayune,* June 16, 1975.

Martinez, Al, "The Vision They Create is Most Spectacular," *Los Angeles Times,* September 23, 1973.

Matre, Lynn Van, "...And in Elton's Case It's Framed in Feathers, Finery, and Frenzy," *Chicago Tribune,* November 10, 1974.

Matre, Lynn Van, "Superstar in Shining Splendor," *Chicago Tribune,* May 9, 1972.

Matre, Van, "All That Glitters in Elton John's Act is Not Gold...But it Dazzles the Faithful," *Chicago Tribune,* July 18, 1976.

McCollum, Charlie, "Elvis' Popularity Grows by Leaps and Pounds," *The Washington Star,* June 28, 1976.

McCormack, Ed, "Elton's Tour Ends: Tears, Lennon, and Whatever Gets You Through the Night," *Rolling Stone,* January 2, 1975.

McDonough, Jack, "Talent in Action: Elton John/Kiki Dee," *Billboard,* November 2, 1974.

McGrath, Mick and Quigley, Mike, "This is Your Song: The Elton John Interview," *The Georgia Straight,* April 11, 1971.

McGrath, Rick and Quigley, Mike, "This is Your Song: The Elton John Interview," *Georgia Straight,* April 11, 1971.

McKaie, Andy interview with Elton John and Bernie Taupin, *To Be Continued...* box set (U.S.)

McLain, Daisann, "Someone Saved His Life Tonight," *Feature,* January, 1979.

McLaughlin, Peter and Liff, Mark, "225,000 Rock With Elton to Roll in $," *New York Daily News,* September 14, 1980.

McLeod, Pauline, "Elton," *London Daily Mail,* November 6, 1978.

Me, Myself and I, television documentary, VH1, 2008.

Means, Andrew, "Magna Carta and the Gentle Sound," *Melody Maker,* January 23, 1971.

Meldrum, Ian, "Ian Meldrum's Keyhole News," *Go-Set,* March 2, 1974.

Meldrum, Ian, "The Weather Was Nothing! It Was Elton, Nigel and Dee Who Blew Everyone's Cool," *Go-Set,* 1971.

Meldrum, Ian, "To: Mr. Reg Dwight, Alias Elton John," *Go-Set,* January, 1973.

Mendelssohn, "Elton John," *Rolling Stone,* November 12, 1970.

Michaelway, "Elton a Hit in France," *Billboard,* September 18, 1971.

Mills, Bart, "Kiki Dee's Career Hits High Notes Under Elton John's Wing," *Chicago Tribune,* January 9, 1977.

Mitch, "Front Row Reviews: Elton John, Randwick Racecourse," unknown Sydney publication, March, 1974.

Morecambe & Wise Christmas Special, December, 1977.

Mulligan, Jess, interview with Clive Franks and Ricky Ball, *Radio New Zealand* radio show, 2015.

Murray, Charles Shaar, "Elton John: *Don't Shoot Me, I'm Only the Piano Player (DJM),*" *New Musical Express,* January 27, 1973.

Murray, Charles Shaar, "Elton John: *Rock of the Westies,*" *New Musical Express,* October 25, 1975.

Murray, Charles Shaar, "Step Right Up and Feel the Man's Muscles: Honky Château," *Creem,* June, 1972.

Myers, Paul, *It Ain't Easy: Long John Baldry and the Birth of the British Blues,* Greystone Books, Douglas & McIntyre Publishing, 2007.

Nagar, Larry, "Singing Animals Are Only Human," *Philadelphia Daily News,* July 6, 1994.

Nash, Jess, "Losing Elton in the Lost City," *Creem,* March, 1994.

Ness, Chris Van, "Elton John," *Los Angeles Free Press,* May 21, 1971.

New York Times, "Crowd of 400,000 Sets Record for Park," September 14, 1980.

Newman, Del, *A Touch From God: It's Only Rock and Roll,* Apex Publishing Ltd., 2010.

Newman, Gerald and Bivona, Joe, *Elton John,* New American Library, 1976.

Norman, Philip, "Playing It the Way It Was at the Top," *The Times* (London), June 23, 1975.

Norman, Philip, liner notes, *To Be Continued...* box set (U.K.), Rocket Records, 1991.

Norman, Philip, *Sir Elton,* Sidgwick & Jackson, 2001.

Nunes, Jose Manuel, "Lisbon," *Billboard,* August 28, 1971 & October 2, 1971.

Nutter, David, and Taupin, Bernie and John, Elton, *Elton: It's a Little Bit Funny,* Viking Press, 1977.

O'Brien, Connan television interview with Elton John, *Late Night with Conan O'Brien,* NBC-TV, November 15, 1996.

O'Casey, Matt (dir.), *Days of Our Lives,* BBC-Two, 2011.

O'Connor, John J., "Goodbye to Norma Jean..." *New York Times,* May 17, 1974.

O'Flaherty, Pete, "Elton John Tours Scotland with Simon Dupree—1967," 2013.

O'Haire, Patricia, "Madman Plays Carnegie Hall," *New York Daily News,* November 22, 1972.

O'Hanton, Terry, "Elton's Secret Agony," *London Sunday Mirror,* January 27, 1991.

O'Neill, Terry, *Eltonography: A Life in Pictures, Sir Elton John,* Evans Mitchell Books, 2008.

O'Neill, Terry, *Two Days That Rocked the World: Elton John Live At Dodger Stadium,* Iconic Images, edited by Carrie Kania, Design Direction by Stephen Reid, 2015.

Olson, Catherine Applefeld, "Elton On Stage and Screen," *Billboard,* October 4, 1997.

Orange, Julia, "...And a Star on Hollywood Boulevard," *Rolling Stone,* December 4, 1975.

Page, Mike Flood and Salewicz, Chris, "Elton John: Renaissance Man of Pop," *Let It Rock,* September, 1973.

Palmer, Robert, "Rock Concert: Elton John in Central Park," *New York Times,* September 14, 1979.

Palmer, Tony, "The New Elton John Won't Have to Be a Clown," *New York Times,* May 12, 1974.

Pang, May and Edwards, Henry, *Loving John,* Warner Books, 1983.

Parets, Jeff, "The Eye of the Acoustic Storm: Supertramp/Roger Hodgson," *Acoustic Storm,* March 16, 2010.

Paris, Tony, "High Frequencies: Iggy Pop – The Atlanta love affair continues," *Creative Loafing,* October 5, 2017.

Parkinson, Judy, *Made in England,* Michael O'Mara Books Limited, 2003.

Parry, Ryan, "'I Discovered Sir Elton and Put Him on the Path to Fame...'," *Dailymail.com,* April 8, 2016.

Pavone, Barbara, "Stuart Epps Toured America With Elton John...," *The Rock and Roll Report,* November 5, 2009.

Peebles, Andy, *The Elton John Tapes: Elton John in Conversation with Andy Peebles,* St. Martin's Press, 1981.

Perry, Roger, "Chairman Elton," *London Sunday Times,* September 9, 1978.

Pevney, Joseph (dir.), *Hardy Boys and Nancy Drew Meet Dracula, Part I,* ABC-TV, September 11, 1977.

Pidgeon, John, "Elton John: *Don't Shoot Me I'm Only The Piano Player,*" *Let It Rock,* April, 1973.

Pipolo, Pat, "Elton's Chart Challenge," *Record World,* January 31, 1976.

Polack, Andy, "Remember David's Mum? Say Hello to Reggie's Dad," *New Musical Express,* May 29, 1976.

Pond, Steve, "Elton John's Subdued Return," *Rolling Stone,* November 15, 1979.

Ponsford, Kenneth, "Stag," *Honour Before Honours,* Pinner Grammar Recollections, 1937-1982.

Pope, Mal, *Old Enough to Know Better,* Y Lolfa, 2010.

Pousner, Michael, "It's Elton's Show—And He Runs It," *New York Daily News,* August 5, 1976.

Prentice, Thomas, "Can TV's Mr. Jingle Rock Elton John Back to the Top of the Hit Parade?" *Daily Mail,* September 5, 1978.

Prentice, Thomson, "Can TV's Mr. Jingle Rock Elton John Back to the Top of the Hit Parade?" *London Daily Mail,* September 5, 1978.

Puterbaugh, Parke, "Elton John," Rock 'n' Roll Hall of Fame Annual Induction Dinner program, 1994.

Radio interview with Elton John, Bernie Taupin, Gus Dudgeon, John Reid, Steve Brown and Paul Buckmaster, WBBM-FM Chicago, 1974.

Radio interview with Elton John, WRKO Boston, "Christmas from Barbados," December, 1975.

Record World, "Elton's Albums: An Appraisal," January 31, 1976.

Record World, "Weston Describes the Troub Engagement," January 31, 1976.

Rees, Dafydd and Crampton, Luke, *VH1 Music First Encyclopedia,* DK Publishing, 1999.

Reisfeld, Randi and Fields, Danny, *Who's Your Fave Rave?,* Boulevard Books, 1997.

Rensin, David, "Elton John at the Hollywood Bowl," *Rolling Stone,* October 11, 1973.

Review, "Come Back Baby," *Record Retailer and Music Industry News,* July 22, 1964.

Richards, Alan, review, *Taupin, Crawdaddy,* 1972.

Riddell, Mary, "Yes, We Remember Shy Little Reg," *London Daily Mirror,* June 20, 1986.

Robins, Wayne, "Elton John: *Captain Fantastic and the Brown Dirt Cowboy,*" *Creem,* August, 1975.

Robins, Wayne, "Elton John: *Goodbye Yellow Brick Road,*" *Creem,* January, 1974.

Robinson, Lisa, "Elton John Tells All to Our Lisa," *The Chicago Sun-Times,* July 18, 1976.

Rock Scene, "Elton John Conquers New York," March, 1978.

Rock Scene, "Making *Tommy,*" July, 1975.

Rockett, Louise, "Blue Max Staff Remember Magical Elton John Concert in Lahaina," *LahainaNews.com,* February 17, 2011.

Rockwell, John, "Elton John in a Smooth Show at Garden," *New York Times,* August 12, 1976.

Rockwell, John, "Flamboyant, Vulnerable Star Was in Eclipse," *New York Times,* May 23, 1979.

Rogers, Byron, "Captain Fantastic He Is," *London Daily Telegraph,* April 30, 1976.

Rohter, "Elton John: The Music Machine," *Washington Post,* July 1, 1976.

Rohter, Larry, "Elton John: Why Fans Are Hooked on His Act," *Washington Post,* June 29, 1976.

Roland, Paul, *Elton John,* Proteus Books, 1984.

Rosen, Craig, "Bernie Taupin: The Billboard Interview," *Billboard,* October 4, 1997.

Rosenthal, Elizabeth J., "Elton Goes Pinky," *Hercules,* Number 35, June, 1996.

Rosenthal, Elizabeth J., *His Song: The Musical Journey of Elton John,* Billboard Books, Watson-Guptill Publications, 2001.

Ross-Leming, Eugenie and Standish, David, "The Elton John Interview," *Playboy,* January, 1976.

Salewicz, Chris, "Elton John Without the Glitz," *Musician,* March, 1987.

Salewicz, Chris, "The Rise and Fall of Reginald Dwight," *Q,* December, 1986.

Savage, Mark, "Elton John: On the Yellow Brick Road," BBC News, March 24, 2014.

Sandall, Robert, "Ray Cooper: Who Are Those Blokes Up There With Ray?" *Q,* October, 1990.

Santelli, Bob, "Elton John Q&A at Capitol Records," April, 2013.

Scoppa, Bud, "Elton John: *Blue Moves,*" *Phonograph Record,* November, 1976.

Scoppa, Bud, "Elton John: *Caribou,*" *Phonograph Record,* August, 1974.

Scott, Ken and Owsinsky, *Abbey Road to Ziggy Stardust: Off the Record with The Beatles, Bowie, Elton...,* Alfred Music, 2012.

Searl, Hanford, "John Gig Best Rock Show to Play Vegas,'" *Billboard,* October 25, 1975.

Sekuler, Eliot, "John Reid Tells His Side of the Story," *Record World,* January 31, 1976.

Sexton, Paul, "Around the World," *Billboard,* October 4, 1997.

Shaw, Greg, "*Captain Fantastic*: Elton John," *Phonography Record,* June, 1975.

Shaw, Greg, "Elton John: *Captain Fantastic,*" *Phonograph Record,* June, 1975.

Shears, Richard, "Silent Year for Elton," *Daily Mail,* January 3, 1987.

Sheff, David, "Rock's Bernie Taupin Sings His Own Lyrics Now But He Hasn't Written Elton a Dear John," *People,* June 23, 1980.

Short, Don, "Elton Escapades," *London Sunday Mail,* June 22, 1975

Short, Don, "My Fan, the Princess," *London Sunday Mirror,* June 29, 1978.

Silver, Jr., Murray M., "Interview with: Nigel Olsson," *Modern Recording,* June, 1979.

Sischy, Ingrid, "Elton John: 150% Involved," *Interview,* April, 1995.

Smeaton, Bob (dir.), *Classic Albums: Elton John—Goodbye Yellow Brick Road,* documentary, Eagle Rock Entertainment, 2001.

Smith, Joe, edited by Fink, Michael, *Off the Record: An Oral History of Popular Music,* Warner Books, 1988.

Smith, Robin, "Star Spangled Piano," *Record Mirror,* May 7, 1977.

Snow, Mat, "Elton John," *Q,* January, 1995.

Snyder, Patrick, "A Piece of the Rock of the Westies," *Rolling Stone,* December 4, 1975.

Snyder, Patrick, "Taupin Speaks Through Elton John's Mouth," *Rolling Stone,* fall, 1977.

Snyder, Tom television interview with Elton John, *Tomorrow Show,* NBC-TV, fall, 1976.

Sorel, "Prude of the Week," *The Village Voice,* November 15, 1976.

Spencer, Bright, *Essential Elton,* Chameleon, 1998.

Spencer, Neil, "As Elton Backs Government Labour Rock Ads Spark RAR [Rock Against Racism] Protest," unknown publication, 1979.

St. Michael, Mick, *Elton John,* Smithmark, Brompton Books Corp., 1994.

Staff writer, "Elton John Corrals Over $1-Mil in Dodger Stadium Concert Gigs," *Variety,* October 29, 1975.

Stambler, Irwin, *The Encyclopedia of Pop, Rock and Soul,* St. Martin's Press, 1989.

Stanton, Tom and Turano, James, "A Little Bit of Hope," *East End Lights,* No. 29, winter, 1998.

Stanton, Tom and Turano, James, "Clive Franks: He's Seen More Elton Shows Than Anyone in the Universe," *East End Lights,* No. 34, spring, 1999.

Stanton, Tom and Turano, James, "Lennon, Moonie and Dee: Nigel Recalls Friends, Idols," *East End Lights,* No. 30, spring, 1998.

Stanton, Tom, "A Star Was Born, But Not Overnight," *East End Lights,* No. 8, summer, 1992.

Stanton, Tom, "Sedaka Wonders Whether Breaking Up With Rocket Was Wise Thing To Do," *East End Lights,* No. 14, Spring, 1994.

Stanton, Tom, "The Tom Robinson Tracks," *East End Lights,* No. 34, spring, 1999.

Stark, David, "The Manager: John Reid Has Spent a Quarter-Century Steering the Career of Elton John," *Billboard,* October 4, 1997.

Stein, Cathi, *Elton John: Rock's Piano Pounding Madman,* Popular Library, 1975.

Stewart, Dave, *Sweet Dreams Are Made of This: A Life in Music,* NAL, 2016.

Stewart, Rod, *Rod—The Autobiography,* Three Rivers Press, 2013.

Stewart, Tony, "Elton John: Rainbow Theatre, London," *New Musical Express,* May 14, 1977.

Stoop, Norma McLain, "John Reid: The Right Way In," *After Dark,* March, 1976.

Sutcliffe, Phil, "Elton John Mk II," *Juke,* April 15, 1977.

Sutcliffe, Phil, "The Real Elton John Stands Up—'Hoorah!'" *Sounds,* December 18, 1976.

Swan, "Elton John (Rainbow, London)," *Variety,* May 18, 1977.

Swartley, Ariel, review, *Blue Moves, Rolling Stone,* December 30, 1976.

Swenson, John, "Elton John: A Few Moments of Candor on the Yellow Brick Road," *Crawdaddy,* February, 1974.

Symonds, David radio interview with Elton John, *Symonds on Sunday,* BBC, July 20, 1969.

Tannebaum, Rob, "Bring Back the Old Elton," *New York Post,* October 19, 1988.

Tatham, Dick and Jasper, Tony, *Elton John,* Octopus Books Ltd. in association with Phoebus, 1976.

Taupin, Bernie, 'Sideways' by John, Elton, Aldridge, Alan & Dempsey, Mike eds. Cape Jonathan, *The One Who Writes the Words for Elton John,* Knopf, 1976.

Taupin, Bernie, *A Cradle of Haloes: Sketches of a Childhood*, Aurum Press, 1988.

Taupin, Bernie, liner notes, *Rare Masters* box set, Polydor, 1992.

Television broadcast live from Edinburgh Playhouse Theatre, Edinburgh, Scotland, BBC-TV, September 17, 1976.

The New Yorker, "The Talk of the Town," December 23, 1974.

Thodoris, A., "Interview: Derek Shulman (Gentle Giant)," *Hit Channel,* April 22, 2014.

Thomas, Deborah, "Sending Himself Up...The Rocket Man," *London Daily Mail,* December 12, 1972.

Tiegel, Eliot, "Odetta, Johhn, Coorder [sic]: 1 Plus & 2 Maybes," *Billboard,* December 5, 1970.

Time, "The Bash," review of the *Tommy* film premiere party, March 31, 1975.

"Time of Your Life" television documentary, BBC-TV, 2013.

Tiven, Jon, "Elton John's *'Captain Fantastic and the Brown Dirt Cowboy'*/The Story of a Million $ Friendship," *Circus Raves,* August, 1975.

Toberman, Barry, *Elton John: A Biography,* George Weidenfeld & Nicolson Limited, 1988.

Tobler, *Elton John: 25 Years in the Charts,* Hamlyn, 1995.

Tobler, John, "Elton John: *Blue Moves,*" *ZigZag,* December, 1976.

Tobler, John, "Elton John: *Captain Fantastic and the Brown Dirt Cowboy,*" *ZigZag,* November, 1975.

Tobler, John, "Elton John: Hammersmith Odeon, London," *ZigZag,* January, 1975.

Tobler, John, "Elton John: *Rock of the Westies,*" *ZigZag,* February, 1976.

Tobler, John, "Part One: Paying Dues," *ZigZag 25,* No. 25, 1972.

Tobler, John, "The Elton John Story: Final Part," *ZigZag,* April, 1973.

Tucker, Ken, "Art in the Right Place," *Entertainment Weekly,* March 31, 1995.

Turano, James, "A Tale of Taupin's Tealby Tile," *East End Lights,* No. 37, winter, 2000.

Townshend, Pete, *Who I Am: A Memoir,* Harper Perennial, 2013.

Trakin, Roy, "Elton John: Concert in Central Park, September, 1980," *Musician,* January, 1981.

Trynka, Paul, "Goodbye Reg, Hello Elton," *The Guardian,* March 18, 2007.

Tucker, Ken, "Elton Takes a Dive," *Rolling Stone,* September 23, 1976.

Turano, James, "1976," *East End Lights,* No. 25, winter, 1997.

Turano, James, "Dudgeon on the Record," *East End Lights,* No. 13, winter, 1993.

Turano, James, "Mover/Can-Can Fantastic," *East End Lights,* No. 42, 2001.

Turner, Steve, "Bernie Taupin: The B-Side of Elton John," *Beat Instrumental,* February, 1972.

Turner, Steve, "Elton John: *Don't Shoot Me I'm Only the Piano Player,*" *Beat Instrumental,* January, 1973.

Tyler, Andrew, "Davey Johnstone, Straight Man in Elton's Camp," unknown publication, 1973.

Uhelszki, Jaan and Bangs, Lester, "The Elton John Interview," *Creem,* May, 1975.

Valentine, Peggy, "Elton John: *Madman Across the Water,*" *Sounds,* October 30, 1970.

Valentine, Peggy, "Elton John: The Great White Hope," *Sounds,* October 17, 1970.

Valentine, Peggy, "Elton John: The Record Rise of a Superstar Called Reg," *Disc and Music Echo,* 1971.

Valentine, Peggy, "Elton John: The Tumbleweed Connection," *Sounds,* 1971.

Valentine, Penny, "Elton John: The Record Rise of a Superstar Called Reg," *Disc and Music Echo,* 1971.

Valentine, Penny, "Elton John: *Tumbleweed Connection,*" *Sounds,* 1971.

Valentine, Penny, "Elton: Earthquake in LA," *Sounds,* November 4, 1972.

Valentine, Penny, "The Sounds Talk-In: Elton John," *Sounds,* December 26, 1970.

Viceroy, Daniel, "Elton Chers Spotlight," *Woodmore TV Review,* February, 1975.

Variety, "Elton John Says He's Quitting Road," November 9, 1977.

Video interview, "James Newton Howard—Elton Tale," *Yamaha All Access,* 2010.

Wale, Michael, "Elton John," *The Times* (London), June 8, 1972.

Wale, Michael, "Garden Party: Crystal Palace," *The Times,* (London), August 2, 1971.

Walker, Michael, *Laurel Canyon: The Inside Story of Rock-and-Roll's Legendary Neighborhood,* Faber & Faber, 2007.

Wansell, Geoffrey, "Elton John, a Long Way From a Pound a Night, Plus Tips, in Northwood," *The Times* (London), June 21, 1975.

Warburton, Nick, "Bluesology," *garagehangover.com*, 2015.

Waters, Harry F., "Cher and Cher Alone," *Newsweek,* 1975.

Watts, Michael, "Oh, You Pretty Thing," *Melody Maker,* January 22, 1972.

Webb, Julie, "Elton John: Undedicated Performer," *Hit Parader,* October, 1972.

Welch, Chris, "Elton John: Belle Vue, Manchester," *Melody Maker,* December 8, 1973.

Welch, Chris, "Elton John: Caribou," *Melody Maker,* June 15, 1974."

Welch, Chris, "Elton John: Hammersmith Odeon, London," *Melody Maker,* January 4, 1975.

Wendeborn, John, Rock Singer Justifies Full House," *The Oregonian,* October, 1975.

Wheeler, Stephen P., "Bernie Taupin: The Brown Dirt Cowboy Rides Again," *Music Connection,* October 30-November 12, 1989.

Whitaker, James, "Sorry to Elton for Drug Boob," *London Daily Express,* May 4, 1977.

White, Timothy, "The Poignancy of Tzuke," *East End Lights,* No. 10, winter, 1993.

Whitburn, Joel, "Joel Whitburn's Record Research Report," *Billboard,* July 13, 1974.

Whitburn, Joel, *Top Pop Singles 1955-1996,* Record Research Books, 1997.

White, David, "Corporal Loudmouth," *Rock Australia Magazine,* June 28, 1975.

White, Timothy, "Elton John: The Billboard Interview," *Billboard,* October 4, 1997.

Wigg, David, "About My Young Elton," *London Daily Express,* May 29, 1979.

Wigg, David, "Exit Elton," *London Daily Express,* November 4, 1977.

Wilde, Jon, "Elton the Magnificent," *Uncut,* September, 2001.

Williams, Richard, "Elton John," *Melody Maker*, February 13, 1971.

Wilson, Brian with Gold, Todd, *Wouldn't It Be Nice: My Own Story,* HarperCollins, Publishers, 1991.

Wilson, Tony, "Genius with Feathers," unknown Australian publication, February, 1974.

Wishart, John, "Elton Moves On," *Record Mirror,* October 21, 1978.

Wislon, John radio interview with Bernie Taupin, *Front Row,* BBC, June 14, 2006.

Wolfinden, Bob, "Kiki Dee: The Life Story of a Hot Girl," *New Musical Express,* October 5, 1974.

Zito, Tom, "Boring Music, Bad Attitude," *The Washington Post,* October 1, 1973.

Zollo, Paul, "Bernie Taupin's Words of Wisdom," *Musician,* January, 1998.

ABOUT THE AUTHOR

David John DeCouto lives and breathes in Chandler, Arizona. Besides *Captain Fantastic: Elton John in the '70s,* he is also the author—along with Rock and Roll Hall of Fame photographer James Fortune—of *Celebration Day: Shooting Led Zeppelin in America 1973/1975, 36 Rocks Per Roll: A Photographer's Odyssey Through the '60s & '70s,* and *Venus & Mars: Paul McCartney Over America '75/'76.* David's upcoming works include a novel, *Killing Time,* and *Faithless Prayers,* a collection of new and selected poems. Between vinyl, 8-tracks, cassettes, CDs and digital downloads, David has purchased *Goodbye Yellow Brick Road* more than a dozen times over. Tell no one.